Jason Goroncy

T&T Clark Studies in Systematic Theology

Edited by
John Webster
Ian A. McFarland
Ivor Davidson

Volume 20

Hallowed Be Thy Name

The Sanctification of All in the Soteriology of P. T. Forsyth

by
Jason Goroncy

BLOOMSBURY
LONDON • NEW DELHI • NEW YORK • SYDNEY

Bloomsbury T&T Clark
An imprint of Bloomsbury Publishing Plc

50 Bedford Square
London
WC1B 3DP
UK

1385 Broadway
New York
NY 10018
USA

www.bloomsbury.com

First published 2013
Paperback edition first published 2014

British Library Cataloguing-in-Publication Data
A catalogue record for this book is available from the British Library.

ISBN: HB: 978-0-567-06682-4
PB: 978-0-567-65719-0
ePDF: 978-0-567-40253-0
epub: 978-0-567-17439-0

Library of Congress Cataloging-in-Publication Data
Goroncy, Jason
Hallowed Be Thy Name/Jason Goroncy p.cm
Includes bibliographic references and index.
ISBN 978-0-567-06682-4 (hardcover)
2012045678

Typeset by Newgen Imaging Systems Pvt Ltd, Chennai, India
Printed and bound in Great Britain

To Judy and Sinead, who thrive in the love and hope of holiness;
and to Tui, for whom the great eternities of holy love have come home.

Contents

Acknowledgments

This study has nurtured in its author a peculiar combination of reverence, jealousy and condolence for any who would undertake the assignment of academic writing and, more particularly, a new admiration for those having to live with such authors and their projects. My principal thanks, then, is directed to Judy and Sinead, who have both borne the long hours of my absence and a presence too often more associated with tiredness than with the energy to which this project seeks to bear witness. I am also indebted to my doctoral supervisor, Trevor Hart, whose friendship and inspiration helped make this project a joy to work on, and to my doctoral examiners, Ivor Davidson and Tom Smail†, whose comments about this project were encouraging and constructive. I am thankful to the team of the New Creation Teaching Ministry for first introducing me to Forsyth, and to many others who have offered support and assistance along the way: Dean Carter† and Noel Due for their encouragement to pursue doctoral work in the first place; Willy Carter-Golin and family, for making available to me Dean's notes on Forsyth, Lidgett and Denney; Michael Partridge, for his enthusiastic counsel on this assignment; Rindy Hoegger and members of the Clarendon Park Congregational Church, members of Shipley United Reformed Church, and of Emmanuel Church, Cambridge, for their assistance with unearthing historical material from cobwebbed and long-abandoned cupboards and boxes, and for keeping alive those chapters in their oral story in which Forsyth features; Bradford Library, Dr Williams's Library (London), and the university libraries in Aberdeen, Manchester, Leicester, Göttingen, Edinburgh and St Andrews for making material available that genuine devotees of Forsyth can only drool over; Catherine van Dorp, Richard Floyd, Jim Gordon, Warwick Johnson, Jill Pope, Paul Moser, André Muller and Stanley Russell for casting their eyes over earlier drafts of this book; Alan Torrance, Robin Parry, Alan Sell, Bruce Hamill, Frank Rees, Graham Redding and Murray Rae, for their friendship and encouragement to 'keep writing', and, in some cases, to 'stop writing'. Finally, my memorable three years of research in St Andrews, where this project was brought to birth, was made considerably more rewarding because of a supportive postgraduate and worshipping community, particularly Chris and Lisa Chandler, Luke and Holly Tallon, Theng Huat and Cheng Ping Leow, Gisela Kreglinger, Kevin and Gwen Diller, Daniel and Adriel Driver, Aaron and Kerri Kuecker, Darren and Cara Schmidt, Annice and Rory Macleod, Alasdair and Cathie Macleod, Drew and Melanie Lewis, Andrew and Julie Torrance, and Bruce and Linda Baker. Anything worthwhile requires a community.

Abbreviations

Scriptura Forsyth

'Adam'	'The First and Second Adam'
'Allegory'	'An Allegory of the Resurrection'
Art	*Religion in Recent Art: Being Expository Lectures on Rossetti, Burne Jones, Watts, Holman Hunt, and Wagner*
'Atonement'	'The Atonement in Modern Religious Thought'
'Attacks'	'The Attacks on the Churches'
Authority	*The Principle of Authority in Relation to Certainty, Sanctity and Society: An Essay in the Philosophy of Experimental Religion*
'Baldwin Brown'	'Baldwin Brown: A Tribute, a Reminiscence, and a Study'
Brown	*Baldwin Brown: A Tribute, a Reminiscence, and a Study*
'Catholic Threat'	'The Catholic Threat of Passive Resistance'
'Centre'	'At the Centre of Me'
Charter	*The Charter of the Church: Six Lectures on the Spiritual Principle of Nonconformity*
'Charter of Missions'	'The Charter of Missions'
'Chinese 18 Jan'	'Chinese Labour in the Transvaal'. 18 January 1906
'Chinese 20 Jan'	'Chinese Labour'. 20 January 1906
'Chinese 25 Jan'	'Chinese Labour in the Transvaal'. 25 January 1906
'Chinese 26 Jan'	'Chinese Labour'. 26 January 1906
'Chinese 29 Jan'	'Chinese Labour in the Transvaal'. 29 January 1906
'Christian Principle'	'Christ and the Christian Principle'
'Christianity of Christ'	'The Christianity of Christ and Christ our Christianity'
'Christmas'	'The Christening of Christmas'
'Christ's Person'	'Christ's Person and His Cross'
'Church and Society'	'The Church and Society – Alien or Allied?
'Church Fabric'	'The Significance of the Church Fabric'
'Church, State, Dogma'	'Church, State, Dogma and Education'
'Church Theory'	'The Need of a Church Theory for Church Union'

Congregationalism	*Congregationalism and Reunion: Two Lectures*
'Conquest of Time'	'The Conquest of Time by Eternity'
'Conversion'	'The Conversion of the "Good"'
Cruciality	*The Cruciality of the Cross*
'Distinctive Thing'	'The Distinctive Thing in Christian Experience'
'Effects of War'	'Some Effects of the War on Belief'
'Efficiency and Sufficiency'	'The Efficiency and Sufficiency of the Bible'
'Empire'	'The Empire for Christ'
'Evangelical Basis'	'The Evangelical Basis of Free Churchism'
'Evangelical Churches'	'The Evangelical Churches and the Higher Criticism' (Anderson)
'Evangelical Faith'	'What is the Evangelical Faith?'
Evolution	*Christian Aspects of Evolution*
'Experience'	'Our Experience of a Triune God'
'Faith and Mind'	'Faith and Mind'
Father	*God the Holy Father*
'Final Seat of Authority'	'The Cross as the Final Seat of Authority' (Anderson)
'Foolishness'	'The Foolishness of Preaching'
'Forgiveness'	'The Problem of Forgiveness in the Lord's Prayer'
'Forsyth and Campbell'	'"Dr. Forsyth and Mr. Campbell", Letter'
'Forsyth on Preaching'	'Principal Forsyth on Preaching'
Freedom	*Faith, Freedom and the Future*
'Fund'	'The Fund and the Faith'
'Gate'	'Christ at the Gate'
'Genius'	'Christ – King or Genius?'
'God, Sin'	'God, Sin, and the Atonement'
'Hell'	'"The Bible Doctrine of Hell and the Unseen": Sermon by the Rev. P. T. Forsyth, Preached in the Bradford Road Congregational Church, Shipley, Nov. 23rd'
'Higher Criticism'	'The Evangelical Churches and the Higher Criticism'
'Ibsen's Treatment'	'Ibsen's Treatment of Guilt'
'Immanence'	'Immanence and Incarnation'
'Immortality'	'The Argument for Immortality Drawn from the Nature of Love: A Lecture on Lord Tennyson's "Vastness"'
'Inner Life'	'The Inner Life of Christ'
'Institute Library'	'The Rev. P. T. Forsyth, MA, on "Contents of the [Saltaire] Institute Library"'

'Insufficiency'	'The Insufficiency of Social Righteousness as a Moral Idea'
'Intellectualism'	'Intellectualism and Faith'
Intercessory Services	*Intercessory Services for Aid in Public Worship*
Jesus	*The Preaching of Jesus and the Gospel of Christ*
'Jowett'	'The Chairman's Mantle: Dr Forsyth to Mr Jowett'
Justification	*The Justification of God: Lectures for War-Time on a Christian Theodicy*
'Land Laws'	'Land Laws of the Bible'
'Letter 1877'	'Letter'. *English Independent*, 1877
'Letter 1911'	'Letter'. *British Weekly*, 1911
'Letter to Nicoll'	'Letter to William Robertson Nicoll, 25 November'
'Liberal'	'Why am I a Liberal?'
'Liberty and Limits'	'Liberty and Its Limits in the Church'
Life	*This Life and the Next: The Effect on This Life of Faith in Another*
'Love of Liberty'	'The Love of Liberty and the Love of Truth'
Maid Arise	*'Maid, Arise': A Sermon to School Girls. Preached in Shipley Congregational Church, Sunday 28 July 1878*
'Majesty'	'Majesty and Mercy'
Marriage	*Marriage: Its Ethic and Religion*
Mercy	*Mercy the True and Only Justice: A Sermon Preached in Shipley Congregational Church, on the Missionary Sunday, September 30, 1877*
'Metaphysic'	'Faith, Metaphysic, and Incarnation'
'Ministerial Libraries'	'Ministerial Libraries: V. Principal Forsyth's Library at Hackney College'
Missions	*Missions in State and Church: Sermons and Addresses*
'Missions'	'Missions the Soul of Civilisation'
'Moral Principle'	'The Cross of Christ as the Moral Principle of Society'
'Moralization'	'The Moralization of Religion'
'Mystics'	'Mystics and Saints'
'Nationality'	'Christianity and Nationality'
'New Theology'	'The "New Theology": Mr Campbell's Teaching Criticised: A Repudiation'
'New Year'	'A New Year Meditation'
'Newest Theology'	'The Newest Theology'

Old Faith	*The Old Faith and the New*
'Ordination Address'	'Ordination Address, 20 October'
'Orthodoxy'	'Orthodoxy, Heterodoxy, Heresy and Freedom'
'Paradise Lost'	'"Milton's Paradise Lost": Lecture by the Rev. P. T. Forsyth, M.A.'
'Paradox'	'The Paradox of Christ'
'Paralytic'	'The Healing of the Paralytic'
Parnassus	*Christ on Parnassus: Lectures on Art, Ethic, and Theology*
Person	*The Person and Place of Jesus Christ: The Congregational Union Lecture for 1909*
'Pocket of Gold'	'"A Pocket of Gold". Review of *The Way, the Truth, and the Life*, by F. A. J. [sic] Hort'
'Positive Gospel'	'The Need for a Positive Gospel'
Prayer	*The Soul of Prayer*
Preaching	*Positive Preaching and the Modern Mind*
'Present Unrest'	'The Attitude of the Church to the Present Unrest'
'Principle of Liberty'	'Congregationalism and the Principle of Liberty'
'Protestantism'	'The Protestantism of the Protestant Religion'
'Public Impotence'	'The Public Impotence of Religion'
Pulpit	*The Pulpit and the Age*
'Rallying Ground'	'A Rallying Ground for the Free Churches: The Reality of Grace'
'Reading the Bible'	'A Few Hints about Reading the Bible'
'Reality'	'The Reality of God: A War-time Question'
'Regeneration – I'	'Regeneration, Creation, and Miracle'
'Regeneration – II'	'Regeneration, Creation, and Miracle: Second Article'
'Religious Strength'	'The Religious Strength of Theological Reserve'
'Revelation'	'Revelation and the Person of Christ'
Revelation	*Revelation Old and New: Sermons and Addresses*
'Robert Browning'	'Teachers of the Century: Robert Browning'
Rome	*Rome, Reform and Reaction: Four Lectures on the Religious Situation*
'Sacramentalism'	'Sacramentalism the True Remedy for Sacerdotalism'
Sacraments	*The Church and the Sacraments*
'Sanctification'	'Christ our Sanctification'
'Sects and Wars'	'Churches, Sects and Wars'
'Self-Denial'	'Self-Denial and Self-Committal'

'Sinless'	'The Preaching of Jesus and the Gospel of Christ. [VII:] The Meaning of a Sinless Christ'
'Slowness'	'The Slowness of God'
Socialism	*Socialism, the Church and the Poor*
Socialism and Christianity	*Socialism and Christianity in Some of Their Deeper Aspects*
Society	*The Church, the Gospel and Society*
'Soul of Christ'	'The Soul of Christ and the Cross of Christ'
'Spiritual Experience'	'The Place of Spiritual Experience in the Making of Theology'
'Spiritual Needs'	'The Spiritual Needs in the Churches'
'Strength'	'The Strength of Weakness'
'Sunday Schools'	'Sunday Schools and Modern Theology'
Theology	*Theology in Church and State*
'Thomas Hardy'	'The Pessimism of Mr Thomas Hardy'
'Unity and Theology'	'Unity and Theology: A Liberal Evangelicalism the True Catholicism'
'Valedictory Address'	'"Valedictory Address", delivered in June, 1909, based on 1 Corinthians 4:1'
'Veracity'	'Veracity, Reality, and Regeneration'
War	*The Christian Ethic of War*
'Way of Life'	'The Way of Life'
'Workers'	'Rev. P. T. Forsyth on "The Workers of the Future"'
Work	*The Work of Christ*
World-Commonwealth	*The Roots of a World-Commonwealth*

Foreword

Despite a brief renaissance of interest in his thought at the end of the twentieth century, the work of Peter Taylor Forsyth remains largely forgotten in the second decade of the twenty-first. Yet for those who have not forgotten him, returning to his writings again and again for theological enrichment and spiritual insight alike, he remains one of the genuinely great theologians of the modern era, if greatness be measured here by the scale and nature of response to the major theological questions which dominated not just a former generation, but every generation since, and not merely by the prejudices and conventions embodied in the received canons and curricula of historical theology. The theological pyrotechnics erupting on the European mainland in the immediate wake of the 1914–18 war no doubt deserve their prominent place in such narratives, but it is a pity that they have all too often displaced the attention due to a series of first-rank British theologians, the Scots among whom in particular (Denney, Mackintosh, Caird as well as Forsyth himself) were already engaging critically and constructively with the best and worst of the Germanic Protestant tradition, sometimes anticipating quite uncannily some of the key moves made with much more noise and to much more acclaim on the other side of the North Sea, whether in Basel, Marburg or elsewhere. Admittedly, Forsyth's writings are also difficult to read in their way, at least at first, and especially in a culture which can hardly cope with any gratification deferred beyond the second clause or so of a sentence. And yet, idiosyncratic and verbose though they often are, and difficult too in their unashamed grappling with theological and religious issues resistant to any easy or trivial treatment, Forsyth's works quickly reward the patient reader, opening up a distinctive vista on the world as viewed through the eyes of a Christian faith steeped in the heritage of both Scripture and tradition, and relentless in its imaginative and intelligent interrogation of these to illuminate and account for the fundamental moral realities of human life lived not just in the world but in the presence of a God best characterized as 'holy love'.

Like much of the best Christian theology across the centuries, Forsyth is at his most relevant when he refuses to pursue relevance as an end in itself, choosing instead to remain faithful to his calling to articulate often unpopular and unpalatable truths as he perceived them, nonetheless, to be. His conflict with the so-called New Theology of his day (which was in reality, he believed, little more than the residue remaining after a biblically informed faith had been filtered through the mesh of contemporary intellectual prejudices and dogmas) is for that very reason still instructive and inspiring both in its method and its content for those who would wrestle afresh with parallel questions in our own day. Forsyth, though, is anything but conservative in his disposition, occasionally sailing rather too close to the wind of independent thought for some of those whose theological commitments were finally to the letter of some orthodox -ism or other rather than to the disruptive effects of an evangelical encounter with the cross of Christ and its radical implications for our thinking about all manner of subjects. So, Forsyth is refreshingly hard to classify in theological terms. And his thought is organic rather than logically systematic: Everything finally holds together, but hardly anything can be considered and defined in neat isolation or squeezed into a box for convenient containment and analysis in the abstract. This being the case, there are various possible routes into the larger body of Forsyth's thought, though all will find their way eventually (and sooner rather than later) to its doctrinal heartbeat and centre of gravity – the cross of Christ, the place where both simple faith and theology (which is simply 'faith thinking') are driven ever and again to their knees. Interpretations unduly constrained by the limits of traditional creedal or doctrinal categories, though, may nonetheless find themselves struggling to keep up, and frustrated by the semantic excess and overspill.

As even a fleeting glance at some of his writings quickly reveals, Forsyth was particularly fond of the Lord's Prayer, rejuvenating its familiarity dulled phraseology with readings which are frequently striking both for their apparent novelty and for the sense of self-authenticating authority that they bear. It is fitting, therefore, that in this fine new study of Forsyth's theology, Jason Goroncy proposes the 'hallowing of God's name' as affording one fruitful point of entry into the larger body of that theology as a whole. Forsyth's own distinctive reading of the relevant dominical petition fuses together aspects of his doctrines of God, the atonement and redemption, the person of Christ, the Church, and creation and the last things, where the hallowing of God's name (by a reciprocal holiness issuing from the side of the creature) is first envisaged and purposed, and then finally secured, a triumph of holy love which is in a deep sense demanded as much for God's own sake as for ours. Dr Goroncy's expertise and authority as an interpreter both of Forsyth and of the wider cultural and theological milieux within which his writing must be situated is more than apparent on every page, but it is combined wonderfully with an accessibility and elegance of written style which makes reading a genuine pleasure and learning a happy by-product of the whole enjoyable process.

If there is hope yet for a renewed lease of interest in P. T. Forsyth's substantial contribution to Christian theology (and it is to be hoped, both for the sake of theology and the life of the church that there may indeed be such), such hope lies in innovative and engaging readings of his work such as this one which, quite apart from its merits and importance as a study of Forsyth himself, brings to the fore in a thoroughly Forsythian manner the unashamed but intelligent articulation of insights earthed in the heart of the Christian gospel, making them available to a church (and a world) sorely in need of the peculiar word of judgement and grace, and grace *through* judgement, which that gospel alone entails. This is a book which requires no recommendation other than its own excellence, but it gives me enormous personal pleasure to recommend it nonetheless.

Trevor Hart
Professor of Divinity
St Mary's College
St Andrews

Prolegomenon

The year that Richard Wagner began writing the libretto that would become *Der Ring des Nibelungen* witnessed great turmoil in Europe. Karl Marx's *Manifesto* trumpeted the ultimate triumph of the proletariat and the creation of a classless, lawless and socialist utopia. February witnessed Paris' revolt against King Louis Philippe which led to France's Second Republic with 'Prince' Louis-Napoléon Bonaparte elected as its first president. The following months saw revolution in Hungary, pro-republic demonstrations in Stockholm and the Matale Rebellion against British rule in Ceylon. At the same time, prophets like Søren Kierkegaard scornfully dismissed revolutionist dreams and the new *Zeitgeist* as leading to nothing but a new form of servitude under regimes that surpassed anything yet known in their brutality and claims to unbridled power.

The year was 1848. On 12 May, some 915 kilometres away (in a land under the burden of a disastrous potato famine) and as far away again culturally, one was born who would see as deeply into the true nature of life as Kierkegaard had done, sharing the Dane's critical diagnoses of human self-confidence, his faith in God, and his conviction that the way to true life would take one through the crucible of suffering of the kind with which God was personally familiar. Peter Taylor Forsyth was born in Aberdeen to Isaac Forsyth (a merchant, book courier and then postman who made 11 shillings a week, and who loved reading) and Elspet McPherson (the housekeeper to Peter Taylor). Forsyth, the first of five children, was baptized at Old Machar, by the Rev. W. Grant. The family resided at 100 Chapel Street, Aberdeen. The home has since been demolished.

1

Coming into Focus: Finding Lenses

The object of Christianity is . . . the glorifying of the Father, the hallowing of his name.[1]

Once one has removed the glasses prescribed for the intellectual dispositions of modernity and replaced them with those especially adjusted for Forsyth's nonpareil idiosyncrasy, then, for the most part, his corpus is not difficult to read. His words and the realities to which they bear witness, however, require time – considerable time. A faithful reading resists the soundbite theology too common to his reception, and to our age. It also requires a certain level of fitness, and a willingness to feel one's way around his landscape. The content of his theology is as demanding and its application as taxing as that Word he seeks to publish. Certainly, it is an unfortunate choice of phrase to speak of 'the simplicity of Forsyth's system'.[2]

To some readers, Forsyth's writing appears to lack an obvious unity and coherence. But studies by Gwilym Griffith, William Bradley, Robert McAfee Brown, John Rodgers, Archibald Hunter, Donald Miller, Browne Barr, Robert Paul, Clifford Pitt, Angus Paddison, Noel Due, Alan Sell, Colin Gunton, Trevor Hart, Leslie McCurdy, Justyn Terry and others suggest otherwise. This essay builds on their labours. Specifically, it explores the question of whether sanctification – or 'hallowing' – may provide a fruitful lens through which to read and evaluate Forsyth's theology. It is certainly not the only lens available. Equal attention could be paid to the themes of authority, Hegelian dialectic, divine kenosis, theodicy, evangelical experience or to the relationship between divine and creaturely freedom, for example. But contrary to Terry's claim that Forsyth 'has relatively little to say regarding sanctification itself',[3] I believe that the schema of hallowing saturates Forsyth's corpus, providing a most profitable lens through which

[1] *Person*, p. 77.

[2] Rufus Theodore Burton, 'Glorious in Holiness: The Holiness of God in the Reformed Tradition' (unpublished doctoral dissertation, University of London, 2004), p. 123.

[3] Justyn Terry, *The Justifying Judgement of God: A Reassessment of the Place of Judgement in the Saving Work of Christ* (Milton Keynes: Paternoster, 2007), p. 103.

to approach Forsyth's work, and serving as a central referent for his thought in a way that takes due account of his broad vision and interests. The latter is not altogether surprising for, more than most theologians, Forsyth helps us comprehend holiness as a reality of utmost practical import.

Robert McAfee Brown correctly observes that, for Forsyth, 'the central fact of the Christian gospel is God's gracious action in Christ'.[4] But central facts are not identical to those realities which undergird and motivate them. This essay will explore what Forsyth considers to be *God's* central concern and will argue that it is, in all its profundity, the hallowing of God's name. This is the prime concern, Forsyth insists, not only of the Gospel writers, but also of St Paul. Indeed, Forsyth insists, 'all the Pauline Atonement is in "Hallowed be Thy name"'.[5] The incarnation of the Word in Mary's womb, and the arrival of the Spirit, represent God's self-determination to answer what Karl Barth refers to as the Lord's Prayer's 'primary petition'.[6] Christian dogmatics contends that this petition is asked *and answered* by, in and through one who, though not of this world, has, in the fullness of holy love, audaciously identified himself with it. This one too has a 'name': Jesus, who in the Spirit, presents the Father with 'a perfectly holy Humanity',[7] hallowing God's name *in* the earth. This hallowing action, wholly and exclusively the work of God, transforms humanity's locus and constitution before God, and commands, combs and creates corresponding action. Holy Scripture's way of describing this is to speak of human creatures being made 'participants' in the divine nature (2 Pet. 1.4). However one interprets such participation, the hallowing of God's name is the fashion by which God claims creation for such service and glory. To comprehend Forsyth's theology as an exposition, a preachment, of the first petition of the Lord's Prayer, therefore, is to do more than position Forsyth in a theo-cultural context. It is to understand more fully the ministry of Jesus Christ as the fullest expression of God's creative love, and creation as the beloved of God.

Why is this question worth pursuing? Three reasons might be noted: First, there is a gap in Forsythian studies hereabouts. Indubitably, this in itself is insufficient reason to proceed, but hallowing is so central to Forsyth's thought that it is difficult to believe that such an approach has largely been neglected.[8] Secondly, The Lord's Prayer – from which the grammar of 'hallowing' most obviously comes – clearly informs Forsyth's

[4] Robert McAfee Brown, *P. T. Forsyth: Prophet for Today* (Philadelphia: Westminster Press, 1952), p. 50.

[5] Forsyth, in Robert Mackintosh, 'The Authority of the Cross', *Congregational Quarterly* 21 (1943), pp. 209–18 (214). Forsyth makes numerous direct references to this petition: *Authority*, pp. 45, 378; *Cruciality*, pp. 7, 39, 204, 209; *Father*, pp. 5, 24; *Jesus*, pp. 20, 25, 71, 74; *Justification*, pp. 11, 25, 107, 125, 150–51, 155, 165, 169, 194; *Missions*, p. 336; *Person*, p. 40; *Preaching*, p. 107; *Prayer*, pp. 28–29, 36, 75–76; *Sacraments*, p. 255; *Society*, pp. 11, 14; *War*, pp. 39, 53, 58, 141, 184; *Work*, pp. 150–51, 205; cf. *Freedom*, pp. 36–37, 261, 268; *Marriage*, p. 150; *Missions*, p. 334; *Person*, pp. 77, 120, 313; *Theology*, p. 27; *passim*.

[6] Karl Barth, *Church Dogmatics IV.2* (ed. Geoffrey W. Bromiley and Thomas F. Torrance; trans. Geoffrey W. Bromiley; Edinburgh: T&T Clark, 1958), p. 501.

[7] *Person*, p. 313.

[8] Two notable exceptions are Clifford A. McKay, 'The Moral Structure of Reality in the Theology of Peter Taylor Forsyth' (unpublished doctoral dissertation, Vanderbilt University, 1970) and Trevor A. Hart, 'Morality, Atonement and the Death of Jesus: The Crucial Focus of Forsyth's Theology', in *Justice the True and Only Mercy: Essays on the Life and Theology of Peter Taylor Forsyth* (ed. Trevor A. Hart; Edinburgh: T&T Clark, 1995), pp. 16–36.

theology, not only his soteriology (which is the focus of this book) but also his ecclesiology, and his understanding of the role of the State, of marriage and of the arts, *et cetera*. Particularly, its opening petition is so prevalent in Forsyth's writing that it invites consideration as an interpretive cue for engaging with his entire corpus. Thirdly, Forsyth's readers could use some help in seeing the systematic nature of his project. This thematic approach may reveal that Forsyth is somewhat less unsystematic than he has often been accused, though one must be careful to qualify terms here, and not overstate the case. The question of whether or not this is a subtle attempt to unfairly 'systematize' Forsyth can only be answered by the reader. For my part, I trust that I have not done so.

The study will adopt the following trajectory:

Chapter 1 will attend to questions of methodology and to what kind of theologian Forsyth is. Some attention will be given to Forsyth's writing style, apart from which an appreciation of his theology is incomplete. Chapter 2 will position Forsyth in the social context of his day, introduce the theological landscape and grammar from which he expounds his notion of reality as fundamentally moral, and identify some of the key but neglected voices that inform such a vision. Chapter 3 will explore the principal locale wherein the first petition of the Lord's Prayer is answered; namely, in Jesus Christ who is holiness incarnate, the kingdom in person, and God's perfectly obedient Son who, in confessing holiness 'from sin's side', bears its judgement against sin and creates a new humanity. Chapter 4 will examine Forsyth's moral anthropology: specifically, the self-recovery of holiness in the human conscience. It will outline that humanity is created, elected and sanctified to mirror the God of holy love and to be God's counterpart in creation. And it will probe Forsyth's understanding of the human conscience as our moral centre, as the reflection of where humanity's unity lies, and as the locus of divine judgement. The chapter will conclude with a brief review of the experience of the new conscience in relation to matters of perfection, faith, suffering and ethics. Chapter 5 will inquire whether Forsyth's theology of hallowing finally requires him to embrace dogmatic soteriological universalism.

I. Serviceableness and circumscription

Typically, assessments of Forsyth's theology have proceeded along thematic lines: notably christology, authority, revelation, art criticism, sacraments, homiletics and scripture.[9] Mostly, this approach has served well to introduce readers to Forsyth's theological trajectories. However, such efforts have in some cases and to various degrees

[9] For example, Colin E. Gunton, 'Authority and Freedom: P. T. Forsyth's *The Principle of Authority*', in *Theology Through the Theologians: Selected Essays 1972–1995* (Edinburgh: T&T Clark, 1999), pp. 221–42; George Pattison, *Art, Modernity and Faith* (London: SCM Press, 1988), pp. 78–99; Jeremy Begbie, 'The Ambivalent Rainbow: Forsyth, Art and Creation', in *Justice the True and Only Mercy: Essays on the Life and Theology of Peter Taylor Forsyth* (ed. Trevor A. Hart; Edinburgh: T&T Clark, 1995), pp. 197–219; James Michael Gray, 'An Atonement Theology for South Africa: Preaching the Cross Using Insights from the Atonement Theology of P. T. Forsyth' (unpublished doctoral dissertation, University of St Andrews, 2000).

tendered to smother the broader and creative sub-structure of Forsyth's thought. Less constraining contributions have been offered in edited volumes by Trevor Hart and Alan Sell, and in Leslie McCurdy's commendable study on 'Holy Love'.[10] Forsyth's theology encourages such an approach. The appearance of these essays has made evident that while there will remain a place to explore a theologian's thought along more traditional or creedal lines, we have reached a certain level of exhaustion in so evaluating Forsyth's work. Approaching Forsyth's work through the lens of hallowing recognizes a unity and coherence to what might otherwise seem to be an unstructured corpus. However, we must beware of over-reaching here, or of forcing valuable insights into a convenient system. Life is not like that, and neither will fidelity to Forsyth's writing allow us to so proceed.

'We cannot merely repeat, but must translate what he said and did, even as he was no mere "repeater" but always a translator. We can, however, let him serve as a warning sign and a corrective. For our faithfulness to the fathers of the faith does not consist in our copying them but in our comprehending them.'[11] So wrote Helmut Thielicke regarding C. H. Spurgeon. Thielicke's words remind us that, quotable as Forsyth is,[12] we honour his ideas best not merely by reproducing them, but by engaging with them, by moving beyond them, just as Forsyth moved beyond his teachers. To be sure, my concern in this present study is to present Forsyth's thought faithfully and, as I am able, to let Forsyth speak for himself; at times I attempt to translate him for our age. Where I do have reservations about Forsyth's thinking, and insofar as they are germane to our study, these will be raised and responses offered.[13]

I am concerned to plug some holes in Forsyth scholarship, but with a view to showing how such plugs inform the broader landscape of Forsyth's soteriology. I am not especially concerned to impose a pattern of consistency on Forsyth's thinking. Indeed, for this enthusiast of paradox, such an attempt would prove futile.[14] Instead, I wish to accept the fragmentary and occasional nature of his writings, the density of his thought and the capital of his experience. Jim Gordon's treatment of James Denney identifies a major shortcoming that attends many essays that seek to systematize

[10] Trevor A. Hart (ed.), *Justice the True and Only Mercy: Essays on the Life and Theology of Peter Taylor Forsyth* (Edinburgh: T&T Clark, 1995); Alan P. F. Sell (ed.), *P T Forsyth: Theologian for a New Millennium* (London: The United Reformed Church, 2000); Leslie C. McCurdy, *Attributes and Atonement: The Holy Love of God in the Theology of P. T. Forsyth* (Carlisle: Paternoster, 1998).

[11] Helmut Thielicke, *Encounter with Spurgeon* (trans. John W. Doberstein; London: James Clarke & Co., 1964), p. 44.

[12] So Charles S. Duthie, 'The Faith of P. T. Forsyth', *British Weekly*, 17 December 1964, p. 9: 'The trouble about quoting from Forsyth is that once you start, it is very difficult to call a halt.'

[13] One recalls here words by Slavoj Žižek in his 'Foreword: Hallward's Fidelity to the Badiou Event', in *Badiou: A Subject to Truth* by Peter Hallward (Minneapolis: University of Minnesota Press, 2003), p. xii: Fidelity is 'not dogmatic allegiance and blind repetitive résumé. Philosophical fidelity is not fidelity to all that an author has written, but fidelity to what is in the author more than the author himself (more than the empirical multitude of his writings), to the impulse that activates the author's endless work'.

[14] It seems that Forsyth, like the Apostle Paul, uses paradox 'because he wants to make sure that God's way cannot be mentally digested and that Christ's death cannot be announced except through the rhetoric of exaggeration'. Jean-Noël Aletti, 'God Made Christ to be Sin (2 Corinthians 5:21): Reflections on a Pauline Paradox', in *The Redemption: An Interdisciplinary Symposium on Christ as Redeemer* (ed. Stephen T. Davis et al.; Oxford: Oxford University Press, 2004), p. 120.

thought without reference to context: 'It flattens the intellectual topography of ideas, making it impossible to appreciate the contours, scale and perspective which indicate how the landscape took shape.'[15] While I hope that this study resists such crude 'decontextualized reconstruction', Forsyth studies (including this one) would be well served by the publication of an intellectual biography along the lines of Gordon's work on Denney, or Gabriella Fiori's on Simone Weil.[16]

II. Past receptions

Forsyth's contemporaries and Britain's neglect

'We students worshipped him, and would not have exchanged our poverty-stricken little Hackney College, with him as its Principal, for Oxford, Harvard and Heidelberg rolled into one.'[17] So penned H. F. Lovell Cocks, one of the longest surviving of Forsyth's students, who died in 1983. Cocks' words recall for us that despite his critics, Forsyth was a much loved and popular teacher whose impact on his first generation of students is clear.[18] Sydney Cave, for example, who became Principal of New College London, was not the first Nonconformist to decline Oxbridge; but that he did so in order to sit under the Aberdonian at Hackney College speaks volumes of Forsyth's draw.[19] Although receiving widely sourced praise as 'the most able theologian associated with the evangelical movement at the turn of the century',[20] as the 'greatest of Free Church theologians' in the Edwardian Age,[21] and as that 'outstanding Congregationalist theologian',[22] the bulk of Forsyth's theological output has largely gone ignored. British

[15] James M. Gordon, *James Denney (1856–1917): An Intellectual and Contextual Biography* (Milton Keynes: Paternoster, 2006), p. 8.

[16] Gabriella Fiori, *Simone Weil: An Intellectual Biography* (trans. J. R. Berrigan; Athens/London: University of Georgia Press, 1989). I have sketched the beginnings of such in Jason A. Goroncy, 'Preaching *sub specie crucis*: An Introduction to the Preaching Ministry of P. T. Forsyth', in *'Descending on Humanity and Intervening in History': Notes from the Pulpit Ministry of P. T. Forsyth* (ed. Jason A. Goroncy; Eugene, OR: Pickwick Publications, 2012), 2013.

[17] H. F. Lovell Cocks, 'P. T. Forsyth, "A Voice from A Better Future"', *British Weekly*, 6 May 1948, p. 7.

[18] See H. F. Lovell Cocks, 'The Message of P. T. Forsyth', *Congregational Quarterly* 26, no. July (1948), pp. 214–21 (214); H. F. Lovell Cocks, *The Wondrous Cross* (London: Independent Press, 1957), p. 17; Alan Green, 'Personal Memories of P. T. Forsyth', *British Weekly*, 13 May 1948, p. 11; Sidney F. Wicks, 'He Loved the Children in Cheetham Hill: A Tribute to Dr Peter Taylor Forsyth, Great Theologian', *Manchester City News*, 23 September 1949, np; T. Hywel Hughes, 'Dr. Forsyth's View of the Atonement', *Congregational Quarterly* 18 (1940), pp. 30–37.

[19] Alfred Cave, Sydney's uncle, was a student at New College between 1866 and 1872. Forsyth proceeded him there upon his acceptance in probation in September 1872. In 1899, Alfred Cave and Forsyth addressed the Second International Congregational Council in Boston. Cave spoke on 'The Living Christ', and Forsyth on 'The Evangelical Principle of Authority'. Forsyth succeeded Alfred Cave as principal of Hackney College upon Cave's untimely death on 19 December 1900; Forsyth taking up charge in the Spring of 1901.

[20] Stephen R. Holmes, 'British (and European) Evangelical Theologies', in *The Cambridge Companion to Evangelical Theology* (ed. Timothy Larsen and Daniel J. Treier; Cambridge: Cambridge University Press, 2007), p. 250.

[21] Adrian Hastings, *A History of English Christianity 1920–1990* (London: SCM Press, 1991), p. 108.

[22] Hans Urs von Balthasar, *Mysterium Paschale: The Mystery of Easter* (trans. Aidan Nichols; Edinburgh: T&T Clark, 1990), p. 35.

evangelicalism's relationship with neo-orthodoxy may be partly responsible. But why has interest in Forsyth's work generally lagged in Britain whereas interest in Barth seems to have taken deeper root, shaping more significantly the landscape of British theology, especially in Scotland?[23]

Until relatively recently, Nonconformist theologians have typically struggled to be taken seriously in Britain, particularly south of the border. The dominance of Anglicanism, and its somewhat triumphalistic stance, made it impervious to Nonconformist contributions.[24] Moreover, being so self-contained, Conformists disdained Nonconformity for social reasons, and so, with some exceptions, rarely bothered with Dissenting thought. Had Forsyth been a Presbyterian and remained in Scotland, the reception of his thought may well have been otherwise. Forsyth was also the victim of other circumstances. As will be noted in due course, he was a demanding theologian, both conceptually and stylistically, and was swimming against a doctrinal stream even among fellow Dissenters. While Forsyth may have been what the mind of his time needed, he was not what it wanted. Those, however, who took the time to comprehend his thought discovered in him deep theological acumen, a catholic spirit and rugged footing for life and for ministry.

Post-war interest and beyond

Forsyth once suggested that his words could not be fully appreciated until intellectualism had been cured, and that that cure would have to wait on history. I will not speculate here about whether Forsyth's *kairos* has come. I will recount, however, an event that

[23] See D. Densil Morgan, *Barth Reception in Britain* (London/New York: T&T Clark, 2010). Morgan treats Forsyth on pp. 67–68; also Alister E. McGrath, *T. F. Torrance: An Intellectual Biography* (Edinburgh: T&T Clark, 1999), pp. 32, 115–17, 121–25. R. F. Thompson cites F. W. Camfield's (one of Forsyth's former students) communication from late 1939 about Barth's and Brunner's knowledge of Forsyth: 'I have not come across any books or articles which tend to draw out the relationship between Forsyth and Barth, and I do not know that any have been written. Of direct connection there is none, for I have recently asked both Barth and Brunner whether they had heard of Forsyth and neither of them had'. Robert Franklin Thompson, 'Peter Taylor Forsyth: A Pre-Barthian' (unpublished doctoral dissertation, Drew University, 1940), pp. 177–78. Writing around the same time, Lovell Cocks wrote: 'Karl Barth's son tells me that the work of Forsyth has only recently been brought to the attention of his father'. Cited in Thompson, 'Forsyth: A Pre-Barthian', p. 179. Brunner's ignorance of Forsyth is odd given he spent almost a year in England (1913–14) when Forsyth was at the peak of his theological career. To be sure, Brunner's time in England was concerned primarily with learning English. He was also more interested at that time in governmental theory (socialism and democracy) than in theology. However, by the time he came to pen the first volume of his *Dogmatik: Die christliche Lehre von Gott* (1946), he had read Forsyth. See Emil Brunner, *The Christian Doctrine of God, Dogmatics Volume 1* (trans. Olive Wyon; London: Lutterworth Press, 1949), p. 92; Emil Brunner, *The Christian Doctrine of Creation of Redemption, Dogmatics Volume 2* (trans. Olive Wyon; London: Lutterworth Press, 1958), p. 315. Brunner also praised Forsyth in a 1961 television interview. When asked, 'Who do you think is our greatest British theologian of recent times?', Brunner, after a brief compliment about Dodd, stated, 'As for my field, systematic theology, I would mention a man who died about forty years ago, P. T. Forsyth'. Emil Brunner, 'Emil Brunner on his Faith and Work: Television Interview with Vernon Sproxton', *The Listener* 65 (1961), pp. 307–08 (307, 308).

[24] See Colin E. Gunton, 'The Nature of Systematic Theology: Anselm of Canterbury, Samuel Taylor Coleridge and the Possibility of an English Systematic Theology', in *Theology Through the Theologians: Selected Essays 1972–1995* (Edinburgh: T&T Clark, 1999), p. 2.

took place on the evening of 10 June 1948, when staff, students and other interested parties gathered in College Hall of New College, London (formerly Hackney and New College) to celebrate the 275th anniversary of the College's founding by John Lawrence of the Harmondsworth Charity on 17 May 1673. Among the names of the 'pious Founders and Benefactors' that were commemorated that evening, two were given special mention: Alfred Cave and Forsyth. Of Forsyth it was noted:

> P. T. FORSYTH was in that great Scottish succession of poor boys who at all odds won themselves an education, though his physical delicacy handicapped him in his student days, as it did throughout his life, without frustrating his purpose. His warfare accomplished, he had fought a good fight, and we are entered into his conquest; the fruits of his victories are ours and his influence deepens, rather than lessens, through the years.
>
> He was a brilliant scholar, and upon his death the Governors of the then New College, London, said he was the College's 'most distinguished alumnus'. He was a great preacher; in that and in his teaching the Cross was crucial. He had a questing, penetrating mind and a gift of flashing wit. Out of his own experience he became skilled in spiritual things.
>
> We of New College, London, remember with particular pride that there were always those, chiefly connected with the College, who knew him, in his earthly life, to be a prophet. At this first Commemoration since the centenary of his birth we are thankful that his teaching is now being more and more widely understood and appropriated. We rejoice in the honour of his name.[25]

Certainly, while Forsyth hoped to influence his own generation more than he did, it was the next generation (introduced to his thought though the re-publication of a number of his works to mark the centenary of his birth) who most valued and evaluated his work, whether in Britain, North America or Japan.[26] By 1946, all of Forysth's books

[25] Anonymous, '275th Commemoration' (London: New College, 1948), p. 3.

[26] See Forsyth Society, *Forsyth-kenkyu [Forsyth Studies]* (Tokyo: Forsyth Society, 1932–35); Saburo Ishijima, *Gaisetsu Forsyth-shingaku* (Tokyo: Nagasaki-shoten, 1938). And Japanese interest in Forsyth's work has continued. See Hiroshi Ōmiya, *Fōsaisu Shohan* (Hito to shisō shirīzu; Tōkyō: Nihon Kirisuto Kyōdan Shuppanbu, 1965); Kazoh Kitamori, *Theology of the Pain of God* (Richmond: John Knox Press, 1965), pp. 51, 56, 60, 83, 181; Masaichi Takemori, 'Scottish Theology and the Church and Theology in Japan', *Theological Studies in Japan* 14 (1975), pp. 16–17, 161–77; Akio Hashimoto, 'An Analysis of the Theology of Pain of God', *ATA Journal* 3, no. 2 (1995), pp. 49–69 (61); Yasuo Furuya, *A History of Japanese Theology* (Grand Rapids: Wm. B. Eerdmans, 1997), pp. 33, 48–50; Hisakazu Inagaki and J. Nelson Jennings, *Philosophical Theology and East-West Dialogue* (Amsterdam/Atlanta: Rodopi, 2000), pp. 24, 98–99, 105, 108, 123; J. Nelson Jennings, *Theology in Japan: Takakura Tokutaro (1885–1934)* (Lanham: University of America Press, 2005), pp. 171–77; Yutaka Morishima, 'God's Holiness in P. T. Forsyth: Through Influence of R. W. Dale', *Theological Studies in Japan* 46 (2007), pp. 101–18; Hiroshi Ōmiya (ed.), *Fōsaisu shingaku gairon: jūjika no shingaku* (Tōkyō: Kyōbunkan, 2011); J. Nelson Jennings, 'Who Did They Say That He Is?: Four Hopeful and Suffering Generations of Japanese-Reformed Christologies', *Global Missiology* 4, no. 8 (2011): http://ojs.globalmissiology.org/index.php/english/article/view/610/1533. See also Naoya Kawakami's dissertation on the reception of Forsyth's thought in Japan, published as 日本におけるフォーサイス受容の研究　-神学の現代的課題の探求 (Tokyo: Christian Literature Society of Japan, 2012).

were out of print, but in 1952, Robert McAfee Brown noted that increasing numbers of American seminary students were embracing Forsyth as 'one who can rescue them either from an outworn liberalism or from a stale orthodoxy', and who provided them with a 'positive gospel'.[27] The following year, Ray Allen observed something of a renaissance of interest in Forsyth, and attributed it in part to Forsyth's being 'a Biblical theologian'.[28] Another reason for the renewed assessment of Forsyth's theological achievement was the discovery that he had anticipated many themes which engrossed Barth in his own protests against the liberalism (Ritschlian and other) that so dominated the theological landscape at the dawn of the twentieth century.

Brown over-optimistically suggests that the impact of two world wars has 'removed the heady optimism that seemed in Forsyth's lifetime to make his "positive gospel" redundant to forward-looking Christians'.[29] However much the machineries of violence – whether state-sanctioned or otherwise – destabilize human pride and underscore humanity's moral crisis, the feeling is always too short-lived. It is for this reason, among others, that the gospel which Forsyth so faithfully bears witness to will continue to remain as fresh and as germane as ever. Recent studies suggest an unabated interest in Forsyth in the English-speaking world,[30] and Gunton highlights Forsyth's abiding theological merit for students of British theology:

[27] Brown, *Prophet for Today*, p. 10.

[28] Ray Maxwell Allen, 'The Christology of P. T. Forsyth' (unpublished doctoral dissertation, Duke University, 1953), 289. Allen's was one of at least ten doctoral dissertations to be completed on Forsyth in the 1940s and 1950s. Details in Leslie McCurdy, 'Bibliography', in *Justice the True and Only Mercy: Essays on the Life and Theology of Peter Taylor Forsyth* (ed. Trevor A. Hart; Edinburgh: T&T Clark, 1995), pp. 301–03.

[29] Robert McAfee Brown, 'P. T. Forsyth', in *A Handbook of Christian Theologians* (ed. Martin E. Marty and Dean G. Peerman; Cleveland: World Publishing, 1965), p. 147.

[30] See Richard L. Floyd, *When I Survey the Wondrous Cross: Reflections on the Atonement* (San Jose: Pickwick Publications, 2000); Sell (ed.), *PT Forsyth: Theologian for a New Millennium*; D. W. Widdicombe, 'Theology and Experience: Methodological Issues in the Theology of P. T. Forsyth' (unpublished doctoral dissertation, Oxford University, 2000); Jason A. Goroncy, 'Bitter Tonic for Our Time – Why the Church Needs the World: Peter Taylor Forsyth on Henrik Ibsen', *European Journal of Theology* 15, no. 2 (2006), pp. 105–18; Jason A. Goroncy, 'Fighting Troll-Demons in Vaults of the Mind and Heart – Art, Tragedy and Sacramentality: Some Observations from Ibsen, Forsyth and Dostoevsky', *Princeton Theological Review* 13, no. 1 (2007), pp. 61–85; Terry, *The Justifying Judgement of God*; Jason A. Goroncy, 'The Elusiveness, Loss, and Cruciality of Recovered Holiness: Some Biblical and Theological Observations', *International Journal of Systematic Theology* 10, no. 2 (2008), pp. 195–209; Angus Paddison, 'P. T. Forsyth, "the Positive Gospel", and the Church', *Ecclesiology* 5 (2009), pp. 28–47; Theng Huat Leow, '"The Cruciality of the Cross": P. T. Forsyth's Understanding of the Atonement', *International Journal of Systematic Theology* 11, no. 2 (2009), pp. 190–207; Jason A. Goroncy, 'The Final Sanity is Complete Sanctity: Universal Holiness in the Soteriology of P. T. Forsyth (1848–1921)', in *'All Shall Be Well': Explorations in Universalism and Christian Theology, from Origen to Moltmann* (ed. Gregory MacDonald; Eugene, OR: Cascade Books, 2010), pp. 249–79; Matthew Lee Sanders, 'Subordinate but Equal: The Intra-Trinitarian Subordination of the Son to the Father in the Theologies of P. T. Forsyth and Jürgen Moltmann' (unpublished doctoral dissertation, University of St Andrews, 2010); Theng Huat Leow, *The Theodicy of Peter Taylor Forsyth: A 'Crucial' Justification of the Ways of God to Man* (Eugene, OR: Wipf and Stock, 2011); Jason A. Goroncy, '"Tha mi a' toirt fainear dur gearan": J. McLeod Campbell and P. T. Forsyth on the Extent of Christ's Vicarious Ministry', in *Evangelical Calvinism: Essays Resourcing the Continuing Reformation of the Church* (ed. Myk Habets and Bobby Grow; Eugene, OR: Pickwick Publications, 2012), pp. 253–86; Jason A. Goroncy (ed.), *'Descending on Humanity and Intervening in History': Notes from the Pulpit Ministry of P. T. Forsyth* (Eugene, OR: Pickwick Publications, 2013).

> The weakness of the English tradition is that it has produced few of the ability of Scotland's P. T. Forsyth and T. F. Torrance, both of whom are at the very least – like or dislike the content of their theologies as you may – theological talents whose intellectual achievement will continue to live, and on whom a continuing stream of secondary works is to be expected, rather than, say, the occasional doctoral thesis.[31]

III. Forsyth as 'Theologian of the Cross': *Per Crucem ad Lucem*

Forsyth as 'positive' theologian

The Church's theological enterprise, Forsyth boldly intones at the close of the nineteenth century, is in need of reform. Wooed by the 'gnosis of speculation, the occultism of science, the romance of the heart, the mysticism of imagination',[32] it has developed severe laryngitis, lost its footing and failed to maintain the integrity it once carried into the new age. There is no question that the well-worn path of dieting on the gnostic course with its due eloquence, taste and confidence fosters popularity because 'it expresses the formless longings and dim cravings of the subjectivity of the day', but 'accommodation theology' has no future.[33] It does not help that 'vague and romantic intuitions' have borrowed Christianity's mantle and simulated the 'voice of the authentic Word', but the Church's laryngitis, Forsyth contends, is due to a loss of authority and trust in its own historic, foundational and ethical evangel grounded in the incarnate and crucified God.[34]

The Church now faces a situation not unlike that of the fourth century when Athanasius led the charge against that Gnosticism which presented Christianity as culturally noble, philosophically comprehensive, ethically efficient, religiously pluralistic and apotheosically humanitarian, confident of a brave and better future. It was Athanasius, Forsyth contends, who saved the day by carving his distinguished position 'out of the principle of the experienced redemption of a ruined world'. To do this, he, like Forsyth, gravitated towards St Paul 'as the supreme devotee, organ and expositor of Christ' who captured and converted his day's speculation, even coining 'a new metaphysic'.[35]

Raising a road between the twin heresies of 'orthodoxy' and 'liberalism', Forsyth does not, however, recommend a retreat into the past, whether to the first, fourth or sixteenth century. To be sure, he wants the Athanasian Christ but is somewhat less enthusiastic about the Athanasian Creed.[36] He proposes, instead, a positive theology which is related to the genius of the past but unafraid of currents of contemporary

[31] Colin E. Gunton, 'The Nature of Systematic Theology: Anselm of Canterbury, Samuel Taylor Coleridge and the Possibility of an English Systematic Theology', in *Theology Through the Theologians: Selected Essays 1972–1995* (Edinburgh: T&T Clark, 1999), p. 4.

[32] *Preaching*, p. 80.

[33] Ibid., pp. 80, 196.

[34] Ibid., p. 80.

[35] 'Forsyth on Preaching', p. 83.

[36] See *Jesus*, p. 64; *Justification*, p. 87; 'Metaphysic', p. 701; *Person*, p. 229; *Preaching*, p. 70.

thought. Although Congregationalism wades firmly in a Reformation stream, Forsyth is never one to romantically postulate a disentombment of the Reformation or a 'very narrow' Calvinism: 'Nothing is more fatal to the progress of any form of truth than its idolatry, its canonisation, the enthronement in the Church for all time of a rule of faith'.[37] He calls (uniquely for a Nonconformist[38]) for a respectful unsphering of the spirit of John Calvin (along with that of Jonathan Edwards, both 'spiritual giants of the race'), and for a sympathetic appreciation of Calvin's thought coupled with scientific continuity and reinterpretation. Forsyth's confidence in the everlasting gospel, however, means that he is not content to let the grammar employed in the past be redeployed to speak on his behalf in a time of crisis – a crises that came to its head with the loss of confidence in liberal Protestantism, with its failure to speak to a world whose confidence in progress had been buried in the 'chaotic, crater-ridden, uninhabitable, awful . . . abode of madness'[39] – the No Man's Lands of Flanders and France.

> The changeless Gospel must speak with equal facility the language of each new time, as well as of each far land. If it be missionary to every soul it is also missionary to the whole soul of history. There is an ironic, socratic docility in the everlasting Gospel. It must be flexible if it is to search and permeate. It must be tractable and reasonable because it is so supreme and sure. It must have the power to vary, and to meet the forms of thought and life which it does so much to produce. We could never preach to the time if our Gospel had but a lapidary and monumental eternity.[40]

Forsyth entreats that we do theology from Calvin's 'atmosphere of Christian experience'. Calvin's theology – together with Edwards', Dante's, Milton's and Kierkegaard's – was 'like the wounds of Christ, graven on [his] heart and on the palms of [his] hands'. While we ought to modify Calvinism's way of securing it, 'we must ask what their profound and solemn minds aimed at, and what they strove by their system to guarantee'.[41] Thus the requisite continuity with the past is provided not by baptizing Western culture but by recalling the world back to its roots in the gospel itself. At the centre of this recalling, Forsyth believes, was recovery of the cruciality of holiness. This principle of faith – articulated by the Apostle Paul, lost in the rationalization of Chalcedon which 'obscured Redemption' behind the metaphysics of the Incarnation,[42] and recovered in the Reformation – was largely lost again, Forsyth detects, and Forsyth is one of a band who calls for a finishing of the Reformation not through some extraneous

37 *Work*, p. 62; 'Theology in the Future', p. 451.

38 There are few examples of nineteenth-century nonconformist commendations of the Reformation, nor indeed (thanks to Harnack's *History of Dogma*, 1894), of any period in Church history. Here, Forsyth's *Rome, Reform and Reaction* (1899) is quite exceptional.

39 Letter of Wilfred Owen to Susan Owen, dated 4 February 1917, in Wilfred Owen, *The Collected Letters of Wilfred Owen* (ed. Harold Owen and John Bell; Oxford: Oxford University Press, 1967), p. 431.

40 *Preaching*, pp. 140–41.

41 Ibid., p. 93.

42 'Principle of Liberty', p. 512.

principle like or from culture, but through that which arises out of the gospel's own intrinsic power and positive word. Forsyth argues that in Calvin we are given 'a gospel deep enough' with 'all the breadth of the world in its heart'.[43] He also acknowledges that although a modernized 'New Calvinism' is necessary[44] (e.g. a re-forming of the 'intolerable' doctrine of predestination[45]), it requires arduous moral effort: 'it is not easy ... to think our way out of Calvinism into truth more modest and no less mighty ... [It] is laborious moral effort, as well as mental energy, which enables us to keep in the front of our interest that issue of God's freedom, and yet to secure it by other doctrines than those which have now become untenable'.[46] That noted, 'It is better to have the dogma of Melanchthon, or even Calvin, than of Wellhausen or Schmiedel'.[47]

The theology of Forsyth's time was, not unlike the theology of every time it seems, somewhat discombobulated. At a time when Forsyth attacked the amorality of established theology and raised a near-lonely voice in plea for a staurocentric theology of redemption, misidentified and easy optimism was about to be crushed under the press of catastrophic historical events. His plea employed philosophical presuppositions that were more contemporary and more morally sensitive than the philosophical outlook of the subjectivism, liberalism and shallow humanitarianism around him which make religion 'no more that the crown of humanity and the metropolitan province of the world'.[48] However, to describe Forsyth, as Bradley does[49] – as a mediating theologian – is to misjudge Forsyth's theological locale. His is not only far removed from the mediating theology of the mid-nineteenth century, but it also expresses no interest in mediating between positions. His concern is neither to preserve the truths of a 'stiff old orthodoxy'[50] nor to dismantle liberalism per se; nor is he interested in promoting a new system of theology. His concern is, rather, to unleash the reserve of evangelical faith with a new pronunciation – theology with 'a change of accent'.[51] In Theodor Kaftan's terms, Forsyth's is a 'modern theology of the ancient faith'.[52] Still, we must not disregard the mature Forsyth's (post-1891) grounding of his theology in the moral structure of reality foreign to both orthodoxy's negativism and liberalism's hollowness. A few years in the pastorate taught Forsyth that the 'sunny liberalism' he once embraced had no word for the real *moral* location wherein human persons live.

43 *Work*, p. 62.
44 *Freedom*, pp. 254–94.
45 Ibid., pp. 262–64, 302.
46 *Preaching*, p. 98.
47 *Person*, p. 263.
48 *Cruciality*, p. 6; John Huxtable, 'Forsyth, Peter Taylor (1848–1921)', in *Oxford Dictionary of National Biography* (ed. H. C. G. Matthew and Brian Howard Harrison; Oxford: Oxford University Press, 2004), 20:442.
49 William L. Bradley, *P. T. Forsyth: The Man and His Work* (London: Independent Press, 1952), pp. 113–14.
50 'Present Unrest', p. 214.
51 Allen, 'The Christology of P. T. Forsyth', p. 11; cf. Gerald B. Smith, 'The Modern-Positive Movement in Theology', *The American Journal of Theology* 13 (1909), pp. 92–99.
52 Theodor Kaftan, *Vier Kapitel von der Landeskirche* (Schleswig: Julius Bergas, 1903); Theodor Kaftan, *Moderne Theologie des alten Glaubens* (Schleswig: Julius Bergas, 1905). Cf. Theodor Häring, *The Christian Faith: A System of Dogmatics* (trans. John Dickie and George Ferries; vol. 1; London: Hodder & Stoughton, 1915), pp. 122–23.

Written off by the sterile orthodox for espousing the value of biblical criticism, and by theological progressives for promoting an 'out-of-date' gospel, Forsyth carves his own path and refuses to be pigeonholed. His own name for his position is 'heterodox' – the preservation of 'a positive core and a flexible casing'[53] – and he regards himself as a 'large and generous *evangelical*',[54] which he earnestly desires that the Church might again become. He considers himself advancing not a 'theology' but a gospel earthed in the economy of the supreme holiness of God's love. And he champions a return to the personalism and evangelical authority which made the Reformation truly reforming: 'new life and not a new creed, a new power and not a new institution'.[55] British theology, at the time recovering from a stiff and hackneyed orthodoxy, tended to misconceive vagueness for breadth and maudlinism for love. Such sentimentalism, Forsyth insists, threatens to kill the gospel. Conversely, the pastoral task that makes the Church, and the revelation which defines it, is not the 'success' of its members in living up to some religious expectations – as in the prodigal's elder brother in Luke 15 – but rather grace, and that of a kind which regenerates. Accusing his age of being 'unreal, sentimental and impressionist', Forsyth instead seeks to 'go to the bottom of things'[56] and re-ground Christian dogmatics in the positive authority of the great eternities announced in the apostolic word. This is where we must 'continually return, to adjust our compass and take our course . . . It is more than our base, it is our source'.[57] And Forsyth's yearning for ministers of the Word is that 'when we are tired of trying to *impress* people, we may return to the doctrine of a Gospel which regenerates both us and them'.[58] This is part of Forsyth's enduring allure. While some of his ideas deserve more attention,[59] and others are distracting,[60] his theocentric vision resists being contained or defined by passing fads or scaled down to capitulate to human systems.

Forsyth is equally concerned that he communicate this word to the deepest needs of his age utilizing the grammar of his age – grammar which he discerns to be that of the ethical:

> As Anselm co-ordinated his Gospel to the ideas of his age about monarchical honour, or Grotius to those of his time about the moral order, so we adjust our

[53] 'Orthodoxy', p. 322.
[54] Ibid., p. 325.
[55] *Preaching*, p. 210; cf. 'Letter 1877', pp. 1231–32; 'Religion and Reality', p. 548.
[56] *Society*, p. 100.
[57] *Freedom*, pp. 119, 120.
[58] 'Spiritual Needs', p. 255.
[59] For example, (i) a clearer account of the relationship between the moral and the mystical nature of Christian faith and of the Church sacraments; (ii) a more positive account of Jesus' full humanity and of the relationship between Jesus' teaching/healing and his death/resurrection; (iii) a clearer account of the relationship between christology and pneumatology; (iv) greater attention to the matter of the present session of the ascended Son; (v) some assessment of how his social and public theology informs – and is informed by – things nearer to the centre of his thought and the wider global context; (vi) the matter of Israel and the notion of covenant so central to the Bible's witness; (vii) his invaluable conception of pastoral ministry requires especial transposing for contemporary situations.
[60] For example, (i) his relative neglect of the Gospels in preferencing the Epistles; (ii) his sexual stereotyping and the grammar of 'feminine' faith and 'female Christianity'.

> theology to the more spiritual ethic of holiness which the Gospel has brought to pass, and to the new reading of the New Testament. We construe it in terms of holiness, confessing in the act the growing effect on the Church of the Holy Ghost, with His Word for every age, and His deepening of them all.[61]

Anticipating other Nonconformists who aver that 'no movement as fruitful and abiding as Protestantism ever nourished itself in negations',[62] Forsyth champions a 'positive' theology which issues out of the gracious experience of faith as God's act, and faith's dynamic and vital moral reality of relations between persons. Only thus, Forsyth insists, can theology take seriously the moral crisis facing the race and bear witness to God's resolution of such in Christ. He rejoices that the 'pooh-pooh school of Christians' sponsored by their 'cheery prophets' seems to be losing strength, and now abound 'only in the less intelligent denominations'.[63] And he defines 'positive Christianity' thus:

> Positive Christianity then is Christianity which recognizes the primacy of the moral in the shape of life, and of holy life. It is Christianity which first adjusts man to the holy and then creates the holy in man, and does both through the Cross with its atoning gift of eternal life. It is evangelical Christianity – Christianity not as a creed nor as a process but as a Holy Spirit's energy and act, issuing always from the central act and achievement of God and of history in the Cross of Christ.[64]

That Independency understands theology to be the expression rather than the essence of faith is, according to Forsyth, part of its strength: 'Rooted in that freedom we theologise as it compels. For it is the compulsion of a new freedom and not of a new scheme, of a final gospel and not a fixed law'.[65] Thus the moral arena of the will comes to the fore in Forsyth's thinking, as positivity describes the demands on God and human persons and recognizes the cruciality of a redemption that will affect both parties. While he rejects Albrecht Ritschl's gospel as unevangelical, Forsyth does not follow Barth in discarding his former teacher altogether, for he sees in Ritschlian moralism something too requisite to abandon – his world-embracing notion of the kingdom. Just as Ritschl's failure was an evangelical one, Barth's, Forsyth might suggest, was an ethical one. What the Church must recover, Forsyth proposes, is a theology as ethical as it is evangelical and as evangelical as it is ethical. To therefore accuse Forsyth's moralizing of dogma as both narrowing and trivializing 'the Holy', as does Gerhard Forde,[66] is to undervalue Forsyth's confidence that the ethicizing of religion is no prompt application to present

[61] *Authority*, pp. 330–31. This is Forsyth's only direct reference to Grotius. Stott lists Forsyth among twentieth-century theologians (such as Warfield and Brunner) who have taken up Grotius' vision. John R. W. Stott, *The Cross of Christ* (Leicester: IVP, 1986), p. 122.

[62] R. Newton Flew and Rupert E. Davies (eds), *The Catholicity of Protestantism, Being a Report Presented to His Grace the Archbishop of Canterbury by a Group of Free Churchmen* (London: Lutterworth, 1951), p. 14.

[63] 'Pessimism', p. 44.

[64] *Preaching*, p. 139.

[65] *Freedom*, p. 120.

[66] Gerhard O. Forde, 'The Work of Christ', in *Christian Dogmatics* (ed. Carl E. Braaten and Robert W. Jenson; Philadelphia: Fortress, 1984), 2:34.

problems, nor the reduction of religion to ethics, nor faith to cold morality. Rather, by concentrating religion in a crisis between holiness and its opposite – namely, sin – it gives to religion a moral nature, core, focus and soul so absent in liberalism, and so incongruous and repugnant not only to liberalism's 'God' but also to the unfree 'God' of conservative 'orthodoxy' whose entry into and overcoming of the crisis birthed by sin's entry into God's creation is tragically inconspicuous.

Forsyth as 'biblical' theologian

While Forsyth's writings are not bruised with the exegetical work of Calvin or Barth, they nevertheless betray a profound wrestling with Scripture and a mind irrigated with its words, images and themes, not least that of holiness.[67] Strictly, Forsyth may not write as a biblical theologian,[68] but at least one New Testament professor observes that Forsyth 'bottoms all his theological thinking' upon Scripture and that his biblical scholarship was 'twenty or thirty years ahead' of most of the exegetes of his day.[69] Forsyth never wrote a commentary, but this expository preacher – a third of whose library was in German, who read numerous biblical journals every week and who championed the value of biblical criticism to a British audience still hard of hearing – was clearly on top of his game. He is no hypocrite when he writes, 'No man should ask for a public hearing on a theological question unless he has mastered his New Testament at first hand.'[70]

Forsyth is no bibliolatrist, however. An infallible book implies that our primary need is intellectual rather than moral. He believes that it should be difficult for us not to believe in verbal inspiration,[71] but the locus of belief is not the Bible but that word of grace which both creates the Bible and to which the Scriptures faithfully bear witness by the determination of the Spirit. The text itself is of secondary value to the holy intent of its inspiration, Forsyth insists. It is the communication of the gospel itself which elevates the Bible 'above a mere chronicle of events to be dissected and discussed by scholarly pedants'[72] and sets it free to be a 'sacrament' and 'sermon' of the good news.[73] Still, one wishes that Forsyth had shared more with us not only the finished fruit of

[67] That there are over 260 references to the ἁγιάζω word group in the NT (the קדשׁ group occurs over 770 times in the Hebrew Scriptures, and over 700 times in the LXX) testifies to the fact that holiness, sanctification and consecration are central themes therein.

[68] See Samuel J. Mikolaski, 'The Theology of P. T. Forsyth', *Evangelical Quarterly* 36 (1964), pp. 27–41 (36).

[69] Archibald M. Hunter, *P. T. Forsyth: Per Crucem ad Lucem* (London: SCM Press, 1974), p. 31; cf. Archibald M. Hunter, 'P. T. Forsyth Neutestamentler', *The Expository Times* 73 (1962), pp. 100–06; George D. Jackson, 'The Biblical Basis of the Theology of P. T. Forsyth' (unpublished doctoral dissertation, Princeton Theological Seminary, 1952); George D. Jackson, 'The Interpreter at Work: XIV. P. T. Forsyth's Use of the Bible', *Interpretation* 7 (1953), pp. 323–37; Angus Paddison, 'P. T. Forsyth, Scripture, and the Crisis of the Gospel', unpublished paper, University of Nottingham, 2008, pp. 2–22. Not all agreed: See, for example, W. H. Griffith-Thomas, 'Notices of Recent Publications', *Bibliotheca Sacra* 75 (1918), pp. 604–07 (607).

[70] *Preaching*, p. 70.

[71] See ibid., pp. 9–11, 26; *Parnassus*, p. 243; *Authority*, p. 63.

[72] Stephen W. Sykes, 'Theology Through History', in *The Modern Theologians: An Introduction to Christian Theology in the Twentieth Century* (ed. David F. Ford; Oxford: Blackwell, 1997), p. 232.

[73] *Authority*, pp. 134–35, 372–74; 'Sects and Wars', p. 620; *Sacraments*, p. 132; *Society*, pp. 68–69, 80, 125–27; 'Reading the Bible', pp. 530, 542–43; 'Efficiency and Sufficiency', pp. 28–29.

his Bible reading, but also the processes of his mind given to disciplined and attentive exegesis of Holy Scripture. In this sense, one might well wish to look to additional places than Forsyth alone for providing a model for doing systematic theology. But this, in turn, presses further the question, in what sense we can describe Forsyth as a 'systematic' theologian at all?

Forsyth as 'systematic' theologian

> *There are different ways of understanding the adjective 'systematic', and not all are equally helpful.*[74]

The unsystematic tenor of Forsyth's theology has been duly documented.[75] He probably would not have been disturbed by the judgements insofar as he was suspicious of systems and there is something about his approach that makes his work less dated than most. He most certainly would have been concerned, however, if his readers deduced from his aversion to 'systems' that his thought is not governed by and around certain crucial commitments at the heart of Christian truth. At the very least, Forsyth invites a reconsideration of what the adjective 'systematic' in 'systematic theology' might mean. Not only does he believe that the reduction of religion to a system eviscerates it but he also deems that no system is fit for the task of stinging 'the mind and conscience of the evangelicals out of their Hegelian day-dreams into a sense of theological reality and crisis'.[76] One here recalls Frederick Maurice's words regarding his father:

> His thoughts and character were not . . . built up like rows of neatly ordered bricks. Rather, as each new thread of thought was caught by the shuttle of his ever-working mind, it was dashed in and out through all the warp and woof of what had been

[74] Trevor A. Hart, 'Systematic – In What Sense?', in *Out of Egypt: Biblical Theology and Biblical Interpretation* (ed. Craig G. Bartholomew and Anthony Thiselton; Milton Keynes/Grand Rapids: Paternoster/Zondervan, 2004), p. 341.

[75] See H. Hamilton, 'A Review of *Lectures on the Church and the Sacraments* by P. T. Forsyth', *Journal of Theological Studies*, no. 19 (1917), pp. 91–94 (91); W. H. Leembruggen, 'The Witness of P. T. Forsyth – A Theologian of the Cross', *Reformed Theological Review* (1945), pp. 18–46 (34); F. W. Camfield, 'Peter Taylor Forsyth', *The Presbyter* 6 (1948), pp. 3–10 (9–10); Harry Escott (ed.), *Peter Taylor Forsyth (1848–1921), Director of Souls: Selections from His Practical Writings* (London: Epworth, 1948), pp. 10–12; R. E. Higginson, 'The Theology of P. T. Forsyth and its Significance for Us Today', *The Churchman* (1959), pp. 66–75 (74); Samuel J. Mikolaski, 'P. T. Forsyth', in *Creative Minds in Contemporary Theology* (ed. Philip Edgcumbe Hughes; Grand Rapids: Wm. B. Eerdmans, 1969), p. 310; Colin E. Gunton, 'Foreword', in *Justice the True and Only Mercy: Essays on the Life and Theology of Peter Taylor Forsyth* (ed. Trevor A. Hart; Edinburgh: T&T Clark, 1995), p. xiii; Colin E. Gunton, 'The Real as the Redemptive: Forsyth on Authority and Freedom', in *Justice the True and Only Mercy: Essays on the Life and Theology of Peter Taylor Forsyth* (ed. Trevor A. Hart; Edinburgh: T&T Clark, 1995), p. 37; Alan P. F. Sell, 'P. T. Forsyth as Unsystematic Systematician', in *Justice the True and Only Mercy: Essays on the Life and Theology of Peter Taylor Forsyth* (ed. Trevor A. Hart; Edinburgh: T&T Clark, 1995), pp. 134–35, 144; John Thompson, 'Was Forsyth Really a Barthian Before Barth?', in *Justice the True and Only Mercy: Essays on the Life and Theology of Peter Taylor Forsyth* (ed. Trevor A. Hart; Edinburgh: T&T Clark, 1995), p. 238; *passim*.

[76] Gwilym O. Griffith, 'Peter Taylor Forsyth', *The Christian World*, 13 May 1948, pp. 1–2 (1); cf. 'Intellectualism', p. 328.

> laid on before, and one sees it disappearing and reappearing continually affecting all else, having its colour modified by successive juxtapositions, and taking its own place in the ever growing pattern.[77]

Evident here is something germane to the English tradition itself – a tendency to 'rest its laurels' on historical and exegetical skills rather than on those of systematics. And while Forsyth does not share this tradition's 'nationalist fear of continental thought',[78] he is suspicious of 'systems' which aim at a certain level of watertightness, not least because such systematizations tend to overlook the limits set by the nature of the subject itself – namely God. He is also aware that the theologian's task is far from complete when the historian and exegete has set down her pen. Carved out *against* his rejection of G. W. F. Hegel's monism, Friedrich Schleiermacher's pessimism, Gotthold Lessing's historiographical scepticism, and *from* which he develops his principle of authority, moral reality and a proper distinction between creation and God, Forsyth represents a third way: the interpretation of all history, thought and action in light of God's self-disclosure in Christ, the 'continuous evangelical centre'[79] from which all *dogma*, *doctrine* and *theology* are developed, and to which the preacher, like the underside image of Martin Luther in Lucas Cranach's 1547 altarpiece in Stadtkirche St. Marien in Wittenberg, bears witness. Standing undeliberately in the tradition of Augustine of Hippo and of Gregory of Nyssa, Forsyth takes seriously what Rowan Williams refers to as 'the oddity of the world, its irreducibility to the tidy patterns of logic'[80] and 'premature harmonies',[81] and, like Saint John of the Cross, 'the Christian suspicion of conceptual neatness, of private revelation and religious experience uncontrolled by the reference to the givenness of Christ's cross'.[82] Furthermore, by seeing things whole, rather than in isolated clumps, Forsyth avoids the Enlightenment's traps of artificial disentanglement. Insofar as he does this, Forsyth fulfils Brunner's characterization of systematic theology. Thinking of Irenaeus, Brunner contends that to be a systematic theologian is 'to perceive connections between truths, and to know which belongs to which'.[83] So Samuel Mikolaski's assessment: 'History and experience, criticism and faith, process and morality were not for [Forsyth] mutually exclusive ideas but realities properly belonging together in evangelical faith and witness'.[84] By not succumbing to the provisionality of any 'system', but rooting theology in the blood-satiated divine economy, Forsyth is at once deeply and 'thoroughly systematic',[85]

[77] Frederick Maurice (ed.), *The Life of Frederick Denison Maurice, Chiefly Told in His Own Letters* (London: Macmillan and Co., 1884), 1:147.
[78] Gunton, 'Nature of Systematic Theology', p. 14.
[79] 'Newest Theology', p. 581.
[80] Rowan Williams, *The Wound of Knowledge: Christian Spirituality from the New Testament to St. John of the Cross* (Cambridge: Cowley Publications, 1991), p. 79.
[81] Rowan Williams, *On Christian Theology* (Oxford: Blackwell, 2000), p. 50.
[82] Williams, *The Wound of Knowledge*, p. 180.
[83] Emil Brunner, *The Mediator: A Study of the Central Doctrine of the Christian Faith* (trans. Olive Wyon; London: Lutterworth Press, 1934), p. 262.
[84] Mikolaski, 'Forsyth', pp. 310–11.
[85] Alan P. F. Sell, *Testimony and Tradition: Studies in Reformed and Dissenting Thought* (Aldershot: Ashgate, 2005), p. 179.

evangelical, trinitarian, ecclesial, ecumenical and catholic. Few have voiced it more exactly than J. K. Mozley:

> The student of this remarkable thinker [Forsyth] feels that language is taken by force, and strained to its utmost capacity for the expression of the conceptions which raise themselves from the great deeps of a mind wherein the Christian has triumphed over the philosopher, and then served himself of his adversary's weapons. Systematic is not a word that one would naturally apply to Dr. Forsyth; yet I know of no theologian of the day who has fewer loose ends to his thought. To adopt a phrase of his own he never attempts to set up in his theology a subsidiary centre, but at every point which he reaches in the gradual development of a position, or by some bold coup de main [vigorous attack], one knows that there is a straight line back, as from any point on the circle's circumference to its centre, to that which is the moral and therefore the only possible centre of the world – the Cross of Christ.[86]

Barth is characteristically helpful here too:

> Let us remember first an old hermeneutical rule which says that there is no law concerning the sequence of theological topics. You can begin theology anywhere, however you like. We are allowed to begin here, or there. Let us hope that we do not do it arbitrarily, but it can be done! Each specific doctrine or topic in theology is to be understood, let us say, as a point on the periphery of a circle, a point which points to the focus and common center. So, you can begin here, or here, or here, and you always have the same subject-matter with which to deal. Each doctrine or topic can be treated and explained adequately if it is clearly such a finger pointing towards the center. The criterion is that a point must point! If we look here, and here, and here but not at the same center, then all is wrong everywhere . . . Systematization is always the enemy of true theology.[87]

An appreciation of Forsyth's theological presentation requires that we recognize the distinction he proposes between *Dogma*, *Doctrine* and *Theology*. This is most clearly outlined in *Theology in Church and State* (1915). Briefly put, *Dogma*, for Forsyth, nearly always refers to the one compressed statement of the gospel. Forsyth suggests that this could be John 3.16, 2 Corinthians 5.18–19 or Romans 1.16–17. It should be brief, but the important thing is its finality. It forms the basis for doctrine and theology. *Dogma* is that which 'holds the Church rather than is held by it'.[88] To employ an imperfect analogy from the world of botany, *Dogma*, if you like, is the tree's root system and trunk. It is *Dogma* that (i) makes the Church the Church; (ii) secures the Church's freedom and rights from State interference; (iii) forms the basis of ecumenical union and survival;

[86] John Kenneth Mozley, *The Doctrine of the Atonement* (New York: Charles Scribner's Sons, 1916), p. 182.
[87] Karl Barth, 'A Theological Dialogue', *Theology Today* 19, no. 2 (1962), pp. 171–77 (173–74).
[88] *Theology*, p. vi.

and (iv) provides the only basis by which churches might serve together in ministry and mission. *Doctrine* refers to the expansion, clarification and development of *Dogma*. It is indispensable for the Church's practical unity and for protection against other 'gospels'. To continue with the botanical analogy, *Doctrine* refers to the tree's branches. It has a relationship integral to the trunk, but no one branch is indispensable to the life of the tree and can (indeed must) be pruned or lopped if the life of the tree is at stake. It has no finality (as *Dogma* does) and requires editing and revision in new circumstances. *Theology* is the prime necessity for *Doctrine*, for 'it is theology which prepares the material for the doctrine by which the Church preaches its dogma'.[89] Forsyth also distinguishes between primary and secondary theology. Primary theology is that which is verifiable by experience. Secondary theology is that which is a scientific exposition of primary theology. Secondary theology is verified by thought. Moreover, secondary theology is necessary for the Church, its life and witness, but not for the individual. Primary theology is personal, experiential. It forms part of the very act of revelation upon which secondary theology reflects. Primary theology is sacramental itself. Secondary theology describes the sacrament given in primary theology. Primary theology is a theology of experience. Secondary theology is the experience of theology, what Forsyth calls 'faith thinking'. Theology, therefore, is something like the tree's leaves. Departure from the Church's *Doctrine* or *Theology* ought not to be considered as heresy. The Church's *Dogma*, its positive faith, is the only criteria for truth. Forsyth avers that we ought to be free to modify, re-evaluate and/or disregard our doctrines and theology against the Church's *Dogma*. When such modification, re-evaluation and/or disregard actually reduces or extinguishes the *Dogma* and replaces it with a new dogma (even under the banner of 'freedom') then this is heresy (rather than freedom). Thus heresy, for Forsyth, is not an abandonment of the creeds but abandonment of the positive faith to which the creeds point.

On the basis of Forsyth's own confession that he is concerned with postulating 'a minimal creed, an ample science, a maximal faith',[90] Allen concludes that Forsyth's theology cannot be considered a system at all.[91] But this is to miss Forsyth's point which concerns the futility of building a theology on the 'foundations of the present', on those systems which he suggests 'do not last', are built 'but to house a generation or a couple', and so are 'all revisable, all on lease'. Instead, and following 'our fathers', Forsyth posits that we ought to be building as did our forebears; *In aeternum pinxerunt*.[92] They built towards finality and universality – specifically, the universality and finality of God's action in Jesus Christ. Herein is a practical theology positing salvation not as a matter of scientific enquiry charged to satisfy all human curiosity, but of personal relation to the gospel: 'A few mighty cohesive truths which capture, fire, and mould the whole soul are worth much more than a correct conspectus of the total area of divine knowledge'.[93] By so undertaking the theological task, Forsyth encourages an opening up rather than a closing down of

89 Clifford S. Pitt, *Church, Ministry and Sacraments: A Critical Evaluation of the Thought of Peter Taylor Forsyth* (Washington: University Press of America, 1983), p. 85.
90 *Preaching*, p. 86.
91 Allen, 'The Christology of P. T. Forsyth', p. 281.
92 Literally, 'They built/made to last forever.'
93 *Preaching*, p. 86.

exploratory space and so promotes situations wherein the deepest of theological truths might mesh with 'the texture of reality as we experience it, which is open-ended, complex and often elusive, resisting our efforts to pin it down'.[94]

Forsyth as 'staurocentric' theologian

> *The scriptural basis for Christian belief in the triune God is not the scanty trinitarian formulas of the New Testament, but the thoroughgoing, unitary testimony of the cross; and the shortest expression of the Trinity is the divine act of the cross, in which the Father allows the Son to sacrifice himself through the Spirit.*[95]

The Ritschlian school posted a legitimate protest against the automation of redemption via a crude orthodoxy ending in simplistic moralism. But the path it took trivialized the reality of sin, the authority of God's Law, and the muscle of the demonic, and reduced Jesus at best to a mere representation of God's universal love and at worst to nothing more than another martyr. Various strands of like theological liberalism had taken deep hold of both academy and Church in the Europe of Forsyth's day. But there were other strands too and, within a couple of years of the 1877 Leicester Conference,[96] Forsyth follows Martin Kähler's lead in rejecting the nineteenth century's high point of theological interest in the life of Jesus, a call also taken up in early twentieth-century attacks on liberalism's 'sacred biographies' as fanciful and subjective.[97] 'I regard the entire "Life of Jesus" movement as a blind alley', wrote Kähler, who restored the Passion and Easter narratives to their Pauline centrality, reducing the rest of the Gospels to 'extended introductions'.[98]

Forsyth's 'Scottish Christocentrism'[99] does not necessarily mean that he neglects other parts of the Christian story, however.[100] Still less does his staurocentricism equate to stauromonism. Rather, Forsyth proceeds on the basis that each truth of that metanarrative receives its most concentrated and illumined expression, dignity and interpretation in Christ's cross. So the cross becomes Forsyth's 'abiding obsession',[101]

[94] Hart, 'Systematic – In What Sense?', p. 342; cf. Jürgen Moltmann, *The Trinity and the Kingdom: The Doctrine of God* (trans. Margaret Kohl; Minneapolis: Fortress, 1993), p. xi: 'systems do not present themselves for discussion'.

[95] Bernhard Steffen, *Das Dogma vom Kreuz. Beitrag zu einer staurozentrische Theologie* (Gütersloh: Bertelsmann, 1920), p. 152.

[96] On the Leicester Conference, see Mark Hopkins, *Nonconformity's Romantic Generation: Evangelical and Liberal Theologies in Victorian England* (Milton Keynes: Paternoster, 2004), pp. 85–121.

[97] Charlotte Allen, *The Human Christ: The Search for the Historical Jesus* (Oxford: Lion Publishing, 1998), p. 69.

[98] Martin Kähler, *The So-Called Historical Jesus and the Historic Biblical Christ* (trans. Carl E. Braaten; Philadelphia: Fortress Press, 1964), p. 46. cf. *Person*, pp. viii–ix, 123; Joseph Estlin Carpenter, *The Historical Jesus and the Theological Christ* (London: Philip Green, 1911).

[99] Hans Schwarz, *Theology in a Global Context: The Last Two Hundred Years* (Grand Rapids: Wm. B. Eerdmans Publishing, 2005), p. 381.

[100] Garvie suggests that Forsyth's de-emphasis on Jesus' earthly ministry borders on irreverence. Alfred Ernest Garvie, 'Placarding the Cross: The Theology of P. T. Forsyth', *Congregational Quarterly* 21 (1943), pp. 343–52 (351).

[101] Escott (ed.), *Director of Souls*, p. 13.

and the 'inspiring motive of every book' he penned.[102] It 'dominates and saturates' Forsyth's theological canvas, weaving itself in and out of everything he wrote, whether on theological method, theology proper, evil, art, war, poverty, politics or marriage: 'the cross is never set off in some convenient niche as merely a part of a total theological system; it underlies, overarches, and permeates every aspect of Forsyth's thinking'.[103] Forsyth is in many respects, as Mozley asserts, 'a man of one idea – the Cross. But that idea, or rather act and fact, was for him so universal and eternal, all-compassing, all-penetrating, all-absorbing, that he was able to combine a great simplicity with a great subtlety and richness'.[104] The Moderator of the General Assembly of the Presbyterian Church of Wales, T. Charles Williams, spoke for not a few when, in his moving tribute upon Forsyth's death in 1921, he articulated: 'No one has ever made preaching a bigger thing, nor the Cross more real and central to me than he did'.[105] And Forsyth's 'closest friend and colleague in the later years', his own son-in-law and Professor of New Testament Exegesis at New College and Hackney College, Herbert Tom Andrews, described Forsyth as 'the prophet of the Cross':

> For him the Cross was everything – 'his rock, his reality, his eternal life.' Apart from the historic act of redemption, there was nothing in Christianity that counted for very much with him. He used all the weapons in the prophet's armour to confound his opponents. People thought sometimes that some of his blows were too hard, but he felt that he was fighting for the very life of the Faith, and that he had no option but to contend to the uttermost for his soul's convictions.[106]

It helps, I think, if we recognize that for Forsyth, 'cross' is often theological shorthand employed to describe the whole soteriological centre in Jesus Christ – his birth, public ministry, the passion narrative, the historical event of Calvary itself, the resurrection, Christ's cosmic victory and Christ's reign. Still, Forsyth probably over-employs the grammar of 'cross'. Griffith's suggestion, that by doing so, Forsyth skates very close to encouraging a return to an 'impersonal transactionalism in which the machinery of salvation obscures the Divine Saviour'[107] certainly overstates the case, however.

[102] Hughes, 'Forsyth's View of the Atonement', p. 31.

[103] Brown, *Prophet for Today*, p. 78.

[104] John Kenneth Mozley, *The Heart of the Gospel* (London: SPCK, 1925), p. 109; cf. Georg Wilhelm Friedrich Hegel, *Lectures on the Philosophy of Religion* (trans. E. B. Speirs and J. Burdon Sanderson; London: Kegan Paul, Trebch, Trübner, & Co., 1895), 3:86.

[105] T. Charles Williams, 'A Tribute from Wales, by the Rev. T. Charles Williams, M.A.', *British Weekly*, 17 November 1921, p. 154.

[106] Cited in Jessie F. Andrews, 'Memoir', in *The Work of Christ* by P. T. Forsyth (London: Independent Press, 1938), p. xxviii; cf. James Denney, *The Atonement and the Modern Mind* (London: Hodder & Stoughton, 1910), pp. 1–2; E. Hermann, 'Studies of Representative British Theologians: VI.–Peter Taylor Forsyth, D.D.', *Homiletic Review* 66 (1913), pp. 179–85 (182); Thomas Hywel Hughes, *The Atonement: Modern Theories of the Doctrine* (London: George Allen & Unwin, 1949), pp. 39–40; Thomas D. Meadley, 'The "Obscurity" of P. T. Forsyth', *Congregational Quarterly* 24 (1946), pp. 308–17; N. H. G. Robinson, 'The Importance of P. T. Forsyth', *The Expository Times* 64 (1952), pp. 76–79; H. H. Scullard, 'Principal Forsyth', *London Quarterly Review* 137 (1922), pp. 104–06 (105); Robert E. Ziegler, 'P. T. Forsyth and His Theology', *Methodist Quarterly Review* 62 (1913), pp. 455–63 (456).

[107] Gwilym O. Griffith, *The Theology of P. T. Forsyth* (London: Lutterworth Press, 1948), p. 94.

Overplayed or otherwise, Forsyth is concerned that the Church's compass is being rerouted from its perennial interest in Christ's work and the holy love of God it declares towards, at best, second-order issues, issues of leaves and twigs rather than roots and trunks. And he calls upon us to shed the husk in order to grow the tree.[108] Such a commitment is profoundly informed by Forsyth's view of history. Forsyth recognizes only two possible ways to view history. History is either 'an organism evolving on certain lines, laws, or ideals' or it is a 'supreme conflict of the good will to secure its goodness universally in collision with various forms of evil'.[109] He insists we choose between these two schemes. The basis of that choice, however, must be theological – it must rest on the finality of Jesus Christ who is the centre of the soul and of human history, the 'Alpha and Omega of grace',[110] and the creator of faith. 'When your happy world goes to pieces', he writes, 'you cannot believe in a moral world except in the faith of such a revelation as took effect in the moral redemption of the universal conscience, and which secured for ever the holiness of God out of the worst that man can do'.[111]

> The whole world is re-constituted in the Cross as its last moral principle, its key and its destiny. The Cross is at once creation's fatal jar and final recovery. And there is no theodicy for the world except in a theology of the Cross. The only final theodicy is that self-justification of God which was fundamental to His justification of man. No reason of man can justify God in a world like this. He must justify Himself, and He did so in the Cross of His Son.[112]

Here Forsyth is nothing if not practical.[113] The cross is not only the locus of God's self-justification but it also gifts confidence in God's efficacy and determination to fully sanctify creation, realities confirmed in the evangelical experience of forgiveness which transforms the moral centre of reality – the human conscience and will.

When Forsyth speaks of the centrality of the cross of Christ, he has more in mind than where a particular doctrine is situated in a religious schema. For Forsyth the cross is the centre not only of thought, but of life itself. It is the centre of history and of the conscience – God's and ours. And it is central precisely because it is the action *of God* bearing responsibility for the covenant-deranging power of sin and founding a new humanity reconciled to God.[114] Thus is God's name hallowed. The cross is not only the foundation of the Church's existence but also the concentration of 'the life-power of the

108 See 'Atonement', pp. 62–63; 'Evangelical Churches', p. 29.
109 *Authority*, p. 202.
110 *Preaching*, p. 87.
111 *Justification*, p. 152.
112 Ibid., p. 122. On Forsyth's theodicy see Noel Due, 'Theodicy and Atonement' (Conference paper presented at P. T. Forsyth Colloquium, University of Aberdeen, 29 June 1993) and Leow, *The Theodicy of Peter Taylor Forsyth*.
113 The practical nature of Forsyth's theology has sometimes gone underappreciated. Forsyth's own pastor, J. Baldwin Brown, once quipped in *The English Independent* (22 November 1877, p. 1293), 'Those who have known [Forsyth] as I have, through many years and in trying times, will sustain my witness that he is an earnest, high-minded, and faithful man, with his heart set on the work of the ministry. But he is also, I should say – I hope he will forgive me; the world has held many noble men of that type – one easily fascinated by, and led after, impracticable ideals'.
114 See *Work*, p. 56.

moral world', 'the sole meaning of Christ Himself. Christ is to us just what His cross is'. Forsyth continues:

> All that Christ was in heaven or on earth was put into what He did there. And all that man's moral soul needs doing for it eternally was done centrally there. Neither cross nor Christ is simply a historic fact by which we order our mental calendar; they make the sun in our heaven, the force in our world. They make our vital centre, not as mere facts, but as sacraments; not for their occurrence, but for their significance; not because we reckon from them, but because we live from them.[115]

The cross is holy love being realized decidedly and unconditionally, an event not only within human history but within God's own trinitarian life where God 'goes out to save us into His own holiness'.[116] Stated otherwise, the cross is the happening of a 'creative synthesis' (*Schöpferische Synthese*) of powers (as Wilhelm Wundt would have it),[117] God's and the new humanity therein created. Forsyth contends, moreover, that in the action of the cross there exists between Christ and humanity not only 'an organic moral connection and a spiritual solidarity' but, more particularly, that such solidarity births 'a moral effect on Humanity' which in its antedated action on us – 'judging, melting, changing us' – forms part of Christ's offering to God which includes humanity implicitly and proleptically, and creates a new people of faith, filled by the Spirit with 'the power of responding' to God.[118]

> [Christ's] offering of a holy obedience to God's judgment is therefore valuable to God for us just because of that moral solidarity with us which also makes Him such a moral power upon us and in us. His creative regenerative action on us is a part of that same moral solidarity which also makes His acceptance of judgment stand to our good, and His confession of God's holiness to be the ground of ours.[119]

To this we shall return in Chapters 3 and 4.

Sparks from the anvil: Reckoning with Forsyth's style

> *The prophet is human, yet he employs notes one octave too high for our ears. He experiences moments that defy our understanding. He is neither a 'singing saint' nor a 'moralizing poet', but an assaulter of the mind. Often his words begin to burn where conscience ends.*[120]

[115] *Cruciality*, p. 44.
[116] Ibid., p. 116.
[117] Cited in 'Veracity', p. 209; cf. Robert W. Rieber and David Keith Robinson (eds), *Wilhelm Wundt in History: The Making of a Scientific Psychology* (New York: Kluwer Academic, 2001), pp. 129–32.
[118] *Work*, pp. 15, 192.
[119] Ibid., pp. 190–91. There are some Maurician echoes here. See Frederick D. Maurice, *The Lord's Prayer* (London: John W. Parker, 1851), p. 21.
[120] Abraham Joshua Heschel, *The Prophets* (vol. 1; New York: Harper & Row, 1962), p. 10.

Some of Forsyth's students were surprised to hear that others regarded their teacher's books difficult to read:

> About his books. I question whether those who knew him only through his books could ever really know him. It was [a] surprise to me when I first discovered that many people regarded his books as difficult. To me they have always been the most readable of theological books. The explanation doubtless is that I had learned, a little at least, to know the man. He took pains to make his thought plain to us students. Though probably our understanding may often have been misunderstanding![121]

Most reviewers, on the other hand, comment negatively on his writing style.[122] Forsyth-patron Alan Sell notes that 'a characteristic pitfall' is Forsyth's tendency to overstate his case by needless disjunction: '"both . . . and" do not come easily to him'.[123] Even Forsyth's close friend, James Denney, confessed to finding *Missions in State and Church* 'very difficult to read', and asked 'If this is how one feels who is heartily at one with the writer, how must it strike an unsympathetic reader?'[124] Moreover, regarding *Positive Preaching and the Modern Mind*, Denney wrote, 'The peculiarity of [Forsyth's] style is such that only people who agree with him strongly are likely to read him through.'[125] While the assessment that Forsyth's overall thought is 'remarkably free from inconsistencies'[126] remains a sound one, criticisms of his style are too numerous to discard. Most criticisms, however, betray a failure to account for the occasional and

121 From an anonymous (nd), and unpublished letter headed 'Dr. Forsyth' in Dr Williams's Library, London. The letter has a pencil inscription – 'Elliot?', possibly the student's name.

122 See, for example, reviews and essays by James Warschauer, A. R. Whatley, H. Hamilton, E. Albert Cook, Fort Newton, R. W. Stewart, A. J. Gossip, Thomas D. Meadley, Charles S. Duthie and Warren Wiersbe, which are listed in the bibliography. Also J. K. Mozley, 'Preface by the Rev. Dr. J. K. Mozley', in *The Church and the Sacraments* by P. T. Forsyth (London: Independent Press, 1947), p. viii; R. E. Higginson, 'Peter Taylor Forsyth: Prophet and Pastor, 1848–1921', *English Churchman and St James' Chronicle*, 1 July 1955, pp. 309, 315 (315); Donald G. Miller et al., *P. T. Forsyth: The Man, the Preachers' Theologian, Prophet for the 20th Century: A Contemporary Assessment* (Pittsburgh: Pickwick Press, 1981), pp. 16–21, 39–40, 72; W. J. F. Huxtable, 'P. T. Forsyth: 1848–1921', *Journal of the United Reformed Church History Society* 4 (1987), pp. 72–78 (74); Noel Due, 'Foreword', in *The Preaching of Jesus and the Gospel of Christ* by P. T. Forsyth (Blackwood: New Creation Publications, 1987), p. vii; Iain R. Torrance, 'Dominated by His Own Illustrations? P. T. Forsyth on the Lord's Supper', in *Justice the True and Only Mercy: Essays on the Life and Theology of Peter Taylor Forsyth* (ed. Trevor A. Hart; Edinburgh: T&T Clark, 1995), p. 59; Dale A. Johnson, *The Changing Shape of English Nonconformity 1825–1925* (New York/Oxford: Oxford University Press, 1999), p. 157; Clyde Binfield, 'Peter Taylor Forsyth: Pastor as Principal', in *P T Forsyth: Theologian for a New Millennium* (ed. Alan P. F. Sell; London: The United Reformed Church, 2000), pp. 21, 32; David R. Peel, 'PT Forsyth on Ministry: A Model for Our Time?', in *P T Forsyth: Theologian for a New Millennium*. (ed. Alan P. F. Sell; London: The United Reformed Church, 2000), pp. 177–80; *passim*. Particularly helpful here is Harry Escott's treatment in his edited volume *P. T. Forsyth and the Cure of Souls: An Appraisement and Anthology of His Practical Writings* (London: George Allen & Unwin, 1970), pp. 17–21.

123 Sell, *Testimony and Tradition*, p. 176.

124 James Denney, *Letters of Principal James Denney to W. Robertson Nicoll, 1893–1917* (London: Hodder & Stoughton, 1920), pp. 118–19.

125 Ibid., p. 97.

126 Frank F. Jones, 'The Christological Thought of Peter Taylor Forsyth and Emil Brunner: A Comparative Study' (unpublished doctoral dissertation, University of St Andrews, 1970), p. 472.

preached-genre of the bulk of Forsyth's work, prepared in the midst of busy college life and denominational responsibilities, and, more particularly, of the impossible task of speaking and writing about the cross unparadoxically. Even Forsyth's most systematic work, *The Person and Place of Jesus Christ*, was not, he recalls, 'meant for scholars, but largely for ministers of the Word which it seeks in its own way to serve'. His stated aim was to 'be as popular as the subject and its depth allowed', and confesses that the lack of bibliographical apparatus is not only because it is unnecessary for lectures, but also because it would give the book 'an aspect of erudition which its author does not possess'.[127]

We might note too that many criticisms of Forsyth's writing style betray a disregard for Forsyth's theological methodology which avoids philosophizing and whose target is the human imagination. A generation whose reading diet has included the likes of Karl Barth and Rowan Williams as ingredients for the main course ought to find Forsyth's grammar palatable enough and his disallowing of logic – other than the *sui generis* logic of the *logos ensarkos* – to dictate the direction in his argument sufficient attraction to keep reading.

But the failure to understand this 'patently original thinker'[128] is due more to the taxing nature of his gospel, and to a decline in affinity to the evangelical experience out of which he wrote than it is of his writing per se.[129] 'The merchantmen of these goodly pearls must be seekers; and without even divers they cannot be had.'[130] Still, the demand of his writing upon the reader is something of which he was aware: 'I own I tax you, and I am sorry, but it has taxed me more.'[131] Eugene Peterson concludes: 'Here is a no-nonsense theologian who goes for the jugular.'[132] Forsyth's daughter, Jessie Andrews, notes that though her father could certainly write simply (never simplistically), when writing for trained theological minds he 'demands everything we have of mental and spiritual gasp'. When writing, this master of English prose was wrestling – like Jacob at Peniel – with thoughts mysterious, unconquerable and beyond human mastery; and he wrote with 'a physical and nervous intensity which shook the desk, and which after an hour or two left him utterly spent, stretched out white and still upon his study couch, until the Spirit drove him back to pen and paper'.[133] Such intensity was the fruit of the subject itself; 'the Browning of theology'[134] entertaining no illusions that the truth of the

127 *Person*, p. viii. Camfield suggests that there were practical, rather than theological or philosophical reasons for why Forsyth never embarked on a systematic theology. He writes: '... the truth is that the thought of Forsyth required that "treatise" which he never gave. Partly, one suspects, from chronic ill-health, and partly, through a disinclination to, and perhaps incapacity for, the work of research ...'. Camfield, 'Forsyth', p. 9.

128 David W. Bebbington, *Evangelicalism in Modern Britain: A History from the 1730s to the 1980s* (London/New York: Routledge, 2005), p. 141.

129 So too Thomas F. Torrance, *The Christian Doctrine of God, One Being Three Persons* (Edinburgh: T&T Clark, 2001), p. xi: 'I would claim ... that the difficulty of my style is sometimes due to the difficulty of the subject-matter!'

130 *Person*, p. vii.

131 *Cruciality*, pp. 171–72.

132 Eugene H. Peterson, 'Foreword', in *The Soul of Prayer* by P. T. Forsyth (Vancouver: Regent College Publishing, 2002), p. 5.

133 Andrews, 'Memoir', p. xxvi.

134 John Bishop, 'P. T. Forsyth: "Preaching and the Modern Mind"', *Religion in Life* 48 (1979), pp. 303–08 (305).

gospel might be lubricated for easier swallowing: 'it is not the simple things that make the soul. The greatest powers are those that break through language and escape'.[135]

Like St Hilary and Calvin, Forsyth knows that witness to the cross is ultimately beyond human speech (*ineffabili quodam modo*),[136] ought to be felt more than analysed (as with Kierkegaard), even as the outworking of the atonement itself involves (demands) words. Thus Forsyth strains and tortures language itself, utilizing every human discipline available to him in order to shed light – or rather expunge the light that is there – on one or other facet (vista and panorama) of the cross. He writes fugue-like, developing endless variations on the one immense theme of inexhaustible grace (while opening up space for other voices to contribute). Certainly 'a reader would have to work very hard to exit from a Forsyth text in absolute ignorance of the author's intention'.[137] Furthermore, Forsyth never constrains himself to only reading, learning and engaging with 'theologians'. No arena of human activity is off limits to him. Instead, Forsyth makes every thought an agent of a redeemed personality bearing faithful witness to a waxing world reconquested for God.

Like Dostoyevsky, Forsyth is a poet's theologian: he believes that theologians, like 'first rate poets, must deal with human life. They may not deal with bloodless abstractions or scientific systems whether of anthropology, cosmology, or theology; they must deal with life'.[138] This also means that he continually employs the grammar of 'gospel', 'religion', 'moral', 'revelation', 'cross' and 'redemption' to encompass a broad possibility of meanings. This does make reading Forsyth unnecessarily onerous at times, but it is also part of the sheer delight of being swept along with waves of such a breathtaking freedom. Just as Ritschl's fate was 'never to be long satisfied with his teachers',[139] Forsyth's fate was never to be long satisfied with the ideas and formulations of those who had gone before him, no matter how greatly he respected and valued their contribution. So Donald MacKinnon: 'Forsyth explicitly preferred a theology that could flirt with the mythological in its insistence on the primacy of narrative, to one tainted by what he called "Chalcedonianism", which seemed to subordinate the concrete reality of Christ's agony in Gethsemane and Calvary to a "bloodless ballet of impalpable categories"'.[140]

To borrow another image, Forsyth is concerned to paint for us a living picture which we are personally invited to enter. Those who accept his invitation must take account of his technique. One of his techniques is to use very broad brushes which leave very broad brushstrokes. Some of these strokes are called 'holiness', 'moral' and

[135] 'Way of Life', p. 86.

[136] See John Calvin, *Institutes of the Christian Religion* (ed. John T. McNeill; trans. Ford Lewis Battles; The Library of Christian Classics; Philadelphia: The Westminster Press, 1977), 2.17.2; Hilary of Poitiers and John of Damascus, *Hilary of Poitiers, John of Damascus* (ed. Philip Schaff and Henry Wace; trans. E. W. Watson and L. Pullan; A Select Library of the Nicene and Post-Nicene Fathers of the Christian Church, Second Series; vol. 9; Edinburgh: T&T Clark, 1898), I.37; II.2.

[137] Alan P. F. Sell, 'P T Forsyth: Theologian for a New Millennium?', in *P T Forsyth: Theologian for a New Millennium* (ed. Alan P. F. Sell; London: The United Reformed Church, 2000), p. 238.

[138] 'Immortality', pp. 360–61.

[139] James Orr, *The Ritschlian Theology and the Evangelical Faith* (London: Hodder & Stoughton, 1897), p. 13.

[140] Donald M. MacKinnon, 'Aspects of Kant's Influence on British Theology', in *Kant and His Influence* (ed. G. M. Ross and T. McWalter; Bristol: Thoemmes, 1990), p. 356.

'the cross'. They are strokes repeatedly brushed, sometimes to the point of exhausted blurring. Forsyth certainly could have used more brushes – and different kinds – than he does. But we must resist analysis of a single brushstroke, or approaching his work as one would the fine lines germane to continental philosophy. To understand a Forsyth requires standing back and looking at the way his copious amounts of paint lavishly but carefully blend into a single work. This way of doing theology resists those kinds of analysis all too common in academic attempts to systematize the divine economy, and a theologian's attempts to bear witness to those actions. In this study, I am concerned to provide an interpretation of Forsyth's canvas; not definition of any (or every) particular brushstroke.

Nevertheless, Forsyth's blurring of the distinction between (and interchangability of the grammar of) 'the holy', 'the moral' and 'the ethical', for example, makes it difficult to identify concepts for independent religious and ethical consideration. This may have been Forsyth's point; that there can be no stand-alone 'religion' or stand-alone 'ethics', but only ethical theology and theo-ethics, and that attendance to one is always to attend the other also. Put otherwise, Christian theology is always ethics. To be sure, dogmatics and ethics are not entirely the same thing, but there can be no responsible dogmatics that is not also concerned with ethics, and no responsible ethics that is not equally concerned with dogmatics. Unhinged from one another, both become retarded at best, and tyrants at worst. Ethics, moreover, is part of the doctrine of God precisely because, as Barth noted, God makes himself responsible for us.[141] Certainly, Forsyth's presentation of the moralizing of dogma does not call for a philosopher's definition and resists certain kinds of logical analysis. But does Forsyth try to make too few words do too much, and in so doing, shut down discussion at precisely those points wherein he means to open things up? He may be correct when he insists that 'what Christianity means by the holy is best expressed in ethical terms as the absolute moral Reality',[142] but what can such a statement actually mean?

Still, not all were deterred by Forsyth's style. Reflecting on a photograph of Forsyth, the President of the Literary and Philosophical Society comments in *The Wyvern*:

> Ministers achieve success in their labours by the soundness of the doctrine they set forth, by their energy and earnestness, and by the attractiveness of their manner and style. And any one of these is often sufficient to make a popular teacher of religion: the pastor of the Clarendon Park Church has them all. He is very broad in his beliefs, but he never gets away from the foundation facts of religion . . . Of Mr. Forsyth's energy and enthusiasm in the good cause there can be no doubt. It is impossible to listen to him without catching the seriousness of his themes, and realising that the preacher is pouring out his inmost feelings. Then again, the rev. gentleman has a most happy style. His sermons are not only literary, but even poetical. He is apt indeed in his phrases, and uses exceedingly forceful and elegant English.[143]

141 Barth, *CD* II/2, §36.
142 *Authority*, p. 4.
143 Anonymous, 'Our Photograph', *The Wyvern*, 25 November 1892, p. 67.

2

The Moral Is the Real: Location, Landscape, Appropriation

The universe is active and mighty. We are surrounded by things that have a vital interest in us. All things work. We were made for and are called to action. The universe is not only operant, but co-operant. The whole universe not only speaks to us, but works out a mighty purpose with us.[1]

I. Location

To understand Forsyth we must first place him as a man of his time, a high Victorian Congregational minister of Word and Sacrament turned Edwardian college principal, a Scotsman who had lived in London for longer than he had lived in Aberdeen (and far longer than anywhere else), of wide experience and considerable contemporary influence, as providentially out of step as only a man so formed could be.[2]

Sensibility and sentiment, Idealism and Romanticism, in Victorian and Edwardian Britain

Broadly put, Victorian and Edwardian[3] society was characterized by an inherited appreciation of 'sensibility' and 'sentiment' seeking re-expression in a new age of expanding population, spreading industrialization, declining church attendance, and an increase in urbanization, mobility, unemployment and middle-class wealth. Philip Davis describes the period as, after the Reformation, 'a second great, and perhaps final, crisis for the Western conscience'.[4] It was indubitably an age of anguish, of agnostics

[1] Forsyth, 'Sermon on Romans 8.28', in Goroncy (ed.), *'Descending on Humanity'*, 2013.

[2] Binfield, 'Pastor as Principal', p. 16.

[3] Because Victorianism so dominated the Edwardian period, here I shall coalesce Victorian and Edwardian periods (1830–1914) under the name 'Victorian'.

[4] Philip Davis, *The Victorians* (Oxford: Oxford University Press, 2002), p. 102.

and honest doubters symptomatically suspended between belief and disbelief, an age 'Wandering between two worlds, one dead|The other powerless to be born',[5] wherein society's mood reverberated 'all the loneliness of humanity amid hostile forces . . . concentrated upon the individual soul, which must struggle alone, with what of courage it can command, against the whole weight of a universe that cares nothing for its hopes and fears'.[6] Notwithstanding, the mood of many in the last quarter of the nineteenth century was also optimistic, a mood by-and-large shared by Nonconformists. Sell observes 'a feeling of relief and satisfaction that some of what were regarded as the rougher edges of Calvinism had been smoothed out; that shriller exponents of the higher biblical criticism had not after all scuppered the faith; and that the idea of evolution had been cashable in terms of God's providential and progressive way of going about his creative work'.[7]

The publication of *On the Origin of Species* (1859) and *Essays and Reviews* (1860) attests that evolutionary theory was an important element in the *Weltanschauung* of the time resulting in a perception that Christianity and progress were inseparable. This fuelled the modernist project, the civilizing/missionary agenda of Victorian Christianity, and found expression in trade unionism, Marxism and liberal Protestantism, and in a new stress on immanentism, incarnational theology, idealism, fraternity and church unity. Not only did the Church, Darwin's evolutionary hypothesis, and Mill's liberal utilitarianism contribute to society's shape, but they also continued to shape the response. While censuses indicate that less than half the population (and less than ten per cent of the urban poor) regularly attended church services, Victorian Britain still possessed a deeply religious consciousness. Over a third of the books published between 1836 and 1863 were religious, and religious newspapers and tracts flourished. It was not only middle-class Evangelicals who spoke of 'duty' and 'earnestness'; so too did agnostics and working-class radicals. Yet while church leaders sought to keep these words grounded in a religious milieu, the increasing influence of utilitarianism meant that the goal of human existence had shifted from one of divine service striving towards perfection, to coaxing imperfect people to feel comfortable. Still, utilitarianism and the mainstream Church shared at least three common assumptions: (i) the primacy of the individual, (ii) the possibility, and duty, of improving the human condition, and (iii) the need for individual asceticism. These also bore similar fruit in philanthropic activity and social reform. This sense of vocation was perhaps 'the most marked character in Victorian religion'.[8] The period also witnessed a modifying of Enlightenment thinking

[5] Matthew Arnold, 'Stanzas from the Grande Chartreuse', in *Dover Beach and Other Poems* (London: Dover, 1994), p. 71. Also cited in *Father*, p. 88. See Richard J. Helmstadter and Bernard Lightman (eds), *Victorian Faith in Crisis: Essays on Continuity and Change in Nineteenth-Century Religious Belief* (Houndmills: Macmillan, 1990); Anthony Symondson (ed.), *The Victorian Crisis of Faith* (London: SPCK, 1970); Timothy Larson, *Crisis of Doubt: Honest Faith in Nineteenth-Century England* (Oxford: Oxford University Press, 2006).

[6] Bertrand Russell, *Mysticism and Logic, and Other Essays* (London: Longmans, Green and Co., 1918), p. 57.

[7] Alan P. F. Sell, 'The Theological Contribution of Protestant Nonconformists in the Twentieth Century: Some Soundings', in *Protestant Nonconformity in the Twentieth Century* (ed. Alan P. F. Sell and Anthony R. Cross; Milton Keynes: Paternoster, 2003), p. 35.

[8] Owen Chadwick, *The Victorian Church* (vol. 2; London: Adam & Charles Black, 1970), p. 466.

with the invigorating cultural atmosphere of Romanticism.[9] Reason began to lose its grip to emotion and spirit as poetic and sublime as nature itself. In an age of mechanical materialism it was the poets who became the new priests.[10]

The three common assumptions identified above betray a shared moral idealism which grew out of explorations and redefinitions of Hegelian metaphysics and ethics,[11] and a romantic sentimentalism nurtured by the largely evangelical belief in the sanctity of the home. The practice of daily private and family prayer, supplemented by spiritual reading[12] and weekly sermons, helped to define a 'holy home', and generated a strong bond between Victorian parents and their children, for whom holiness conventionally meant tidy hair and an ordered bedroom. Prominent in both secular and religious literature were themes of sexual promiscuity and alcohol – partly a reaction against the wantonness and drunkenness so noticeable in Victorian cities. Reticence, therefore, became a phase in the 'history of the battle for refinement and civilization, and above all the better protection of women, against promiscuity, animalism, brutality and grossness'.[13] Thinking about holiness, when it happened, largely identified it with piety. It found voice in predominantly *negative* form in matters related to sex and alcohol, in censorship of literature and the arts, and in a loss of a sense of play which affected dress, conversation, intellectual speculation, church liturgy and games. Where it did not largely seek such new depth was in a *positive* recovery of holiness. This neglect provides a key to understanding the psyche of morality that characterized Victorian sensibilities. Though fascinated by holiness, Victorians were also hostile to it; a hostility that fruited in doubt and anxiety, rather than in wonder and joy. Victorian aversion for the 'holy' had its roots, on the one hand, in an Enlightenment spirit which insisted on a certain autonomous self-regulation. On the other hand was a romanticism which longed for a notion of the sublime and for an alternative to crude secularist visions of reality.

9 For Forsyth's critique of this trend, see *Father*, pp. 26–27; 'Intellectualism', p. 313; *Jesus*, p. 25; *Parnassus*, p. 277; *Preaching*, p. 111; *Revelation*, pp. 17–18; *Society*, pp. 101–02; cf. Karl Barth, *Protestant Theology in the Nineteenth Century: Its Background and History* (trans. J. Bowden and B. Cozens; London: SCM Press, 1972), p. 225. On the difficulty of defining Romanticism, see Isaiah Berlin, *The Roots of Romanticism* (ed. H. Hardy; London: Chatto & Windus, 1999), pp. 1–20.

10 Indeed, Silvester Horne suggests that the influence of Browning upon English Nonconformity was greater than that of Dale and Spurgeon. Silvester Horne, *A Popular History of the Free Churches* (London: James Clarke & Co., 1903), p. 421. And Forsyth also noted that 'It is a very remarkable feature of our non-theological age that its two very greatest *poets* [Browning and Tennyson] are not only theological in their spirit, but almost aggressively so. Theology, driven from life and science, has taken refuge with poetry.' 'Immortality', p. 361; See Percy B. Shelley, *Works of P. B. Shelley* (Hertfordshire: Wordsworth Editions, 1994), p. 605; G. Haydn Huntley, 'Notes on Victorian Art', *College Art Journal* 4, no. 3 (1945), pp. 127–31.

11 See Berlin, *Roots of Romanticism*, pp. 139–41.

12 John Vine Hall's tract 'The Sinner's Friend' (1821) had by 1845 sold 800,000 copies and by 1867 more than 1.5 million copies. *Pilgrim's Progress* too was a favourite for 'the kitchen, the servant's hall and cottage'. Chadwick, *Victorian Church*, 2:467.

13 George K. Clark, *The Making of Victorian England* (Cambridge: Harvard University Press, 1962), p. 126; cf. Sue Morgan, '"Wild Oats or Acorns?": Social Purity, Sexual Politics and the Response of the Late-Victorian Church', *Journal of Religious History* 31, no. 2 (2007), pp. 151–68; William A. Madden, 'Victorian Morality: Ethics Not Mysterious', *The Review of Politics* 23, no. 4 (1961), pp. 458–71 (460).

Tired of moral precepts and attitudes which represented Christianity as 'just human nature at its best',[14] and God's kingdom as 'just our natural spirituality and altruism developed',[15] – and knowing the stakes – Forsyth reacts strongly, accusing his generation of succumbing to cheap comforts, of muffling the moral note, of seeking a form of idealized Christianity divorced from a historic and perennial Christ and of interpreting sin 'in a softer light than God's'.[16]

The requisition of holiness: Forsyth's call for a theological re-centring of holiness

While Forsyth remains a product of his context, his foremost contributions are unveiled insofar as he transcends it. Nowhere does he do this more overtly or more creatively than in his thinking on holiness. From our brief aperçu of Forsyth's cultural context, we can surmise at least two trends. First, Victorian notions of holiness were mostly associated with the negative, and were often reduced to one's conduct. Antithetically, Forsyth presses that persons, society and indeed the whole creation require salvation not from morality ('because we can only be saved by the moral') but from 'mere moralism, from a religion three parts conduct'.[17] Secondly, Victorian speech concerning holiness is chiefly applied to *human* activity.[18] Forsyth challenges both tendencies: holiness is a fundamentally positive notion applying not primarily to personal conduct, but to God and to God's self-imprinting on reality. 'It is not from [Christ] that holiness has become for the world a negative idea, cloistered and feeble.'[19] And as early as his 1891 Chairman's Address for the Leicestershire and Rutland Congregational Union,[20] Forsyth reclaims holiness vocabulary as a distinctly *theo*-logical reality and as the key ingredient of a satisfactory response to romanticized permutations of God. While in 1902 he perceives in Newman and the Oxford revival (along with John Wesley and the Evangelical revival) 'God's answer' to the 'Deism outside, and drought within' the English church,[21] his 1905 account of contemporary Christianity highlights what he considers the poisonous fruit of Victorian romanticism:

> One reads somnambulant sermons about coming into tune with the infinite, about cultivating the presence of God, about pausing in life to hear the melodies of the everlasting chime, and all the rest of the romance of piety breathed beneath the

[14] *Work*, p. 9.
[15] Ibid., p. 10.
[16] *Person*, p. 13.
[17] *Work*, p. 81; cf. 'Final Seat of Authority', p. 591. Forsyth compares the '"eminent Christians" in Victorian days' with the first-century's pharisees. 'Conversion', p. 763.
[18] God's holiness was assumed. See John Henry Newman, *Discourses on the Scope and Nature of University Education* (Dublin: James Duffy, 1852), pp. 92, 448; Thomas Carlyle, *Past and Present* (Boston: Little, Brown, 1843), p. 77.
[19] 'Allegory', p. 318.
[20] Published as *The Old Faith and the New*. This pamphlet publicly marks a shift in Forsyth's theological locale.
[21] 'Allegory', pp. 314–15.

> moon in the green and pleasant glades of devotion – all without a hint of the classic redemption, or even of the Christ, whereby alone we have access to any of the rich quietives of faith. The preacher has glimpses of the paradise, but no sense of the purgatorio. He has the language but not the accent of that far heavenly country. Oh! but we want men who have been there and been naturalized there. We want more than romantic and temperamental piety. We want the accent of the Holy Ghost, learned with a new life at its classic capital – the cross.[22]

After three generations of besottedness with God's love, Forsyth believes that in most circles, ironically, justice has not been done to God's love because of the downplaying of God's holiness, the absence of which has 'slackened and flattened the whole tone and level of Christian life'.[23] By despoiling and excoriating love of its holiness, by repudiating the moral note and the Scriptures' own stress on God's holiness, his and earlier generations had, he believes, dwarfed sin, God's wrath and judgement, and thereby distorted the moral majesty of divine love. What Forsyth bears witness to is no self-absorbed obsession with personal holiness, but a love of God's and an awareness that therein lay creation's hope, for apart from love's holiness there is no restraint to human wickedness, nor hope that the Holy One may conquer all. Yet such is the aversion to God's holiness that 'it is hard to reconcile even the Churches to-day' to it.[24] Consequently, Forsyth observes an age impoverished in moral imagination, the ramifications of which exceed the theological realm.[25] He calls on preachers to 'saturate . . . people in the years that are to come as thoroughly with the idea of God's *holiness* as they have been saturated with the idea of God's love'.[26] This is Forsyth's theme in his 1897 sermon, 'The Holy Father', and continues throughout his ministry, revoiced in 1916 in *The Justification of God* where he attributes the shock brought to popular Christianity because of World War I, among other factors, to 'the loss of the sense of the holy God amid the fair humanities of new religion'.[27] This loss, he believes, manifested itself ecclesiologically in the form of irreverent worship, sentimental piety, ethical laxness and a replacing of the biblical idea of God's wrath for 'the slack God of the period'.[28] Forsyth's resolve is that *holy* love and the primacy of the moral – not war, economics, debates about biblical criticism or liturgy or the relationship between science and faith,[29] or social

22 *Society*, pp. 101–02. He voiced similar concern in 'Allegory', p. 317; and again in July 1908 in an address to the Third International Congregational Council at Edinburgh. *Cruciality*, pp. 48–50; cf. 'Lay Religion', p. 779; 'Veracity', p. 198.

23 *Work*, p. 241; cf. *Preaching*, p. 232; 'Immortality', p. 364. Forsyth, indubitably, was not alone here. See Thomas Chalmers' *Bridgewater Treatise* in Francis H. E. Bridgewater, *The Bridgewater Treatises on the Power, Wisdom and Goodness of God as Manifested in the Creation* (Philadelphia: Carey, Lea & Blanchard, 1836), p. 166.

24 *Society*, p. 30.

25 See 'Revelation', p. 121; *Sacraments*, pp. 36–37; Roy Hattersley, *The Edwardians* (London: Abacus, 2004), pp. 364–65.

26 *Work*, pp. 78–79.

27 *Justification*, p. 109.

28 *Cruciality*, p. 38.

29 See Frank M. Turner, 'The Victorian Conflict between Science and Religion: A Professional Dimension', *Isis* 69, no. 3 (1970), pp. 356–76.

questions[30] – be restored as the 'ruling interest'[31] of the Church's life, worship, polity, relation with the state, mission and theology. 'In front of all our prayer or work stands "Hallowed be Thy name".'[32]

Forsyth unremittingly presses that the Church's first word is not that God is merciful but that God is holy: 'Christianity is concerned with God's holiness before all else; which issues to man as love, acts upon sin as grace, and exercises grace through judgment.'[33] Accordingly, he insists, everything in Christian theology ought to begin and end with God's holiness and with the revelation of such in the divine economy. Holiness is 'the most quick and piercing, the most subtle, pervasive, and permanent'[34] power we know. To bring sin and grace home, holiness must come home first.[35] This is not merely pragmatic hamartiology. Forsyth believes that *from* holiness, and *for* holiness' sake, God brings creation home.

While Forsyth accentuates that the focus of the Church's thinking should not be determined by the concerns of World War I, he does hope (against the trend among many Nonconformists) that the trenches of war – the 'revelation of the evil power, the man of sin'[36] – might burn in on us the primacy of holiness not as a bourgeois concern with respectability but as the moral reality undergirding all life. Forsyth understood World War I to be the outworking of holiness' lesser judgement on the 'sinfulness of sin', a favourite phrase of his.[37] Into a world lulled by the idea that sin is harmless, impotent and irrelevant, 'God enters the pulpit, and preaches in His own way by deeds. And His sermons are long and taxing, and they spoil the dinner. Clearly God's problem with the world is much more serious than we dreamed.'[38] 'If such a war as this do [*sic*] not make us face reality, what will?', he asks in 1918.[39] The long absence of this tone, he believes, has 'lowered the whole temperature and authority of religion'. The war's service as a

[30] Forsyth's day witnessed a significant programme of social improvement that employed 'holiness' terminology, but it was of a sort almost entirely bereft of the type of which Forsyth speaks. For this reason, Forsyth contends, the Church has lost the very reality that founded it and for which it exists, and so its authority to act socially. See *Socialism* and *Socialism and Christianity*; cf. Edith C. Batho and Bonamy Dobrée, *The Victorians and After: 1830–1914* (London: The Cresset Press, 1950), pp. 178–81.

[31] *Cruciality*, p. 38; *Father*, p. 77; *Freedom*, p. 268.

[32] *Cruciality*, p. 39.

[33] Ibid., p. 5; cf. *Freedom*, p. 292; P. Bonnard, 'Holy', in *Vocabulary of the Bible* (ed. J.-J. von Allmen; London: Lutterworth, 1958), p. 166: 'Yahweh is holy inasmuch as He imparts Himself, inasmuch as He wishes men to share in His own divine life as He brings them within the scope of His judgment and mercy. His holiness is dynamic, exacting; it confronts man to pour upon him a new life.'

[34] *Missions*, p. 335.

[35] See *Cruciality*, p. 40; *Missions*, p. 231.

[36] *Sacraments*, p. 37.

[37] See *Authority*, p. 45, *Cruciality*, p. 200; *Father*, p. 117; *Work*, p. 180.

[38] *Justification*, p. 28; cf. *World-Commonwealth*, pp. 4–5. Forsyth was not the only one who had hoped that the horrors of war might sponsor moral awakening: Rudyard Kipling's *Recessional*, John Ruskin's warrior ethics, William James' *The Moral Equivalent of War*, and the 1916 Keswick Convention are further examples. See also Sell, 'Theological Contribution', pp. 39–42; Walter B. Sloan, *These Sixty Years: The Story of the Keswick Convention* (London: Pickering & Inglis, 1935), p. 74; Alan Ruston, 'Protestant Nonconformist Attitudes towards the First World War', in *Protestant Nonconformity in the Twentieth Century* (ed. Alan P. F. Sell and Anthony R. Cross; Milton Keynes: Paternoster, 2003), pp. 240–63; Guy Kendall, *Charles Kingsley and His Ideas* (London: Hutchinson & Co., 1947), p. 86.

[39] 'Reality', p. 615; cf. 'Effects of War', p. 16.

revelation of human evil, among other things, is that it ends 'the comfortable, kindly, bourgeois, casual Victorian age, so credulous in its humanism'.[40]

The discarding of holiness in 'The New Theology'

The Oxford-trained and Anglican-confirmed Reginald John Campbell (1867–1956) was among Congregationalism's most admired sons.[41] In 1895, Campbell became pastor of the Union Street Church (Congregationalist) in Brighton, and in 1903 accepted a call to one of the world's most prestigious pulpits, City Temple in London, where his popularity only grew as his thrice-weekly sermons were read by tens of thousands. He served at City Temple until 1915. The Victorian spirit, immersed in scientific determinism and biblical uncertainty, was most conducive to Campbell's gospel which represents a stream of Ritschlianism of substantial concern to Forsyth.[42] For his part, Campbell rejects traditional dogmatic formulations and seeks 'a restatement of the essential truth of the Christian religion in terms of the modern mind',[43] looking to science to supply its facts.[44]

Drawing on Schleiermacher, Caird, Ritschl, Gore, Fairbairn and Hegel, and motivated by a desire to make Christianity more palatable – thereby, Campbell believed, enabling the Church to fulfil its 'true mission of saving the world'[45] – Campbell posited what he dubbed 'The New Theology'. By late-1906, the New Theology became the centre of a theological tempest which echoed throughout Britain and the world.[46] It was, arguably, 'the dominant religious question in England in 1907'.[47] Campbell articulated his thoughts in the *Examiner* and the *London Daily Mail*:

[40] *Sacraments*, p. 37; cf. *War*, p. 21.

[41] See Clyde Binfield, *So Down to Prayers: Studies in English Nonconformity 1780–1920* (London/Totowa: J. M. Dent & Sons/Rowman and Littlefield, 1977), p. 213; Keith Robbins, 'The Spiritual Pilgrimage of the Rev. R. J. Campbell', in *History, Religion, and Identity in Modern Britain* (London/Rio Grande: The Hambledon Press, 1993), pp. 133–48. The Congregational minister Sydney Cave notes, however, that Campbell 'was not one of ourselves, and, in spite of his great popularity, was ill at ease in English Nonconformity'. Sydney Cave, 'Dr. P. T. Forsyth: The Man and His Writings', *Congregational Quarterly* 26 (1948), pp. 107–19 (113).

[42] Forsyth's engagement with Campbell helped form the vigorousness of his expression and the reiteration of his theological centre, not least in his consideration of the relation between liberty and authority in the Church. See *Freedom*, pp. 192, 207, 213, 216–17, 289–90, 293, 318, 354–55; *Authority*, pp. 79, 215, 219–20, 224, 230, 246–62, 290, 299, 321, 325; *Congregationalism*, pp. 52, 63–64; *Society*, pp. 5, 48, 62, 71–73, 107; *passim*.

[43] Reginald J. Campbell, *The New Theology* (London: Chapman & Hall, 1907), p. 3; cf. Keith W. Clements, *Lovers of Discord: Twentieth Century Theological Controversies in England* (London: SPCK, 1988), p. 27.

[44] Campbell, *The New Theology*, p. 15.

[45] Ibid., p. 11.

[46] British newspapers, revelling in the controversy, published hundreds of letters a week regarding the New Theology, including many from South Africa, India, Japan, North America and Continental Europe. Cave recalls the controversies: 'I hope that some of those now writing Ph.D. theses in "The Theology of P. T. Forsyth" will explore the columns of the religious weeklies of that time. If they do, they will discover an extraordinary confusion'. Cave, 'Forsyth', p. 114.

[47] Peter Hinchliff, *God and History: Aspects of British Theology, 1875–1914* (Oxford/New York: Clarendon Press/Oxford University Press, 1992), p. 215; cf. B. G. Worrall, 'R. J. Campbell and His New Theology', *Theology* 01 (1970), pp. 312–18.

> The starting point of the New Theology is belief in the immanence of God, and the essential oneness of God and man . . . We believe man to be the revelation of God, and the universe to be the one means to the self-manifestation of God. The word 'God' stands for the infinite reality whence all things proceed . . . Our being is the same as God's, although our consciousness of it is limited . . . There is thus no real distinction between humanity and deity . . . Every man is a potential Christ, or rather a manifestation of the eternal Christ . . . Sin is simply selfishness. It is an offense against the God within. We believe that Jesus is and was divine, but so are we. His mission was to make us realise our divinity and our oneness with God.[48]

The British Weekly, Nonconformity's unofficial mouthpiece, raised a campaign against Campbell accompanied by unsubstantiated threats of a possible heresy trial. In the following year, in response to growing criticism,[49] Campbell published his crudely polemical and hastily written defence, *The New Theology*, in an attempt to clarify his position and because his supporters ('The Progressive League') felt that his thinking 'ought to be dealt with in some comprehensive and systematic way'.[50] If Campbell thought the publication of *The New Theology* would quell the storm, he was tragically mistaken. While drawing momentous positive response (particularly from lay people), for its overwhelming number of critics[51] the publication served only to confirm all suspicions of Campbell's jumbled immanentist, neo-platonic, gnostic[52] and quasi-pantheistic[53] thinking – what Campbell referred to as spiritual monism or 'Higher Pantheism'.[54] In *The New Theology*, he argues that certain traditional tenets

[48] Cited in *The British Weekly* (17 January 1907), p. 414; cf. Campbell, *The New Theology*, pp. 76, 94. These were not original ideas, nor unique to Campbell; see G. Glen Wickens, *Thomas Hardy, Monism, and the Carnival Tradition: The One and the Many in the Dynasts* (Toronto: University of Toronto Press, 2002), p. 66.

[49] As to what amount of this hostility directed against Campbell was due to his socialist leanings is difficult to ascertain, though this at least fuelled the controversy, especially among Nonconformists. See David Bebbington, *The Nonconformist Conscience: Chapel and Politics, 1870–1914* (London: George Allen & Unwin, 1982), pp. 158–59; John W. Grant, *Free Churchmanship in England 1870–1940: With Special Reference to Congregationalism* (London: Independent Press, 1955), pp. 139–41. Forsyth was fearful of attempts to acquire the Church for social ends, naming it the most recent form of Erastianism. See *Sacraments*, pp. 9, 118, *Freedom*, p. 285; *Socialism*, pp. 28, 50–52; *Society*, pp. 15–18, 54–57, 63–64, 94, 96.

[50] Campbell, *The New Theology*, p. v. See T. Rhondda Williams, *The Evangel of the New Theology* (London: Percy Lund, Humphries, 1905); Joseph Warschauer, *The New Evangel: Studies in the 'New Theology'* (London: James Clarke, 1907). Warschauer later rejected the New Theology.

[51] The New Theology came under broad criticism from theological conservatives like George Barrat, Silvester Horne, R. F. Horton, and from liberals such as W. F. Adeney. See also D. L. Higgins, *Is it Christianity?: An Examination of a Book Entitled 'The New Theology,' by the Rev. R. J. Campbell* (London: G. Morrish, 1911); W. Lieber, *The New Theology or the Rev. R. J. Campbell's Main Conclusions Refuted* (London: R. & T. Washbourne, 1907); Henry Varley, *The New Theology and Mr. R. J. Campbell's Teachings Examined and Criticised* (London: A. Holness, London Bible and Book Saloon, 1907).

[52] Forsyth considered the New Theology to be a revived Gnosticism. 'Immanence', pp. 57–58.

[53] Cf. Campbell, *The New Theology*, pp. 16–25, 65, 74–75. He charged traditional Christian belief with a practical dualism. Campbell, *The New Theology*, pp. 4, 81, 94.

[54] Campbell, *The New Theology*, p. 35; cf. Reginald J. Campbell, *Thursday Mornings at the City Temple* (London: Macmillan, 1908), p. 151. Campbell reveals his indebtedness to James Ward's *Naturalism and Agnosticism*, and to Spinoza, in Reginald J. Campbell, *A Spiritual Pilgrimage* (New York:

such as the Fall, the scriptural basis of revelation, the blood-atonement, the meaning of salvation, the punishment of sin, and heaven and hell are both 'misleading' and 'unethical'.[55] Moreover, Campbell reduced the notion of sin to not being true to one's self,[56] and Jesus to little more than the exemplar human being whose mission is to display 'what we potentially are'.[57] When Campbell posits that faith in Jesus is faith in one's own Christhood,[58] he betrays a failure to appreciate the nature of the incarnation as *sui generis*. Given his reductionist christology, it is no surprise that Campbell discards the centrality of holiness as effortlessly as Ritschl does. In one of the very few references to holiness in *The New Theology*, Campbell accuses Roman Catholics and those whose theological genealogy runs through the Puritans of espousing 'the "awful holiness" of God' and of conceiving of God's holiness as mercilessly inflexible.[59]

The New Theology controversy exposed the egregious liberalism within the Free Churches, causing evangelicals to clarify and defend their faith, rather than to assume it. Campbell indeed represents the very sentimentalizing of Christianity and the subversion of holiness that Forsyth severely opposes.

In his Hull speech at the Union meeting in 1910, Forsyth spoke of

> adventurers who set up violently to discredit and revolutionise belief, not only without mastering the subject, but without having mastered a single theological classic or studied thoroughly and critically a single book of the Greek Testament. We ought to repel with warmth the claims to teach of men who inhale their theology out of their age, as orchids grow with their roots in the air, instead of planting it in historic revelation, like the tree of life.[60]

Although Forsyth, who 'preferred to avoid names and personalities and treat movements', insists that this reference was not to Campbell specifically but to those lay amateurish intellectuals from the literary and scientific community who 'have no honest place in an evangelical church', most, including Campbell himself, took it as an attack on Campbell.[61] Certainly Campbell had good reasons for thinking so. Forsyth, in his capacity as Chairman of the Congregational Union of England and Wales (a position he held from 1905) and as the leading adversary of Campbell's New Theology, had three years earlier retorted, 'it is not easy from [Campbell's] utterances

D. Appleton & Co., 1916), pp. 96–97. In 1904, Campbell wrote to a friend that 'God and the universe were not separate entities. Whatever else He may be, He is the universe, too, and, therefore, is one with all sentient life'. Cited in Albert H. Wilkerson, *The Rev. R. J. Campbell, the Man and His Message* (London: n.p., 1907), p. 50. Six years after the publication of *The New Theology*, Forsyth suggests Campbell departed Congregationalism because 'He craved for more mystic depth, atmosphere and control.' 'Spiritual Needs', p. 251.

55 Campbell, *The New Theology*, p. 9.

56 See ibid., pp. 146, 213–17.

57 Ibid., p. 84.

58 Ibid., p. 174.

59 Ibid., p. 60.

60 'Forsyth and Campbell', p. 172.

61 See H. C. Waddell, 'Is P. T. Forsyth Coming to His Own?' *Biblical Theology* 7 (1957), pp. 35–39 (38); Denney, *Letters of Principal James Denney to W. Robertson Nicoll*, pp. 79, 85–87, 107, 148.

to place him for a week at a time'.[62] He is 'like a bad photograph – underdeveloped and overexposed',[63] lacking clarity and explicitness.[64] After only a few days, however, a more composed Forsyth charged that although Campbell's ideas if taken to extreme are neither trinitarian nor theist – 'there is a group among us who are making a deliberate and organised attempt to assert for Unitarianism or Arianism a right within the liberties of Congregationalism'[65] – they do at least rescue us 'from a distant deism'.[66] However, in 'Immanence and Incarnation', Forsyth contends that immanence, as conceived by Campbell, fails to engage the existential bite and depths of human tragedy.[67] Moreover, Campbell's immanence theology both 'discourages the sense of guilt and the miracle of grace' and 'destroys the fundamental relation of God to the world as Creator to creature'.[68] It is not immanence we require but incarnation, not an idealized Sonship but a historic and reconciling Redeemer.

Forsyth laments the 'sense of wonder' eroded from a modern religion that has become too absorbed with love's immanence, too intoxicated with natural, poetic and aesthetic pursuits to contain the divine. He also considers liberalism's aesthetically determined morality too far removed from that 'moral amazement and awe which are inseparable from the mystery of grace. It has ceased to be to us a most strange thing that God should love, forgive, and save us'.[69] Writing in 1917, he says,

> It is not a new theology we need so much as a renovated theology, in which orthodoxy is deepened against itself, and not pared away... We have had many new theologies in the last hundred years. Theological enterprise has been turning them out freely. But the vein of liberalism, which thus followed on the old Orthodoxy... is now exhausted of religious ore. The spring has given out (to change the image), and the stream runs thin, and whispers softly among little pebbles, though once it roared among great boulders now left behind in the hills . . . We need that the

[62] 'Forsyth and Campbell', p. 172.

[63] *The Christian World* (31 January 1907).

[64] The New Theology's defeat within Congregationalism was chiefly due to Forsyth. Campbell later came to agree with Forsyth, confessing of *The New Theology*: 'It was much too hastily written, was crude and uncompromising in statement, polemical in spirit and gave a totally wrong impression of the quality of the sermons delivered week by week from the City Temple pulpit'. Cited in Cave, 'Forsyth', p. 115.

[65] 'Forsyth and Campbell', p. 172.

[66] 'Immanence', p. 48.

[67] Originally published in the *British Congregationalist* 24 (January 1907), pp. 77–78, the article is republished in *The Old Faith and the New Theology*, pp. 47–61.

[68] 'Immanence', p. 49.

[69] Ibid., p. 54. Forsyth's adoption of 'aesthetic' terminology requires some clarification. 'Aesthetics' refers to more than the harmony, symmetry and beauty of the senses. It extends to the symmetry of the rational order itself and is used occasionally in this sense to represent the principle of ordered, arranged thoughts. As a purely sensual notion, aesthetics is a 'peril to religion'. *Authority*, p. 105. He laments that 'we are still at a stage where the aesthetic imagination of nature is more active than the moral imagination of sanctity' and reminds that we ought not champion aesthetics or feeling towards the dear and desirable, but rather an aesthetic of conscience and 'obedience towards the holy and imperative'. *Sacraments*, pp. 290, 294; cf. *Sacraments*, pp. 16, 280; *Congregationalism*, p. 77; *Society*, p. 23.

> Gospel we offer be moralised at the centre from the Cross, and not rationalised at the surface by thin science.[70]

In a two-pronged critique of Victorian fascination with Romantic interpretations of creation's value, and of Campbell's neo-Hegelian pantheism, Forsyth presses that while the popular escape into cosmic emotions and contemplation of nature's grandeurs 'may enlarge the intelligence and calm the mind it cannot satisfy the soul. If your soul is wrong all nature cannot put it right'.[71]

Cognizant that 'the exclusion of those deemed to be Babylonians does not destroy the Babel in the souls of those who are left',[72] Forsyth was one of the very few pastor-critics who maintained friendship with Campbell throughout this difficult period.[73] Far from seeking to crush Campbell personally, the maturer Forsyth sought to reason with him. Less than a month after he wrote 'Immanence and Incarnation', Forsyth penned another article about Campbell's theology, this time to London's *Daily Chronicle*, wherein he says of Campbell:

> [His] motives are high, his enthusiasm is pure, his quality of mind is *spiritual* and sympathetic, his spirituality is ethical, his expression is lucid and consecutive, his temper of discussion is faultless . . . But, apart from his personality, it is quite impossible for those who take Christian truth seriously to treat his views with respect. It is not a question of heresy. It is a question of intellectual levity and temerity. It is a question of lack of knowledge, with no sense of the lack . . . Mr. Campbell gives no sign of even faintly realising the pain and anxiety produced by some of his wild public statements on those who worship Christ as Saviour . . . [and he is] grossly and absurdly inconsistent. But we should empty many saddles if men were shot for inconsistency. The man who worships Christ in sincerity and truth I dare not disown. And he has the true secret if he will let it carry him whither it would. Mr. Campbell does not understand the Cross, though he responds to it. He does not grasp its first theological principle. And he will never have a moral or rational basis for his worship of Christ till he does.[74]

It could be that Forsyth's concern for Campbell was partly motivated by his own inner fight against the powerful ghost of subjective neo-Hegelianism that formed part of his own early over-sentimentalist thinking.[75] What he considered in Campbell to be

[70] *Sacraments*, p. 20.

[71] Unpublished sermon on 2 Corinthians 4.17–18, in Goroncy (ed.), *'Descending on Humanity'*, 2013. It is likely that Campbell's pantheism would have recalled in Forsyth's mind the Leicester Conference, and the paraded pantheism in a paper delivered by James Allanson Picton.

[72] *Sacraments*, p. 75.

[73] Forsyth had once hoped that Campbell might succeed him at Emmanuel Church. Campbell refused. Campbell, *Spiritual Pilgrimage*, p. 83. The New Theology controversy cost Forsyth 'in nervous exhaustion more than anyone outside could imagine' both in terms of physical and emotional health, and in the heavy responsibility he felt as College Principal for the future 'career of some of our men'. Andrews, 'Memoir', p. xxi.

[74] 'New Theology', np.

[75] See *Maid Arise*, np.

dangerous to the age and for the Church, he knew not only because he had subsequently been made 'an object of grace' but because he had first experienced Campbell's other 'gospel'. He had been where Campbell was. Although Campbell initially seemed unable to distinguish between an attack on this theology and that on his person,[76] Forsyth's unwavering affection was such that it assisted Campbell to eventually publicly repudiate his New Theology (he recalled *The New Theology* in 1911), make a strong christocentric statement at the 1911 Congregational Union meeting,[77] resign from City Temple (1916) and be re-ordained as an Anglican priest.[78] This theological shift is reflected in his mature writings, some of which echo Forsythian themes:

> That consuming fire is eternal as God himself; it is because he is; it is that which was from the beginning, is now, and ever shall be, world without end. In that scorching, purifying blast everything shrivels up and perishes which does not pertain to Christ and the kingdom of Christ in the heart of man. Oh, if there be one thing for which we ought to rejoice and praise God without ceasing, it is that eternal fire which will burn up all the foulness and rottenness, all the wickedness and hate, all the shame and wrong from which our souls have ever suffered. It is not evil that will have the last word, but good, not sorrow but joy, not sin, but holiness.[79]

As testimony to the reconciliatory nature of the brand of holiness that Forsyth was committed to expounding and living,[80] history records that in 1922 Campbell spoke at the dedication of a memorial to Forsyth, offering a tribute that during those tumultuous years (1907–11) Forsyth had been nearer to him than most of his own supporters and

[76] Nicoll characterized Campbell as a man of moods and inspirations, poorly trained, badly read and entirely out of his league for the level of debate he had chosen to engage in. W. Robertson Nicoll, 'City Temple Theology', *British Weekly* 24 (1907), pp. 437–38. And Forsyth may have had Campbell in mind when he wrote that the task of restating Christian truth should be done by 'competent and reverent people and not by amateurs, with but a natural religion and a poor education or none on the subject; for the worst heresy is quackery'. *Person*, p. 240.

[77] See Anonymous, 'Autumnal Assembly', *British Weekly*, 19 October 1911, p. 90, and Forsyth's warm response in 'Letter 1911', p. 100. Campbell's statement was published as far abroad as New Zealand: 'During a discussion at the conference of the Congregational Union of England on the "Historical Basis of Christianity," Rev. R. J. Campbell – the well-known minister of the City Temple, Holborn Viaduct, London, and author of "The New Theology" – declared that "Christianity was impossible without a living personal Christ." Amid cheers, Dr P. T. Forsyth, Principal of the Hackney Theological College, ex-chairman of the Union, and author of numerous theological works – declared that, after hearing what Mr Campbell had said, the sharp contentions which had existed between that gentleman and himself for the past five years were at an end.' Anonymous, 'The New Theology', *Wairarapa Daily Times*, 30 October 1911, p. 2.

[78] See Campbell, *Spiritual Pilgrimage*, pp. 253–76; Reginald J. Campbell, *The Call of Christ: Sermons Preached on Various Occasions, Chiefly in Advent and Lent* (London: Skeffington & Son, 1932).

[79] R. J. Campbell, 'Sermon on The Eternal Fire'. Cited in G. A. Gaskell (ed.), *Dictionary of the Sacred Languages of All Scriptures and Myths, Part 2* (Whitefish: Kessinger, 2003), p. 276.

[80] For example, at a time when the relationship between Anglicanism and the Free Church was far from cordial, Forsyth penned *The Charter of the Church* and *Rome, Reform and Reaction*. While lesser theologians on both sides sought to win applause by mere denunciation of the other, Forsyth's works are models of courteous polemic which deal not with individual abuses but with broader principles.

that he had always been conscious of Forsyth's personal concern for him.[81] Such is the shape that holiness takes in the world.

II. Landscape

The elusiveness of a concept

Given the centrality of divine and creaturely holiness in Holy Scripture, Christian theologians have surprisingly made relatively little of the idea in their theology proper. While copious material is available on God's righteousness, faithfulness and love, the extra-biblical tradition betrays something of a lack of sustained reflection on holiness, specifically divine holiness. Where such is offered, the tradition characteristically conflates holiness into concepts of righteousness, goodness, truth and glory (most often using specifically judicial language) or of God's perfections. Alternatively, holiness is used to consummate, unify and harmonize all incomparable divine attributes. Most seem content to work with the uncertain etymological meaning as it relates of God's 'otherness', 'his sheer difference from everything else'.[82] This otherness expresses itself both negatively and positively. Negatively, in its rejection of all that is opposed to God; positively, in the sanctifying of things and creatures other than God. Typically, what most definitions fail to offer, however, is any clarity over the prime locus of holiness' revelation via christology.[83]

Forsyth and Otto: Holiness as 'Incarnation' or 'Idea'

Rudolph Otto's (1869–1937) designation of 'the holy' as *mysterium tremendum* (what Goethe termed the 'daemonic'[84]) is not without its usefulness (as helpful descriptors of Isaiah 6 and Luke 2.9, and as a reminder that religion is more than disguised morality, for example), though it is less helpful than has often been considered.[85] Otto has overstated and oversimplified his case, partially because of an over-dependence, of which he is aware, on the residual *rationalism* of Immanuel Kant and Jakob

81 Anonymous, 'The Addresses Delivered at the Unveiling of the Tablet Erected in the College Library, to the Memory of Rev. Peter Taylor Forsyth, MA, DD, 11 May 1922' (New College Library, University of London, 1922), pp. 5–10.

82 Colin E. Gunton, *The Christian Faith: An Introduction to Christian Doctrine* (Oxford: Blackwell, 2002), p. 49. God's otherness is partly a function of his election of a people for the sake of the world. Thus, 'to call God the Holy One *of Israel* implies presence, not absence, insiderness, not outsiderness'. Christopher R. Seitz, *Word Without End: The Old Testament as Abiding Theological Witness* (Grand Rapids/Cambridge: Wm. B. Eerdmans, 1998), p. 23.

83 See 'Christ's Person', p. 21; Goroncy, 'The Elusiveness, Loss, and Cruciality of Recovered Holiness', pp. 195–209.

84 See Angus Nicholls, *Goethe's Concept of the Daemonic: After the Ancients* (Rochester: Camden House, 2006); Ronald D. Gray, *Goethe: A Critical Introduction* (Cambridge: Cambridge University Press, 1967), p. 112.

85 See Owen Rogers Jones, *The Concept of Holiness* (London: George Allen & Unwin, 1961); Helmer Ringgren, *The Prophetical Conception of Holiness* (Uppsala: A.-B. Lundequistska Bokhandeln, 1948), p. 10; Colin Crowder, 'Rudolph Otto's *The Idea of the Holy* Revisited', in *Holiness Past and Present* (ed. S. C. Barton; London/New York: T&T Clark, 2003), pp. 22–47.

Fries.[86] While holiness certainly carries connotations of the mystery of divine power, it is far from the naked omnipotence that Otto describes. Not only does the New Testament call for a more christocentric definition, but Otto's notion of holiness is far too entrapped in a subjectivist framework to truly shed light on the broader spectrum of biblical teaching on holiness.[87] Yet for all his Kantianism, Otto remains suspicious of Forsyth's approach of employing holiness as a moral category which serves to qualify the nature and *telos* of God's love, accusing this route of narrowing and trivializing the Holy. That said, long before Otto, Forsyth was speaking of the 'idea of the holy',[88] challenging his romantic-love-besotted generation with the truth that 'the holiness of God is the real foundation of religion'.[89] Forsyth insists that love, grace, faith and sin mean nothing apart from God's holiness – as they arise from it, return to it, satisfy it, show it forth, set it up and secure it ubiquitously forever. The Forsythian notion of holiness as the creative power of God has not always been understood, however, even by those otherwise sympathetic to his theological programme. Those who wish to underscore that 'raw' holiness terrifies and repels rather than appeals and wins, for example, have strayed somewhat from the path that Forsyth – for whom holiness is intensely personal, creative and determined to create that which it seeks and seek that which it creates – is concerned to walk.

With the tradition, Forsyth maintains that holiness has no meaning apart from God. God is ontologically holy. Indeed, holiness is the one thing about God that is without parallel in the created order. It ought then come as no surprise that holiness can only be conceived by revelation – by giving itself to us. That God does precisely this is an expression of God's freedom to be *for* and *with* the creature. That this 'giving' happens in the beloved Son is assurance that divine holiness is that which stoops down to us in a merciful voyage of anguish (to borrow a phrase from H. R. Mackintosh[90]) and at great cost. Put otherwise, God's holiness never means that God is less gracious; a truth that Ritschl fails to grasp. Here Forsyth reveals a development in the idea of holiness absent in Otto's *mysterium tremendum*, Paul Tillich's 'the divine' or 'the *quality* of that which concerns man ultimately'[91] and Jacques Derrida's 'unscathed which is safe and sound'.[92] Forsyth offers us not the results of a particular reading of a universal religious phenomenon but a specifically *Christian* understanding of holiness – that is, one determined by the evangelical centre of the divine economy; namely, Jesus Christ. That

[86] Rudolph Otto, 'Foreword by the Author', in *The Idea of the Holy: An Inquiry into the Non-Rational Factor in the Idea of the Divine and its Relation to the Rational* (London: Oxford University Press, 1931), p. vii. On Otto's relationship to Fries, see Philip C. Almond, 'Rudolf Otto and the Kantian Tradition', *Neue Zeitschrift für Systematische Theologie und Religionsphilosophie* 25, no. 1 (1983), pp. 52–67; Philip C. Almond, 'Rudolph Otto: The Context of His Thought', *Scottish Journal of Theology* 36 (1983), pp. 347–62 (354–55).

[87] See Friedrich Schleiermacher, *The Christian Faith* (ed. H. R. Mackintosh and J. S. Stewart; trans. D. M. Baillie; Edinburgh: T&T Clark, 1928), pp. 341–45; cf. Owen Ware, 'Rudolph Otto's Idea of the Holy: A Reappraisal', *The Heythrop Journal* 48, no. 1 (2007), 48–60.

[88] *Authority*, pp. 188, 191; *Justification*, pp. 107, 117, 121; *Preaching*, pp. 199, 211, *Sacraments*, p. 89.

[89] *Cruciality*, p. 38.

[90] Hugh Ross Mackintosh, *The Christian Experience of Forgiveness* (London: Nisbet, 1927), p. 191.

[91] Paul Tillich, *Systematic Theology* (vol. 1; London: Nisbet & Co., 1955), p. 239.

[92] Jacques Derrida, 'Faith and Knowledge: The Two Sources of "Religion" at the Limits of Reason Alone', in *Religion* (ed. Jacques Derrida and Gianni Vattimo; Cambridge: Polity Press, 1998), p. 36.

said, the charge that Forsyth's presentation of holiness is insufficiently trinitarian, and particularly that it is pneumatalogically undersupplied is deserving.[93] Any criticism of Forsyth's trinitarianism, however, must be assessed in the context of Forsyth's age. While there was some early interest in trinitarian theology among Nonconformist theologians in the 1930s (by H. Wheeler Robinson and Robert Franks, for example) any serious endeavours (such as those offered by Colin Gunton, Paul Fiddes and others) post-dated Forsyth's death by half a century or more. Even as consequential a theologian as Wilhelm Herrmann has little in his *Dogmatik* devoted to the Spirit.[94] While Forsyth believes that the prevalent Ritschlianism demotes the role the Spirit, he generally reflects the West's pneumatalogical poverty adjusting his sights on the second article of the Creed – the Word enfleshed, crucified, proclaimed and inscribed. To be fair too, Forsyth was fighting other battles, and the dangers regarding identification of the Spirit with Hegel's and Romanticism's *Geist*, and that with history itself, were never far away. Indeed, Forsyth explicitly warns of those who are 'full of *Geist* . . . but not full of the Holy Ghost'.[95] This is aptly illustrated in the charges of pantheism laid against Schleiermacher in the early 1800s when he began to recover a sense of the uncreated Spirit who enlivens all things. Whether in the face of the New Theology controversy Forsyth was concerned that a similar charge may be made against him, or simply because he was part of that mainstream of theological conversation wherein pneumatology is less explicit, Forsyth insists on the closest possible relation between cross and Spirit and consistently identifies the Spirit's sanctifying work closely with christology: 'if ever divine holiness is to be produced in man it can only be produced by God's act through Christ in the Holy Spirit'.[96] Forsyth contends, moreover, that it is by the Spirit that God 'knows Himself',[97] that God has self-consciousness, and that it is this same Spirit who in the determination of grace is both active throughout the Christian experience and who makes all things new. Forsyth is concerned too about the mysticalization of the moral impulse in faith that considers the Spirit and the Spirit's sanctification as a 'second revelation' or new dispensation apart from, or subsequent to, Christ. He believes that whenever we detach the Spirit from the Spirit's 'real source' in the cross we encourage antinomianism and isolate faith from life.[98] The other charge that can be laid fairly against Forsyth is that his pneumatology is too subsumed under ecclesiological boundaries: 'The Holy Spirit can act upon the main stream of human history only by spiritual communities.'[99] He concedes that the Spirit has 'action and

[93] See Gunton, 'Real as the Redemptive', p. 54; Stephen W. Sykes, 'P. T. Forsyth on the Church', in *Justice the True and Only Mercy: Essays on the Life and Theology of Peter Taylor Forsyth* (ed. Trevor A. Hart; Edinburgh: T&T Clark, 1995), pp. 13–14; Terry, *The Justifying Judgement of God*, p. 102.

[94] Wilhelm Herrmann, *Systematic Theology (Dogmatik)* (trans. Nathaniel Micklem and Kenneth A. Saunders; London: George Allen & Unwin, 1927), pp. 145–48.

[95] 'Regeneration – I', p. 640.

[96] *Work*, p. 72. Furtherore, Forsyth emphasizes that it is by the Holy Spirit that we make our theories of atonement, and that the Spirit guides God's people in the exegesis and proclamation of Scripture. *Freedom*, pp. vii, 7, 11–16, 19–20, 26–35, 39, 42, 83–84, 91, 102, 119, 143, 306–07; 'Protestantism', p. 4; *Society*, p. 125.

[97] *Person*, p. 116.

[98] *Work*, p. 218; cf. *Authority*, p. 116; 'Fund', p. 219; *Art*, p. 82.

[99] *Charter*, p. 61.

effect outside the churches'[100] but unfortunately he never adequately unpacks the implications of such a commitment.

While general consensus supports that the notion of 'otherness' is not absent, Forsyth posits that it is more proper to define God's holiness by considering its expression in the divine economy as it takes shape in history, centrally in the incarnation of the Son, but also in the sending of the Spirit, and in God's election of a people whose *telos* is life formed after God. Certainly, as I have already noted, Forsyth never considers God's holiness in abstraction from God's sanctifying activity in Jesus Christ. Holiness is that which suckles on Mary's breast, is crucified under Pontius Pilate and which goes on bearing witness to God's creative suffering amid the world's ruin. In this vein, 'holiness is not anything that can just be shown; it must be done'.[101] Holiness is action, manifested in creating, sustaining, judging and delivering: 'God evinces his holiness in his actions, which mediate the historical and cosmic presence of God together with his absolute transcendence'.[102] Divine holiness *must* find expression, must exert itself in action. It is not enough that God's love be emptied out on creation. The Creator must personally carry the evil for which the Creator is held liable. Hence, God in Christ is God's own theodicy; God alone can do full justice to God's own name, and do so 'from sin's side'.[103] Holy love proceeds to establish command of all in order to present humanity to God 'presanctified'.[104] Though transcendent, here is no remote or static god of the deists or the epicureans. The influence here of the Baden School theologian Ernst Troeltsch (1865–1923), whose writings are familiar to Forsyth,[105] is apparent:

> The divine holiness is no moralism. God did not give the world his law and then abandon it; instead, he searches for the creature with love and passion, creating the very holiness that he demands. Here we find no cold law, no crushing commandment that seeks fulfilment in human compliance; we find a holy love that embraces us and incorporates us into itself, thereby bringing us to faith.[106]

Where, O holiness, is your 'definition'?

Despite the pervasiveness of the grammar and idea of holiness throughout Forsyth's corpus, Forsyth's readers search in vain for a definition of holiness per se:

> The holiness of God is beyond our definition, for it is God the holy; and we cannot define a person, far less the absolute Person. It is not simply His perfection either in thought or act. Its appeal is to something beyond both mind and will. It carries us

[100] Ibid.
[101] *Justification*, p. 167.
[102] Thomas Söding, 'Heilig, heilig, heilig. Zur politischen Theologie der Johannes-Apokalypse', *Zeitschrift für Theologie und Kirche* 96 (1999), pp. (49–76) 56.
[103] *Cruciality*, p. 182; cf. *Justification*, p. 125.
[104] *Work*, p. 225.
[105] *Authority*, p. 153; 'Christian Principle', p. 142; *Freedom*, pp. 60, 75, 89–90, 123, 128, 150; *Person*, pp. 248, 267, 347; *Preaching*, p. 152.
[106] Ernst Troeltsch, *The Christian Faith* (ed. G. von le Fort; trans. G. E. Paul; Minneapolis: Fortress, 1991), p. 119.

> deeper into God and man. We cannot define it, we can but realise it. And, as it is the last reality, we can but realise it in the last and highest energy of the soul. It is that in God which emerges upon us and comes home to us only in our worship.[107]

Forsyth contends that holiness has to do first and foremost with God. Its language is not borrowed from the realm of human experience and is consequently (and uniquely) free from all logic of metaphor. Unable to be either translated or substituted for any other word, its meaning therefore can only be determined within the dynamic of theology which it both reveals and mediates, even while it veils its principal subject. Unsurprisingly, therefore, the vocabulary of divine holiness is most clearly preserved in the language of liturgy and prayer – in those arenas of human activity where God is spoken to rather than spoken about, where God is realized and praised rather than analysed and appraised, and where the burden of precise definition and explanation is not only less pressing, but if pressed could be disadvantageous and distorting. Forsyth cautions that any attempt to define holiness with the precision of thought that systematic theology characteristically strives for is futile. What holiness does, he argues, is to direct us towards reality itself rather than towards carefully formulated 'truth' statements. Consequently, his grammar regarding holiness tends to be more impressionistic than descriptive. This mirrors the task, he argues, of theology anyway – it is more an energy of the soul than an activity of the mind. That reality is personal means that it is described by the relations of obligation, obedience, worship and love.

'To the theologian the changeless holiness of God stands for the like capital to that which the physicist finds in the uniformity of nature.'[108] Holiness is 'the most perfect and real thing in the universe'.[109] It has to do, in other words, with divine ontology: 'no word more so, nor indeed any other as much'. [110] McCurdy and Burton[111] mistakenly argue that, for Forsyth, holiness is a divine 'attribute'. Forsyth, for his part, insists that holiness 'is no attribute of God, but his very essence . . . It is not a quality in God, but the being of God, in which all else inheres'.[112] Indeed, it is reckless, Forsyth believes, to speak of God having attributes *in se*. And even more certainly the charge of a 'crisis of attributes'[113] in Forsyth's God betrays a failure to understand his thought at this point. Forsyth is very cautions about the grammar of attributes, arguing that what he might

107 *Authority*, p. 418; cf. *Preaching*, pp. 138–39. Some theologians have sought to distinguish between God's 'essential holiness' and his 'moral holiness'; that is, between ontology and economy. See James Marsh, *Select Practical Works of Rev. John Howe and Dr. William Bates* (New York/Burlington: G. & C. & H. Carvill/Chauncey Goodrich, 1830), p. 57; John Rogerson, 'What is Holiness?', in *Holiness Past and Present* (ed. S. C. Barton; London/New York: T&T Clark, 2003), pp. 3–21. And Douglas has argued that holiness means not only separation to divine service, but also wholeness/completeness. Mary Douglas, *Purity and Danger: An Analysis of Concepts of Pollution and Taboo* (London: Routledge, 2002), p. 52.

108 *Cruciality*, p. 147.

109 *Jesus*, p. 88; cf. *Jesus*, p. 47; *Work*, p. 204.

110 Norman H. Snaith, *The Distinctive Ideas of the Old Testament* (London: Epworth Press, 1947), p. 21.

111 McCurdy, *Attributes and Atonement*, p. 208; Burton, 'Glorious in Holiness', pp. 120, 122–29.

112 *Revelation*, p. 62; cf. *Preaching*, p. 145. On the divine attributes see *Authority*, p. 418; *Person*, pp. 197, 309; *Work*, pp. 117–18.

113 Stott, *The Cross of Christ*, pp. 129–31; McCurdy, *Attributes and Atonement*, pp. 148, 277; cf. *Jesus*, p. 110.

consider an attribute is actually God himself 'in a certain angle and relation'.[114] His concern is clearly articulated when he insists that an attribute is not 'something loose within God which He could manipulate – as though the attributes of God were not God Himself, unchangeable God, in certain relations. The attributes of God are not things within Himself which He could handle and adjust. An attribute of God is God Himself behaving, with all His unity, in a particular way in a particular situation'.[115] Holiness is '[God's] name, and being, and infinite value'.[116] Holiness is not an isolated attribute magnified, but 'God's very essence and nature: changeless and inexorable'.[117] It is God's self-satisfaction, the actuality of the triune life. 'By holiness is not meant anything so abstract or subjective as mystical absorption, but the whole concrete righteousness of existence, self-sustained at white heat. For our God is a consuming fire.'[118] God does not do 'holy things'. God acts, and those acts are congruous with who God is. Just as Forsyth considers God's love not as an attribute but as God loving, so too he considers holiness as 'the whole God himself as holy'.[119]

'In the Bible', Forsyth says, 'things, or places, or people are holy which are set apart for God; God is Holy as He is set apart for Himself. Things are holy as they are for God; He is holy as He is for Himself'.[120] And again: 'For the creature to be holy is *to be for God*; for God Himself to be holy is *to be God*.'[121] Holiness, in fact, is God's chief concern precisely because it is so absolutely personal, describing God's very life and self-giving in electing, recalling and perfecting prodigals for 'personal intercourse with the Holy' wherein thoughts and feelings are exchanged.[122] Consequently, Forsyth resists speculating on what holiness is *in se*, and concentrates on pronouncing on what holiness *does*: 'Holiness is not mere purity or saintliness; it is kingship, moral kingship, the moral absolute taking slow, costly, invincible possession of its own. It carries with it the patience which is sure of its achieved reversion of the world, the portentous meekness (not without irony) which inherits the earth and has the world in fee.'[123]

Forsyth also understands that holiness can finally leave nothing outside its reach. Holiness is all that creation will be in the fullness of time when at last it corresponds in its own proper creaturely way to all that God is. This is because, as Rowan Williams

[114] *Person*, p. 309.

[115] *Work*, p. 117.

[116] *Life*, p. 29. The most likely root for *shēm* is from the Arabic *wšm*, which means to mark or brand. The close connection between name and existence (Deut. 7.24; 9.14; 29.20 and 1 Sam. 24.21 suggest that to 'cut off the name' is to eliminate the person – and their line – forever), character and reputation (e.g. 1 Sam. 25.25) suggests that to defile God's name is to threaten to destroy God's existence. Hence the cruciality of Jesus' ministry as the hallower – a battle for the very being of God. Kaiser notes that 'in some passages *shēm Yahweh* is so inextricably bound up with the being of God, that it functions almost like an appearance of Yahweh (Ex 23:20–21; Isa 30:27)' and that the tabernacling of the Name at various places in the OT acts 'almost like a Christophany'. Walter C. Kaiser, '(shem) name', in *Theological Wordbook of the Old Testament* (ed. Gleason L. Archer et al.; Chicago: Moody, 1980), p. 934.

[117] *Cruciality*, p. 205.

[118] Ibid., p. 159, fn. 1; 'Insufficiency', p. 607, fn. 1.

[119] *Work*, p. 118.

[120] *Life*, p. 28.

[121] Ibid., p. 29.

[122] *Work*, p. 68.

[123] 'Religion and Reality', p. 551

observes, God cannot bear to be separated from the reflection of himself and 'goes eagerly in search of it, hungry to find in the created "other" the reality of his own life and bliss'.[124] Or, in Forsythian parlance: 'if the holiness do not go out to cover, imbue, conquer, and sanctify all things, if it do not give itself in love, it is the less holy'.[125] It would not, in other words, be absolute, authoritative and self-satisfied. Moreover, holiness alone can achieve such an end with all intact, for 'only the holy can love for ever and for ever subdue the loveless; only the holy can thoroughly forgive so as to make His holiness dear'.[126]

God's conscience

> *If your heart condemn you, His condemnation is greater than that of your condemning heart. Do you consider His conscience? His conscience has to be pacified as well as His heart indulged. And if His conscience be not met, ours is not sure.*[127]
>
> *... all begins and ends there – in a theology of the conscience of God.*[128]

One of the most fascinating features of Forsyth's theology proper is the notion that God has a conscience.[129] Such a notion does raise a question, however. For while this is probably an acceptable homiletical phrase, is the application of such grammar (more or less univocally to God and to humans) any more than an impossible anthropomorphism in strict theology? Rodgers argues that Forsyth's locution of a divine conscience is shorthand for 'God's faithfulness to himself, to his absolute possession of himself, to the utter seriousness with which he regards himself'.[130] True enough, but such a definition falls short of exhausting Forsyth's meaning. Put simply, for Forsyth, 'God's conscience' is synonymous with holiness. This is evident, for example, when Forsyth articulates his belief that liberalism's bane is that it fails to grasp 'the idea of the holy as the changeless thing in God, God's conscience, the immutable thing in the universe, the ruling principle of religion, and the organizing principle of its truth as theology'.[131] Consequently, liberalism (Kantian and other) dulls the reality of sin 'which is the central issue of all ethic because it turns on the relation of the conscience to the conscience of God', and so marauding that which makes grace grace.[132]

124 Rowan Williams, *Ponder These Things: Praying with Icons of the Virgin* (Norwich: Canterbury Press, 2002), p. 27.
125 *Life*, p. 29.
126 Ibid.
127 *Work*, pp. 166–67.
128 *World-Commonwealth*, p. 4.
129 The only other place of which I am aware where the idea is present is in Horace Bushnell, *The Vicarious Sacrifice Grounded in Principles of Universal Obligation* (New York: Charles Scribner and Co., 1866), p. 238. 'The conscience of God is only the fact itself of his moral nature.' On a popular level, José Saramago suggests God has a guilty conscience, which is why God gets no sleep – that God might 'avoid the nightmares of remorse'. José Saramago, *The Gospel According to Jesus Christ* (trans. G. Pontiero; San Diego: Harcourt Brace & Co., 1994), p. 193.
130 John H. Rodgers, *The Theology of P. T. Forsyth: The Cross of Christ and the Revelation of God* (London: Independent Press, 1965), p. 34.
131 *Authority*, p. 191; cf. *World-Commonwealth*, p. 3.
132 *Cruciality*, pp. 31–32.

Although Forsyth rarely alludes to the *imago dei*, it is in his examination of God's conscience that the thought enters: 'If there is a difficulty due to man's moral psychology, the root of it is really in God's, who so made man in his image that the transgressor's way is hard.'[133] Hart properly observes that conscience is 'not just that in humans which keys them directly into the moral order in and through which God addresses them, but [it is] something which both share in common.'[134] Creation's moral fabric, Forsyth contends, is created by the consummation of God's holy conscience in the eternal action of God's love and for the reflection of such. The atonement, therefore, represents the undivided, changeless, self-sustained and absolute conscience of God accounting for itself. Indeed, not only is God's conscience the 'ethic of eternity',[135] and 'the supreme conscience of the world',[136] but what is happening in the Divine Conscience's 'greatest Act'[137] is definitively the satisfaction, justification and reconciliation of two consciences – God's and humanity's. It is most certainly not the 'rapt commingling of two beings, or the infusion of one nature into another'.[138] Rather, it is the 'adjustment, the pacification, of conscience, and especially God's'.[139] And the hypostatic union means that the justification of two consciences takes place inescapably in the one person who is (as Forsyth would have it) 'the soul and conscience of the race'[140] and in whom reconciliation is not (as the Ritschlians would have it) about two hearts making up, or sympathetic adjustment wherein humans open themselves up to God, but is a matter of two consciences making good.[141]

Forsyth accuses of treason those new humanists who would speak of a general conscience of the nation detached from its 'one public focus of moral creation and inspiration' in Christ, and insists that we comprehend it, instead, evangelically and christologically; as, in other words, 'the crisis and regeneration of the universal conscience of the world by the eternal conscience of a God of holy love'.[142]

> Christ was and is the conscience of mankind and of God. He called Himself man's final judge. Was he deluded? He stands in the whole race as conscience does in each man. But He also means that the Eternal conscience is the Eternal love, that judgment is, in the heart of it, grace, that the judge is on our side and is our Redeemer. It is only love that can do justice, it is only grace that can right all wrong.[143]

133 'Christ's Person', p. 8.
134 Hart, 'Morality, Atonement and the Death of Jesus', pp. 19–20.
135 *Cruciality*, p. 25.
136 *War*, p. 133.
137 Ibid., p. 115.
138 *Congregationalism*, p. 30.
139 *Cruciality*, p. 116; cf. *Authority*, p. 415.
140 *Justification*, p. 220; cf. *War*, p. 53.
141 'Christ's Person', pp. 7–8. There is no sense of equality here. 'The God of the conscience' (*Authority*, p. 365), the 'holy conscience' (*Justification*, p. 88), remains the absolute conscience who exerts divine authority over and upon the guilty human conscience, and offers it a new authority. Neither is God's conscience latent in its creaturely counterpart, but it is 'revealed to it in history' (*Authority*, p. 401) – that is, 'fontally and creatively' in the moral focus and crisis of God's own conscience in the practical action of the cross. *Jesus*, p. 97.
142 *Justification*, p. 96.
143 *Cruciality*, p. 132.

We must not read Forsyth here as conflating God's conscience with some Kantian notion of abstract moral reality. Forsyth's insistence on God's personal and living nature, and the stress he lays on the active obedience of the incarnate Son (as opposed to Kant's more static depiction), mean that we ought not to conflate the two. Indeed, Christian hope and ethics proceed on the basis that the two not be fused.

> If He, the great one conscience of the world, who had the best right and the most occasion in all the world to complain of God for the world's treatment of Him – if He hallowed and glorified God's name with joy instead (Matt. xi. 25–27; Luke xxiii. 46), there is no moral anomaly that cannot be turned, and is not by long orbits being turned, to the honour of God's holy love, and the joy of His crushed and common millions.[144]

God's holy love

> *The gospel of God's holy love in the form of forgiving grace is the greatest miracle in the world. It is the most wonderful, inexplicable and supernatural thing in the world that the holy should forgive the unholy, the anti-holy.*[145]
>
> *Your holy love condemns us all, it slays|the self-claimed virtue that insults your name|the worthless pride we wear|your holy love alone has power to raise|our self-inflicted souls from death and shame|to save us from despair.*[146]

The notion of the divine conscience is, in Forsyth's mind, indispensable from that of 'Holy Love'. But the notion of 'Holy Love' – a phrase not unique to Forsyth[147] – can be and has been understood in a variety of ways. Thomas Oden, for example, speaks for not a few when he argues that Christ's death was to 'bring together the holiness and love of God as they cohere eternally in God'.[148] But such is not Forsyth's view. For Forsyth, holiness and love are not *brought together* at all – ever! Rather, in the face of evil, the divine economy manifests the holiness of love.

'Holy Love' so dominates Forsyth's mature thought that one recent enthusiast penned, 'If I were forced to name one twentieth-century Nonconformist theologian who, more decisively than any other has driven to the heart of the gospel of God's holy love, my choice would fall upon P. T. Forsyth'.[149] Although, as Forsyth concedes, 'the God of holy love is a paradox',[150] if God be not holy love in his eternity, then his love towards us economically would be without ontological foundation. God is holy love towards us

144 *Justification*, p. 125.

145 'Foolishness', p. 153.

146 Alan Gaunt, 'For PT Forsyth, 1848–1921', in *PT Forsyth: Theologian for a New Millennium* (ed. Alan P. F. Sell; London: The United Reformed Church, 2000), p. 5.

147 The expression also finds voice in Germans Isaak Dorner, Martin Kähler, Gottfried Thomasius, Karl Nitzsch, and in Scots Andrew Davidson, Robert Flint, Thomas Erskine and James Denney, all of whose work was familiar to Forsyth.

148 Thomas Oden, *Life in the Spirit, Systematic Theology* (vol. 3; Peabody: Prince, 2001), p. 250.

149 Alan P. F. Sell, *Nonconformist Theology in the Twentieth Century: The Didsbury Lectures 2006* (Milton Keynes: Paternoster, 2007), p. 163.

150 *Life*, p. 28.

because God is holy love *in se*, that is, in God's own triune *koinonia*. From the life of holy perichoretic hospitality, God creates, loves, sanctifies. Indeed, Forsyth insists that God's love is love precisely because God has power to subdue all things to the holiness of love. God's love, in other words, is nugatory unless it go out in gracious judgement to undo its antithesis. God's is a love, as another has recognized, of 'cauterising holiness'.[151] A failure to move against sin would be neither loving nor holy. As Anders Nygren reminds us, 'Only that love which pronounces judgment on all that is not love is in the truest sense restoring and saving love. And, conversely, no judgment pierces so deep as the judgment of Love. That which cannot be won by the reckless self-giving of love cannot be won at all; there remains only Judgment'.[152] Or as Barth reminds us, 'It would be a strange love that was satisfied with the mere existence and nature of the other, then withdrawing, leaving it to its own devices'.[153] Holy love relinquishes sinners in their sinning at the same time as it moves savingly towards them to reconcile, transform, liberate and enable.

In Forsyth's moralizing of dogma, there is no crisis of attributes between divine love and holiness, or a need for re-adjustment between wrath and propitiating love.[154] Christ does not, as Milton has it, step into the breach to 'end the strife of mercy and justice in thy face discern'd'.[155] Forsyth's point, with Wilhelm Herrmann, is that with God we have to do with a unity of Person, and not, as John Stott suggests, with 'a conflict of emotions, a strife of attributes . . . "duality" within God'.[156] Accordingly, responsible theology is unconcerned with an isolating investigation of the divine perfections uprooted from the self-revealing identity and unity of the Triune God in God's economy.[157] This is, is part, what motivates Forsyth's claim that love is not an attribute of God, but is simply God loving. Neither is holiness an attribute, but it is 'the whole God Himself as holy. There is nothing in the Bible about the strife of attributes'.[158] Moreover, Forsyth avers that love without holiness lends itself too easily to unreality, sentiment and dissimulation, just as sovereignty abstracted from grace lends to despotism,[159] and that holy love is one self-qualifying word and not a conflation of two separate ideas: 'The great triumphant

[151] John Arthur Thomas Robinson, *In the End, God: A Study of the Christian Doctrine of the Last Things* (London: James Clarke & Co., 1950), p. 104.

[152] Anders Nygren, *Agape and Eros* (vol. 1; London: SPCK, 1932–39), p. 75.

[153] Karl Barth, *Church Dogmatics III.1* (ed. G. W. Bromiley and T. F. Torrance; trans. J. W. Edwards et al.; Edinburgh: T&T Clark, 1958), p. 95.

[154] Forsyth does employ the grammar of 'adjustment' as it pertains to the pacification of God's conscience (*Cruciality*, p. 116), but he qualifies the language over against notions of vengeance or pacification. Judgement involves readjustment in God's dealing with humanity, rather than a change in God's attitude.

[155] John Milton, *The Paradise Lost* (ed. James Robert Boyd; New York: A. S. Barnes & Co., 1867), p. 132.

[156] Stott, *The Cross of Christ*, p. 130; cf. Herrmann, *Dogmatik*, p. 122. Shaw is mistaken to see in Forsyth's theology 'almost a dualism' between God's holiness and love. J. M. Shaw, 'The Theology of P. T. Forsyth', *Theology Today* (1946), pp. 358–70 (369).

[157] The grammar of attributes, too, tends to close down rather than open up enquiry into persons, whether human or divine. See Adolf Schlatter, *Das christliche Dogma* (Stuttgart: Calwer Verlag, 1977), p. 356; Russel F. Aldwinckle, *More Than Man* (Grand Rapids: Wm. B. Eerdmans, 1976), p. 194; Thomas A. Smail, *Once and For All: A Confession of the Cross* (Eugene, OR: Wipf and Stock, 2005), p. 130.

[158] *Work*, p. 118; cf. *Authority*, p. 418; *Cruciality*, p. 78; *Revelation*, p. 62; *Work*, p. 105.

[159] *Cruciality*, p. 173; cf. Robert W. Dale, *Christian Doctrine: A Series of Discourses* (London: Hodder & Stoughton, 1894), pp. 241–42.

reality in love, the divine thing in it, is its moral righteousness and invincible holiness. Holiness is the antiseptic in love which saves it from its own weakness'.[160]

Hughes suggests that Forsyth's emphasis on divine holiness is 'one of the primary weaknesses of Forsyth's view' because it opposes the New Testament notion of love.[161] Pitt and Ferré too suggest that Forsyth undermines divine grace and love by making these dependent on holiness' satisfaction, implying that Forsyth's God is selfish because ultimately concerned not with the plight of 'the miserable sinner' but with 'himself and his infrangible holiness'.[162] But this is to grossly misrepresent Forsyth who employs the moral category of holiness to qualify the nature, authority and goal of God's love. Holy love, Forsyth insists, is 'the tenderness of the Holy, which does not soothe but save. It is love which does not simply comfort, and it is holiness which does not simply doom. It is holy love, which judges, saves, forgives, cleanses the conscience, destroys the guilt, reorganises the race, and makes a new world from the ruins of the old'.[163] Only this manner of love has the promise and puissance of the indestructible life of which the New Testament speaks. Holiness, moreover, is what gives God's love 'divine value'.[164] God's love is holiness 'brimming and overflowing', just as God's holiness is God's 'morally perfect' love. The perfection of holy love speaks in the overflow of redemption where the redeemed witness the nature of love's perfection 'not in amount but in kind, not as intense but as holy', not as remote or merely pure but as that loving authority asserting itself in redeeming grace. Holiness is grace; the universal, omnipotent, final, insuperable, invincible and absolute love of God overcoming every possible enemy, subduing the whole moral world, and establishing itself 'in Satan's seat' through atonement. Holiness is love labouring to secure the 'final settlement of all things'.[165] Indeed. Forsyth argues that God's love, however intense or well-meaning, could not be trusted if God 'let His holiness go'.[166] Holiness, in other words, is that in God's love which finds and assures it. Our only guarantee of the deathlessness of God's love is God's holiness which called for Christ's cross. If God had compromised on holiness there, Forysth avers, then we could never be sure that God would not also compromise on love. Thus to think of God's love as *holy* love is immensely practical: 'If God's love were not essentially holy love, in course of time mankind would cease to respect it, and consequently to trust it.'[167]

Where do we find this holy love that is at the centre of all things and the source of Christian ethic? Forsyth's answer: 'neither in the affections nor the intuitions of the individual heart, but in Christ', and specifically in Christ's cross.[168] The cross is the

160 'Religion and Reality', p. 552.
161 Hughes, *Atonement*, pp. 41–42.
162 Pitt, *Church, Ministry and Sacraments*, p. 41; cf. Nels Ferré, *The Christian Understanding of God* (New York: Harper, 1951), p. 116. Forsyth is ably defended in Kenneth Hamilton, 'Love or Holy Love? Nels Ferré versus P. T. Forsyth', *Canadian Journal of Theology* 8 (1962), pp. 229–36.
163 *Missions*, p. 233; cf. *Preaching*, pp. 145, 242–43; 'Christ's Person', p. 11, 'Paradox', pp. 130–31; 'Atonement', p. 66; *Work*, p. xxxi.
164 *Cruciality*, p. 205.
165 'Christ's Person', p. 11; cf. Thomas F. Torrance, *Divine and Contingent Order* (Edinburgh: T&T Clark, 2005), p. 136.
166 *Father*, p. 24.
167 *Work*, p. 117.
168 *War*, p. 136.

demonstration – and actualization – of God's heart in history which is, in Calvin's words, 'that nothing might stand in the way of his love toward us'.[169] In the cross, God's love for God's self, God's name and God's authority, and also God's love for rebels, is taken up and met in one just action wherein God self-exhibits God's very nature as unconditioned holy love. The cross, in other words, is the *fruit* of holy love. That is why the doctrine of the Trinity is not only the theological exegete necessary to make sense of the atonement, but the atonement is necessary to reveal to and define for creatures the love of the one God.[170] The holy love that is the perichoretic life has, by the grace of the Father in the action of the Son and by the mission of the Spirit, overflowed freely towards those outside God's community so that creation may participate in the communion that God has ever known *in se*. Indeed, it is for this that God spoke creation into being.

Where Ritschl's system forces a crisis of divine attributes, positing a God who 'suffers from schizophrenia, and is not quite in control of himself'[171] but who ultimately subsumes all under the umbrella of love, Forsyth contends that holiness is the only real foundation of religion and life. Even if some sentimental notions of love 'found no difficulty placed by the holy law of God's nature in His way of forgiveness' to forgive arbitrarily, holy love cannot. Indeed, those brands of love which know no moral hesitation about mercy are fundamentally immoral: 'There are conditions to be met which reside, not in man, but in the very nature of God Himself'.[172] So, against his former teacher, Forsyth shouts:

> Love is but [holiness'] outgoing; sin is but its defiance; grace is but its action on sin; the cross is but its victory; faith is but its worship. This holiness is no attribute of God, but his very essence . . . It is not a quality in God, but the being of God, in which all else inheres. God is Holy Love. To bring sin home and grace home, then the Holy must be brought home.[173]

'There is more in God than love. There is all that we mean by His holy grace. Truly, "God is love." Yes, but the kind of love which you must interpret by the whole of the New Testament.'[174] Such holy love, as already indicated, is always for creation, and finds its synthesis in the movement wherein creation is brought to share in the burning purity of God's all-constraining being. Stated otherwise, 'Holy love is the only love that, having loved the world from the beginning, loves it to the end in a kingdom of peace, power and joy.'[175]

[169] Calvin, *Inst.*, 2.17.2.
[170] See Jürgen Moltmann, *The Crucified God: The Cross of Christ as the Foundation and Criticism of Christian Theology* (trans. R. A. Wilson and John Bowden; London: SCM, 1974), pp. 240–49.
[171] R. P. C. Hanson, *God: Creator, Saviour, Spirit* (London: SCM, 1960), pp. 45–46; cf. Karl Barth, *Church Dogmatics II.1* (ed. G. W. Bromiley and T. F. Torrance; trans. T. H. L. Parker et al.; Edinburgh: T&T Clark, 1957), pp. 380–81.
[172] 'Atonement', p. 66; cf. Denney, *Atonement*, pp. 81–82.
[173] *Revelation*, p. 62; cf. *Cruciality*, p. 39.
[174] *Work*, p. 26.
[175] 'Things New and Old', p. 276.

Truth, being and reality: The moral is the ontological

We must in our hearts believe in a world saturated with moral purpose, and not a brute or casual world.[176]

The entire cosmos is one vast burning bush, permeated by the fire of the divine power and glory.[177]

What I hope is becoming clear by now is that, for Forsyth, holiness is a moral power which constitutes and directs all being, binding a coherent universe in such a way as all remigrates to its source in God. And while Forsyth nowhere attempts any constructive explication of this moral metaphysic, he consistently exposits the claim that holiness is not merely *a* religious idea, but *the* religious idea, and one of utmost practical import. Forsyth believes that for too long the tradition has placed the nature of religion in the region of theory wherein the question 'Is it true?', that is, 'Does it conform to our a priori rational principles and standards of science and philosophy', became definitive. With Kant, however, comes 'a new order of things' for which Forsyth is grateful, and with the coming of that 'new order' Forsyth over-optimistically intones 'the night of Rationalism' is over, and philosophy reconstituted on that which provides for the whole of life and crowns all our spiritual effort. Forsyth believes that although Kant got hampered by disrupting circumstances, 'his route was right', for Kant taught us that Christianity is exhausted neither with the rational, the aesthetic, the 'orthodox', nor the purely ethical, though it is the latter that best expresses its true nature.[178] This residual Kantianism does not lead to Forsyth's abandonment of the rational, however, so much as a reprioritization of categories, challenging those attempts to bypass the religious experience of grace as the determining factor in deciding the question for philosophy.

Although Forsyth only makes two direct references to Grotius,[179] John Stott and Stanley Russell properly observe in Forsyth some indebtedness to the Dutch lawyer's preoccupation with the public vindication of divine justice and law.[180] However, as we shall see, Forsyth does not share Grotius' belief that judgement is undertaken by One who is *personally* unaffected by sin. For Forsyth, the law is not something external to God's self, but the expression of divine presence in the world, and consequently 'cannot be treated as less than inviolate and eternal' lest God be 'false *to Himself*'.[181] While Forsyth does not grant to God's law any externality that must be fulfilled, there remains a genuine Creator–creation correspondence which is given more concrete form not in Grotius but through Forsyth's debt to Hegel for whom the *world* 'confronts [God] as an other'.[182] And Forsyth draws upon Hegel's interpretation of the maintenance of the moral order by the state in order to provide the substratum of – and to make

[176] 'Gate', p. 181.
[177] Kallistos Ware, *Through the Creation to the Creator* (London: Friends of the Centre Papers, 1997), p. 9.
[178] *Authority*, p. 4.
[179] Ibid., p. 330; *Justification*, p. 171.
[180] Stott, *The Cross of Christ*, p. 122; Stanley Russell, 'Spoiling the Egyptians: P. T. Forsyth and Hegel', in *Justice the True and Only Mercy: Essays on the Life and Theology of Peter Taylor Forsyth* (ed. Trevor A. Hart; Edinburgh: T&T Clark, 1995), p. 228.
[181] 'Atonement', p. 79.
[182] Merold Westphal, *Hegel, Freedom, and Modernity* (Albany: State University of New York, 1992), p. 12.

plausible – his own understanding of the moral order and transposition of such to that of the genus of the Holy.

Kant and Hegel coalesce in Forsyth for whom the doctrine of creation is woven into the entire tapestry of Reality as moral. The upshot of this, for Forsyth, is that the 'cosmic order of holiness' *corresponds* with God in holiness, truth, righteousness, goodness and love.[183] It is the protraction of God's moral personality into the creaturely purview, creation being (in some sense) the *sine qua non* for God whose eternal will is to find holiness' self echoed in the entire existence of a moral world. This commitment finds expression in a variety of ways throughout Forsyth's corpus. To draw attention to just one example, Forsyth's 1884 sermon 'Pessimism' argues that the centre and secret of Christianity lies in the miracle of forgiveness. This is the key, he contends against Arthur Schopenhauer, to why Christianity, with all its melancholy, cannot be pessimistic. Forsyth then reveals what he believes undergirds this reality: 'It is in the moral world we read the secrets which make all the mysteries of life tolerable and just.'[184] Clearly, the accenting of the moral is no mere speculative fascination for Forsyth, but rather informs his desire to interpret life *sub specie crucis*. And it reflects his conviction that basic to all reality is 'the absolute righteous reality – i.e. the Holy God, the Holy Trinity' with whom the 'welfare of the universe is bound up'.[185] Hart summarizes Forsyth's position:

> [The moral order] is objective and universal, and is not to be tampered with. It is not a bylaw arbitrarily imposed and therefore readily suspended; it is an eternal and unchangeable ordinance the demands of which must be met. It inheres in the very nature of reality, is as much part of the fabric of the universe as the molecular structure of hydrogen or the force of gravity, and it cannot be set aside or indeed broken without the moral structure of reality being placed at risk. Thus, when its laws are broken, restitution must follow; holiness, says Forsyth, must assert itself in the face of evil, must *heal* itself . . . God, therefore, could not waive his moral order, but must honour it, for the guilt of humanity is no mere matter of private and personal affront, but rather of a public justice, a public truth, in which God must safeguard not his own honour or his own feelings, but truth itself.[186]

Clearly for Forsyth, the moral represents not only the *substance* of the Triune life but also the *eternal act* of the divine modes of being prosecuting their 'eternal converse', communicating their eternal powers, self-donating in Christ and ordering all after their likeness.[187] In this sense, Forsyth can speak of Christ as the world within the world, the

[183] *Cruciality*, p. 138; cf. Eberhard Jüngel, *Justification: The Heart of the Christian Faith – A Theological Study with an Ecumenical Purpose* (trans. J. F. Cayzer; Edinburgh: T&T Clark, 2001), p. 104.

[184] 'Pessimism', p. 43. There are some echoes here of Windelband's 1876 essay 'Pessimismus und Wissenschaft', republished in Wilhelm Windelband, 'Pessimismus und Wissenschaft', in *Präludien – Aufsätze und Reden zur Einleitung in die Philosophie* (Tübingen: Verlag von J. C. B. Mohr [Paul Siebeck], 1911), pp. 195–220.

[185] *Cruciality*, pp. 147–48.

[186] Hart, 'Morality, Atonement and the Death of Jesus', pp. 27–28.

[187] 'Christ's Person', p. 15.

'positive moral destiny' awaiting all things, the truth which the world is working out, and the order within all order who prescribes all order at last.[188] To so comprehend reality is to 'open Christianity with its own key'.[189] Forsyth contends that it takes moral revelation (i.e. the experience of forgiveness) to construe that the movements of the Great Reality in history are not noetic processes but are fundamentally moral movements; that is, movements full of holy commands, acts and power. Furthermore, that life's last reality is moral extends to the conviction that revelation comes home through moral crisis wherein the soul 'fights for its moral life', and where we touch – and are touched by – that which leaves us permanently changed.[190] This moral order is 'our one modern certainty',[191] more permanent and more reliable than either materiality or ideas. This is not to suggest, however, that creation is somehow shut down or turned *in se*. Rather, as N. H. G. Robinson observes: 'In Forsyth's system morality is not closed but open. It does not set up a law but offers at most a guiding, interpretive, but, above all, illuminable principle. It does not detract from revelation but provides the means for its exaltation'.[192] That all reality is at core moral both reflects God's holy nature, and confesses creation's supreme interest. Moreover, in a world principally moral, the only certainty, Forsyth contends, is evangelical, creative and teleological, taking command not principally of thought, but of conscience and will.

Forsyth's insistence that the action and unity of the moral order is testified to in the human conscience betrays his indebtedness to Immanuel Kant, Joseph Butler and F. D. Maurice. That 'morality is the nature of things' (Butler)[193] is not an indication or description of morality's content but of its status as reality. That the locus of this revelation is the new conscience indicates that the moral is never theoretical nor (contra Hegel) merely rational or speculatively necessary, concerned with mere ideas, energies or movements. Rather, the moral is profoundly and unavoidably concerned with actions, persons, faith, free grace, and relations, even while its attendant theological discourse requires the resources of imagination that Hegel and others may, from time to time, provide. Consequently, following Kant, Forsyth contends that persons be treated as ends in themselves and not merely as instruments to ends beyond themselves. This characteristic of reality concerns the dynamic of obligation and responsibility, and raises a challenge to Forsyth's readers of holding in tension the desire to categorize reality while not distorting the critical quality of the moral as creative and dynamic personalism; readers must neither strangle Forsyth's thought into rationalist casts, nor abandon critique in favour of description.

However, Forsyth moves beyond Kant's idealism (which, in effect, drives God out of the world) when he insists that creation is incomprehensible apart from Jesus Christ.

188 'Distinctive Thing', p. 487.
189 'Moralization', p. 162.
190 'Religion and Reality', p. 551; cf. *Society*, p. 29; *Work*, pp. 57, 163.
191 *Cruciality*, 50.
192 N. H. G. Robinson, *Christ and Conscience* (London: James Nisbet, 1956), p. 142.
193 *Parnassus*, p. 274; cf. *Authority*, p. 179; Andrew M. Fairbairn, *The Philosophy of the Christian Religion* (London: Hodder & Stoughton, 1902), pp. 83–93. Forsyth resists unpacking Butler's statement but simply develops his thoughts from Butler's regulative referent. (Forsyth probably first read Butler's *Sermons* while at Aberdeen.)

Creation's moral movement, meaning and destiny are ruled, revealed, reconstituted and determined in and by Christ in whom the whole creation praises God, certain that whatever has come and gone, 'it was worth all it endured to serve with such praise. Yea, it would go through it again at the Father's will. In him the whole creation sees of the travail of its soul and is satisfied'.[194] In other words, the moral order is not only the 'ultimate interpretive key for making sense of the cross',[195] but the cross is also the interpretive key for understanding the moral order. It was the lack of this note, Forsyth believes, that made Edwardian theology 'so impotent to speak to nations or to achieve anything beyond ambulance work'.[196]

The concern here is to trumpet the view that creation is a work of One who 'can do only the things that are congruous with His moral, His holy nature and purpose'.[197] Consequently, it possesses throughout a moral glory, dignity, accountability and *telos*. This suggests a number of things: that the creation is 'very good' and fit, both aesthetically and functionally; that God exercises authority over creation;[198] that the creation, though distinct from God, is never a strange thing to God, nor God to it (there is no Deistic schism between God and creation);[199] that creation is the imposing of order into formless chaos; and that creation's end is to reflect God's own moral glory back to God and, incredibly, to 'justify Him for ever'.[200] Because holiness' 'must' is the exhibition, reception and return of itself from the side of its other – because 'holiness alone answers holiness'[201] – the 'purpose of a world created by a holy God must be holiness, the reflection and communion of His own holiness'.[202] Whether God can secure this 'holy destiny' in the face of that sin which mocks and smites holiness is 'the ultimate question in life' because it concerns final moral authority.[203] When Forsyth witnesses to creation as 'a fullness flushed and glorious in power',[204] and to 'the wealth of Nature's beauty' as 'but the reflection of the immanent beauty of the Infinite Spirit, who moves and lives and has His being in it all',[205] he is replacing a metaphysic of abstract ontology with a metaphysic of energy, of power, of personality, of a 'living, rich, and inexhaustible whole'.[206] Indeed, according to Forsyth, a 'metaphysic of things' rather than of personality, society and history is

194 *Justification*, p. 127.
195 Hart, 'Morality, Atonement and the Death of Jesus', p. 18.
196 Cited in Higginson, 'Theology of P. T. Forsyth', p. 69. See *Society*, pp. 96–97.
197 *Person*, p. 228.
198 This need not infer that 'there is no struggle here, no anxiety, no risk'. Walter Brueggemann, *Theology of the Old Testament: Testimony, Dispute, Advocacy* (Minneapolis: Fortress Press, 1997), p. 153.
199 See *Parnassus*, pp. 20–21; 'Christ's Person', p. 5.
200 *Freedom*, p. 272.
201 *Person*, p. 327.
202 Ibid., p. 228.
203 Ibid.; cf. *Authority*, pp. 66–67, 405.
204 *Justification*, p. 62.
205 *Parnassus*, p. 80.
206 *Justification*, p. 62; cf. *Sacraments*, p. 268; 'Veracity', pp. 208–09. The context here is Forsyth's criticism of Hegel's 'pure', 'encyclopedic' and 'architechtonic' thought as unable to cope with the wealth of the whole because it is neither full nor creative nor personal enough. We must pass from 'energetic idealism to personal idealism'. *Justification*, p. 63. This leads to some overstatements; for example, 'Christianity and Society', p. 4: 'Christ is God by his eternal personal relation to the divine holiness, rather than by his essential relation to the divine substance.'

merely 'hollow shells of ruined towers that let heaven be seen through their cracks rather than their windows'.[207]

Although God's holiness does not isolate God from creation, it does differentiate God from it. Still, Forsyth speaks of holiness organizing God into the world, lifting God above the instinctive and passionate; and drawing God down 'from the lonely majesty of Omnipotence, and Omniscience, and all the abstract purities that cow and crush us'. So understood, holiness is 'majesty made intimate in moral mercy'.[208] God is not content to remain holy alone, but seeks – and creates – corresponding holiness from the creaturely side. It is this offering that constitutes human hallowing and which, it seems, human beings uniquely among all God's creatures are suited to render. So Hart:

> What [God] desires most, and enjoys most, in his creation, is not its staggering beauty or its physical complexity and intricate eco-systems, but this reflection of his own inner nature; the rendering back to him of love in holiness from humankind. It is for this that he longs; it was in order to share and to enjoy this with another that he created at all, and it is this which he is determined to find . . . not in any narcissistic sense, but because [holiness] longs to share what is good with another, and will not tolerate that which would spoil or deface that goodness.[209]

Atonement, therefore, is the 'moral remedy' for a world that has refused to be God's correspondent.[210] It is the action in which such refusal is met with breach-healing grace, creation's destiny being intractably bound with the Father's giving the Son up to be the historic witness to and warranty of holy love's triumph. For since the enmity between God and creation affects moral relations, there can be no reconciliation by divine fiat. Instead, the God who comes preaching peace to us (Eph. 2.17) proclaims peace on the basis of divine action wherein the strife is not simply overpowered or erased, but converted and its victims recovered.

> The unholy must be restored to holiness. It is unmade but to be remade. And there is none but the Holy creative enough to do this. And He must – by the necessity of His holiness. The same Holy who is imperative as law is also creative as life; He is creative and restorative by a necessity moral and not physical, of impulse and not pressure.[211]

Clearly there is no sense here that the creation is left to run mechanistically, or that judgement is purely the 'automatic recoil' of God's moral order upon sinners.[212] Rather, holy love issues in wrath-bearing divine enfleshment precisely because God is *personally* against sin. For Forsyth, grace is not like the sentimental love of an indulgent parent. It

[207] 'Regeneration – I', p. 631.
[208] *Authority*, p. 187.
[209] Trevor A. Hart, 'Atonement and Worship', *Anvil* 11, no. 3 (1994), pp. 203–14 (205).
[210] *Missions*, p. 77.
[211] *Justification*, p. 67.
[212] *Work*, p. 239.

is the holy love of One who cannot abide sin but who cannot abandon creation either. Grace provides not only impetus but personally goes into battle against sin in order to refashion creation. Holy love is creation's final teleology and its deep entelechy or realization.

Such a reading assists us to interpret human experience. We sense that there is both blessing and curse upon creation and that sin affects more than our relationships (comprehensively conceived) but in some way also creates a wrong note, an ugly mistrust, that echoes throughout a morally sensitive order. Forsyth's doctrine of creation helps us to plot human actions and their consequences within a broader moral reality and not simply as part of the physical scaffolding of cause and effect. This is not to obviate materiality or to raise difficult issues to ethereality, however. So Forsyth observes creation's moral sensitivity as reflected in Israel's relationship with the land in his essay 'Land Laws of the Bible', arguing that 'land, people, and Deity made one organic whole'.[213] He had illustrated the darker elements of this over 20 years earlier via his exegesis of Holman Hunt's 'The Scapegoat' which depicts the 'accursed lake and dismal swamp' of creation that 'carries for ever the record of sin's dead level and its bitter end . . . The very life of vegetation has become contaminated with curse'.[214]

> But with all this salt ooze and lifeless waste the curse is not complete, nor the dreariness raised to the agony of utter woe. Some feeling thing must reflect and realise it all in consciousness. It must rise in appeal and prayer to the living God through its reflection in a life. Curse must become lonely agony, and agony must pass by innocence into atonement. Another life than the mere glow of nature must redeem the mysterious curse upon nature.[215]

Here, Forsyth avers that creation does not possess the ability to self-heal, to self-recuperate, to overcome those powers which arrest its development to secure its own end. As fundamental as the moral order is, it has no successful power of self-assertion against its enemy. Forsyth asks rhetorically,

> Now, if that order be broken, how can it be healed? If I slit the canvas of this tent it can be patched. I make a fissure, but it is not irremediable. I simply get some one to stitch it up. At the worst I can have a new width put in. But if the moral order, and its universal solidarity, its holiness, is broken, how can that be healed? That cannot be patched up. It is not merely a rent in a tissue, a gap in a process, which the same process goes on to heal into a scar.[216]

Here Forsyth departs from the monists – naming Eduard von Hartmann in particular – and presses for the necessity of divine donation, of God the holy who besets us before and behind, and who not only waits for us and works in us by way of repair, redemption

[213] 'Land Laws', p. 497.
[214] *Art*, p. 184.
[215] Ibid., p. 185.
[216] *Work*, p. 123.

and reconciliation but who alone can realize holiness' self and complete creation in the face of all antitheses. Here is a doctrine of creation that takes questions of justice and suffering seriously. Forsyth can even speak of the 'justice of the universe'[217] into which the redeemed human conscience is integrated and re-established. To pray 'Thy kingdom come' this side of Easter, therefore, is both a prayer of hope for the consummation, sanctification, redemption and final restitution of all things, and a prayer of thanksgiving that God has already acted to 'edenize' the whole creation and will continue to defang every antithesis of holiness that tries to ruin that work. Appreciating the moral nature of creation and history also means reading 'the secrets which make all the mysteries of life tolerable and even just. It is there, in conflict with good and evil, that we find the means of dealing with pleasure and pain'.[218]

Clearly, the brand of moral seriousness that Forsyth identifies in Butler and Kant – and, as we shall see, in Adolf Schlatter and Wilhelm Windelband – characterizes his own work. And this, funded by philosophical and theological realism, has extensive ramifications. The finality of the moral provides for Forsyth a way of construing history and society in light of the evangel. Therein alone can we envision the possibility of erecting human community and a social ethic which is enduring and loving, and therein alone can the Church find her authoritative and practical voice. Such an approach to social ethics renders Forsyth's voice perdurably relevant.

Dynamism, morality and monism

Forsyth's creation theology reflects the widespread peace that late-Victorian Nonconformity had made with evolutionary thought: 'Creation means life, movement, evolution', albeit with a 'shut and sealed' future.[219] Conservatives such as Charles Hodge and B. B. Warfield, and Aberdeen Free Church College professor James Iverach, had also expounded the view that evolutionary theory could be compatible with a theistic notion of design. And Henry Drummond's popularity on both sides of the Atlantic (his *Natural Law in the Spiritual World* already had 19 editions by 1887!) and his 'law of biogenesis' is further testimony to the widespread acceptance of evolutionary theory among evangelicals. For his part, Forsyth's insistence that the Church today is holier than in the first century may also betray such acceptance.[220] Certainly, Forsyth publicly commended Darwin's *Origin of Species* and *Origin of Man* (*Descent of Man*) in his 1878 lectures on the 'Contents of the [Saltaire] Institute Library'.[221]

217 *Authority*, p. 268.

218 'Pessimism', p. 43; see also p. 44.

219 *Justification*, p. 44; see also p. 48; 'Slowness', p. 220; *Preaching*, pp. 228–29; David Bebbington, *Victorian Nonconformity* (Milton Keynes: Paternoster, 2007), p. 54; David N. Livingstone, *Darwin's Forgotten Defenders: The Encounter between Evangelical Theology and Evolutionary Thought* (Grand Rapids: Wm. B. Eerdmans, 1987), pp. 100–05, 115–22; James R. Moore, *The Post-Darwinian Controversies: A Study of the Protestant Struggle to Come to Terms with Darwin in Britain and America, 1870–1900* (Cambridge: Cambridge University Press, 1979); James Iverach, *Christianity and Evolution* (London: Hodder & Stoughton, 1900), p. 107.

220 See *Society*, p. 25.

221 'Institute Library', p. 4.

While withstanding any illegitimate extension of biological evolutionary theory into non-biological domains, the notion of evolution appeals to Forsyth because it affords a more plastic view of the world and a more subtle providential working of the Spirit, provided that persons are not sacrificed to a system, or the Incarnation to immanence or that categories like sin, judgement and redemption are not displaced by mere process. He is concerned that theology does not place us in a *natural movement* between the finite and the infinite which would depreciate the value of the spiritual *act*, rendering us independent of grace.[222] Although he doesn't draw the distinction, Forsyth is really tackling nineteenth-century confidence in the 'superstition' of inevitable progress as it found voice in neo-Hegelian dialectic, in Romanticism, Idealism and materialism, as evidenced for example in the work of Thomas Carlyle, John Ruskin and the Transcendentalists. Objecting to Hegel and von Hartmann, Forsyth observes how German idealism is preoccupied with monistic process rather than with the moral notions of personality, freedom, crisis, sin and sanctification. Such a shift towards monism leaves persons with too impersonal an authority, 'tends to erase moral distinctions',[223] devours the moral value of history and undermines the value of the creature as *one who acts*: 'The chief practical objection to putting a principle in front of a person is that the religious life thereby becomes a one-sided process rather than a mutual act, an evolution rather than a communion; and thus it loses its ethical value, and is relegated to the pensive and passive side of our nature'.[224] Forsyth is concerned that we are not 'simply carried along on the crest of a wave'[225] but are rather constituted by the eternal, divine and moral acts of One who does not leave in trail a pile of victims. And Forsyth is equally concerned to punctuate the indispensable value of the moral acts of *human* persons, apart from which faith is meaningless. The temptation to make progress automatic is, in Sell's words, to 'skirt the historic redemptive act, minimise humanity's moral need, and open the door to salvation by education or social improvement rather than by radical rescue'.[226]

While positing genuine correspondence between God and creation, Forsyth is careful to clarify his own position against that of both Hegel and von Hartmann. Rather than emphasize the 'immanence of God in nature' he suggests we might better speak of 'the immanence of the Kingdom of God' breaking into history. Such a route, he insists, makes possible 'the true escape from Monism':[227]

> A solution of the world which is determined to be theoretic above all must end in Monism, which is the death of religion; but if it be moral, if it be religious, it must begin with the experienced and certain fact of the divided conscience, a standing

[222] See *Preaching*, p. 146; *Person*, pp. 344–45; 'Metaphysic', p. 719; *Justification*, 25; 'Religion and Reality', p. 549; *Monism*, pp. 7–8, 12–15. The latter is a paper read before the London Society for the Study of Religion, 2 February 1909, printed for members only. A copy is in Dr Williams's Library, London.
[223] 'Regeneration – II', p. 89; cf. 'Immanence', p. 48; *Justification*, pp. 56–68.
[224] 'Christian Principle', p. 149.
[225] *Work*, p. 67.
[226] Sell, *Testimony and Tradition*, p. 176.
[227] 'Religion and Reality', p. 552. On God's immanence see *Work*, pp. 240–42; 'Immanence', pp. 48–61; *Parnassus*, pp. 20, 32, 53; *Person*, pp. 314–16, 353; *Authority*, p. 416; *Revelation*, p. 19; 'Christian Principle', pp. 137–38, 158; *passim*.

> state of collision, war, and sin. It begins with a state of the consciousness anterior to its branches as theoretic, aesthetic, or ethical, a state underlying all these. It must begin with that fundamental antinomy of the conscience which emerges in the conflict of 'must' and 'ought', of instinct and obligation, of natural law and moral norm.[228]

This is not to conceive God as the custodian of an independent moral order, or of the moral as a third hypostasis or reality distinct or apart from God or creation. The only ontological distinction that exists is that between God and God's works. There are no half-divine/half-created beings or abstract metaphysical forces that fill some 'windless vacuum'[229] between God and God's works. And although God and creation know their own proper space, that space is both maintained and crossed *by God* in God's second and third modes of being by which creation is enabled to be itself. This promise of space sponsors a footing for Christian ethics, and for genuine communion between persons, though, in itself, does not make such possible. This communion is made possible, rather, only in Christ in whom the 'moral soul and self find the moral reality for which it craves'.[230] The event of creation therefore is God's making accommodation within God's own triune life that others might share in holy love. Here there is neither collapse in the Creator–creation distinction, nor ontological remoteness between God and creation (it is precisely this proximity that makes the introduction of sin so painful and offensive); creation per se is both a *communicatio idiomatum* and an invitation to participate in God's holiness without being ingurgitated into God's life. Creation's *raison d'être*, in other words, is that there might in a creaturely, finite and moral way be a reflection of the eternal, infinite and moral relationship that the Son and the Father enjoy in the Spirit. This relationship depends, Forsyth believes, on the moral integrity and hallowing of creation.

This dynamic view of creation extends to Forsyth's sponsorship of the doctrine of *creatio continua*, that God's way with creation 'is the way of growth, of progress, of evolution, and all by way of humiliation'.[231] Creation is no ready-made 'completed system of reality', an 'unfinished world'.[232] Rather, with Schlatter, Forsyth presses that creation is ever that which is becoming, because a creation that God had finished with would be dead. *Creatio continua* means that *God* is continuously enabling creation to bring forth what God ever intends it to be and what it could never generate of itself: 'He is Creator in His nature; wherever He is and works there is creation'.[233] Providence, therefore, is not merely part of how a faithful Creator acts in the world but is itself creation; God's unfolding unto the end that which is permanent. Also, 'History is no mere preparation for the Kingdom, it is the Kingdom in the making. The actual world is not only the workshop of God. It is His building in process'.[234] To be sure, there can

228 *Authority*, p. 5.
229 Ibid., p. 408.
230 *Parnassus*, p. 273.
231 'Empire', p. 305.
232 *Authority*, pp. 188, 183.
233 'Empire', p. 305; cf. Adolf Schlatter, 'Genesis' (unpublished lecture. Landeskirchliches Archiv Stuttgart, 1881), pp. 14–15, 37.
234 *Sacraments*, p. 126.

be no suggestion that it is anything or anyone other than God who is the norm that makes process progress. Forsyth contends that the Hegelian tendency to discard such hands-on involvement 'drops us to a moving series of integrations and eliminations, with no law but causation, no values but those that are relative, and no standard to measure whether movement is progress, or evolution is development to any end'.[235] Thus Forsyth not only avoids the deist tendencies in much religious ethics but he also avoids the criticism that *creatio continua* promotes a relativism which renders moral judgements hollow.[236] Such an either/or is, as Forsyth maps, unnecessary.

Forsyth insists that while evolutionary theory can supplement the doctrine of creation, on its own it is over-optimistic and inadequate, offering 'no sure footing'[237] in a moral world. Nor does it deal justly with the moral crisis of a race needing redemption. The rectification of the present state of things is no mere straightening of a tangle that Meliorism (i.e. the notion that the world, or society, may be improved and suffering alleviated through rightly directed human effort) might be competent to undertake, but the justification on a transcendent plane of righteousness, the moral adjustment of humanity and God in one final and eternal act which God undertakes at massive cost to God's self.[238] Here again, Forsyth distances himself from those Hegelian notions wherein creation takes its origin 'not from a personal absolute at the beginning of the series, but from an idea of some monistic kind which only acquired the self-consciousness of personality at the end of the series as Man'.[239] Forsyth does, however, follow Hegel in his insistence that the continuous struggle between the human spirit and the remainder of creation forms the backdrop for how we read the whole history of art, culture and progress as God's work. This is an example of the fact that while there is no shortage, even within Congregationalism, of hand-wringing lament that the old faith is being trumped by the new, some, like Forsyth, insist that despite the discomfort God, and not evil, is responsible. Certainly, the language of responsibility needs to be handled carefully lest we articulate that God is responsible for sin. A thoroughgoing determinism (which, as we shall see in the following chapter, robs obedience of its moral force) makes God directly responsible for sin, whereas to the extent that we take freedom seriously in a non-compatibilist sense then we have to deal with a responsibility that is more removed. Even so, God has finally brought the state of affairs into being as we have it and, if one wants to maintain both God's sovereignty and God's love, then God knew that God was doing it and that it was worth doing and therefore God takes responsibility for all that God has made.

235 *Justification*, p. 202.

236 See Wilhelm Windelband, 'Was ist Philosophie? (Über Begriff und Geschichte der Philosophie)', in *Präludien – Aufsätze und Reden zur Einleitung in die Philosophie* (Tübingen: Verlag von J. C. B. Mohr [Paul Siebeck], 1907), pp. 24–77; John Polkinghorne, 'Kenotic Creation and Divine Action', in *The Work of Love: Creation as Kenosis* (ed. John Polkinghorne; Grand Rapids: Wm. B. Eerdmans, 2001), p. 96.

237 *Parnassus*, p. 263.

238 See *Justification*, p. 69; cf. William James, *The Varieties of Religious Experience: A Study in Human Nature, Being The Gifford Lectures on Natural Religion Delivered at Edinburgh in 1901–1902* (New York: Longmans, Green, and Co., 1920), p. 91.

239 'Christian Principle', p. 164; cf. James Baldwin Brown, 'Latter-Day Prophets', *The Evangelical Magazine, and Missionary Chronicle* 10 (1868), pp. 20–27 (23).

Forsyth's most sustained criticism (and appreciation) of evolutionary theory (albeit as a philosophy rather than a science)[240] appears in his essay *Christian Aspects of Evolution*, wherein he contends that the theory offers no teleological explanation to human life. Having no goal, history and creation's moral *telos* testify against the randomness of evolution. It shares with the sciences an inability to address questions of purpose, and has a lack of moral vigour insofar as it provides no precept or obligation to act morally and substitutes moral effort for a process (so failing to adequately address questions of suffering), offers no power for repentance, devalues life, and sponsors despair, pessimism and indifference (at best) to the spiritual effort that human beings ought to undertake. Furthermore, evolutionary theory fails to account for the lapses and stagnations in the race's development, which lead to a diminution of the importance of the present replacing it with a strong utilitarianism that treats nothing as an end in itself. This leads to a hardening and flattening of life.[241] Evolutionary theory's main flaw, however, is that it fails to understand creation as moral.

Forsyth also considers the doctrine of *creatio ex nihilo* as naïve 'as if it were a magician's power to bring out blossoms with a wave of his hand, or place coins suddenly where there were none'.[242] As with evolutionary theory, the difficulty with *creatio ex nihilo*, according to Forsyth, is that there is an almost entire absence of any 'acquaintance with moral ideas':[243]

> Creation seems to be thought of entirely out of reference to the idea of moral freedom. It seems to be regarded as the production of a thing instead of a *soul*, and as the making of that thing out of nothing. But, in the first place, nothing could be made out of nothing. The original nothing was not there. There was always and everywhere the Being of God Himself. Creation out of nothing is a phrase with no meaning. It is unthinkable. It is that meaninglessness that has driven many into Pantheism, and especially into the crude form of it, which says that every thing is made of God.[244]

This charge of pantheism (no doubt dispraising Hegel and Campbell's 'New Theology') appears to be because pantheism blasphemously blurs the divine–creature distinction, denies true creaturely *and divine* freedom, moral sense and value and offers 'a spurious appearance of unity'.[245] Yet Forsyth's thought itself journeys surprisingly close to pantheism when he insists that far from the creation being God's external and mechanical product (which God could destroy and remake), God has so created

240 For example, Forsyth appeals to evolutionary theory, among other things, to argue for the superiority of monogamy over polygamy in marriage, and in defence of Liberal over Conservative politics. *Marriage*, pp. 30–32; 'Liberal', p. 4.

241 See *Evolution*, pp. 8, 17–18, 23, 26–27, 32, 34–35, 37; *Authority*, p. 77; *Life*, pp. 13–14.

242 *Authority*, p. 157.

243 Ibid. There is no evidence that Forsyth considers the two alternatives: (i) the forming of the created order out of pre-existent 'stuff', as in Platonism and Process Theology; or (ii) interpreting creation as some kind of emanation of the divine (panentheism), though his strong insistence on the divine–creation distinction categorically rules out the latter.

244 Ibid., p. 158; cf. 'Things New and Old', p. 276.

245 *Justification*, p. 73.

that the very existence and certain future of materiality is intractably and eternally bound up with God's own life. The life of the universe is, as Forsyth would have it, 'the immanence of the Transcendent'.[246] Such a commitment to radical correspondence finds expression too in Forsyth's relating creation to the *creatio fidei*. Created in moral freedom, creation's unity and freedom must be seen and accomplished in the light of true moral choice. God's creative activity in creation is in essence the same as God's creative activity in the creation of faith, which is 'our true adjustment to the ultimate moral reality, which is Christ'.[247]

Blaspheming the name: Sin's 'collision with the holy'[248]

> *... if sin be but a peripheral affair there is no adequate motive for the kenosis of a being with the divine intimacy of even an Arian Christ.*[249]

'People live so decently and feebly', Forsyth opines, 'that they do not believe that it is possible to hate God'.[250] And from his latter days: 'It is very freely lamented in religious circles that no feature in the moral physiognomy of the day is more marked than the decay or absence of the sense of sin'.[251] Remarkably, as Forsyth observes, this absence of a sense of sin is coupled with significant interest in the person and teachings of one 'in whom that sense was overwhelming'. Churches and pulpits ring with a 'note of self-satisfaction' rather than repentance. That we have 'erred and strayed' is the proclamation, but we are not rebels or miserable offenders in whom is no health.[252] Forsyth warns that while there are churches that seem to live in an atmosphere of urbane liveliness, 'where all is heart and nothing is soul', so long as the confronting reality of holiness is abandoned in the Church's liturgical life, it will not be long before the going power flags, and the petrol gives out in the desert.[253] Sin's minimizing, he avers, belittles God's holiness, and so perverts creation, devalues salvation and impoverishes human dignity.

Whether sin is conceived as a *necessary* product of humanity's sensuous nature, existing solely in human consciousness (as for Schleiermacher), or as a necessary step in humanity's evolution as self-conscious spirit (as for Hegel) or as a natural form of ignorance and a necessary stage in human development (as for Ritschl), or as anti-creational, unfaithfulness, disbelief and rebellion (as for Calvin), Scripture offers no definition of sin. What we are given instead are descriptions. For example, the Bible speaks of transgressions, evil, iniquity, lawlessness, thanklessness, disobedience, separation, rebellion, and moral corruption, et cetera. Nevertheless, sin remains a subject of theological and existential curiosity. Forsyth rightly rejects the endeavour

[246] Ibid., p. 75.
[247] *Father*, p. 120.
[248] *Cruciality*, p. 116.
[249] 'Love of Liberty', p. 166.
[250] *Society*, p. 98.
[251] 'Sinless', 288; cf. *Work*, p. 229.
[252] 'Sinless', p. 288; cf. *Jesus*, p. 25.
[253] *Jesus*, p. 119.

to understand sin by considering abstract religious notions of goodness, justice or shalom, or by turning to social anthropology or psychology, or by systematizing and standardizing various biblical texts, or by (as R. J. Campbell attempts) justifying it. Sin is a mystery. It is insane, 'utterly irrational',[254] inexplicable, distorting, deceptive and disenabling of self-revelation. It is 'the absolute contrary of everything God meant'.[255] Yet insofar as sin can be accounted for, it is only from the side of forgiveness wherein it is, as Barth would have it, 'unmasked, discovered and judged'[256] in the context of Christ's victory over the last enemy. So too Forsyth understands sin, not by regarding the First Adam but by hearing the Second clothed in his gospel, by seeing what sin means *for Christ*.[257] In Christ, sin is not only revealed for the cosmically nefarious, pseudo-sovereignty and harrowing execrable blasphemy that it is, but is also destroyed. Indeed, it took One equally incapable of explanation – 'not only beyond it but [as] alien to it' and as 'extra-rational' – to reveal sin *as sin*.[258]

In his 1908 essay, 'The Love of Liberty and the Love of Truth', Forsyth asks, 'Is a religion which treats sin as a factor in God's creation the same religion as that which makes it the one thing that would destroy creation if it did not compel creative resource to rise to redemption?'[259] He proceeds to witness to sin as God's antithesis which could not stop at indifference but goes on through aversion to hate and threaten attack on the entire moral fabric of the universe, a fabric that cannot be tampered with or suspended but at cost not only to creation, but also to God. As he would write elsewhere, sin is not only 'the wrongest thing with the world', and the 'most vile, not because it is ugly, but because it is guilty' of blaspheming holiness,[260] but sin also finds its voice as God's antithesis. Where sin brings only confusion, disorder and contradiction, holiness means order, integrity and healing. Sin disfigures humanity, putting it outside the camp where there can be no community life. Sin destabilizes and makes everything unreliable and untrustworthy. Within the chaos of sin's fracture and its untruth there remains nothing to give life any meaning, while anger and violence erupt from the seed of discontent and self-assertion. As dire as this diagnosis sounds, the reality is substantially worse:

> There is that in us and in our sin which is in its very essence intractable to all the processes of a reconciling idea; something which, to the end, by its very nature, refuses to be taken up as a factor into the largest and most comprehensive procession of divine action; something which can never be utilized, but can only be destroyed in a mortal moral war; something which, *if God cannot kill it, must be the death of God*.[261]

254 *Father*, p. 74.
255 'Missions', p. 273.
256 Karl Barth, *Church Dogmatics IV.3.1* (ed. G. W. Bromiley and T. F. Torrance; trans. G. W. Bromiley; Edinburgh: T&T Clark, 1999), p. 369.
257 See *Society*, p. 115; *Justification*, p. 156; cf. Dietrich Bonhoeffer, *Christology* (trans. John Bowden; London: Collins, 1966), pp. 37–40.
258 'Reality', p. 610.
259 'Love of Liberty', p. 168.
260 *Justification*, p. 167; 'A Sermon on Philippians 4.4', in Goroncy (ed.), *'Descending on Humanity'*, 2013.
261 *Preaching*, p. 38. Italics mine.

What makes sin so repulsive, so transcendentally evil, is its intent on 'the destruction of the holy'.[262] What makes sin sin is its protest against God's absolute holiness. What may begin as indifference or challenge, the effect of sin upon God is so radically severe that it threatens God's very being. Forsyth believes that sin has not simply challenged an impersonal moral order, as a particular reading of Kant might suggest. Sin has wounded God, sought God's death: 'Sin is the death of God. Die sin must or God'![263] It would be difficult to find a more sober statement about sin. Sin's heinousness is such that Forsyth is compelled to employ language – here more than anywhere else – that lays him open to the charge of dualism. Yet Forsyth's point is precisely the opposite: that God can never be reconciled to sin, that there can be no compromise between sin and holiness. In a moral universe, thesis (holiness) and antithesis (sin) simply cannot cohere. One *must* go. Herein is one of Forsyth's clearest breaks from Hegel's control: that no higher synthesis can at last integrate God and sin: 'Any compromise is a victory for sin.'[264] Consequently, Forsyth calls for an escape from those presentations which reduce sin's cosmic and historic dimensions and retire into a sectarian righteousness which ends in religious egoism, priggery and futility. Understanding grace's staurological shape demands recovering sin's Machiavelianness, its warlikeness, its imperiality and its universality.

> God is fundamentally affected by sin. He is stung and to the core. It does not simply try Him. It challenges His whole place in the moral world. It puts Him on His trial as God. It is, in its nature, an assault on His life. Its total object is to unseat Him. It has no part whatever in His purpose. It hates and kills Him. It is His total negation and death. It is not His other but An other. It is the one thing in the world that lies outside reconciliation, whether you mean by that the process or the act. It cannot be taken up into the supreme unity. It can only be destroyed.[265]

Sin is a *diminutio capitis*, threatening to kill God 'in the eye'.[266] Forsyth, at times, grants to sin an almost separate 'personality'. This comes to the fore in a number of places, usually when distinguishing sin from the sinner. So, he speaks about 'an eternal damnation of sin which sears it out of the sinner',[267] and of how God's wrath sets its sights on sin, and only derivatively upon those who identify themselves with sin.[268] This is also borne out in Forsyth's insistence that Christ was 'made sin' rather than made 'a sinner'. Such a conclusion is motivated by Forsyth's belief that above all else, it is sin itself that must come under God's judgement, and sinners only insofar as they are aligned with sin. That said, Forsyth is equally keen not to separate sin from the 'sinning

262 'Regeneration – II', p. 91.
263 *Justification*, p. 147; cf. *Cruciality*, p. 213; *Work*, p. 131.
264 William L. Bradley, 'Forsyth's Contributions to Pastoral Theology', *Religion in Life* 28 (1959), pp. 546–56 (555); cf. Leow, *The Theodicy of Peter Taylor Forsyth*, p. 233: 'there is no insidious dualism lurking in Forsyth's thought'.
265 *Preaching*, p. 252.
266 *Justification*, p. 148; *War*, 33.
267 *Authority*, p. 120.
268 See *Work*, p. 241.

personality', which would be to see sin as 'a mere abstraction, incapable of rousing the real wrath of God'.[269]

To be sure, Forsyth is adamant that sin is no merely individual matter. Sin is a guilt, and that of the race. But while never individualistic, sin is deeply personal. Notwithstanding what we noted above about sin taking on a separate 'personality', there is in Forsyth no sense of God hating the sin but loving the sinner. This 'meaningless phrase' and 'psychological anomaly' separates and abstracts sin from the 'sinning personality'. Rather, as Forsyth would have it: 'It was I who, at my will's centre, did that thing. It was my will and self that was put into it. My act was not the freak of some point on my circumference. It came from my centre. It was my unitary, indivisible self that was involved and is infected.'[270] Conversely, it requires a personal act to destroy it: 'It was neither in word nor in feeling that we wounded [God's holiness], but in life and deed. It must be acknowledged in like fashion – practically.'[271] Indeed, sin rouses divine wrath precisely because it *is* personal.[272] It is not, as in some recent accounts,[273] some anarchic but finally abstract rebellion against a *principle* of *shalom*: Forsyth's *God* says, 'It was I who, at my will's centre, felt that thing. It affected *me*. Your sin did not just brush up against me. It attacked my centre. It hated me and wanted me dead. And it wanted me dead that it might rule and go after you. That would be the end of us.' Sin 'exists' as God's irreconcilable other, as the 'absolute antichrist' who taxes God to the limit and which ever seeks to foil God's movement towards us in holy love.[274] What comes between us and the Holy Father 'does not come between us and any earthly father – sin. Sin, hell, curse, and wrath!'[275] That the Father's Son is ignored, discarded, denounced, called the agent of Beelzebub, and hustled out of the world in the name of God only seeks to further drive home sin's real agenda, a point powerfully made in Forsyth's sermon on John 16.11.[276]

As one regards sin christologically, one can appreciate that Forsyth's employment of the grammar of 'alienation', 'hostility' and 'antagonist' in order to describe the human position before God is entirely fitting. Citing Kant and Carlyle for support, Forsyth states that 'Man is not a mere runaway, but a rebel; not a pitiful coward, but a bold and bitter mutineer'.[277] And in the face of such hardened mutiny, for God to have simply articulated verbally God's love for the world would have been grossly inadequate, ineffectual and ultimately unloving: 'Something had to be *done* – judging or saving'.[278]

[269] *War*, p. 131. One might argue that Forsyth's granting of sin almost separate personality is chiefly a personification for rhetorical purposes and not a theological dictum.

[270] *Father*, pp. 100–01; cf. *Authority*, p. 404; James Baldwin Brown, *The Divine Treatment of Sin* (London: Jackson, Walford, & Hodder, 1864), pp. 19, 34–37; Robert W. Dale, *The Atonement: The Congregational Union Lecture for 1875* (London: Hodder & Stoughton, 1881), p. 345: 'Sin is a personal act; it has no existence apart from the sinner'.

[271] *Work*, p. 125.

[272] *War*, p. 131; *Authority*, p. 7.

[273] For example, N. T. Wright, *Evil and the Justice of God* (Leicester: IVP, 2006); Cornelius Plantinga Jr, *Not the Way It's Supposed to Be: A Breviary of Sin* (Grand Rapids/Leicester: Wm. B. Eerdmans/Apollos, 1995), pp. 7–27.

[274] *Justification*, p. 147.

[275] *Father*, p. 8.

[276] See *Missions*, pp. 56–57.

[277] *Father*, p. 9.

[278] *Work*, p. 57.

The holy God must go out in judgement against all that mocks and flaunts holiness because God's Godhood is at stake and because God is committed to hallowing all things.

Hallowing the name: Holiness' assiduous answer to sin

> *Every sin is a total violation of the entire holiness of God and must be treated accordingly if we are to have a moral world that is under the hand of a holy God. God has a right – indeed, a duty – to be wrathful regarding violations done to His Holiness, His holy love, and His beautiful creation. He will not have both Man and creation vandalised, much less His own holy Name.*[279]

> *The idea of God's holiness is inseparable from the idea of judgment as the mode by which grace goes into action.*[280]

While the young R. J. Campbell reduces the efficacy of the cross to Jesus' ability to remain pure and unchanged through the worst that evil had to give,[281] Forsyth insists that in the face of sin, holiness *must* exert itself as 'creative reaction' in loving judgement.[282] The nature of holy love is such that 'God could not look on sin without acting on it; nor could He do either but to abhor and curse it, even when His Son was beneath it'.[283] While God's wrath is not one of God's 'permanent attributes', it is not 'uncharacteristic' of divine love.[284] Indeed, God's wrath is the consequence – what Brunner terms 'a subordinate reality' – of God's love.[285] Forsyth suggests that if we spoke more about divine holiness and its judgement, we should say much more when we did speak about God's love. His way of putting it is this: 'Holiness must in very love set judgment in the earth.'[286] So understood, judgement is neither the 'inevitable process of cause and effect in a moral universe'[287] nor is it the 'wholly impersonal [which] does not describe an attitude of God but a condition of men'.[288] Rather, judgement is, Forsyth avers, Holy Love's categorically personal imperative; one that crypto-Marcionism fails to comprehend. Forsyth obdurately rejects any hint that forgiveness means no judgement: 'It carries in one hand peace, in the other a sword. But either hand is the hand of love, love holy, just, and wise'.[289] In other words, God's holiness is expressed in God's being for, and not against, humanity. Like God's glory, it serves the interests of

279 Geoffrey C. Bingham, *Ah! Strong, Strong Love!* (Blackwood: New Creation, 1993), p. 128.
280 *Cruciality*, p. 5; cf. *Jesus*, pp. 74–75.
281 Campbell, *The New Theology*, 126.
282 *Jesus*, p. 87; cf. *War*, p. 52.
283 *Work*, p. 243.
284 Walther Eichrodt, *Theology of the Old Testament* (trans. J. Baker; vol. 1; London: SCM, 1961), p. 289; H. G. L. Peels, *The Vengeance of God* (Leiden: Brill, 1995), p. 289.
285 Brunner, *The Mediator*, pp. 519–21; cf. Barth, *CD* II/1, p. 394; Tony Lane, 'The Wrath of God as an Aspect of the Love of God', in *Nothing Greater, Nothing Better: Theological Essays on the Love of God* (ed. Kevin J. Vanhoozer; Grand Rapids: Wm. B. Eerdmans, 2001), pp. 138–67.
286 *Cruciality*, p. 208.
287 Charles Harold Dodd, *The Epistle to the Romans* (The Moffat New Testament Commentary; New York/London: Harper & Row, 1932), p. 21.
288 A. T. Hanson, *The Wrath of the Lamb* (London: SPCK, 1957), p. 110.
289 'Forgiveness', p. 204.

the creature. And so against 'the colour of the time', Forsyth maintains that there can be no mere wiping of the slate, that sin's blasphemy requires more than a slap on the wrist or even eternal detention to make things right. Things are so gravely 'out of joint that only something deeper than the wrecked world' can mend it.[290] Consequently, he is scathing of that preaching which avoids and disdains the 'moral salt of judgment', averring that just as so-called orthodoxy has tended to divorce love from judgement, 'the central failure of theological liberalism' has been its ignorance and severance of holiness and judgement.[291] And here he invokes Kant's witness concerning those who err by suggesting that God could ignore sin:

> God could do nothing of the kind. So far the omnipotence of God is a limited omnipotence. He could not trifle with His own holiness. He could will nothing against His holy nature, and He could not abolish the judgment bound up with it. Nothing in the compass of the divine nature could enable Him to abolish a moral law, the law of holiness. That would be tampering with His own soul. It had to be dealt with.[292]

This note of judgement so lacking in 'current and weak religion'[293] occupies so prominent a place in Forsyth's teaching that his whole system would disintegrate without it. There can be no question here of sin being ignored or healed, as Allen suggests,[294] or somehow absorbed into creation's ontology. Sin can be given no value by God, nor redeemed or reconciled. As the infernal contradiction of holiness, sin must be judged, condemned, vanquished, 'extinguished'[295] and made nought. Therein alone is holiness re-established 'upon the wreck of sin',[296] and all things re-adjusted to God's conscience. As we shall observe in Chapter 3, judgement for Forsyth always has this prospective thrust; it is adjustment more than vengeance, sanctification more than punishment. It is, following Calvin, the indispensable foundation upon which to establish our salvation and new life of holiness.[297] Judgement is, therefore, to be welcomed as mercy 'unto holy victory and endless peace'. Moreover, 'in face of the horrors, moral and physical, around us, and amid all misgivings, [judgement] is our faith, our stay, and our last word'.[298] Judgement is God answering himself, meeting the demand of his own holiness. In the face of sin, holiness is in conflict for its life, the outcome of which means that God is either 'secured or lost to the world for ever'.[299] Judgement is the 'good news' that God has determined to destroy sin, to hallow the eternal name and to establish

290 *Justification*, p. 194.
291 *Cruciality*, pp. 201–03, 205; cf. *Work*, p. 242.
292 cf. *Work*, pp. 112–13; cf. *Cruciality*, p. 194; *Missions*, pp. 230–31; James Denney, *The Second Epistle to the Corinthians* (London: Hodder & Stoughton, 1907), pp. 212–13.
293 *Cruciality*, p. 9.
294 Allen, 'The Christology of P. T. Forsyth', p. 86.
295 *Jesus*, p. 90; cf. 'Sinless', p. 301.
296 *Missions*, p. 52.
297 Calvin, *Inst.*, 3.11.1; cf. Justyn Terry, 'The Justifying Judgement of God', *Anvil* 22, no. 1 (2005), pp. 29–39.
298 *Justification*, p. 58.
299 Ibid., pp. 147–48.

holy communion with us. And because 'love is not holy without judgment',[300] love has spared us no judgement – it is a '*moral* necessity' – necessary to prove and *hallow* God's love, and raise it 'from the fondness of a blind parent'[301] to the authority in which all things delight and are secure. Put otherwise, God's judgement is no undisciplined fit of divine rage, nor a Hegelian-like process through which sin is overcome (though it is some kind of overcoming), nor an automated response towards sin. Rather, it is the *purposed* and *personal* expression of a Father's love towards armed prodigals for whose sake it is pursued. Creation's future – and God's – is bound up with the outcome of such response and so with Jesus Christ in whom holiness must so die as to put death to death – and so rob sin of 'its chief servant' – and be raised.[302] Clearly, there can be no 'easy forgiveness',[303] all things considered. Forsyth contends that sin's gravity only comes home to us when we see what it took God to deal with it.[304] Yet having so seen, one can only conclude that the cross-resurrection represents God's final verdict on creation, and on God's self. This 'Eternal Deed'[305] represents not only 'the greatest moral Act of Time or Eternity'[306] but also 'the world's great day of judgment'.[307] Final judgement is past. The prince of this world *is* a 'doomed power' whose 'sentence went out in the Cross. And he knows it. Humanity was rescued from him there'.[308] This judgement then becomes the basis of genuine hope, the delight of the redeemed and the motivation for the Church's mission in the world. And so in his sermon on Isaiah 6, for example, titled 'The Missionary's Staying Power', Forsyth gives most space to the point (his fourth) that the great missionary motive of the Church ought to be its enthusiasm for holiness. It was *in* the crucible of holiness that Isaiah received his call, he argues, and it was *for* the sake of holiness that Isaiah was driven forth with enthusiasm and inspiration to serve the holiness of God *to* humanity: 'The age that has lost the sense of God's holiness, and therefore of man's sin, is an age of missionary difficulties which nothing but the restoration of that sense can help.'[309]

Clearly, the cross does not represent a deflection of God's anger, 'as if the flash fell on Christ and was conducted by Him to the ground' while humanity stood in passive safety 'with no part or lot in the incomprehensible process'.[310] Indeed, while God's holiness is secured on Pilate's hill, its sense of judgement also attends a moral experience in terms of God's hardening of the sinner, the locus of which is the human conscience. By moral necessity, humanity ever stands before Christ's judgement seat, and one day all

300 *Work*, p. 85.

301 *Justification*, pp. 63, 117; cf. *Cruciality*, pp. 52–53; *Jesus*, p. 28.

302 *Justification*, p. 148.

303 *Preaching*, p. 201; *Theology*, p. 28.

304 Forsyth's student, Sydney Cave, expresses this well in *The Christian Estimate of Man* (London: Duckworth, 1944), p. 228.

305 *Authority*, p. 7.

306 *War*, 134; See *Work*, pp. 207–11.

307 *Work*, p. 133; cf. *Jesus*, pp. 47, 88–89; *Justification*, pp. 185–86, 190, 195–96; 'Sinless', p. 299; *Missions*, pp. 14, 16, 61–62, 72–78; *Preaching*, pp. 216, 238; *Work*, pp. 160–61; *passim*.

308 *Father*, pp. 72–73.

309 *Missions*, pp. 231–32; cf. 'Missions', p. 273; 'Soul of Christ', pp. 207–09; D. W. Lambert, 'The Missionary Message of P. T. Forsyth', *Evangelical Quarterly* 21 (1949), pp. 203–08; Douglas Webster, 'P. T. Forsyth's Theology of Missions', *International Review of Missions* 44 (1955), pp. 175–81.

310 *Cruciality*, p. 78.

humanity will know it. Concerned that he may here be misunderstood, Forsyth makes the following statement in an Addendum to his fourth lecture in *The Work of Christ*:

> Weigh, as men of real moral experience, what is involved in the hardening of the sinner. That is the worst penalty upon sin, its cumulative and deadening history. Well, is it simply self-hardening? Is it simply the reflex action of sin upon character, sin going in, settling in, and reproducing itself there? Is it no part of God's positive procedure in judging sin, and bringing it, for salvation, to a crisis of judgment grace? When Pharaoh hardens his heart, is that in no sense God hardening Pharaoh's heart? When a man hardens himself against God, is there nothing in the action and purpose of God that takes part in that induration? Is that anger not as real as the superabounding grace? Are not both bound up in one complex treatment of the moral world? When a man piles up his sin and rejoices in iniquity, is God simply a bystander and spectator of the process? Does not God's pressure on the man blind him, urge him, stiffen him, shut him up into sin, if only that he might be shut up to mercy alone? Is it enough to say that this is but the action of a process which God simply watches in a permissive way? Is He but passive and not positive to the situation?[311]

Clearly, for Forsyth, the seat of the human predicament is neither political, economic nor psychological, but is moral. This is unsurprising, given what we have already had cause to note about the basic ontology by which Forsyth construes reality. In personal terms, Forsyth believes that the Word of God brings moral pain 'not of a wrong but of rectifying it; not of grief but of judgment'.[312] Furthermore, this judgement is not adjourned to some oblivious futurity; rather, as Hegel notes, 'the subject is itself drawn into the process; it feels the pain of evil and of its own alienation'.[313] In Forsythian terms:

> When we have entered the kingdom through the great judgment in the Cross, we do not escape all judgment; we escape into a new kind of judgment, from that of law to that of grace. We escape condemnation, for we are new creatures, but chastisement we do not escape. Our work may be burned, to our grief, that we may be saved (I Cor. xi. 32). We are judged or chastened with the Church to escape condemnation with the world.[314]

'There is judgment', as Simpson has it, 'not only at the end of history, but now and always'.[315] The judgement at history's end 'has its prelude in the very midst of life', says Forsyth.[316] Whether as individuals or nations, every day involves the registration of our

[311] *Work*, pp. 241–42.
[312] *Cruciality*, p. 208.
[313] Hegel, *Philosophy of Religion*, 3:97.
[314] *Justification*, p. 181.
[315] A. F. Simpson, 'P. T. Forsyth: The Prophet of Judgment', *Scottish Journal of Theology* 4 (1951), pp. 148–56 (153).
[316] 'Church and Society', p. 43; cf. Rom. 13.2–4.

own judgement, 'that we are creating our own Kharma, that we are writing two copies of our life at once – one of them, through the black carbon of time and death, in the eternal'. Indeed, Forsyth insists that we view history 'as at bottom the action . . . of the divine judgment – so long as we can rise to think it is moral *action* with an end, and not incessant moral *process*'.[317] By so doing, Forsyth confronts the problem which concerns many contemporary would-be theists – the sheer amorality and apparent randomness of the process which seems writ large across the development of our world.

To be the object of divine address is to be judged – experienced negatively in the 'atmosphere of personal guilt' in the conscience, and positively in the declaration of forgiveness.[318] So Simpson observes that 'in conscience man finds that in spite of himself, he is critical of himself. There is in the soul a tribunal, a judge, a judge who is not in our own power, whom we cannot get rid of any more than we can escape our own shadows'. Wherever there is guilt, there is judgement, and the awareness that we are personally responsible for our sin. Accordingly, guilt is 'the last problem of the race, its one central moral issue'.[319] Guilt, put otherwise, is sin's penalty. It is not a self-hardening so much as it is divine pressure to blind, urge and stiffen the sinner – to shut him or her up into sin – that God may shut all up into mercy. With pastoral sensitivity, Forsyth turns to the experience of desertion by God, an experience he describes as 'the worst judgement'. Yet in God's wisdom and grace, forsakenness 'may be [our] sanctification'.[320] Here Forsyth distances himself from Ritschl, for whom wrath was unworthy of a loving and gracious God, averring that despite their severity God's ongoing judgements are the result of paternal love which is 'quite capable of being angry, and must be angry and even sharp with its beloved children'.[321]

Teleological orientation

> *The supreme object of creation and of history . . . is to bring every man before the judgment-seat of the grace of Christ. It is not to provide each with a minimum of three acres and a cow, and keep his pot boiling.*[322]
>
> *True history, we may say, is teleological history.*[323]

In *The Principle of Authority*, Forsyth examines Lessing's famous 'ditch': 'The accidental truths of history can never become proof for the necessary truths of reason.'[324] And although careful to avoid its rationalist implications, Forsyth happily adopts Lessing's distinction between *Geschichte* and *Historie*:

[317] *Justification*, p. 196.
[318] 'Atonement', p. 77.
[319] Simpson, 'The Prophet of Judgment', p. 152.
[320] *Work*, p. 243.
[321] Ibid., p. 105; cf. Albrecht Ritschl, *The Christian Doctrine of Justification and Reconciliation: The Positive Development of the Doctrine* (trans. Hugh Ross Mackintosh and Alexander Beith Macaulay; Edinburgh: T&T Clark, 1900), p. 64.
[322] *Justification*, p. 81.
[323] Ernst Troeltsch, 'The Ideas of Natural Law and Humanity in World Politics', in *Natural Law and the Theory of Society, 1500 to 1800* (ed. Otto Gierke; Boston: Beacon Press, 1957), p. 218.
[324] Gotthold Ephraim Lessing, *Theological Writings* (trans. Henry Chadwick; London: Adam & Charles Black, 1956), p. 53.

> *Historie* is history as it may be settled by the methods of historical science, where our results, like those of all science, are but relative, and either highly or poorly probable. *Geschichte* on the other hand is a larger thing, out of which *Historie* has to sift, but which may embody and convey ideas greater than the critical residum retains power to express.[325]

Historie may contain a mass of empirical and documentable events, but it can neither prove nor provide any sense of meaning to those events, the 'great ideas and powers' (*Geschichte*) that govern.[326] Moreover, while even 'defective documents may be great sacraments',[327] only in Christ does God give the final account of himself and of his purpose for creation and history. Indeed, 'the key of creation', Forsyth avers, 'is its redemption. It can come to itself only by being redeemed'.[328] Forsyth asks: 'Has creation any ground plan else? Plenty of process, but what plan, what goal? The goal to which the whole creation moves – is it not that Eternal Redemption? Does it not all wait and work to the manifestation of the Sons of God?'[329] Forsyth's construing of the cross as redemptive revelation, superhistoric – as *Geschichte* – grants to creation a teleology absent in monist or process theology, or in naturalist histiography. It also serves to bear witness to the ground and centre of evangelical authority in the historic and eternal act of deliverance, and 'prolonged in an infinite number of acts *ejusdem generis* ["of the same kind or class"] in the experience by Christian people of their redemption in Christ',[330] a prolongation, as we shall see in our final chapter, that continues 'post-mortem'. While great spiritual truths belong to, and reach us through, history, affecting, shaping and enhancing us, they are not at the mercy of historical science: 'They are not proofs, but sacraments or sources'. Christ's death does not *prove* anything: 'It is not evidence but action, the outcrop of an eternal act' which sources new life and secures a 'morally safe and finally free' cosmos.[331]

Just as Tillich later suggests that creation's eschatological orientation provides its *raison d'être* – 'Creation is creation for an end: in the "ground," the "aim" is present'[332] – so too Forsyth grants primacy to creation's future when he privileges eschatology for determining the shape of being. This eschatological thrust spans past and future, and provides the brackets for rendering meaningful and coherent the temporal, while granting to the temporal a particular transcendence which brings together in our

[325] *Authority*, pp. 112–13.
[326] We see here Forsyth's indebtedness to Kähler's insistence (against Ritschl) on a Jesus of *Geschichte* rather than of *Historie*. The fact that revelation for Forsyth does not discard *Historie* for *Geschichte* has led some commentators to employ Forsyth's work against Barthians. Hugh Dermot McDonald, *Theories of Revelation: An Historical Study, 1860–1960* (London: George Allen & Unwin, 1963), pp. 89–91. Yasukata has suggested that the distinction between *Geschichte* and *Historie* was not clear-cut until the early twentieth century. Toshimasa Yasukata, *Lessing's Philosophy of Religion and the German Enlightenment: Lessing on Christianity and Reason* (New York: Oxford University Press, 2002), p. 165, fn.58.
[327] *Authority*, p. 114.
[328] *Parnassus*, pp. 262–63.
[329] *Person*, p. 326.
[330] 'Revelation', p. 116.
[331] *Authority*, pp. 114, 251.
[332] Paul Tillich, *Systematic Theology* (vol. 3; Digswell Place: James Nisbet and Co., 1964), p. 424.

imagination all three tenses of time. Refusing to play protology and eschatology off against one another, Forsyth is able to affirm the value to eternity of temporal realities which are in Christ redeemed and transfigured, and not abrogated. To disregard creation's teleological current is to either separate creation from redemption, or nature from supernature, or the first creation from the second, bringing into question the continuity and unity of God's creative activity. As Jürgen Moltmann puts it: 'Only through an understanding of the process of creation as coherent and eschatologically oriented can the concepts of both the unity of God and of the unity of meaning within his creative activity be maintained . . . Creation at the beginning points forward to the history of salvation and both point beyond themselves to the kingdom of glory.'[333] Subjected to frustration, the creation is a groaning womb which can hardly wait for what is coming – the uncovering and birthing of its filial destiny. Forsyth interprets these groans as the warming-up tunes that function as the hope of new tunes and even a complete symphony, as the creation reverberates with the praises and glory of its Creator-Redeemer.[334]

This dynamic element in creation is often neglected in more static treatments. Gunton properly recalls that 'the creation is not a static and tireless lump of matter, but ... something with a direction and a destiny.'[335] But it is not just any destiny: 'Through his Son and Spirit, his two hands, the Father both prevents the creation from slipping back into the nothingness from which it came and restores its teleology, its movement to perfection.'[336] While he lacks the full expression of Gunton's trinitarian grammar, it is the certainty of this perfection that Forsyth assumes when he urges that we understand creation proleptically, as the *act* of One who meets creation from the future and not of a 'spiritual process, or native movement between the finite and the infinite', a move which would render creation independent of grace.

> [We] must begin with the end, taken as a gift. We must carry it back to the beginning. The purpose is not revealed in the process, but the process in the purpose... Creation does not explain Christianity, but Christianity creation ... We began in Him in whom we end ... Our great destiny is as certain as He is absolute and holy.[337]

Here Forsyth's christologically cored and soteriologically driven creation theology is woven in an eschatological shape. The purpose and nature of the creation's origin is rooted and revealed only in its destiny wherein creation comes to itself, realizes its moral soul and is re-created. Only redemption can make sense of the old creation:

333 Jürgen Moltmann, 'Creation and Redemption', in *Creation, Christ and Culture: Studies in Honour of T. F. Torrance* (ed. Richard W. A. McKinney; Edinburgh: T&T Clark, 1976), p. 123.
334 See *Justification*, p. 31; *Prayer*, pp. 23, 58.
335 Gunton, *The Christian Faith*, p. 7.
336 Colin E. Gunton, *Father, Son, and Holy Spirit: Essays Toward a Fully Trinitarian Theology* (London: T&T Clark, 2003), p. 117.
337 *Justification*, pp. 56–57; cf. James Orr, *The Progress of Dogma: Being the Elliot Lectures, Delivered at the Western Theological Seminary, Alleghany, Penns, U.S.A., 1897* (London: Hodder & Stoughton, 1901), pp. 323–24; Alan P. F. Sell, *The Philosophy of Religion 1875–1980* (London: Croom Helm, 1988), pp. 62–68.

'The first creation was the prophecy of the second; the second was the first tragically "arrived".'[338] Indeed, Forsyth believes that God only 'took the responsibility of creating because He knew He possessed the power to redeem and retrieve whatever creation might come to'.[339] Here, soteriology guarantees teleology. Humanity's final confidence that 'victory awaits us' is grounded in the certainty that 'victory is won', apart from which there is 'no teleology of the world'.[340]

With Kierkegaard, Denney, McLeod Campbell and others, Forsyth contends that nothing can be gained by imagining the world to have been something other than we know it to be. One upshot of such a move is that while God was free to create or not to create, by creating *this* world, and not some other one, God commits himself to the Incarnation and the cross, to the judgement and sanctification of all God has made.[341] Like Irenaeus, Forsyth understands that creation's 'purpose and burthen'[342] is in its destiny of redemption. And apart from this 'moral and experient sphere', it has no real meaning.[343]

> The ground plan of an evolving Creation, and indeed of Being, is God's redemptive Will. *Heilesratb ist Schöpfungsplan* [The saving Will is creation's plan]. We are born into a redeemed world. We are created for redemption, created by One who knew in creating that He had in Himself all the resources wherewith to deal with freedom's abuse of His creation. Beneath, behind, and above God the Creator is God the Redeemer. Our final footing in a moral world, i.e. in the universe, is the holy God of its salvation.[344]

Forsyth insists that creation is an act *of love* – 'In Christ we were neither made nor saved to eke out some lack in God, nor to meet some hunger in his being; but of his fulness have we all received. And we are here as the fulness and overflow of his creative love'[345] – but it was *for grace*. Subsequently, the supreme revelation of God's creativity is not in calling forth the world in an act of creative love, but in calling it back *as God found it* as a new creation in grace.

> It is not as if we had a realm of providence in the first creation with a realm alongside it of redemption in the second ... That is a crude and maimed conception of the divine action, and lacks its unity of plan. But the first creation with its providential

338 *Justification*, p. 124; cf. Wolfhart Pannenberg, *Jesus – God and Man* (trans. Duane Priebe and Lewis L. Wilkins; Philadelphia: Westminster Press, 1968), p. 169: 'creation happens from the end, from the ultimate future'.

339 *Justification*, p. 32; cf. *Justification*, pp. 90–91, 155–56; *Authority*, pp. 184, 202–04, 416; *Pulpit*, pp. 5–6; *Mercy*, p. 9.

340 *Justification*, pp. 78, 79; cf. *Work*, pp. 171–72.

341 See *Authority*, pp. 30, 365, 406; *Justification*, pp. 123–24; Denney, *Atonement*, pp. 55–57; James Denney, *The Christian Doctrine of Reconciliation* (London: James Clarke & Co., 1959), pp. 181–82; Sydney Cave, *The Doctrine of the Work of Christ* (ed. Eric S. Waterhouse; London Theological Library; London: University of London Press, 1937), pp. 233, 246.

342 *Sacraments*, p. 282.

343 Ibid., p. 303.

344 *Authority*, p. 184.

345 *Person*, pp. 353–54; cf. 'Metaphysic', p. 713.

> course was made for the second, and only comes home in it, though by the way of creation and not evolution, of redemption and not mere development. Conversely the second creation has all along been reacting on the first and moulding it.[346]

So stated, nature is not the 'mother' but the 'matrix' of Grace. Grace precedes creation, and sin. However original sin may be, grace is more original still. Moreover, grace does not merely prolong nature, but descends upon, acts on and changes it. Grace is the '*primum mobile* [prime mover] of Nature itself'[347] burning itself into the very structure of reality, from which it draws out the creaks and groans for the manifestation of its Hallower. For 'strange grace'[348] is not only creation's ground-plan but also 'Nature's destiny. We are born to be saved',[349] to come to ourselves in a new self.[350] Put otherwise, 'the final key to the first creation is the second; and the first was done with the second in view'.[351] And again:

> The beginning only exists because of the end, and exists to be glorified in the end . . . We were created to be recreated. The new creation is the destiny of the first. And it is the experience of the new creation crowning all that gives us any key to understand what creation everywhere is and intends, what it was the first in a mystery, and aims to be in a manifestation.[352]

Consequently, Forsyth believes that the second creation needed to be not only as wide as the first, but also more creative, meeting not only material chaos but moral crisis, and sanctifying all for which the first was conceived. God's entire resources were not expended in creating; 'The greater part was in reserve to save',[353] to bear the burden of creation's moral struggle, to hallow all things. Forsyth here provides a way of affirming not only the genuine newness of the new creation, but also its simultaneity with the old. And his insistence that creation's relationship with its Creator is teleological properly safeguards both the absolute contingency of the creature and the freedom of the Creator.

Although Forsyth is right to insist that creation's eschatological orientation provides creation's *raison d'être* – that the second creation both shapes and *justifies* the first – his enthusiasm to proclaim the it-is-finishedness of God's work leaves too unclear the teleological thrust of his creation doctrine. His tendency to over-eschatologize may have been avoided had he granted Christ's resurrection greater theological weight,

346 *War*, p. 171; cf. *Authority*, p. 185; *War*, pp. 52, 176, 177; *Life*, pp. 68–69; *Justification*, pp. 32, 58, 155, 192.

347 *War*, p. 171; cf. *Work*, p. 180; 'Valedictory Address'; 'Regeneration – II', p. 97.

348 *Person*, 343.

349 *Life*, p. 69; cf. Brown, *The Divine Treatment of Sin*, 16, 20–24, 53–70.

350 'Regeneration – II', p. 92.

351 *Justification*, pp. 123–24; cf. *Justification*, p. 53; *Evolution*, pp. 9–10, 16–17; James Baldwin Brown, *The Doctrine of Annihilation in the Light of the Gospel of Love* (London: Henry S. King & Co., 1875), p. 115: 'Man [was] made originally for Redemption; the Redemptive purpose cherished by God from eternity; all the forces and influences of the Universe arrayed for its accomplishment.'

352 'Veracity', p. 210.

353 *Authority*, p. 205.

as the anticipatory first fruit in which 'the whole created order is taken up' and 'on whose fate turns the redemption of all'.[354] To be sure, Forsyth gives Jesus' resurrection a more prominent place than did many of his predecessors, and its truth undergirds his christology. Nevertheless, Forsyth can explain Christ's work largely without direct reference to it and he too often reduces Jesus' resurrection to little more than the vindication of Jesus' passion. Christ's victory over death and his present reign as ascended Lord turns our attention back to the divine judgement concerning creation's goodness. It also vindicates the providential unfolding of created order within history, thereby renewing and realigning the natural ordering of human life towards God as its proper *telos* in whom creation is finally sanctified. And because Jesus' resurrected body is both continuous with the old while also of a new materiality (however conceived), the exalted Christ bears witness to creaturely destiny that is continuous with and yet also departs from its antecedent history. Consequently, we may anticipate the redemption of creation as its renewal and completion, but not its restoration; for Christian hope is placed not in a renovated Eden but in a hallowed new heaven and earth.

III. Appropriation

> *Much of our work has been to steal. That does not matter if it is done wisely and gratefully. When a man gives out a great thought, get it, work it; it is common property. It belongs to the whole world, to be claimed and assimilated by whoever shall find.*[355]

Despite the mileage that has been made attributing various sources to Forsyth's theology, it remains that Forsyth rarely reveals who he is responding to or addressing, he rarely identifies the source(s) of his thought,[356] and on most issues displays prodigious independence. Forsyth largely leaves those who wish to identify his sources to 'read between the lines'. So Brown's warning: 'When all is said and done . . . one must be wary of assessing the precise influence of men upon Forsyth's thought.'[357] Attempts to identify sources, therefore, are not only risky, but entail a certain level of guess-work. That said, the identification of some sources for the development of Forsyth's basic ideas regarding sanctification is possible, though readers must recognize that on sanctification, as on just about everything else, Forsyth betrays an indebtedness to a diverse number of thinkers. While Forsyth drank deeply from the Apostle Paul above all else, those themes characteristic of his theology also betray a debt to Anselm of Canterbury, Luther, Kant, Hegel, Carlyle, Ritschl, Troeltsch, Dorner, Kähler, Turner, Dale,[358] Goethe,

354 Oliver O'Donovan, *Resurrection and Moral Order: An Outline for Evangelical Ethics* (Leicester/Grand Rapids: IVP/Wm. B. Eerdmans, 1986), p. 15.

355 *Work*, p. 66.

356 Forsyth recalls that the critical apparatus expected in sustained studies would be 'foreign to the lecture form', which is what most of his books originated as. *Person*, p. viii.

357 Brown, *Prophet for Today*, p. 32.

358 Bradley suggests that it was from Dale that Forsyth first acquired his interest in the atonement, and was introduced to Ritschl's thought, albeit by print, for Forsyth did not meet Dale until the Summer of 1892 when he holidayed in Llanbedr (Wales) for three weeks with Dale and his wife. Bradley, *P. T. Forsyth*, p. 101. See Alfred William Winterslow Dale et al., *The Life of R. W. Dale of Birmingham*

Law,[359] Harnack, Arnold, Eliot, Kierkegaard, Maurice,[360] Fairbairn, Denney,[361] Newman, Schleiermacher, Butler, Nietzsche, Milton, Greenwell, Ruskin, Hardy, Browning, Zahn, Seeberg, Schopenhauer, Ibsen,[362] Lessing, Ihmels, Loofs, Bunsen, Schelling and others.[363] Indeed, sometimes it is more than an echo, and there are occasions when Forsyth offers us extended paraphrases, sometimes running to pages, from German theologians, without so much as an acknowledgment.

Before we turn to consider some of the more important parents of Forsyth's sanctification theology, we ought simply to note that, customarily, Forsyth does not take ideas over from others directly. Instead, he ingests their insights, he breathes deeply of their vapour, but these are transformed in his lungs so that what is expired is no longer pure Kant or Kierkegaard, but is Forsyth.

While exposed to a broad gamut of Continental and British scholarship, there are a few voices in particular that seem to have been of explicit interest to Forsyth, and specifically to his thinking on holiness. Kant, Hegel, Dorner, Ritschl, Kähler, Maurice and Fairbairn all qualify in this regard and have received due attention in the secondary literature on Forsyth. Our focus, however, will be on five no less influential and, I would argue – with the possible exception of Thomas Goodwin – more important figures in a study on Forsyth's theology of sanctification; namely, John Calvin, Thomas Goodwin, James Baldwin Brown, Wilhelm Windelband and Adolf Schlatter. The inclusion of Goodwin in this shortlist betrays the fact, as we shall see, that it is his name that has been identified as the key influence in Forsyth's notion of holiness, a claim I will argue which is to be found wanting. We turn first, however, to Calvin.

John Calvin (1509–1564)

Broadly, Forsyth was indebted to the old orthodoxies, especially the Puritans who 'had a true eye for what really mattered in Christianity' and which drew and sustained

(London: Hodder & Stoughton, 1899), p. 636. In a more recent study, Yutaka Morishima revives the argument that Dale is 'a likely source' of Forsyth's emphasis on holiness in the atonement. See Morishima, 'God's Holiness in P. T. Forsyth', pp. 101–18.

359 *The Soul of Prayer* and 'Christian Perfection', particularly, betray a deep affinity with William Law's work of almost identical titles.

360 'Ministerial Libraries', p. 268: 'I owe a great deal to Maurice; in some respects I owe him everything.'

361 Forsyth once announced that '[Denney] has more important things to say than anyone at present writing theology'. Cited in John Randolph Taylor, *God Loves Like That!: The Theology of James Denney* (London: SCM, 1962), p. 9. While Forsyth confessed, in 1906, to 'have not read Denney with such care' (cited in Mackintosh, 'The Authority of the Cross', p. 211), writing some years after Denney's death, he confessed in an unpublished letter that 'Denney [had] became a court of reference in my silent thought. No man was so needful for the conscience of the Church and the public ... There is nobody left now to be the *theological prophet* and lead in the moral reconstruction of belief.' 'Letter to Nicoll', np. And again: 'Denney is the greatest thinker we have upon our side'. Cited in James Moffatt (ed.), *Letters of Principal James Denney to His Family and Friends* (London: Hodder & Stoughton, 1921), p. 153.

362 On Forsyth's indebtment to Ibsen see Goroncy, 'Bitter Tonic for Our Time', pp. 105–18 and Goroncy, 'Fighting Troll-Demons', pp. 61–85.

363 Wood argues for the primacy of a Hegelian influence on Forsyth. Ralph C. Wood, 'Christ on Parnassus: P. T. Forsyth Among the Liberals', *Literature and Theology* 2 (1988), pp. 83–95; cf. Brown, *Prophet for Today*, p. 31; *Preaching*, p. 195.

him 'amidst much that is hopelessly out of date'.[364] That debt extended no less to the magisterial Reformers, especially to Luther (and Lutheran theology) and Calvin, and over time increasing towards the latter.[365] Forsyth is always quick to distinguish, however, between Calvin and that movement which bears the Frenchman's name, naming the 'second- or third-rate' Calvinism of the seventeenth century a 'very hard-shell kind of Christianity', and reporting that eighteenth-century Calvinism maintained a devotion to an orthodoxy 'whose architecture was of a late, debased, and perpendicular type'. It was Calvinism with 'high sides rather than high summits', 'with a lid on and the air exhausted', of lesser minds and the lay pieties, 'devoid of the grand note it had in Calvin and Edwards. It was Calvinism without the atmosphere of the great tradition of Church and State, which gave an amplitude to theology, and kept it close to history on the one hand and to the Gospel experience on the other'.[366] Similarly, Forsyth describes nineteenth-century Calvinism as 'clotted, and sometimes soured ... [leading] to Unitarianism (through Arianism) in one direction, and into Methodism in the other'.[367] He also describes the teaching out of the London University of his day as having 'a mixed benefit' on Christian ministry, partly because of its moderated Calvinism, 'immoderately diluted, and set in a somewhat amateur philosophy'. They 'respected Mill, loved Tennyson, and trounced Calvin'.[368]

Again, we must be careful of assigning sources too hastily, but there are a significant number of places where Forsyth directly acknowledges his debt to Calvin, and the mature Forsyth's debt to this 'commanding religious genius'[369] has been too neglected by Forsyth scholarship. What Forsyth most values about Calvin is his doctrine of 'the absolute freedom' of a gracious God – not as the 'Eternal Imperative of the conscience' but as humanity's 'Everlasting Redeemer' and Father.[370] Therein, we are given in Calvin a vision of humanity's and human society's *raison d'être* and true freedom: to 'serve the freedom and worship the glory of a holy, loving, and absolute God'.[371] While Forsyth cannot accept all of Calvin's doctrines nor the Calvinistic creed, he joins Dale in stressing that we have much still to learn from Calvin's repudiation of 'an easy good-natured God'[372] and Calvin's witness to the one holy Father who engages an unholy world in order to make it holy and serviceable for himself.

[364] *Society*, p. 121; cf. *Congregationalism*, p. 39; *Freedom*, pp. 42, 47, 107–08, 115; *Justification*, pp. 95–96; *Missions*, p. 95; *Rome*, pp. 29, 58–60; *Society*, pp. 102, 121–22; *War*, p. 107.

[365] On Forsyth's appreciation for the Reformers see 'Atonement', p. 61; 'Sanctification', p. 733; *Work*, pp. 165, 231; *Authority*, p. 71; *Society*, p. 121; *Jesus*, p. 58; 'Gate', p. 182; *passim*.

[366] *Justification*, p. 83; *Work*, p. 71; *Freedom*, p. 169; cf. *Freedom*, p. 347.

[367] *Freedom*, p. 316.

[368] *Freedom*, pp. 176–77. On the changing mood of antagonism towards Calvinism among Victorians and beyond, see James Baldwin Brown, *First Principles of Ecclesiastical Truth: Essays on the Church and Society* (London: Hodder & Stoughton, 1871), pp. 353–60; Alfred Ernest Garvie, *Revelation Through History and Experience: A Study of the Historical Basis of the Revelation of the Godhead* (London: Ivor Nicholson & Watson, 1934), p. xii; Alfred Ernest Garvie, 'Freedom of the Church in Christ', *Congregational Quarterly* 20, no. 2 (1942), pp. 108–14 (113).

[369] *Rome*, p. 29; cf. *Freedom*, pp. 45–50, 71–72, 74, 107–08, 114–16, 120–21, 131, 134–35, 155–56, 159–60, 170, 278, 297; *Missions*, pp. 309–10; *Sacraments*, p. 127; *Theology*, pp. 280, 327.

[370] *Freedom*, pp. 263, 277; cf. *Authority*, p. 377.

[371] *Freedom*, p. 264; cf. *Freedom*, pp. 265–66.

[372] Robert W. Dale, 'On Some Present Aspects of Theological Thought Among Congregationalists', *The Congregationalist* 6 (1877), pp. 1–15 (8).

While Forsyth sees in Luther one who seized on the primacy of God's love, it was Calvin who was apprehended by a 'pre-eminence on the holy' which brought the world's freedom and security.[373] It is through Calvin that Forsyth comes to reinterpret what he had learnt in Kant and Butler both christocentrically and patercentrically. From Calvin, too, Forsyth learns that holiness is love's power to remain, assert and establish itself – 'always come home to itself'[374] – and that holiness can be satisfied with nothing less than the sanctification of all things. With Forsyth, Calvin is keen to assert that while sanctification is a 'natural' impossibility, it is not something that happens 'over our heads' or 'behind our backs' but rather involves human 'voluntary' action, the 'obedience of righteousness'.[375] Also, through the gracious operation of the Spirit, sanctification discloses the eschatological nature of justification and so shapes life towards a righteous end. With prodigious clarity, Calvin asserts that sanctification is not merely the outworking, or sign, of justification and election, but is its purpose and *telos*. It involves our responsible participation in the Spirit who recovers us from the pollution of sin and renews us as fitting covenant partners. Thus the basis of assurance remains Christ who, by the Spirit, confirms our sanctification through the testimony of a good conscience.[376]

Sanctification, therefore, refers to both ontological reality (Rom. 5–6) and eschatological promise (Rom. 8) that finds expression in the earthly sojourn of 'fresh progress' to godliness (vivification), repentance and 'continual warfare with the flesh' (mortification) that will 'end only at death' (Rom. 7).[377] Both Calvin and Forsyth categorically reject 'the illusion of perfectionism': 'Believers are still sinners' who – 'under the cross' – trust the Word of God in the 'continuing occasion for struggle'.[378] Both understand, too, that perfect righteousness does not refer to 'sinlessness' but to 'blamelessness' (in the Hebraic sense) and means responsibility to God (and to God's creation) and service with 'wholeheartedness, integrity, . . . sincerity', and self-denial, which is 'the sum of the Christian life'.[379] Finally, both pronounce that personal sanctification, and the nurture and discipline of the Christian life, takes place within the locus of the visible Church which stands together under the Word of God (publicized from pulpit, font and table)[380] who consecrates God's people for priestly service in the world.

373 *Life*, p. 29.
374 Ibid., p. 30.
375 John Calvin, *Commentary upon the Acts of the Apostles, Volume I* (trans. Henry Beveridge; vol. 18; Grand Rapids: Baker, 2003), p. 218.
376 See John Calvin, *Commentaries on the Epistles to the Philippians, Colossians, and Thessalonians* (vol. 21; Grand Rapids: Baker, 2003), pp. 303–05; John Calvin, *Commentaries on the Epistles of Paul to the Galatians and Ephesians* (trans. William Pringle; vol. 21; Grand Rapids: Baker, 2003), p. 169; Randall C. Zachman, *The Assurance of Faith: Conscience in the Theology of Martin Luther and John Calvin* (Minneapolis: Fortress, 1993), pp. 210–23.
377 Calvin, *Inst.*, 2.8.30; 3.3.9; cf. Calvin, *Inst.*, 2.15.4; 2.16.13; 3.3.20; 3.6.3; 3.20.46; 3.25.6; 4.8.12.
378 Calvin, *Inst.*, 3.8.8; 3.3.10; cf. Calvin, *Inst.*, 3.3.14; 3.8.1–11; Dietrich Bonhoeffer, *The Cost of Discipleship* (trans. R. H. Fuller; London: SCM, 1959), p. 152.
379 Calvin, *Inst.*, 3.7.1–10; cf. Calvin, *Inst.*, 3.23.12–3; *Justification*, pp. 180–81.
380 Calvin, *Inst.*, 4.15.2; 4.16.29.

Thomas Goodwin (1600–1680)

Forsyth's regard for Goodwin is aptly summed up in his naming the puritan 'the apostle and high priest of our confession'.[381] Goodwin, who served as Oliver Cromwell's chaplain from 1656, exemplifies, for Forsyth, theology fittingly done: uninterested in peripherals but arising and expanding from its source – God in action. Dogma first, then doctrine, then theology, as we noted earlier. Thus practised, Forsyth believes, theology is liberated from its metaphysical shackles and becomes 'modern' in spirit. While many of the old 'forms' and 'fittings' remain, Goodwin instils them with new 'current', 'force' and eternal youth.[382] As an alternative to those Reformation sermons which 'shook half-Europe . . . [but] to-day not only read flat, but are intolerable',[383] Forsyth advocates Goodwin as an example of one who promotes positive theology which attends this 'jaded, impotent life with the note of a real, foregone redemption'.[384] Goodwin thus passes Forsyth's 'test of theology': 'its capacity for being preached to the believer's soul . . . that the dogmatic norm is identical with the religious authority in the Gospel'.[385] While grateful for Calvin's systematic treatments whose foundations are indispensable for theology, Forsyth identifies in Goodwin (and other Puritans)[386] the experiential fruit of Calvin's system – truth as alive and not as a 'closed system' (as medievalism and 'debased' eighteenth-century Calvinism had made it),[387] grace not 'secured in a scaffolding of extraneous philosophy' but that which 'carries within itself and its nature its own expansive power', organic form and self-corrective principle. To this gospel Forsyth invites us to 'continually return, to adjust our compass and take our course'.[388] Only thus is freedom (personal, ecclesial and political) secured, and the church catholic shaped after its proper apostolic and evangelical foundation.

Bradley and Sell attribute Forsyth's emphasis on holiness (and Bradley, Forsyth's belief in universal election) to his reading of Goodwin. Sell uncharacteristically overplays his hand when he concludes that Forsyth 'almost certainly derived his conviction that atonement theory must do something to satisfy God's holiness . . . from the Puritan Thomas Goodwin'.[389] The evidence for such a claim is wanting. The fact is that we cannot be certain from where Forsyth garnered this central theme in his theology.[390] Goodwin

381 *Freedom*, 118.

382 *Freedom*, p. 116; *Authority*, p. 272.

383 'Sanctification', p. 733.

384 *Preaching*, p. 158; cf. *Freedom*, p. 97.

385 *Society*, p. 83.

386 See 'Allegory', p. 314; *Congregationalism*, p. 39; *Freedom*, pp. 42, 47, 107–08, 115; *Justification*, pp. 95–96; *Missions*, p. 95; *Rome*, pp. 29, 58–60; 'Sinless', p. 289; *Society*, pp. 102, 121–22; *War*, p. 107.

387 *Freedom*, pp. 97, 99, 113, 169, 347.

388 Ibid., p. 119.

389 Sell, 'Unsystematic Systematician', pp. 117–18.

390 Bradley cites numerous selections from Goodwin's *Expositions on Ephesians* in support, though none of these are conclusive, proving little more than that Goodwin wrote about holiness. Bradley, *P. T. Forsyth*, pp. 102–03. Bradley offers no evidence that Forsyth was familiar with Goodwin before 1891 when Forsyth first emphasized holiness. In fact, Bradley offers no direct evidence at all. Furthermore, none of Forsyth's own references to Goodwin appear in the context of a discussion on holiness. A few appear in discussions of divine love, though unqualified by holiness. Sell seems to merely assume Bradley's conclusions, but proffers no argument nor provides any new evidence. One might also consider Forsyth's indebtment to Edwards, whose teaching on holiness and experience offers an important commentary on what was happening, for example, in the early Keswick Movement. See Jonathan Edwards, *The Works of Jonathan Edwards* (Edinburgh: Banner of Truth Trust, 1998), 1:101; 2:257–77.

is a candidate, but certainly not the strongest. Still, the Goodwin-echo *is* evident in the judgement that God could not rest in love for God's children, 'nor heighten it to delight in them, till he had made them blameless in love before him; till he had made them perfectly holy like himself'.[391] The Forsyth–Goodwin association appears also in regard to sanctification. Goodwin's soteriology reflects the Augustinian–Puritan conviction that happiness accompanies knowledge of and communion with God. Sanctifying faith looks to Christ, the objective ground of our election. Indeed, the 'chief thing' in election, the 'end of it', is that God both is and sees God's own unblameable 'holiness and love before him'.[392] This 'seeing' happens only in Christ, apart from whom there can be no thought of our being holy, or, in him, other than holy.[393] While Forsyth nowhere explicates this in Goodwin's terms of a covenant of works, for both, election, adoption, sanctification, regeneration and faith are constituted only in Christ in whom God is the redemptive-historical narrative finding consummation.[394] Thus it is not the promise of redemption per se which is foundational for the Church's hope and consolation, but the actuality of that promise *in the man Jesus*. So Goodwin: 'all the promises in the word are but copies of God's promises made to Christ for us from everlasting'.[395]

Comprehending sanctification to be that process whereby what humans are objectively in Christ is made real subjectively, Goodwin construes holiness both as 'imperfect' (though known 'in truth and sincerity')[396] and as 'perfect', as that which humans are 'ordained to in the world to come' and which constitutes a perfection that God can 'fully and perfectly delight in'.[397] Therefore, while believers know a *pugna spiritualis* [spiritual battle] through the 'bloody wounds and gashes'[398] of Romans 7, they look towards holiness' full eschatological triumph.[399] 'We are sanctified by degrees', 'by parcels in the possession' of glory reserved for a latter day.[400] This aligning of sanctification with faith resembles Forsyth's essay on 'Christian Perfection'. The sanctified life is 'nothing but sheer faith . . . and no mixture of law, or works, or qualifications, or anything else in it'.[401]

Goodwin's doctrine of sanctification, however, exposes a more announced pneumatology than Forsyth articulates.[402] Sanctification, for Goodwin, is the 'writing in the heart . . . not with ink, but with the Spirit of the living God'.[403] Sanctification

[391] Thomas Goodwin, *The Works of Thomas Goodwin* (ed. Thomas Smith; Nichol's Series of Standard Divines, Puritan Period; Edinburgh/London/Dublin: James Nichol/James Nisbet and Co./W. Robertson, 1845), 1:81.

[392] Ibid.

[393] See ibid., pp. 86, 88.

[394] Goodwin, *Works*, 1:13–14, 66, 82, 127–28, 131, 135, 142, 209, 215, 220, 229, 254, 291, 415, 424; Goodwin, *Works*, 2:137, 233, 244, 246, 315, 318, 329, 336, 383, 421–24; Goodwin, *Works*, 4:14–15.

[395] Goodwin, *Works*, 5:139.

[396] Goodwin, *Works*, 1:80.

[397] Ibid., 80; Goodwin, *Works*, 2:438; cf. Goodwin, *Works*, 2:315.

[398] Goodwin, *Works*, 3:448.

[399] Goodwin, *Works*, 1:82.

[400] Goodwin, *Works*, 2:335; cf. Goodwin, *Works*, 7:129–336.

[401] Goodwin, *Works*, 1:444; cf. Goodwin, *Works*, 1:424, 460, 463, 501; Goodwin, *Works*, 3:450.

[402] See Goodwin, *Works*, 1:231, 233–34, 238, 241, 247, 254, 270, 503; Goodwin, *Works*, 2:308, 352. Goodwin develops Calvin's views on sanctification and the sealing of the Spirit in his *Exposition of the Epistle to the Ephesians*, a study which Forsyth referred to as Goodwin's 'magnificent homiletic'. *Freedom*, 117. See Goodwin, *Works*, 3:231–350; 359–403; 432–506; Goodwin, *Works*, 8:338–419.

[403] Goodwin, *Works*, 1:230; cf. Goodwin, *Works*, 1:360.

is nothing short of 'a resurrection', requiring the same pneumatalogical energy that creates faith and raised Jesus from the dead.[404]

James Baldwin Brown (1820–1884)

In September 1872, upon Forsyth's return from Göttingen (a common destination for young Nonconformist theological students at the time), he was accepted on probation (he was fully admitted in 1873) at New College (London) to study theology. While his health continually restricted his attendance at classes, and he seems to have felt a 'misfit' who was increasingly 'wasting his time' there (which led to his resignation in 1874, before completion and in circumstances difficult to square with sound order[405]), there are two lasting results of his time at New College. First, he met Maria Hester (Minna) Magness (1850/51–94), the devout, 'intellectual and cultured' Anglican whom he married in 1877.[406] Secondly, he came under the influence of James Baldwin Brown, Congregationalism's mediator of Maurice.[407] In fact, it may have been Brown who first drew Forsyth to London, Forsyth travelling the six and a half miles out to Brixton every Sunday to hear the devout Maurician who he later describes as 'the greatest Independent of our times', indeed, the greatest since the seventeenth century.[408]

> To us juniors he was always young, and always, till he became ill, accessible. It was new life to come from the dogmatists with their exclusions, their system of

[404] Goodwin, *Works*, 1:440; cf. Goodwin, *Works*, 2:13.

[405] See Extract from 386 Council Meeting minutes from Council of New College, 'New College London', np.

[406] Andrews, 'Memoir', xii. The wedding was conducted by Brown in a small church near Notting Hill Gate, London, close to Minna's Bayswater home. It seems that both Forsyth and Minna had been previously engaged to others: 'A man named Watt (a former Lord Mayor of Aberdeen) had been a reporter while young, in London, at Forsyth's Church. He heard that Forsyth was engaged to his landlady's daughter (Christina Glegg). There was a "breach of contract" (a deadly sin in those days: see the court costs awarded in the *Manchester Examiner*). Watt wondered whether this accounted for the change in theology from Liberalism to orthodoxy'. William L. Bradley, 'Wm. Bradley to D. J. Carter'. Unpublished letter, 12 September 1990, np. In a letter to Bradley (who was, according to Jessie Andrews, 'amazing in terms of his ability to find information about the family'), Jessie had noted that her mother (Minna) was engaged to a Church of England Missionary, but this contract was broken: 'how they disentangled themselves and managed to get engaged to each other I have no idea; it is a shocking affair, and is not to go into any life of my father!' Jessie F. Andrews, 'Jessie Forsyth Andrews to Wm. Bradley'. Unpublished letter, 4 September 1948, np.

[407] Frederick J. Powicke, 'Frederick Denison Maurice (1805–1872): A Personal Reminiscence', *Congregational Quarterly* 8 (1930), pp. 169–84 (172): 'I may be wrong, but I incline to say that the majority of our younger ministers in 1877 bore the Maurician stamp, if under that description may be included what they drew from Thomas Erskine, McLeod Campbell, A. J. Scott, and George MacDonald. These, I am sure, were the favourite authors of my own friends in the ministry; and the man to whom we looked up with enthusiastic trust as leader was James Baldwin Brown, who knew Maurice personally, corresponded with him, and sympathized fully with the spirit and scope of his teachings and very strongly with his efforts in favour of the working classes . . . He was the Charles Kingsley of the Free Churches, the mediator of Maurice to them'.

[408] 'Baldwin Brown', pp. 139, 142; cf. Elizabeth Baldwin Brown (ed.), *In Memoriam: James Baldwin Brown* (London: James Clarke, 1884), pp. 6–9, 19–21; James Baldwin Brown, *The Home: In Its Relation to Man and to Society* (London: James Clarke & Co., 1884). Although Brown's thought was less substantial than Fairbairn's, Brown's influence on English Congregationalism was earlier and more pronounced.

> checks and air of suspicion, to this great generous believer and comprehensive anti-comprehensivist . . . He had something of Maurice's suspicion of popular religion, and was inclined to think there must be something good, and for the hour very necessary, in a man whom the societies and denominations united to taboo.[409]

Theologically liberal, the young Forsyth found it difficult to receive a pastoral call. It was not only due to Brown's influence that Forsyth received his first call to a full-time pastoral charge (where he was ordained by both Brown, and by the Principal of New College, the Rev. Dr Samuel Newth) at Shipley in 1876,[410] but Brown also arranged for Forsyth's next church, at Hackney, to first hear Forsyth in 1879 when circumstances in Yorkshire became increasingly awkward (partly due to a sermon wherein Forsyth denied substitutionary atonement).[411] In between, the heterodox Brown, in his capacity as chairman-elect of the Congregational Union, supported Forsyth and others (though not their position) at the Leicester Conference of 16 October 1877 against his more 'orthodox' seniors. Forsyth later recalls not only Brown's charismatic personality, but also his kindness, courage and collegiality.[412] We know that Forsyth consulted Brown by mail regarding a number of matters, including religious communion with Unitarians. Could it be that Brown's ongoing friendship, support and counsel had such a profound impact on the young pastor that Forsyth was compelled to reassess his own theology alongside that of Brown's? We may never know.

Though he receives only one mention in Forsyth's books,[413] and while there is no direct evidence that Forsyth's thinking on holiness per se came from his pastor,[414] many of the themes central to Brown's theology indisputably inform Forsyth's own theology of holiness. Hopkins is not entirely out of line, therefore, to refer to Forsyth as Brown's 'disciple'.[415] For Forsyth and others, part of the lure in Brown is an experientially verifiable emphasis on conscience, a serious regarding of sin and the atonement, a conviction about the centrality of divine fatherhood, a hope in the all-conquering love of God and an accent on a spirituality free from a slavish dependence on Scripture. Moreover, Forsyth finds in Brown some anti-Hegelian currency, exemplified in Brown's dreading of 'the drift of a current' in place of 'the action of a will'.[416] As Hopkins notes, 'People were looking for an ethically-satisfying theology that would also be invulnerable to the assaults of philosophy, criticism and science, and the efforts of Maurice, Brown and their like were the most attractive on offer'.[417]

409 'Baldwin Brown', pp. 135, 138.

410 While at Shipley, Forsyth at once began to make a name for himself as a 'challenging and unconventional preacher' (A. Martin, 'Peter Taylor Forsyth', *The Messenger* (1942), p. 557), attracting such unconventional folk that his church became known as 'The Cave of Adullam', and was rejected by the Yorkshire Congregational Union. See Goroncy, 'Preaching *sub specie crucis*', 2013.

411 See James Baldwin Brown, 'Letter', *English Independent*, 22 November 1877, p. 1283.

412 See 'Baldwin Brown', pp. 133–42. Forsyth attended Brown's funeral on 30 June 1884, and on 6 July 1884 preached a sermon (based on 2 Kgs 2.12) dedicated to Brown at St Thomas' Square, Hackney.

413 *Rome*, p. vii.

414 This is not to say that Brown neglects holiness; for example, see James Baldwin Brown, *The Soul's Exodus and Pilgrimage* (London: Smith, Elder and Co., 1862), p. 177.

415 Hopkins, *Nonconformity's Romantic Generation*, p. 33.

416 Brown (ed.), *In Memoriam*, p. 28.

417 Hopkins, *Nonconformity's Romantic Generation*, p. 43.

Other Brownite themes that reverberate in Forsyth's work include a preferencing of moral grammar over metaphysical, that creation is with a view to redemption, the distinction between 'sin' (as racial) and 'guilt' (as personal), the universality of guilt and its irreconcilability to God,[418] a concern for human freedom and 'the responsibility which it brings',[419] a sympathy for patripassianism,[420] the twofold movement within Christ's person (that in Christ, 'man was dealing with the Father, and the Father was dealing with man in Him'[421]), that the restoration of righteousness is essential for the human conscience and 'lies deep in the nature of God',[422] the divine–human relationship defined in filial terms, a distrust of democracy,[423] a rejection of ecclesiastical and biblical infallibility,[424] a hermeneutical priority of Epistles before Gospels, an opposition to the 'deadly error'[425] of conditional immortality and of the papacy, the necessity within the gospel itself for the Church to concern itself with issues of social justice and of national importance,[426] a resemblance in literary style (notably the second-person form and 'involved, antithetical constructions'[427]), a love for St Bernard,[428] and a preference for formal, liturgical public prayer. Like Forsyth, Brown draws deeply not only from Maurice but also from the wells of the Romantic poets and essayists: Goethe, Shelley, Keats, Coleridge, Emerson and, especially, Carlyle. And, like Forsyth, Brown considers himself 'not a member of a purely worldly profession . . . but a preacher of the living Word, into the proclamation of which I can throw as much of earnestness and life as I have in myself'.[429] Still, Forsyth never adopts his pastor's (or anyone else's) entire system. The 'post-conversion' Forsyth, for example, does not follow Brown's lamenting of liberalism but rather advocates a much more carefully nuanced appreciation and firmer repudiation of liberal theology. Nor is he nearly so negative towards Calvinism and higher criticism as Brown.[430]

418 James Baldwin Brown, *The Doctrine of the Divine Fatherhood in Relation to the Atonement* (London: Ward, 1860), pp. 29–30; James Baldwin Brown, *The Divine Life in Man* (London Ward & Co., 1859), pp. 106–07; Brown, *The Divine Treatment of Sin*, pp. 34–37.

419 James Baldwin Brown, *Misread Passages of Scripture* (London: Hodder & Stoughton, 1869), p. 72.

420 James Baldwin Brown, *The Divine Mystery of Peace* (London: Jackson, Walford, & Hodder, 1863), pp. 39–40.

421 Brown, *The Doctrine of the Divine Fatherhood*, p. 39.

422 Brown, *The Divine Treatment of Sin*, pp. 16, 19, 86.

423 James Baldwin Brown, *The Perfect Law of Liberty: An Address* (London: Unknown, 1878), p. 44.

424 Brown, *First Principles of Ecclesiastical Truth*, pp. 3–125.

425 James Baldwin Brown, *Stoics and Saints: Lectures on the Later Heathen Moralists, and on Some Aspects of the Life of the Mediæval Church* (Glasgow/New York: James Maclehose and Sons/ Macmillan and Co, 1893), p. 268; cf. Lefferts Augustine Loetscher, 'Brown, James Baldwin', in *The New Schaff-Herzog Encyclopedia of Religious Knowledge* (ed. Johann Jakob Herzog et al.; Grand Rapids: Baker, 1977), p. 276.

426 For example, Brown took an active interest in the relief of the labouring classes during the Lancashire cotton famine.

427 Bradley, *P. T. Forsyth*, p. 100.

428 Brown, *Stoics and Saints*, pp. 139–70.

429 Brown (ed.), *In Memoriam*, p. 4; cf. See 'Veracity', pp. 193–216.

430 Brown, *First Principles of Ecclesiastical Truth*, p. 172; James Baldwin Brown, *The Risen Christ the King of Men* (ed. Elizabeth Baldwin Brown; London: T. Fisher Unwin, 1887), pp. 270–74. An exception appears in Brown, *The Divine Treatment of Sin*, p. 5.

Brown's intellectual quest, influenced by A. J. Scott,[431] paves an emphasis on the priority of the incarnation for theology,[432] by which Brown means the totality of Christ's ministry, though with a particular focus on Christ's death: 'what we call His life was but a death after all, while His death was His life'.[433] The cruciform shape of the Father's love that was so absent in Ritschl is boldly trumpeted in Brown's preaching. Although Forsyth expresses greater caution about the gospel-sufficiency of the Luke 15 parable than does his former pastor,[434] the accent on divine fatherhood in Brown's theology had an enduring impact on Forsyth. Against those who construed the divine–human relation as primarily that of king–subject, or in primarily legal terms, Brown recalls the unconditionality of divine Fatherhood (perhaps 'the most vital theological question of [the] day' upon which rests the whole structure of redemption),[435] that the 'Holy and Righteous Father' is not conditionally converted from alienation to reconciliation by 'the awful spectacle of unutterable, unmeasurable pain'[436] but is already entirely *for* creation. The atonement represents, therefore, the changeless will of 'the righteous and holy Father ... establish[ing] a way by which He might meet and clasp His recovered sons'.[437] As tragic, disordering, deathly and unordained as it was, Brown considers the Fall as progress, development, as upward into a new relationship of grace. It is not in Eden but in the wilderness that the prodigal who broods over the experience of free will learns that if the father should in pity receive her again, then their fellowship will be richer and more joyous than it could ever have been had she never left Eden. Brown sees in Christ's death no hiding of the heinousness of sin in order that reconciliation may be 'pleasant and facile'. Rather, sin – the one 'thing' in the universe that cannot be redeemed – is exposed and condemned. And because there is no room for sin 'in the Father's bosom', Jesus stands before the Father to confess sin – its guilt and its misery – with human lips 'as Divine lips alone could utter'. In this twofold

[431] Contrary to Johnson, Hopkins asserts the priority of Scott over Maurice as Brown's greatest influence. Hopkins, *Nonconformity's Romantic Generation*, pp. 19–22. See John Hunter, 'Alexander John Scott', *Expositor* 21 (1921), pp. 386–400, 450–62.

[432] Forsyth said of Brown's theology: 'Everything centred in the Incarnation, in the historic God'. 'Baldwin Brown', p. 134.

[433] James Baldwin Brown, *Aids to the Development of the Divine Life* (London: Henry James Tresidder, 1862), p. 12; cf. James Baldwin Brown, *The Battle and Burden of Life* (London: Hodder & Stoughton, 1875), p. 111.

[434] Luke's parable (15.11–31) is a dominant recurring theme in Brown's sermons, without laying the criticism of crosslessness upon it that Forsyth does. Brown, *Aids to the Development of the Divine Life*, pp. 9–10; Brown, *The Divine Mystery of Peace*, pp. 7, 22, 29, 81, 85; Brown, *The Divine Treatment of Sin*, pp. 6–8; Brown, *The Doctrine of Annihilation*, pp. 100, 114–15, 118–19; James Baldwin Brown, *Studies of First Principles, No. 3, First Principles of Politics* (London: M. Tayler, 1848), p. 13.

[435] Brown, *The Divine Mystery of Peace*, p. 26; cf. Brown, *The Divine Mystery of Peace*, p. 50. Brown hoped that changes in the British penal system would sponsor better understanding of the divine–human relationship. Brown, *The Divine Life in Man*, pp. 26–27.

[436] Brown, *The Divine Mystery of Peace*, pp. 66, 31. Brown considered Campbell's *The Nature of the Atonement* to be the greatest theological work since the Reformation. Brown, *The Divine Life in Man*, pp. 115–16; Brown, *The Divine Mystery of Peace*, p. 55.

[437] Ibid., p. 29; cf. Brown, *The Doctrine of the Divine Fatherhood*, p. 38; *Work*, p. 180. The strongest (and fairest) criticisms of Brown's theology here appear in John Howard Hinton, 'Strictures on Some Passages in the Rev. J. B. Brown's *Divine Life in Man*', *Baptist Magazine* 52 (1868), pp. 134–37. This article represents the beginnings of a break between (the more liberal) Congregationalists and (the doctrinally conservative) Baptists.

confession sinners are assured that God, in forgiving, has dealt fully with sin and that in a manner consistent with God's own nature, that sinners are reconciled to God, and that the Father's forgiveness is 'absolute and final . . . the word of the very justice and holiness of God'.[438] Brown also wholeheartedly repudiates the high Calvinist doctrine of limited atonement, noting that 'it would be hard perhaps to frame any doctrine more essentially unchristian'.[439]

Forsyth shares with Brown a commitment to expounding the deep ethical note in Christianity so characteristic of mid- to late-nineteenth-century thought and spurred on by Ritschl. Brown rejects any sense that human beings can be 'saved by ideas, as Athens has taught us'; it is only the 'solid substance of Divine fact which is behind ideas . . . which sanctifies and saves'.[440] Here, the *telos* of divine holiness and the liberation of the human conscience are constitutive of the one movement of God upon which the 'welfare of the universe' depends. While Christ's sacrifice is necessary 'to declare God's righteousness in the forgiveness of sins',[441] redemption is not God's *response* to evil. Rather, 'the need of being a Redeemer lies deep in the nature of God, and not only was man's sin foreseen, but all things were ordered with a view to the great drama of Redemption, from before the foundation of the world'.[442]

Resembling McLeod Campbell's rejection of Protestantism's all-too-common demarcation between justification and sanctification, Brown asserts the intrinsic bond between legal and ethical righteousness. Consequently, he rarely employs the grammar of 'sanctification' but prefers instead to speak of 'righteousness'. Where Brown's accent differs most here from Forsyth, and betrays another debt to A. J. Scott, is in granting a greater role to the Spirit, who 'completes the manifestation of God in the Incarnation'.[443] Pneumatology, Brown avers, is 'the essential complement of the Cross, and it is the glory of Christianity and its power'.[444] That this power is at work in and through the conscience is 'the great condition of the reality of the Christian life'.[445] The Spirit, Brown insists, creates belief in the atoning God – the 'meeting of the Father in the sacrifice which He has Himself offered for the sin which He puts away in Christ' – bringing peace, assurance and the 'first cry, "My Father"'.[446] Moreover, the Spirit is the guarantee that the world did not lose the divine presence with the ascension but has, rather, gained a divine presence 'more real, more vital, more abiding' than was possible in

438 Brown, *The Divine Mystery of Peace*, pp. 30, 55–56; cf. Brown, *Soul's Exodus*, pp. 228–29; Brown, *The Doctrine of the Divine Fatherhood*, p. 38.

439 Brown, *First Principles of Ecclesiastical Truth*, p. 351.

440 James Baldwin Brown, 'Our Theology in Relation to the Intellectual Movement of Our Times', *Congregational Yearbook* (1879), pp. 51–77 (70).

441 Brown, *The Doctrine of the Divine Fatherhood*, p. 32.

442 Brown, *The Divine Treatment of Sin*, p. 16. See *Authority*, pp. 19, 72, 172, 184, 202–05; *Justification*, p. 63; 'Metaphysic', p. 718; *Person*, p. 320.

443 Brown, *The Divine Mystery of Peace*, p. 65.

444 James Baldwin Brown, *Light on the Way: Brief Discourses* (London: James Clarke & Co., 1886), p. 290.

445 James Baldwin Brown, *Studies of First Principles, No. 1, Voluntaryism: An Appeal from the Custom to the Conscience of the Church* (London: The Author, 1848), p. 7; Brown, *The Divine Mystery of Peace*, pp. 3, 5.

446 Brown, *The Divine Mystery of Peace*, pp. 67–68, 76; cf. Brown, *The Divine Mystery of Peace*, pp. 83–86.

Jesus' earthly ministry.[447] It is also by the Spirit that Christ continues to share in the sorrow, struggle and suffering of the world.[448] The Spirit who acts on human spirit never smothers creaturely freedom, however: 'The God who made us free, respects our freedom, and will have us to be free subjects of the heavenly kingdom, through the comfort of the Holy Ghost.'[449] This assertion extends to Brown's positing a purgatorial space where the moral education of unbelievers might continue post-mortem. While he maintains that one's fate is undetermined by divine decree, and he rejects both annihilationism and universalism,[450] he upholds in hope that 'the love which won the sceptre on Calvary will wield it as a power, waxing ever, waning never, through all the ages; and that the Father will never cease from yearning over the prodigals, and Christ will never cease from seeking the lost, while one knee remains stubborn before the name of Jesus, and one heart is unmastered by His love'.[451] We shall return to this subject in the final chapter.

Wilhelm Windelband (1848–1915)

While the word 'Heiligkeit' (or a cognate) appears in some post-Enlightenment German philosophical literature (in Kant, Schleiermacher, Hegel and Nietzsche, for example) and in some poetry (in Goethe and Hölderlin, for example), the grammar of 'holiness' attracted very restricted currency in pre-twentieth-century Germany, and none of the examples noted here employ the word in Rudolph Otto's sense. In the early twentieth century, however, the notion of *Heiligkeit* gained prevalence through the work of the Baden school neo-Kantian philosopher Wilhelm Windelband, most accessibly in his essay 'Das Heilige' which appeared in the 1902 and 1907 editions of his two-volume *Präludien* (which first appeared in 1884) and then again in *Einleitung in die Philosophie* (1914). It was translated as 'The Sacred' in the 1921 English edition.[452] In this essay, Windelband (who was born one day before Forsyth[453]) argues that *Heiligkeit* does not refer directly to any special class of universally acceptable values, such as those which constitute logic, ethics and aesthetics, but that the true, the good and the beautiful together are related to a 'suprasensuous reality', a moral reality that transcends the mind, will or feelings. Windelband names this 'suprasensuous reality' *Heiligkeit*, which is not only a higher reality but also the 'metaphysical anchorage' from which all values – logical, ethical and aesthetic – derive their validity.[454] While

[447] Brown, *The Divine Mystery of Peace*, p. 71.
[448] Ibid., p. 89.
[449] Ibid., 80, cf. Brown, *The Divine Mystery of Peace*, p. 77.
[450] Sellers wrongly identifies Brown as a universalist. Ian Sellers, *Nineteenth-Century Nonconformity* (Foundations of Modern History; London: Edward Arnold, 1977), p. 26.
[451] Brown, *The Doctrine of Annihilation*, pp. 118–19; cf. Catholic Church, *Catechism of the Catholic Church* (Homebush: Society of St Pauls, 1994), p. 165.
[452] Wilhelm Windelband, *Präludien – Aufsätze und Reden zur Einleitung in die Philosophie* (vol. 1; Tübingen: Verlag von J. C. B. Mohr [Paul Siebeck], 1907), pp. 414–50; Wilhelm Windelband, *Einleitung in die Philosophie* (Tübingen: J. C. B. Mohr [Paul Siebeck], 1914); Wilhelm Windelband, *An Introduction to Philosophy* (trans. Joseph McCabe; London: T. Fisher Unwin, 1921), pp. 324–33.
[453] 11 May 1848. Windelband completed his doctoral thesis, 'Ueber Lehren vom Zufall' at Göttingen in 1870 under the direction of the monist Rudolf Hermann Lotze. Forsyth was at Göttingen in 1872.
[454] Windelband, *Introduction to Philosophy*, p. 325.

Nathan Söderblom[455] and Rudolph Otto would later employ the grammar of 'holiness' merely as a key to interpreting the deepest of religious phenomena, Windelband posits that *Heiligkeit* alone is the final ontological reality and as such stops the world from being 'a world of contradiction'. Conscience alone can know this, he insists, but even conscience's experience of truth, goodness and beauty beyond all the chances of space and time is possible only in virtue of a still deeper and personal relation constituted by *Heiligkeit* itself. *Heiligkeit* must be given a name: 'God'.[456] God alone, who is 'just as real as conscience', transcends belief which may in the end be no more than opinion or illusion. Holiness alone, Windelband avers, is the energy that determines all value, serves as a precondition for philosophical enquiry and renders relativism impossible.[457] There is only God *das heilige*, from whom and for whom exist those created realities which are by virtue of their relation with God. Consequently, 'the essential thing [for philosophy] is to inquire to what extent man belongs to this suprasensuous vital order which forms the essence of every religious affirmation'.[458]

Although Forsyth only refers to Windelband once in his major works,[459] the Baden School – and Windelband in particular – are the most prominent of the philosophical influences on Forsyth's comprehension of holiness. Repeatedly, we hear echoed in Forsyth's work the Baden *Weltanschauung* – the accent on 'the primacy of the willing subject over all knowledge and all speculative constructions of reality',[460] that the world subsists under moral precepts, that the historical process is infused with 'ideal' purposes, that the monism of immanent *Geist* is as repugnant as is the idea of an inevitable sequence of material causality, that the willing personality is primary although volition does not run riot, that cultural life is to be measured by enduring and universal values, that historical events are not only unique but also laden with teleological import, that

455 Nathan Söderblom, 'Holiness', in *Encyclopædia of Religion and Ethics* (ed. James Hastings; Edinburgh: T&T Clark, 1913), 6:731–41.

456 Here Windelband is by no means a typical neo-Kantian who were, on Windelband's assessment, on average 'strongly empiricist and agnostic'. Cited in Klaus Christian Köhnke, *The Rise of Neo-Kantianism: German Academic Philosophy between Idealism and Positivism* (ed. Richard Rorty et al.; trans. R. J. Hollingdale; Cambridge: Cambridge University Press, 1991), p. 262; cf. Wilhelm Windelband, *Die Geschichte der Neueren Philosophie in ihrem Zusammenhange mit der Allgemeinen Cultur und den besonderen Wissenschaften, Erster Band: Von der Renaissance bis Kant* (vol. 1; Leipzig: Druck und Verlag von Breitkopf und Härtel, 1878), pp. 114–51; Friedrich H. Tenbruck, 'Geschichte und Geschichtsschreibung der Philosophie am Beispiel des Neukantianismus', *Philosophische Rundschau* 35 (1988), pp. 1–15.

457 Windelband, 'Was ist Philosophie?', pp. 24–77.

458 Windelband, *Introduction to Philosophy*, p. 332. We see this religious a priori affirmed by another Baden School theologian, Ernst Troeltsch, though without Windelband's personalism and specific content. See Ernst Troeltsch, 'Zur Frage des religiösen Apriori', in *Gesammelte Schriften* (Tübingen: J. C. B. Mohr [Paul Siebeck], 1913), pp. 754–68. Willey and Ringer are critical of what they understand to be Windelband's dissolving 'real problems' (i.e. political and social problems) into 'spiritual and moral categories'. Thomas E. Willey, *Back to Kant: The Revival of Kantianism in German Social and Historical Thought, 1860–1914* (Detroit: Wayne State University Press, 1978), p. 133; Fritz K. Ringer, *The Decline of the German Mandarins: The German Academic Community, 1890–1933* (Hanover/London: Wesleyan University Press, 1990), p. 121. Still, it must be observed that neo-Kantianism's commitment to the ethical drew neo-Kantians into the orbit of practical socialism, evident also in Forsyth.

459 *Authority*, p. 5, fn. 1.

460 Richard Kroner, *Kant's Weltanschauung* (trans. John E. Smith; Chicago: University of Chicago Press, 1956), p. vii.

knowledge of God is possible only because of God's prior claim on human being, that rational intuition which privileges the intellect over the moral and bypasses the will is to be rejected, that knowing is a creative act wherein the intellect is active as synthesizing but not as intuiting essence, and that knowing is an act no less creative than the initial grace of creation itself (and so to be received and celebrated with gratitude). 'If the study of science, society, or history employs purely arbitrary constructs, then the universal and necessary character of knowledge maintained by Kant dissolves into subjectivity.'[461] It was precisely this arbitrary notion of truth that Windelband sought to defeat with his philosophy of norms, and which – because grounded in universal *Heiligkeit* – Forsyth seems to have found so constructive.

Adolf Schlatter (1852–1938)

If Windelband encouraged the philosophical ground upon which Forsyth would explore his theology of sanctification, it was the St. Gallen-born pietist Adolf Schlatter who sponsored the biblical substratum for such an undertaking.[462] Few contemporary theologians were more important to Forsyth's thought or earned such august acclaim from him: 'Of all living theologians there is no one more learned, more acute, more profound, more original, more devout, more sober, terse, and suggestive than Prof. SCHLATTER [*sic*], of Tübingen. None has an experience more veteran or more wise, whether of current thought or Christian life.'[463] Forsyth welcomes Schlatter's theology as one for whom there is a positive correspondence between historical facts and personal experience. Schlatter's objectivity was, Forsyth believes, desperately required in an age given to extravagant subjectivity more humanist, temperamental and pious than Christian, certain and faithful. He praises Schlatter's distrust of that natural and rationalist mysticism which seeks spiritual intimacy apart from the positive and creative content in the act of God in Christ, thereby following Schlatter's emphasis on 'theology as irreducible to the merely conceptual, or experiential'.[464]

In Schlatter, Forsyth recognizes one in whom the a priori idealism of Hegel and the neo-Hegelians is overcome, and holiness' journey of thesis–antithesis–synthesis is properly rooted in the history of God and of God's people. Whether of the Kantian or Hegelian type, idealism's contempt for creaturely particularity finds no ally in Schlatter or Forsyth, not least because such practically push God out of the world, leaving 'no

[461] Willey, *Back to Kant*, p. 133.

[462] And that not only on sanctification. In 1912, Forsyth identifies work by Schlatter (on the theological right) along with Paul Feine (*Theologie des Neuen Testaments*, 1911) (in the centre), and Heinrich Weinel (*Biblische Theologie des Neuen Testaments. Religion Jeus und des Urchristentums*, 1911) (on the left), as 'the most recent and competent work on the New Testament'. *Authority*, p. 126.

[463] 'Religious Strength', p. 577. Forsyth's praise for Schlatter was not unique. Fritz Barth, who was successor to Schlatter at Berne, encouraged his son Karl to study under Schlatter at Tübingen in 1907, which Karl did briefly before moving to Marburg in 1908 to be with Herrmann.

[464] Markus Bockmuehl, *Seeing the Word: Refocusing New Testament Study* (Grand Rapids: Baker, 2006), p. 147. Forsyth does not, unfortunately, follow Schlatter's lead (and that of Johannes Weiss, Hermann L. Strack, George Foot Moore, Samuel Krauss, Francis Crawford Burkitt, Paul Billerbeck, Claude Joseph Goldsmid Montefiore, Joseph Klausner and Albert Schweitzer) in stressing the Jewish dimensions of Jesus' kingdom pronouncements.

space for knowledge of God'[465] and so sponsor a disregard for divine action in the world and the consequent turn inward (to psychology and secular anthropology, to 'the "I" as a moment of its own spiritual life'[466]) as the foundation for dogmatics. The moment the divine economy is negated as constituent of divine revelation, the latter is sought apart from or behind God, leaving theology in contradiction to its own object. In 'denial of God . . . every so-called knowing of God, which claims to have come about without God, collapses because of this antithesis.'[467] Such a shift disintegrates the theological task to descriptions of God which merely 'list his attributes' and proffer 'general ideas through which the richness of the divine acting is to be grasped and ordered'. These descriptions, Schlatter contends, 'provide us merely with abstractions' uprooted from the 'actualities in which they have their ground'.[468] So holiness, for Schlatter as for Forsyth, is indiscernible – a mere abstraction – apart from the divine economy when God's work 'happens to us'.[469] Implicit here is Schlatter's conviction (again, with Forsyth) that God's action is not that of raw causal omnipotence, but is of that 'way of grace'[470] which creates life and awakens the will: 'God's relationship to us is intended to be of that kind which develops between persons, not only between forces and substances, not only between natural factors . . . God is an I and reveals himself to me as an I in that he presents me with an I and thus becomes a Thou to me.'[471] As we shall see in the next chapter when we consider the matter of conscience as the locus of sanctification, Forsyth follows Schlatter's conviction concerning the indispensability of real historical encounter for doing theology, *and* that such experience's value lay in the superhistoric nature of its content. Careful to note that Voluntarism means only the primacy and not the monopoly of the will, Forsyth also identifies in Schlatter one who properly distinguishes between the intellect and the will: 'The intellect may be an instrument of the will, but it is not its creature.' Full thought requires action and not merely receptivity. The pursuit of truth is a 'moral act and discipline'.[472]

Schlatter's provision of the biblical substratum for Forsyth's thinking on holiness is most apparent in Forsyth's essay on 'Christian Perfection', and in some passages in *This Life and the Next* where Forsyth paraphrases (unacknowledged) from *Das christliche Dogma*. I am not claiming that Forsyth's theology moved in a different direction subsequent to his reading of Schlatter (this cannot be proven); certainly by the time Schlatter's *Das christliche Dogma* appeared in 1911, Forsyth had already cemented holiness at the centre of his theology (although it was to intensify from 1912). But the similarities between the two at numerous points are too obvious to ignore, and

465 Adolf Schlatter, *Die philosophische Arbeit seit Cartesius: Ihr ethischer und religiöser Ertrag* (Giessen: Brunnen-Verlag, 1981), p. 129.

466 Adolf Schlatter, 'Wesen und Quellen der Gotteserkenntnis' (unpublished lecture, Bern. Landeskirchliches Archiv Stuttgart, 1883), p. 44.

467 Schlatter, *Das christliche Dogma*, p. 103; cf. Schlatter, *Das christliche Dogma*, p. 354; Adolf Schlatter, *Romans: The Righteousness of God* (trans. Siegfried S. Schatzmann; Peabody: Hendrickson, 1995), p. 226.

468 Schlatter, *Das christliche Dogma*, p. 12.

469 Ibid., p. 11; cf. Schlatter, *Das christliche Dogma*, pp. 14, 100–03; Adolf Schlatter, *Die christliche Ethik* (Stuttgart: Calwer Verlag, 1986), pp. 258–61.

470 Adolf Schlatter, *Einleitung in die Bibel* (Stuttgart: Calwer Verlag, 1923), p. 24.

471 Adolf Schlatter, 'Die Unterwerfung unter die Gotteswirklichkeit', *Die Furche: Akademische Monatsschrift zur Förderung einer Deutschen christlichen Studentenbewegung* (1911), pp. 6–17 (9–10).

472 *Authority*, p. 102. Here Forsyth credits Schlatter's *Das christliche Dogma* I. §D.

Forsyth's own confession of his dependence on Schlatter (such confessions are rare in Forsyth's work) only serves to bolster my claim regarding Schlatter's influence on Forsyth's thought.

Section 40 of *Das christliche Dogma*, titled 'Der Heilige', begins by observing 'holy' as a word of adoration (*Anbetung*), which is first God's attribute and is then transferred onto everything which is God's – things, times, actions and people which stand in solidarity with God, those things which are given to, and exist for, God and which reflect God as God's possession and servant.[473] The notion, therefore, of holiness as separation is maintained, and yet the negative associations of separation are met with positive ones, the voluntary nature of which finds its *telos* in service to God. Schlatter speaks of the simultaneity of humbling and exaltation, of holiness creating consciousness of otherness *from* God while also providing certainty of entrance (*Zugang*) *to* God. He notes that the term 'holy' is distorted if it only retains one or other characteristic. If only the former, then it awakens only our flinching fear. If only the latter, religious pride is fostered.[474] Most interesting for our purposes is Schlatter's notion of holiness as 'movement' (*Bewegung*), wherein holiness 'enriches and completes' (*bereichert und vollendet*) itself. For Schlatter, this movement finds its end in the praise of God's mercy, which is holy to us, and which sanctifies us.

Schlatter returns to this theme in §107, titled 'Die Heiligung', where he presses for the Church's necessary belief in sanctification, by which he means that God's grace adapts itself to, and enters into, the actual situation of our present condition and so arranges things that our actions correspond to the divine will. Moreover, he insists that we must speak of sanctification in terms of stages and of growth; we grow in sanctification, some more than others. And history's restlessness provides the context in which such growth occurs.

Schlatter follows the Reformed distinction between justification and sanctification, stressing that both have their origin in God's mercy and not in creaturely achievement, and their solidarity in the finished gift of God.[475] He contends, furthermore, that justification must prove itself in actual sanctifying consequences in our history. Otherwise, it becomes a bare promise, an abstraction, meaningless and incomplete – issuing, often, in an inert piety which neither thinks, loves nor acts, but only seeks itself and thereby loses itself.[476] He insists that the key to understanding the relationship between sanctification and justification is Jesus Christ, in whom the reality of justification acquires concrete form and through whom humanity is baptized in the sanctifying Spirit, an act which effects confidence (*Zuversicht*) in Jesus. While Schlatter observes that the concept of holiness plays a more dominant role in the New Testament when compared to that of justification,[477] he maintains that neither justification nor sanctification is more dispensable than the other. There is no tension between the two, nor is the divine gift 'divided in parts'[478] as if one only the reason and the other only

473 Echoed in *Life*, pp. 28–29.
474 See Schlatter, *Das christliche Dogma*, p. 147.
475 See ibid., p. 472.
476 Ibid., pp. 468–69.
477 Adolf Schlatter, *The Theology of the Apostles: The Development of New Testament Theology* (trans. Andreas J. Köstenberger; Grand Rapids: Baker, 1998), p. 249.
478 Ibid., p. 248.

the consequence. Rather, both demonstrate God's 'one-time decision' to join creaturely being with an eternal reason and perfect goal.[479]

The tradition's description of sanctification 'needs supplementing', Schlatter believes, because while it grasps the mortifying integrant of sanctification, it has tended to neglect the vivifying aspects. Grace not only 'exterminates our blindness' and separates us from the profane, but also reveals our duties, overcomes our lovelessness and motivates us towards life, all of which happens in communion with Christ in whom we are given to share in God's 'integrity, purity, and majesty'.[480] By limiting sanctification to its negative aspects, theology not only undermines the ongoing liveliness of that communion, but also sponsors a reduction of God's creative work to something akin to the recovery of the patient to a former condition and so neglects its eschatological movement, its 'promise of perfection'.[481] 'Our lives remain poor, if we have no higher goal than the containment of our desires' (*Eindämmung unserer Sinnlichkeit*).[482] Just as justification gives justice to the sinner, so too sanctification includes one as an agent of the divine teleological will. The details of how this *telos* will be realized in the course of our history are hidden from us, but faith trusts in the God who is determined to make us fit for holiness.[483] Sanctification, therefore, never negates the peculiarity of our present historical situation, or of our obligation to live today in accord with the divine promise,[484] or of our present being-in-*koinonia*. Indeed, Schlatter warns that attempts to imagine for ourselves an ideal by which believers hope to complete their sanctification apart from the relationships by which being is defined are counterproductive and inducing of sin. He insists that grace places persons into Christian community with its communal work and culture, and that ascetics, who in the interest of their sinlessness divorce themselves from others, deny their own sanctification.[485] Enough has been noted here to identify in Schlatter's thought some key refrains that weave their way into Forsyth's mature work.

This chapter has been concerned to locate Forsyth's theology of sanctification upon a broad canvas laden with the cultural, etymological and theological content that informs his soteriology. Behind Forsyth's appropriation and contribution, however, stands the holy God and the absolute question of the soul:

> [The] first, last, and supreme question of the soul, of religion when it is practical, is not, '*How* am I to think of God? – He or It?' but it is, 'What does He think of me? How does It treat me?' More positively it is, '*How* shall I be just with God? How shall I stand before my judge?' That is the final human question – how to face the eternal moral power. What is it making of us? What is He doing with us? What is He going to do?[486]

It is these questions that concern the remainder of this study.

479 Schlatter, *Das christliche Dogma*, p. 469; Schlatter, *The Theology of the Apostles*, p. 249.
480 Schlatter, *The Theology of the Apostles*, p. 248.
481 Schlatter, *Das christliche Dogma*, pp. 470, 472.
482 Ibid., p. 471.
483 Ibid., p. 473.
484 Schlatter, *The Theology of the Apostles*, p. 249.
485 Schlatter, *Das christliche Dogma*, p. 474.
486 *Cruciality*, p. 119.

3

Thy Kingdom Come. Thy Will Be Done, on Earth as it Is in Heaven

On the very front of [Christ's] prayer the Father's desecrated name had to be hallowed by its practical confession in a perfect holiness of response, before the Kingdom should come either in earth or heaven. And that is the nature of Atonement – the practical hallowing of God's name in Humanity by the Son of God and in the sight of God.[1]

The best exposition of the Lord's Prayer is the life, death and Resurrection of him who taught it.[2]

Jesus Christ occupies *the* central place in Forsyth's theology. Appropriately, therefore, dissertations, essays and broader theological treatments spare no ink addressing Forsyth's christology, and particularly his staurology. Even those whose focus is other than christology proper – for example, those assessments of Forsyth's thought on ecclesiology, homiletics, missiology, theological method, ethics or holy love, et cetera – cannot avoid due attendance to his christology. Wherever one begins with Forsyth's thought, all is examined *sub specie crucis*. This study is no exception. Resisting retracing those steps that others have trod, our concern here is to hone in on a somewhat overlooked aspect of Forsyth's christology – the notion of Christ as hallower, the one in whom the first petition of the Lord's Prayer finds its prime and definitive response.

Few, if any, theologians have more recognized this vista of christology. For Forsyth, salvation means hallowing – the making secure and praising of holiness as the very power of love. And repeatedly, Forsyth articulates that the determining centre of history is the cross which hallows God's 'sole and suzerain name',[3] not as an act of naked omnipotence but foremostly as the climax of Jesus' lifelong and loving obedience. The transformative power of this act within and for God reverberates throughout creation, bearing witness to God's love, faithfulness and moral victory.

1 *Jesus*, p. 108.

2 T. W. Manson, 'The Lord's Prayer: II', *Bulletin of the John Rylands University Library of Manchester* 38 (1955–56), pp. 436–48 (448).

3 *Revelation*, p. 66.

This chapter introduces Forsyth's understanding of the kingdom of God, offers some observations on the christological shape that holiness assumes in the world and explores the importance of Christ's obedience as a key motif in Forsyth's christology. It also attends to Forsyth's presentation of the cross as a threefold cord – as triumph, satisfaction and regeneration – through which runs the thread of holiness; Christ in his cross (i) *positively* satisfies God's holiness by confessing holiness from sin's side; (ii) *negatively* satisfies holiness by bringing holiness' antithesis under judgement, and (iii) *creatively* satisfies holiness by creating a new humanity wherein holiness is echoed, prized and praised.

I. 'Thy Kingdom Come'

> *At some risk of being misunderstood I will venture to say that the chief of the wider needs in current religion is the moralization of the idea of God through His Kingdom; its translation to experience, and to the central experience – that of the conscience. It is the standing need, indeed, of an atonement – to do justice to the holiness of God in the central human situation. This is the chief interest of the New Testament. And it is the element in any religion that fits it for such a moral crisis as history has reached.*[4]

The hallowing of all things begins in the 'pure event'[5] wherein *God happens* to us in human flesh, God's reign is proclaimed and enacted, and the world re-constituted towards God's appointed destiny. Familiar with Schweitzer and Ritschl, united with Herrmann, and anticipating Otto, Dodd and Barth, Forsyth urges that the kingdom or reign of God is 'more than a social idea', 'a thing' or a human creation.[6] Rather, it is history's final goal, the 'last moral realm',[7] the greatest interest on earth, the inner truth and moving spirit of all Society, the secret of humanity and the principle of our evolution. It is that for which creation travails, the emergence into the purview of history of sanctifying sovereignty and moral command. It pertains to the growth or the inroad of God's will on earth as in heaven, and to the King who *must* act if he is to be King of the world.[8] So Forsyth suggests that we get nearer the meaning of the word 'kingdom' when we substitute it for 'sovereignty'.[9]

> [The] phrase 'as in heaven so on earth' belongs to each of the three first petitions, and not only to its next neighbour. 'Hallowed be Thy Name' as in Heaven so on

[4] 'Moral Principle', p. 9.

[5] Alain Badiou, *Saint Paul: The Foundation of Universalism* (trans. Ray Brassier; Palo Alto: Stanford University Press, 2003), pp. 48–49.

[6] *Life*, p. 60; *Marriage*, p. 26; cf. Markus Barth, 'P. T. Forsyth: The Theologian for the Practical Man', *Congregational Quarterly* 17 (1939), pp. 436–42 (437); Herrmann, *Dogmatik*, p. 44. Forsyth does, sometimes, equate the kingdom of God with 'Christian civilization'. See, for example, *World-Commonwealth*, p. 4.

[7] 'Moral Principle', p. 10.

[8] 'Church and Society', p. 43; 'Christ's Person', p. 13.

[9] See *Authority*, p. 380; *Socialism*, p. 48.

> Earth; 'Thy Kingdom come' as in Heaven so on Earth. As if it should say, 'There is a realm at the heart of things where all is already won and well, all is Yea and Amen. And access to it is not barred to faith on earth. And it is the real workshop of history.'[10]

It is not as if God first redeemed, and, having thus prepared the ground, brought in the kingdom. Rather, God redeems *by* bringing in the kingdom. We err, therefore, when we reorder the first and second petitions of the Lord's Prayer. God's cross is not the preliminary of the kingdom, the clearing site for the heavenly city, but the kingdom breaking in, the city itself descending out of heaven. In Christ, God inaugurates the eschatological future, not in the sense that the old creation in any way serves as a precondition for the new, but in the sense, as Hart observes, 'that the new has already begun to create its own presence in the midst of the old by assuming it and drawing it into new self-transcendent anticipation of what it will ultimately be'. It is 'God's skilful modulation from the key of death into the key of life'.[11]

Forsyth is convinced – as few exegetes in his day were – that God's kingdom is not merely some vision of eschatological reality but is that already realized in Jesus. To witness the narrative of Jesus' life, death and resurrection is to witness nothing short of the reality and sovereignty of God. Jesus *is* the kingdom – first and foremost. 'The Gospel of the Kingdom was Christ in essence; Christ was the Gospel of the Kingdom in power . . . Christ was the publication, the establishment of the Kingdom . . . It is wherever he is. To have him is to ensure it.'[12] The kingdom's coming, in other words, *is* the decisive action of 'man in God and God in man',[13] the hypostatic union meeting between the historic and the absolute, between Time and Eternity.

Forsyth identifies the kingdom's source and constitution neither with Jesus' teaching – which was merely 'illustrative' and which 'failed' to effect the 'attention and conversion of Israel'[14] – nor with Jesus' calling of the disciples, nor with Jesus' resurrection – 'which was but God's seal set upon a greater work already finished' – nor with Pentecost – 'which was but the sequel and emergence of the great achievement in its social power'. In what one might well consider an unjustified reductionism, Forsyth is suspicious even of identifying the kingdom generally with Christ's person per se lest the kingdom appear an inert thing. Instead, he identifies the kingdom particularly with Christ's obedience manifest in the creative deed of the cross: 'The cross is the real foundation of the Kingdom. *There* was condensed the conscience of Christ and the holiness of eternity – and there arose, in consequence, the ethic of human society. The Kingdom was expounded, indeed, by parables, but it was founded on the cross, and upon the holiness which made the central issue of the cross.'[15] For Forsyth, the whole

[10] *Life*, pp. 60–61.

[11] Trevor Hart, 'Imagination for the Kingdom of God? Hope, Promise, and the Transformative Power of an Imagined Future', in *God Will Be All In All: The Eschatology of Jürgen Moltmann* (ed. Richard Bauckham; Minneapolis: Fortress, 2001), pp. 73, 74.

[12] *Person*, p. 123.

[13] *Society*, p. 23.

[14] Forsyth in Mackintosh, 'The Authority of the Cross', p. 213.

[15] *Society*, p. 19; cf. 'Christ's Person', pp. 3–22; *Life*, pp. 63–67; *Old Faith*, p. 26; 'Moral Principle', p. 17.

nature of Christian certainty and of Reality itself is 'dominated and determined by its christology'.[16] In Christ, God 'revolutionises the eternal foundations of our moral world' and the whole of human society, altering not only the way God relates to creation, but also the ethical foundations of creation itself.[17] To remove the cross from the centre of the moral universe is to make it a chimera, history an enigma and progress irrational.

Forsyth always has broader societal consequences in mind. God's kingdom may not be 'of this world, but it is *for* it'.[18] Forsyth therefore emphasizes the manifestation of God's kingdom in the creature where holiness finds its correspondence through the creation of a new conscience, and of the new ethic of the race. He believes that that which is eternally mirrored in the Godhead must find its creaturely fulfilment and echo. Insofar as this happens, creation finds itself, discovers that it is never itself an absolute source, and that creaturely life is necessarily dependent and responsive. In bringing the kingdom, therefore, Christ 'did not come to make a society God could live in, but to bring a God that society could live in, to make God the real King, shaping His own society from within'.[19] So understood, the kingdom proceeds holiness' satisfaction: 'Hallowed be Thy Name' is the kingdom's one condition.

II. Holiness incarnate

Holiness is revealed in the divine economy, the locus of which was that nation birthed from slavery by God's mercy and liberated to live as the holy nation among all nations to bear witness to the one true God (Exod. 15.11; 19.5–6). In the Incarnation, that locus *shifted* and 'even intensified'[20] as an 'unearthly holiness'[21] moved through history in one who 'was and *is* the holiness of God'.[22] At Pentecost, that locus *extended* to those whom Jesus is not ashamed to call his brothers and sisters.

While some argue that holiness is not only 'the quality peculiar to [God's] very essence'[23] but finally an incommunicable quality, Forsyth posits that in Jesus Christ, God's incommunicability is communicated: 'The unapproachable approaches, enters, tarries, lives, dies, conquers among us and in us . . . subdues all things to its sanctity, and establishes its good and blessed self in us and on us all.'[24] Rejecting the impersonal Aristotelian formulations of holiness which found voice in Plotinus and Baruch Spinoza and later in Protestant and Roman scholasticism which posited God as 'the Supreme Being, inviolable, self-sufficing, and splendid', Forsyth gives holiness a 'true Christian sense'[25] when he regards Jesus as 'God's holiness in human

16 *Authority*, p. 188.
17 *Cruciality*, p. 212; *Society*, pp. 20–27.
18 *War*, p. 179.
19 *Socialism*, pp. 48–49.
20 Herrmann, *Dogmatik*, p. 99.
21 'Paradox', p. 119.
22 *Justification*, p. 125.
23 Gerald L. Bray, *Holiness and the Will of God: Perspectives on the Theology of Tertullian* (London: Marshall, Morgan & Scott, 1979), p. 66.
24 *Authority*, p. 6.
25 *Society*, p. 19.

form'.[26] Approached christologically, holiness refers not to the calm balance and self-possession of an infinite Eternal Being but rather is 'more akin to the self-conquest, self-bestowal, and self-effectuation which belong to an eternal moral personality'.[27] It is the sum of all God's action and relation to the world, the acknowledgment of which must be made in like action.

Stephen Barton argues that holiness concerns both '*who God is*' and '*where he is to be found*', a sense of God's transcendent incomparability as well as God's accessibility 'arising out of his covenantal love and mercy'.[28] Forsyth agrees, although he neglects to unpack the radical implications of such a move. A survey of the ἅγιος (holy, dedicated) word group in the New Testament, for example, suggests a number of christological implications, some of which are undeveloped by Forsyth.[29] For example, the radical redefining of sanctification that forms a central part of Jesus' ministry to second temple presumptions, not least those practices that excluded disreputable people from eating at the table of 'the righteous', is all but neglected by Forsyth. Forsyth is right to press that, in Jesus, holiness is not relaxed but brought near to those who were formerly on the outer, but he accounts too little for Jesus' entering the matrix of Israel's cultic society and deliberately setting about to actively embody holiness and bring 'unholy' outcasts into the sphere of God's holiness, thereby transforming those he is in contact with. While holiness' victory was not secure until the cross–resurrection–ascension, Jesus' hospitality with 'sinners' is of the one action. Forsyth makes too little of those Synoptic accounts which promote Jesus' making himself not only common but also ceremonially unclean – bringing himself under the curse and judgement of God.

Clearly, Forsyth's sights are set elsewhere. Just as Jesus – in his last hours – was engrossed with the Father's will and the hallowing of his Father's name, Forsyth insists that Christianity's 'first necessity' lay in God's holiness.[30] Forsyth sees in the atonement that action whose 'first business',[31] 'prime regard',[32] 'first charge',[33] 'supreme interest'[34] and 'first concern'[35] was not simply the forgiving love of God, but the holiness of such love, and the practical effectuation and establishment of that holiness upon the annihilated 'kingdom of the unholy'.[36] Against Ritschl and Marcus Dods[37] (who

[26] *Person*, p. 347.
[27] *Society*, p. 19.
[28] Stephen C. Barton, 'Dislocating and Relocating Holiness: A New Testament Study', in *Holiness Past and Present* (ed. S. C. Barton; London/New York: T&T Clark, 2003), p. 195.
[29] See Goroncy, 'The Elusiveness, Loss, and Cruciality of Recovered Holiness', pp. 195–209.
[30] Forsyth in Mackintosh, 'The Authority of the Cross', p. 216.
[31] *Cruciality*, p. 209
[32] Ibid., p. 5.
[33] *Sacraments*, p. 34.
[34] *Revelation*, p. 60.
[35] *Society*, pp. 11–12; *Cruciality*, p. 6; *Justification*, p. 37; *Preaching*, pp. 173, 223; cf. *Parnassus*, p. 263; *Sacraments*, p. 34; *Socialism*, p. 57.
[36] *Society*, p. 21.
[37] Ironically, Dods' reduction of the atonement to a mere 'demonstration' of God's righteousness that makes it 'possible and safe' for God to forgive occurs in a collection wherein Forsyth contributes his clearest statement on the atonement as objective, securing that which it sets out to secure. Marcus Dods, 'The Atonement in Modern Religious Thought', in *The Atonement in Modern Religious Thought: A Theological Symposium* by Frédéric Louis Godet et al. (New York: Thomas Whittaker, 1901), p. 181.

posit an atonement-less reconciliation), Forsyth stresses that vertical and horizontal reconciliation is 'impossible except as that holiness is divinely satisfied once for all on the cross'.[38] Consequently, Forsyth insists that christology must attend to that which does most justice to God's holiness and 'takes profoundly and seriously the hallowing of his name'.[39]

III. Christ the hallower

> *The benefit from Christ is not exhausted in the satisfying of the heart or in the pacifying of the conscience. Christ does more than fill or fortify us; he sanctifies.*[40]

Answering the Lord's Prayer from God's side

> *The holiness that atones, though it return from the race that rebelled, must . . . be the gift of the holiness atoned. For if holiness could be satisfied by anything outside itself it would not be absolutely holy.*[41]

From 1878/79, Forsyth avows that the gospel's foundation concerns neither humanity's demand on God nor God's demand on humanity, but supremely God's demand on himself, a demand 'from God's side'.[42] Whatever else God might do, God owed it to himself to 'save' the holy name and purpose,[43] to self-propitiate, to self-atone,[44] to find holiness' self.[45] Indeed, Forsyth insists that God's 'first charge' and due is to God's own insatiable holiness.[46] And he cites Ezekiel 36.22 – 'I do not this for your sake, but for My holy name which ye have profaned'[47] – insisting that 'God would not be God if He loved His own holy nature less than man'.[48] It is, in other words, 'Divine requirement' that moves Christ.[49]

[38] *Cruciality*, p. 5. This notion was articulated by Tertullian. Satisfaction remains the appropriate word so long as we remember that it is God and not something external to God that needs to be satisfied. The 'necessity' of the atonement 'arises within God himself'. Ronald S. Wallace, *The Atoning Death of Christ* (London: Marshall Morgan and Scott, 1981), p. 113.

[39] *Cruciality*, p. 7.

[40] *Person*, p. 280.

[41] *Work*, pp. 207–08.

[42] *Cruciality*, p. 29; cf. *Justification*, p. 40. Forsyth also insists that Christ's dealing with the Father was largely hidden, like a stable iceberg, taking place independently of our knowledge, and 'behind our backs'. *Father*, p. 19. This sponsored the charge that Forsyth advocates a 'transactional theory which operates outside personality' (Escott (ed.), *Director of Souls*, p. 28), a charge ably rejected in Samuel J. Mikolaski, 'The Nature and Place of Human Response to the Work of Christ in the Objective Theories of the Atonement Advanced in Recent British Theology by R. W. Dale, James Denney and P. T. Forsyth' (unpublished doctoral dissertation, University of Oxford, 1958), pp. 85–87.

[43] See 'Metaphysic', p. 713; 'Majesty', p. 307.

[44] *Justification*, p. 94.

[45] *Jesus*, p. 21.

[46] Ibid., p. 74.

[47] Ibid., p. 75.

[48] *Father*, p. 65.

[49] *Society*, p. 11.

Forsyth counts it 'a solemn and fortifying thought that interior to all space, time, and history there is a world where God's name is perfectly hallowed, His will fully done, and His Kingdom already come'.[50] Unless God's name be hallowed, Forsyth avers, the entire moral fabric of reality is compromised and the whole moral demand on creation is slackened, along with love's value. Only when God places holiness' self into a theodicy that hallows God's own name can all be well with the world. Consequently, but by no means mechanically or involuntarily, Jesus grew to recognize, seek and win holiness as the constituent ingredient of his establishing of God's kingdom. Unsurprisingly, therefore, Forsyth insists that liberalism's gospel of self-salvation must be rejected, God alone can satisfy the moral order God never disturbed, and pay the cost God never incurred. The Hegelian resonance here is palpable: 'God cannot find satisfaction through anything other than Himself, but only through Himself'.[51] And again: '. . . the life of Spirit is not the life that shrinks from death and keep itself untouched by devastation, but rather the life that endures it and maintains itself in it. It wins its truth only when, in utter dismemberment, it finds itself . . . Spirit is this power only by looking the negative in the face, and tarrying with it. This tarrying with the negative is the magical power that converts it into being.'[52]

In 1885, some years before preaching 'The Holy Father' before the 1896 Autumnal Assembly at Leicester, Forsyth was already speaking of the living God as 'the dying God' who in the holiness of the cross *finds himself*.[53] With Fairbairn, Forsyth insists that the atonement cost the Father as much as, if not more than, it did the Son.[54] Forsyth never qualifies exactly what he means by this language, but simply employs the strongest possible grammar to insist that in the cross the Father spares nothing, sacrifices *himself*, and stakes his whole being and purpose for holiness' satisfaction. There is nothing Sabellian here: the Father did not suffer *as* the Son, but *with* the Son. Forsyth's point is that the Father and the Spirit are not spectators of the Son's anguish, nor merely recipients of his sacrifice, but full participants: 'They were involved in it'.[55] This undergirds Forsyth's avowal that unless forgiveness actually costs the forgiver *personally* then the act is vacated of all moral value, rendering it effectively worthless as an act of love. This conviction also informs Forsyth's concern regarding the use of Luke 15 as a parable of the gospel.

[50] *Justification*, p. 151.

[51] Hegel, *Philosophy of Religion*, 3:95–96; cf. Georg W. F. Hegel, *Encyclopedia of the Philosophical Sciences. Part 3: The Philosophy of Spirit* (trans. William Wallace and A. V. Miller; vol. 3; Oxford: Clarendon Press, 1892), §554.

[52] Georg W. F. Hegel, *Phenomenology of Spirit* (trans. A. V. Miller; New Delhi: Motilal Banarsidass, 1998), p. 19.

[53] *Pulpit*, p. 8.

[54] *Society*, p. 29; cf. Andrew M. Fairbairn, *The Place of Christ in Modern Theology* (London: Hodder & Stoughton, 1893), pp. 483–84: 'Theology has no falser idea than that of the impassibility of God . . . To confine the idea of sacrifice to the Son is to be unjust to His representation of the Father. There is a sense in which the Patripassian theory is right.'

[55] *Missions*, p. 29; cf. *Cruciality*, p. 61; *Justification*, p. 169; *Revelation*, p. 10; 'Sermon on 1 Peter 4.19', in Goroncy (ed.), *'Descending on Humanity'*, 2013; John S. Lidgett, *The Fatherhood of God in Christian Truth and Life* (Edinburgh: T&T Clark, 1902), p. 392. Mozley helpfully traces the beginnings of a reaction against traditional notions of impassibility from the nineteenth century in Pringle-Pattison, William James and Horace Bushnell. See John Kenneth Mozley, *The Impassibility of God: A Survey of Christian Thought* (Cambridge: Cambridge University Press, 1926).

Forsyth is alert to how closely he sails to the rocks of patripassianism. Far from being apologetic about it, however, he rejoices in it, seeing therein neither incongruity nor undermining of Christian truth – it took the action of the Trinity, even 'the death of God', to justify the triune name, and to realize creation's destiny in holy love.[56] The charge that Forsyth is guilty of patripassianism[57] fails to appreciate Forsyth's concern that any separating of the action of the 'Persons' is to suggest individualization in the godhead, so driving a wedge between the 'Persons' and undermining God's united resolve. Such a charge also tends to overlook the support in Forsyth's day for a renewed Arianism. Maintaining (at this point) an Alexandrian/Athanasian orthodoxy, Forsyth contends that God could be satisfied by no 'outside party'.[58] Human redemption was not 'wrung' out of unwilling holiness, nor was it purchased by a 'mere bystander or third person with good offices between God and man'.[59] Rather, it is the gracious outworking of the Holy Trinity given fully to us. God does not woo us by 'proxy', love us by 'deputy' or 'sacrifice by substitute'.[60] The only apostle God sends is God's self. God did not simply send the Son, but 'He came as the Son'.[61] The 'object' and 'agent' of judgement, therefore, are one. To support this claim, Forsyth never tires of quoting 2 Corinthians 5.18–19, claiming that in Christ, *God* self-expends for us in order to reclaim us for holiness and that in Christ, holiness 'takes its own consequences in an evil world', suffering, dying and saving.[62] Sparing nothing, *God sacrificed himself*, staking God's whole being and 'His whole campaign with the world' upon this act.[63]

Answering the Lord's Prayer from sin's side

> *Whenever he, the Holy One, is numbered with the human race, he is numbered with transgressors.*[64]
>
> *The holiness of love's judgment must be freely, lovingly, and practically confessed from the side of the culprit world. It must be answered with perfect holiness, i.e. with the Supreme Act of God and man in history, the Supreme Act of the world's King and conscience.*[65]

The cross' value lay in it being not only the act *of God* performed *ab extra* upon humanity, but also in it being that act of God done *ab intra*, from within the limitations of the human situation. The hallowing of God's name is achieved through the Son's taking on fallen flesh and in the power of the Spirit offering *from the side of*

[56] See *Justification*, pp. 145, 164; Hegel, *Philosophy of Religion*, 3:91, 92, 98.
[57] For example, Brown, *Prophet for Today*, p. 178.
[58] *Justification*, p. 169.
[59] *Jesus*, p. 89.
[60] *Authority*, p. 372; *Father*, p. 64; cf. *Work*, pp. 150–52; *Father*, p. 4.
[61] *Father*, p. 64.
[62] *Revelation*, p. 11.
[63] *Justification*, p. 147.
[64] Søren Kierkegaard, *Gospel of Sufferings* (trans. A. S. Aldworth and W. S. Ferrie; London: James Clarke & Co., 1955), p. 73.
[65] *Justification*, p. 167.

creation – 'not only out of a non-holy chaos, but out of an anti-holy crisis'[66] – the fitting response to, and confession of, God's holiness. From as early as his 1895 sermon, 'The Divine Self-Emptying', and again in an 1898 Cambridge sermon, Forsyth presses that the effectiveness of Christ's ministry depends on his taking for his vocation 'not some division or aspect of human life, but human life, and human sorrow, and human sin' in their fullness,[67] no matter how awkward such identification might be for him. The hallowing of God's name was achieved 'amid the extreme conditions of sin and suffering';[68] holiness' final self-witness issued from the depths of human sin and 'amid sin's last wreck, penalty, and agony'.[69] Here Christ is presented as one who has become (as in Holman Hunt's 'Scapegoat') an 'innocent creature' whose groans are 'an *organic part* of the great and guiltless sorrow which bears and removes the curse of the world'.[70] This is the ultimate act of worship.

Drawing upon *Cur Deus Homo*, Forsyth argues that satisfactory honouring is imperative, but not to 'outraged dignity' or 'talionic [retaliatory] justice'.[71] Avoiding Anselm's 'excessive objectivity',[72] Forsyth posits that holiness gives atonement objective value. With Forsyth, Anselm asserts that atonement must come 'from sin's side'; yet given humanity's moral quagmire, the undoing of the effects of sustained blasphemy 'from the sinner's side' is, for those blinded and bound by sin, impossible, let alone that done 'on the scale of the race' as Forsyth insists is required.[73] Additionally, Forsyth contends that even if we could amend the breach, amendment is not reparation; and even the most sincere repentance cannot attain to the measure of the broken law or even gauge how great the damage has been against our own souls, and against our 'injured, neglected, sin-stung God'.[74]

Forsyth preserves Anselm's view that for God to simply forgive would be dishonourable,[75] and that Christ is the sole means by which holiness answers itself from sin's side. But by highlighting (feudal) honour rather than holiness, Anselm – according to Forsyth – 'put theology on a false track', sponsoring a compounding of sin rather than sin's full abrogation. Moreover, Forsyth contends, Anselm fails to grasp the *personal* nature of Christ's sacrifice, its concern with holy obedience. Anselm's Christ acts entirely over our head, without any real reference to the human nature wherein the benefit is to take effect and so leaves us mere beneficiaries. Middle Age soteriology, with its prime concern for a monarch's dignity, required, Forsyth believes, the ethical

66 'Regeneration – II', p. 91.

67 Anonymous, 'First Impressions: Dr. P. T. Forsyth at Cambridge. Signed, "A Country Cousin"', *The Rosebud*, 15 December 1898, np; cf. Donald M. MacKinnon, *Borderlands of Theology* (ed. George W. Roberts and Donovan E. Smucker; Philadelphia/New York: J. B. Lippincott Company, 1968), p. 102.

68 *Work*, p. 222.

69 *Father*, p. 10.

70 *Art*, pp. 181–82.

71 *Cruciality*, pp. 40–41. Anselm's model is closer to Forsyth's than many traditional theories of penal exaction. See Hart, 'Morality, Atonement and the Death of Jesus', p. 32.

72 Paul S. Fiddes, *Past Event and Present Salvation: The Christian Idea of Atonement* (London: Darton, Longman and Todd, 1989), p. 106.

73 *Jesus*, pp. 108–09.

74 *Father*, p. 11.

75 Anselm, *Cur Deus Homo?* (Edinburgh: John Grant, 1909), pp. 44–47.

advances of Protestant orthodoxy which placed the making of satisfaction in the moral and personal realm of the conscience.

The nineteenth and early twentieth centuries witnessed an assault on penal theories, and that not only among liberal theologians.[76] While not wholly joining this assault against 'the old view',[77] Forsyth moves closer to those 'new' christologies proposed by Moberly and McLeod Campbell.[78] This is evident, for example, when he writes that 'It is a matter not so much of substitutionary expiation . . . but of solidary confession and praise from amid the judgment fires, where the Son of God walks with the creative sympathy of the holy among the sinful sons of men'.[79] So radical is this sympathy that it is not only 'the Word made flesh' but specifically 'the Son made sin' who meets the conditions of holy love.[80] This is a centrepiece of Forsyth's christology. Rejecting neither the penal nor the substitutionary elements within Christ's sacrifice, Forsyth offers a shift away from those '*quid pro quos*' and 'dubious ethics of substitution' that tend to vacate the action of genuine personality and reduce it to an external transaction or 'mere distributive equity'.[81] And he moves cautiously[82] in the direction of Abelard, whose contribution finds voice in Grotius, Ritschl and Schleiermacher. By so doing, Forsyth loads the grammar of 'substitution' with positive and creative value. Apparent here too is the fact that Forsyth consistently has an eye on the long-term practical implications of theology for both the Church and the wider public. The shift from a legal to an ethical emphasis in his atonement theology reflects this. He is concerned that stress on the legal places Society on the legal level and the Church in the binds of legalism. He also believes that the old non-ethical and 'hard-shell' orthodoxies, 'where divine justice is satisfied by penalty instead of divine holiness by sanctity', have tended to encourage a low public ethic.[83]

Forsyth welcomes the shift from judicial to ethical categories because it serves the Church's preaching to an age that conceives religious questions in moral, aesthetic and relational terms. He finds in the German Mediating theologians, particularly Dorner, the ethical and universal-representative weight he seeks: that God's work is 'carried out by the God-man in an ethical way' and for ethical ends.[84] Moreover, there is an almost aesthetic quality in Forsyth's atonement theology. It is concerned, as Hart notes, with 'that which God feels when he finds himself in the world through the presence of reciprocal holiness. It is divine self-fulfilment in relationship with a holy other'.[85] The cross is where God is not only self-satisfied, but feels so.

[76] For example, Thomas Vincent Tymms, *The Christian Idea of Atonement: Lectures Delivered at Regent's Park College, London, in 1903* (London: Macmillan, 1904), p. 167.
[77] *Work*, p. 164; cf. *Justification*, pp. 167–69.
[78] Forsyth is not fully supportive of McLeod Campbell's theology, however. See 'Pocket of Gold', p. 187; Goroncy, '"Tha mi a' toirt fainear dur gearan"', pp. 253–86.
[79] *Work*, pp. 225–26.
[80] *Preaching*, p. 124; cf. 'Foolishness', p. 153.
[81] 'Sunday Schools', p. 126; *Father*, p. 4.
[82] See 'Moral Principle', p. 17; 'Christ's Person', pp. 4–7; 'Final Seat of Authority', p. 606.
[83] *Society*, p. 32.
[84] Isaak August Dorner, *System of Christian Ethics* (ed. A. Dorner; trans. C. M. Mead and R. T. Cunningham; Edinburgh: T&T Clark, 1887), pp. 348–49.
[85] Hart, 'Morality, Atonement and the Death of Jesus', p. 32.

While in 1905 Forsyth dismissed Anselm's theory as 'now out of date' and of little more than 'historic value' because it ignores the moral for the purely juridical and so fails to satisfy the modern conscience,[86] five years later (possibly after engaging with Dorner's work) he positively weaves Anselmian theory into 'the threefold cord' (triumph, satisfaction, regeneration) of the atonement. Four factors inform this move: (i) Forsyth's fidelity to Scripture; (ii) his conviction that no one group of metaphors can exhaust the atonement's meaning;[87] (iii) his desire to communicate the gospel to as wide an audience as possible: while 'the destruction of evil, the satisfaction of God, and the sanctification of men' are all 'sides' of the one action, 'some souls . . . will gravitate to the great Deliverance, some to the great Atonement, and some to the great Regeneration';[88] and (iv) a conviction that the juristic is a real element in Christ's death and that discarding it threatens to abandon the 'one revelation of that irrefragable holiness of God which must be expressed in judgment and confessed from its midst'. Forsyth identifies the dilution of this aspect of christology as beginning in Schleiermacher and concluding in Ritschl, averring that this defect in modern theology has impoverished and beclouded true religion, robbing it of 'the power of moral conviction by reducing the idea of sin and dismissing the note of guilt. It makes grace not so much free as arbitrary, because it does not regard in its revelation what is due to the holiness of God'.[89]

Kenosis: The divine self-emptying

Christ's answering of the Lord's Prayer 'from sin's side' finds most radical and creative expression in Forsyth's modified kenoticism. And few have articulated the doctrine's value for Forsyth more precisely than Mozley when he writes that for Forsyth, 'the doctrine of kenosis is no mere way out from an impossible position, but an absolute necessity if the life of Christ is to have full moral value'.[90] To be sure, British formulations of the doctrine generally tend to be less speculative and less sacramentally loaded than German ones[91] but they are no less innovative and they certainly represent a significantly more mediatorial christology for that. But what of Forsyth's presentation? While the affinity in Forsyth's kenoticism with that of Charles Gore has been noted,[92] the affinity

[86] *Art*, p. 259.

[87] See *Work*, pp. 199–235. Also Colin E. Gunton, *The Actuality of Atonement: A Study of Metaphor, Rationality and the Christian Tradition* (Edinburgh: T&T Clark, 1988), pp. 27–52.

[88] *Work*, pp. 202, 233.

[89] Ibid., pp. 228–29.

[90] John Kenneth Mozley, 'A Review of *The Person and Place of Jesus Christ*, by P. T. Forsyth', *Journal of Theological Studies* 12 (1911), pp. 298–300 (300).

[91] For example, Alexander Balmain Bruce, *The Humiliation of Christ In its Physical, Ethical and Official Aspects* (Edinburgh: T&T Clark, 1895), pp. 4–21, 164–72; Charles Gore, *The Incarnation of the Son of God; Being the Bampton Lectures for the Year 1891* (London: John Murray, 1891), pp. 169–73; Charles Gore, *Dissertations on Subjects Connected with the Incarnation* (London: John Murray, 1895), pp. 94–97, 202–25; Thomas R. Thompson, 'Nineteenth-Century Kenotic Christology: The Waxing, Waning, and Weighing of a Quest for a Coherent Orthodoxy', in *Exploring Kenotic Christology: The Self-Emptying of God* (ed. C. Stephen Evans; Oxford: Oxford University Press, 2006), pp. 74–111. For a helpful summary of the work of major German kenoticists see Martin Breidert, *Die kenotische Christologie des 19. Jahrhunderts* (Gütersloh: Gütersloher Verlagshaus Gerd Mohn, 1977).

[92] Bradley, *P. T. Forsyth*, p. 94.

is tenuous as they represent two types of kenoticism. As A. B. Bruce notes, Gore's kenoticism is 'Real but Relative', while Forsyth's is 'Real but Potential'.[93] Moreover, the originality of Forsyth's presentation of the doctrine suggests significant independence of thought. Indeed, as far as I am aware, Forsyth nowhere makes direct reference to Gottfried Thomasius (arguably the most influential of the German kenoticists for the British scene) or to Wolfgang Friedrich Gess, nor to the British kenoticists A. J. Mason, D. W. Forrest, W. L. Walker, R. L. Ottley and Thomas Adamson.[94]

Certainly Forsyth's commitment to kenoticism, a notion that he (and later H. R. Mackintosh) ably defended in Britain against waning popularity, ensured its survival until the years immediately after World War II, when it finally fell out of favour with the publication of Donald Baillie's *God was in Christ*.[95] Baillie's critique is aimed at the older kenotic theories that practically reduced the incarnation into a theophany. Oddly, Baillie never refers to Forsyth's version of the theory. Forsyth, for his part, is already alert to the criticisms and 'many difficulties' that 'arise readily in one's own mind' concerning kenoticism[96] but remains persuaded that kenoticism offers the most compelling account of the incarnation. The presentation is most ably expounded in his 1909 Congregational Union lectures published as *The Person and Place of Jesus Christ*; however, the seeds of Forsyth's convictions were in place by his 1895 sermon, 'The Divine Self-Emptying'.[97] In both places is evidence not only of Forsyth's awareness that he is navigating between 'a choice of difficulties' but also of his taking pains to isolate himself from kenoticism's more vulnerable aspects, not least Thomasius' belief that the relative attributes could be simply severed (rather than self-retracted).[98] Indeed,

93 Bruce, *The Humiliation of Christ*, p. 179.

94 Robert Lawrence Ottley, *The Doctrine of the Incarnation* (London: Methuen, 1895); Arthur James Mason, *The Conditions of Our Lord's Life on Earth: Being Five Lectures Delivered on the Bishop Paddock Foundation, in the General Seminary at New York, 1896; to which is Prefixed Part of a First Professorial Lecture at Cambridge* (London/New York/Bombay: Longmans, Green and Co., 1896); Thomas Adamson, *Studies in the Mind of Christ* (Edinburgh: T&T Clark, 1898); David William Forrest, *The Christ of History and of Experience* (Edinburgh: T&T Clark, 1901); W. L. Walker, *The Spirit and the Incarnation in the Light of Scripture, Science, and Practical Need* (Edinburgh: T&T Clark, 1907).

95 Donald Macpherson Baillie, *God was in Christ. An Essay on Incarnation and Atonement* (London: Faber & Faber, 1948), pp. 94–98.

96 *Person*, p. 294; cf. James Denney, *Studies in Theology* (London: Hodder & Stoughton, 1906), p. 57.

97 For an evaluation of Forsyth's kenoticism see Floyd, *When I Survey*, pp. 39–54; 'The Work of Christ in the Thought of PT Forsyth: Kenosis and Plerosis Revisited', in *PT Forsyth: Theologian for a New Millenium* (ed. Alan P. F. Sell; London: The United Reformed Church, 2000), pp. 131–52; Adrian Giorgiov, 'The Kenotic Christology of Charles Gore, P. T. Forsyth and H. R. Mackintosh', *Perichoresis: The Theological Journal* 2, no. 1 (2004), pp. 47–66 (56–59). Forsyth's kenoticism has not gone uncriticized. See, for example, Bradley, *P. T. Forsyth*, p. 210; Charles W. Hodge, 'Review of *The Person and Place of Jesus Christ*', *Princeton Theological Review* 8 (1910), pp. 688–93. Hodge is less critical of Forsyth's kenoticism in another review of the same book. See Charles W. Hodge, 'Review of *The Person and Place of Jesus Christ*', *Bibliotheca Sacra* 67 (1910), pp. 363–64 (363).

98 See Gottfried Thomasius, 'Christ's Person and Work. Part II: The Person of the Mediator', in *God and Incarnation in Mid-Nineteenth Century German Theology* (ed. Claude Welch; A Library of Protestant Thought. New York: Oxford University Press, 1965), p. 48. Thomasius argues that Christ's divine nature assumed a sleep-like unconsciousness during his incarnation which effectively excluded him from the Trinity. Forsyth rejects any suggestion that the Incarnate Son was any less divine. Forsyth charges much kenoticism with a neglect of the accompanying *plerosis*, a neglect which leads to a weak ethic, asceticism and 'self-occupied piety'. *Person*, p. 329.

the latter is so much so that some have concluded not only that Forsyth's kenoticism is kenoticism 'with a difference, for it is construed in moral rather than in metaphysical language' but even that Forsyth is 'not really a kenotic theorist' at all.[99]

One difference worthy of note between Forsyth's presentation of the doctrine in his earlier thought (e.g. his sermons 'God the Holy Father' and 'The Divine Self-Emptying') and that in his 1909 lecture is that in the latter, Forsyth does not attend to the common objection posed by anti-kenoticists regarding the status of the Logos as cosmic sustainer during his earthly life. In his sermon on John 17.11, 'God the Holy Father', preached before the 1895 Congregational Union Autumn Assembly, however, Forysth affirms (with Gore) a double consciousness of the Logos in terms of an extra-Calvinisticum, and so by implication rejects the Lutheran notion of the *communicatio idiomaticum*.[100] Whether this then strictly undermines the doctrine of kenosis as a system is unimportant to Forsyth, though Thomasius had already pathed the way in that direction. Certainly, Forsyth's acceptance of the 'extra' makes him less a target of anti-kenotic criticism than Thomasius, Hofmann, Liebner, Frank, Ebrard, Martensen and Gess (in Germany) or Gore, Fairbairn, Weston, Gifford and H. R. Mackintosh (in Britain) were.[101]

Where Forsyth finds his distinct voice, however, is with the construal of the doctrine in radically dynamic rather than in static terms. And this involves two firm convictions. First, there is, as we shall soon see, his resolve that we not attend to the doctrine of *kenosis* in isolation from its corresponding reality or movement in Christ's *plerosis*. Secondly, Forsyth's two-*act* (rather than two-*nature*) christology concerns the 'contraction' or compression of the divine attributes. The notion, he contends, bears witness to God's true omnipotence; its value lay in it being a moral achievement on God's behalf – a theological commitment which enables Forsyth to take seriously the *non posse peccare* in Christ's moral struggle.[102]

Forsyth's kenotic christology is at its most creative when he identifies it not with God's stooping *from* himself but *in* himself – an act of 'heart and will, of free resolve, of self-limitation, self-contraction as it were, self-divesting, self-humiliation, self-subordination'.[103] Divine kenosis is neither sentiment, weakness nor an 'occasional mood', but is 'the great ethical act, which forms the real connection . . . and the *reconciliation* between God and man'.[104] Moreover, God's self-limitation 'in the freedom of holiness'[105] is a revelation of divine power rather than a curtailment of it, the supreme demonstration of God's freedom, 'the greatest thing the greatest will could do',[106] and

[99] Floyd, *When I Survey*, p. 39; Colin E. Gunton, *The Barth Lectures* (ed. Paul H. Brazier; London/New York: T&T Clark, 2007), p. 167; cf. David F. Wells, *The Person of Christ: A Biblical and Historical Analysis of the Incarnation* (Westchester: Crossway Books, 1984), pp. 136–38; Donald G. Bloesch, *Jesus Christ: Saviour and Lord* (Christian Foundations; Carlisle: Paternoster Press, 1997), p. 61.

[100] See *Father*, pp. 18, 22; cf. Gore, *Dissertations on Subjects Connected with the Incarnation*, p. 93.

[101] Loofs has suggested that the acceptance of the 'extra' is the necessary concession for kenoticists lest the doctrine of divine immutability be reduced to nought. Friedrich Loofs, 'Kenosis', in *Encyclopedia of Religion and Ethics* (ed. James Hastings; Edinburgh: T&T Clark, 1914), 7:687; cf. Thomasius, 'The Person of the Mediator', p. 56.

[102] See *Person*, pp. 296–99, 341.

[103] *Father*, p. 38; cf. *Father*, pp. 36–40, 83.

[104] Ibid., p. 39.

[105] *Person*, p. 311.

[106] *Father*, p. 38.

the highest example of Christ's divinity: 'Among the infinite powers of the Omnipotent must be the power to limit Himself, and among His glories the grace to bend and die. Incarnation is not impossible to the Infinite; it is necessary. If He could not become incarnate His infinitude would be partial and limited. It would not be complete. It would be limited to all that is outside human nature'.[107] Here Forsyth follows Hegel's rejection of any dualism between God and creation, and that it is the nature of the Absolute to become incarnate; there is 'an act of going out on the part of God into finitude, a manifesting of God in finitude, for finitude, taken in its proper meaning, implies simply the separation of that which is implicitly identical but which maintains itself in the act of separation'.[108]

Omniscience's self-contraction means that while Jesus knew what was required of him, he was not always 'fully conscious of all He was' nor could he have known the consequence that his obedience would have for God or for the world.[109] As Donald MacKinnon attests, 'All had to be received, as it were, step by step from the Father in the manner accepted . . . Christ entered upon the road into the unknown – a way that led to a place of disintegration, where the limitations of human knowledge were suffused by a sense of the ultimately impenetrable'.[110] This is what it means, it seems, for holiness to own itself under the 'unspeakable load' of human limitation; an 'essential part' of which entailed Christ bearing God's judgement 'alone with the Father veiled, the future veiled, and . . . with some *explicit* sense veiled to Himself of that value which the occultation of His glory and knowledge was having for God and for man'. As a sheep before his shearers is silent, Christ was 'silent in the agony of knowing only the Father's will and not the Father's way'.[111] The point here is that if Christ was to master the race, he could only do so through voluntary renunciation into genuine human life, effecting the will of infinite love from sin's side and mastering all that sets itself against God's name.

Forsyth himself saw relatively early on in his ministry that one cannot take the incarnation seriously if the Son appears in the divine economy in a form radically other than that which he appears in the immanent Trinity. The Son's kenosis is the externalization in creaturely space and time of an eternal happening or movement in the Godhead and is not indicative simply of some temporal segment in God's history. The self-emptying of God in Jesus is not only the gracious provision of epistemological access to the divine life,[112] but is also an eternal happening in the final reality itself as

[107] Ibid., p. 33.
[108] Hegel, *Philosophy of Religion*, 3:38.
[109] *Jesus*, p. 31; cf. 'Higher Criticism', p. 39; *Father*, pp. 21–23, 32–36; *Jesus*, pp. 44, 50, 64–65, 69–70, 104; *Person*, pp. 301, 310–11, 317–18; 'Revelation', p. 131.
[110] Donald M. MacKinnon, 'Teleology and Redemption', in *Justice the True and Only Mercy: Essays on the Life and Theology of Peter Taylor Forsyth* (ed. Trevor A. Hart; Edinburgh: T&T Clark, 1995), p. 109; cf. 'Revelation and Bible', p. 245.
[111] *Father*, pp. 21–22.
[112] So Hans Küng, *The Incarnation of God: An Introduction to Hegel's Theological Thought as Prolegomena to a Future Christology* (trans. J. R. Stephenson; Edinburgh: T&T Clark, 1987), p. 451: '"The Godhead" was manifested "bodily" in the depths of the flesh and not in a God who dwells in spurious sublimity; and the πλήρωμα [*pleroma*], the fullness of the Godhead, was revealed in the emptying of his κένωσις [*kenosis*]'.

self-emptying, self-giving, self-limiting, self-filling and self-receiving.[113] Forsyth was one of the first kenoticists to articulate this clearly – that to speak about kenosis is, first and foremost, to say something about God *in se*, and only secondarily about the shape of God's life in Jesus of Nazareth. There is a correspondence here at this point too between the kenotic reality which is the divine life and the suffering which such life undergoes as it comes into contact with whatever holy love would seek to own and to overcome. The Father's grief in the Spirit at the death of the Son is indicative that kenosis runs through the life of all three modes of being and is not a movement in any way restricted to the history of the second.

Equally firm is Forsyth regarding the claim that whatever 'external' or 'physical' attributes the Son leaves behind in his humiliation, the one thing that God cannot set aside – and remain God – is holiness. So when God takes on flesh in order to confess holiness 'from sin's side', God is never less than holy in so doing. Holiness, it seems, is a reality – alongside love, justice and truth – that provides a continuum between the Son's eternal and incarnate life, and preserves God's immutability. Because kenosis is the expression of *who God is*, there is no violation of God's immutability. At this point, Forsyth distinguishes himself from F. L. Godet's and Charles Gore's contention that 'the Word in His kenosis strips Himself *even of His immutable holiness*, His infinite love, and His personal consciousness, so as to enter into a human development similar to ours'[114] and follows the view more akin to that of Thomasius and Fairbairn who posit that in the Incarnation God's 'external' or 'metaphysical' attributes (omnipotence, omniscience, omnipresence) – those attributes that pertain to God as Creator – are limited, restrained, self-reduced, self-retracted or veiled, while the 'internal' or 'ethical' attributes (love, truth, et cetera) – those that constitute the Godhead itself – are retained.[115]

As with other doctrines in the tradition, Forsyth is unapologetic in the freedom with which he modifies ideas. He modifies older kenoticisms and follows Hegel and Kähler in recasting the older orthodoxies when he urges a preference for discarding the two-natures formula ('we have long ceased to think of two persons, or two consciousnesses') in favour of a more dynamic proposal of two *acts* – a shift made in such a way that preserves 'the full value of the orthodox Christology'.[116] This accounts for the hypostatic realism and 'mutual involution' of a twofold vertical movement of *kenosis* and *plerosis* in a single, active, free and responsible personality raised to the whole scale of the human conscience and of God's.[117] In this twofold movement, the

[113] See John Macquarrie, 'Kenoticism Reconsidered', *Theology* 77 (1974), p. 124; Karl Rahner, 'On the Theology of the Incarnation', in *Theological Investigations* (London: Darton, Longman & Todd, 1966), 4:114–15.

[114] A. J. Maas, 'Kenosis', in *The Catholic Encyclopedia: An International Work of Reference on the Constitution, Doctrine, Discipline, and History of the Catholic Church* (ed. Charles G. Herbermann et al.; New York: Robert Appleton Company, 1913), 8:617. Italics mine.

[115] See *Person*, pp. 309, 313; Fairbairn, *The Place of Christ*, pp. 476–77. Note that Forsyth's use of the word 'attribute' is not always consistent here. For example, *Person*, pp. 308–09.

[116] John K. Mozley, 'Christology and Soteriology', in *Mysterium Christi: Christological Studies by British and German Theologians* (ed. G. K. A. Bell and D. Adolf Deissmann; London: Longmans, Green, 1930), p. 183.

[117] *Person*, p. 333.

human is distinguished by the emergence of personality through moral struggle, and the divine through an act of self-retraction. Both movements coexist and cooperate in a common objective of hallowing God's name through divine–creaturely reconciliation and the annihilation of sin. God and humanity come together in this moral movement; that is, in a meeting of action. Hallowing is action. In Christ are two personal movements representing both parties – the actively productive God and the actively receptive and responsive humanity. Thus is created the response that holiness seeks from sin's side, and that by not bypassing the will of the human subject. This means that God's reception of humanity and humanity's reception of God is created and achieved in the one twofold movement of descent and ascent in Jesus Christ. In him alone is holy hospitality secure.

With Kant and Herrmann, Forsyth rejects the mainstream metaphysical philosophizing of the divine essence (as in Fairbairn[118]) and follows Bruce and Gore in preferring an ethical emphasis beginning with the actual historic humiliation of 'God self-humbled to man's level'.[119] The self-retraction or potentiality ('perhaps the most slippery term in the whole vocabulary of philosophy'[120]) of God in his second mode of being certainly strains traditional understandings of the triune relationships; but, in Forsyth's defence, it (i.e. what John Donne would describe as 'immensity cloistered'[121]) does so no more than the event of the incarnation itself. Forsyth correctly presses that the 'infinite mobility' that attends the divine self-determination includes the ability for the infinite to reduce itself to the finite. To undertake christology with abstract metaphysics of divine being – no matter how 'Chalcedonian' – is, Forsyth urges, to fail to allow our theologizing about God to be guided and structured by the historic act itself. The meaning of divine kenosis is determined, not through formal analysis of an a priori decision for 'depotentiation' (to borrow Donald MacKinnon's word), but only by discovering God's self-definition in the economy. Kenosis, as MacKinnon too reminds us, is not only 'an ontological mystery' but also 'the principle that bids us measure the Logos-Christ by the *Christus-patiens*'.[122] It is the facts to which Chalcedon seeks to bear witness that are sacrosanct, not the metaphysics.[123] Still, Forsyth concedes that

> Some metaphysic is here involved . . . but it is a metaphysic of the conscience. It starts from the conviction that for life and history the moral is the real, and that the movements of the Great Reality must be morally construed as they are morally

[118] Fairbairn, *The Place of Christ*, pp. 475–76.

[119] Bruce, *The Humiliation of Christ*, p. 167.

[120] Andrew Seth Pringle-Pattison, *The Idea of God in the Light of Recent Philosophy* (Oxford: Clarendon Press, 1917), p. 106; cf. Gore, *Dissertations on Subjects Connected with the Incarnation*, p. 97.

[121] John Donne, 'La Corona', in *The Poems of John Donne: Letters to Several Personages. Funeral Elegies. Divine Poems. Elegies upon the Author* (ed. Charles Eliot Norton and James Russell Lowell; New York: The Grolier Club, 1895), 2:144. See Hugh Ross Mackintosh, *The Doctrine of the Person of Jesus Christ* (Edinburgh: T&T Clark, 1913), p. 470.

[122] Donald M. MacKinnon, 'Philosophy and Christology', in *Essays in Christology for Karl Barth* (ed. T. H. L. Parker; London: Lutterworth, 1956), 80; MacKinnon, *Borderlands of Theology*, p. 114. See also Donald M. MacKinnon, 'Kenosis and Establishment', in *The Stripping of the Altars* (Suffolk: Collins, 1969), pp. 13–40.

[123] See *Justification*, pp. 91, 93; 'Metaphysic', pp. 712–15; *Person*, pp. 69, 71–72, 177, 223–24, 229–31, 305, 307, 319, 323–24, 330, 333, 339, 343–48; *Sacraments*, pp. 33, 197–98; *War*, p. 188; *passim*.

> revealed. The spiritual world is not the world of noetic process or cosmic force, but of holy, i.e. moral, order, act, and power.

Forsyth then proceeds to both clarify and to defend his position:

> Now concerning the union of the two natures in Christ the old dogma thought in a far too natural and non-moral way. Its categories were too elemental and physical. It conceived it as an act of might, of immediate divine power, an act which united the two natures *into* a person rather than *through* that person. It united them miraculously rather than morally, into the existence of the incarnate personality rather than by his action. The person was the resultant of the two natures rather than the agent of their union. They were united into a person whose action only began after the union, and did not affect it. It began (according to the dogma) in the miraculous conception, which was not an ethical act, rather than in the grace of the eternal son, who, for our sakes, from rich became poor. There can be no unity of spirits like God and man except in a moral way, by personal action which is moral in its method as well as in its aim.[124]

Forsyth's efforts to communicate to his age the facts to which Chalcedon is equally concerned to witness to are to be commended. That said, it seems to me that Forsyth's efforts here are somewhat as fixed by his age as those he criticizes. Nineteenth-century philosophy stamped by personalism found evangelical appeal and articulation in the vernacular parlance of personal-ethical experience rather than more speculative abstraction. Certainly, Forsyth stops too short in working out some of the implications of his position. While he does concede the need to adopt some form of metaphysics for christology – letting in through the back door with his language of 'modes of being'[125] what he dismissed out the front door – and while his preferencing of a metaphysic of the conscience is successful insofar as he shows that there is finally no antagonism between ethics and metaphysics, he is largely unsuccessful in establishing clearly the relation between the metaphysics and the psychology.

To be sure, and unlike some earlier kenoticists, Forsyth is not claiming that christology be reduced to experiential or ethical categories. Neither is he simply being lazy, avoiding the hard intellectual work that witness to the incarnation calls for. In my view, Forsyth's is a largely successful attempt to make intelligible the New Testament's presentation of the incarnation as the event of God actualized in real human history. Also, as Gunton helpfully observes,

> Forsyth's demand for a metaphysic of conscience is to be understood in the light of his positive assessment of the work of Schleiermacher and his successors. [Forsyth] sees the great nineteenth-century theologians as critics of the tendency to treat Christology scholastically, with the result that for him the formulas of the

[124] *Person*, pp. 222–23.
[125] Ibid., p. 307.

> tradition become not the vehicles of a saving experience but simply intellectual counters.[126]

That said, Forsyth's kenotic theory, despite its careful and less speculative presentation, still serves to 'illustrate that those who attempt to avoid ontology run the risk of doing ontology badly'.[127]

Pertinent here is Gunton's further objection against Forsyth's route, a route which, Gunton argues, threatens to sponsor an essentially dualistic christology. Gunton contends that far from replacing a two-nature doctrine, kenotic theories actually presuppose such, before proceeding to suggest that they 'cannot go so far as Chalcedon but must in some way qualify the assertion of unity so that it is not quite so bald'. He continues:

> Unlike Chalcedon, which says that in the one Christ there are, simply given, the two realities, make of them what you will, [kenoticists] say, 'Chalcedon gives us two realities in one. We know (or believe) that this is impossible. Let us therefore qualify this full-blooded assertion and hold that the divine Son is not present in his fullness, but only almost so.' It is the kenotic theorist who rationalizes Christology, not the Chalcedonian Definition. He also in effect divides the Son from the Father, by saying that God cannot empty himself and still remain God.[128]

While I agree with Gunton that this course represents one often undertaken by kenoticists, the suggestion that it represents Forsyth's account of the doctrine is untenable. Forsyth's presentation neither rationalizes christology, nor divides the 'Persons'. Nor does it negate in any way the claim that, in Barth's words, 'God is always God even in His humiliation'.[129] Forsyth would want to underscore the tradition's claim that, in the incarnation, 'the divine being does not suffer any change, any diminution, any transformation *into something else*'.[130] He would, however, immediately qualify that such a claim does not mean that God remains unchanged as a result of the free and gracious decision to take on flesh. It is true (with Thomasius) that divine enfleshment does not mean that God reaches into something wholly other than himself. While God's becoming human represents a new experience for God – one which introduces into the divine life a mode of relationality which must find expression from within the human situation – what God finds in the depths of that situation is God's self. Also, with the tradition, Forsyth is insistent that, in Barth's words, 'the deity of Christ is the one unaltered because unalterable deity of God. Any subtraction or weakening of it would at once throw doubt upon the atonement made in Him. He humbled Himself, but He did not do it by ceasing to be who He is. He went into a strange land, but even

126 Colin E. Gunton, *Yesterday and Today: A Study of Continuities in Christology* (London: Darton, Longman and Todd, 1983), p. 171.

127 Ibid., p. 172.

128 Ibid.

129 Karl Barth, *Church Dogmatics IV.1* (ed. G. W. Bromiley and T. F. Torrance; trans. G. W. Bromiley; Edinburgh: T&T Clark, 1961), p. 179.

130 Ibid. Italics mine.

there, and especially there, He never became a stranger to Himself'.[131] Or, as Forsyth would put it: 'The suicide of God is no part of the kenotic idea, which turns but on self-divestment as a moral power of the eternal Son; who retains his consciousness but renounces the conditions of infinity and its precreate form.'[132]

Where Gunton's charge does find some traction, however, is precisely in that locale left too vacuous in Forsyth's presentation of the doctrine. Gunton writes:

> It seems . . . not inappropriate to speak of a self-emptying of God, but only if it is understood in such a way as to be an expression rather than a 'retraction' of his deity. The self-emptying is part of God's fullness, for the heart of what it means to be God is that he is able to empty himself on behalf of that which is not himself. In other words, it is part of his love, through which he comes among us in our time and history to transform our existence from within.[133]

While Forsyth does prefer the language of 'self-retraction' and 'potentiality', he is not unsympathetic with the motivation expressed here by Gunton. His underdeveloped account of the doctrine, however, leaves his christology vulnerable and, at this point, less satisfying than it might have been. In his defense, however, Forsyth is significantly more suspicious than are many kenoticists of sponsoring a kenotic 'system' or 'principle' that one can then employ as a grid to interpret events beyond the *sui generis* act of divine enfleshment.

Having considered Forsyth's presentation of God's self-emptying, we turn now to the doctrine's requisite correspondent – Christ's *plerosis*.

The death of 'a good Kantian'? or, plerosis on the Friday

'The key to history is the historic Christ above history and in command of it, and there is no other.'[134] By undertaking christology so superhistorically, does Forsyth's Jesus truly enter into the realm of God-abandonment – the unresponsive silence of heaven – as, for example, St Mark's Jesus does? Does Forsyth's Christ look more like Holman Hunt's romanticized Jesus than he does Isaiah's suffering servant? Is it true, as one commentator avers, that in Forsyth's christology, '*Christus Consummator* overshadows *Christus Revelator et Exemplar*'?[135]

No harsher sustained criticism has been issued in pen towards Forsyth's theology than that by John Forster who contradictorily accuses Forsyth *both* of having too great an emphasis on the historical Christ (so betraying his close affinity with Ritschlianism) *and* of treating history as 'pseudo-historic', and so dehistoricizing grace.[136] The charge

131 Ibid., pp. 179–80.
132 *Person*, p. 296.
133 Gunton, *Yesterday and Today*, p. 172.
134 *Justification*, p. 218.
135 Ebenezer Griffith-Jones in 'Dr Forsyth on the Atonement', *The Expositor, 7th Series* 9 (1910), pp. 307–19 (315).
136 John Forster, 'Dr. Forsyth on the Authority of Grace', *Primitive Methodist Quarterly Review* 29 (1907), pp. 286–300 (291, 299).

of pseudo-historicity is made more substantially by Gerhard Forde, who is otherwise largely sympathetic to Forsyth's programme. Although not unaware that the decisiveness of Christ's sacrifice necessitates a high christology,[137] and while he falls short of accusing Forsyth of positing a *theologia gloriae* (the ultimate sin for a Lutheran!), Forde insists that Forsyth's christology is too high:

> As in other systems, *theology* rescues Jesus from death. Christ dies in obedience, quite conscious of the system. The cry of dereliction is not what it seems: not the anguished cry of a dying man but the concrete confession of the holy God's repulsion of sin. It is doubtful that the New Testament would sustain such an interpretation. Jesus dies too much like a good Kantian. There are still too many roses on the cross.[138]

One of the limitations of the *Christus Victor* motif so dominant in Forsyth is that a pseudo-docetic, monophysite or Platonic translation of it threatens to sever Christ's triumph from the earthbound reality of what took place during those hours when 'darkness came over all the land' (Mt. 27.45). When such severing occurs, Christ 'escapes into an intangible up in the air kind of world where great forces of divine and demonic power struggle for domination in a way more reminiscent of Captain Kirk and Star Wars than of the gospel story'.[139] Certainly, when theologians cut the metaphor loose from its narrative, they inevitably distort the meaning of what took place and undermine its pertinency. On this matter, more than on most, Forsyth's mature thought betrays a radical reaction to his 'liberal' days. Around the time of the 1877 Leicester Conference, in a speech entitled 'Free Trade in Theology', he urged his colleagues to rely less on the Apostle Paul and 'lean simply on Christ'.[140] After his 'conversion', however, Forsyth becomes more Pauline and begins to anticipate the best insights of C. H. Dodd and others who contend that we cannot expect to find in the Gospels bare facts unaffected by the interpretation borne by the *kerugma* of the early Church.[141] 'The Gospels', Forsyth writes, 'float in the Apostolic Gospel. Not only is Luke Pauline but even Mark. We have in the New Testament but apostolic Christianity, i.e., a theological Christianity, Christ interpreted in that apostolic way'.[142] Now while few would argue

137 See Gerhard O. Forde, *Theology is for Proclamation* (Minneapolis: Fortress Press, 1990), pp. 70–72.

138 Forde, 'The Work of Christ', pp. 34–35; cf. Gerhard O. Forde, *On Being a Theologian of the Cross: Reflections of Luther's Heidelberg Disputation, 1518* (Grand Rapids: Wm. B. Eerdmans, 1997), pp. 69–102; Alfred Ernest Garvie, *The Christian Certainty Amid the Modern Perplexity: Essays Constructive and Critical Towards the Solution of Some Current Theological Problems* (London: Hodder & Stoughton, 1910), pp. 460–63; A. S. Peake, *Recollections and Appreciations* (ed. W. F. Howard; London: The Epworth Press, 1938), p. 193; I. Howard Marshall, *The Work of Christ* (Carlisle: Paternoster, 1994), p. 9.

139 Smail, *Once and For All*, pp. 69–70. Pelikan suggests that Forsyth's *The Work of Christ* renders Aulén's typology 'quite irrelevant'. Jaroslav Pelikan, 'Foreword', in *Christus Victor: An Historical Study of the Three Main Types of the Idea of the Atonement* by Gustaf Aulén (New York: Macmillan, 1969), p. xviii.

140 Cited in Leslie Stannard Hunter and John Hunter, *John Hunter, D.D., A Life* (London: Hodder & Stoughton, 1921), p. 42; See also 'Letter 1877', pp. 1202–03, 1231–32.

141 Charles Harold Dodd, *The Apostolic Preaching and its Developments: Three Lectures with an Appendix on Eschatology and History* (London: Hodder & Stoughton, 1936), chapter 2.

142 *Authority*, p. 140.

that Forsyth operates from elsewhere than St Paul's centre – the cross – Forsyth does not explicitly place this centre within Paul's narrative world – creation, covenant, Israel, et cetera. Thus, it is argued, despite his concern to emphasize to the contrary, Forsyth's theological centre is vulnerable from being dehistoricized.

It is not difficult to conceive how the casual reader may concur with Forde's evaluation, and statements from Forsyth's pen such as 'the value of our Lord's actual flesh and blood was little before God'[143] do not help to allay the charge. Certainly Forsyth's (over)reaction to the Young Hegelians' atheistic New Testament scholarship's enthusiasm with recreating 'lives' of the historical Jesus does not help either.[144] Neither does his commendable effort of moralizing dogma with a view to returning *ecclesia* and *societas* to their proper footing and authority in the cross. Perhaps if Forsyth had further developed his thinking on Christ's obedience along stronger covenant lines and those of Christ as Israel's – and so the world's – one true covenant-keeping Representative (a notion, it must be said, that is not entirely absent in his thought[145]), then he may have better staved off the criticism of sponsoring idealistic christology.

Forde fails, however, to account for at least two significant factors in Forysth's presentation. First, Forsyth's disassociation at this point from Hermannesque mystic christology which sits loose from real history. Secondly, Forde omits the decisive two-act movement of *kenosis* and *plerosis*, wherein there is 'mutual interplay, mutual struggle, and reciprocal communion', and which takes seriously *both* the initiative, creation and productive action of God, and the 'seeking, receptive, appropriative action of groping, erring, growing man'.[146] Forsyth insists that a Christ merely kenotic would be merely negative; the self-humbled One must also realize himself, win himself back in a moral reconquest. Thus Forsyth identifies growth in Christ – what Hegel in his own thinking on the kenosis of substance refers to as 'growth into self-consciousness'[147] – culminating in the perfecting of his own soul and the full realization of his stauro-teleological mission – the plerotic climax: 'The diminuendo of the Kenosis went on parallel with the crescendo of a vaster Plerosis.'[148] Forsyth

[143] 'Sacramentalism', p. 265.

[144] See *Cruciality*, pp. 95–107, 169; 'Intellectualism', pp. 326–27; *Person*, pp. 49, 52, 274; *Freedom*, p. 240; *Authority*, pp. 221–22, 306; *Jesus*, pp. 39–40; 'Inner Life', pp. 149–52. Forsyth appropriately names Strauss and Baur in this context (*Authority*, p. 125; cf. David Friedrich Strauss, *Das Leben Jesu kritisch bearbeitet* (Tübingen: C. F. Osiander, 1835–36); David Friedrich Strauss, *Die christliche Glaubenslehre in ihrer geschichtlichen Entwicklung und im Kampfe mit der modernen Wissenschaft dargestellt* (Tübingen: C. F. Osiander, 1840–41), 2:2336; and David Friedrich Strauss, *Das Leben Jesu für das deutsche Volk bearbeitet* (Leipzig: Brockhaus, 1864), which saw its thirteenth edition by 1904) and in two places, at least, (*Authority*, p. 267; *Justification*, pp. 209–10) confesses his preference for Nietzsche's interpretation of life as a vast depth and a throbbing reality over Strauss' reconstituted Hegelianism wherein everything is fitted into a neat system. Forsyth describes Schweitzer's *Quest* as 'very remarkable'. *Work*, p. 163n. Forsyth's regard for Kähler's Christ of faith (as the true *geschichtliche*) over against Strauss' *historisch* is apparent here. Kähler claims that 'the entire life of Jesus movement [is] a blind alley'. Kähler, *Historical Jesus*, p. 46.

[145] See *Cruciality*, pp. 193–94; *War*, p. 148; 'Conversion', p. 763.

[146] *Person*, p. 336; cf. *Art*, p. 197; H. F. Lovell Cocks, 'Books on the Person of Christ: P. T. Forsyth's *The Person and Place of Jesus Christ*', *Expository Times* 64 (1953), pp. 195–98 (197–98).

[147] Hegel, *Phenomenology of Spirit*, p. 457.

[148] *Person*, 311; cf. Hegel, *Philosophy of Religion*, 2:255; C. F. D. Moule, 'The Manhood of Jesus in the New Testament', in *Christ, Faith and History* (ed. S. W. Sykes and J. P. Clayton; Cambridge: Cambridge University Press, 1972), pp. 98–99.

combines the two 'movements': the cross is both 'the nadir of that self-limitation which flowed from the supramundane self-emptying of the Son' and 'the zenith of that moral exaltation which had been mounting throughout the long sacrifice of [Christ's] earthly life'.[149] Here there is for Christ a becoming what he eternally is. Also, in Christ, God is seeking humanity and humanity God. Few kenoticists hold this double-movement together as carefully as Forsyth, who allows neither movement to eclipse the other, and whose Jesus experiences genuine history and growth as he learns to taste the acquired divinity he had eternally known, winning by faith what was his own by right. Not until the very end was Christ perfectly sure, nor did his hope fade that the Father might find another way.[150]

Forsyth certainly could have further annotated the relationship between Christ's *plerosis* and Christ's ascension, how Christ's ongoing life and activity crowns (rather than ends) his incarnation, and how these relate to the life of the believing community that is lifted beyond itself (not out of itself) to participate in the Triune life. But his accentuation on the cross as 'deed' helps to keep his presentation of the atonement 'from seeming to speak of things that take place in eternity'. Forsyth's Jesus dies on earth, among sinners, his whole life 'rooted in the organic context and moral necessity of [Israel's] history'.[151] No charge that Forsyth's atonement theology is *ahistorical* or *suprahistorical* has considered his chapter, 'Christian Ethic Historic and National', in *The Christian Ethic of War*, wherein Forsyth explores the value of the 'world event . . . in a national situation',[152] in Israel between two criminals, and without aureole.

Although Forsyth makes no direct mention of Mark 15, he does offer some direct comment on Jesus' cry of dereliction. Against liberalism's vacuity, Forsyth urges that for the 'pale and blood-stained Jew',[153] death meant 'disheartenment, failure, desertion, heartbreak'. More than any other, Jesus enters the quagmire of humanity's despair, the history constituted as a conveyor-belt of corpses, and drinks to the dregs the 'cup of divine anger which the sinner must drain'.[154] In order to save, Christ enters humanity's grave, goes down into the experience of nothingness and dread, into death, into hell, into the furnace of God's own wrath, into the radical depths of its wound.[155]

> The revelation of the Father had to speak that tongue. The God who saves to the uttermost saves from the uttermost. He is the God of the God-forsaken, the Father of the fatherless . . . When our soul awoke in hell He was there. The faith of the

[149] *Person*, p. 232.
[150] 'Inner Life', p. 162.
[151] *Cruciality*, p. 193.
[152] *War*, pp. 146, 139.
[153] 'Strength', p. 87.
[154] Hans Urs von Balthasar, *Mysterium Paschale: The Mystery of Easter* (trans. Aidan Nichols; Edinburgh: T&T Clark, 1990), p. 123.
[155] See 'Genius', p. 441; cf. Friedrich Nietzsche, *Thus Spoke Zarathustra: A Book for Everyone and No One* (trans. R. J. Hollingdale; London: Penguin, 1969), pp. 278–79. I use the word 'hell' cautiously here, aware, as Balthasar reminds us, that difficulties attend calling this suffering 'hell', 'for there is no hatred of God in Jesus, only a pain that is deeper and more timeless than the ordinary man could endure either in his lifetime or after his death'. Hans Urs von Balthasar, *You Crown the Year With Your Goodness: Sermons Through the Liturgical Year* (trans. Graham Harrison; San Francisco: Ignatius Press, 1989), p. 85.

> saved may be radiant, but the faith of the Saviour, and the saving hour, had to be a darkling faith.[156]

While genuine victory 'over the evil power or devil'[157] is certain, *Christus Victor* need not be understood triumphalistically. The victory procured in Jesus' all-or-nothing campaign is won by harnessing his real power to take the form of a slave and submitting to the worst his enemies can deliver. It is precisely because Jesus willingly enters the dreadful depths of godforsakenness in order to bear sin's judgement, and because he does so from the side of fallen and fractured humanity (though steadfastly refusing to be fallen and fractured in it) that his death satisfies God.[158] Moreover, in the triumph of Christ's will over sin and its guilt, humanity sees God's purpose for the world and God's principle throughout history. *Christus Victor* is *Christus Doulos*.

IV. Christ as obedient: 'To obey is better than sacrifice'

The nature of Christ's obedience

> *The secret of the Incarnation lies in the personality of Christ, whose centre is the holy Will.*[159]

Forsyth locates his staurology not in the precincts of temple sacrifice but in the territory of moral action. Averring that any one atonement theory is distorted by isolation, he weaves three traditional strands – triumph, satisfaction and regeneration – into one comprehensive cord, convinced, following Calvin, Kähler, Schlatter and Lidgett, that their unity and value lay in Christ's perfect obedience. Christ's obedience, Forsyth insists, is 'the atoning thing' in every major atonement motif, 'the only idea which unites justification and sanctification and both with redemption'.[160] It is neither the degree of suffering nor the amount of blood which is of prime value to God, but the conformity to God's gracious will – 'the suffering being only the condition not the sacrifice'.[161] Moreover, it is not obedience (as a subjectivity) per se that is of value but obedience replete with moral content and fervour which issues from its object and his demands. Indeed, in itself, obedience may be no more than resignation, docility and, even, immoral.[162] There is nothing in the Father's perfect Word that is not answering the Father in their history with the world as it is drawn out by the Spirit. The obedience manifest in the divine economy is an unbroken prolongation – now from the inside of the conditions of sin – of that which marks the triune life *in se*, and so constitutes Christ's whole personality as 'absolute sonship'.[163]

156 *Missions*, p. 30.
157 *Work*, p. 199.
158 'Christ's Person', p. 16.
159 'Sacramentalism', p. 265.
160 *Work*, p. 222.
161 Forsyth in Mackintosh, 'The Authority of the Cross', p. 216.
162 See 'Moral Principle', pp. 19–20.
163 *Person*, p. 285; cf. Hugh Ross Mackintosh, *The Person of Jesus Christ* (Edinburgh: T&T Clark, 1912), p. 402.

> Such a relation as we believe our Saviour now bears to the Father could not have arisen at a point of time. It could not have been created by his earthly life. The power to exercise God's prerogative of forgiveness, judgment, and redemption could never have been acquired by the moral excellence or religious achievement of any created being, however endowed by the spirit of God.[164]

Just as Eberhard Jüngel contends that 'the highest and final statement which can be made about the being of God is: God corresponds to himself' (*Gott entspricht sich*)[165] – and that no less so in the economy – so too Forsyth understands that any division between the Trinity *in se* and the Trinity *ad extra* only serves the interests of Arianism.

Justyn Terry argues that Forsyth's attempt to unite the different aspects of atonement under the rubric of obedience 'does not succeed'. If this is indeed Forsyth's final proposition, then Terry is correct, but if obedience serves the greater notion of hallowing, as I argue, then Terry's criticism is unjustified. By positing judgement as 'the paradigmatic metaphor for atonement, with victory, redemption and sacrifice as subordinate metaphors to it',[166] Terry suggests that justification rather than sanctification is the end goal of God's work. I believe that such a move risks reinforcing a primarily legal rather than filial relationship between God and humanity and of forcing needless lines in the *ordo salutis*. Avoiding such a demarcation, Forsyth follows Calvin in understanding justification and judgement as beginning in God's election to be for God and for humanity with an end in the glory of holiness. Against Terry, I want to suggest that for Forsyth hallowing, and not judgement, is 'the paradigmatic metaphor' (if we need one!) for understanding Christ's work. This not only underscores the closest possible relation between divine ontology and divine action (something Forsyth is keen to do) – that God's being *is* God in action – but also avoids the dead end that Terry would lead us into. For by making judgement (as Terry understands it) the key metaphor, Terry then has to find a way of accounting for the human response to and participation in Christ's saving work, an account which is then fundamentally a *separate work*. Forsyth, conversely, by interpreting the proper human response to have already been offered vicariously in Christ's twofold movement, keeps the unique act of the atonement and its subsequent action in the life of God's people grounded firmly in the one person and action of Jesus Christ and so bears witness that, from first to last, grace is grace.

Forsyth also insists that the Son's eternal obedience is inconceivable 'without some form of subordination' which, in the very nature of God, implies no inferiority. The Son's is a self-subordination, a willing and free service, as it is for all true human being: 'If man is to be holy as He is holy, our self-subordination to each other is not necessarily inferiority, nor need obedience be slavery. There is an obedience bound up with the supreme dignity of Christian love, so that where most love is, there also is most obedience'.[167] Here Forsyth relates the beauty of the Son's equality

[164] *Person*, p. 269.

[165] Eberhard Jüngel, *God's Being is in Becoming: The Trinitarian Being of God in the Theology of Karl Barth* (trans. John Webster; Grand Rapids: Wm. B. Eerdmans, 1976), p. 36.

[166] Terry, *The Justifying Judgement of God*, p. 171.

[167] *Marriage*, pp. 70–71.

with, and obedience to, the Father with the willing service God intends the people of God to render. 'Subordination is *not* inferiority . . . it *is* godlike', 'imbedded in the very cohesion of the Eternal Trinity', and subsequently inseparable from the unity, fraternity and true equality of human community. To obey is divine.[168] Manifest in the incarnation is an unbroken continuum of eternal ontological obedience offered now amidst the conditions of sin, death and judgement. As already noted, the Son's obedience is not merely a feature of his earthly session, as if he were undergoing a performance for the benefit of those he represents, or as if it were a necessary compromise or feature of his being immersed in the human state of affairs. Rather, the obedience expressed in the incarnation is revelatory of the life which characterizes the triune relations *in se*, relations exemplified by subordination and superordination proper to love – that is, a subordination and superordination which implies neither inferiority nor superiority and which underscores the claim that the greatest among persons is the one who serves. Such service takes different shapes for God in God's three modes of being, and is no less about the Father's and the Spirit's kenosis than it is about the Son's.

The 'very crux of the Cross, the spot of final victory',[169] however, was Christ's loving trust and trusting love when no love was felt, when love was doing everything but rejoicing, when all his lovers failed him and things that had gone from bad to worse seized their worst, when every reason for loving traitorous humanity had evaporated. Here was love completely given to hallowing the name of one who seemed to have vacated the cosmos, love with no feeling of sympathy, where compassion was beclouded, inspiration sucked dry and where all that survived was pure fidelity.

There is no break here between the *logos ensarkos* and the *logos asarkos*: Christ's action as the human Son of God arose out of, and expressed faithfully, what he is first and foremost – the Father's ever-receptive Son in whom obedience is 'his divinest achievement' – and out of which 'grew his vast creative, commanding, and even coercive, effect upon the world'.[170] Moreover, divine enfleshment is the result of an eternal decision, its consequent sacrifice beginning before creation, and itself the result of the Son's supreme obedience.

> There was a Calvary above which was the mother of it all. His obedience, however impressive, does not take divine magnitude if it first rose upon earth, nor has it the due compelling power upon ours. His obedience as man was but the detail of the supreme obedience which made him man . . . Unlike us, he *chose* the oblivion of birth and the humiliation of life. He consented not only to die but to be born. His life here, like His death which pointed it, was the result of his free will. It was all one death for him. It was all one obedience. And it was free. He was rich and for our sakes became poor. What he gave up was the fulness, power, and immunity of a heavenly life. He became 'a man from heaven'.[171]

168 *Father*, p. 42.
169 'Moral Principle', p. 20.
170 *Person*, p. 352.
171 Ibid., pp. 270–72.

Jesus' identification with sinners in the baptismal waters of Adam's fall therefore is met with the Father's oft-spoken word: 'This is my beloved Son, with whom I am well pleased' (Mt. 3.17). The Spirit then leads the newly coronated Son-Messiah into the wilderness to be tempted by the devil. The one declared Son of God at the baptism will now display the obedience that such Sonship entails, even unto death.[172]

> Never was man's composure of self-certainty like this Man's. The awful hour troubled Him, but it did not appal Him. He suffered, but He never complained. He quailed, but He never broke. He halted, but He never went back. He lost His joy of God, but never His faith. He realized the vastness of His task, and He rose to it; the agony of it, but He went through. The eternity in Him was always equal to the hour when it came. He was despised, rejected, forsaken, but always the King.[173]

Here it is not Christ's sufferings but what Joseph Ratzinger calls Christ's 'unrestricted Yes to God's will' that makes Jesus Lord.[174] Jesus' whole life was an outworking of Hebrews 10.9, 'Here I am, I have come to do your will'. 'His meat and drink', Forsyth insists, 'was to do the will of the Father'.[175] Crediting Schleiermacher with removing the barrier between Christ's active and passive obedience, Forsyth rejects such distinction which is sometimes made in Reformed theology in favour of what Ritschl calls the 'unbroken continuity' in Christ's 'distinct personal life'.[176] Christ's whole life was redemptive. With Ritschl, Calvin, Mozley and McLeod Campbell, Forsyth underscores the organic unity of the Son's life and work as one active offering to the Father. 'We can no longer separate Christ's life of obedience from His expiatory death. He was obedient, not simply *in* death, but *unto* death . . . His whole person was expiatory in its ultimate function and supreme work'.[177]

> The great confession was made not alone in the precise hour of Christ's death, although it was consummated there. It had to be made in life and act, and not in a mere feeling or statement; and for this purpose death must be organically one with the whole life. You cannot sever the death of Christ from the life of Christ. When you think of the self-emptying which brought Christ to earth, His whole life here was a living death. The death of Christ must be organic with His whole personal life and action. And that means not only His earthly life previous to the Cross, but His whole celestial life from the beginning, and to this hour, and to all eternity.[178]
>
> The Cross is latent in Christ's Person as the oak in the acorn. The acorn must end in the oak and come to itself there, unless it rot or be crushed. And the whole energy

[172] See *Father*, pp. 64–65; *Cruciality*, p. 199; *Work*, pp. 146, 183; David Peterson, *Hebrews and Perfection: An Examination of the Concept of Perfection in the 'Epistle to the Hebrews'* (Cambridge: Cambridge University Press, 1982), pp. 74–103.
[173] 'Paradox', pp. 135–36.
[174] Joseph Ratzinger, *Jesus of Nazareth* (trans. Adrian J. Walker; New York: Doubleday, 2007), p. 17; cf. *Work*, pp. 200–02, 206, 221–23; 'Christ's Person', p. 18.
[175] 'Paradox', p. 114.
[176] Ritschl, *Justification and Reconciliation*, p. 443; cf. 'Regeneration – I', p. 632; 'Christ's Person', p. 3; *Cruciality*, pp. 178, 193.
[177] 'Atonement', p. 69; cf. Calvin, *Inst.*, 2.16.5.
[178] *Work*, p. 153.

> of Christ blossoms in the Cross not as a mere possibility nor as an idea, but as an entelechy, a ruling end, a destiny – as the result not of a mere moral process, but of purposed action.[179]

Christ's obedience, Forsyth insists, is a necessary condition for his offering up vicarious and satisfactory confession. It involves *one* act of reparation sufficient to take away the world's sin and create a new humanity which shares in the obedience, freedom, confession and praise of the human conscience of God. To this end, 'Christ did not go to His death with His eyes shut. He died because He willed to die, having counted the cost with the greatest, deepest moral vision in the world'.[180] And not only the incomparable cost but also the joy of the new creation that was before him, a joy in holiness' triumph: 'It *was* hard for God to redeem, however freely He might forgive, and the whole travail of Creation was the reflection of the Divine pain and sorrow in the joyful task.'[181] In Christ, the holy love of God is manifest throughout the earth, and mirrored back to its source from the new humanity he creates. And while the final chapter of this study shall consider Forsyth's doctrine of election more fully, germane here already in Forsyth's thinking about Christ's obedience is the claim that as for all election, Christ's too is 'an election in love to obedience, and service, and even death, for the rest'.[182]

The limitation of Christ's obedience

Forsyth is aware of the destructive effects of Socinus' ultra-rationalistic teaching not only in the sixteenth and seventeenth centuries, but also in the Unitarianism and modified Arianism of post-Restoration England up to, and including, his own day.[183] Finding fresh voice in nineteenth- and twentieth-century theology through Schleiermacher, Socinianism pressed that Christ so satisfied God by his obedience that he obtained *apart from the cross* the remission of sins and eternal salvation.[184] Conversely, Forsyth contends that obedience that stops short of Good Friday can finally deliver nothing. While Jesus' whole incarnate life is a worshipful offering to God brimming with soteriological import, Gethsemane reveals the necessity of the coming cross as the climax of an obedient life, apart from which his obedience would be of no soteriological value for humanity. Only at the cross does Christ finally find his tongue and take command of the 'deep eloquence of moral things'.[185] Or, as Forsyth

179 'Christ's Person', p. 4.
180 *Work*, p. 27; cf. *Jesus*, p. 107.
181 'Baldwin Brown', p. 141.
182 *Authority*, p. 360.
183 *Freedom*, pp. 121–22.
184 Thomas Rees, *The Racovian Catechism, with Notes and Illustrations* (London: Longman, Hurst, Rees, Orme, and Brown, 1818), p. 304. The Socinian background to Schleiermacher is noted in David Friedrich Strauss, *The Christ of Faith and the Jesus of History: A Critique of Schleiermacher's Life of Jesus* (trans. Leander E. Keck; Philadelphia: Fortress, 1977), pp. 60–61.
185 *Cruciality*, p. 45; cf. *Father*, pp. 26, 40–41; 'Metaphysic', p. 718; 'Intellectualism', p. 327; *War*, pp. 77, 93–94, 140–41, 145–46, 151, 153, 157–58, 169, 187–88, 190; *Justification*, pp. 25, 147–56, 166–67, 181, 218; *Sacraments*, pp. 35, 59, 240, 255–56; *Society*, pp. 19, 32, 94, 98, 121; *Revelation*, pp. 14, 22; *Jesus*, pp. xxii, 2, 10, 16–17, 24–25, 28, 33, 36.

noted elsewhere: 'Gethsemane was not wholly adequate because there the nadir was not touched. The real nadir – the hinge of all – was in the dereliction . . . I would say the recognition of God's holiness was not uttermost, was not complete, till the last extremity of suffering experience for a holy soul was reached in the sense of forsakenness.'[186]

The value of Christ's obedience

> The *precious and sacred thing was [Christ's] holy, God-beloved will and its complete obedience of faith. There is the nerve of personality, there is the seat of sanctity. There the great, eternal, final Redemption transpired. The value of the cross lies in its value as an act of Christ's soul and will.*[187]

There is a fourfold movement within the one act of grace: (i) The Father speaks; (ii) The Son hears/receives the Father's words; (iii) The Son does what the Father says, answering the Father by his act; and (iv) The Father receives the gift; that is, receives his Son and his work. So understood, obedience's value is not in the depth of agony but in the height of surrender. It is obedience that atones, that turns an execution into a sacrifice, a judicial act of a human court into a personal and perichoretic exchange between Father and Son, and through which 'the many are made righteous' (Rom. 5.19) and God's kingdom established on earth as in heaven.

Forsyth follows Schlatter, who contends that Jesus' obedience meant the revelation of righteousness, that Christ's obedience in death provides 'its sanctity and effectiveness and . . . turns it into the realization of righteousness'.[188] Furthermore, the gift is valuable because it is voluntarily 'offered up' and not extracted against his will. It was Christ's will that hung on Calvary's tree; a detail, for Forsyth, for why the cross is more virtuous and valuable that the virgin conception.[189] What is offered up in Christ's death is 'life in its most intimate, spiritual, and moral form'. God is not seeking equivalent pain as if Christ's work was to 'suffer in a short time . . . the pains of the endless hell which we had earned'.[190] Rather, he who heard the Father's word was, in the Spirit, completely given to it, and called upon all his resources in order to answer. The Father receives the Son's work – his offering in the Spirit – and in him, the creation he hallows.

Drawing on the Levitical sacrifices for support, Forsyth avers that it was obedience – a will fully, freely and lovingly engaged with God's and not some *ex opere operato* manipulation – that gave the sacrifices their value. Forsyth recalls that the Old Testament sacrifices were not 'desperate efforts and surrenders made by terrified people in the hope of propitiating an angry deity' but were 'in themselves prime acts of obedience to God's means of grace and His expressed will'.[191] 'The

186 Forsyth in Mackintosh, 'The Authority of the Cross', p. 217.
187 'Sacramentalism', p. 265.
188 Schlatter, *Romans*, p. 131; cf. Adolf Schlatter, *Die Theologie des Neuen Testaments, Volume 2: Die Lehre der Apostel* (vol. 2; Calwer: Verlag der Vereinsbuchhandlung, 1909), p. 262; Adolf Schlatter, *The History of the Christ: The Foundation for New Testament Theology* (trans. Andreas J. Köstenberger; Grand Rapids: Baker, 1997), pp. 306, 352.
189 See *Father*, pp. 40–41.
190 *Cruciality*, p. 191.
191 *Work*, p. 90.

sacrifices were consecrated by self-sacrifice. It was the offerer's will that lay on the altar. What was precious was not the thing, not the elements, but the act.'[192] In Christ's obedience, the essence of all sacrifice – self-surrender to God – was lifted out of the 'Old Testament garb of symbolism' and made a moral reality.[193] Moreover, it is argued, not only does God provide the sacrifice for the covenant people, but God also creates the obedient will which gives the sacrifice its value. While sinners will make costly sacrifices, such do not unaided 'go to the very centre of our life'[194] – the will. Indeed, the will is the last thing that sinners will let go, precisely because it is the one place, we believe, where we can hold out against God. It is the last citadel of the self, 'our dearest life, the thing we cling to most and give up last. Our will alone is our ownest own, the only dear thing we can and ought really to sacrifice. The blood as life [see Lev. 17:11] means the central will, the self-will, the whole will, in loving oblation. This is the sacrifice even in God'.[195] To speak of Christ's death therefore is to recall one who 'drew upon the very citadel of His personality and involved His total self'.[196] We must not confuse his death with martyrdom.[197] Reflecting again on the Old Testament sacrifices, Forsyth writes:

> To obey everywhere is better than sacrifice. The good priest would have said that as honestly as the good prophet. For the ritual was but an act of obedience. That was its real worth. It was only hearty obedience, and not mere compliance, that gave sacrifice any divine value, and raised it above being a mere subsidy from us, or a mere exaction by God.[198]

Throughout his sojourn, Christ fully identified with the claims of holiness upon the race. And as the shadow of Calvary grew closer, he became the race's contradiction, creating no mere prerequisite or condition for the possibility of human obedience, but creating human obedience itself by taking up humanity's response to God into himself – and so into a deeper and broader movement of response within God's being – a response which then elicits a corresponding obedience in those who by the Spirit repeat that perfect confession, 'Our Father, hallowed be thy name'.

While Forsyth's kenoticism takes seriously that the eternal Son 'learned' what obedience entailed on the stage of fleshly suffering (Heb. 5), it also posits that there is a sense in which Christ's obedience was not only different from but also 'easier' than

192 *Cruciality*, p. 189.
193 *Work*, p. 164.
194 *Cruciality*, p. 194.
195 Ibid., pp. 192–93; cf. *Sacraments*, p. 258; *Society*, pp. 80–81.
196 *Cruciality*, p. 195.
197 See ibid., pp. 14, 68; *Father*, p. 70; *Preaching*, p. 245; *Society*, p. 26. From the second century BCE until the Middle Ages the sanctification of the divine Name became synonymous with martyrdom. So Gen. Rab. 4:2. R. Nehemiah (mid-second century) notes that Abraham was willing to die in battle against foreigners in Genesis 14 in order to sanctify God's Name. See also 1 Macc. 1.60–63; 2 Macc. 6–7; 4 Macc; Josephus, *Ant.* 12:255–56; Josephus, *Apion* 1:43; 2:218–19, 233–35; Phil, *Leg. Gai.* 117, 192, 215, 233–36; Esther M. Menn, 'Sanctification of the (Divine) Name: Targum Neofiti's "Translation" of Genesis 38.25–26', in *The Function of Scripture in Early Jewish and Christian Tradition* (ed. C. A. Evans and J. A. Sanders; Sheffield: Sheffield Academic Press, 1998), pp. 221–32.
198 *Cruciality*, p. 198.

ours, 'for we start from no such unity with the Father'.[199] Unlike ours, however, Christ's obedience 'was effective for salvation'. It is Christ's obedience that makes ours possible as Christ reproduces his obedience in the new humanity his obedience creates.

> Our great act of obedience is to give up the hope of any similar and rival obedience, of any obedience so comparable or parallel to His that we could harbour the jealous complaint that He had an advantage . . . Our one obedience is to welcome His obedience as the gift of God, which we must accept, enter, and share as a new and saving obedience. The obedience of faith is faith as obedience. It is faith's nature, not its result.[200]

Forsyth contends that Christ did not feel that he was meeting some 'divine necessity' in God, so much as offering full, perfect and practical confession of God's eternal holy nature, and bringing home to human creatures the effect on him of the holiness of God's love. Such holiness is 'the one object for which man exists or the world'.[201]

> God has power to secure that the perfect holy obedience of heaven shall not be eternally destroyed by the disobedience of earth. He has power to satisfy Himself, and maintain His holiness infrangible, even in face of a world in arms. But satisfied He must be. For an unsatisfied God, a dissatisfied God, would be no God. He would but reflect the distraction of the world, and so succumb to it. But a holy God could be satisfied by neither pain nor death, but by holiness alone. The atoning thing is not obedient suffering but suffering obedience. He could be satisfied and rejoiced only by the hallowing of His name, by perfect and obedient answer to His holy heart from amid conditions of pain, death, and judgment. Holy obedience alone, unto death, can satisfy the Holy Lord.[202]

According to Forsyth, when God saw Christ's 'holy Humanity', that is, saw humanity sanctified, the travail of God's 'Own Soul' was satisfied.[203] 'It was not even the death that saved, but the living act of obedience in it. It was Christ's recognition of it as a divine necessity, which was God Himself meeting the law of His nature and satisfying in man His own holiness.'[204]

However inadequate an analogy creaturely personality is to God, and however much God's personhood transcends (and is in some respects radically unlike) ours and is thus 'inadequate' to the reality of or as a vehicle for God, in Christ creaturely personality is not incompatible but is mutually capable of love and grace. Therefore, whatever difference we maintain between creatureliness and divinity, the attendant obstacles are overcome *by God* in Christ. Jesus is not only the first and final word to humanity concerning God's faithfulness and love, but also the pledge *to God* of

199 'Revelation', p. 128.
200 Ibid.
201 *Cruciality*, p. 72.
202 *Work*, pp. 205–06.
203 *Person*, p. 351.
204 'Revelation', p. 142.

humanity's sure and faithful response to that love in a change of will and life. Just as Jesus' baptism inaugurates him into a ministry in which he is publicly both the eternal Son in whom the Father is well-pleased (so representing the covenant-keeping God) and also the one who fully identifies himself with an estranged Israel (so representing covenant-breaking humanity), Jesus carries this twofold respons-ability in his person throughout his ministry. In his one person, and from the depths of what Barth calls 'the inferno of His complete solidarity with all the sin and weakness and misery of the flesh', Jesus Christ vicariously speaks and acts humanity's 'Yes' to God.[205] Finally, here is one from the sin-gnarled stock of Adam, provided by God, who loves the Lord his God with all his heart, soul, mind and strength, and who loves his neighbour – indeed, his enemies – as himself. Coming 'into the place which Adam occupied' here is one who 'took part of the same flesh and blood of which the children partook, but he sinned not. He fulfilled all righteousness'.[206] At last, here is one in whom the two consciences of the unilateral covenant might be reconciled, who so represents *both* sinful humanity *and* the holiness of God that he is able to engage fully with the moral maelstrom that confronts them both and make the necessary adjustment between them in the one personality.[207] Once and for all, God could look again on humanity and repeat not only that ancient declaration, 'God saw all that he had made, and it was very good' (Gen. 1.31a), but also extend *to humanity* the baptismal (and transfiguration) words spoken over God's only begotten Son's life, 'This is my beloved Son, with whom I am well pleased' (Mt. 3.17; 17.5; Mk 1.11; Lk. 3.22; 2 Pet. 1.17).

In Christ, God is met with a love equally holy, a love opprobriously foreign to sinful human beings but which will not rest until such a declaration is made from sin's side. The confession of faith from the lips of the dying Christ facing nothing but a real sense of disaster and abandonment represents (among other things) God's own identifying love in and for humanity labouring under the surd and inexplicable brute fact of alienation. Moreover, in Christ, 'man's centre and God's coincide',[208] God and humanity 'dwell in each other in mutual personal satisfaction, full and joyful, evermore delighting in each other, and saying each to the other, "Holy, Holy, Holy, Heaven and earth are full of Thy glory"'[209] in such a way that humanity is gathered up into the space of the triune life but without loss of creaturely status, nor blurring of the Creator–creature distinctives. As Paul Fiddes articulates: 'The room that God makes for us within God's own self is not a widening of the gap between individual subjects, but the opening up of intervals within the interweaving movements of giving and receiving.'[210]

Forsyth contends that in order to be of final value Christ's atoning judgement must also attend to the guilty conscience and create from within the very Bastille of guilt a

205 Karl Barth, *The Epistle to the Romans* (trans. E. C. Hoskyns; Oxford: Oxford University Press, 1968), p. 105.
206 William Hanna (ed.), *Letters of Thomas Erskine of Linlathen* (Edinburgh: David Douglas, 1884), p. 287.
207 'Moral Principle', pp. 17–18.
208 *Work*, p. 184.
209 *Cruciality*, p. 218.
210 Paul S. Fiddes, 'The Quest for a Place which is "Not a Place": The Hiddenness of God and the Presence of God', in *Silence and the Word: Negative Theology and Incarnation* (ed. Oliver Davies and Denys Turner; Cambridge: Cambridge University Press, 2002), p. 54.

confession of God's holiness. This too is part of Christ's one work of reconciliation and is not its mere sequel: 'The effect of His Cross is to draw us into a repentance which is a dying with Him, and therefore a part of the offering in His death; and then it raises us in newness of life to a fellowship of His resurrection.'[211] The value of Christ's death for God and for humanity is, Forsyth repeatedly insists, in the act itself in which Christ confesses God's holiness, bears and judges sin and creates a new humanity in himself. Christ represents and meets holiness' two demands: an answering holiness in love, and a judgement on 'those who do not answer but defy'.[212] Central to this twofold movement is the threefold satisfaction of holiness – positive, negative and creative. Positively, through its confession of God's holiness, the atonement reveals, establishes and puts into historic action the changeless grace of God. Negatively, the revelation and establishment of holiness happens through the revelation of sin's sinfulness and sin's judgement. Creatively, the atonement constitutes a new humanity in perfect tune with God's will. We discuss these three movements in the next section.

V. The cruciality of the cross: The self-recovery of holiness

'The train of history is not simply late, but there has been an accident, and an accident due to malice and crime',[213] such that if God's name is ever to be hallowed, God will have to do it:

> Only one who incarnated God's holiest will as His son alone did could produce and establish in men for ever the due response to that will – the response of their whole and holy selves. Holiness alone answers holiness; and only the Holy God could make men holy; it could be done by no emissary of His. We cannot be sanctified by commission or deputy. No intimation of Himself by God (through the holiest of creatures) could effect such an end.[214]

The one who perfectly confessed God's holiness on the scale of our sin alone has the power to reproduce in sinful humanity the brand of holiness which alone satisfies God. Moreover, or so Forsyth argues, the cross reflects an act within the godhead itself, the 'obverse of a heavenly eternal deed', the result in created time of an eternal decision.[215] Any creaturely hallowing, therefore, happens only *in* and *because of* Christ who first hallowed God and humanity. Creaturely hallowing is, therefore, an 'Amen' to the all-sufficient, all-pervasive, all-victorious, it-is-finished reality of Christ's own hallowing of the Father's name. One hallows God when one faithfully participates in the history of Jesus Christ in whom the Triune God embraces and hallows the world.

And so we turn now to an explication and examination of Forsyth's presentation of Christ's threefold confession of holiness: (i) as *positively* recognizing the authority of

[211] *Work*, p. 194.
[212] Ibid., p. 206.
[213] 'Final Seat of Authority', p. 606.
[214] *Person*, p. 327.
[215] Ibid., p. 271.

God the holy; (ii) as *negatively* confessing that holiness in sin-bearing judgement; and (iii) as *creatively* constituting a new humanity which participates in divine holiness. This threefold work dominates Forsyth's extempore lectures given from rough notes to a group, mainly of young ministers, connected to Revd Dr G. Campbell Morgan's annual conference at Mundesley, Norfolk, and then revised for publication as *The Work of Christ*:

> [Christ's] obedience was the Holy Father's joy and satisfaction. [God] found Himself in it. And it was also the foiling and destruction of the evil power. And it was farther the creative source of holiness in a race not only impressed by the spectacle of its tragic hero victorious, but regenerate by the solidarity of a new life from its creative Head. The work of Christ was thus in the same act triumphant on evil, satisfying to the heart of God, and creative to the conscience of man by virtue of His solidarity with God on the one side, and on the other with the race.[216]

Honouring the Church's long-held tradition, and seeing these three strands 'wonderfully and prophetically entwined in 1 Cor. i. 30',[217] Forsyth here identifies the 'three great aspects' of Christ's work as (i) triumph, (ii) satisfaction and (iii) regeneration: 'The first emphasises the finality of our Lord's victory over the evil power or devil; the second, the finality of His satisfaction, expiation, or atonement presented to the holy power of God; and the third the finality of His sanctifying or new-creative influence on the soul of man'.[218] It is to these three movements that we now turn: to the cross as (i) satisfying the heart of God; (ii) triumphing over evil; and (iii) creating a new humanity.

The positive satisfaction of holiness: confessing holiness 'from sin's side'

> *What God seeks is not a religious tribute or present, costly but partial; His self-complete holiness requires, to meet and satisfy it, a total holy self, in a real act or deed of gift once for all, the absorption and oblation of the whole self in a crucial and objective achievement.*[219]
>
> *What is required is not an equivalent penalty, but an adequate confession of His holiness.*[220]

'If God save us in Christ', writes Forsyth, 'he saves us not first for our happiness or comfort but first for His kingdom, for His holy power, purpose, and service'.[221] Against the charge that Forsyth promotes God as 'the Arch-Egoist, the Cæsar of heaven',[222] Forsyth presses that humanity could not honour a God who owed nothing to himself.

216 *Work*, p. 224.
217 Ibid., p. 200.
218 Ibid., p. 199.
219 *Cruciality*, p. 182.
220 *Work*, p. 169.
221 *Authority*, p. 374.
222 *Life*, p. 27.

'That would not honour the God Christ preached . . . The holiness of God is the self-respect of an absolute universal; and it is the death of Egoism, and the very stay and cohesion of social and cosmic existence'.[223] Both creation and God, therefore, have a stake in the priority of divine holiness.

Forsyth even presses that God 'required' Christ's death, 'not simply as a lever to lift man but as a function of the self-respect of the Absolute, for His personal satisfaction and the hallowing of His eternal name'.[224] Forsyth avers that the foundation of all reality is bound up with holiness whose demand and deed are both unsparing. Moreover, the incarnation represents a moral necessity for God more than it does a rescue from humanity's predicament, though the two are not at all unrelated. In the cross, God 'found Himself',[225] creation's moral order was restored, the dread knot drawn into a tight snarl by humanity's blasphemous misuse of divinely given freedom was undone, and the saved conscience reintegrated into the justice of the universe.

It was principally the Father and what was owed to him that filled the Son's thoughts at the end. Forsyth recalls that as much as the Father's love is ever for the world, what he loves most is not his prodigal, nor even his saint, but his delightsome Son who is the most 'perfect and perpetual reflection' of his own holiness and 'in whom His satisfaction is eternal'.[226] Consequently, Christ was self-constrained, 'constituted by His very holiness', to atone.[227] The Holy Father looks at the Son, sees himself reflected and is well pleased, even 'satisfied'. There is nothing contractual here, as though the Son were undergoing an eternal performance review. Rather, the reflection of the Father's holiness is ever the delight of the Son whose words and actions are given by the Father. Moreover, the Father's pleasure and the Son's joyful obedience do not undergo any shift in the Son's enfleshment. Indeed, the Father continues to delight in, and to see himself in, his holy Son, and the *Word* of God continues, in the Spirit, to return the words and action of God to God's self. And because of the identity of the Word, this twofold action defines God's relationship with the world. In this way, the Word, Forsyth insists, constitutes 'the last reality' – that a 'perfectly holy God' should make atonement for an unholy world in the 'perfectly holy Son'. In this action, holiness is met by 'a holiness equal to its own'.[228]

It was the holiness that makes sin so sinful that demanded confession, 'the due and understanding acknowledgment of the holiness offended'.[229] Before all else, Christ's cross was 'an offering made by God to His own holiness', the finished and effectual restitution of God's holiness upon 'the ruins of the evil power'.[230] Holiness must have its due. And because it is most important to God that God's name be hallowed, this is the first function of God's cross. God's holiness therefore necessitates Christ's work, calls for it and provides it. This, for Forsyth, is another way of saying that that holy, righteous,

223 'Sinless', p. 301.
224 Ibid., p. 297; cf. 'Inner Life', p. 155; 'Christ's Person', pp. 7–8.
225 *Society*, p. 30; cf. *Jesus*, p. 25; *Work*, p. 204.
226 *War*, p. 179.
227 'Inner Life', p. 159.
228 Ibid., p. 159.
229 *Work*, p. 189.
230 *Society*, p. 26; cf. *Cruciality*, pp. 50–51.

good and eternal Law must be upheld and cannot, under any circumstance, be waived, warned off or bought off in its claim, that in God's own eternal nature the Law has 'an undying claim to which [God] must *give effect* in due judgment somewhere, if He is to redeem a world'.[231] The implementation of divine holiness by judgement therefore is as essential to universal and eternal Fatherhood as is the outflow of God's love. It is not enough that God be holy. God's holiness must be met and confessed from creation's side, by a love equally holy – even if God personally has to do it.

> God is always the author of His own satisfaction: that is to say, His holiness is always equal to its own atonement. God in the Son is the perfect satisfaction and joy of God in the Father; and God holy in the sinful Cross is the perfect satisfaction of God the holy in the sinless heavens. Satisfaction there must be in God's own nature, whether under the conditions of perfect obedience in a harmonious world, or under those of obedience jarred and a world distraught.[232]

Christ's death, therefore, is not only the making of 'our bad cause His own'[233] but also a gift, as it were, of God's grace to God's self. It is God's perfect recognition of God's own holiness, meeting God's own charge against us and bearing God's own judgement against sin. It is the kingship of sovereignty meeting an equally holy kingship of subordination. It is God's pledge to God – and to us – of the universal triumph of holy love. God's name is hallowed as God realizes God's own holiness in the other. This, Forsyth insists, God achieves by 'really judging and subjugating once for all the unholy thing everywhere, killing it in its eye', and ousting Satan's kingdom with God's. 'It could be done only by bringing to practical effect an answering and trusting holiness on a world scale amid the extremest conditions created by human sin, by bringing universal sin to the final light and fire of the eternal holiness it challenged, by showing both sin in its radical sinfulness and destroying it in the searching and consuming fire of holy heavenly love on earth'.[234]

Forsyth swears that God is not reconciled by any third party: 'God came, He did not send'.[235] It was God who acted in Christ; God, and not the truth about God, who is our salvation. Revealed here – perhaps more than anywhere else – is Forsyth's commitment to the homoousion of Alexandrian and Athanasian christology. Rejecting the notion of conditional forgiveness as it found voice, for example in W. H. Fremantle[236] – the Dean of Ripon 'who had been one of the pillars of Evangelicalism and a vigorous denouncer of "Essays and Reviews"'[237] – Forsyth declared at the opening address of the Third

231 *Father*, p. 10.
232 *Work*, p. 205.
233 'Sinless', p. 304.
234 Ibid., p. 299; cf. *Authority*, p. 158; *Parnassus*, p. 227; 'Holy Father', p. 94; 'Christian Principle', p. 149.
235 'Christianity of Christ', p. 263.
236 William Henry Fremantle, 'The Atonement in Modern Religious Thought', in *The Atonement in Modern Religious Thought: A Theological Symposium* by Frédéric Louis Godet et al. (New York: Thomas Whittaker, 1901), pp. 168, 169: 'the death of Christ . . . is the means of securing the mercy and favour of God, of procuring the forgiveness of sins'.
237 Anonymous, 'Death of Dr. W. H. Fremantle: Dean of Ripon for 20 Years', *The Times*, 26 December 1916, p. 4.

International Congregational Council at Edinburgh in July 1908: 'Procured grace is a contradiction in terms. The atonement did not procure grace, it flowed from grace.'[238] And, in 1914: '[The Cross] was God at this gracious work, not waiting to be gracious. It was his grace in historic and decisive operation, it was not an external and prior contribution which made the action of grace possible.'[239] So Forsyth does not speak of God 'being reconciled' but of God 'reconciling' – 'living, dying, and redeeming' – lovingly going out towards sinners.[240] What was historically offered *to* God was eternally offered *by* God. God did not send an agent, a function or a factor. Rather, in Christ, the whole Godhead was involved in our redemption. Father and Spirit were neither spectators nor sympathizers of the Son's agony but agents in it. Indeed, Forsyth argues that the significant thing in the atonement happened 'within the Godhead's unity', in a personal exchange of worship between Father, Son and Spirit; the cross being an open window into the very heart of the Trinity.[241] Atonement therefore takes place not only on the cross but within the inner being of God. One commentator charges Forsyth here with appearing to 'know almost too much about the Trinitarian "family"';[242] however, anything less than what Forsyth is proposing might suggest schism in the Triune relations, indifference in God towards us and an unjust wrath heaped upon an innocent victim. If the cross is not equally the Father's act then it represents only 'unrelieved darkness and despair',[243] undermining Christian assurance and hope. It is at this point that Forsyth distinguishes between 'evangelical' and 'humanist' Christianity. The former contends that the prime doer in Christ's cross was God: Christ was *God* reconciling, *God* doing the very best for humanity. '"God was in Christ reconciling", not reconciling through Christ, but actually present as Christ reconciling, doing in Christ His own work of reconciliation'.[244] As early as his ordination in 1876, Forsyth confesses of 2 Corinthians 5.19a that he would 'be prepared to stake the whole of Christianity upon [this] one short, simple and mighty creed'.[245] The 'humanist', conversely, believes, according to Forsyth, that Christ was merely a human being doing his very best before God, and in so doing serving as a model for our emulation.

Forsyth urges that more than the confession 'I have sinned' is required by divine holiness. Indeed, such a confession is a 'poor acknowledgment' of God's holiness because it was not words or feelings that wounded God, but action. Confession then entails life and deed. Christ's confession, therefore, is immensely practical – acknowledging God's holiness with the same kind of practical reality in which sin is done. So conceived,

238 *Cruciality*, p. 78. Sell reckons this 'the most important single sentence in the whole of twentieth-century theology'. Sell, *Nonconformist Theology*, p. 172.

239 'Regeneration – I', p. 632.

240 *Jesus*, p. 23; cf. Thomas Erskine, *The Unconditional Freeness of the Gospel: In Three Essays* (Edinburgh: Waugh and Innes, 1873), pp. 80, 93.

241 *Cruciality*, p. 78.

242 Jones, 'The Christological Thought of Peter Taylor Forsyth and Emil Brunner', p. 426.

243 Thomas F. Torrance, 'The Goodness and Dignity of Man in the Christian Tradition', in *Christ in Our Place – The Humanity of God in Christ for the Reconciliation of the World: Essays Presented to Professor James Torrance* (ed. Trevor Hart and Daniel Thimell; Exeter/Allison Park: Paternoster Press/Pickwick Publications, 1989), p. 378.

244 *Work*, p. 152.

245 'Ordination Statement', p. 4.

salvation is not an idea, nor a group of words, but an act which confesses holiness from sin's side, and by so doing re-establishes holiness in the created order.

What Moberly calls 'a perfectly adequate holiness; a response worthy of the holiness of God'[246] alone satisfies holiness. Neither pain, penalty, passionate remorse, repentance, verbal acknowledgment, good deeds nor ritual can satisfy the claim of holy law. Holiness alone, and that on the same scale as the law disregarded, can do that. And because Christ alone can feel holiness' full response in judging sin, he alone is uniquely placed to confess and honour it. Such 'adequate confession' must come from sin's side, from the lips – nay, the life – of a 'perfectly holy man' who in his own personal holiness represents the entire race – the conscience of humanity – before God. 'It is not enough that the eternal validity of the holy law should be declared as some prophet might arise and declare it, with power to make the world admire, as the great and sublime Kant did.'[247] Neither is it enough if holiness be confessed abstractly. This is because, Forsyth insists, wounded holiness is wounded *personal* holiness and as such can only be met by a holiness equally personal and – if it is to be filled with soteriological import – holiness which represents *both* the sinful race *and* the One wounded. As we shall now see, such confession also involves judgement; indeed, the acknowledgment that judgement itself is holy, wise, good and converts into blessing, vertical and horizontal reconciliation, and the disarming of sin's power.

The negative satisfaction of holiness: Confessing holiness in sin-bearing judgement

> *In His Cross He confessed and satisfied the holiness of God in a way so intimate, so absolute, that it was also the radical exposure of sin in all its sinfulness, and thus it became its destruction. If the sinless could not confess sin, He exposed it. He could, and did, confess the holiness which throws sin into complete exposure and ruin.*[248]

> *Christ accepted the judgment holiness must pass upon sin, and did so in a way that confessed it as holy from amidst the deepest experience of it, the experience not of a spectator but a victim. His obedience was not merely a fine, perfect, and mighty harmony of His own with God's blessed will; but it was the acceptance on man's behalf of that judgment which sin had entailed, and the confession on man's behalf in a tremendous act that the judgment was good and holy. For the holiness of God makes two demands: first, for an answering holiness in love, and second, for a judgment on those who do not answer but defy. And Christ met both, in one and the same act.*[249]

Forsyth maintains that in Christ there is a twofold judgement that takes place – the world passed judgement on God and God passed judgement on the world. Moreover,

[246] Robert Campbell Moberly, *Atonement and Personality* (London: John Murray, 1901), p. 99.
[247] *Work*, pp. 126–27.
[248] *Preaching*, p. 172.
[249] *Work*, p. 206.

Forsyth's notion of judgement involves a twofold word: (i) the demonstration, securing and establishing of God's holiness, and (ii) holy love's victory over sin. Just as Anselm sought to expose the Abelardian tendencies of his time by arguing that it is impossible for God to treat sin *as if it were not sin*, Forsyth exposes liberalism's tendency to ignore responsibility to divine holiness. And he does so without severing holiness from love, as 'severe orthodoxy' has done.[250] Of essence to Christ's confession of holiness was, Forsyth believes, 'the securing and establishing of God's holy and righteous judgment throughout the moral world to its victory in love'.[251] What Christ 'recognized' was not sin's equivalent punishment, but sin's due judgement, penalty and condemnation – the consequence attached to sin *by God*.[252] Holiness recognizes sin – indeed it 'makes sin sin'[253] – and exerts its power in Christ who spreads sin out, draws it to himself as a magnet, provoking sin to its hideous climax, revealing the full gravity of the human situation, bears it and carries it to its execution. It is not enough that evil should be restrained: 'Holiness had to be set up and secured in history.'[254]

Forsyth's second book, *Religion in Recent Art*, did not appear until after he had begun his successful ministry at Clarendon Park in 1888, but it already betrayed certain of Forsyth's convictions about the cross that were never to leave him, thus cautioning against any suggestion of a radical shift of theology from his 1891 'conversion' onwards. Developed from both his 1887 lectures to 'a promiscuous audience'[255] at the Workingman's Club in Manchester, and his hearing of Richard Wagner in Bayreuth in 1882, Forsyth offers in this book one of the best interpretations of Hegel's *Æsthetik* available in English. The final two chapters are devoted to Wagner. Earlier chapters trace the spiritual evolution of art through Dante Gabriel Rossetti, Edward Coley Burne-Jones, George Frederick Watts[256] and William Holman Hunt, who 'represents the best that has yet been done by Protestant Christianity in the way of Art. It is Art inspired by the spirit of the Resurrection rather than of the Crucifixion'.[257] The spiritual power of Hunt's work is evidenced in a painting like 'The Scapegoat' of which Forsyth offers 'a *tour de force* of twentieth century art criticism'.[258] Forsyth sees in this work the despised Christ travailing under the load of the world's sin, knowing the horror of despair and confronting it 'head on'. Like Hunt's goat, Christ enters into hell, into the miasmal jungle of death, into the *eretz gezerah* ('place of cutting off'[259]) where there is 'no life, but total curse, and hard, hopeless blight',[260] carrying sin's curse 'amid fearful

[250] 'Christ's Person', p. 8.
[251] *Justification*, p. 108.
[252] 'Atonement', p. 85.
[253] *Father*, p. 8; cf. 'Paradox', p. 129; *Missions*, pp. 56–57.
[254] *Preaching*, p. 223.
[255] *Art*, p. vii.
[256] Watts once pronounced Forsyth as 'the only man in England who thoroughly understands my work'. Cited in Leembruggen, 'Forsyth', p. 24.
[257] *Art*, p. 155; cf. Peter Fuller, *Theoria: Art, and the Absence of Grace* (London: Chatto & Windus, 1988), p. 145: Hunt 'had done what no other artist had ever done for Christianity; he had shown that it is not necessary for an artist, who is a Christian, to be a Catholic'.
[258] Fuller, *Theoria*, p. 145.
[259] On whether Lev. 16.22 is better translated as 'a distant place', see Gordon J. Wenham, *The Book of Leviticus* (Grand Rapids: Wm. B. Eerdmans, 1979), pp. 233–35.
[260] *Art*, p. 185.

loneliness and agony, into the presence of God by confession full and complete; where the sin, being thus exposed, was purged and burned away in the forgiving love of God who is a consuming fire'.[261] In the passion, sin moves to place Christ into the darkness, to isolate him from his community and from God. But in Christ's truthful confession, sin is exposed and guilt removed. Or, as Dietrich Bonhoeffer would put it, in Christ, 'the unexpressed [is] . . . openly spoken and acknowledged. All that is secret and hidden is made manifest'.[262] If death is judgement, then, as Forsyth writes in another place, Christ's was

> the death of death . . . because He tasted the death in death, and visited the caverns of horror that underlie the soul, and are seldom entered even by the dying man. He tasted the death of the universal soul – death eternal . . . He tasted death as it can only be tasted by the moral delicacy of the High and Holy One, who feels Himself in the atmosphere of base, revolting sin, of moral atheism, ashiness, mustiness, torpor, dust . . . He tasted the death of the million, death 'for every man', the death which is the death of all of us.[263]

One consequence of such a commitment, as we shall see more fully in the final chapter, is that 'Death and Hell should be no more'.[264] *As death*, Christ's was itself, as Forsyth understands it, a receiving of the guilty verdict upon those he identified with.[265] Forsyth insists that Christ's identification with sin meant a moral process wherein evil was mastered in the 'Armageddon of [Christ's] soul'.[266] That Christ took on mortal (i.e. deathly) flesh and died with it (i.e. came under God's judgement) is of the utmost soteriological significance. That this judgement is also pronounced in his resurrection provides a foundation for Christian hope. Certainly Forsyth could make more of this prospective element of judgement announced in the resurrection than he does. However, it is not that he discards such a theological claim so much as he underscores with such unrelenting volume the *death* of Christ, sounding that Christ's death has meaning for us because he redeems from our situation, absorbing into his own person the judgement due to humanity. The suffering that Christ endured was the penalty of sin itself (rather than God's punishment[267]). Moreover, while Christ's suffering was penal it was not, for Forsyth, penitential. It was attended by not one hint of one self-accusation. As we have already noted, at no stage did Christ ever feel that God was punishing him, even though it was 'sin's Nemesis' and consequence – the penalty attached by God – that

[261] Ibid., p. 186.

[262] Dietrich Bonhoeffer, *Life Together* (trans. John W. Doberstein; New York: Harper & Row, 1954), p. 112.

[263] *Father*, pp. 52, 53, 55.

[264] 'Hell', p. 4.

[265] The question this raises as to why then we must go on to face our own 'ending time' is attended to by Karl Barth in *Church Dogmatics III.2* (ed. Geoffrey W. Bromiley and Thomas F. Torrance; trans. Harold Knight et al.; Edinburgh: T&T Clark, 1960), pp. 587–640.

[266] 'Regeneration – I', p. 635.

[267] Forsyth distinguishes between 'punishment' and 'penalty' in *Work*, pp. 162–65; cf. John McIntyre, *The Shape of Soteriology: Studies in the Doctrine of the Death of Christ* (Edinburgh: T&T Clark, 1992), p. 44; James Denney, *The Christian Doctrine of Reconciliation* (London: Hodder & Stoughton, 1917), pp. 272–73.

he bore and recognized.[268] Here Forsyth also distinguishes between punishment and judgement. Only judgement can establish holiness upon the wreck of sin. Punishment has no such value, a distinction often missed by Forsyth's critics.[269]

Christ brought sin before God, aggravated it, made it exceedingly sinful, drove it to a crisis through which it was condemned and extinguished it in principle and for eternity, lest it 'lift its head and hide the grace it could not kill'.[270] This, Forsyth insists, is what the confession of holiness entails, a confession wrought by one sympathetic enough with humanity to 'do it from their side' and sinless enough to know 'what sin meant for God'.[271] To be sure, Forsyth contends that it was both metaphysically possible and ethically impossible for Christ to sin. While Christ felt the full lure of sin, he did not yield to it. But he is no less human for that, for 'what is truly human is not sin. Sin is no factor of the true humanity'.[272] Moreover, in Jesus, we see sin's effects *on God* – 'see it slay Christ, and then dissolve and die in His atoning prayer ... The sinless is the only being on earth who ever really understood what sin meant. He alone, whom it never soiled, could carry it before God in all its foul horror'.[273] Here Forsyth follows Hegel who presses that Christ died no natural death but 'the aggravated death of the evil-doer ... in Him humanity was carried to its furthest point'.[274] The debt to Hegel is further realized when Forsyth follows Hegel's contention that in Christ's death God makes death itself an aspect of God's own eternal life. It is God who dies on the cross, but because God remains the living One even in death, Christ's death is the death of death itself, the negation of negation. In becoming as sin, God makes himself identical with his antithesis – his extremest opposite, with what is alien to himself – in order to annihilate it. In perfect freedom, God dies, expending (emptying) himself into his opposite – sin and death – in order to bring an end to his own negation. 'In this death [God] comes to Himself'.[275] As Slavoj Žižek expresses it: 'In the standard form of atheism, God dies for men who stop believing in Him; in Christianity, God dies *for Himself*'.[276] The death of God, therefore, means God's life and death's death. The 'self-abrogation of the determinations of the antithesis' constitutes the 'affirmation' of life.[277]

This constitutes, as Forsyth understands it, the final judgement – 'the crisis of all crises for history', the world's 'last' and 'great day' of judgement, the 'moral Armageddon of the race'[278] – of all that is opposed to the triumph of God's hallowing of all things. Any future judgement is but the outworking of Christ's cross in detail. The cross denotes

[268] 'Atonement', p. 85.
[269] See William Wilson, *Dr. Forsyth and the War: A Pacifist's Reply* (London: Headley Bros., 1917), pp. 3, 10, 19.
[270] *Jesus*, p. 90.
[271] *Work*, p. 189.
[272] *Person*, p. 302.
[273] 'Paradox', p. 130.
[274] Hegel, *Philosophy of Religion*, 3:89; cf. Hegel, *Philosophy of Religion*, 3:90; Denney, *The Second Epistle to the Corinthians*, p. 220: '... in Christ on His cross, by divine appointment, the extremest opposites met and became one incarnate righteousness and the sin of the world'.
[275] Hegel, *Philosophy of Religion*, 2:221.
[276] Slavoj Žižek, *The Puppet and the Dwarf: The Perverse Core of Christianity* (Cambridge: MIT Press, 2003), p. 15.
[277] Hegel, *Philosophy of Religion*, 1:196, 204.
[278] 'Moral Principle', p. 11.

holy love's dealing with a Lancelot race until the confession of holiness required for the ongoing life of that race itself is owned and perfectly praised. 'God could not forgive until man confessed and confessed not only his own sin but confessed still more – God's holiness in the judgment of sin. The confession also had to be made in life and action, as the sin was done.'[279]

Only then has judgement done its perfect work. Not until sin had done its worst, and had in that culminating act been foiled, judged and overcome could creation – and God – be reconciled. Pastorally, this means that God deals with sinful hostility and not merely with sluggishness and passive dullness of heart. In Christ, God has provided for humanity *and for himself* One who does justice to what is most perfect and real in the universe – the holiness of God's love. In the obedient Son, God's love is hallowed, for it 'must be hallowed, even if [God] spare not His Son. His Son spared not Himself in the hallowing of that name. It was the first function of His Cross'.[280] So understood, judgement's *telos* is not condemnatory but soteriological. So Forsyth notes that in the Old Testament judgement is 'not a terror . . . but the grandest hope'.[281] This is because it is precisely through the 'negative side of judgment' that holiness determines its end, perfectly finds, delights in and satisfies itself – repairs itself 'amid the conditions of universal sin'.[282]

It is not enough that the whole human race – or even its perfect representative – should come confessing, 'We have offended against Thy holy law.' To be sure, such confession would recognize the rightful place of God's law, 'but it would not give it its own, it would not bring to pass that which is essential to holiness, namely, judgment'.[283] Moreover, it would fail to establish the very holiness it seeks to set up throughout creation. For the actual adjustment of all things under the joyful aegis of holiness, judgement is the divine 'must', as necessary to the securing of human dignity as it is to the securing of the world itself and of the eternity of divine being.

> We need a religion which decides the eternal destiny of man; and unless holiness were practically and adequately established – not merely recognised and eulogised, but established – there could be no real, deep, permanent change in the world or the sinner. The change in the treatment of us by eternal grace must rest on judgment taking effect. Man is not forgiven simply by forgetting and mending, by agreeing that no more is to be said about it.[284]

It was not 'mere clamant justice', therefore, that God meted out on sin but the 'law of hungering holiness'.[285] Judgement, in other words, is no corollary or by-product of the gospel, but is intrinsic to it. Here Forsyth departs from Grotius whose reductionist staurology of a 'penal example or object-lesson' substitutes 'a device of God for an

279 *Work*, p. 152.
280 *Justification*, p. 11.
281 *Work*, pp. 127–28.
282 Ibid., p. 135; *Jesus*, p. 88.
283 *Work*, p. 127.
284 Ibid., pp. 128–29.
285 'Atonement', p. 68.

element in Him. Judgment is an essential element in Fatherhood, and not a corrective device'.[286] Forsyth contends that while justice might be satisfied with penalty, the *only* satisfaction to holiness is holiness. He believes too that 'the old non-ethical and "hard-shell" orthodoxy, where divine justice is satisfied by penalty instead of divine holiness by sanctity, has tended to concur with a low public ethic'.[287] 'Justice wants penalty, holiness wants holiness in the midst of penalty'.[288] Apart from judgement, there is no guaranteeing the enduring reality and irresistible sovereignty of holy love, nor surety that God is not other than he has shown himself to be in Jesus Christ, nor that the revelation of God's passion for universal righteousness and sanctification is adequately met.

Forsyth maintains that God would not, and could not, save humanity by lessening the gravity that attends guilt. And as only the God-Man could, he did not shrink from his calling and so converted the suffering he endured *from* the worst the world had to give into a suffering *for* the world through which he gave all that God had to give. When Christ touched sin, therefore, he touched it as Redeemer. His suffering would have been decidedly and prodigiously different had he not faced sin as its destroyer, but his final word to every boastful and dissonant voice was 'No. You shall not be at all'. So understood, judgement is grace. As Schlatter has it: '[Jesus] had always been ready to sanctify God's righteousness, even by his own death, and had always seen in the execution of justice the complete act of grace'.[289]

In order to be conquered, sin had first to be expressed. This expression is the fruit of the economy of holiness itself which makes sin 'so sinful' and its 'wickedness so furiously to rage' against God. This is what holiness does as it comes in 'close quarters with human sin'.[290] In Christ, God brought all sin to one concentrated point and 'dealt with it as a unity', forcing a 'final crisis of the universal conscience to decide it for good'. God in Christ, and Christ in God, 'forced battle unto victory once for all, for the race and for eternity'.[291] The manifestation of this concentration is physically and morally violent. This does not mean that violence is part of God's ontology or that violence *itself* gives efficacy to the atonement, but that in the face of sin's violent worst, it is morally proper, Forsyth believes, that God should redeem through an act that exposes the violence of sin. There can be no talk of a transaction (or deception) taking place either with God, or behind God's back (with the Devil, for example[292]) because the submission to judgement is undertaken by 'a conscience unblunted in its moral perceptions'.[293]

> As Judge of all the earth, as the Conscience of the conscience, Christ is absolute in His judgment, unsparing and final in His condemnation. But as the second

[286] *Justification*, p. 171, fn. 1.
[287] *Society*, p. 32.
[288] *Father*, p. 11.
[289] Schlatter, *The History of the Christ*, p. 317.
[290] *Cruciality*, p. 194.
[291] Ibid., p. 117.
[292] Forsyth does suggest in one place, however, that 'there is a certain truth (if we will be very careful with it) in the early Christian fantasy that Satan was befooled by the patient naïveté of Christ. That is the irony of history . . .'. *Justification*, p. 205.
[293] 'Atonement', p. 75.

> Adam and Man of men He attracts, accepts and absorbs in Himself His own holy judgment; and He bears, in man and for man, the double crisis and agony of His own two-edged vision of purity and guilt. He whose purity has the sole right to judge has by the same purity the only power to feel and realise such judgment.[294]

In his death, Christ 'absorbed' sin's punishment entirely. The 'sin of sins' is now 'fixed refusal of that Grace',[295] a sin which remains, at least in theory, the absurd possibility. In Anselm's words, 'God cannot properly leave anything uncorrected in His kingdom ... To leave sin unpunished would be tantamount to treating the sinful and the sinless alike, which would be inconsistent with God's nature. And this inconsistency is injustice.'[296] Clearly, Forsyth insists, what happened in Christ was no case of wiping a slate clean. 'Sin is graven in. You cannot wipe off sin' which goes into the 'tissue of the spiritual being'. Nor was it a case of 'destroying an unfortunate prejudice we had against God', or of simply righting a misunderstanding. 'Sin ... alters things for both parties. Guilt affected both God and man.'[297] Put otherwise, the good news announced in Romans 8.1 is therefore good news *for God* too.

> All sin inflicts a death on God. It is a *diminutio capitis*. It reduces His headship. It imposes on Him a limitation which is quite unlike all His other determinations in that it is not self-determined, and is therefore absolutely intolerable. If His self-determining power were not capable of a determination mightier than the alien one from sin, sin would conquer, and death would reign. But the meaning of the Incarnation is that God was capable, in His self-emptying in Christ, of a self-limitation, *i.e.* a self-mastery of holy surrender, whose moral effect was more than equal to the foreign invasion by sin. He died *unto* sin, as man dies *by* it ... All sin aims at a destruction of God, which His eternal holy life repels; were it unrepelled by the reaction of judgment it would extinguish God. But the reaction and the judgment is that of loving holiness. It is saving judgment. His holiness so dies as to inflict on sin a death which it has not power to repel ... God in Christ so met the one enemy as to turn upon him His own weapon of death. God so died as to be the death of death. He commands His Own negation – even when it pierces as deep within Himself as His Son. He surmounts the last, the most limiting, phase of finitude – evil. He could so identify Himself with sin and death, His absolute antitheses, that He conquered and abolished both, in an act which brings to a point the constant victory of His moral being. The destiny of the world is whatever does most justice to the nature of God, and most glorifies it. And that is, of all things in the world, the atoning Cross of Christ – where therefore the teleology and the theodicy of the world lies.[298]

294 'Atonement', pp. 81–82.
295 *Work*, p. 156.
296 Anselm, *S. Anselmi Cantuariensis Archiepiscopi Opera Omnia* (ed. F. S. Schmitt; vol. 2; Edinburgh: Nelson, 1946), I.12. Anselm was the first to formulate this as 'injustice'. See George Cadwalader Foley, *Anselm's Theory of the Atonement: The Bohlen Lectures, 1908* (New York: Longmans, Green, & Co., 1909), p. 173.
297 *Work*, p. 84.
298 *Justification*, pp. 148–49

Forsyth's presentation of the atonement clearly defends the view that as one in whom sin found its full concentration, Christ assumed the very antithesis of holiness. Christ does this, Forsyth argues, by surmounting 'the last, the most limiting, phase of finitude – evil'. Christ, in other words, not only absorbed the full force of judgement – divine and human – but carried into that judgement a humanity upon which stood God's verdict of 'guilty'. In a rare footnote, Forsyth reveals the source of his thinking here to be Hegel's *Religionsphilosophie* (ii, 249ff.) wherein Hegel speaks of 'an act of going out on the part of God into finitude, an act of manifestation in finitude', finitude implying that 'separation of what is implicitly identical, but which maintains itself in the act of separation'.[299] In Christ, as Hegel has it, the 'Universal puts itself into antithesis with itself' in order to return to himself through the act which abolishes the 'rigidity of the antithesis'.[300] And again:

> It is their [i.e. those who stand over against the divine process] finitude which Christ has taken upon Himself, this finitude in all its forms, and which at its furthest extreme is represented by Evil; this humanity, which is itself a moment in the divine life, is now characterised as something foreign to God, as something which does not belong to His nature; this finitude, however, in its condition of Being-for-self, or as existing independently in relation to God, is evil, something foreign to God's nature; He has, however, taken our finite nature in order to slay it by His death.[301]

That on this point Hegel's words are replayed through Forsyth's voice there can be no argument. Humanity is judged in our Judge's submission to that sentence passed vis-à-vis holiness' verdict. Coming from a region 'deeper than sin or grief could shake', Christ drew on the whole Trinity to be made sin for us. But in being 'made sin', treated as sin, the 'Eternal Son, who knew no sin in His experience', experienced sin as God does (and as only God can!), and sin's effects as humans do: 'He felt sin with God, and sin's judgment with men. He realised, as God, how real sin was, how radical, how malignant, how deadly to the Holy One's very being.'[302] By living in full consent with God's will, the incarnate Son fully identifies with besmirched humanity under judgement, turning the place of rejection and death into the locus of acceptance and life. In order 'to come really near mankind'[303] God literally died our death.

> He stood in the midst of human sin full of love to man, such love as enabled Him to identify Himself in the most profound, sympathetic way with the evil race; fuller still of love to the God whose name He was hallowing; and, as with one mouth, as if the whole race confessed through Him, as with one soul, as though the whole race at last did justice to God through His soul, He lifted up His face unto God and said,

[299] Hegel, *Philosophy of Religion*, 3:38. The ET of the passage to which Forsyth refers is found in Volume III.

[300] Ibid., pp. 87, 111.

[301] Ibid., pp. 92–93.

[302] *Work*, p. 82; *Cruciality*, pp. 212–13.

[303] *Missions*, p. 10.

> 'Thou art holy in all Thy judgments, even in this judgment which turns not aside even from Me, but strikes the sinful spot if even I stand on it.'[304]

Yet while Christ was beside humanity in court justifying the world, he was foremostly on God's side in the issue, representing God, confessing God's holiness in judgement, 'and justifying [God's] treatment of sin. Justifying God!'[305] 'It was one of us that was labouring, fighting, trusting, dying, conquering; but it was Godhead as one of us.'[306] Inclining towards monophysitism insofar as Christ is here presented as being more priest than victim, Forsyth urges that 'our Redeemer must save us by his difference from us, however the salvation get home by his parity with us. He saves because he is God and not man.'[307] And again: Jesus 'stood for the hallowing of God's name as He had stood all along, whether in His rebukes of the Pharisees or in the cleansing of the Temple ... He stood on God's side against men, even while He stood for them.'[308] As determined as Forsyth is here to safeguard the sheer freedom and graciousness of grace, he does not do so at the expense of articulating with like verve that Christ did not fully enter 'the penumbra of our penalty' in order that – 'from the very midst and depth of it' – the confession and praise of God's holiness might 'rise like a spring of fresh water at the bottom of the bitter sea, and sweeten all.'[309] In other words, Forysth does not abrogate the absoluteness of divine gratuity by playing it off against what must be confessed from below. Not only is the possibility of overcoming such a counterbalance made possible by God, but it is precisely through such that, as Hegel also insists, 'everything established, everything moral, everything considered by ordinary opinion as of value and possessed of authority' is thoroughly brought to its terminus.[310]

Clearly, therefore, there must be no nonsense about God judging Christ. What God judged was not Christ but sin upon Christ's head.

> The Saviour was not punished, but He took the penalty of sin, the chastisement of our peace. It was in no sense as if *He felt* chastised or condemned (as even Calvin said), but because He willingly bowed, with a moral understanding possible only to the sinless, under the divine ordinance of a suffering death and judgment which was holily ordained to wait on the sin of His kin.[311]

It has been suggested that the distinction Forsyth draws between *bearing sin's penalty* and *being punished* is ambiguous and perhaps little more than a semantic device.[312] The distinction, however, is more important than is sometimes supposed. The Father is never anything but 'well pleased' with his Son. Yet Christ was 'made sin' for us in a way that he could never have been if he had been made 'a sinner'. Sin is here personified.

304 *Work*, p. 150.
305 *Cruciality*, p. 213; cf. 'Distinctive Thing', p. 498.
306 *Father*, p. 40.
307 *Person*, p. 342; cf. 'Christianity of Christ', pp. 255–56; 'Genius', pp. 436–37.
308 *Jesus*, p. 20.
309 *Cruciality*, p. 79; *Work*, p. 148.
310 Hegel, *Philosophy of Religion*, 3:91; cf. Hegel, *Philosophy of Religion*, 3:96.
311 *Cruciality*, p. 215.
312 Sell, 'Unsystematic Systematician', p. 121.

Christ is 'made sin' because it is sin itself that 'had to be judged, more even than the sinner'.[313] This does not undermine the substitutionary nature of Christ's death, but rather stresses that Christ becomes the proper recipient of holiness' judgement: 'God made Him sin, treated Him as if He were sin; He did not view Him as sinful. That is quite another matter. God made Him to be sin – it does not say He made Him sinful. God lovingly treated Him as human sin, and with His consent judged human sin in Him and on Him.'[314] Christ, in Forsyth's presentation, represents sin and confesses God's holiness from within the 'penumbra' of world judgement,[315] thereby subverting sin as the antithesis of holiness. By confessing holiness on sin's behalf, as it were, Christ does not redeem sin or transform it into something else (something that could be redeemed, for example). Rather, the confession itself is sin's suicide. The logic at work here is this: The moment sin confesses holiness, sin is expunged. By equating (with both paradox and metonymy) Christ with sin (rather than only with the sinner), Christ's death *is* the death of sin. The judgement therefore that fell 'where it was perfectly understood, owned, and praised' was accompanied by judgement's sanctifying effect through which holiness is given at last its own. Thus the twin-goal – that holiness might be perfected in judgement, and humanity become the righteousness of God – occurs in one place; namely, in Jesus Christ.

The creative satisfaction of holiness: Confessing holiness in the new humanity

> *If holiness can be satisfied with nothing but holiness it can only be with a holiness which itself creates. God alone can create in us the holiness that will please Him. And this He has done in Jesus Christ incarnate. But it is in Jesus Christ as the creator of man's holiness, not as the organ of it, as man's sanctifier, and not merely man's delegate. Christ is our reconciler because on the Cross He was our redeemer from sin's power into no mere independence or courage or safety, but into real holiness; because the same act that redeems us produces holiness, and presents us in this holiness to God and His communion . . . Christ's holiness is the satisfying thing to God, because it is not only the means but also the anticipation of our holiness, because it carries all our future holiness latent in it and to God's eye patent; because in His saving act He is the creative power of which our new life is the product. It is not only that Christ conquered for Himself and emerged with His soul for a prey, but, He being what He was, His victory contained ours. If He died all died. It was not only that all the sin of the world, pointed to its worst, could not make Him a sinner. It was that by all the holiness of eternity He had power to make the worst sinners saints.*[316]

A most substantial accent of Forsyth's notion of holiness is also its most creative: holiness' potential for self-recovery. By explicating holiness in terms of personality,

[313] *Work*, p. 83.
[314] Ibid., pp. 150–51.
[315] Ibid., p. 147.
[316] Ibid., pp. 208–09.

Forsyth witnesses to holiness' creative desire: 'The Cross of Christ is not merely the holy summit of the moral order. *Sub specie æternitatis*, it is its creative source.'[317] Holiness does not overcome its antithesis by merely destroying it, but also through a recreation of those for whom sin has become a way of being. Judgement is holiness' mandatory response to its antithesis, but judgement alone does not present the positive obedience and recognition which holiness claims. The self-recovery holiness seeks, in other words, is not exhausted until it finds itself realized fully from creation's side. This is creation's *telos*, *raison d'être* and consummation, and occupies 'God at his most godlike work'.[318]

> Christ's work was above all creative. It had not simply a creative element in it, as our moral victories have, but it was the crowning act of the Holy One on a first creation's wreck. It was the work of the God who created man for the active commission of His own holiness, and who carried creative action to its last form, its true close, and its inner significance by the Cross; so that Christ's work was the new creation for which the first was made, and not merely the last wave of the first.[319]

In 1897, the Principal of New College London, R. Vaughan Pryce, published a paper in which he argued that no witness to Christ's work is complete if it obscures its moral end: 'Its aim is to produce holiness'.[320] Forsyth concurs, articulating that the purpose and goal of human history is the creation of a new sanctified humanity, 'a new life, a new moral self, a new consciousness of moral reality', out of the wreck of sin.[321] This is 'the passion of Christ writ large' and whose work is 'the new creation *in nuce*',[322] 'a new creation in history, at once moral and mystical, individual and universal'.[323]

Forsyth believes that Christ did not find an already existing public, but 'like a great new poet He had to make His own constituency'.[324] This new humanity is, for Forsyth, foremostly a reference to the Church, 'the greatest thing in the universe'.[325] The Church, he argues, is not an entity that can be situated in binary polarity vis-à-vis the world. Rather the creation of the Church inaugurates the apocalyptic creation of a new and holy order arising from the ashes of the cross. It is 'the final and direct object' of God's election because each soul in the Church represents a 'cell' of that great Society God is creating.[326] To be the Church, therefore, is to be that *qahal* in which the human race has been transformed from negative into positive service. It is also to be hopefully oriented towards that *telos* when all created reality is liberated from the old order and integrated

317 *Justification*, p. 199.
318 'Regeneration – I', p. 635.
319 Ibid., p. 638.
320 R. Vaughan Pryce, 'The Redemptive Work of the Lord Jesus Christ', in *The Ancient Faith in Modern Light* (ed. T. Vincent Tymms et al.; Edinburgh: T&T Clark, 1897), p. 226.
321 Allen, 'The Christology of P. T. Forsyth', p. 157; cf. 'Sacramentalism', p. 268.
322 *War*, p. 189; *Person*, p. 280.
323 'Regeneration – I', p. 632; cf. 'Church Fabric', p. 416.
324 'Christianity of Christ', p. 258.
325 *Work*, p. 5.
326 *Authority*, p. 353; *Society*, p. 31.

into the new. It is not to be a mere remnant of the race but its destiny. Forsyth resists the temptation to draw too ontological a distinction between world and Church as if they are two separate entities occupying some univocal metaphysic. He also resists any suggestion that the Church is the continuation of the Incarnation. Instead, the creation of the Church marks the beginning of Christ's apocalyptic annihilation of the old world, the creating of a new order of being in which all created reality is integrated into the communion of the triune God through union with Christ who takes the form of *de*formed humanity that humanity might be *re*formed from ugliness and *con*formed to the *imago Christi*. The new humanity created in Christ implicitly, but realized proleptically in the Church (as humanity's firstfruits), is central in and indispensable to Forsyth's thinking about holiness. The Church, Forsyth claims, constitutes holiness answering the holiness that made it.[327] This too is part of Christ's offering to God. Employing a eucharistic cadence, we might say that in the Incarnation, God *took* humanity, *blessed* it, *broke* it and then *gave* it to himself sanctified. The grammar of 'satisfaction' is most appropriate in this context. That Christ is 'the only real and fundamental reconciliation'[328] is beyond debate. That Christ offered his body as a living sacrifice, as holy and pleasing to God, as his act of worship, serves to make our so doing possible.

> We hallow into worship all our subjective experience by His objective work and its real presence. He not only stirs our emotions by His memory, but being in us, mingled with our experience, He consecrates them and carries them to God. He makes worship of them by creating them, and by incorporating our act with its parent act, with the sole, sufficient, and all-hallowing act of worship ever done to God, namely, His own soul's obedience, agony, victory, and praise. No religious excitement or energy is worship till sanctified thus, either within our knowledge or beyond.[329]

As ecclesial head, Christ presents to the Father a 'perfect racial obedience' for his 'complete joy and satisfaction'. 'God's holiness found itself again in the humbled holiness of Christ's "public person." He presented before God a race He created for holiness.'[330] Hart helpfully observes:

> In some sense . . . the 'objective' aspect of the atonement in Christ is precisely the vanguard, the firstfruits, the security of the ultimate return, the 'subjective' realisation of holiness in us, the historical or eschatological manifestation of the kingdom of the world. Only then will God truly be satisfied. Only then will his joy be complete. Only then will God have done justice to himself, and to his decision to create.[331]

[327] *Sacraments*, p. 25; cf. 'Reading the Bible', p. 541.
[328] 'Things New and Old', p. 275.
[329] 'Sacramentalism', pp. 270–71.
[330] *Work*, p. 129.
[331] Hart, 'Morality, Atonement and the Death of Jesus', p. 35.

As radically new as the original creation was, the new creation is more radical still, demanding much more of God. Forsyth highlights Christ's cross as a cosmic, eschatological act wherein God fulfils his eternal purpose of recreating creation for holy communion and does not 'simply prophesy it'.[332] In presenting himself, Christ offers 'implicitly and proleptically the new Humanity His holy work creates',[333] his self-presentation constituent of his office as Representative Man. It ought be noted, however, that while Forsyth regards 'representation' as more ethical and constitutional than 'substitution', he argues that understanding Christ's work as *only* representative is inadequate. With W. B. Pope[334] and J. S. Lidgett, Forsyth preferred the word 'Representative' to 'Substitute', but he was not enamoured of either. R. S. Paul certainly overplays his cards when he states that Forsyth 'would not use the word "substitution"'.[335] Forsyth's main concern with the grammar of representation is that it is too suggestive of the idea of a 'spiritual protagonist' who draws power and authority democratically from those represented. For Forsyth, Christ's 'relation to us is royal' and not elective. As humanity's 'federal person', Christ is 'head of the human race by his voluntary self-identification', 'all humanity is in him and in His act'.[336] Hence Forsyth's preference for the word 'Surety'.

One reason for Forsyth's early hesitation about penal theories is their fundamentally backward vista. Within their own terms of reference, penal models leave us pardoned criminals but not participants in God's new work. Conversely, cruciform justice is not only punitive but also transformational, bringing a new holy race to 'permanent, vital, life-deep communion with the holy God'.[337] To be sure, there is a narrative continuity between the old and the new. The 'new' humanity is the healed and restored 'old', born again in holiness with the promise of no return. This continuity depends entirely upon the continuous activity of the Triune God. Understood christologically, however, there is no metaphysical dualism here between Adam and Christ. Rather, there is a dialectical or teleological dualism that is determined by a movement from one to the other. From a race of armed rebels, Forsyth argues, God made a people at one with him, and who mirror back to him the covenant love and holiness that constitute his life. This is the foretaste and 'eternal guarantee of the historical consummation of all things some great day'.[338]

Human sanctification is understood by Forsyth to be the fruit of Christ's 'once for all' (Heb. 10.10) offering: 'Our sanctification is already presented in our justification.'[339] What Christ has already secured, humanity must (in Christ and by the Spirit) take possession of. This, too, Forsyth insists, is God's work – grace creating in humanity

332 *Work*, p. 212.
333 Ibid., p. 192.
334 See William Burt Pope, *The Person of Christ: Dogmatic, Scriptural, Historical. The Fernley Lecture of 1871, with Two Additional Essays on the Biblical and Ecclesiastical Development of the Doctrine, and Illustrative Notes* (London: Wesleyan Conference Office, 1875), p. 51.
335 Robert Sydney Paul, *The Atonement and the Sacraments: The Relation of the Atonement to the Sacraments of Baptism and the Lord's Supper* (London: Hodder & Stoughton, 1961), p. 235.
336 *Work*, pp. 210, 172, 159.
337 Ibid., p. 81.
338 Ibid., p. 130.
339 Ibid., p. 194.

the response God freely seeks. Righteousness is no 'legal fiction', therefore, but, in Christ, becomes a constituent actuality of the new humanity. So, too, is humanity's sanctification more than a 'moral fiction'; Christ has become for us wisdom from God, righteousness, sanctification and redemption (1 Cor. 1.30).

During the second century, Irenaeus explored the implications of what it means for 'the long history of the human race' to have been 'recapitulated' in Christ that we might regain 'what we had lost in Adam'.[340] Forsyth, who one suspects probably read the Fathers through the Harnack school, particularly such volumes as Loofs' *Leitfaden*,[341] believes that this short-changes Christ; Christ, Forsyth contends, does more than restore humanity to an edenic state. Rather, in Christ, God creates of 'men like Paul, and far worse men than Paul'[342] something 'new', a new humanity – norm, ethic, penitence and conscience – to echo, and commune with, the conscience of God. And through the Spirit, God makes 'unwilling givers'[343] joyously willing subjects of his praise. The new humanity created in the cross confesses the holiness of God by accepting and praising the very cross which brought an end to its old existence and created it anew.

In his post-ordination address at Shipley in 1876, Forsyth joins his former pastor in asserting that 'Man cannot "sink into himself and rise redeemed"',[344] but, having sunk into Christ in whom human sanctification is latent, redemption is irrevocable. Elsewhere, Forsyth clarifies this idea:

> This ideal perfection, being of pure free grace, is not the vision foreseen by God of our moral effort's final success. But it is the finished and foregone gift of God in Christ through our faith, and the thing which alone promises the final success of any moral efforts. In giving Christ He gave us all things – *i.e.* perfection. It is not our moral success that is presented as perfection to God even in anticipation; it is God's present to us of perfection that makes moral success possible.[345]

Christ's work satisfies because it anticipates and effects creatures becoming holy. Here Forsyth unites the subjective elements of sanctification with its objective givenness. Sanctification is a finished work being finished. This involves a transference and repetition within the human creature, a finding of its correspondent home, and a realization in humans of the experience of holy love amid the conditions of sin. It is, moreover, from first to last, an act of inexplicable grace, of God calling his children to sanctity and graciously giving them what he commands (1 Thess. 4.3–7; 5.23–24). '*The same act* as disburdens us of guilt commits us to a new life. Our Saviour in His salvation is not only our comfort but our power; not merely our rescuer but our new life.'[346] Christ does not simply pluck us out of Satan's hands, as it were, but he gives us to God. In Christ, humanity is not simply liberated from slavery, but is committed to

340 Irenaeus, *Adversus haereses* (ed. Adelin Rousseau and Louis Doutreleau; Sources chrétiennes; vol. 211; Paris: Éditions du Cerf, 1974), 342.1–344.13 (3.18.1).
341 See *Sacraments*, pp. 269, 271.
342 *Work*, p. 84.
343 Anselm, *Cur Deus Homo?*, p. 29.
344 'Ordination Statement', p. 4; cf. Brown, *Stoics and Saints*, p. 87.
345 *Father*, pp. 120–21.
346 *Work*, p. 182.

a positive liberty. Christ, Forsyth writes, does not 'simply cancel the charge against us in court and bid us walk out of jail, He meets us at the prison-door and puts us in a new way of life'.[347] The new *modus vivendi* is synonymous with discipleship. It is, both in its beginning and in its continuation, wholly enclosed by the fact that the one who has fully embraced the Father's will is in our place. If there is a corresponding human obedience, therefore, it is not with a view to securing fellowship with God. Rather, as John Webster notes, it is because this movement and direction is one which has already been established in Jesus that it can now be 'echoed, filled out and attested in our own obedience. To obey Jesus' command is to follow him; it is not to start a fresh movement but to enter into one which precedes us and catches us up into itself'.[348]

Hastings Rashdall's famous sermon 'The Abelardian Doctrine of the Atonement', preached at Oxford in 1892, contended that the justifying effect of Christ's work is not 'mere legal fiction' but real; it 'really does make men better', and not simply supply the ground why they ought to be.[349] Rashdall (and here we could also name R. S. Franks and V. F. Storr, among others) reflects the Darwinian- and Hegelian-inspired optimism in human progress, notions that were to be all but buried under the rubble of two world wars. Although Forsyth did not share the savour of naïve optimism at work in the wider culture, it was this regenerative aspect that informed the third note – with *Christus Victor* and Anselmian articulations – of Forsyth's threefold chord of Christ's cross-work. Though certainly no less, more than a change of temper from one of alienation to peace and confidence is in view here. Indeed, the atonement's work is not done until there is created a 'reciprocal communion' between humanity and God.[350] Therefore, with both Hegel and Ritschl in his sights, Forsyth presses that reconciliation involves two *persons* – two wills – and not 'an order or a process on the one hand and a person on the other'. Furthermore, this reconciliation involves 'a real and deep change' in the relationship – a change which involves not just humanity but also God. This is because, as David W. Simon reminded Robert W. Dale (his academic colleague at Spring Hill College) in their famous debate on the atonement, we are dealing with 'living persons', with organic relations, and not with abstract processes or ideas. So Forsyth: 'Any reconciliation which only means change on one side is not a real reconciliation at all'.[351] Full harmony of mind and heart and will defines the divine–human relationship. Besides, for God to forgive but to then leave the forgiven unchanged apart from some forensic standing would be to invite the estrangement and war of the past to erupt again in the future.

347 Ibid., p. 202.

348 John Webster, 'Discipleship and Obedience', *Scottish Bulletin of Evangelical Theology* 24, no. 1 (2006), pp. 4–18 (6).

349 Hastings Rashdall, *Doctrine and Development: University Sermons* (London: Methuen & Co., 1898), p. 137; cf. Hastings Rashdall, *The Idea of Atonement in Christian Theology* (London: Macmillan, 1919); Robert S. Franks, *A History of the Doctrine of the Work of Christ in its Ecclesiastical Development* (Edinburgh: Thomas Nelson, 1918); Vernon F. Storr, *The Problem of the Cross* (London: John Murray, 1919).

350 *Work*, p. 57; cf. John S. Lidgett, *The Spiritual Principle of the Atonement: As a Satisfaction Made to God for the Sins of the World: Being The Twenty-Seventh Fernley Lecture Delivered in Leeds, July, 1897* (London: Chas. H. Kelly, 1907), p. 367.

351 *Work*, p. 75. See Johnson, *English Nonconformity*, pp. 153–55; Dale A. Johnson, 'Fissures in Late-Nineteenth-Century English Nonconformity: A Case Study in One Congregation', *Church History* 66, no. 4 (1997), pp. 735–49 (745–46); Dale, *The Atonement*, pp. xlii–xliii.

Christ's holiness-confessing action did not end on the cross but the 'exhaustless energy of His saving act'[352] continues in his ascended, priestly and ecclesial humanity wherein humanity participates in the perfection of Christ's ongoing work of hallowing God's name in all the earth. The ancient call 'you shall be holy, for I am holy' (Lev. 11.45) is not a call to independent response to what God has done. Rather, it is both a command and an invitation to participate in Christ's perpetual hallowing of the Father's name. As Forsyth argues, 'Nothing short of living, loving, holy, habitual communion between His holy soul and ours can realise at last the end which God achieved in Jesus Christ.'[353]

Christ's work, in addition, has a moral effect on humanity. His satisfaction to God, in other words, is not isolated from the objects of God's love but includes 'our responsive union'. Indeed, 'our repentance and our sanctity are of saving value before God' precisely because they are 'produced by the creative holiness of Christ'.[354] In Christ, in other words, God creates in us what God promises for us. Repentance therefore takes place in the twofold movement of Christ's humanity: 'As the sole organ of this repentance Christ represents us before God, no less than He represents God to us; and so He is the sole condition of our repentance being saving repentance with God.'[355] So understood, the new humanity requires no response from ourselves to advance it out of the purview of possibility into that of actuality. Yet Forsyth also wants to insist that that death is creative and has a necessary subjective element to it – authoring in sinners the appropriate response of repentance that holiness seeks. At this point, Forsyth certainly echoes Dorner's conviction that while the end is already latent in the finished work of the cross, God's good purposes of creative love are realized through a cooperative divine–human effort by which love is organized into the life of the world. This goal involves three components: (i) the realization of a living intercourse between God and humanity through which the 'full reality' of human religious capacities – namely, holiness and blessedness – are attained; (ii) the right regulation of developed human energies towards virtuous ends; and (iii) the moral upbuilding of human life in moral communities where subjective moral capacities find objective existence, and imperfect communities 'arrive at true reality'.[356]

Forsyth's christology provides the necessary objectivity required for a credible atonement theology. Christ's death, as we have seen, is constitutive for sanctification rather than merely illustrative. Also, avoiding the mechanical characteristics of many substitutionary theologies, Forsyth posits a rich moral canvas that takes seriously both the chorus of Scripture and the experience of believers. He adequately accounts for the human appropriation of God's sanctifying work and provides pastoral instruction for the shape that such appropriation might take so that human society might live and flourish – subjects we will attend to more fully in the next chapter.

352 *Work*, p. 170.
353 Ibid., p. 58.
354 Ibid., p. 213. Warfield misunderstands the relationship between repentance and forgiveness in Forsyth's theology. Benjamin B. Warfield, 'Modern Theories of the Atonement', in *Studies in Theology* (vol. 9; Grand Rapids: Baker, 2003), pp. 283–97.
355 'Revelation', pp. 142–43.
356 Dorner, *System of Christian Ethics*, pp. 283–84.

4

Hallowed Be Thy Name: Holiness' Self-Recovery in the Human Conscience

'The Holy Lord shows His holiness in righteousness', says Isaiah . . . If such righteous holiness be the nature of the last reality, and therefore of the last worship, it gives us the last standard of man's worth.[1]

I. Recovering Forsyth's vision of humanity

Humanity as moral

Samuel Mikolaski is not alone when he laments that what often passes as counselling, effectively emasculates the moral life and treats persons 'granularly' rather than as 'part of the solidaric racial life'.[2] Forsyth also bemoans that too often psychology impairs positive faith, operates as a 'moral anæsthesia',[3] and resolves religion into either subjectivism or symbolism that undermines the full complexity of human personhood, personhood which at core participates in the moral ontology of all that is. Supporting this assessment stands his conviction (informed by Butler and Kant) that it is the *moral self* which 'makes man man'.[4] His theological anthropology is replete with such phrases as 'humanising means moralising' and 'my real, surest me' is my moral self, claims that recall for the reader Schleiermacher's rejection of scientific reconstructions of human being.[5] All endeavours to discard our true moral being, therefore, are futile because, as Forsyth claims, we 'cannot escape from ourselves'.[6] We are not merely atoms, but are essentially consciences which cohere in a moral reality in relationship not only

1 *Authority*, p. 66.
2 Samuel J. Mikolaski, *The Grace of God* (Grand Rapids: Wm. B. Eerdmans, 1966), p. 76.
3 *Authority*, p. 408; cf. 'Metaphysic', p. 697.
4 *Father*, p. 9; cf. *Mercy*, p. 14; *War*, p. 27; *Preaching*, pp. 36, 117–19; 'Lay Religion', p. 773; *Authority*, pp. 317–18, 416–17.
5 *Freedom*, p. 185; *Person*, p. 197. See Friedrich Schleiermacher, *Brief Outline on the Study of Theology* (trans. Terrence N. Tice; Richmond: John Knox Press, 1966), §32, p. 167.
6 *Justification*, p. 200.

with a cosmic moral order and other creaturely personalities, but with a universal moral personality – the Holy, the moral Absolute, infinite Love. The truth of this moral milieu, Forsyth insists, poses the chief problem for democracy, which tends to reduce human society to a mass of 'clotted' individuals, and for capitalistic consumerism which shrinks persons into machine cogs.[7]

To be truly human is to participate in holiness, truth and love, to correspond to the whole dynamic of God's being and character, and that in a fully creaturely way. Thus does Forsyth witness to the practical recognition of the human predicament as one that is fundamentally moral, weighing the centre of gravity in his theology towards the conscience and holiness more than to the heart and affections (and still less to outward behavioural forms). Addressing a 'respectable' and 'self-respecting' Edwardian readership, Forsyth observes with passionate realism:

> The moral crisis of society is in a region which you may know little of. You are bred, perhaps, in the sober, unbitten, and untragic atmosphere of intellectual West Ends, where evil is a study and not a curse. You have never felt the bottom drop out of your own soul, the ground give way beneath your own moral nature, while flying voices scream that Macbeth has murdered sleep.[8]

To construe human persons not as metaphysical substances, nor as consumers, nor as 'property',[9] but as *moral* personalities is to recognize an ego-alter dialectic with obligations to self, to others and to God. Certainly this necessitates the grammar of metaphysics, but it is, for Forsyth, the 'metaphysic of the conscience'[10] that is paramount here and which serves to plot and assess human existence and action primarily on a moral rather than a physical, aesthetic or psychological map. The key to history, therefore, is not human marionettes, but a plexus of wills – human and Divine – fully and freely engaged with one another. Whenever history is refracted through the prism of personal reality, its key is to be 'sought in the will as free and not as the puppet of ideas nor as a vortex of force'.[11] With his former pastor (J. Baldwin Brown), what Forsyth dreads is 'the drift of a current, not the action of a will'.[12] Forsyth believes that the collapse of the Hegelian synthesis and the hopelessness of process advance the realization that ideas are not the prime movers they are thought to be. Taken alone, Hegel's ideas

> bleached all the complexion out of history, and left but a pale form, moving but anaemic. They had a far more vital and organic connection with their personal agents than Hegel allowed; these were not mere wires on which the ideas travelled nor vortices where they met. Man was made a living soul by a life-giving Spirit, he was not the pawn of a moving process even of thought.[13]

7 'Moral Principle', p. 12. See also 'Moral Principle', pp. 12–19; *Socialism*, pp. 15–16, 20–21, 57; *Missions*, p. 173.
8 *Cruciality*, p. 155.
9 'Land Laws', p. 504.
10 *Person*, p. 222.
11 *Justification*, p. 51.
12 Brown (ed.), *In Memoriam*, p. 28.
13 *Justification*, p. 51.

Accordingly, for Forsyth, history is constituted by a succession of personal moral acts (the adjective is as important as the noun here), supremely demonstrated in Christ's obedience unto death. What constitutes an act as moral is its active resolve of a moral problem raised by God's holiness. On an eternal scale, therefore, the action of the cross is interpreted as universal because it affects the universal conscience.

To speak of humankind as moral is to testify to more than that human persons live – veritably battle – with ethical and social responsibilities. To be sure, Forsyth urges that to be a moral creature means to be capable of making choices that comport with the claim and 'ought' of God; that is, with God's law in the light of God's covenantal goodness, or, in Kant's words, with the *categorical imperative*. But it is deeper still: 'Morality is the expression of our personality; and to grow moral means to grow in personality, and not merely in a certain exercise of personality. It is our creative action.' This amounts to human souls 'co-operating with the holy energy of God and fulfilling [their] redeemed destiny'.[14] While there are some resonances here with eastern language about synergism and participation in the divine 'energies', Forsyth's theology of grace construes 'energy' in moral rather than metaphysical terms. Positive Christianity, he argues, recognizes this moral ontology, and adjusts to it. Anything less is to dislodge Christian faith from its one fixed and certain thing in all the world – a real place in the ethical sphere in which we are not merely sensitive atoms influenced by God, but moral beings judged by God.

Manifest here is Forsyth's conviction that human beings 'were made with a moral nature for supremely moral issues'.[15] To disguise this truth behind some brand of post-Hegelian idealism, or to investigate this reality within the boundaries of empirical science alone, is to defraud human nature of real ontology, rob human persons of obligation, responsibility and freedom and to hand persons over to 'the vagrancy of the moment's appetite and the slavery of chance desires'.[16] Such constitutes a commitment to embrace the chimerical, 'severed from the great moral whole which gives [us our] reality', thereby undermining the whole economy of the human soul and its freedom, and cheating faith of its 'one creative, authoritative, life-making, life-giving, life-shaping power'.[17] Conversely, Forsyth's morally determined anthropology is in concordance with the ruling locale that sanctification occupies in his thought:

> The source and sublimate of the moral is the holy, which in God's righteous love is calling to man's warm conscience, to his moral heart, and calling for the whole man, the whole soul, the whole personality, and not merely a faculty of it, nor for its behaviour. It calls for the response known as faith, in which the personality assigns itself to the grace of the Holy in an act of committal which is holy as He is, and which has all actual sanctity latent in it, and all conduct.[18]

One example of where this is observed is in the *ecclesia* where dialogical and perichoretic selves reflect the Triune God in whose image we are made and by whom we are called

[14] *Preaching*, p. 139.
[15] *Marriage*, p. 120.
[16] Ibid., p. 121.
[17] *Preaching*, p. 146.
[18] *Justification*, p. 108.

to express life in a holy society. This Maurician accent on community is important for Forsyth, sponsoring his conviction regarding the race's unity before God and his profession of the atonement's universal scope.

Moreover, to accentuate the moral is to bear witness to the fundamentally *personal* nature of reality. This is because, Forsyth avers, the decisive moral issue for creation concerns the clash of Conscience and conscience, Will and will, each with a claim on the other. The absolute authority that our conscience accounts to is *our* Other. And it is precisely because we inhabit a moral world that that claim must be met: 'It will not do simply to draw the edges together by mere amendment, to have God here and man there, and gradually bring them together till they unite. It is two moral persons with moral passions we have to do with. It is moral relationship that is in question, communion, trustful mutuality, is the object of the divine requirement.'[19] In clarifying the nature of the divine–human *koinonia*, Forsyth turns, appropriately, to christology: interpreting the hypostatic union morally rather than metaphysically, Christ's union with us constitutes not the mystical interfusion of two substances but real intercourse between persons, wills witnessing to the ontology of all things.[20] The relevant point here is one of analogy: that is to say, just as in the hypostatic union the union is moral rather than metaphysical, so too of the union between Christ and believers.

It is imperative that we understand what Forsyth is *and is not* affirming here: in no sense is he suggesting that human beings are called to be morally 'successful' in the sense of attaining some idealized vision of perfect conduct or character. There is a perfection, but it is a perfection of faithful relations and not of performance (which, as Bonhoeffer observed, 'necessarily leads to perfectionist sectarianism'[21]). Moreover, it is the prius of this relationship with God for which humankind is created moral, plunged into moral nemesis and secured by a moral crisis wherein humanity is forgiven and converted, and that not by scaling heaven by our intrinsic moral strength but rather by the gracious action of one who Francis Thompson referred to as heaven's hound[22] – Jesus Christ – who not only 'fully set out man's moral idea, excellence and resource'[23] but who also revealed the shape of true human being.

Humanity created for holy communion: Holiness' self-reflection

Hebrews 12.10 makes the astounding claim that believers are to share (μεταλαβεῖν) in God's holiness, a holiness which Forsyth insists desires to 'establish itself in the unholy by gracious love'. This suggests that holiness is not contented by remaining remote but only as it finds and asserts itself in redeeming grace, as it goes out and comes home via the costly overturning of 'Satan's seat'.[24]

What we also discover in Forsyth's thought is that not only do holiness and morality have no meaning apart from God's conscience, majesty and kingship, but that without

19 *Work*, p. 124.
20 See 'Mystics', p. 402.
21 Bonhoeffer, *Sanctorum Communio*, p. 141.
22 Forsyth references Thompson's poem, 'Hound of Heaven', in *Father*, p. 8.
23 'Adam', p. 347.
24 *Preaching*, p. 145.

holiness no one shall see the Lord in history.[25] It was *in* the 'moral medium of holiness'[26] that humanity was created. And it was *for* such holiness that humanity was destined, elected, judged, redeemed and hallowed, that humanity might mirror God's holy love back to God's self from the side of creation. Here the source and *raison d'être* of the creation and redemption find unison: the joyful participation of the redeemed in the overflowing harmony of God's life. In this action, God's image and glory in humanity are reflected back to God through the incarnate Son, and in the new community he creates. So whereas for Jonathan Edwards, for example, this action is 'simply [God's] own love reflected and returned to him',[27] for Forsyth, such love is defined specifically in terms of *holiness'* yearning to find its creaturely correspondent. Nevertheless, with an Edwardsian tone, Forsyth recalls, 'We were created by God not out of his poverty and his need of company, but out of his overflowing wealth of love and his passion to multiply joy.'[28] It was precisely this passion that stayed the determination of the obedient Son in his ministry – and especially in his death – as he realized for humanity and transferred to humanity the reality of holy love amidst the conditions of sin and 'the penalty of loveless defiance'.[29] Such passion refused to be satisfied until it saw from sin's side a holiness like its own – 'and not merely a merit deserving holiness'[30] – that God might look upon humanity and declare over human history those words which God spoke over Christ's whole life, 'Behold, my servant whom I have chosen, my beloved with whom my soul is well pleased' (Mt. 12.18).

So against Kant's insistence that 'God alone is holy, and [that] man can never become so, but the ideal is good',[31] Forsyth, in a fairly original explication of the wonderful exchange, insists that Christ laid his 'holiness on us', absorbing us 'into His satisfaction to God'. Certainly 'in the empirical sense we are no more made righteous than [Christ] was made sinful. But we are as closely incorporated in the holy world as He was in the sinful'. In this sense, 'our holiness is not ours, in the same sense as our sin was not His'.[32] Nevertheless, this 'borrowed' holiness compares in kind (though not in measure) to God's. God alone is self-sufficiently holy, but God wills that creation shares in, knows, and delights in, divine holiness – that is, in 'the most majestic thing about God'.[33] Forsyth here exposes Otto's attempt to define holiness phenomenologically as 'the totally other' and insists that the Church has done a disservice to the divine disclosure itself by treating holiness as 'rare, aloof and saintly' as opposed to 'warm, brotherly [and] social'.[34] Furthermore, he contends that holiness corresponds to 'the total action of the spiritual world both in us and around . . . We find ourselves before and within a

25 *Justification*, p. 117.
26 *Work*, p. 202.
27 Cited in T. A. Schafer, 'Jonathan Edwards and Justification by Faith', *Church History* 20 (1951), pp. 55–67 (62).
28 *Life*, p. 13.
29 *Father*, p. 11.
30 *Jesus*, p. 109.
31 Immanuel Kant, *Lectures on Ethics* (ed. P. Heath and J. B. Schneewind; trans. P. Heath; Cambridge: Cambridge University Press, 1997), p. 229.
32 *Work*, p. 227.
33 *Revelation*, p. 88.
34 *Congregationalism*, p. 40.

holy God, a spiritually moral personality, self-determined and self-complete'.[35] The fact that holiness is only found 'within' God, however, is a reminder that creatures have no intrinsic holiness, and that to be holy is to be *for* God; that is, 'according to His relation to us'.[36]

Forsyth's ubiquitous claim is that because holiness is the 'fundamental principle' of God's 'whole saving revelation and economy of love',[37] holiness is inextricably bound up with God's purposes for creation. These purposes, he insists, are so utterly non-negotiable and personally invested that not only is creation's holiness at stake, but so is God's. Citing an unnamed source, Forsyth writes,

> 'The dignity of man is better assured if he were broken upon the maintenance of that holiness of God than if it were put aside just to give him an existence' . . . just to let him off with his life. This holy order is as essential to man's greatness as it is to God's; and that is why the holy satisfaction Christ made to God's holiness is in the same act the glorifier of the new humanity. Any religion which leaves out of supreme count the judging holiness of God is making a great contribution to the degradation of man.[38]

Forsyth presses that persons are good not in happiness but in perfection; that is, in holiness. Such 'moral harmony' is attained through God's creative action whereby we are reconciled with the 'Eternal Conscience with which we have for ever to do'.[39] Humanity is not forgiven 'by forgetting and mending',[40] by agreeing that no more be said about sin, but only by an objective, final and fully vicarious atonement from which no sin is excluded and through which the hegemony of God's antithesis is ruined. This adequate and worshipful answering of holiness to the Holiness that made it corresponds with humanity's full participation in 'personal intercourse with the Holy', [41] an intercourse which involves the exchange of thoughts and feelings as well as service, worship and holy communion – which is our true greatness and joyful satisfaction. Thus to pray for deliverance from evil is not simply to pray to be taken 'out of hell', but to pray to be taken 'into heaven',[42] into the reign of God, into discipleship, into the eucharistic 'realization of complete sonship, its powers and its confidences'.[43] It is 'not enough' that we should worship and pay homage to a loving God. 'That does not satisfy the love of God. Nothing short of living, loving, holy, habitual communion between His holy soul and ours can realise at last the end which God achieved in Jesus Christ.'[44] Forsyth's point

35 *Preaching*, p. 229.
36 *Authority*, p. 5.
37 *Life*, p. 29.
38 *Work*, p. 128; cf. 'Insufficiency', p. 601; 'Atonement', p. 66; *Work*, p. 85; *Authority*, p. 67; 'Charter of Missions', p. 309; 'Evangelical Faith', p. 239.
39 'Forgiveness', p. 206.
40 *Work*, p. 129.
41 Ibid., p. 68.
42 Ibid., p. 202.
43 *Prayer*, p. 58.
44 *Work*, p. 58.

is that while humanity may be incomparable with God, humanity is not incompatible, and that 'in Christ the compatibility becomes full communion'.[45]

> To treat a living person as an end, to seek him for himself, has but one meaning. It is to love him, to have our desire and energy rest in him, to have our personal finality in him. So it is that we need and seek God, not His help nor His gifts – even of sanctity, but Himself. His great object with us is not our sinlessness but our communion. 'Give me thy heart'. He does not offer us communion to make us holy; He makes us holy for the sake of communion.[46]

Forsyth insists that 'we do not need God chiefly as a means even to our own holiness. But we need God for Himself. He Himself is the end. We need chiefly communion with Him', a communion which is not 'confined to the perfectly holy but is open to all in faith, and possible along with cleaving sin'.[47] Certainly, holiness involves no hint of Pharisaism, for 'God alone could duly hallow God in man'.[48] Here Forsyth reminds us that holiness can never be divorced from the cross, not even in eternity: 'we shall never be so good and holy at any point, even in eternity, that we shall not look into the Cross of Christ as the centre of all our hope in earth or heaven'.[49] Forsyth is quick to recall that sanctified people are those 'fully indwelt' by one who became our 'sole creditor' in his hallowing work. Consequently, believers ought not let the devotional aspect of sanctity exhaust the word's meaning, as if holiness were but prayer to God and not principally God's action on us. The New Testament meaning of 'saints' is 'not the holy, but those who have been chosen by the Holy, and ear-marked for His purpose'.[50] This suggests that human holiness is creational, ecclesial and eschatological, hence the deep pain when persons are 'out of ontological, covenantal peace and activity'.[51]

To be sure, to be creatures *of* and *for* holy love involves a reorientation of one's love, a reorientation from being simply impressed by Christ (sentimentalism) to being compelled habitually to 'cultivate in the Spirit the power of seeing into Christ and into His Cross'.[52] And the 'real test' of such reorientation comes when one loves one's enemies: 'The love of our enemy is only the love of our neighbour true to itself through everything . . . And there is only one source in the world to feed it and keep it alive – which is God's love of His bitter enemies, and His grace to them in repaying their wrong . . .'.[53] Clearly, while holiness is immensely personal, Forsyth resists those attempts to make it atomic, private, cellular, monastic and doctrinaire. Instead, he sponsors the view that personal sanctification is inextricably bound up with that of the

45 *Person*, p. 353.
46 *Father*, p. 103.
47 Ibid., p. 103.
48 *Person*, p. 120.
49 *Work*, p. 154.
50 *War*, p. 56.
51 Geoffrey C. Bingham, *Everything in Beautiful Array* (Blackwood: New Creation, 1999), p. 63.
52 *Work*, p. 50. On sentimentalism see *Congregationalism*, p. 70; *Justification*, p. 86; *Life*, p. 13; *Marriage*, p. 148; *Missions*, p. 66; *Preaching*, pp. 120–21; *Revelation*, pp. 26–27; 'Revelation', p. 101; *Society*, p. 103; *War*, p. 168.
53 *Cruciality*, pp. 166–67.

world and adopts a posture that works out in the world: 'for my righteousness is Christ, and He is no private possession. My holiness is my hold of Him who is the holy destiny of the world. I cannot be right or holy in Christ if I am not waiting, praying, working in some way for social righteousness, reform, and brotherhood'.[54] For Forsyth, the initial locus of this holy-making activity in the human person is the conscience – the subject to which we now turn.

II. Forsyth on the human conscience: Moral centre, consanguinity and sphere of redemption

Conscience as moral centre and locus of judgement

> *PT Forsyth never wrote a book on the conscience, but few seem to have understood it better than he did. He said that conscience makes us man, makes us one, and makes us eternal. He appears to be saying that of all creatures man is endowed the conscience, and without conscience he is not truly man. He is also saying that it is one of the most dynamic factors common to every human being, and that transcending class, language, race and creed it gives us that by which we can understand humanity . . . Man is really what his state of conscience is.*[55]

So pervasive is the moral ontology Forsyth adopts that he contends that human persons do more than possess a conscience: We are a conscience.[56] Misinterpreted, there is an uncomfortable reductionism here; a further example of Forsyth trying to do more with a word than is helpful. However, palpable here is Forsyth's recognition (influenced mostly by Luther, Kant and Maurice) that conscience is that arena of created capacity of awareness of one's being woven into a complex of relationships with persons, history, creation and God. He properly determines that a Christian theology of conscience is best articulated when we resist isolating conscience and treating it as a phenomenon in itself and we expound it as one feature within a broader moral landscape.[57] Still, Forsyth insists, conscience is a person's 'most human and universal part' arranging each person in their 'own gracious order and place'. It does 'not appeal simply to the pneumatics, psychics, or illuminates naturally [those] so selected and disposed'.[58] While physiologically the conscience is found in the prefrontal cortex, theologically it is humanity's moral centre, the place in the moral order wherein God's holiness finds its 'echo, or even . . . facet, of [God's] own righteousness'.[59] Consequently, it is, according to Forsyth, the prime locus of redemption. So Forsyth's preference for speaking of the redeemed *conscience* rather than of the redeemed *person*, and redemption as the

54 'Sanctification', p. 734.
55 Geoffrey C. Bingham, *The Conscience – Conquering or Conquered?* (Blackwood: New Creation, 1987), pp. xi, 2.
56 *Cruciality*, p. 127; cf. *Authority*, p. 169; 'Veracity', p. 206.
57 See John Webster, 'God and Conscience', in *The Doctrine of God and Theological Ethics* (ed. Alan J. Torrance and Michael Banner; London/New York: T&T Clark, 2006), p. 147.
58 'Orthodoxy', p. 325.
59 'Sinless', p. 301.

transformation not primarily of the mind but of the conscience. By so locating the seat of 'evangelical experience' in the human conscience, Forsyth here echoes Ritschl and Hermann; it is in the conscience, in our 'moral centre, where men are made men or marred'.[60] Thus divine enfleshment was with a view to dealing a deathblow to the sinful conscience and not only to the 'heart and its aches', for God 'had to do with our tragic guilt more than [with] our tragic lot'.[61] Against his former teacher, however, Forsyth insists that everything that enhances native purity, extenuates sin, diminishes guilt and sets over us nothing but a Ritschlian-like divine father only belittles God's true greatness: 'It is a tremendous power to be capable of sin against God. It betokens, as nothing else but holiness can do, the greatness of the soul, and its place and its issues.'[62] And again:

> The prime question of the soul which the Cross answers is not the filial question of a child-heart simply to be met by the mere revelation of a Father correcting our bewilderment; nor is that the question answered in the discourses of Christ; but it is everywhere the moral question of an adult conscience, the question of sinful man before his Judge, to be answered by a justification and a real redemption.[63]

With Maurice and Butler, Forsyth asserts that the conscience is our 'common starting ground. Man is more than a consciousness, he is a conscience. He is not only aware of himself, he is critical of himself'.[64] 'Our judicial self'[65] not only *can* stand in the tribunal's dock but *must*. There our thoughts and actions, which refuse to be silenced, are 'ranged before it' and 'judgment is passed . . . upon what we have been and done'.[66] The Kantian reverberation is unmistakable. Forsyth asks,

> Who is this judge that follows us like our shadow? We did not appoint him. We did not give him his place. He is there in spite of us. He is no fiction of our imagination, else we would not be so afraid of him; we would not so dread our own creature. We fear him because he is in a position to threaten us or to ennoble us; because he does not suggest, but command.[67]

While morality may or may not involve religion, the conscience, Forsyth insists, involves God. Indeed, 'conscience is the Word of God within us'. Accordingly, moral responsibility finally means 'responsibility *before God*'.[68] There is 'no crevice of the

60 *Sacraments*, p. 298.
61 'Intellectualism', p. 320; cf. Søren Kierkegaard, *The Concept of Anxiety* (trans. Reider Thomte; Princeton: Princeton University Press, 1980), pp. 104, 162.
62 *Missions*, p. 32.
63 *Jesus*, p. 58.
64 *Cruciality*, p. 127; cf. Frederick D. Maurice, *The Conscience: Lectures on Casuistry, Delivered in the University of Cambridge* (London: Macmillan and Co., 1872), pp. 1–23.
65 *Cruciality*, p. 128.
66 Ibid., p. 127.
67 Ibid., pp. 130–31.
68 Ibid., p. 132. Italics mine.

universe into which the culprit could creep and reckon on escape'.[69] Or, as Kant would have us believe:

> Conscience represents the divine tribunal within us: first, because it judges our dispositions and actions according to the purity of the law; second, because we cannot deceive it; and last, because we cannot escape it, since, like the divine omnipresence, it is always with us. It is thus the representative within us of divine justice, and hence must on no account be injured.[70]

Forsyth's equating of the conscience with the Word here risks misunderstanding. His point is not that particular accusations of conscience are the Word of God per se, but that *in* these accusations the person (as a creature of law) cannot circumvent moral responsibility. In other words, the conscience gives voice to humanity's moral nature, regardless of social and historical locale, and decrees that remission of sin alone is not enough. What is demanded is judgement – the justification of God and humanity. Here Forsyth re-sounds the Psalmist (96.11–13) in understanding judgement as that to be looked for with hope and joy because judgement is principally concerned with vindication, glory, the establishment of righteousness and the healing of that which is broken. 'Judgement is adjustment far more than vengeance. It is sanctification more than punishment.'[71] Consequently, neither penalty, remorse, repentance, verbal acknowledgment nor ritual can satisfy the claim of holy law. Holiness alone, and that on a scale commensurate with 'the one holy law which was broken', can satisfy the conscience and so carry assurance to the human person (and to God).[72] By gracious moral necessity, therefore, humanity lives under judgement which establishes God's holiness in the face of sin and thereby heals creation. Moreover, such judgement is worked out not only in the cross but also in the human conscience – in its guilt – and in the events of history. Clearly, nothing can satisfy the human conscience that does not first satisfy the conscience of God.

> Conscience has always mistrust in the background if grace is mere remission. Mere remission of sin does not satisfy even us . . . Conscience has in trust God's law and its majesty, which must be made good, as mere remission does not make it . . . How may I be sure that I may take the grace of God seriously and finally, how be sure that I have complete salvation, that I may entirely trust it through the worst my conscience may say? Only thus, that God is the Reconciler, that He reconciles in Christ's Cross that the judgment of sin was there for good and all . . . Nemesis on us is hallowed as a part of the judgment on Him to whose death we are joined . . . Thus the severity of conscience becomes the certainty of salvation.[73]

[69] Ibid., pp. 131–32.
[70] Kant, *Lectures on Ethics*, p. 134; cf. *Justification*, p. 20; *Cruciality*, p. 127.
[71] *Jesus*, p. 47.
[72] *Work*, p. 126.
[73] Ibid., pp. 167–69; cf. 'Unity and Theology', p. 72.

Exemplified here is Forsyth's conviction that humanity's primary need is neither knowledge nor direction but a sure footing in life and in death. Christ meets this need, advocating for us as 'in God, not against God . . . [and] against our accusing conscience'. Christ, put otherwise, is the 'human conscience of God', and so our Surety, 'more sure and merciful and universal than our conscience' is.[74] As such, he is God's own 'Self-justification to the world'.[75] And in him, the crisis of the human conscience is answered in such a way that a unity is formed between God's conscience and ours: 'The moral malady of the race is mastered by the Saviour of the conscience . . . The conscience cries for forgiveness, and history brings to it the cross.'[76] Accordingly, the new conscience, even in the face of *Anfechtung*, confirms the verity of our sanctification as it looks to God's sanctifying work. The testimony of a good conscience confirms that our faith is sincere and not feigned. Furthermore, the testimony of a good conscience not only speaks about God's grace towards us, but also about the sincerity of our response to that grace. It thereby builds on the foundation of God's self-witness to us in the gospel (testified to in baptism) and although it cannot replace that foundation, it testifies to the truth of it. In this liberty, the believer knows in her conscience that she is bound to God through the inner witness of the Spirit.

In the same year that Forsyth began at Emmanuel Church, he penned 'Mystics and Saints' in response to the charge of mysticism laid against him, arising out of his *Faith and Criticism* essay. Therein, he contends that conscience serves as the final certainty by which we test all else, acting as the place of authority, truth and judgement. It is the 'authority for truth no less than action'.[77] However, the conscience can operate as this standard only because Christ sits on 'the throne of conscience, in absolute command of our whole moral self'.[78]

What Forsyth offers us is an account of Christian conscience in which christology, pneumatology, scripture, creation, ecclesiology, eschatology and theo-anthropology are integrated in such a way that the grammar employed to describe God's acts in history is undetached from human experience and faith's practices. This 'moral space'[79] is the proper theological backdrop against which a christologically determined account of conscience, moral reckoning and faith's action can be adequately translated. Forsyth demands that we understand God's creative, reconciling and perfecting work as the determining locale for human activity, defining humanity in reference to God rather than in categories such as reason, will or consciousness. Here his attention to the primacy of the moral and the conscience simultaneously betrays an anti-Enlightenment agenda (with its centre of gravity in reason) and a qualifying of Ritschl's presentation. For while Forsyth accepts Ritschl's emphasis on moral primacy as centred in the human will and conscience, he faults Ritschl for overemphasizing the moral response of the human subject. Also, Ritschl's twin *foci* of cross and kingdom, Forsyth charges, leads to a

74 *Father*, p. 93.
75 *Justification*, pp. 14, 183.
76 *Cruciality*, p. 133.
77 'Mystics', p. 402.
78 'Intellectualism', pp. 325–26.
79 John Webster, *Word and Church: Essays in Christian Dogmatics* (Edinburgh: T&T Clark, 2001), p. 234.

synthetic separation of religion and ethics. Both of these distortions arise from Ritschl's divorcing these realities from the christological foundation required to sustain them. Moreover, Forsyth invites us to understand the *ecclesia* and its work in the context of this moral field, both anticipating and provisionally embodying the shape and fruit of a hallowed society.

Conscience as reflection of the ground of our racial consanguinity

... the conscience is the real focus of human unity.[80]

The Justification of God includes a lengthy discussion on the 'what' and 'where' of human unity. Forsyth begins by asking, 'Why should we think mankind a unity? It is not natural to the struggle for life. It is not how we begin. We begin as warring atoms.'[81] He then proceeds to investigate whether the race's unity can be established from our ideas, passions or sympathies. His answer: 'No'. Next, he explores whether it may be found in our history, in a common progenitor or a 'single and common creation'. Again, the answer is negative. What then of our 'conjectural future'? Shall we find our unity in 'a common destiny – a goal of values if not a scheme of operations'?[82] Disavowing Hegelian notions of progress, again Forsyth rejects this hypothesis. Our racial unity, he insists, is found neither in our past, nor our future, still less in any self-projected goals or hopes that we might share. Neither can our common sin provide any such basis in a positive sense. Rather our unity is a graced unity, a creation of holy love. So too in *The Cruciality of the Cross*: 'Only at the centre of the cross does the man find himself in his kind, and both in God.'[83] The implication here is that racial unity is neither biological nor aesthetic, but moral, found in our corporate sanctification in redemption and in the life of God's community – both its divine and human counterparts. Such unity, Forsyth insists, emerges in the 'unity of conscience': 'It is in the conscience, where man is member of a vast moral world.'[84] Here humanity stands or falls together, in the race's witness to the one power over it, to Christ who gathers up the race's conscience, and who, in his own soul, sets it in the active light of God's own conscience. Accordingly, the only universal religion is that which prioritizes the conscience and its redemption.

The conscience is not, therefore, the *ground* of our racial unity. By itself, the human conscience but bears witness to our racial guilt and division. The ground of our racial consanguinity is found in our deliverance from guilt, in forgiveness, in Jesus Christ and in what God has done in and through him for humanity's conscience. Humanity is 'most surely one' only as a *redeemed* conscience.[85] 'Such ... is the Christian faith ... Guilt is ... the last problem of the race, its one central moral crisis; and the Cross that

[80] 'Church Theory', p. 358.
[81] *Justification*, p. 17.
[82] Ibid., pp. 17–18.
[83] *Cruciality*, p. 43.
[84] *Work*, p. 122; cf. Dietrich Bonhoeffer, *Ethics* (ed. Eberhard Bethge; trans. N. H. Smith; London: SCM, 1955), pp. 211–16.
[85] *Justification*, p. 81.

destroys it is the race's historic crisis and turning-point.'[86] Humanity is made one by that which overcomes its guilt.

Moreover, whereas the ground of our racial unity is in guilt's overcoming and the forgiveness of sins, its source is God's own unity, and its power God's holiness. It is to this 'one power over it'[87] that the conscience bears united witness – to Christ who gathers up humanity's conscience and sets it in the active precinct of God's conscience (holiness). Here, in 'what is done with [humanity's] conscience by the power it owns supreme', humanity is one. Human unity, therefore, is constituted in God's giving and saving grace, in deliverance, forgiveness, reconciliation and regeneration:

> We do not achieve unity by our resource, we receive it as a gift to our spiritual poverty, and as a creation out of our last distress of dissolution. Our destiny is found in our tragedy and not in our idyll, not in our hour of triumph but in our depth of distress. If man is one *in* conscience, he is not one *by* conscience; for by itself it reveals guilt and division. The unity is a unity effected *by* God *in* conscience, in the tragedy of our conscience, and not simply its voice or law. It is His gift of release to conscience, His reconstruction of it. It is not at last a matter of our conscience but of Christ in our conscience. It is a divine reconciliation, but a reconciliation of the conscience more even than of the affections ... It is the reconciliation given to the conscience of the race by a holy grace, which must judge conscience, but which judges it in Christ and upon Him.[88]

The key to human unity, therefore, is not the first Adam but the second, in whom we participate in a 'unity refused by our first origin'.[89] The entire race is reconstituted in Christ, whose life is not only manifested in the individual conscience (albeit not yet fully in each person) but whose nature also lays upon each person an ek-static obligation in the Spirit.[90] Further, because creation is sustained as the action and unity of God's moral order, the crisis precipitated by its brokenness is no private anxiety, but a racial disjuncture rippling through all creation. Certainly, social evils and 'individual' sins are inseparable; both are the outworking of human guilt, which is 'at bottom' a moral (and so a religious) rather than a sociological or political problem.[91] Accordingly, Forsyth insists that a *private* conscience is a contradiction in terms, an 'impossible thing' which ends only in self-will and the ruin of community.[92] The 'atomic conscience'[93] is not only the particularization of the racial conscience but is also the province wherein persons understand themselves to be members of a 'vast moral world'.[94] Unfortunately,

[86] Ibid., p. 19; cf. 'Religion and Reality', p. 551; Karl Heim, *Jesus the World's Perfector: The Atonement and the Renewal of the World* (trans. D. H. van Daalen; Edinburgh/London: Oliver and Boyd, 1959), p. 15: 'Guilt alone is the absolute evil, the absolutely terrible and unbearable, the simply irrevocable loss.'

[87] *Justification*, p. 187.

[88] Ibid., pp. 20–21; cf. 'Revelation', p. 108.

[89] *Justification*, p. 18.

[90] See Thomas Erskine, 'Letter to Mrs Schwabe, 14 December 1853', National Library of Scotland, Manuscript, 9747–33.

[91] *Cruciality*, p. 118.

[92] *War*, p. 65.

[93] Ibid., p. 68.

[94] *Work*, p. 133.

Forsyth nowhere makes clear what the relationship between the individual and the racial conscience is, though his way of speaking about it sometimes suggests something analogous to the Jungian 'collective unconscious', *mutatis mutandis*.[95] At bottom, Forsyth's point, however, is that if one desires to 'find the trunk out of which all the loves and practices of humanity proceed' one must 'go to conscience at the centre. That is where the unity of Humanity lies',[96] not in basic affections or in the 'palpable relationships of natural life',[97] nor in that which can be engineered like machinery. So Forsyth's challenge to preachers: 'What have you to preach if you have no gospel that goes to the foundations of human conscience? . . . The most universal God is one that goes there, not to the heart in the sense of affections, but to the conscience.'[98]

Forsyth's claim concerning the race's unity in the new conscience is confirmed not merely by Christian tradition, but in 'all deep and earnest experience'.[99] Indeed, this is where God's final revelation is effected – at the depth of our moral despair, rather than at the height of our aesthetic pride and cultured insight. And while Forsyth recognizes that Christianity is 'direct personal communion with Christ',[100] in that action in which he knew himself turned from 'a lover of love to an object of grace' he identifies that what happened to and in him happened to the race *in toto*.[101] This new relation of the conscience as universal, he believes, is concomitantly the proleptical form of the final relation of humanity to God and the anticipation of holiness' full teleological achievement.

To recapitulate, the conscience's unity – indeed the unity of all things, God and creation – is not revealed in a native cohesion or state but in its Lord, his hallowing action and creative effects. What Keats called the 'conscience-calmed'[102] would take a world-redemption to secure but, having been secured, would answer holy love's will and purpose, creating a moral totality around Christ's redeeming conscience and his reconciliation. Our racial consanguinity is the unity of 'Christ in our conscience' and the sole foundation for confidence in human unity (and for its certain future) is the 'moral certainty of God's conquering holiness' in the human conscience.[103] This is the 'solidary moral destiny which saves and completes' creation.[104]

The self-recovery of offended holiness provides surety to God's own conscience, which is then the unifying factor mediated by the Spirit in the human conscience as 'a will in relation to a Will'.[105] This is no mere movement but the battle which 'must be won' as it confronts the crisis created by God's holiness. It is the loss of this creative note, Forsyth contends, that encourages division and strife. Conversely, only that which

95 See Carl Gustav Jung, *Collected Works: The Archetypes and the Collective* (trans. R. F. C. Hull; Bollingen Series; vol. 9, Part 1; London: Princeton University Press, 1968), pp. 42–43.
96 *Work*, p. 122; cf. *Life*, p. 26; 'Nationality', p. 385; *Sacraments*, p. 53.
97 *Work*, p. 122.
98 Ibid.
99 *Justification*, p. 19.
100 *Rome*, p. 93.
101 *Preaching*, p. 193; cf. 'Faith and Mind', pp. 642–43; 'Church Fabric', p. 416.
102 John Keats, 'This Living Hand, Now Warm and Capable', in *Selected Poems* (trans. John Barnard; London: Penguin, 2007), p. 237.
103 *Justification*, p. 21.
104 *Authority*, p. 187.
105 *Justification*, p. 20.

undoes and destroys guilt 'in its very exposure' and secures holiness in the conscience – God's and humanity's – is the world's solution: 'The solution of life is not to be found in grappling with pain, but in the conflict with sin.'[106] To be sure, here is a further example of Forsyth's tendency to overstate his case by needless disjunction. His point, however, is that conscience rests where eternity rests, 'in the Being, Will, and Act of the Self-existent, Whose Being is Holiness and Whose Will is Grace, and Whose Act is the New Creation of the New Humanity'.[107]

Conscience as locus of sanctification

> Human nature's a funny thing. Hard to get rid of. The more you pick at it, the faster it heals. Look at my son in law. He seemed happy to do anything: chuck off his Christian clothes, drink bull-beer, wear a tail. All I asked. I thought Old Adam was gone for good – but here he is again. It's no good, son in law. You've got chronic human nature. You need the operation.[108]

So voiced the old man of the mountain to the young Peer Gynt; to which Peer replied, 'You're drunk . . . You're out of your mind.'[109] Few have been able to articulate the severity of the human maelstrom that Ibsen paints here. Too often, however, Peer's words are taken as the final word, even as good news. But Forsyth – 'the Ibsen of British theology'[110] – joins the old man: 'Human Nature is a good fellow enough – when you don't cross him, or meddle with his bone. Then he is less divine than canine.'[111] Here Forsyth not only identifies the demand for 'the operation', but he announces that we live in a post-operation world. The 'last moral issue of the whole world'[112] has been adjudicated. Moreover, the Word who comes clothed in his gospel does not range history's far-flung fields, but attends to its 'moral centre, to the site both of its power and its impotence, to the conscience'. Only when that is set right will all be 'right in tail'.[113] Forsyth's co-commitment to the priority of the moral and to Christ's headship of humanity leads to his claim that if the hallowing of all things is to occur then the foremost locus of God's sanctifying action is the sinful conscience. If God can master (but not concuss) this moral centre of creation and creative region of all history, then all else will follow. In other words, Forsyth's claim is that to heal here is to initiate the healing of all things. Conversely, to leave conscience uncured, or to hope that some nameless antibiotics might emerge over time to 'do the job' is to be blinded to the veracity of the situation, a situation created, sustained and exacerbated by the holiness of the God who desires us:

[106] 'Pessimism', p. 43.
[107] 'Veracity', p. 206.
[108] Henrick Ibsen, *Peer Gynt* (trans. K. McLeish; London: Royal National Theatre/Nick Hern, 1990), p. 34.
[109] Ibsen, *Peer Gynt*, p. 34.
[110] Hermann, 'Representative British Theologians', pp. 179, 180.
[111] *Socialism*, p. 28.
[112] *Congregationalism*, p. 16.
[113] *Justification*, p. 80; cf. 'Veracity', pp. 212–13.

> What crushes my conscience is not a taunt from another individual, however great, but an indictment from the moral universe. I did not break a by-law, nor transgress a regulation; I collided with the moral unity of things, with the absolute holiness of God. I have to do with Him, and He with me. All the holiness of God bears down on my soul. Not His power, His influence, but His holiness. I am not a sensitive atom affected by Him, but a moral monad judged by Him. The question of personal religion therefore (the prime question, if not the first), the matter of most urgent certainty, is, How do I stand before my Judge?[114]

In answering, Forsyth turns to Christ's action of interposing God's 'perfectly holy conscience' onto the 'helplessly guilty conscience of man'.[115] He insists that humanity's greatest need *and foremost resentment* is that which comes to our moral centre in the darkest, most despairing and most terrible hour, 'the hour of our guilt'. That same holiness which 'makes our guilt' (as well as our best repentance) sanctifies us and in that same bloody action the moral world is at once confounded, crowned and recreated.[116] Implicit here is that Christ is uniquely able to deal with the 'most real and the most needed'[117] thing of all – the soul's moral reconstruction.

> The spiritual authority of the long future rests where rests the effectual power to judge, forgive, and redeem the evil conscience. And this is true whether what we feel most is sin or sympathy . . . The final reality of life is in its tragic conflict of good and evil, God and sin. It lies in the practical region, not in the ideal; and in the region of the practical conscience paralysed by its own failure, schism, and wickedness.[118]

Christ 'must be the authority owned by the conscience'.[119] This is the first calling of Christian religion: not aesthetic, but ethical and practical. Eucatastrophic grace attends not primarily our intellect, but our guilty conscience. Thus Forsyth urges pastors-in-training, 'For God's sake do not tell poor prodigals and black scoundrels they are better than they think, that they have more of Christ in them than they know, and so on. The conscience which is really in hell is the first to be angered at ingenuities and futilities like these, the more exasperating because of the poetic quarter-truth they contain.'[120]

Beginning with Kant's axiom that 'there is nothing in the world which can be termed absolutely and altogether good, a good will alone excepted',[121] Forsyth posits the standard of reality in the moral personality. And writing in the current of Oswald

114 *Authority*, pp. 40–41. Forsyth identifies Wagner as one artist, among 'probably no artist of any kind', who perceives this. *Art*, p. 235.
115 *Authority*, p. 58.
116 *Revelation*, p. 22.
117 *Society*, p. 93.
118 Ibid., p. 97; cf. 'Unity and Theology', p. 77.
119 *Authority*, p. 303.
120 *Preaching*, p. 106.
121 Immanuel Kant, *The Metaphysic of Ethics* (trans. J. W. Semple; Edinburgh: Thomas Clark, 1836), p. 1; cf. Kant, *The Metaphysic of Ethics*, pp. 59–73.

Spengler's ideas, Forsyth stresses that the real subject of history is human life, will and conscience and not an evolutionary scheme of birth, bloom and death.[122] The human will, however, is the one thing we have not given to God, and now cannot give, of ourselves. We are like Tolkien's Frodo who, when the crunch comes, cannot give up the ring he has so faithfully carried through three volumes. Something must happen to take it from him. To capture that citadel draws upon all of holy love's resources in the Incarnation. God alone has 'the power that heals the conscience by calamity, wipes out guilt, and creates in us and for us the only condition, the moral condition, for the final realisation of our [and God's] ideals'.[123]

Sanctifying grace frees humanity not simply from what crushes happiness, but, more importantly, from 'something which loads our conscience and mars our perfection'.[124] What Forsyth repeatedly refers to as the 'evangelical experience' is nothing less than the residency of Christ in the conscience as humanity's King conquering, regenerating and sanctifying humanity from its moral centre: 'We are not found for ever till we are plucked by the conscience from the fearful pit and the miry clay; not till we hunger for holiness as once we did for love and joy, and yet find holiness our dread; not till we thirst for peace with a judging God more than ever we craved for our young ideals in a splendid God.'[125] Citing Schlatter's *Briefe über Dogma* in support, Forsyth maintains that real authority must be experienced in life and contact with history; that is, it is authority *within* and *for* experience. He is careful, however, to distinguish this from the authority *of* experience.[126] Experience's real value, in other words, lies in the superhistoric nature of its content. Johnson explains:

> Just as Kierkegaard essayed a decisive repudiation of subjectivism, and did so in the name of 'subjectivity'; so Forsyth attempted a final break with the tyranny of experience that had gripped Protestant theology at the turn of the century, and did so in the name of 'the evangelical experience'. He posited a clear-cut definition between the human seat and the divine source of authority, designating the former 'experience', and the latter 'the experienced'; and then insisted that the primacy of concern must be shifted to the latter.[127]

Forsgiveness, Forsyth contends, is the one 'truly supernatural' thing that 'releases us from the State conscience',[128] creates a new conscience for a universal public and inaugurates

[122] See *Justification*, p. 50; cf. Oswald Arnold Gottfried Spengler, *The Decline of the West: Form and Actuality* (vol. 1; London: George Allen & Unwin, 1922).

[123] 'Ibsen's Treatment', p. 119. Forsyth's confidence was not always so God-directed. See 'Workers', p. 4.

[124] *Jesus*, p. 3.

[125] 'Experience', pp. 241–42.

[126] See *Authority*, pp. 30, 79–81, 96–98, 104, 153–56, 178, 211, 301–02, 329, 333–34, 371–74, 384–87; 'Metaphysic', pp. 716–17; *Freedom*, pp. 184–87, 276; *Person*, pp. 94, 194–210, 221, 243–46, 249–54, 281–82; *Revelation*, pp. 13, 68–80, 104; 'Revelation', pp. 111–12; *Rome*, pp 41, 137, 147, 233, 243; *Sacraments*, p. 16; *Society*, pp. 83, 85, 90, 94, 107, 125; *passim*.

[127] Robert Clyde Johnson, *Authority in Protestant Theology* (Philadelphia: Westminster Press, 1959), p. 100.

[128] 'Evangelical Basis', p. 684. The term 'conscience' attracted growing secular usage among Nonconformists, particularly following the Parnell crisis (1889–90) when 'the Nonconformist Conscience' was used in relation to Nonconformists' tactics of using the Irish leader to drive Liberalism irreversibly into sectarian politics. See John F. Glaser, 'Parnell's Fall and the Nonconformist Conscience', *Irish Historical Society* 12 (1960), pp. 119–30.

the reconstituting of human society. The source of this action is God's insatiable determination to hallow 'to the uttermost', to find himself in the worship of the cross, and there to establish the kingdom.[129] Indeed, Forsyth insists that the cross meant more for the God whose first concern is his own holy name than it did for humanity. But if creation is to be sanctified, and God's name hallowed in the earth, then that work must attend to the human conscience.

III. Forsyth on the 'new' conscience – the conquering and sanctification of humanity's moral centre

> *Is the Christian conscience but the natural refined, or is it the natural reborn? Christ's relation to the conscience – is it to develop its culture or to reconstitute its power? Is it to subtilise its acumen, or is it to give it a new quality and a new principle corresponding to the new centre on which it is set and the new life which Christ now lives in us – a life new in proportion as He is of God more than of man?*[130]

Forsyth distinguishes between the 'natural' conscience as that objectively guilty (something akin to how Luther describes the conscience under law), and the 'new' or 'evangelical' conscience as that which, by the Spirit, is in harmony with Christ and made to share in God's sanctifying life and activity. The life of the new conscience is characterized above all by faith stilled and established in forgiveness and certain that there is no pending condemnation. In the Holy Spirit, the new conscience looks away *from* itself and *to* its objective ground – Christ, the Conscience of God enfleshed, the 'living Word' who has become the conscience's new lord, judge and redeemer, 'a Conscience within our conscience'.[131] Here, Forsyth reflects the New Testament, and particularly St Paul, who assigns conscience and faith in close relation, often speaking of them in the one breath (e.g. 1 Tim. 1.5, 19; 3.9; cf. Heb. 10.22), and Dorner who insists that the 'properly guided' conscience seeks Christ and thereby becomes 'the very soul of sanctification'.[132] So construed, the notion of conscience is properly subsumed in Christian dogmatics under the rubric of faith.

As Christ sits on conscience's throne 'in absolute command of our moral self'[133] we are not simply quickened, but changed, made certain that only he who can master sin and guilt can master us, and so life, society and history. The conquering of humanity's conscience in the cross of God reconstructs humanity's moral world, authority and compass, and lifts persons from a centre in their own egoism and plants them with Christ in God whose holiness does not isolate but surrounds one with persons destined to reflect and share it.

[129] *Society*, p. 30.
[130] *Life*, p. 72.
[131] *Father*, p. 96.
[132] Dorner, *System of Christian Ethics*, p. 226.
[133] 'Intellectualism', pp. 325–26.

In Christ's moral treatment of our quagmire we are given 'not an impression of personal influence, which might evaporate, but a faith of central personal change'[134] and are 'taken into a share of His superhuman life. That is our salvation'.[135] Thus:

> I do not merely feel changes; I am changed. Another becomes my moral life. He has done more than deeply influence me. He has possessed me. I am not his loyal subject, but his absolute property. I have rights against King Edward, however loyal I am, but against Christ I have none. He has not merely passed into my life as even a wife might do, but he has given me a new life, a new moral self, a new consciousness of moral reality ... There has been what I can only call a new creation, using the strongest word in my reach. I owe him my total self. He has not merely healed me, in passing, of an old trouble, but He has given me eternal life. He has not only impressed me as a vision might ... but he has done a permanent work on me at my moral centre. He has made a moral change in me which, for years and years, has worked outwards from the very core of my moral self, and subdued everything else to its obedience. In my inmost experience, tested by years of life, he has brought me God.[136]

Forsyth relates such staurological action with pneumatology, with the Spirit who converts and sanctifies humanity for communion with the Conscience of God.

> The final moral conviction cannot be brought about by the conscience alone, but by God's Spirit in the conscience ... Salvation, if it means anything real, means a new heart; and the new heart is not simply a new affection, but a new relation, a new man, the conscience forgiven, recreated, and reassured before God by the atoning, reconciling act of God ... That is what gives the great accent of reality.[137]

Another name for this accent is 'grace'. Grace is not medicine for disease – 'more than disease ailed us'[138] – but mercy to recalcitrant consciences whom Christ irresistibly calls from out of the tomb of their own betrayed testimonies with a word of revolutionary power, effecting in human nature a rebirth into a new life under a new Lord: 'The new master made a new man, and not a reformed man.'[139] The new has not been created *ex nihilo*, but is the old with a new impulse, complexion, perspective, hope and controlling interest; the old finally come to its own via the crisis of death and resurrection. And the result is 'a new sense of freedom and soul-possession'.[140] Here freedom is conceived not as a capacity or attribute that one might possess or claim as a singular human identity but rather as a relation between persons, a relation that takes a particular shape both before God and before others. Forsyth employs a rare citation, quoting with approval

134 'Distinctive Thing', p. 489.
135 *Work*, p. 216.
136 *Person*, pp. 197–98; cf. 'Genius', p. 437.
137 *Missions*, pp. 64, 65.
138 *Sacraments*, p. 298.
139 *Father*, p. 77.
140 'Regeneration – II', p. 92.

a Fellow and Classical Tutor of Hertford College, Oxford, E. A. Burroughs: 'The very citadel of personality is invaded. An *alter ego* appears where before the *Ego* sat enthroned. And the Ego loves to have it so.'[141] In Christ, Holy Love has asserted the divine right to reign within and over us, to invade our personal life and increasingly sensitize our conscience to sin, effecting grief for holiness stained and wounded. This 'saved and enlightened conscience',[142] 'washed in pure water',[143] recognizes – albeit through a glass darkly – things as they really are and assures believers that their sanctification is found in God's self-sanctification. Moreover, in this action, believers are made aware that their sanctification signals by way of anticipation the sanctification of the race.

Forsyth associates the new conscience with a newly constituted relationship in which believers are known fully and transformed for loving service. When Christ comes to our home 'in its very sanctum, and to [our] conscience in its very adytum',[144] our consciences are liberated and re-orientated for true vocation in God's service. The freed conscience, in other words, rejects calls to autonomy and lives for fellowship with the eternal Conscience who has reconstituted it with 'a new moral motive'.[145] The new conscience also lives for fellowship with others, recognizing, as Bonhoeffer would put it, that 'being free means "being-free-for-the-other", because I am bound to the other. Only by being in relation with the other am I free'.[146] Essentially, the new conscience lives for and delights in holiness, and so hates sin, especially that which hides itself under the guise of perfectionism or espouses an alternative set of moral judgements. Rather than creep back under the way of legalism and self-justification, the new conscience 'turns to grave moral power'.[147] Obedience becomes attractive, and conscience a matter of delight, for in the new conscience God is hallowing God's own name. Echoing Kant, Forsyth contends that whereas the old conscience aggressively spurned and mocked God's law, the new conscience rejoices in law as the practical shape of loving service, true liberty and responsibility.[148] Addressing young men sometime after 1901, Forsyth avowed, 'Manliness is a matter neither of health, youth, nor success. It is not simply fresh air religion. It is a matter of the conscience. And the conscience is not something to brandish and talk about so much as to live by, taking on loyalty, duty, responsibility and service. No conscience is worth much, and no courage, except as an obedience.'[149] In obedience, the new conscience 'meets that Grace with faith in it, with self-committal' and is awake to One who 'must establish holiness in command everywhere'.[150]

141 'Regeneration – I', p. 639; cf. Dietrich Bonhoeffer, *Act and Being* (ed. W. W. Floyd; trans. H. M. Rumscheidt; Dietrich Bonhoeffer Works; vol. 2; Minneapolis Fortress Press, 2000), pp. 137–43; Dietrich Bonhoeffer, *Ethics* (ed. Clifford J. Green; trans. Reinhard Krauss et al.; Dietrich Bonhoeffer Works; vol. 6; Minneapolis: Fortress, 2005), p. 277.

142 *Authority*, p. 77.

143 *Jesus*, p. 120.

144 *Authority*, p. 169. An 'adytum' is a sacred place (in ancient worship) forbidden to the public.

145 *Sacraments*, p. 24; cf. 'Revelation', p. 108; cf. *Society*, p. 82; Dietrich Bonhoeffer, *Discipleship* (ed. G. B. Kelly et al.; Dietrich Bonhoeffer Works; vol. 4; Minneapolis: Fortress, 2000), p. 107.

146 Dietrich Bonhoeffer, *Creation and Fall: A Theological Exposition of Genesis 1–3* (ed. John W. de Gruchy; trans. Douglas Stephen Bax; Dietrich Bonhoeffer Works; vol. 3; Minneapolis: Fortress Press, 2004), pp. 62–63.

147 *Revelation*, p. 123.

148 See Kant, *Lectures on Ethics*, p. 133.

149 'Moral Manhood', p. 153.

150 *War*, p. 174.

Sanctification and trust: On 'Christian Perfection'

> *A human being is holy, not because he or she triumphs by willpower over chaos and guilt and leads a flawless life, but because that life shows the victory of God's faithfulness in the midst of disorder and imperfection. The church is holy . . . not because it is a gathering of the good and the well-behaved, but because it speaks of the triumph of grace in the coming together of strangers and sinners who, miraculously, trust one another enough to join in common repentance and common praise – to express a deep and elusive unity in Jesus Christ, who is our righteousness and our sanctification. Humanly speaking, holiness is always like this: God's endurance in the middle of our refusal of him, his capacity to meet every refusal with the gift of himself.*[151]

In 'A New Year Meditation' from January 1895, Forsyth recalls not only that 'the soul has its own chronology' but also that 'there are stages . . . in our spiritual progress'.[152] Sanctification, it is argued, is not the automatic continuum of a unitary process but a series of new departures, crises and invasions. While orientated around the new moral ontology secured in the cross, perfection describes the 'new life of faith' attached to but not growing out of the old person or resources. And sanctification describes the 'growth of our faith in forgiveness'.[153] The righteousness for which believers labour, therefore, is 'already holiness in being'.[154]

Forsyth interprets life *coram Deo* as one of continuous responsibility to the Word of God whose speech is commanding. We do not stand back from the world and survey it from a distance, but instead embrace our role in the divine drama and give ourselves to it. Here Forsyth betrays his own commitment to Voluntarism and follows Kant's position that the central expression of human freedom is moral action, that daily bread involves doing God's will and that obedience is the fruit of God's sanctifying work.

In the previous chapter, we noted that Christ's obedience brought about the creation of a new humanity (the firstfruit of which is the Church). Now we must note Forsyth's stress on the continuity of the old with the new as part of that creative work. The new humanity does not negate the old community, or annihilate it and replace it with another, but grows up within it 'without destroying the old'.[155] In Christ, the old and new are united and 'all things (even the oldest) are not destroyed, but made endlessly new'.[156] Interpreted individually,

> In Him our old selves are not lost and parted with, but renewed. It is a new birth; but it is *we*, our inalienable, identical selves, who are born again. It is not somebody else that is born and starts into being in our place. Thus He makes a new world – so new that there is no difference greater than between the new

[151] Rowan Williams, *Open to Judgement: Sermons and Addresses* (London: Darton, Longman & Todd, 1994), p. 136.

[152] 'New Year', p. 29. For a helpful introduction to Forsythian spirituality see Gordon Mursell, *English Spirituality from 1700 to the Present Day* (London/Louisville: SPCK/Westminster John Knox, 2001), pp. 393–404.

[153] *Authority*, p. 24; *Society*, p. 94.

[154] *Society*, p. 30.

[155] 'Paradox', p. 112; cf. 'Christianity and Society', p. 5.

[156] 'Paradox', p. 113.

> humanity and the old. Yet He makes it out of the old. The old is not swept away as by total deluge, and a new race suddenly created on the earth. The new humanity grows from old history.[157]

The life of human hallowing is akin to Forsyth's description of true prayer as the thought of God pressing into action. We cannot truly pray and remain idle. Eventually we find ourselves in 'interwork'[158] with God, albeit in a way more befitting that hallowed name that God has attached to us. To pray, therefore, is to engage in eschatological activity. It is precisely because eternity exists prior to time, the future before the present, the Sanctifier before the sanctified, that the promise of sanctification remains an eschatological one. While sanctification only finds its fulfilment eschatologically, the continuity between the 'then' and the 'now' is such that the prayerful life lived in the 'now' bears on the 'then'. The 'then' is 'the benediction of those that overcome', the flush and glory of moral victory which presses upon us now to unveil the future and assure those who wait in faith for the coming day.[159]

Evident here is Forsyth's conviction that holiness seeks satisfaction through reciprocation – creatures being drawn into God's own triune interpenetration. It recalls that one of the most compelling features of Forsyth's theology is his claim that 'however inadequate earthly personality is to heavenly, they are not incompatible, and they are capable of the supreme mutual act of love and grace'.[160] It is precisely this event that we witness in the twin movements in Jesus Christ. So viewed, it is inadequate, therefore, to define holiness as merely the absence of sin. While sanctification remains the work of the Holy Trinity (in election, reconciliation and perfection), that work is such that the human subject is renewed for a positive life of loving obedience, liberating authority, and eternal worship, the content of which is faith and the character of which is at every moment both mortifying and vivifying.

Akin to Kierkegaard's *Fear and Trembling*, Forsyth's 1899 essay 'Christian Perfection' reveals a critical rejection of both Hegel's *sittlichkeit* (ethical life)[161] and Kant's 'categorical imperative'.[162] And anticipating R. Newton Flew's work,[163] Forsyth rejects

157 Ibid.

158 *Prayer*, p. 57.

159 See Forsyth's undated sermon on Revelation 2.28 in Goroncy (ed.), *'Descending on Humanity'*, 2013. Forsyth's doctrine of progressive sanctification is staple Reformed Protestant, and is in harmony with Articles XVI and XVII of the *Principles of Religion* of the 'Declaration of the Faith, Church Order, And Discipline of the Congregational, or Independent Dissenters, Adopted at the Annual Meeting of the Congregational Union May, 1833'. See David W. Bebbington et al. (eds), *Protestant Nonconformist Texts, Volume 3: The Nineteenth Century* (Aldershot: Ashgate, 2006), p. 42.

160 *Person*, p. 339.

161 As developed in Georg W. F. Hegel, *Elements of the Philosophy of Right* (trans. H. B. Nisbet; Cambridge Texts in the History of Political Thought; Cambridge: Cambridge University Press, 1991), pp. 187–380 (§§142–360).

162 See also 'Christianity and Society', pp. 19–21. Purkiser charges Forsyth's essay with being 'neither perfection nor Christian'. Westlake Taylor Purkiser, *Sanctification and its Synonyms* (Kansas City: Beacon Hill Press, 1961), p. 77n.

163 R. Newton Flew, *The Idea of Perfection in Christian Theology: An Historical Study in the Christian Ideal for the Present Life* (Oxford: Oxford University Press, 1934), p. 399. According to Turner, Flew found Forsyth 'exhilarating'. John M. Turner, 'Theologian of Righteousness: Peter Taylor Forsyth (1848–1921)', *Methodist Sacramental Fellowship Bulletin* 199 (1990), pp. 1–14 (4).

any metonymy between 'perfection' and 'sinlessness'. For Forsyth, perfection is neither sinlessness nor the comprehensive achievement of human character but is thoroughly evangelical, concerned with faithful relations between divine and creaturely persons, and manifested in one who loves and trusts. So while believer and unbeliever remain sinners, the difference between them is that the believer trusts in, and looks to, Christ who is, in his person, our sanctification. Forsyth insists that the difference between the believer and the non-believer at this point is one of attitude, affinity, verdict on and treatment of sin, and of things called sin: 'The world sins and does not trouble; it even delights in it . . . But with the Christian man there is a new spirit, a new taste, bias, conscience, terror, and affection . . . He may indeed lapse . . . [but] the loyalty of his person is still true, and his course in the main is right, whatever deviations the storms may cause, or however the calms may detain and irritate him.'[164] Such constitutes the 'mystery and the power of Christianity' not as mere religious sympathy or affection, but as faith allied with the good conscience's certainty of forgiveness.[165] 'Christian faith is . . . absolute faith in Christ. The soul intrusts itself to God-in-Christ for ever.'[166] '"My will at all costs" – that is to be weak. "Thy will, not mine" – that is to be strong.'[167] Such 'self-surrender' or 'resignation' is, as Schopenhauer also saw, the final goal and inmost nature of all holiness.[168] Or, in Kierkegaard's words, 'What is obedience other than to let God ordain!'[169] Indeed, Forsyth follows Kierkegaard in positing that there is no higher life than that of faith. Faith, the highest – and hardest – thing, is 'fundamental to the Christian consciousness . . . affecting daily life at every point, its content being the entire essential reality of the individual's existence'.[170] On any 'normal' day, there is no contradiction between faith and the ethical. There are times, however, when the two create discord, when the philosophers' God meets head-on the God of Abraham and Isaac. What or Who one trusts *in that moment* betrays who one *is*, and *whose* one is. To be sure, determining when that moment is genuinely 'that moment' is impossible. Indeed, if 'that moment' could be defined, it would cease to be 'that moment'. Forsyth's point, however, is that faith is not akin to the detached curiosity of a spectator who is little more interested if her team scores the next goal than that she not miss her train. Faith means taking sides, and then staking all on the decision. Bonhoeffer articulates the same point thus: 'It is a Christian insight that the person as conscious being is created in the moment of being moved – in the situation of responsibility, passionate ethical struggle, confrontation by an overwhelming claim; thus the real person grows out of the concrete situation.'[171] Forsyth insists that Christ forces the last stand and

164 *Father*, pp. 109–10.
165 *Rome*, p. 92.
166 'Metaphysic', pp. 703–04.
167 'Strength', p. 87.
168 See Arthur Schopenhauer, *The World as Will and Idea* (trans. R. B. Haldane and J. Kemp; vol. 1; London: Routledge & Kegan Paul, 1883), pp. 75, 199, 371, 526.
169 Kierkegaard, *Gospel of Sufferings*, p. 57; cf. Søren Kierkegaard, *Fear and Trembling and The Sickness Unto Death* (trans. Walter Lowrie; Princeton: Princeton University Press, 1954), pp. 44, 62, 95.
170 Walter Lowrie, 'Fear and Trembling: Translator's Introduction', in *Fear and Trembling and The Sickness Unto Death* by Søren Kierkegaard (Princeton: Princeton University Press, 1954), p. 15.
171 Dietrich Bonhoeffer, *Sanctorum Communio: A Theological Study of the Sociology of the Church* (ed. Clifford Green; trans. Reinhard Krauss and Nancy Lukens; Dietrich Bonhoeffer Works; vol. 1; Minneapolis: Fortress Press, 1998), p. 49.

verdict of the conscience for himself or for his enemies. So when we arrive at 'the last great battle, the choice is narrow but vast, brief but yet endless, and as strait as it is sublime'.[172] The choice is that between the crucified God and no God. Faith meets Christ neither with intuition nor assent, but with decision, resolve and committal. Grounded in the unfailing faithfulness of God, faith is always answering back, an energy of the will reciprocating the entire personality that has come to us in grace. To believe, therefore, is to act. Moreover, it is not a response to an irresistible law of our nature, but the free choice of our will to God's, a choice free because created by God: 'We believe in the grace of Christ crucified only by a miracle. Human nature is against it. Faith is something created in us by the nature of that act, rather than accorded by us on any kind of evidence.'[173] Clearly Forsyth understands the Christian life not as that in which believers are insulated in a passivism, but rather as that in which believers embrace all things from a standpoint of faith, even if sin ensues. Luther's words to Philip Melanchthon, dated 3 August 1521, come to mind here:

> God does not save people who are only fictitious sinners. Be a sinner and sin boldly, but believe and rejoice in Christ even more boldly, for he is victorious over sin, death, and the world. As long as we are here [in this world] we have to sin. This life is not the dwelling place of righteousness, but, as Peter says, we look for new heavens and a new earth in which righteousness dwells. It is enough that by the riches of God's glory we have come to know the Lamb that takes away the sin of the world. No sin will separate us from the Lamb, even though we commit fornication and murder a thousand times a day. Do you think that the purchase price that was paid for the redemption of our sins by so great a Lamb is too small? Pray boldly – you too are a mighty sinner.[174]

Indeed, as Forysth insists, the knowledge of sin is parasitic upon our growth in grace. 'The height of sinlessness means the deepest sense of sin.'[175]

Faith, as articulated by both Forsyth and Luther, is the 'divine foolishness' that upsets the laws of systematic reasoning and glories in weakness. It is the 'secret assurance of inexhaustible power which can afford to set forth its infirmities in the world's very face' making one feel victories at precisely those times when most confuted by 'all the tests of world or Church'. Furthermore, this faith is the 'kind of strength which does not appear till every other power has gone in. When all the common stars have gone down, the sun of this strength arises with healing in his wings'.[176] It is 'the eye that sees when all other eyes fail that we look to for help'.[177]

Repudiating the suggestion that sanctification means self-consecration – 'it is a dangerous thing to . . . work at your own holiness'[178] – Forsyth urges believers to 'seek

[172] *Jesus*, p. 97.
[173] *Authority*, p. 163.
[174] Martin Luther, *Luther's Works, Volume 48: Letters I* (ed. Helmut T. Lehmann; Philadelphia: Fortress Press, 1999), pp. 281–82.
[175] *Father*, p. 102; cf. 'Thomas Hardy', p. 211.
[176] 'Strength', p. 85.
[177] Ibid., p. 86.
[178] *Work*, p. 71.

first for the kingdom and sanctification will be added ... sail by the Cross and you will sail into holiness'.[179] He warns of the unreliability of emotions and pleads that only the objective work of the cross can leave believers confident that all past and future sin is taken up into God's redemption, that the great transaction of our moral lives is *a done thing*: 'Faith's greatest conquest of the world is to believe, on the strength of Christ's Cross, that the world has been overcome, and that the nations which rage so furiously are still in the leash of the redeeming God.'[180] Forsyth can, therefore, press that faith is not a *condition* of the subjective aspect of justification apart from which our being made holy is thwarted, but it *is* itself the subjective aspect of justification; it is the human response to God's *finished* work, the acceptance of the truth regarding our being and the point at which what is truly complete perturbs our existence and hurls us into actuality. Here again, Forsyth echoes both Calvin and Schlatter: that our individual experiences are indissoluble with the 'full depth of their source'.[181] By pressing for the essential unity of justification and sanctification, Forsyth is led to argue that faith *is* the perfection of the Christian life: 'To be perfect is to be in Christ Jesus by faith. It is the right relation to God in Christ, not the complete achievement of Christian character.'[182] The obedience of faith is the intelligent committal and adoring 'surrender of the will' to the living, saving God made known in Jesus Christ by the Holy Spirit: 'That is Christian perfection.'[183]

It is clear that the faith of which Forsyth speaks is authored by God: 'The great change was not a somersault I succeeded in turning, with some divine help; it was a revolution effected in me and by him, comparable only to my entry on the world.'[184] There is no whiff of Pelagianism here! Indeed, faith, in James Fraser of Brae's words, 'hath beggary stamped upon it'.[185] Forsyth insists that it is no more possible for the 'natural' person to believe what God has done in Christ than to do it.[186] This is where we are compelled to recognize what Troeltsch calls an 'abruptly Transcendental Ethic',[187] the work of the Spirit who not only creates the appropriate response in us but also creates 'the very capacity for response'.[188] God creates *in* us what God

179 'Final Seat of Authority', p. 597.
180 *Justification*, p. 158.
181 Schlatter, *The Theology of the Apostles*, p. 249; cf. Calvin, *Inst.*, 3.11.6; *Authority*, p. 45; *Work*, pp. 129, 215. Forsyth turns to Ritschl to correct Schleiermacher at this point. See 'Spiritual Experience', p. 185; *Authority*, pp. 372–73. Allen mistakenly argues that Forsyth's Ritschlianism means that Forsyth encourages believers to *base* their 'faith and theology on the personal experience of receiving the benefits of Christ's work'. Allen, 'The Christology of P. T. Forsyth', pp. 86–87. Forsyth is pleased to cite at length (376 words in one place!) the preface to Melanchthon's 1521 *Loci*, but neither he nor Melanchthon confuse the *experience* of the work with the *work itself*. *Person*, pp. 199, 220–21.
182 *Father*, p. 119; cf. Schlatter, *Romans*, p. 150.
183 *Father*, p. 126; cf. *Prayer*, p. 68; 'Intellectualism', p. 6; Sermon on Mark 14.3, in Goroncy (ed.), *'Descending on Humanity'*, 2013; 'Ordination Address', np.
184 *Person*, p. 199; cf. 'Distinctive Thing', p. 491; *Authority*, pp. 9, 27, 59, 120–21, 157–58; 'Spiritual Experience', p. 184; *Father*, p. 75; *Cruciality*, p. 190; *Sacraments*, pp. 220–21, 230; *Jesus*, pp. 80–82.
185 Cited in John Brown, *Gospel Truth Accurately Stated and Illustrated by the Rev. Messrs. Jamers Hog, Thomas Boston, Ebenezer and Ralph Erskine, and Others; Occasioned by the Republication of the Marrow of Modern Divinity. With Various Improvements* (Edinburgh: Archibald Fullarton and Co., 1817), p. 438.
186 *Authority*, p. 27.
187 Cited in 'Veracity', p. 212.
188 *Work*, 10.

promises *for* us. This is 'the Creator's self-assurance of His own regenerative power'.[189] The Spirit who 'proceeds from the Cross' recreates and redeems persons 'into the very power of realizing it'.[190] The alternative, Forsyth avers, would 'destroy grace' and suggest that one could satisfy God if only God would but dispense 'time to collect the wherewithal'.[191]

The ministering theologians' burden, therefore, is 'an objective gospel, which descends on our experience both to kindle and to correct it'.[192] Clearly, the object of faith is neither a Book nor a Church, but Christ (the 'true authority over the soul and conscience') who is received as the Word of God in the preaching of the cross.[193] Such reception is ecclesial, and is nurtured and sustained through the reading of Scripture. Indeed, no inner process, nor other spiritual discipline or methodology of cultivating subjective holiness could serve the pursuit of personal holiness as much as being given over to a preoccupation with Christ's mind in the sacrament of Scripture.

Sanctification and a suffering biography

We are in the world to act and take the consequences.[194]

Schopenhauer, a thinker of some interest to Forsyth,[195] once observed that the 'overcomers' and 'holy' people of this world are those who possess an 'excellent form full of deep life'; they stand before us 'in perfect virtue, holiness, and sublimity, *yet in a state of supreme suffering*'.[196] Indeed, so closely did Schopenhauer identity holiness with suffering that he concluded that we cannot help regarding every sorrow that exists as at least a potential advance towards holiness, and, on the contrary, pleasures and worldly satisfactions as a retrogression from holiness.[197] Another from whom Forsyth drew significantly was Pascal who, in his *Letters to Mademoiselle de Roannez*, wrote that 'two things are necessary for sanctification – sufferings and joys'.[198] Forsyth agrees, and, with Kierkegaard too, is scathing of those who paint a picture of the life of faith devoid of both true joy and, particularly, of spiritual struggle, accusing such a portrait of lacking moral depth and without a taste of reality. Forsyth abhors 'natural religion of the cheerful, sunny, young and American type, which has never "descended into Hell" or

189 Ibid., p. 212.
190 *Preaching*, p. 236.
191 *Work*, p. 212.
192 'Spiritual Experience', p. 186.
193 *Rome*, p. 136.
194 *Cruciality*, p. 121.
195 See *Art*, pp. 33, 210–23, 231–44, 271, 278; *Freedom*, p. 144; *Justification*, p. 224; *Parnassus*, p. 206; *Prayer*, p. 85; *Preaching*, p. 207.
196 Schopenhauer, *The World as Will and Idea*, 1:120. Italics mine. See also Schopenhauer, *The World as Will and Idea*, 1:420, 528; Arthur Schopenhauer, *The World as Will and Idea* (trans. R. B. Haldane and J. Kemp; vol. 3; London: Routledge & Kegan Paul, 1909), p. 457; Søren Kierkegaard, *Practice in Christianity* (trans. Howard Vincent Hong and Edna Hatlestad Hong; Princeton: Princeton University Press, 1991), pp. 186–99.
197 Schopenhauer, *The World as Will and Idea*, 1:513; 3:462.
198 Blaise Pascal, *Letters* (ed. Charles W. Eliot; trans. M. L. Booth; vol. 48/2; New York: P. F. Collier & Son, 1909–14), p. 20.

found the absolute triumph in the absolute tragedy',[199] and embraces the ingredients of the pilgrim's progress in the soul's pursuit and battle for reconciliation with God. 'There is no greater division within religion than that between Emerson and Kierkegaard, between a religion that but consecrates the optimism of clean youth, and that which hallows the tragic note, and deals with a world sick unto death. We choose the latter.'[200] So, in an unpublished sermon, Forsyth insists that 'God has given men feet not wings, and the order is fight not flight. We reach heaven step by step, fighting all the way. What we need most of all for this life is the courage of the prosaic.'[201] Such fighting involves suffering, not as the *price* of glory but as the *way* of glory. Such is holiness' way in this world, and so for this reason alone is to be embraced:

> To make us partakers of God's holiness: there are no cheap absolutions. Hold out. Do not spoil God's sculpture. Lend yourself like living marble, 'living stones'. Do not be stubborn to the potter, as intractable clay. God is not making casts but men. Forward the Maker's work. Rise to it, as the audience rises to the speaker who is moulding them. Yield yourselves servants of righteousness. You were hearty enough as servants to unrighteousness. If you cease to be martyrs, you cease to be sons.[202]

By the time Forsyth, the first of five children, was ordained in 1876 he was already well acquainted with hardship. His father, Isaac (d. 1880), a merchant, book courier and then postman, supported the family on a mere eleven shillings a week, while his mother, Elspet McPherson, supplemented their income as a housekeeper to Peter Taylor, a well-to-do retired shoemaker. Three of Forsyth's siblings had died: Isaac (b. 1852), Jessie (b. 1853) and Elizabeth Ann (b. 1856) who died at age 2. In 1851, when Forsyth was 3, Elspet began to take in boarders, and the family moved to Marischal Street, Aberdeen, near the docks. After attending the local parish school (1853–) and then Aberdeen Grammar School (where he was Dux in 1864), Forsyth, in October of that same year, sat for the annual Bursary Competition at Aberdeen University. He was placed twenty-first in a class of 204, thereby winning the Cargill Bursary which secured him £20 per year for the next four years. Although unable to complete his third year due to illness, he went on to graduate with first-class honours in Classical Literature, and tied for first place in Moral Philosophy at Aberdeen University in 1869. The 1866 interruption, however, was to be something of a pattern for the remainder of his life. In September 1872, Forsyth was accepted on probation at New College, London, where he began the following February, but did not complete the full course of study due to ill health. In 1874, the year after meeting his wife-to-be, Minna Magness, ill health (and boredom) forced his resignation from New College. We know little of his movements between 1874 and 1876, the year he was ordained into his first full-time pastoral charge at Shipley. Yet it is of little surprise that Forsyth

199 'Positive Gospel', p. 65; cf. 'Thomas Hardy', pp. 193–219; Goroncy, 'Bitter Tonic for Our Time', pp. 106–07; Goroncy, 'Fighting Troll-Demons', pp. 66–80.

200 *Authority*, p. 203; cf. *Parnassus*, p. 83.

201 Sermon on Philippians 4.4, in Goroncy (ed.), *'Descending on Humanity'*, 2013.

202 *Revelation*, p. 90.

concludes his ordination statement with words that betray not only the influence of Carlyle, but a familiarity with suffering: 'Battle is the condition of life, but it is battle where the issues are already foreclosed and the end sure to the eye of faith. Conflict is life, suffering is food, death is victory; the cross ends in the empty tomb.'[203] So too his confession elsewhere: 'I cannot remember since boyhood passing a day without pain.'[204] Little wonder that after the Rev. John Hunter led a prayer for Forsyth, and the obligatory hymn was sung, J. Baldwin Brown described Forsyth as 'a good soldier in Jesus Christ'.[205] Little wonder too that Forsyth once described Newton's Olney hymn – 'Prayer Answered by Crosses' – as 'almost holy writ',[206] and as 'one of the greatest and most realistic utterances of Christian experience' representing 'the course our sunny liberalism must take as it passes from a trout stream of the morning to the river of God which is full of deep water'.[207] To be sure, Forsyth suffered from not infrequent descents into hypochondriasis. Still, it was his conviction that 'Christ had endured his cross in such a way that no other cross could finally threaten any of Christ's disciples'[208] that enabled him to endure and grow through suffering.

Forsyth's 'conversion' to 'positive' faith also cost him greatly: 'I cannot myself claim to have been free born in this faith; with a great price have I procured its freedom.'[209] The stand Forsyth took for the gospel during the New Theology controversy, for example, cost him dearly, re-introducing the pain of the cross he preached as he was attacked for rejecting those beliefs which he once espoused. Not only did many of his friends from the Leicester days spurn him, but so did many of his 'liberal' friends. Yet he confessed in 1891,

> Spiritual profit is inseparable from spiritual pains . . . obscurity is not fatal to a gospel . . . The obscurities of faith are the reservoirs of faith. From the arduous hills our help cometh. It is by the deep sea and the steep mountains that we recruit our liberty and our power. It is not, indeed, by the obscurities that we are saved, but it is not by what passes for the simplicities that we are girt up and sanctified.[210]

In addition to the usual strains that attend manse and college life, Forsyth endured some further difficulties. In 1894 Minna suddenly become an invalid. Forsyth was

203 'Ordination Statement', p. 4. While it is beyond the scope of this study, it would be interesting to probe further Forsyth's relationship and debt to Carlyle. At this point, however, we might simply raise the question of whether Forsyth isn't adopting a certain stylistic idiom in order to say something which, in the end, calls into question the very framework that provided that language with its native setting. That Forsyth can talk with such a Carlylean accent about conflict as life, etc., while championing a soteriology so fundamentally at odds with Carlyle's own framework is a further reminder of the freedom with which Forsyth stole and adapted ideas from a broad range of sources and bent them to suit his own purposes.

204 *Missions*, p. 41.

205 'Ordination Statement', p. 4.

206 *Preaching*, p. 195.

207 Ibid., p. 106.

208 D. Mackenzie Brown, *Ultimate Concern – Tillich in Dialogue* (New York: Harper & Row, 1965), p. 145.

209 *Person*, p. 255.

210 'Robert Browning', pp. 451–52.

unwell most of that year and, following doctor's advice, took three months off for complete rest. In his first week at Emmanuel Church (Cambridge), where he served until 1901, Minna died of paralysis and Forsyth entered another period of deep depression, not leaving his bed for a fortnight.[211] This experience birthed the verses on 'The Healing of the Paralytic'[212] which were later published in the *British Weekly*. While raising his school-aged daughter Jessie alone, Forsyth's health deteriorated and he was forced to severely curtail his pastoral work; during this time he received loyal support from Emmanuel Church. In 1905, eight years after he married Miss Emily Bertha Ison, Forsyth was seriously ill most of the year, as he was again in February 1907. In 1920, the year before his death, Forsyth regularly fell ill and his strength gradually declined.

In his 1878 sermon on 'The Strength of Weakness', Forsyth describes 'the sanctifying influence of perpetual pain'. He has in mind here the thorn in the flesh which is an impulse to patience, and those who 'under pressure of bodily weakness . . . give up every suggestion of natural ambition' and who thereby come to 'accept a life other than the life they had framed'.[213] These 'fragments of the true cross' (as opposed to those sought by the 'relic-mongers') issue in the sanctifying effects of that cross – namely, 'gentle intelligence', 'sweet will', hope amid hopelessness.[214] The cross and the existential reality of human sorrow are ever coupled; and one is able to bear sorrow 'who sees his God sorrow with him'.[215] Put otherwise, the infinite of pain and the infinite of glory meet in 'a suffering God'.[216] What is evident here is that the reality of the brand of holiness that Forsyth is committed to espousing means that no matter how arduous the present, it can be lived and accepted when it leads towards a goal which is, in Ratzinger's words, 'great enough to justify the effort of the journey'.[217]

211 Waddington records that in 1888, just prior to his call to Clarendon Park, Leicester, Forsyth was 'in a very delicate state of health', to the point that initially 'the deacons did not recommend an invitation'. Norah Waddington, *The First Ninety Years* (Leicester: Clarendon Park Congregational Church, Leicester, nd), p. 4. Five years later, in 1893, she notes that 'Mr. Forsyth's health was proving unsatisfactory with consequent depression and he appealed for the sympathy of the congregation in these circumstances' (p. 8). Jones notes that the four years following Minna's death were marked for Forsyth 'by great physical and nervous weakness, with even the threat of a lapse into hypochondria'. Jones, 'The Christological Thought of Peter Taylor Forsyth and Emil Brunner', p. 10. Following an interview with Mrs Jessie Andrews on 7 December 1968, Jones notes that Forsyth's (second) marriage to Emily Bertha Ison (b. 1866/67) of Oxford in 1897 was 'the real turning point of Forsyth's life . . . This charming and devoted woman was a true helpmate and unfailing inspiration, helping her husband to focus on the future rather than the past. There followed for him a great upsurge of physical and intellectual vigour'.

212 'Paralytic', p. 4.

213 'Strength', p. 86.

214 Forsyth lists numerous homely examples. 'Strength', p. 86.

215 Ibid., p. 87.

216 Ibid.

217 Joseph Ratzinger, 'Encyclical Letter Spe Salvi of the Supreme Pontiff Benedict XVI to the Bishops Priests and Deacons Men and Women Religious and All the Lay Faithful on Christian Hope, Given in Rome, at Saint Peter's, on 30 November, the Feast of Saint Andrew the Apostle, in the Year 2007, the Third of My Pontificate', n.p. [cited 5 December 2007]. Online: www.vatican.va/holy_father/benedict_xvi/encyclicals/documents/hf_ben-xvi_enc_20071130_spe-salvi_en.html.

Sanctification and the cruciform ethics of holiness

> *Free Church theological colleges were not places for the safe grazing of academic sheep, neither were they early staging posts for deaneries or public schools or bishop's palaces. They were the nerve centre of the Reformed enterprise, their principals an apostolic succession of true bishops, men for the moment as well as men of moment.*[218]

We have already noted that while immensely personal, holiness is never private but is inextricably bound up with the sanctification of the world: that Christ is no 'private possession', and so to be 'right or holy in Christ' means 'waiting, praying, working in some way for social righteousness, reform, and brotherhood',[219] and that our most deliberate moral efforts can 'fructify to true personality only in a social *milieu*'.[220] Against the tide of Victorian Christianity, Forsyth trumpets that God's claim upon human being and activity concerns the freedom given in Jesus Christ who is 'not there to enable Humanity to be all that it aspires to be, but to effect in Humanity the Kingship of God. Faith is realising not only that we are there by salvation, but that we are saved for God's absolute service and God's holy honour. Faith makes us servants more than beneficiaries, and trustees more than grantees'.[221] Revising Ritschlian value-judgements, Forsyth contends that God's greatest service to us also sets up God's deepest claims. Grace not merely lifts us out of despair, as it were; it releases us into the 'bondservice of Christ' in order that we may live within the joyful communion of holiness and its 'entire obedience'.[222] But against those who would reduce the Church's *raison d'être* to the functions of mission, a reduction which merely finances and ratifies the urge towards activism and leads to faith running on empty, Forsyth issues the following warning:

> Christian philanthropy is the finest thing in the history of the world (except the Church's whole history). But it has been the work of the Church, whose faith has produced so much else. There is no tenderness, either to the sinner or to the child, so tender as that which melts upon them from the Church's passion of holiness to God. For the sake of the good works themselves, the first need is to restore to the Churches that sanctity which has ebbed from so many of the bustling communities, but which is the only permanent source of love, help, and brotherly kindness. This, rather than efficiency, is the one note of the true Church.[223]

Forsyth warns that working at holiness can be 'fatal', and he criticizes those popular forms of devotion which are 'pursued as a spiritual luxury rather than worn upon faith

[218] Clyde Binfield, 'Peter Taylor Forsyth, 1848–1921, Minister of Emmanuel Church, Cambridge, 1894–1901: Sermon Preached to Mark the Sixtieth Anniversary of His Death' (unpublished sermon; Emmanuel Church, Cambridge, 1981), p. 4.

[219] 'Sanctification', p. 734.

[220] 'Genius', p. 433.

[221] *Authority*, p. 376.

[222] Ibid.

[223] 'Attacks', p. 614.

like a spiritual halo as unfelt as our hair'. It is not hard to take up 'Christian work', he says. But it is hard to really pray, to not evade the 'arduous toil of spiritual concentration'.[224]

The new conscience with which we have already been concerned emerges in a 'new ethic of the race',[225] a new order, ideal, standard and final mode of holiness which is not merely a new morality such as the Sermon on the Mount (which cannot, according to Forsyth, form the basis of anything but legalism[226]), but a new 'personal intercourse' between God and humanity bearing co-witness to the truth that God has carried human society into the holiness of God's cross.[227] Forsyth perceives here that one of the problems with Rome is that there 'the gospel became a new law; and virtue became a thing of order, instead of a thing of the new conscience'.[228] This is precisely why, he insists, the Church required Luther who 'never began with the idea of reconstructing the Church, but with the experience in him of a new conscience, of a new conception of religion, of grace and faith'.[229]

The creation of the new conscience enables persons and communities to engage the ontology of the universe, and to engender its ethical shape in our world. So Forsyth expressed support for Socialists' efforts such as the great Dock Strike in 1889, and for the Church's new sense of social responsibility expressed in practical concern locally for the poor and disregarded, and globally, for example, in his public opposition (in 1904) to the importation of Chinese labour into the Transvaal on the grounds that it was a disguised form of slavery, an issue he revisited in 1906.[230] Also, between 1885 and 1889, Forsyth was actively involved in political debate, writing political and social essays for the *Manchester Examiner* under the pseudonym 'Publicola'. 1886 saw the publication of his lectures on *Socialism and Christianity in Some of Their Deeper Aspects* and, in 1888, Forsyth lectured on 'The Relation of the Church to the Poor' before the Lancashire Congregational Union. Influenced by Gore and the Anglican CSU, Forsyth essentially theologized T. H. Green's doctrine of the positive state and the efficacy of legislative action. Recalling Forsyth's ministry at Manchester 28 years after his death, Sidney F. Wicks, the editor-in-chief of the *Manchester City News* and ex-student of Forsyth's at Hackney College, observed that it was Forsyth's 'love of the poor and humble and ignorant that was the chief mark of his ministry in Cheetham Hill. Above all he loved and understood children'.[231] Once, and at a time when he was chairman of the Congregational Union, Forsyth erupted, 'Do not take my arm and lead me away to the dwellings of the pound-a-weeks and the nothing-a-weeks and tell me if I want realities to consider there. Long ago I was there, and worked there, and considered there, and have been considering ever since'.[232] Forsyth knows nothing of

224 *Preaching*, p. 123.
225 *Cruciality*, p. 53.
226 See 'Sects and Wars', pp. 621–22; *War*, pp. 22–23, 41, 66, 86, 137–39.
227 'Mystics', p. 401.
228 *Rome*, p. 91.
229 Ibid., pp. 64–65; cf. 'Lay Religion', p. 767; 'Evangelical Basis', p. 684.
230 See *Socialism*, p. 32; 'Chinese 18 Jan', p. 4; 'Chinese 20 Jan', p. 12; 'Chinese 25 Jan', p. 11; 'Chinese 26 Jan', p. 7; 'Chinese 29 Jan', p. 7.
231 Wicks, 'He Loved the Children', np. An example of Forsyth's ministry with children during this period is evident in his *Pulpit Parables for Young Hearers*, co-authored with Rev. J. A. Hamilton.
232 *Society*, p. 96.

a Christianity divorced from the demands of justice and righteousness which he calls 'applied holiness'.[233]

> We are not really saved if we are saved into neglect of a social salvation. The Gospel preached to the soul must be a Gospel which leaves the saved soul much more concerned than he used to be about the saving of civilization, the salvation of the just as well as of the lost, and the restoration of the poor as well as of the wicked.[234]

That Forsyth's concern spanned the whole of society was because 'his gospel was big enough to handle it'.[235] In the face of the exploitations that attend local and global communities and economies, Forsyth contends that a holy Church has a duty to challenge injustice wherever it exists. 'It has to declare that certain things, like a living wage for the workers, are a first charge on industry; that proper housing is essential for the family life that is the backbone of Society; that due rest, and especially a day of rest, is also needful; that Capitalism must be modified if it is always dogged by masses of unemployed, and that Labour must regard contracts and keep its word even to its own hurt.'[236] Forsyth's sympathies for the newly formed Labour Party[237] were clear, although he never confused the sympathies that ennobled the movement (which he fully supported) with the kingdom of God itself (as some others had done), and he discouraged the Church to resist ever aligning itself with any political party. No political issue was worth rending the Church over. Rather,

> [The Church's] business is to substitute for the lust of power the passion for righteousness . . . She must lend her sympathy and influences to every effort by the labourer to be less of a serf and more of a man, freely bargaining with what he has to sell, and cherishing a standard of life, and not a mere existence. To buy in the cheapest market and sell in the dearest is an economic principle which the Church must oppose when the commodity is human life or human labour. Cheapness here is bought far too dear at the cost of human dignity. And our prosperity is unblest if it do not at the same time make it more possible for all who produce it to live in conditions becoming men and women, and cherish the hopes and interests of a self-respecting Humanity. The Christian principle is to buy and sell under conditions that make life worth living in the sight of God. It is the Church's duty to saturate Society with such convictions and ideals . . .[238]

233 *War*, p. iii. One reviewer goes too far when he writes that Forsyth had an 'angry . . . yearning for social justice'. Neal C. Gillespie, 'Review of *P. T. Forsyth* by Archibald M. Hunter', *Church History* 44, no. 2 (1975), pp. 274–75 (275).

234 *Preaching*, p. 178.

235 Martin Bleby, 'Publisher's Note', in *The Principle of Authority in Relation to Certainty, Sanctity and Society: An Essay in the Philosophy of Experimental Religion* by P. T. Forsyth (Blackwood: New Creation Publications, 2004), p. vii.

236 'Church and Society', p. 43.

237 The various socialist organizations and trade unions that had cooperated intentionally since the late nineteenth century officially came together as 'The Labour Party' on 15 February 1906 under Keir Hardie's leadership. Forsyth refers sympathetically to Hardie in *Freedom*, pp. 52, 285.

238 'Church and Society', p. 43.

5

Thine Is the Kingdom, the Power, and the Glory. Amen

True holiness . . . hallows everything.[1]

The purpose of a world created by a holy God must be holiness, the reflection and communion of His own holiness. Can God secure it? . . . That is the ultimate question in life . . . And to that question Christ and His cross are the answer, or they have no meaning at all. They reveal in their foregone victory the omnipotence of holiness to subdue all natural powers and forces, all natural omnipotence, to the moral sanctity of the Kingdom of God. And if they do not reveal that we are left without any ground of certainty about a holy ending for the world at all . . . It is a tremendous claim. And the improbability of it is either a pious absurdity; or it is the quiet irony of a God who has it already done in the hollow of His hand.[2]

'A Christian Minister has no need to explain his reasons, in these days, for directing the attention of his congregation to the subject of the following discourses.'[3] So penned J. Baldwin Brown in the Preface to his published lectures on annihilationism and God's love. The lectures attend to two of the more voluminous theological debates of the nineteenth century – the everlasting punishment of the unrepentant, and the immortality of the soul.[4] These debates crossed cultural, denominational and

[1] Martin Buber, *Between Man and Man* (trans. Ronald Gregor-Smith; London/New York: Routledge, 2002), p. 67.

[2] *Person*, pp. 228–29.

[3] Brown, *The Doctrine of Annihilation*, p. v.

[4] English Congregationalist Edward White attracted attention in 1846 with his defence of the doctrine of conditional immortality, and from the 1870s onwards annihilationism gathered increasing popularity. See Charlotte E. Woods, *Memoir and Letters of Canon Hay Aitken* (London: C. W. Daniel Co., 1928), pp. 174–81; Joseph Agar Beet, *The Last Things* (New York: Eaton and Mains, 1898), pp. 194–229; Joseph Agar Beet, *The Immortality of the Soul: A Protest* (London: Hodder & Stoughton, 1901), pp. 55–87; cf. J. S. Banks, *Words on Immortality* (London: Charles H. Kelly, 1902), p. 28; Lyman Abbott et al. (eds), *That Unknown Country: Or, What Living Men Believe Concerning Punishment After Death Together with Recorded Views of Men of Former Times* (Springfield: C. A. Nichols & Co., 1889), especially chapters 4, 6, 9, 51; Richard Whately, *A View of the Scripture Revelations Concerning*

theological lines,[5] and promoted re-evaluation not only of eschatology, but also of other areas of theology as well.

The nineteenth- and early-twentieth-century Church also witnessed and adopted many of the onslaughts and intrusions of Enlightenment thought. The literature unanimously underscores the mounting influence of biblical criticism, swelling confidence in scientific theory, rising convictions about the imaginative value of religious language and concerns to rethink traditional 'orthodoxies' about a God whose 'divine decrees of election and reprobation had an iron fixity and mechanical action of the laws of the Newtonian universe'.[6] These attended – and contributed to – an increasing agnosticism in Victorian England concerning the afterlife, and precipitated a new resolve to work out the gospel's social implications in the present, a resolve emboldened by optimism in secularized visions of inevitable progress (in both its Hegelian and biological forms).[7] Certainly, William Gladstone spoke for many when he suggested that the doctrine of hell had been relegated to 'the far-off corners of the Christian mind ... there to sleep in deep shadow as a thing needless in our enlightened and progressive age'.[8]

Certainly from about 1800, debates concerning the final fate of the impenitent were hotly contested (and not only by Unitarians who took a particular interest in such) and questions of an *apokatastasis*, annihilationism and the possibility of post-mortem probation were all posed as theologically viable options for Christians. Along with reworked doctrines of election, justification and atonement, there were,

a Future State (Philadelphia: Lindsay & Blakiston, 1857), p. 181; Charles Frederic Hudson, *Debt and Grace: As Related to the Doctrine of a Future Life* (Boston: John P. Jewett and Company, 1859), pp. 160–356; William E. Gladstone, *Studies Subsidiary to the Works of Bishop Butler* (Oxford: Clarendon Press, 1896), pp. 184, 195–97, 241; Joseph Parker, *The People's Bible: Discourses upon Holy Scripture* (vol. 1; London: Hazell, Watson and Viney, 1897), pp. 222–23; J. J. Stewart Perowne, *Immortality: Four Sermons Preached Before the University of Cambridge* (Cambridge: Deighton, Bell, and Co., 1869), pp. 31–32, 63; John Hancock Pettingell, *The Theological Trilemma. The Threefold Question of Endless Misery, Universal Salvation, or Conditional Immortality (i.e., the Survival of the Fittest), Considered in the Light of Reason, Nature, and Revelation* (New York: Sherwood & Co., 1878); Edward White, *Life in Christ: A Study of the Scripture Doctrine on the Nature of Man, the Object of the Divine Incarnation, and the Conditions of Human Immortality* (London: Elliot Stock, 1875); Le Roy Edwin Froom, *The Conditionalist Faith of Our Fathers, Vol. 2: From Repression and Obscurity to Restoration, Gathering Momentum and Status, Accelerated Acceptance and Expansion Spiritualism Climaxes the Conflict* (Washington: Review and Herald, 1955).

[5] For example, the German Reformed theologian Wilhelm Herrmann (in *Dogmatik*, p. 110) and the North American Wesleyan Methodist J. A. Beet (see *The Last Things*, p. xviii).

[6] Geoffrey Rowell, *Hell and the Victorians: A Study of the Nineteenth-Century Theological Controversies Concerning Eternal Punishment and the Future Life* (Oxford: Clarendon Press, 1974), p. vii.

[7] Something of this now-faded moral and political idealism has been preserved for us in a no-holds-barred advance in scientific-technological progress and an obsession with economic growth. Nineteenth-century confidence in evolutionary progress largely replaced neo-platonism's cycle of divine emanation and return which had influenced Universalists of previous centuries. Rowell identifies several prevalent concerns in response to this re-examination: (i) a connection between belief in an infallible Bible and belief in hell, (ii) a fear of theological vocabulary being rendered meaningless, (iii) a concern that moral sanctions were being undermined, and (iv) a concern that the Church's authority was being sabotaged by liberalism more generally. Ibid., p. 123. Watts has argued for a connection between declining belief in hell and decay in church attendance, a connection Bebbington suggests Watts exaggerates. Michael R. Watts, *Why Did the English Stop Going to Church?* (London: Dr Williams's Trust, 1995); Bebbington, *Victorian Nonconformity*, p. 55.

[8] Gladstone, *Studies Subsidiary to the Works of Bishop Butler*, p. 206.

also, no shortage of theories of punishment that flirted with deterrence, prevention and purgatorial rehabilitation schemes. Part of the fall-out of such debates was a substantial abandonment of the traditional doctrine of eternal punishment. Nevertheless, hell remained – at least officially – a component of Christian dogma, predominantly serving as a moral sanction and witnessing to the abiding magnitude of ultimate ethical axioms.[9] There continued to be a robust defence of the notion that 'the impenitent wickedness of which a man is consciously guilty can lead to nothing but damnation',[10] evident in the 1846 Evangelical Alliance Basis of Faith, and in the conservative preaching of this period.[11] There was, however, a growing sense even among evangelicals that the doctrine of everlasting punishment be not given undue weight. Generally, evangelicals continued to endorse the reality of hell, but even one as conservative as C. H. Spurgeon was able to quote approvingly Henry Ward Beecher that the future of the impenitent was God's business and not ours.[12] Evangelicals, by and large, no longer dwelt on hell's prospects, or to its attendant details, and certainly did not relish them. Increasingly, there prevailed an italicizing of God's love and a hope that 'there may be some transcendent manifestation of the Divine grace in reserve, of which as yet we have no hint'.[13]

Such was this emphasis that it was not uncommon to reject the doctrine of everlasting punishment entirely and, for many, both High and Broad Churchmen, to embrace (at least) a modified universalism.[14] Nurtured in Romanticism's humanitarianism and in the faint trust of the 'larger hope' expressed in Tennyson's *In Memoriam* – that requiem penned for the poet Arthur Henry Hallam and commended by Forsyth as that which 'ought to be read and studied to-day more than ever before'[15] – theologians of the calibre of F. D. Maurice, T. R. Birks, A. R. Symonds and Angus Mackay were among those who pressed in this direction, while some such as Andrew Jukes and Samuel Cox embraced

[9] For a rebuttal of the view that universalism undermines ethics, see Sydney Herbert Mellone, *Eternal Life Here and Hereafter* (London: The Lindsey Press, 1916), pp. 272–73. For a critical response to Mellone, see Ebenezer Griffith-Jones, *Faith and Immortality: A Study of the Christian Doctrine of the Life to Come* (London: Duckworth, 1917), pp. 242–43.

[10] Robert W. Dale, *Christ and the Future Life* (London: Hodder & Stoughton, 1895), p. 99.

[11] For example, Richard C. Morgan, *The Life of Richard Weaver, the Converted Collier* (London: Morgan and Chase, 1861), p. 100; Chas. H. Fowler, 'Punishment Is Not the Great Aim or Design, but an Incident, of God's Moral Government; yet it is so Important, that the Doctrine Concerning Hell is Fundamental in Methodist Teaching', in *That Unknown Country: Or, What Living Men Believe Concerning Punishment After Death Together with Recorded Views of Men of Former Times* (ed. Lyman Abbott et al.; Springfield: C. A. Nichols & Co., 1889), p. 303.

[12] Charles H. Spurgeon, 'Preface', in *The Duration of Future Punishments: Two Lectures to the Students at the Metropolitan Tabernacle* by William Barker (London: Passmore & Alabaster, 1865), p. v; cf. Handley C. G. Moule, '"Detached Remarks on the Doctr[ine] of Future Punishment", Lecture Notebook, Handley Moule Papers' (unpublished papers; Ridley Hall, Cambridge, nd).

[13] Dale, 'On Some Present Aspects of Theological Thought', p. 14; cf. Stanley N. Gundry, *Love Them In: The Life and Theology of D. L. Moody* (Chicago: Moody Press, 1999), pp. 97–100.

[14] Ludlow identifies four main sources of eighteenth- and nineteenth-century universalism: (i) liberal humanism, (ii) mysticism, (iii) a reaction again Calvinism's double-predestination, and (iv) a strong interest in egalitarian political aims, such as opposition to slavery. Morwenna Ludlow, 'Universalism in the History of Christianity', in *Universal Salvation? The Current Debate* (ed. Robin A. Parry and Christopher H. Partridge; Carlisle: Paternoster, 2003), p. 204.

[15] *Life*, p. 11; cf. *Art*, pp. 62, 140, 213, 256; *Parnassus*, p. 59; *Preaching*, p. 5; *Freedom*, pp. 172, 177, 249; *Society*, p. 121; *Work*, p. 17.

universalism in more dogmatic forms.[16] Birks, for example, hypothesized that the 'lost' might even enjoy a sense of heavenly blessedness simultaneous with their experience of punishment. Though this did not go unchallenged by his evangelical colleagues, the fact that it did not lead to his dismissal as the honorary secretary of the Evangelical Alliance suggests a significant shift in outlook. A confessed universalist, Hannah Whitall Smith was even invited to preach at the 1874 Broadlands Keswick Convention,[17] and Samuel Cox, who was editor of the *Expositor*, maintained his Nottingham Baptist congregation's confidence even while advocating unbridled universalism.[18]

Within this climate, Forsyth carved out his own eschatological vision motivated by the weight of God's holiness, and given concrete shape in the hallowing activity of One who entered 'the sphere of sin's penalty and the horror of sin's curse, in order that, from the very midst and depth of it, His confession and praise of God's holiness might rise like a spring of fresh water at the bottom of the bitter sea, *and sweeten all*'.[19] The remainder of this study will explore the final three words of this claim: of holiness which does not relent until *all* is sweetened. I will outline something of that vision as it pertains to the subject of hallowing with particular focus on Forsyth's account of universalism. And I will enquire as to whether or not his public agnosticism regarding dogmatic universalism finally compromises his theology of holiness.

I. For the sins of the world: 'So that by the Grace of God He Might Taste Death for Everyone'

Forsyth's rejection of limited atonement

[Jesus] did save a world. He did think in wholes.[20]

. . . every single soul is saved in an act which was the organic salvation . . . of the whole race.[21]

[16] See, for example, Thomas Rawson Birks, *The Victory of Divine Goodness* (London: Rivingtons, 1867); Alfred Radford Symonds, *The Ultimate Reconciliation and Subjection of all Souls to God Under the Kingdom of Christ* (London: Hamilton, Adams, R. Gladding, 1873); Andrew John Jukes, *The Second Death and the Restitution of All Things* (London: Longmans, Green, and Co., 1867); Samuel Cox, *Salvator Mundi: or, Is Christ the Saviour of All Men?* (London: C. Kegan Paul and Co., 1878).

[17] See Hannah Whitall Smith, *The Unselfishness of God and How I Discovered It: A Spiritual Autobiography* (Victoria: Shirley Sloan, 2008), pp. 72, 179, 193–94, 223. First published in 1903.

[18] See Cox, *Salvator Mundi*, pp. 172–97. For a survey of some of the literature see David Hilborn and Don Horrocks, 'Universalistic Trends in the Evangelical Tradition: An Historical Perspective', in *Universal Salvation? The Current Debate* (ed. Robin A. Parry and Christopher H. Partridge; Carlisle: Paternoster, 2003), pp. 219–44; Joseph H. Leckie, *The World to Come and Final Destiny* (Edinburgh: T&T Clark, 1922), pp. 252–73. See also the work of Thomas Baldwin Thayer, James Brown and David Thom as noted in the bibliography.

[19] *Work*, p. 148. Italics mine. On the matter of Forsyth's soteriological universalism, see also Goroncy, 'The Final Sanity is Complete Sanctity', pp. 249–79. Forsyth was not, of course, the only Nonconformist to affirm the universal implications of Christ's work. There was, among others, the work of David Worthington Simon, R. Vaughan Pryce, W. F. Adeney and Forsyth's student H. F. Lovell Cocks.

[20] 'Conversion', p. 760.

[21] *Preaching*, p. 178.

Like Calvin, McLeod Campbell, Dale and Baldwin Brown,[22] Forsyth underscores that Christ's death is not merely *potentially* universal in scope but is so *actually* and *efficiently*: Christ experienced 'in a Divine life the universal death'.[23] Forsyth's rejection of the doctrine of limited atonement is informed primarily by five factors: (i) his belief in the universality of God's paternal love, (ii) his staurology, (iii) his conviction regarding the solidarity of the race, (iv) his eschatological claim that 'all time and space is the content of eternity',[24] and (v) his reading of Scripture. Redemption, conceived broadly, concerns the 'last things', 'the goal', 'the end' and the 'consummation', and Forsyth believes that God's action in history's centre is not resigned until everything – and everyone – is readjusted, reconciled to the Godhead who is 'perpetually recalling, or exalting, everything into fusion with itself'.[25] The potential for something – or someone – to escape such action would be so catastrophic as to be unthinkable. Not only, he insists, would the existence of an unreconciled part of creation be a continual threat to God's being – as holiness, love and fidelity – but such would also undermine confidence in Christian assurance.

Forsyth consistently, also, draws attention to the universality of judgement: 'In the Cross the *world* was doomed to – salvation. *All* were shut up unto sin, that there might be mercy on *all*'.[26] And in another place: 'The good are condemned with the bad, the bad are saved with the good. All were shut up unto judgment that mercy might be on all'.[27] He resists speculating on futurist eschatologies, or preaching either christological representation or punishment for a select group only. Instead, Christ is the 'sole and exclusive includer of all'.[28] Forsyth praises his former pastor, J. Baldwin Brown, for 'recognising the growing demand of the future for a social salvation', and that the Christ who died was the 'Brother of the human race and not of a chosen few'.[29] He also joins Brown in crediting the decline in nineteenth-century Calvinism with the ascension of the conviction that there can be no place for a theology which treats pagan nations as outside God's love and care.[30] The human race, Forsyth presses, is not only committed to 'salvation in advance', but is 'baptised into Christ's death'.[31] Christ's judgement-bearing is, therefore, 'not only of every soul, but of the whole soul ranged before the whole God and the holy God', putting the race in right relation to God.[32] This serves as a key for understanding Forsyth's hopeful universalism, and makes his denial of a dogmatic *apokatastasis* all the more perplexing. For in the one sentence Forsyth can speak of Christ absorbing not only the sin of every person – and all sin

[22] See John Calvin, *Concerning the Eternal Predestination of God* (trans. J. K. S. Reid; London: James Clarke and Co., 1961), pp. 148–53; George M. Tuttle, *So Rich a Soil: John McLeod Campbell on Christian Atonement* (Edinburgh: Handsel, 1986), pp. 42–54.

[23] *Father*, p. 47.

[24] *Justification*, p. 10.

[25] *Work*, p. 69.

[26] *Preaching*, p. 247. Italics mine. Cf. 'Liberty and Limits', p. 503.

[27] 'Conversion', p. 768.

[28] *Missions*, p. 206.

[29] *Brown*, p. 8.

[30] Brown, *First Principles of Ecclesiastical Truth*, p. 353.

[31] *Revelation*, p. 36.

[32] *Cruciality*, p. 171; cf. 'Insufficiency', p. 612.

itself – but also of the possibility of the ongoing existence of 'the sin of sins', the 'fixed refusal of grace'.[33]

Forsyth's rejection of double-predestination

Our subject unequivocally echoes Ritschl's, Schleiermacher's and Brown's reaction against the doctrine of double-predestination as, in Ritschl's words, an 'unwarranted overstepping of theological competency to define the Biblical thought of divine election more precisely by filling out, through rational processes, the opposite thought of reprobation'.[34] Indeed, Forsyth consistently rejects those schemes that subordinate grace to a non-christologically determined doctrine of election, thereby avoiding the trap of reading back into God's saving purposes the possibility of eternal rejection. He argues that when understood in light of God's final revelation in Christ (and certainly not in light of the law of natural selection) the doctrine of predestination is good news: 'The object of God's will and purpose of love is mankind as one, mankind as an organism, mankind in its totality.'[35] The great doctrines of redemption are not 'peculium of groups' as if divine election concerned a particular section of humanity.[36] Each person, therefore, is entitled to call themselves God's elect, and to locate security in 'the changelessness of the eternal nature and the indefectibility of the divine purpose'. Forsyth asks, 'How then can there be talk about a will of God for the perdition of any? Faith realizes the will of God in Christ as pure salvation – and my salvation. Damnation is not preached enough, but from a Christian Gospel eternal and destined damnation is excluded.'[37] And so in an early sermon, he asks:

> Can it be just that God should bring beings into the world unprotected by an infinite armour of foresight against the infinite chances and temptations to wrong, and yet hold them liable to infinite punishment when they had gone wrong? . . . Punish a man for his sin, that is just; punish him for ages (if in that other world you can reckon time), that may be just; but make no end of punishing him for that sin, reduce him from a man to a devil and keep him there, let him become for ever vile, mainly because he was ignorant to start with, that is not just . . . Preach the eternal, unappeasable wrath of God upon lost souls and you offer men a devil to worship.[38]

[33] *Work*, p. 156.

[34] Ritschl, *Justification and Reconciliation*, p. 126; cf. 'Paradise Lost', p. 4; Brown, *The Doctrine of Annihilation*, pp. 9–10. On Schleiermacher, see Matthias Gockel, 'New Perspectives on an Old Debate: Friedrich Schleiermacher's Essay on Election', *International Journal of Systematic Theology* 6, no. 3 (2004), pp. 301–18; Matthias Gockel, *Barth and Schleiermacher on the Doctrine of Election: A Systematic-Theological Comparison* (Oxford: Oxford University Press, 2006); Jason A. Goroncy, '"That God May Have Mercy Upon All": A Review-Essay of Matthias Gockel's *Barth and Schleiermacher on the Doctrine of Election*', *Journal of Reformed Theology* 2, no. 2 (2008), pp. 113–30 (114–15).

[35] *War*, p. 118.

[36] Ibid.

[37] *Authority*, p. 355.

[38] *Mercy*, pp. 9, 14.

And years later in his Yale lectures, he articulated at some length his conviction that the doctrine of predestination ought to find voice in the pulpit. Indeed, as one reviewer noted, this is one of the reasons that Forsyth broaches the topic at all – to 'tell us how to preach predestination still'.[39]

Another error that Forsyth identifies in the double-predestination schema is the construal of death as the terminus of God's electing work. Double or 'absolute predestination',[40] is 'a nightmare which grew from the association of the truth of election with the falsehood of death's finality . . . Take [Calvin's] doctrine of election, relieve it of the notion of death's absolute arrest, and you have a great panorama of development' which opens the possibility of endless growth beyond death.[41]

Forsyth argues that the doctrine of double-predestination arises not from grace but from an experience of the world which is then read back into a theory of divine causation. This posits practically two causes, two wills, and two gods, and reduces Christ to a 'mere provision' or 'engine' of God 'by which the happy lot of the one class can be brought to effect'. This process is 'totally wrong' and 'a false orthodoxy', and is largely responsible, Forsyth believes, for the 'popular debasement of Christ, and for current heresy and unbelief'. Instead, he argues, Christ is the 'one source' and expression of God's one holy and loving will. Here, Forsyth shares Tillich's anxiety about the 'demonic implications' of the doctrine of double predestination which introduce an 'eternal split into God himself'.[42] Moreover, Forsyth presses that 'what our faith answers in [Christ] is election as Love's mode of action, God's election of *the world* to salvation, and its effective and solidary salvation accordingly'. There can be no talk of God's damnation of any: 'Faith knows much of predestination, but nothing of a predestination of some to bliss and some to perdition. And when the Bible speaks of election it is never the election to heaven or hell.'[43] Instead, in Christ, *the race* has been 'fore-ordained', 'fore-saved' and 'justified . . . before the day of Time'.[44]

Ultimately, therefore, one cannot choose to be godless for it is precisely those that God elects. The intractable choice, therefore, is made void by God's will and action. 'What therefore God has joined together, let no one separate' (Mk 10.9). To be sure, God's predestination can be met with resistance and denial, but whether holiness' determination to realize itself in *all* creation can be finally compromised remains a question I will discuss below. All we need to note here is that *there can be no ultimate dualism* and that *predestination always means life*, even if some for a time choose death.

39 Anonymous, 'A Review of *Positive Preaching and the Modern Mind* by P. T. Forsyth', *Expository Times* 19 (1907), pp. 98–99 (98); cf. *Positive Preaching*, pp. 94–97; F. D. Coggan, '"Under-estimated Theological Books": A Review of *Positive Preaching and the Modern Mind* by P. T. Forsyth', *Expository Times* 72 (1961), pp. 324–26 (325).

40 *Authority*, p. 359.

41 *Life*, pp. 16, 17.

42 Tillich, *Systematic Theology*, 3:434.

43 *Authority*, p. 359. Italics mine.

44 *Preaching*, p. 96.

Forsyth's rejection of annihilationism

> *That nothing walks with aimless feet|That not one life shall be destroy'd|Or cast as rubbish to the void|When God hath made the pile complete.*[45]

The nineteenth century certainly accommodated its share of Annihilationists – Ritschl, Dale and Drummond among them;[46] but, following Baldwin Brown, Forsyth insists that it is 'our weakness, not our strength, that consents to the agnosticism of the grave, to death as complete erasure'.[47] And he faults the burdened West's pessimism for being 'drawn to the Buddhistic idea of the human soul's extinction'.[48] Forsyth also believes that any Christian warrant for believing in immortality on the basis of some inherent aspect of creatureliness which provides 'a mere asbestos . . . for future flames, or for the happier incandescence' is lacking.[49] Instead, immortality is God's gift announced in Christ's resurrection, and pertains to God's incessant gift of life 'and not to an infinite lease of life which [God] signed at the beginning'.[50] It is, therefore, theological, soteriological, religious, and not principally anthropological or philosophical. 'A sure belief in immortality . . . is not founded on the nature of the psychic organism, but on its relation to Another'.[51] Clearly, God has a stake in our continuation, and the 'miserable doctrine of annihilation'[52] contradicts God's purposes and love's 'inability to surrender what it possesses'.[53] The faithful Creator will bring all creation to its goal in holy communion, the durability of which is ensured in God's own eternity and in God's unwillingness to abandon his beloved.

While some have suggested the possibility of human beings so dedicating their lives to subhuman activities and to refusing all signposts to God's love that after death they become, by their own effective choice, decreated,[54] Forsyth refuses to concede such an end: Jesus liberates humanity from all that leaves us imperilled to the nothingness of our choices that he might be Lord of both the living and the dead (Rom. 14.9).[55] Holy love is not content ever to discard any part of creation. Forsyth, therefore, would reject Richard Bauckham's suggestion that God might 'create some creatures for a temporary

[45] Alfred Tennyson, *In Memoriam* (Boston: Ticknor and Fields, 1861), p. 121 (stanza LIII).
[46] Ritschl, *Justification and Reconciliation*, pp. 125–39, 323. Dale et al., *Life of R. W. Dale*, pp. 110, 149, 313; Henry Drummond, *Natural Law in the Spiritual World* (London: Hodder & Stoughton, 1883), pp. 226–28. The doctrine had historical support too in Justin Martyr, Arnobius and Irenaeus. See also Edward William Fudge, *The Fire That Consumes: The Biblical Case for Conditional Immortality* (Carlisle: Paternoster, 1994), and John W. Wenham, 'The Case for Conditional Immortality', in *Universalism and the Doctrine of Hell: Papers Presented at the Fourth Edinburgh Conference in Christian Dogmatics, 1991* (ed. Nigel M. de S. Cameron; Carlisle/Grand Rapids: Paternoster/Baker, 1992), pp. 161–91.
[47] *Father*, p. 67.
[48] *Work*, p. 171.
[49] *Life*, p. 46.
[50] Ibid., p. 22; cf. Andrew Seth Pringle-Pattison, *The Idea of Immortality* (Oxford: Clarendon Press, 1922), pp. 195–201.
[51] *Life*, p. 20.
[52] 'Hell', p. 4, citing Brown, *The Doctrine of Annihilation*, p. vi.
[53] Fairbairn, *The Place of Christ*, p. 464.
[54] N. T. Wright, *Surprised by Hope* (London: SPCK, 2007), pp. 191–92, 195.
[55] *Authority*, p. 417.

purpose that, once fulfilled, leaves no room for their eternal preservation'.[56] Indeed, Forsyth argues in his 1877 Shipley sermon: 'Purity which is infinite is purifying also, and is not content till it has subdued all things to itself, and given of its fulness to all who are morally poor . . . It longs and yearns; it waits, it prays, it strives; it soothes, and when need is, it burns; it has colour, and soul, and life.'[57] Here Forsyth's thoughts most closely resemble those of Andrew Fairbairn who compared annihilationism to 'a ruthless remedy, somewhat in the manner of a rude physician, who, in order to stay the disease, killed his patient'. He continues: 'The annihilation of the creature either now or at any moment even inconceivably distant, were a confession by the Creator of utter helplessness, an acknowledgment that the universe, or a part of the universe, had so broken down in His hands that He knew no way of mending it but by ending it.'[58]

Despite the initial attraction of the annihilationist position as that which (i) at least leaves every room of the universe without spot or blemish, and (ii) is more theologically and morally plausible than the 'sheer pointlessness'[59] of everlasting punishment, it comes at the expense of granting evil a final victory. If annihilationism is to be defended it must face the demons it creates: (i) that evil has claimed a victim in the creation – in Lewis' terms, that 'the demand of the loveless and the self-imprisoned . . . should be allowed to blackmail the universe . . . that Hell should be able to *veto* Heaven';[60] (ii) the possibility that being itself can be unmade; (iii) that there is a limit to the recreative power of divine love over the recalcitrant will, that divine victory is attained via 'the destruction of the soul which does the evil';[61] (iv) the expiration of love – that 'if our beloved were extinguished in death, the fact would be signalled from the unseen by the expiring of our love in the seen';[62] and (v) that even if God could purge the bitter memories of that defeat from the minds of human creatures, God could not do so from God's own mind. While (according to Forsyth[63]) the author of the Apocalypse may have held such a position, annihilationism amounts to calling off creation, and results from a morbid fascination with nothingness rather than existence, both factors fundamentally at odds with the moral ontology with which Forsyth operates, and with the tenor of the remainder of the New Testament.

Forsyth's employment of 'universal' grammar

Forsyth's adoption of the grammar of the 'universal' and 'the many' reflects that employed within Scripture itself. Little surprise then that he credits St Paul with being 'the first to

56 Richard Bauckham, 'Eschatology in *The Coming of God*', in *God Will Be All In All: The Eschatology of Jürgen Moltmann* (ed. Richard Bauckham; Minneapolis: Fortress, 2001), p. 12; cf. Harold Knight, *The Hebrew Prophetic Consciousness* (London: Lutterworth Press, 1947), p. 173.

57 *Mercy*, p. 11.

58 Fairbairn, *The Place of Christ*, p. 466.

59 Brian Hebblethwaite, *The Christian Hope* (Basingstoke: Marshall, Morgan & Scott, 1984), p. 216.

60 C. S. Lewis, *The Great Divorce* (London: Geoffrey Bles, 1946), p. 111. Swinburne's defences of annihilationism fail to deal with this objection. Richard Swinburne, *Providence and the Problem of Evil* (Oxford: Clarendon Press, 1998), p. 201; Richard Swinburne, *Responsibility and Atonement* (Oxford: Oxford University Press, 1998), pp. 182, 197.

61 'Hell', p. 4; cf. John Baillie, *And the Life Everlasting* (New York: C. Scribner's Sons, 1936), p. 294.

62 'Immortality', p. 363.

63 'Hell', p. 1.

construct a philosophy of History' through his 'theology of universal redemption'.[64] We have already noted Forsyth's attention to the conscience as 'the great universality' and to God's conscience as 'the final universality'.[65] He also refers to 'Christian Universalism' as that which has 'a moral interior, and finds in the conscience the true unity of the race'.[66] He shares a conviction regarding the universality of deepest reality in evangelical experience,[67] and of Christ's 'universal kingship' which is concerned with his 'universal mission' brought to a 'universal . . . head in the Cross'.[68] Christ himself is described as a 'universal person', and the adjective is also attached to his 'life', 'personality', 'soul' and 'kingship'.[69] The cross is Christ's universal 'work',[70] 'moral conquest',[71] 'certainty',[72] 'act',[73] and 'the real secret of Christ's universalism'.[74] It is an act of 'universal judgment'[75] wherein Christ shared 'a universal moral death'[76] turning 'a universal curse into a universal blessing'.[77] Forsyth also speaks of 'the miracle of universal grace',[78] of the universality of reconciliation,[79] redemption,[80] salvation[81] and regeneration,[82] and of the soteriological ground-plan of the creation with which it 'groans toward the manifestation of a universal and holy reality'.[83] More significantly for our study, Forsyth couples 'universal righteousness' and 'eternal holiness',[84] contending for 'the victory of perfect holiness for an end of universal holiness'.[85] This is what Denney (who is no universalist) might call 'Christianising the universe'.[86]

To be sure, 'universal' grammar need not necessitate universal*ism*. Forsyth also speaks of 'universal fatherhood',[87] of God as universal,[88] of the 'universal soul',[89]of the

64 *Sacraments*, p. 101. Contra Stephen T. Davies, 'Universalism, Hell and the Fate of the Ignorant', *Modern Theology* 6, no. 2 (1990), pp. 173–86 (176); I. Howard Marshall, 'Universal Grace and Atonement in the Pastoral Epistles', in *The Grace of God, the Will of Man: A Case for Arminianism* (ed. Clark H. Pinnock; Grand Rapids: Zondervan, 1989), p. 61; N. T. Wright, 'Towards a Biblical View of Universalism', *Themelios* 4, no. 2 (1978), pp. 54–58 (55).

65 *Preaching*, p. 213.

66 'Nationality', p. 385.

67 *Authority*, pp. 23, 60, 82–83, 188, 312, 355.

68 Ibid., pp. 11, 12, 29.

69 *War*, pp. 148, 187; 'Atonement', p. 86; *Authority*, p. 416; *Justification*, p. 218; *Sacraments*, pp. 59, 255; *Preaching*, pp. 151, 153, 237.

70 *Authority*, p. 119.

71 *War*, pp. 77, 145, 187, 188.

72 *Parnassus*, p. 263.

73 'Regeneration – I', p. 632.

74 *Preaching*, p. 213.

75 *Cruciality*, p. 171; 'Insufficiency', p. 612.

76 *Father*, p. 58.

77 *Missions*, p. 17.

78 *Authority*, p. 153.

79 *Parnassus*, p. 264.

80 *Father*, pp. 58, 70; *Sacraments*, p. 101; *Parnassus*, p. 264; *Preaching*, pp. 9, 181.

81 *Authority*, p. 132; *Justification*, pp. 10, 161; *Person*, p. 171; *Work*, p. 116.

82 *Sacraments*, p. 225.

83 *Authority*, p. 107.

84 *Preaching*, p. 200.

85 *Society*, p. 32.

86 James Denney, *Jesus and the Gospel: Christianity Justified in the Mind of Christ* (London: Hodder & Stoughton, 1908), p. 37.

87 *Preaching*, p. 219.

88 Ibid., p. 241.

89 *Authority*, p. 281.

'universality of the Gospel',[90] of the 'universality of Christian faith' (a faith 'universalised' by the cross[91]), of 'universal judgment',[92] universal redemption,[93] of the moral as the 'universal reality',[94] of 'universal history',[95] of universal ethics,[96] of the necessity for a 'universal way' to, and 'universal note' of, proclamation,[97] of the 'universalism of modern missions',[98] of the 'universal Spirit',[99] of the 'universal reign of unmodified law',[100] of baptism as bearing witness to the 'grand universal of regeneration',[101] of the 'universal society' of the Church',[102] of the universality of Christian revelation as final,[103] of God's 'universal Kingdom'[104] and 'universal counsel',[105] of God as the 'absolutely universal',[106] the world's 'universal Redeemer'[107] and of the 'universal empire' of holiness which 'makes the universal and infinite power to be truly God'.[108]

The language of 'universal', in other words, pervades Forsyth's mature writing. But lest we too quickly conclude on matters where Forsyth would bid us to remain somewhat agnostic, in his critique of metaphysics, for example, Forsyth reminds us that universality is not the same as speaking of the whole but is only a factor of the whole: 'It may be . . . a very thin universal without the content and wealth of a whole'.[109] He charges that even metaphysics as architectonic as Hegel's cannot be truly universal because it is not dynamic, creative or full enough. Copious examples could be cited, but the point is clear enough: Forsyth understands God's way with creation in universal terms. God's hallowing activity clearly has universal scope. Notwithstanding the pervasiveness of the grammar of the universal, however, the implications of such in Forsyth's thought are far from automatic.

The cross as (practically) final . . . the new beginning

> *A moral salvation, the final and foregone conquest of guilt by judging Grace and searching Love, is our only warrant* in extremis *for believing in the radical order and final purpose of the world.*[110]

90 *Justification*, pp. 21, 40; cf. *Preaching*, pp. 58, 72, 182; *Sacraments*, pp. 6, 53, 119, 126.
91 *Authority*, pp. 163, 183, 364, 416; *Justification*, p. 46; *Preaching*, p. 222.
92 *Justification*, p. 56.
93 *Sacraments*, p. 294.
94 *Authority*, pp. 196, 198.
95 Ibid., p. 205; *Sacraments*, p. 101.
96 *Preaching*, p. 213. Ethics, Forsyth contends, can only become 'really universal' when there is a rise towards holiness.
97 *Authority*, pp. 207, 215.
98 Ibid., p. 351.
99 *Preaching*, p. 43.
100 Ibid., p. 198.
101 *Sacraments*, p. 225.
102 Ibid., p. 124; cf. *Authority*, pp. 213, 229; *Charter*, pp. 38–39, 58–60, 78; *Preaching*, pp. 64, 72; *Work*, p. 44; *Sacraments*, pp. 6, 31, 45, 47, 49–50, 65, 106–07, 180; *Congregationalism*, pp. 14, 21–23, 55–57; *Revelation*, pp. 37.
103 *Authority*, pp. 213–14; *Justification*, p. 43.
104 *Authority*, pp. 229, 253, 319; *Justification*, p. 41; 'Nationality', p. 385; *Preaching*, p. 222.
105 *Justification*, p. 10.
106 *Authority*, p. 186.
107 Ibid., p. 299.
108 Ibid., p. 355.
109 *Justification*, p. 62.
110 Ibid., p. 78.

Forsyth neither trivializes nor minimizes the seriousness of sin, nor God's holiness and justice, nor final judgement and the threat of hell. Neither does he emasculate or marginalize the atonement from the centre of the Christian story. If Forsyth has a vision for universal sanctification, it is because of – and not in spite of – his conviction that what God has done in the crucified Christ is a teleological *fait accompli*; everything is decided in the cross (*crux probat omnia*). Here alone, history's *telos* is finally unveiled, the *eschaton* arrived, evil's death warrant signed, the end's new beginning begun, God's decisive move made, and all things recapitulated into the triumph of that holiness which is the last reality. The cross is where 'all things are (so to say) tied up'.[111]

> All history, through His great act at its moral centre, is, in God, resolved into the harmonies of a foregone and final conquest. And our faith is not merely that God is with us, nor that one day He will clear all things up and triumph; but that for Him all things are already triumphant, clear, and sure. All things are working together for good, as good is in the cross of Christ and its saving effect.[112]

Articulated here is a commitment to the claim that the world is not *being* redeemed 'as the number of believers grow'.[113] Unlike every human enterprise, the world's redemption through Christ's hallowing work has been accomplished *de facto*: 'In the universal Christ the world is chosen for salvation, and is saved in principle, and shall be saved in fact.'[114] Whatever remains to be realized, therefore, is an unfailing work – there can be no uncertainty whether God's kingdom will succeed. This is because of the only two parties involved – God and humanity – the final party in the matter is God. 'And God has done His part . . . The effectual thing is done. Whatever more He does is to only carry home what he has done; and all we can do is to take it home. We can but appropriate his gift of a final, a complete Christ.'[115]

While Forsyth believed that Europe in 1914 witnessed 'the man of sin' breaking the 'restraints that kept him from being revealed till his appointed Day',[116] it would be a mistake at this point to too haphazardly accuse Forsyth of advancing a classic over-realized eschatology. Not only is he acutely aware of the sin that remains at the door, but also that the eruption of the kingdom inaugurated in the incarnation finds its *telos* in a different world: 'The greatest revelation of all is yet to come.'[117] 'It is too great for earth. There is not room enough in this world for God's eschatology.'[118] In the unsolved contradictions of history, even a reconciled world is not yet the new world, but only its beginning. Only in the new world, Forsyth avers, will we rest from our vertical ascent, with its labour and sorrow, and cease to be nomads of progress.

111 *Justification*, p. 81.
112 *Cruciality*, p. 62.
113 *Revelation*, p. 37.
114 *Authority*, p. 357.
115 *Revelation*, p. 37.
116 'Effects of War', p. 19.
117 Ibid., p. 20.
118 *Justification*, p. 163.

Only in the new world are human persons 'set to acquire spiritual wealth, and to build the city of God on His shining tableland'.[119] This is the new reality that has begun in the Easter action where we are given eternity in a point condensed and creative and which will reach its satisfying homecoming in another world.

Responsible theology is, at core, concerned to direct us to revelation's teleological direction, unveiling creation's purpose, presenting us with the future in advance, as it were, and building on the supremacy and finality of intelligent action towards a moral horizon, towards the consummation of life. It is not framed under the aegis of rationality, secular politics or science, but under the sponsorship of the holy whose word it serves and to whose self-fulfilment it bears witness. It understands that the world is not merely God's expression, but God's action, conflict and conquest. 'What theology has in charge', Forsyth avers, 'is the message of a final and holy consummation, awaiting history, yet anticipated in history, in the consummate, victorious Christ. It is the prepayment of our divine destiny. We see not yet all things put under either God or man but we see Jesus, faith's source and consummator alike'.[120] 'We see not yet all things righteous, but we see Christ, to Whose holy "Yes" all righteous things are for ever sure.'[121]

II. Revising election

Forsyth's doctrine of sanctification cannot be comprehended apart from his doctrine of election. And election, he urges, involves three concentric spheres gathered around a fixed point. Foremostly, election concerns Jesus Christ. Next, it concerns that 'vast totality'[122] of souls elected in Christ, the first fruit of which is the Church. Finally, it concerns the individual soul. So A. E. Garvie's description of Forsyth's doctrine of election as 'the individual application of the universal purpose of salvation in Christ'.[123] To these three we now turn.

Christ, 'Captain of the elect'

> *[Christ] is the supreme object of the divine election, 'the Captain of the elect', the object . . . of an eternal election.*[124]

There are strong echoes of Goodwin, and indeed of the Reformed tradition generally, in Forsyth's conviction that 'divine initiative is everything', that it is in the divine

119 Ibid.
120 *Preaching*, p. 210.
121 'Sanctification', pp. 733–34.
122 *Authority*, p. 354.
123 Alfred Ernest Garvie, 'A Cross-Centred Theology', *Congregational Quarterly* 22 (1944), pp. 324–30 (325–26). Garvie was Chairman of the Scottish Congregational Union in 1902, and Professor of the Philosophy of Theism, Comparative Religion, and Christian Ethics at Hackney College and New College, Hampstead, from 1903. He succeeded Forsyth as Principal of New College from 1907 and of Hackney College from 1924.
124 *Person*, p. 286.

freedom that 'all our hopes begin',[125] and that humanity's final interests and liberation are prescribed. As Forsyth would have it, 'Nothing can make man free which does not secure in advance the freedom of God.'[126] Consequently, 'Nothing must be done to imperil the absoluteness, the freedom, of God, His creative initiative on grounds entirely within Himself.'[127] Some form of Calvinism is, therefore, 'indispensable and immortal'.[128] Behind such a claim lies Forsyth's conviction that the essence of Calvinism lay not in the doctrine of predestination per se but rather in the doctrine of God and specifically in the 'absolute freedom of God's grace'.[129] Such priority does not 'concuss our personality',[130] but neither does it merely 'refurbish' it or 'release its best powers'.[131] Because Forsyth understands and thinks about freedom – whether divine or human – in a fully christological way, his account of freedom avoids the problems posed by those accounts which are articulated in abstract metaphysical terms and independently of the concrete reality and revelation of how God has actually exercised and self-communicated freedom in the one man, Jesus Christ.

Forsyth stands with the tradition in maintaining that election is God's method and way to God's goal. He defines election as 'the one compendious *actus purus* of God, the act whose participation makes all action divine, the act of incessant free choice, wherein His will is not simply mighty but absolute'.[132] Evangelical faith has always confessed that it is the Son who is from eternity elected to be the one mediator between God and humanity, the one in and through whom the Triune life would embrace human existence and raise humanity to participate in the divine movement. So Schlatter: 'The Son's eternal communion with the Father comprises our election.'[133] So too Forsyth understands that not only has God, in eternity, elected humanity for adoption in Christ, but also that Christ himself is the primary object of God's electing love and so the ground of our election. There is no word which precedes Christ, nor which exists behind him. Jesus is the first, final and only beloved Word of God's election.

By comprehending both freedom and election christologically, Forsyth circumvents the pattern of those who would divide the human race into two groups – one the object of grace and the other the object of wrath. 'From the beginning, from the heart of God, from Christ', he insists, all humanity was 'destined for God's will and redemption'.[134] Furthermore, humanity is elected not as an assembly of isolated entities, nor by 'a love distracted and dissipated into millions of points without concentration or unity',[135] but in Jesus Christ who is 'the personal embodiment of God's personal purpose and choice with persons, the Captain of the elect, the eternal object of God's choice, and God's own perfect and perpetual answer to His own will'.[136]

125 *Work*, p. 69.
126 *Preaching*, p. 97.
127 *Person*, p. 344.
128 *Authority*, p. 255.
129 *Freedom*, p. 263.
130 *Preaching*, p. 44.
131 *Person*, p. 96.
132 *Authority*, p. 352.
133 Schlatter, *Das christliche Dogma*, p. 479.
134 *Preaching*, p. 96; cf. 'Church, State, Dogma', p. 831.
135 'Metaphysic', p. 706.
136 *Preaching*, pp. 95–96; cf. Dorner, *System of Christian Ethics*, p. 350.

Forsyth understands that there is no dark decree lurking behind God's election in Christ. He thereby avoids the causo-logical problems that attend federal Calvinism which tend to foster, among other ugly ideas, a hidden Nestorian dualism between Christ's two natures, and even to encourage a form of Arianism and Socinianism wherein Christ's atoning work is regarded as a divinely sub-contracted activity ultimately separate from God's intrinsic person, nature and character. This means that Forsyth's understanding of the Christian life is not vulnerable to the more contractual, mechanical, legalistic and introspective forms such as took hold in his native Scotland sponsored by the intrusion of federal theology into Reformed, and dogmatized in the Westminster Standards. Forsyth agrees that Calvin was right to direct us to Christ as the objective mirror of our election,[137] but wrong to suggest that that mirror reflects two groups – the elect and the reprobate. To look to Christ in his cross is to see the human race apart from which one's own existence is impossible. Moreover, it is to be transformed from crippling soteriological anxiety to liberating assurance. In Christ, all are entitled to find security in God's changelessness and in the indefectibility of God's purposes – to say 'I am chosen and elect of God'. In fact, the refusal to declare so is 'the sin of unfaith', and that precisely, Forsyth argues, because Christ is the Saviour of the whole race 'and not of a section of it'.[138]

Circles of election: The Church as the firstfruits of the new creation

> *The Church is not a mere coterie of faddists, the mere assembly of people who happen to be drawn together by a common interest; the Church is an essential factor in the whole history of humanity, and it contains the key to it all.*[139]

Forsyth follows Ritschl's twofold belief that 'the community to which the sacrifice of Christ stands in necessary relation, extends over the whole human race',[140] and that the divine election of the Church is (as for Israel) an 'election by love for communion and service' – for bearing prophetic witness to God's works and words towards the nations, and for calling the world back to faith in the God in whom alone there is unfeigned hope for all creation:

> [D]ivine leadership means service, sacrifice, help, uplifting, redemption, the Cross. The elect are there for burden. Burden is the badge of the best – not to exploit and exterminate, but to lift and rescue. If any are higher on the hill it is that they may turn to redeem and not to rend, to carry and not to devour. We are elected, individually or in races, not to primacy, but only to priority, and to *a priority* of service.[141]

137 Calvin, *Inst.*, 3.24.5.
138 *Authority*, p. 354.
139 'Church Fabric', p. 416.
140 Ritschl, *Justification and Reconciliation*, p. 130.
141 *Authority*, p. 360; cf. 'Conversion', p. 764; Gregory MacDonald, *The Evangelical Universalist* (Eugene, OR: Cascade Books, 2006), pp. 74–105, 118–19, 167.

While offering little sustained reflection on Israel's election per se, Forsyth does, however, understand Israel's calling and equipping as that directed not to its 'own circle' or 'simply for the good of their own souls'. Rather, Israel's election concerns 'a special, corporate, and official vocation' of being the 'select witnesses of [God's] revelation to all the world, vehicles of His self-interpretation, and stewards of His universal salvation'.[142] Here Forsyth trails Schleiermacher, Birks and Brown, and anticipates Barth, Moltmann and others, in understanding both Israel and the Church – 'the modern Israel'[143] – as those circles of election who exist for wider circles, 'rippling out from the central happening of Christ's crucifixion and raising'.[144] Indeed, both Israel and the Church deny their election when they attempt to claim Messiah and his kingdom as their domesticated champions. And Forsyth looks forward to the day when the Church 'shall include the whole family of God',[145] shall 'cover Humanity',[146] 'humanity as one whole'.[147] So he speaks of God's 'preference', of God's 'predetermining choice', and of 'the divine order of the world', insisting that while it is impossible for us to comprehend the reasons for such ordering, predestination of some sort is indispensable for religion. Nevertheless, while 'relative predestination is a tolerable mystery, absolute predestination is intolerable'. Again, Forsyth makes this claim on the basis of a conviction that predestination is not about monopoly, but priority: 'The chosen are but preferred, not secluded. The left are but postponed, not lost. Every man in his own order – in a historic process not ended by death . . . Some races have a hegemony, some individuals have a start. But for what? Not for privilege, not for prerogative, not out of favouritism, not for immunity, not for dominion, but for leadership.'[148]

Descriptions of the Church as 'the greenhouse in and by means of which the green shoots of God's purposes in and for creation are brought on',[149] or as that 'microcosm in which the divine purpose in reclaiming the entire creation is anticipated and through which . . . that purpose is furthered'[150] aptly reflect Forsyth's position. The Church is more than the sum of those thus far converted. It is the new humanity *in utero*, the human race foretasted proleptically, presented to the world by God as the future in advance – as the 'final and universal certainty'.[151] But for now,

> the converted are still the few. It pleases God to work by an elect in every age, and, therefore, Christianity must be as slow as the God who took that way. It must be

[142] *Authority*, p. 132.
[143] 'Church Fabric', p. 415.
[144] Jürgen Moltmann, 'Hope and Reality: Contradiction and Correspondence', in *God Will Be All In All: The Eschatology of Jürgen Moltmann* (ed. Richard Bauckham; Minneapolis: Fortress, 2001), p. 82; cf. Schleiermacher, *The Christian Faith*, p. 548; Thomas Rawson Birks, *The Victory of Divine Goodness* (London: Rivingtons, 1870), p. 208; Brown, *The Doctrine of Annihilation*, p. 100; Barth, *CD* IV/2, p. 645.
[145] 'Religious Communion', pp. 1202–03.
[146] 'Genius', p. 436.
[147] 'Missions', p. 275.
[148] *Authority*, pp. 359–60.
[149] James D. G. Dunn, *The Epistle to the Colossians and to Philemon* (New International Greek Testament Commentary; Carlisle/Grand Rapids: Paternoster/Wm. B. Eerdmans, 1996), p. 96.
[150] Andrew T. Lincoln, 'The Letter to the Colossians', in *The New Interpreter's Bible: Second Corinthians – Philemon* (The New Interpreter's Bible; Nashville: Abingdon, 2000), p. 611.
[151] *Parnassus*, p. 263.

> slow if it is going to gather up all; it must be slow if it be the appeal of the cross to souls that live by something else than the *panem et circenses* – soup and circuses, beer and bets.[152]

Evident here is Forsyth's belief that love – which is 'the principle of election' – works in a preferential, historic and evolutionary way according to the moral principle and order prescribed by absolute holiness and human freedom. But it is always an 'election of some from others *for* others, to bring others in, and not leave them out, far less cast them out'.[153] Moreover, the reason the world will not be a failure for God is precisely because humanity's redemption is not limited to a 'group of people saved in an ark of some kind'.[154] 'It is', Forsyth avers, 'society that is being saved, and not only a group of individuals, an elect out of society'.[155] The Church, therefore, must be reckoned not only as 'the final and direct object of God's choice',[156] but also as the next circle of election, the 'earnest' and 'inchoate stage of the New Humanity and of the Great History that is to be'.[157] It is that community 'ear-marked' for holiness, and for whom '*every soul is born*',[158] the firstfruits of a race wherein 'there is no soul for which [holiness] is not the last and most practical question of its being'.[159]

To anticipate our discussion below, Forsyth believes that the redemption worked out via succeeding circles of election in history extends post-mortem. Some are elected for witness to God's grace this side of death, some on the other. But finally, God's election comes home to all.

> One elect succeeds another, and each lives for all in rising cycles. From the non-elect in one stage comes the elect for the next. And so on, in an ascending series of elects, till the whole human lump is refined, till all are brought in – the worst and most intractable last, since freedom may not be forced. There is all eternity to do it in. Here time is no longer. The ungathered fruit of one age yields seed for the next. What seems the wreck of one civilization is but the shaling of the next. What seem to us waste products they have means of using and refining behind the veil. And so the elective process goes on – the élite serving the submerged in every cycle – till we all come to the fullness and quality of the universal and eternal Christ . . . But that whole, that goal, is in another world.[160]

152 'Gate', p. 178. Forsyth has mistranslated *panem et circenses* here; it should read 'bread and circuses'.
153 *Authority*, p. 360.
154 *Work*, p. 171.
155 'Final Seat of Authority', p. 608.
156 *Authority*, p. 353; cf. *Life*, p. 63.
157 *Sacraments*, p. 150; *War*, p. 117; cf. Robert W. Jenson, 'Reconciliation in God', in *The Theology of Reconciliation* (ed. Colin E. Gunton; Edinburgh: T&T Clark, 2003), p. 166.
158 *Sacraments*, p. 6; cf. 'Metaphysic', p. 707.
159 *Authority*, p. 354.
160 *Justification*, pp. 161, 163; cf. 'Slowness', pp. 219–20. In an otherwise excellent essay, Hilborn and Horrocks mistakenly observe that the universalist thrust in this passage from Forsyth's *Justification* represents 'a single place in the whole canon of his work to flirt with the possibility of a final restitution'. Hilborn and Horrocks, 'Universalistic Trends in the Evangelical Tradition', p. 240.

Assurance

> *The poet trusts that somehow good will be the final goal of ill; the believer knows that this is how it must be so, for so it is.*[161]

What I hope are evident by now are Forsyth's twin claims: that creation's future is not dependent on an arbitrary course of events, but on divine election as secure as God's self; and that 'Christian universalism turns on a belief, not in the unity of Humanity . . . but in the one final Goal and Judge and Saviour and King of all men'.[162] Christ, in other words, is the pledge *to God* that sanctification is creation's *telos*, and *to us* that the doctrine of election forms the basis of the Christian proclamation of assurance. And because Christ equates to the 'absolute certainty of salvation for the race',[163] each person therefore may call themselves God's elect. Made palpable here is Forsyth's categorical disquiet about an 'overdriven individualism'[164] which seeks self-assurance while being practically unconcerned about God's wider purposes. He believes that the old individualism 'reared under our Election' has done its work for Christianity for the time being, and we are now suffering from its after-effects. 'We do not realise that we are each one of us saved in a racial salvation.'[165] 'I am saved in a saved world.'[166] 'A soul can neither be saved nor sanctified without a world.'[167] Forsyth also believes that individual believers can only know soteriological assurance because they are members of a saved community (the Church) which itself is saved in a universal and racial salvation. By implication, the gospel's object is 'no longer to save a group out of the world, but to save the world itself'.[168] The salvation of one soul can offer no assurance that all are saved, whereas any act which reconciles the entire race also guarantees the sanctification of every member. The human conscience – and God's – can be satisfied with nothing less lest it be beset with eternal qualm.

Forsyth's emphasis on christological and corporate election is never at the expense of the individual who remains the indirect object of election. The 'unspeakable value' of each soul remains an indispensable part of the 'religious value' of the doctrine: 'What is chosen is no Church regardless of single souls, but a Church with the very hairs of its head all numbered', apart from which the Church is a mere 'abstraction'.[169] Furthermore, knowledge of one's election is reached religiously by 'personal and evangelical faith'.[170] Through this experience believers can be confident that Christ

161 *Person*, p. 252.
162 *Justification*, pp. 186–87.
163 *Person*, p. 85.
164 *Intercessory Services*, p. 6.
165 *Freedom*, p. 127; *Work*, p. 114.
166 *Justification*, p. 142; cf. 'Distinctive Thing', p. 495.
167 *Father*, p. 8.
168 *Sacraments*, p. 125.
169 *Authority*, pp. 353, 354.
170 Ibid., p. 356. The relationship between faith and assurance receives particular attention in *The Principle of Authority*. See pp. 17–18, 35–39, 42–43, 46, 49, 52, 55, 59, 81–83, 162, 164, 181–82, 185, 188, 192–93, 198, 320, 328, 331–32, 338–61.

has fulfilled humanity's responsibility, brought perdition to its terminus and replaced 'predestination of some' with 'predestination of all'.[171] It is precisely because the Captain of the elect stands vicariously in every person's place and has overcome the world that believers can 'be of good cheer', recalling that 'the Christian idea is not happiness and it is not power, but it is perfection'.[172] Christian peace, in other words, is not the saint's calm, but filial confidence, even when we are anything but calm: 'Troubled we may be, but sure.'[173] How so? Because the faith that answers grace believes that God does not merely *prove* himself to us, but *comes home* to us in such a way that believers are certain of God's resolve to bring the human will and conscience into unison with the last moral reality.

Repeatedly, Forsyth therefore presses that we ought to be surer of Christ than of self or of the fabric and sense that faith in Christ creates, more certain of that act which creates assurance than of the experience of assurance itself. So Worrall: 'It is important that the believer should be able to say "I am certain", but it is no less essential that he should be able to pass beyond this and say "It is certain".'[174] This is the certainty characterizing faith, which gifts confidence in prayer,[175] and which Forsyth strikingly describes as a sharing in God's self-knowing, and even as a participation in God's own self-certainty. Such sharing is made immanent by faith and is known – whether in God or in us – by the Spirit who searches everything, even the depths of God. The validity of this experience can only be questioned on the basis of something deeper and surer than the rational, on the basis of something identical with reality itself, and without conceding to the disputed regions of intellectualism, evolutionary science or metaphysics, a conviction that not all reviewers appreciate.[176]

Persuaded that we are 'foredoomed to faith' and 'saved . . . before we could be consulted', Forsyth not only staunchly defends paedobaptism, but also underscores that Pelagianism sabotages any possibility of assurance 'unless you presume to be certain that you have done everything you are required to do'.[177] Pelagianism is incongruous with the humility implied in Christian faith which trusts only the 'eternal will and absolute act of God . . . which nothing can unsettle or withstand'.[178] This, Forsyth believes, is where the doctrine of election's true value lies – in the certainty of God's holy and unwavering proclivity for universal sanctification, which can be confounded 'only if God fail'.[179]

171 *Freedom*, p. 125.
172 *Life*, p. 87.
173 *Jesus*, p. 4.
174 B. G. Worrall, 'The Authority of Grace in the Theology of P. T. Forsyth', *Scottish Journal of Theology* 25 (1972), pp. 58–74 (70); cf. *Authority*, pp. 81–82; *Person*, pp. 199, 281–82; *Sacraments*, p. 54; 'Allegory', p. 318; 'Revelation', p. 118.
175 See *Prayer*, p. 57; *Preaching*, pp. 46–47, 136.
176 For example, George Johnson, 'A Review of *A Principle of Authority* by P. T. Forsyth', *Princeton Theological Review* 12 (1914), pp. 125–27.
177 *Sacraments*, p. 219; *Authority*, pp. 349–50.
178 *Authority*, pp. 351–52. Forsyth names three false challenges to assurance: agnosticism, humanist/sentimentalist religion and Roman Catholicism. *Authority*, pp. 349–50.
179 Ibid., p. 350.

III. Pareschatology and the hope of hallowed life

> *That lake of fire is regarded no longer as out of His dominion, beyond the circle of His grace and love. It is His, to be used for His divine purposes.*[180]
>
> *Love alters not with his brief hours and weeks|But bears it out even to the edge of doom.*[181]

While Forsyth had expressed some concern in 1887 that Congregationalism's home missions had relaxed their views 'as to the finality of death for character' and contemplated 'at least the possibility of the redemptive function of hell',[182] he comes by 1916 (in *The Justification of God*) to reject the notion that the state of the soul is irretrievably fixed at death, and to join others (notably Athanasius, Cyril of Alexandria, Kant, Schleiermacher, Kierkegaard, Schelling, Schopenhauer, Dorner and Brown) in their call for a 'larger hope'.[183] This mirrors a growing conviction in Victorian England (spurred by a faith in evolutionary progress and encapsulated in Newman's *The Dream of Gerontius* (1865)) about a general uneasiness with the traditional doctrine of hell and a belief that the intermediate state offers fresh soteriological opportunities for the continuation of what Samuel Cox describes as 'the Divine education and development of the race . . . [being] carried on toward its final issue or goal'.[184] It is this whole-life process, rather than any particular moment before or at death, which is indispensable for being's becoming, which appeals to those for whom sanctification is of foremost

[180] Frederick Denison Maurice, *Lectures on the Apocalypse; or, Book of Revelation of St. John the Divine* (London: Macmillan and Co., 1861), p. 404.

[181] William Shakespeare, *The Complete Works of William Shakespeare* (ed. Williams Aldis Wright; Garden City: Garden City Publishing Company, 1936), p. 1418 (Sonnet 116).

[182] 'Sunday Schools', p. 126.

[183] Brown, *The Doctrine of Annihilation*, pp. ix, 83, 118–19; cf. See Isaak August Dorner, *A System of Christian Doctrine* (trans. Alfred Cave and J. S. Banks; Edinburgh: T&T Clark, 1880–82), pp. 130–35. This view has found more recent support in a number of places; for example, George R. Beasley-Murray, *Baptism in the New Testament* (London/Grand Rapids: MacMillan/ Wm. B. Eerdmans, 1962), p. 258; Donald G. Bloesch, *Essentials of Evangelical Theology, Volume 2: Life, Ministry, and Hope* (San Francisco: Harper & Row, 1982), pp. 226–28; Charles E. B. Cranfield, *First Epistle of Peter* (London: SCM, 1954), p. 91; Charles E. B. Cranfield, 'The Interpretation of 1 Peter 3:19 and 4:6', *Expository Times* 69 (1958), pp. 369–72 (372); Gabriel Fackre, 'Divine Perseverance', in *What About Those Who Have Never Heard?* (ed. John Sanders; Downers Grove: IVP, 1995), pp. 71–95; George Lindbeck, *The Nature of Doctrine: Religion and Theology in a Postliberal Age* (Philadelphia: Westminster Press, 1984), pp. 46–72; Clark H. Pinnock, 'The Finality of Jesus Christ in a World of Religions', in *Christian Faith and Practice in the Modern World: Theology from an Evangelical Point of View* (ed. Mark A. Noll and David F. Wells; Grand Rapids: Wm. B. Eerdmans, 1988), pp. 165–67; Nigel Wright, *The Radical Evangelical: Seeking a Place to Stand* (London: SPCK, 1996), pp. 99–102; *passim*.

[184] Cox, *Salvator Mundi*, pp. 172–73. See James Edwin Odgers, 'Universalism', in *The Encyclopedia of Religion and Ethics, Volume 12: Suffering – Zwingli* (ed. James Hastings and John A. Selbie; Edinburgh: T&T Clark, 1970 (1928)), pp. 530–31; Klaus Schmöle, *Läuterung nach dem Tode und pneumatische Auferstehung bei Klemens von Alexandrien* (Münster: Aschendorff, 1974), pp. 60–62; Philip Schaff (ed.), *Gregory of Nyssa: Dogmatic Treatises, etc* (Edinburgh/Grand Rapids: T&T Clark/Wm. B. Eerdmans, 1997), Great Catechism, VIII; C. S. Lewis, *Mere Christianity* (New York: Macmillan, 1952), pp. 108, 172–75, 182; C. S. Lewis, *Letters to Malcolm: Chiefly on Prayer* (Orlando: Harcourt, 2002), pp. 108–09; Warren H. Lewis (ed.), *Letters of C. S. Lewis* (London: Geoffrey Bles, 1966), pp. 246–47.

concern and offers support for those who contend that there is no feasible way of rendering such an abrupt transition to sanctification in temporal beings. If this desired growth is unattained in this life, then purgatory (or something like it) seems requisite if God is to accomplish his goal with our freedom intact.

Writing in 1918, and acutely aware of 'countless bereaved hearts' resulting from the 'wickedness of war', Forsyth offers no promises that 'every martyr patriot goes straight from the field of death to the side of the Saviour'. Where they do go is to Christ's judgement seat, 'where all must stand'. But while a heroic death does not in itself save, 'it may be the moment of [one's] conversion . . . the first step in a new life which advances faster there than here'.[185] This post-mortem state does not provide the opportunity for sinners to pay for their sins, nor is it a space of probation. Rather, Forsyth believes that 'the crisis of death opens the eyes' of those previously blind, or too stubborn to see.[186] He supposes that death significantly increases sensitivity to spiritual realities: 'Even if a man die indifferent in this life, he comes into circumstances where he ceases to be indifferent. If we believe about a future at all, it will be impossible for an indifferent man to remain indifferent when he has passed on there.'[187] In his Stretton Church burial-ground tribute to lifelong friend Charles Silvester Horne, Forsyth reminds the gathered that 'death is the Great Reconciler', and that some deaths 'do not impoverish life, but enrich it'. He proceeds: 'It is not well at such times to say much about heaven or about the dead. They know more than we do.'[188] In another place, Forsyth presses that 'the souls that go into eternity know themselves as they never did before. The spirit is more to them than ever before. Their spiritual acquirement while they were here opens out upon their sight'.[189] Here those with 'fixed faces, full not of possibilities but of impossibilities [and] . . . drowned beyond recovery in dreams'[190] are granted space and time for healing, growth, repentance, rectification, new perspectives, sanctification, the unwarping of personality, the 'chance of learning the meaning of life's benediction',[191] and, for some, the fulfilling of otherwise abruptly cut-off life.

Manifest here is Forsyth's confidence that, in Christ, our eternity is 'time not simply prolonged, not simply sublimated, but hallowed, morally regenerated for the holy'.[192] There are echoes here too of Kant's (and Plato's) belief that justice and the non-realization of the good in this life demand a doctrine of immortality, that 'the spiritual nature shall have an opportunity for continued development and in which justice shall be vindicated'.[193] Certainly, Forsyth understands time as eternity's

[185] *Life*, pp. 33–34. Forsyth's speculations on post-mortem conversion concern those who die as unbelievers. Forsyth follows mainstream evangelical belief that the righteous are ushered immediately into God's presence.

[186] Ibid., p. 34; cf. Charles Gore (ed.), *Lux Mundi: A Series of Studies in the Religion of the Incarnation* (London: John Murray, 1890), p. 515.

[187] *Work*, p. 165.

[188] Cited in William Boothby Selbie (ed.), *The Life of Charles Silvester Horne, M.A., M.P.* (London: Hodder & Stoughton, 1920), pp. 302, 304.

[189] *Life*, p. 81.

[190] Lewis, *The Great Divorce*, p. 25.

[191] Brown, *The Doctrine of Annihilation*, p. 72.

[192] *Life*, p. 73.

[193] F. Townley Lord, *Conquest of Death: A Christian Interpretation of Immortality* (London: SCM, 1940), p. 60.

servant, citing with approval from Blake's 'Milton' – 'Time is the mercy of Eternity'.[194] Grace makes time both a prophetic and redemptive agent serving to make eternity accessible. The purgatorial 'time' is not empty time, or 'dead' time, therefore, like twiddling thumbs in a dentist's waiting room. Rather, it is time and space filled with Christ's lordship over the dead and the living, and filled with experience of the Spirit, the life-giver. It is time, moreover, when the consequences of sin scaled over by layers of secondary human decision can be dug free. 'It is [God's] powerful patience to wait till a disillusioned world come to drink of Him, despairing of every other spring'.[195] Additionally, the disillusioned and despairing are confronted unambiguously with the regenerating love of God wherein the most malevolent and obstinate of creatures can undergo transformation. Forsyth shares with the Tractarians Pusey, Manning, Newman, Faber, as well as Denney and more recently Hick, the notion that 'beyond this life the process continues in other environments offering other experiences and challenges which open up new opportunities of response and growth'[196] – for learning the lessons of love.

Forsyth's pareschatology attests to the continuity and integrity of creation – its *conservatio* and *concursus* under God. The alternative may be that God becomes a 'demon', contradicting the promise of one who creates for the sake of fulfilment of all created potentialities. Certainly, hope in ongoing growth witnesses to God's regard for persons not merely as they are, but as they shall be.[197] There is enough here to recall that, for Forsyth, death represents (as least in some sense) a continuum, and not a terminus, of life, and that it requires eternity to work through the issues of life. Certainly we cannot judge the progress of the gospel by marks evident in this life alone. We live by faith, not by sight.

> So our fruitless efforts for souls will germinate yonder, as the mummy wheat is said to sprout in soil to-day. Historic Christianity is working its greatest results in the unseen world, and far more mightily, perhaps, there than here, as the spiritual climate is so much more congenial . . . [T]here is a realm far within all that goes on here where [the things of the Gospel] are not neglected, but are ruling, judging, and creative powers.[198]

While post-mortem life is characterized by continual growth, there is no indication that Forsyth's purgatorial vision conflicts with the doctrine of justification by faith, nor

194 William Blake, *Blake: Complete Writings with Variant Readings* (ed. Geoffrey Keynes; Oxford: Oxford University Press, 1969), p. 510; *Life*, p. 81.

195 'Veracity', p. 216.

196 John Hick, *Death and Eternal Life* (London: Collins, 1976), p. 253; cf. Moffatt (ed.), *Letters of Principal James Denney*, p. 17. Hick seems to have a more intimate knowledge of the afterlife than does Forsyth. Here we might also mention the Vicar of Great Staughton, Hunts, who expressed hope in post-mortem 'nurseries . . . and seed-grounds, where the undeveloped may grow up under new conditions – the stunted may become strong, and the perverted restored'. Henry Bristow Wilson, 'Seances Historiques de Genève. The National Church', in *Essays and Reviews* (ed. John William Parker; London: John W. Parker and Son, 1860), p. 206.

197 See George MacDonald, *Unspoken Sermons: Series I, II and III* (Whitefish: Kessinger, 2004), p. 12.

198 *Life*, p. 80.

that he follows some Roman Catholic and Greek Orthodox convictions that 'all those who die at peace with the church but who are not perfect must undergo penal and purifying suffering'.[199] The only suffering involved is the pain of self-discovery. Still less does Forsyth reflect Dante's vision in Part II of *La Divina Commedia*, or entertain the crude eschatological mathematics (e.g. 'Will the redeemed outnumber the damned?') or speculation concerning the geography and purgatorial torments – 'the awful structure of future terror'[200] – engaged in by some Victorian Romanists.[201]

I noted earlier Forsyth's insistence that 'an election to a certain place in this life does not mean that we are condemned to that place for ever. Death does not fix the moral position of the soul irretrievably. Other methods of moral discipline lie beyond'.[202] Forsyth offers no exegetical support for this position, but grounds this hope in God's loving election which refuses to concede that 'all is up' at death, and on a compatibilist notion of free will: 'We are all predestined in love to life sooner or later, *if we will*. An election is to certain stages and methods of endless growth. It is selection for cycles and crises of moral evolution. It is not that some are chosen for eternal life and some are doomed to eternal death' – such would spell what Geiko Müller-Fahrenholz calls 'the triumph of the absurd'.[203] Latent here is the conviction that while death removes us from earthly conditions, it does not remove us from Christ.[204] Indeed, even hell is no point from which there is no return, but remains the purlieu of the possibility of saving mercy in Christ. It is precisely because hell is not the nemesis of hope that it can be part of the gospel.

Unsuprisingly, this 'Protestant reappraisal of purgatory'[205] is among Forsyth's most contentious proposals, and is largely ignored by Forsyth scholarship. While he shares Protestantism's rejection of the whole apparatus of purgatory, Forsyth insists, 'We threw away too much when we threw Purgatory clean out of doors. We threw out the baby with the dirty water of its bath. There are more conversions on the other side than on this.'[206] Forsyth recognizes that the doctrine itself (at least in its traditional forms) lacks biblical support, even if what it contends for does not – its basis in divine patience and in the Church's practice of prayer and the communion of saints. And Forsyth follows the christological and soteriological instincts of the Reformers – even if he rejects their conclusions – when he presses that post-mortem life is neither what Ratzinger refers

199 Loraine Boettner, 'Purgatory', in *Evangelical Dictionary of Theology* (ed. Walter A. Elwell; Grand Rapids: Baker, 1984), p. 897. See Catholic Church, *Catechism of the Catholic Church*, §§1030–32.

200 'Workers', p. 4.

201 See Rowell, *Hell and the Victorians*, pp. 153–79, 215–16; Samuel Taylor Coleridge, *The Table Talk and Omniana* (London: Oxford University Press, 1917), p. 425.

202 *Life*, p. 16.

203 Ibid.; Geiko Müller-Fahrenholz, *The Kingdom and the Power: The Theology of Jürgen Moltmann* (trans. John Bowden; Minneapolis: Fortress Press, 2000), p. 204.

204 See *Justification*, p. 185.

205 Keith G. Riglin, 'The Saints' Everlasting Rest – The Reformed Position', in *Mary for Earth and Heaven: Essays on Mary and Ecumenism* (ed. William McLoughlin and Jill Pinnock; Leominster: Gracewing, 2002), p. 66.

206 *Life*, p. 34. During World War I, the Congregationalist leader J. D. Jones also argued for the notion of probation after death. See Edward Hayes Plumptre, *The Spirits in Prison* (London: Isbister, 1893); cf. James Orr, *The Christian View of God and the World, as Centring in the Incarnation: Being the Kerr Lectures for 1890–1891* (New York: Anson D. F. Randolph and Co., 1893), p. 394.

to as a 'supra-worldy concentration camp'[207] nor is it about works replacing grace. It is, instead, about the triumph of holiness through divine patience, as wood, straw and hay are burned away and sinners are brought to realization that sin is not what we want for ourselves.

It is indicative, too, of the fact that 'God is not in a hurry, even to save'.[208] Divine patience promotes space and time for the creature to develop proper existence, to (in Rowan Williams's words) 'become acclimatized to the fullness of love . . . something like our lungs expanding to cope with a new atmosphere'.[209] In more Forsythian parlance, God's patience serves the ontological structure whereby the purposes of holy love in election might reach their *telos* – the participation in, and reciprocation of, holy love as the free decision of creation, that God may be all in all. Creation exists for this history and remains frustrated until this end is reached.

To affirm the possibility of post-mortem conversion is to confess, also, that God alone – and not death – determines the time when creation reaches its maturity, and to participate in the divine hope to that end. It is to contend too that God's 'grand purpose and justification' depends on bringing the new creation into being 'out of the abuse and wreck' of this one. This determination is secured in the cross of Christ where God's gracious 'hallowing of God's name in all nature and history, and its suborning of all evil to the service, increase, and praise of eternal good' is made public as that requisite aspect of God's will that all be hallowed at last.[210] God's patience is wise because its end is the triumph of God's holiness and justice. God's patience is gracious because it encroaches into human reality. God, Forsyth professes, has all eternity 'to call out living reply from the world'.[211] 'God gives long rests but never lets go.'[212] Or, as Thomas Erskine so beautifully captures it, 'He who waited so long for the formation of a piece of old red sandstone will surely wait with much long-suffering for the perfecting of a human spirit.'[213]

Divine patience also promotes space and time for creatures on earth to develop and to participate in God's hallowing of the dead, a participation that principally takes the form of prayer. Forsyth is viewing life *sub specie aeternitatis* (and not temporally) when he considers praying for the dead 'our supreme link with the unseen'.[214] Prayer is life, communion with the Risen Christ and his Father, life in the Spirit. This life is 'not only an end in itself but *the* end in which the believer eschatologically shares'.[215] An indispensable facet of this life is the communion of saints, one that bridges the living and dead; this is, as Moltmann observes, 'the

207 Joseph Ratzinger, *Eschatology: Death and Eternal Life* (ed. Aidan Nichols; trans. Michael Waldstein; Washington, DC: The Catholic University of America Press, 1988), p. 230.
208 'Majesty', p. 307; cf. 'Things New and Old', p. 274.
209 Rowan Williams, *Tokens of Trust: An Introduction to Christian Belief* (Norwich: Canterbury Press, 2007), p. 149; cf. David Brown, 'No Heaven Without Purgatory', *Religious Studies* 21 (1985), pp. 447–56 (447).
210 *Justification*, p. 155.
211 'Christianity of Christ', p. 252.
212 'Slowness', p. 221.
213 Hanna (ed.), *Letters of Thomas Erskine of Linlathen*, p. 427.
214 *Life*, p. 34. See *Person*, p. 88; *Prayer*, p. 40; *Life*, pp. 34–38.
215 Rodgers, *Theology of P. T. Forsyth*, p. 186.

praxis of resurrection hope'.[216] This praxis, for Forsyth, stems from belief in the consanguinity of the human family, and the triumph of persuasive love which graciously extends beyond the grave: 'In Christ we cannot be cut off from our dead nor they from us wherever they be.'[217] The key phrase here is 'in Christ', for only in the once-dead-but-now-alive one is such communion possible. Only in him, those who pray are assured, when they mention the dead, that all is well.[218]

Commenting on Hebrews 12.22, and drawing upon Origen and Tertullian for support, Forsyth insists that whenever the Church gathers, 'Christ is present, and the angels, and the martyrs, and the faithful, living *and dead*'.[219] In Jesus Christ, the living and the dead remain unforgettably and indestructibly united in love for each other, and in a common hopeful sharing. Consequently, the saints on earth have an obligation in the gospel to pray for those who have died, and who indeed form the largest part of the Church.[220] Such prayer bears witness to the Church's unity and catholicity. And, as we have seen, given that the soul remains unfixed at death – that the tree does not lie as it falls – and there are more conversions on the other side than here, Forsyth gives believers every reason for why such prayer is both God's will and a sign of hope in the God who raises the dead to life. There is no indication that the cross that 'is for ever knocking solemnly at the world's gate' will cease to knock in humanity's grave.[221] But, as we shall see, neither is there any guarantee – for Forsyth – that such knocking will find a positive response from all.

IV. Soteriological universalism qualified

Earlier, I hinted that Forsyth's theology of hallowing suggests and perhaps even demands *dogmatic* universalism. By 'dogmatic' universalism I have in mind that consciously trinitarian and christologically determined soteriology which proposes that all persons will certainly be saved through Christ, though remains agnostic as to any specific timetabling.[222] I am certainly not the first to conclude this about Forsyth's thought. Clifford Pitt, for example, has argued that Forsythian theology 'should lead logically to universalism or to destruction of the finally impenitent'.[223] I have already shown that the latter option is entirely unacceptable to Forysth. It is time now to consider Forsyth's response to the first possibility.

216 Jürgen Moltmann, *The Coming of God: Christian Eschatology* (trans. Margaret Kohl; Minneapolis: Augsburg Fortress, 2004), p. 108; cf. Jürgen Moltmann, *In the End – The Beginning: The Life of Hope* (trans. Margaret Kohl; Philadelphia: Fortress, 2004), pp. 109–11.

217 *Life*, p. 34.

218 Ibid., pp. 36–37.

219 *Sacraments*, p. 66. Italics mine.

220 Denney also defends prayer for the dead, but on creational and experiential, rather than christological, grounds. See Moffatt (ed.), *Letters of Principal James Denney*, pp. 18–19.

221 'Gate', p. 177.

222 See, for example, Jacques Ellul, *Perspectives on Our Age: Jacques Ellul Speaks on His Life and Work* (ed. William H. Vanderburg; trans. Joachim Neugroshel; Toronto: Canadian Broadcasting Corporation, 2004), p. 104.

223 Pitt, *Church, Ministry and Sacraments*, p. 42.

In a relatively small number of passages, Forsyth places certain qualifications on the universalistic thrust of his thought. These are: (i) the possibility of a final impenitence, (ii) the possibility of a future judgement, and (iii) the possibility that the salvation of the race need not include every person. It must be noted that these are, for Forsyth, 'possibilities' or *potential* limitations upon his theology's otherwise universalistic drive. They remain at least theoretical possibilities, however, and so any assessment of Forsyth's soteriology must attend to them. I therefore turn now to consider these three qualifications, as well as offer a brief assessment of Forsyth's public agnosticism about the matter. Attending to some of the problems with Forsyth's three qualifications will then be considered.

The possibility of a final 'No'

> *Love bade me welcome; yet my soul drew back.*[224]
>
> *As long as there is life there is hope – but as long as there is life there is also the possibility of danger.*[225]

I noted earlier Forsyth's confidence that from the vista of the Christian gospel, 'eternal and destined damnation is excluded'.[226] Forsyth proceeds: '*If* every man did as God willed there would be no damnation . . . *If* man heartily believed in God's salvation there could be no perdition.'[227] Such a statement is characteristic of Forsyth's twin convictions: (i) God's desire to save, and (ii) the theoretical possibility of a final impenitence. This possibility is implicit in Forsyth's refusal (with Windelband and Schlatter[228]) to embrace a christomonism that evacuates history and human persons and their actions of all moral meaning. The new humanity is not a *fait accompli* in the cross. Without the unfinished world of 'ought' and its tension with 'is', creation would be shut down to a natural system.

Forsyth contends that the finality of God's redemptive act lies in the quality of the new divine–human relation created and sustained pneumatalogically and which makes possible authentic human response, both positive *and negative*. There must be space in God for the creature to be. This is the point where pantheism always fails.[229] Implicit here is Forsyth's opposition to soteriological schemes drawn along rationalistic rather than voluntaristic lines. Thus his criticism of R. J. Campbell: 'Mr. Campbell, in consistency with the philosophy to which the universe is a divine experiment without the risk of failure, is a convinced universalist. The larger hope is not a hope at all, it is a fact as certain as mathematics. No one can be lost.'[230] Forsyth accuses Campbell

[224] George Herbert, 'Love (3)', in *George Herbert: The Complete English Poems* (ed. John Tobin; London: Penguin, 1991), p. 178.

[225] Søren Kierkegaard, *Christian Discourses and The Lilies of the Field and the Birds of the Air and Three Discourses at the Communion on Fridays* (trans. Walter Lowrie; London: Oxford University Press, 1939), p. 290.

[226] *Authority*, p. 355.

[227] Ibid. Italics mine.

[228] Adolf Schlatter, *Gesunde Lehre: Reden und Aufsätze* (Velbert: Freizeiten-Verlag, 1929), p. 75.

[229] Schlatter, 'Wesen und Quellen der Gotteserkenntnis', pp. 94, 133.

[230] 'God, Sin', p. 670.

of grounding his belief on the assumption that the 'subliminal self' is basic to being, and so cannot be lost. Forsyth assaults Campbell's notion as naïve, as inappropriate to moral relations and as presumptuous for assuming to offer definitive comment on 'the most awful of moral problems'.[231] Evidently, Forsyth resists embracing universal*ism* lest it harden into a dogma or be construed as the *telos* of an indifference and constriction of the automatism of Progress so deeply rooted in late nineteenth-century idealism. He believes that to proclaim an *apokatastasis* as a *necessary* or *inevitable* law of the universe, or as a 'system', is to sponsor another form of annihilationism, that of the will.[232] No matter how debased human beings are, they remain responsible, and only as such are capable of fellowship with God.

> There can, therefore, be no talk of God creating faith in us willy-nilly. That were neither creation, faith, nor salvation. There is no such thing as a faith which could be created and inserted in a soul. There is no such thing as a Spirit which comes like a rushing mighty wind, sweeps the soul of all its contents, and settles in as a totally new tenant. Converts are not changelings. Faith is the soul believing. Its creation can only be some action appropriate to soul – i.e. to freedom. Redemption is recreating a free soul through its freedom. It is converting its freedom, and not its substance. It does not change its natural psychology.[233]

Reflected here is Forsyth's insistence that Christ not only exercises complete faithfulness in God, but also that Christ has faith in human beings and in their will to choose life rather than death.[234] Forsyth is equally confident that no person in the end is ever deprived of the fate they really seek.

Forsyth's presentation reflects Scriptures' confronting even of 'believers' with the possibility of finding themselves on the wrong side of life. Despite holiness' overcoming the distance between humanity and God, Christ's response from the side of sin and making all things fit for holiness' purpose, and despite the gospel's 'objective power' and decisiveness which alter forever our relation to God, Forsyth simultaneously defends that this gospel 'may be rejected or believed'.[235] Clearly, the charge that soteriological universalism denigrates the doctrine of *iustitia fidei* will not stick to Forsyth for whom salvation apart from repentance and faith is untenable. Faith itself is the mode of sanctified existence. There even remains, for Forsyth, the possibility of a permanent 'fixed refusal' – the sin of sins – of a saved world being 'false to itself'.[236] Certainly it is impossible to hear the gospel and remain unchanged. One is made 'either better or worse for it'.[237] Put otherwise, the gospel does not merely enlighten us but effects

231 Ibid.

232 Cf. Fairbairn, *The Place of Christ*, pp. 467–68; Brown, *The Doctrine of Annihilation*, p. 5; Bonhoeffer, *Sanctorum Communio*, pp. 286–88; Karl Barth, *God Here and Now* (trans. Paul M. van Buren; Religious Perspectives Series, Volume 9; London: Routledge & Kegan Paul, 1964), pp. 34–35.

233 *Authority*, p. 159; cf. Herrmann, *Dogmatik*, p. 104.

234 'Strength', p. 86.

235 'Rallying Ground', p. 826 fn.1.

236 *Work*, p. 156; *Revelation*, p. 36; cf. Brown, *The Doctrine of Annihilation*, pp. 129, 119. There is a hint here of Ritschl's view that the only sin that can be properly so named is definitive rejection of Christ. For Ritschl, all other 'sins' are ignorance.

237 *Work*, p. 28.

a crisis: 'To all eternity we are what our sin has made us, by God's grace to it either as taken or refused.'[238]

As a pastor, Forsyth knew firsthand the fix of the 'impenitent temper'.[239] While recognizing the 'absolute power of God's salvation', he imagines that one might become so hardened towards God that one is fixed forever in a state of self-deceit so profound that one is eternally impervious to love; that it is 'in the power of the human soul to harden itself until it become[s] shrunk into such a tough and irreducible mass as it seems the very grace of God could do nothing with'.[240] Rejecting any suggestion that divine sovereignty demolishes or even coerces human 'freedom', Forsyth contends that God respects it and works under its conditions, lest the soul be destroyed: 'The gift of the Spirit overrules natural character, but it does not obliterate it. It transfigures, but does not erase. The will God made so free that it can resist even Himself. It is free enough to resist even His gospel of more freedom and true freedom.'[241] Forsyth urges that this is not a question of God's predestination but concerns the mysteries of eschatology and of human freedom.

> The lost are lost by refusing that gospel in their mysterious and incalculable freedom . . . The self-determining power of the individual is part of the ordered predestination of God, and of the necessity felt by His love to endow man with a freedom like His own if He expected man to respond to His own. Only a fatalist pre-destination, not a personal, excludes such freedom.[242]

Thus we cannot know what the final outcome will be, nor how far God might pursue us despite our unwillingness to cooperate. Still, how can that which has already been overcome in Christ ever be undone? Forsyth cannot here take refuge in God's freedom (as Barth does) to reject dogmatic universalism precisely because, for Forsyth, God's freedom is already bound up in his determination to hallow all things. While Forsyth's 'universalism' lacks the developed groundwork that Barth provides in his doctrine of election and reprobation, at no point does Forsyth threaten to tear open again the abyss of the *decretum absolutum et horribile* as Barth does, as though God's Word towards a person might finally be different from that spoken in Jesus Christ.

The possibility of future final judgement

Forsyth consistently understands judgement against the backdrop of a real, immanent, urgent and eternal moral order. He is reluctant, however, to speculate on any future final judgement, or to detail any eschatology. In fact, as Mozley observes, 'Forsyth had extraordinarily little to say: One has to catch his view from a number, not a large one,

238 *Father*, p. 111; cf. *Missions*, p. 74.
239 *Life*, p. 78.
240 *Work*, p. 161.
241 *Authority*, p. 158.
242 Ibid., p. 357; cf. *Work*, p. 227.

of particular hints.'[243] Still, we can identify three things that Forsyth affirms about future judgement. First, like Dodd, Forsyth believes that the New Testament shifts the focus from the future to the present. Although he never employs the term 'realized eschatology', he does assume an 'immanent teleology of history' secured in the cross which 'presents us in advance with the purpose and destiny of the world'.[244] We ought not to conclude, however, that Forsyth's rendering encourages complacency concerning future judgement.

> The non-intervention of God bears very heavy interest, and He is greatly to be feared when He does nothing. He moves in long orbits, out of sight and sound. But He always arrives . . . The world gets a long time to pay, but all the accounts are kept – to the uttermost farthing. Lest if anything were forgotten there might be something unforgiven, unredeemed, and unholy still.[245]
>
> 'The last judgment' is a phrase which we have almost robbed of its effect because we have used it chiefly for a remote and pictorial future. We have dwelt on the final *date* of judgment, and lost sense of a *state* of judgment, a judgment always there, and always final in its *nature*. We have pictured it in ways which have emptied it of spiritual awe, and reduced it to little more than physical terror and moral impotence.[246]

Forsyth's underlying concern here is to stress the immanence of God's judgement. So his call to young American preachers:

> . . . learn not to say so much to your people of a day of Judgment sure though far. The farness destroys the sureness. Ethicize the reality of judgment. Moralize the eschatology. Couple it up to the hour. Drop, if need be, the drapery of the remote assize. The judge is at the door. Everything comes home. It comes home in calamity if you do not take it home in repentance.[247]

Second, judgement is always a word of mercy and must not be coupled with retribution and damnation.[248] Certainly Forsyth agrees with Maurice that 'Asking God not to judge, is asking utter destruction to ourselves'.[249] But because Forsyth understands judgement christologically, judgement means grace, the stripping away of all our defences against truth. Pitt makes a logico-causal leap here, proffering that those who spurn God's salvation 'must be judged and with a judgement of damnation, unless rebellion is to continue with the universe for all eternity'.[250] But such a leap is unnecessary and threatens to undermine, as Forsyth sees, the finality of God's

243 Mozley, *The Heart of the Gospel*, pp. 103–04.
244 *Justification*, p. 186.
245 *Justification*, p. 207; cf. 'Veracity', p. 216: '[J]udgement leaves nothing unsearched or unsounded, and, therefore, nothing unforgiven'.
246 *Missions*, p. 72.
247 *Preaching*, p. 105.
248 See *Justification*, p. 172.
249 Maurice, *Lectures on the Apocalypse*, p. 400.
250 Pitt, *Church, Ministry and Sacraments*, p. 153.

'last word' of judgement in the cross. By construing judgement as an act of divine mercy, Forsyth reflects Scripture's witness that God's wrath betrays love's unflinching commitment to creation. As *the* 'tragedy of history' the cross represents 'God's saving way with the world'.[251] Thus judgement is simultaneously to be both dreaded and welcomed, for through judgement lies promise that God will not let evil continue indefinitely.[252]

Forsyth also resists the tendency – still prevalent in the nineteenth century – to interpret God's judgements in harsh juridical terms or with the grammar of rewards and punishments. By so doing, he seeks to retain the New Testament's tension between universal restoration and separation, refusing to sponsor any symmetricality between salvation and damnation, or to allow one promise to trump the other. Judgement is always, however, God's penultimate or 'subdominant' word and never the final solution – lest it be a word that speaks of God's failure rather than of God's victory, and by so doing deprive reconciliation of its moral quality.[253] To recall that the nations which forget God shall be 'cast into hell' is simply to witness to the 'rear view of the cross', the 'negative and purgative' elements of God's way towards the kingdom of reconciliation.[254]

Thirdly, Forsyth pleads that the promise concerning future judgement not be evacuated from the pulpit. He applauds the preacher who is aware that the gospel one carries – or, rather, by which one is carried – is that 'whose refusal leaves men more condemned that it found them', that the preacher 'carries peril as well as grace', and that one cannot be a 'true missionary' if one has 'no sense of doom and a wrath to come'.[255] He criticizes preaching which 'lacks the note of doom and the searching realism of the greatest moral seers', naming Shakespeare, Dante, Calvin and Milton.[256] Such preaching robs faith of its energy, virility, command, compass and solemnity. Moreover, it undermines the homiletical task itself insofar as preaching involves confronting the subject with a decision between two genuine and existentially live alternatives. Eternal life is reserved for those who have traversed the valley of decision, for those who are familiar, in T. S. Eliot's words, with 'the last desert between the last blue rocks ... the time of tension between dying and birth'.[257] So while Forsyth

251 *Justification*, p. 170.

252 This problem remains unanswered in Don Carson's defence of hell's eternity on the basis of ongoing sin, a problem addressed by Brown's contention that such a situation would thwart rather than meet the claims of divine justice. Don A. Carson, *The Gagging of God: Christianity Confronts Pluralism* (Grand Rapids: Zondervan, 1996), pp. 515–36; Brown, *The Doctrine of Annihilation*, pp. 96–97.

253 *Justification*, p. 171.

254 Ibid., p. 173.

255 *Missions*, p. 228.

256 *Preaching*, pp. 243–44. See also *Missions*, p. 32. A portrait of Milton appears as one of six stained-glass windows in the apse of Emmanuel Church, Cambridge. See Ann Phillips, *The Bond Memorial Windows* (Cambridge: Emmanuel United Reformed Church, Cambridge, 2002), pp. 8–9.

257 T. S. Eliot, 'Ash Wednesday', in *The Waste Land and Other Poems* (ed. Helen Hennessy Vendler; New York: Signet Classic, 1998), pp. 75, 76.

is (deliberately) scant on the details,[258] he reiterates the New Testament's warnings that rejection of the gospel spells 'doom',[259] 'peril',[260] 'condemnation'[261] and 'wrath to come'.[262]

Of foremost concern for our discussion is that for Forsyth, not all punishment can be shown to be corrective, educative or saving: 'There is plenty of punishment that hardens and hardens'.[263] He is not unaware, in other words, that the word of grace both produces faith and also deepens unfaith, liberates from as well as hardens impenitence: 'If it loose it also binds; and it can do the one only if it do the other – action and reaction being equal. If it draw some near to God, it repels others into distance and estrangement. There is such a thing as the repulsive power of a great affection.'[264] While Forsyth sees this not as a foregone conclusion, he does entertain the possibility that judgement may not be salvific for the finally impenitent – that it may, in the final analysis, be 'death unto death'. He offers no clear word regarding the final annihilation of sin, preferring instead to leave the matter of evil's end to a future life. Does he then open himself to the very charge he articulates against others, of 'taking refuge in an asylum of ignorance, and saving ourselves the trouble of really wrestling with the matter by escaping into a dark and warm mist'?[265]

The possibility of a redeemed race without every member

'The universal destination of Christianity is not impaired by the fact that the members of a Christian nation do not all enter upon the destination which validly obtains for them.'[266] While this notion of Ritschl's only has the 'Christian nation' in view, the idea is reflected in Forsyth's conviction that the salvation of the *race* does not equate to the salvation of every person: 'Christ's work . . . affected a whole race's destiny. The goal was not a vast section of saved individuals, but the salvation of a race of individuals. *Whether that must mean all individuals is [a] matter of dispute*.'[267] This is one of many

258 After a more than 400-page survey of the NT material, Powys also concludes that the NT 'lacks clear and positive expectation' concerning the fate of the unrighteous. David J. Powys, *'Hell': A Hard Look at a Hard Question: The Fate of the Unrighteous in New Testament Thought* (Carlisle: Paternoster, 1998), p. 415.

259 *Prayer*, p. 61; *Parnassus*, p. 132; *Justification*, p. 187; *Person*, p. 257; *Missions*, p. 328; *Jesus*, pp. 47, 52; *Authority*, p. 181; *Revelation*, p. 36. 'Doom' describes what Christ brought upon Israel (e.g. *Justification*, p. 171; *War*, pp. 98, 138, 145, 151–58; *Jesus*, pp. 45, 50, 52, 121–22; *Revelation*, p. 34; *Theology*, p. 158), the Church's failure (*Sacraments*, pp. 59–60; *Freedom*, p. 253; *Missions*, pp. 23, 91, 333; *Preaching*, p. 200; *Authority*, pp. 211, 264; *Revelation*, p. 67; *Rome*, pp. 40, 46, 168; *Theology*, p. 242; *Work*, p. 53), and most usually the 'great doom' which Christ bore (*Preaching*, pp. 8–9; cf. *Cruciality*, pp. 209–10; *Father*, pp. 72–73; *War*, pp. 101, 146, 152; *Missions*, pp. 7, 77; *Preaching*, p. 215; *Jesus*, pp. 69, 71; *Work*, p. 163).

260 *Justification*, p. 82; *Missions*, p. 228; *Revelation*, p. 101.

261 *Justification*, pp. 171, 181; *Missions*, pp. 112, 204, 265; *Person*, p. 39; 'Forgiveness', pp. 206–07; *Work*, p. 29.

262 *Missions*, p. 228.

263 *Work*, p. 161.

264 *Justification*, p. 170.

265 *Authority*, p. 410.

266 Ritschl, *Justification and Reconciliation*, p. 135.

267 *Missions*, p. 241. Italics mine. Similar conclusions are expressed in comments on Romans 11.26 in C. K. Barrett, *Epistle to the Romans* (Black's New Testament Commentaries; London A&C Black,

examples of Forsyth's commitment to countering the rampant individualism infecting late-nineteenth- and early-twentieth-century Congregationalism. Forsyth considers this drift partly responsible for severely undermining congregational catholicity and its 'corporate spirit', concerns held even by many of those who upheld the autonomy of the local church.[268] Mostly, Forsyth's response involves highlighting that persons are by nature social beings who most fully discover their identity as members of a saved race. While calling for the destruction of religious autonomy, Forsyth is sure, however, to press that 'religion is nothing if not individual' and that 'each soul must say "My God," and each conscience hear the words "Thou art the man"'.[269] So he encouraged a gathering of clergy in 1917, 'Keep your individuality, but not your individualism.'[270] But Forsyth progressively abandons the term 'individual' for the term 'personal', concerned that the integrity of subjectivity is forfeited in excessive individualism. For example, he argues in his 1910 lectures at Campbell Morgan's annual conference at Mundesley that 'salvation is personal, but it is not individual . . . It is personal in its appropriation but collective in its nature'.[271] And he repeatedly avers that 'there is no such thing as an absolute individual'.[272] Indeed, individualism is terminal to faith. It was, Forsyth believes, the mainstay of the rationalism and atheism of the French Revolution as well as the father of pacifism and the repudiation of public responsibility; but the Reformation (against some popular readings) stands not for religious individualism but for personal and social religion, the cohesion of Society being no consensus of self-interests.[273]

One of the deficiencies attending the autonomy of 'clotted individualism'[274] is a failure to deliver the freedom it promises, killing – rather than creating – individuality, liberty and personality. It has 'simply bred egoism'.[275] To be cut off from the race's history and organic life, isolated from a common authority and hypnotized in the pursuit of individual freedom is to become the victim of a crowd of individuals too like our vagrant selves, victims of a collective suggestion. True self-realization, Forsyth insists, means to be realized by One who sends us to participate in society as servants of a redeemed sociality. Consequently, one is surprised to encounter Forsyth's questioning that racial redemption does not equate to the salvation of all. By positing that Christ died for all but then denying any necessary connection between Christ's death and universal salvation, Forsyth rejects scholastic Calvinism's tendency to interpret

1957), pp. 223–24; Charles E. B. Cranfield, *The Epistle to the Romans* (vol. 2; Edinburgh: T&T Clark, 2004), 574–77; and A. Andrew Das, *Paul and the Jews* (Library of Pauline Studies; Peabody: Hendrickson, 2003), pp. 96–111. See also Calvin on 1 Timothy 2.4 in John Calvin, *Commentaries on the Epistles to Timothy, Titus, and Philemon* (trans. William Pringle; vol. 21; Grand Rapids: Baker, 2003), pp. 54–55; cf. Katherine Greene-McCreight, *Ad Litteram: How Augustine, Calvin, and Barth Read the 'Plain Sense' of Genesis 1–3* (New York: Peter Lang, 1998), chapter 3.

268 'Church Fabric', p. 417; cf. 'Religious Strength', p. 577.

269 *Charter*, p. 62; cf. 'Self-Denial', pp. 34–35.

270 *Congregationalism*, p. 52.

271 *Work*, p. 119.

272 Ibid., p. 120.

273 See Ibid.; *Revelation*, p. 41; *War*, pp. 17–36; *Socialism and Christianity*, p. 25.

274 *Sacraments*, p. 44.

275 Keith W. Clements, 'P. T. Forsyth: A Political Theologian?', in *Justice the True and Only Mercy: Essays on the Life and Theology of Peter Taylor Forsyth* (ed. Trevor A. Hart; Edinburgh: T&T Clark, 1995), p. 150.

Christ's saving work in logico-causal terms. That Christ's death is sufficient for all is an unequivocal truth of Scripture. That some might not believe remains, for Forsyth, a mysterious possibility (what Calvin refers to as an 'accident'[276]) though not a necessary final outcome: 'Do not go away with the hasty conclusion that the salvation of the race must necessarily mean the salvation at last of every soul in it. You have first to settle the question whether every soul ever born is required for the unity of the race as a whole.'[277] Regarding this point Forsyth has no shortage of sympathetic readers. Noel Due, for example, defends Forsyth's denial of dogmatic universalism arguing that Forsyth is merely giving suitable weight to the apparent paradox in Scripture – that the world has been reconciled and yet only those who believe will be saved. 'Forsyth's contribution', he writes, 'is valuable in that he insists that the enquiry cannot proceed along quantitative terms. Rather the atonement must be understood in *qualitative* categories'.[278]

Forsyth proposes that only when the question of human freedom becomes eschatological may we discuss whether 'a race can be complete with any of its members missing, whether for a species to continue and fulfil its nature every individual must be conserved that it ever produced'. But, he warns, such considerations 'could be very misleading' because it could be importing natural law into the world of spirit whose principle is subverting grace and not nature.[279] 'Neither divine justice nor human freedom can suffer in the process.'[280]

Finally, for Forsyth, universal salvation does not equate to 'the addition of all units', but means universal 'in a solidary sense'. Again, his concern is to reject any notion of soteriological individualism wherein each person authors their own terms with God: 'Salvation by private bargain . . .. is not the New Testament idea.'[281] He therefore rejects, and I think rightly, those attempts to reduce universal reconciliation to 'a piecemeal series of individual repentances and conversions'[282] on the grounds that such moves throw into doubt whether the race as a whole will be saved at last.

Forsyth's public agnosticism

By now, I trust that it is clear that no consensus exists among scholars concerning the question of Forsyth's soteriological universalism. Broadly understood, there are three basic proposals: Garvie and Allen conclude that Forsyth embraces universalism.[283] Bebbington and Due reject this reading.[284] Sell judiciously stops short of concluding whether Forsyth does or does not embrace universalism,[285] identifying themes which

276 Calvin on Mark 4.12 in John Calvin, *Commentary on a Harmony of the Evangelists, Matthew, Mark, and Luke, Vol. 2* (vol. 16; Grand Rapids: Baker, 2003), p. 108.

277 *Revelation*, p. 35.

278 Noel Due, *The Holiness of God in P. T. Forsyth's Theology of Atonement* (Blackwood: New Creation, 1986), p. 51.

279 *Authority*, p. 357.

280 'Hell', p. 4.

281 *Work*, pp. 116, 117.

282 Ibid., p. 114.

283 Garvie, 'A Cross-Centred Theology', p. 326; Allen, 'The Christology of P. T. Forsyth', pp. 287–88.

284 In private correspondence.

285 Sell, *Nonconformist Theology*, p. 152.

'may seem to encourage a universalistic "automaticism" of salvation, or a by-passing of the individual which Forsyth . . . was elsewhere keen to avoid'.[286] On this question, Sell represents Forsyth's position most accurately. However, our concern throughout this chapter is whether Forsyth's theology of divine hallowing not merely suggests but *demands* a commitment to dogmatic universalism. Certainly, consensus about Forsyth's soteriological universalism is hampered by his polemics. It takes little effort to harness a smorgasbord of texts in support of either a more dogmatic or a qualified universalism. Forsyth certainly maintains at least what we might call a *hopeful* universalism, joining at this point a tradition going back to Origen, Clement of Alexandria, Gregory of Nyssa, Ambrose of Milan and Gregory of Nazianzus. And even in his own day, he is far from novel here. Schleiermacher in Germany, and Cox, Maurice and Farrar (among others) in England, provided the intellectual ballast to embrace an unequivocal universalism, even though for Maurice and Farrar the intent was primarily to oppose High Calvinism's doctrine of God and any notion of eternal punishment. Forsyth's brand of universalism is more consciously christological than is either Schleiermacher's or Maurice's, however, and better reflects Brown's whose soteriology is set by his theology of divine fatherhood, and by his conviction that, through Christ's cross and resurrection, death no longer has power to determine human destiny. What is clear is that Forsyth's hopeful universalism is not grounded on vague concepts of God's benevolence, nor on naïve notions of the creature's native goodness, but rather is grounded in holiness' determination of self-realization and is secured in the *kenosis* and *plerosis* of the Son, and by the Spirit who brings to God all that the Son has made alive in his resurrection. We can only speculate about why one whose theology leads us to embrace a more dogmatic universalism refused to publicly posit such a position. And perhaps at this point we might simply recall Karl Barth's own denial of dogmatic universalism made against 'theological consistency' as that which at least serves as a reminder that the leap towards *dogmatic* universalism ought be made with caution.[287]

We have already noted Forsyth's concern to avoid any soteriology that by-passes the human will. But might there not also be other reasons for his public agnosticism? I suggest four.

First, Forsyth is concerned, in 1887, that 'the decay or modification of old notions about the fate of the heathen and their share in hell has seriously affected the foreign mission field, and reduced the number of those who rushed in to pluck brands from the burning'.[288] It is feasible to imagine how such concern might extend to the question of universalism as both a quencher of missionary zeal and a promoter of antinomian lethargy, although it need do neither and may in fact have the opposite effect, encouraging new obligations of proclamation, obedience and service. As much as hell has been employed as a deterrent in the past (even by nineteenth-century Universalists) it is not evident that God's desire for repentance and obedience best results from an exposure to threats and terrors. As Erskine quipped, 'Men cannot be frightened into

[286] Sell, *Testimony and Tradition*, p. 181.
[287] Barth, *CD* IV/3/1, p. 477.
[288] 'Sunday Schools', p. 126.

love.'[289] Equally non-evident is that the kind of love love seeks is achieved when the primary concern is self-preservation, as John William Colenso so eloquently argued, with possibly some effect on Forsyth's own thinking.[290] Such attempts tend to resort to a form of conditionalism seeking an existential foothold in fear and guilt rather than in any true motivation of grace and love. As Otto Weber observes, Romans 11.32 is 'the statement of perhaps the most effective missionary of Christendom!'[291] Still, Forsyth offers sufficient warnings against postponing repentance 'here in the hope of doing it there' in another life,[292] noting that our character here begins our destiny there, so hardening now only deepens the unlikelihood of a softening later on. Certainly by 1909, Forsyth's call of 'must mission' upon the Church is not incompatible with his belief that 'the world at last cannot refuse such a Gospel'.[293]

Secondly, while England had known such movements before, the early nineteenth century onwards witnessed a resurgence of both annihilationism and, increasingly (mostly undogmatic) universalism, chiefly among Unitarians but also among the orthodox. It is reasonable to assume that Forsyth wanted to distance himself from such movements. He would not have welcomed being responsible for encouraging any storms of indignation or inner-denominational furore such as accompanied the publication of Edward White's *Life in Christ* (1846), or the dismissal, in 1853, of that 'proto-martyr of the wider hope',[294] F. D. Maurice, from his professorial chair at Kings College on (unfounded) charges of universalism. One need only recall Forsyth's careful though heart-wrenching response to R. J. Campbell throughout the 'New Theology' controversy. Like Brown, Forsyth had 'no love for the thorny paths of controversy',[295] and would have gladly avoided them had he not felt compelled to tread them.

Thirdly, Forsyth carried keenly his responsibility and influence as college principal and congregational leader and consequently knew when it was prudent to opt for a measure of godly agnosticism. He carefully distinguishes, for example, between heterodoxy and heresy. It is heterodox, he believes, to deny eternal punishment, to regard Christ's death as an object lesson of God's mercy, to deny the Virgin Birth, even to deny a physical resurrection. It is heresy to deny a personal future, to regard Christ's death as mere martyrdom, to deny the Incarnation and to deny that the ascended Jesus

[289] Hanna (ed.), *Letters of Thomas Erskine of Linlathen*, p. 302; cf. Brown, *The Doctrine of Annihilation*, pp. 2–3, 19–51.

[290] A reference in *Missions* (p. 110) reveals that Forsyth had almost certainly read Colenso, whose own work on missions finds numerous echoes in Forsyth's missiology, as well as in Forsyth's thinking of divine Fatherhood, the cross as victory through the destruction of sin, post-mortem remedial process and more 'liberal' attitudes about the treatment of African natives. See John William Colenso, *St. Paul's Epistle to the Romans: Newly Translated and Explained from a Missionary Point of View* (Cambridge: Macmillan and Co., 1861), p. 218.

[291] Otto Weber, *Foundations of Dogmatics* (trans. Darrell L. Guder; vol. 2; Grand Rapids: Wm. B. Eerdmans, 1983), p. 505.

[292] *Life*, p. 78.

[293] *Revelation*, p. 38.

[294] Plumptre, *The Spirits in Prison*, p. viii. On Maurice's universalism, see Bernard M. G. Reardon, *From Coleridge to Gore: A Century of Religious Thought in Britain* (London: Longman, 1971), pp. 187–89.

[295] Brown, *The Doctrine of Annihilation*, pp. 6, 7.

lives on with his people with a personal and royal identity.[296] Concerning Forsyth's public agnosticism, Brown may have pre-empted Forsyth's own feelings when in 1895 he wrote, 'As Chairman for the year of the Board of Congregational Ministers in London, when during three successive meetings the subject [of annihilationism] was very earnestly discussed . . . I took no part in the discussion; indeed, I do not think that large and deep theological questions like this are well suited for debate.'[297]

And finally, Forsyth's rejection of dogmatic universalism is also informed, again echoing Brown and Colenso, by his view that the materials to formulate a dogmatic belief about the last things remain outwith our reach. As Colenso put it: '[T]hese things are too high and too deep for us mortals to profess to comprehend; and so we may leave them calmly in the Hands of Him, who "doeth all things well".'[298] And Brown too:

> We have no power to formulate the doctrine of 'the last things.' Our knowledge must, in any case, be too narrow and vague to make our definitions clear and our dogmas sure; therefore the field of vision is wisely left with the shadows on it, through which we see the sons passing up to complete their training, the rebels passing down to learn all that may be meant by death, and Christ's mercy, pregnant with redeeming influence as ever, folding round and brooding over all.[299]

So too Forsyth: 'We are obliged to leave such questions as universal restoration unsolved.'[300]

V. Problems with Forsyth's qualifications

Forsyth's all-embracing staurology, his trumpeting of divine love's omnipotence, his rejection of limited atonement, his embracing of a doctrine of purgatory (however revised), his hope in post-mortem conversion and his aversion to eschatological dualism all raise reasonable questions about whether his theological project demands the very *apokatastasis* that he finally refuses to affirm. Moreover, his insistence that divine holiness requires the end to its antithesis demands either universalism or annihilationism. Forsyth's rejection of both alternatives is problematic and leaves his entire theological vision vulnerable. And at this point, he is guilty of the very charge that he once accused others of; namely, of stopping 'half-way across the street and run[ning] for refuge to one of those little islands in the middle crowned by a feeble gaslamp where nobody can stay but for a time.'[301] In this section I offer responses to each of Forsyth's three qualifications around the questions of (i) a final rejection of

296 See 'Orthodoxy', pp. 323–24; 'Efficiency and Sufficiency', pp. 25–26. One recalls Luther's note in his Preface to the Romans, 'Every doctrine has its measure, time, and age.' Martin Luther, *Reading in Luther for Laymen* (ed. Charles S. Anderson; Minneapolis: Augsburg, 1967), p. 212.

297 Brown, *The Doctrine of Annihilation*, p. v.

298 Colenso, *St. Paul's Epistle to the Romans*, p. 219.

299 Brown, *The Doctrine of Annihilation*, pp. 129–30.

300 *Work*, p. 161.

301 'Hell', p. 4.

God, (ii) a final judgement which leaves in its wake an eschatological dualism, and (iii) the possibility of a race redeemed short of every person. I shall subsequently explore briefly the question of whether or not Forsyth's soteriological vision finally leaves holiness realized or frustrated.

The possibility of a final 'No'

> *'You must sit down', says Love, 'and taste my meat'|So I did sit and eat.*[302]
>
> *Human treason cannot foil God's plan, In that old victory lies all hope for man.*[303]

The vexed relationship between divine sovereignty and human freedom is a particularly Christian question troubling neither the materialist nor the idealist. This is because, for the Christian, it is grossly misleading to imagine here two irresistible forces pulling in opposite directions precisely because what the greater force desires is not the infringement or violation of the lesser, but its fullest creation. The 1833 Declaration of Faith adopted by the Congregational Churches (and which on this point reflects Forsyth's own moderate Calvinism) asserts that divine activity 'in no way interferes with the system of means, nor with the grounds of human responsibility'.[304] It assumes that creaturely freedom is freedom *in the gospel* – that is, freedom *in Jesus Christ*, – that 'the true freedom of man springs from the holy sovereignty of God, which we only know in Christ, in redeeming action'.[305] Sovereignty and freedom find their meaning in Christ's own journey into the godlessness of the cross and in his resurrection from the dead. Sovereignty and freedom, that is to say, mean the Holy Spirit of grace approaching, crucifying and recreating us in Christ for participation in his own freedom in God wherein we are no longer our own but God's. Grace, in other words, comes not to a sick patient capable of self-recovery if only the right medicine were provided, but to a corpse powerless to come out of its absolute self-centredness and, in Nicholas Berdyaev's words, its 'dark and evil isolation, i.e. final inability to love' – hell.[306] Here grace is all alone to solve – and so overcome – the mystery of evil. Grace – and not modernity's myth of progress, nor its Nietzschian vision of despair and dislocation – is the 'last reality' which shatters the illusion of human independence, the monosyllabic minimalism of the end, and 'overcomes the world for good and all'.[307] Or, as Brian Gerrish articulates it:

> Grace works patiently, in the historical order it has established, toward the goal of universal salvation. Pending the 'absolute end' of grace, its 'relative end' – that is,

[302] Herbert, 'Love (3)', p. 178.
[303] 'Jowett', p. 28.
[304] Congregational Union of England and Wales, 'Declaration of the Faith, Church Order, and Discipline of the Congregational, or Independent Dissenters, Adopted at the Annual Meeting of the Congregational Union, May, 1833', in *Protestant Nonconformist Texts, Volume 3: The Nineteenth Century* (ed. David W. Bebbington et al.; Aldershot: Ashgate, 2006), p. 42.
[305] *Preaching*, p. 43.
[306] Nicholas A. Berdyaev, *The Destiny of Man* (trans. Natalie Duddington; London: Centenary Press, 1937), p. 277.
[307] 'Religion and Reality', p. 554.

> the totality of what it achieves at any moment of time – remains dualistic, dividing the saved from the unsaved. But the limits of history, within which God chooses to work, are wholly subordinate to the ultimate goal of universal redemption beyond history.[308]

Such a 'wholly unlooked for and unpredictable' future contradicts the patterns which we discern in 'the realm of nature and history',[309] but is not hoped for blindly; the reason is announced in the resurrection itself. To play the trump card of human libertarianism is, therefore, as Pringle-Pattison argues, an 'abstraction of the intellect',[310] contradicting all we *know* concerning God's final determination to vacate evil and of what the Church confesses concerning the omnipotence of God's love or the all-constraining power of God's goodness even in the face of human hard-heartedness to turn the most recalcitrant sinner into a freely loving covenant partner. So Forsyth: '[God's] love might be a helpless passion if he had not an equal power behind it. But that power Christ exerts. His Gospel secures not love's exhibition but its final domination of all things and all foes. It does not show something; it does something.'[311]

Forsyth joins astute company when he proposes a kind of 'free-will defence' against dogmatic universalism.[312] This 'most prominent and forceful modern defence of hell', however, is irretrievably problematic.[313] First, there is an implicit assumption (to be sure, much less so in Forsyth than in some others) that creation might be determined apart from God who creates, defines, upholds, reorders, renews and directs humanity to its eschatological destiny. Secondly, the tradition, against Forsyth, has maintained that the possibility of rejecting God is not an act of freedom but of bondage. The possibility of a perpetual 'No' cannot be considered a free choice on the same existential and ontological level as that of a 'Yes' to God because 'Yes' alone has a genuine corresponding referent. A 'No' can only ever amount to a futile attempt to create a counterworld which negates life, ending in radical self-decreation. Rather than make an 'idol of human agency',[314] the tradition insists that freedom means *freedom to be as created by God*, for, as Barth

308 Brian Albert Gerrish, *Tradition and the Modern World: Reformed Theology in the Nineteenth Century* (London: University of Chicago Press, 1978), p. 143.

309 Richard Bauckham and Trevor Hart, *Hope Against Hope: Christian Eschatology at the Turn of the Millennium* (Grand Rapids/Cambridge: Wm. B. Eerdmans, 1999), p. 50.

310 Pringle-Pattison, *The Idea of Immortality*, p. 204.

311 *Justification*, p. 170.

312 On this so-called weak view of hell, see Swinburne, *Responsibility and Atonement*, pp. 180–81, 253; Richard Swinburne, 'A Theodicy of Heaven and Hell', in *The Existence of God* (ed. Alfred J. Freddoso; Notre Dame: University of Notre Dame Press, 1983), pp. 37–54; Eleanore Stump, 'Dante's Hell, Aquinas' Moral Theory, and the Love of God', *Canadian Journal of Philosophy* 16 (1986), pp. 181–96; C. S. Lewis, *The Problem of Pain* (New York: Macmillan, 1962), pp. 126–28; David Fergusson, 'Will the Love of God Finally Triumph?', in *Nothing Greater, Nothing Better: Theological Essays on the Love of God* (ed. Kevin J. Vanhoozer; Grand Rapids: Wm. B. Eerdmans, 2001), pp. 186–202.

313 Lindsey Hall, *Swinburne's Hell and Hick's Universalism: Are We Free to Reject God?* (Aldershot: Ashgate, 2003), p. 2; cf. Geoffrey Bromiley, 'Only God is Free', *Christianity Today* 46, no. 2 (2002), pp. 72–75; Jacques Ellul, *The Politics of God and the Politics of Man* (trans. Geoffrey W. Bromiley; Grand Rapids: Wm. B. Eerdmans, 1972), p. 16.

314 Marilyn McCord Adams, 'The Problem of Hell: A Problem of Evil for Christians', in *Reasoned Faith: Essays in Philosophical Theology in Honor of Norman Kretzmann* (ed. Eleonore Stump; Ithaca: Cornell University Press, 1993), p. 321.

reminds us, 'God did not create a neutral creature, but *his* creature'.[315] True freedom is fitting only in the world of the *Thou*. Here alone there are no tensions between two wills, between grace (which has priority) and free will (which grace creates). Berdyaev, for example, goes massively too far when he argues that the notion of hell is 'ontologically connected with freedom and personality', that human beings therefore have 'a moral right to hell', its existence being 'to save man from being forced to be good and compulsorily installed in heaven'.[316] And similar arguments have been proffered by Hick who insists that a predetermination that creatures endowed with free will shall come to love and obey God would be a 'logical contradiction' and would 'infringe the nature of personal order'.[317] Jeremy Begbie, on the other hand, rightly understands that 'genuine freedom is not constituted by the absence of limits, or by multiplying the number of possibilities open to us; it is realized only in *relation* to real possibilities, by acting in accordance with the way things are'.[318]

Forsyth understands that the relationship between creaturely freedom and the *Thou*-world is bound up in the mystery of grace, and he properly resists all attempts to fashion a schema of logic or of simple cause and effect; grace remains unbound by any laws of non-contradiction. We might even wish to employ here the grammar of paradox. What we cannot do is jettison the priority and authority of grace, and reverse the order; to do so would be to be left with nothing. Christian faith has no other foundation upon which to appeal. If saving faith is 'the gift of God',[319] and God desires that all be saved, then the ongoing reality of the possibility of a final 'No' can only responsibly rest with God. This is particularly so if, as Forsyth claims, we believe because God 'makes us believe – with a moral compulsion, an invasion and capture of us'.[320] Christ, in other words, is more than faith's object; he is also faith's 'cause and creator', the 'author' who 'does not simply elicit' but who effects in us 'a change so total that I could not bring it to pass by any resource of my own'.[321] Christ creates both the response and also 'the very capacity for response',[322] swallowing up every sinful 'No' into his 'Yes', and ending every correlation between 'Yes' and 'No' in his resurrection. The only word that comes

315 Karl Barth, *Table Talk* (ed. John D. Godsey; Scottish Journal of Theology Occasional Papers No. 10; Edinburgh: Oliver and Boyd, 1963), p. 37. To be sure, the tradition does not speak univocally on this matter but also recognizes the very formal, entirely abstract, notion of freedom that I wish to reject here, even if it does this with perhaps a slight sense of irony. Although it usually doesn't push the notion as hard as Berdyaev does, it is, I think, there in Augustine and Aquinas and, in a different way, in Dostoevsky.

316 Berdyaev, *The Destiny of Man*, pp. 266–67.

317 John Hick, *Evil and the God of Love* (London/New York: Macmillan & Co./Harper & Row, 1966), p. 343.

318 Jeremy S. Begbie, *Voicing Creation's Praise: Towards a Theology of the Arts* (London/New York: T&T Clark, 1991), p. 211.

319 *Cruciality*, p. 190; cf. *Person*, p. 198; *Authority*, pp. 9, 59, 120–21, 157–58; *Sacraments*, pp. 220–21, 230; *Jesus*, pp. 80–82; *Father*, p. 75.

320 *Justification*, p. 47. Here Forsyth seems to contradict what he asserts elsewhere. See 'Christian Principle', 150. Evangelical freedom rejects the lie that liberty is 'unformed and unconstrained self-actualization'. John Webster, *Holiness* (Grand Rapids/Cambridge: Wm. B. Eerdmans, 2003), pp. 92–93; cf. *Socialism*, p. 10; 'Love of Liberty', p. 163.

321 *Work*, p. 213; *Jesus*, p. 80; 'Distinctive Thing', p. 490; cf. *Preaching*, pp. 46–47, where Christ is named as faith's creator nine times.

322 *Work*, p. 18.

out of the grave, therefore, is 'Yes'. Indeed, our faith, so understood, is part of *Christ's* offering to God, part of 'God's one pregnant deed and gift to us' in Christ's cross.[323] As Forsyth himself argues, the miraculous revolution effected in us is effected by one whose offering to God of a presanctified humanity comes as a result of 'the *irresistible* power of His own creative and timeless work'.[324] And Forsyth also attributes faith to the 'violent action' of the Spirit who takes us 'by force'.[325]

None of this obviates the 'personal and relational character of creation',[326] however; that love cannot be caused but only rendered freely. As Forsyth proffers in an 1879 sermon, 'the God who has made Hell has made it in a love which it will be seen by all to be utterly ignoble to resist and defy'.[327] Nor does it preclude the mystery of unbelief, of why for some the personal receptivity of, and response to, the miracle of election appears to be non-existent. But if, as Miroslav Volf has argued, 'the will's turning to God and holding onto God is itself God's work',[328] and God's desire is universally salvific, then the end is certain, and the possibility of a final 'No' rendered impossible, even for, as Forsyth concedes, the 'worst and most intractable'.[329] Even Judas the damned must 'take his long journey backward/From darkness into light'.[330] Something like this backwards journey – the undoing of the illusion of freedom which cannot last forever – is requisite if what Forsyth asseverates about holiness' 'must' to find only itself echoed from the side of creation is to be defended.

In the previous chapter, I noted that for Forsyth the will is a monument to our power to resist God, 'our dearest life, the thing we cling to most and give up last'.[331] But it is precisely this giving up of the 'unconquerable will'[332] that must happen lest the universe be subjected to a dualism that threatens to unseat the very holiness that alone can secure its end. Forsyth's own eschatological vision entertains no ongoing reality of anything opposed to holy love. In fact, it is precisely because God's love is the kind of *holy* love of which Forsyth speaks that we can believe in an *apokatastasis panton*, that holy love will not and *can not* leave unsanctified and unredeemed any part of creation.

323 *Jesus*, p. 80.
324 *Work*, p. 225. Italics mine.
325 Ibid., p. 18.
326 Trevor A. Hart, 'Universalism: Two Distinct Types', in *Universalism and the Doctrine of Hell: Papers Presented at the Fourth Edinburgh Conference in Christian Dogmatics, 1991* (ed. Nigel M. de S. Cameron; Carlisle/Grand Rapids: Paternoster/Baker, 1992), p. 31.
327 'Hell', p. 4; cf. Thomas Talbott, *The Inescapable Love of God* (Boca Raton: Universal, 1999), pp. 67–68; Thomas Talbott, 'Reply to My Critics', in *Universal Salvation? The Current Debate* (ed. Robin Parry and Chris Partridge; Carlisle: Paternoster, 2003), p. 264; Robinson, *In the End, God*, p. 123: 'Omnipotent love . . . will take no man's choice from him; for it is precisely his choice that it wants. But its will to lordship is inexhaustible and ultimately unendurable: the sinner *must* yield'. See also Bonhoeffer, *Sanctorum Communio*, p. 288: 'God wants to be the king of his subjects, the father of his children, to rule over spirits whose will is free, and to have community with them – not to be the primordial ground of all being, thus becoming the death of all actual being. God is the God of living persons'.
328 Miroslav Volf, 'The Final Reconciliation: Reflections on a Social Dimension of the Eschatological Transition', *Modern Theology* 16, no. 1 (2000), pp. 91–113 (105).
329 *Justification*, p. 161.
330 Edwin Muir, 'The Transfiguration', in *Collected Poems* (London: Faber and Faber, 1960), p. 200.
331 *Cruciality*, p. 192.
332 Milton, *Paradise Lost*, p. 23. Bk. 1, 106.

If holiness has 'power to subdue *everything* that rises against it',[333] as Forsyth claims, then will it not? Is creaturely freedom really so sacrosanct that not even God is justified in interfering with it? And is not Love's so-called violation of creaturely freedom a 'welcome antidote' to that 'arbitrary stupidity' which refuses to yield?[334]

Forsyth acknowledges the logical inconsistency in his position,[335] but maintains that such logico-causal interpretation effectively shuts down creation, reducing 'living souls' to 'things', and 'converts' into 'changelings'.[336] He would no doubt be quick to remind us of that provisional 'dualism which is the moral foundation of a Christian world' and is expressed in 'paradox':[337] 'What seems to underlie the question is a naïve idea of what is meant by creation – as if it were a magician's power to bring out blossoms with a wave of his hand, or place coins suddenly where there were none . . . Creation seems to be thought of entirely out of reference to the idea of moral freedom.'[338] Here a vestige of Kant's distinction between practical and speculative reason is apparent: that what may not be articulated without contradiction may nonetheless be real. As every Kantian knows, 'the God who is denied as an intellectual truth may be worshipped as a moral reality', that 'faith lives in a vast antinomy' between the dramatic and the intellectual.[339] It is this truth that Forsyth properly seeks to shield, aware that attempts to resolve the antinomy typically distort the mystery of freedom. 'Many systems', he writes, 'try to explain how human freedom and human action are consistent with God's omnipotence and omniscience. None succeed. *How* secondary causes like man are compatible with God as the Universal and Ultimate Cause is not rationally plain. But there is no practical doubt that they are compatible.'[340] Offering no satisfactory solution to the enigma, Forsyth simply affirms what he considers to be the antinomy in which we live: 'Conversion baffles intelligence, but we cannot be converted against our will'.[341] McKay helpfully summarizes Forsyth's position thus:

> Forsyth does not, and evidently cannot, explain the interworkings of will, duty, and conscience that take place when one act becomes the parent of another act between two persons. We are left with the poignant, suggestive relation between God's act and ours that ties the two together, places the initiative on God, and obligates man through faith to participate in the new relation.[342]

While Forsyth's Kantianism finally disserves him here, I believe his instinct is right; faith is not created in us willy-nilly, as if faith could be inserted in a soul, or as if the Spirit would sweep the soul of all its contents and settle in it a totally new tenant. A creation

333 *Prayer*, p. 74. Italics original.
334 Eric Reitan, 'Human Freedom and the Impossibility of Eternal Damnation', in *Universal Salvation? The Current Debate* (ed. Robin Parry and Chris Partridge; Carlisle: Paternoster, 2003), p. 137.
335 See *Authority*, p. 157.
336 Ibid., p. 159.
337 *Prayer*, p. 59.
338 *Authority*, pp. 157–58.
339 'Intellectualism', p. 315.
340 *Prayer*, p. 86; cf. *Authority*, pp. 56–59.
341 *Authority*, p. 300.
342 McKay, 'Moral Structure of Reality', p. 235.

that takes freedom seriously cannot evacuate the new creation from its continuum in history but it is a continuum in which the old has been taken down *involuntarily* into death. In other words, only new creation is free. A generous reader of Forsyth can forgive the rhetoric of a preacher who at times distorts. A more critical evaluator might follow along lines articulated by Forsyth's Polish-born friend, A. E. Garvie: 'Antitheses were not only a too frequent mark of Forsyth's style, but to think in contrasts was an "idiom of his mind", with the result that the *whole* truth was sometimes sacrificed in the assertion of a *part*. In his aversion to some current modes of theology or religion his appreciation of one truth was expressed in his depreciation of another.'[343] A more censorious reading still might consider such theological opaqueness as reason for dismissing his thought altogether.

This introduces a deeper problem, however: that one could finally damn oneself. So Ratzinger: 'Heaven reposes upon freedom, and so leaves to the damned *the right to will their own damnation*.'[344] If the doors of hell cannot be unlocked from the outside, though, then it is creation and not God that finally determines how things will end. If sinners can determine their own destiny, then the nature of the last judgement *as God's* is radically undermined, if not forfeited. God would become the auxiliary who executes the will of those who decide their fate for themselves. So Moltmann: 'If I can damn myself, I am my own God and judge. Taken to a logical conclusion this is atheistic.'[345] And again:

> If God has to abide by our free decision, then we can do with him what we like. Is that the 'love of God'? Free human beings forge their own happiness and are their own executioners. They do not just dispose over their lives here; they decide on their eternal destinies as well. So they have no need of any God at all. After a God has perhaps created us free as we are, he leaves us to our fate. Carried to this ultimate conclusion, the logic of hell is secular humanism, as Feuerbach, Marx and Nietzsche already perceived a long time ago.[346]

Forsyth is aware of the problem of pressing for a notion of creaturely freedom that might be absolute, acknowledging that God faces no light problem:

> There was never such a fateful experiment as when God trusted man with freedom. But our Christian faith is that He well knew what He was about. He did not do that as a mere adventure, not without knowing that He had the power to remedy any abuse of it that might occur . . . He had means to emancipate even freedom, to convert moral freedom, even in its ruin, into spiritual.[347]

343 Garvie, 'Placarding the Cross', p. 350.
344 Ratzinger, *Eschatology*, p. 216.
345 Moltmann, *The Coming of God*, p. 109.
346 Jürgen Moltmann, 'The Logic of Hell', in *God Will Be All In All: The Eschatology of Jürgen Moltmann* (ed. Richard Bauckham; Minneapolis: Fortress, 2001), pp. 44, 45; cf. Nicholas John Ansell, 'The Annihilation of Hell: Universal Salvation and the Redemption of Time in the Eschatology of Jürgen Moltmann' (unpublished doctoral dissertation, Vrije Universiteit/Institute for Christian Studies, 2005).
347 *Justification*, p. 123.

Such patient emancipation reveals 'the costly and inevitable action of holiness in establishing itself everywhere for ever'.[348] Forsyth recalls that God may have to wait long for such to happen, partly because 'it is no slack knot that the Saviour has to undo. All the energy of a perverse world in its created freedom pulled on the tangle to tighten it'. But the knot will be undone. The 'snarl is not beyond being untied'. Why? Because human persons are 'born to be redeemed'.[349] Indeed, redemption is the spinal chord which runs through history. That is why only the new creation can make sense of the old creation. Forsyth reiterates that 'there was moral resource in the Creator equal to anything that might happen to the creature or by him. And that resource is put forth in Christ – in His overcoming of the world on the Cross, and His new creation of it in the Spirit'.[350] The notion that one can finally damn oneself can only be defended on the basis that God has not taken upon himself all of humanity's God-directed rejection. But if in Christ, humanity's rejection of God has been overcome and rejection's attendant isolation has been turned around – as Forsyth seems to suggest – then maintaining the possibility of further rejection can only, it would seem, be defended at the cost of undermining Christ's work. The result of such a move would be to throw humanity back onto itself to, in Barth's words, 'suffer the execution' of the threat alone. But this recalcitrant impenitence is 'the very goal which the godless cannot reach, because it has already been taken away by the eternally decreed offering of the Son of God to suffer in place of the godless'.[351] Or, as Bonhoeffer would express it through the mouth of a fictional character, 'Suddenly, there in the middle of hell, I met – God'.[352]

James Packer (one not well known for his universalist sympathies) recalls what it means to be the object of God's love: 'This is what God does for those he loves – *the best He can*; and the measure of the best that God can do is omnipotence!'[353] No one (as far as I am aware) suggests that such loving omnipotence is pure 'unilateral force', but the alternative that 'omnipotence cannot entail [love's] guaranteed success'[354] is not viable, at least if what Forsyth wants to assert about divine holiness is true. With all due allowance for literary genre aside, critics might suggest that if, when the shepherd finds the one lost sheep, and that sheep then decides that it wants to stay lost rather than come home, then the shepherd – *this Shepherd* – will not only wait *with* that recalcitrant lamb, but also continue to give it every reason to change its mind. But is this where love draws its line? Can this satisfy holiness? Will not 'the hound of heaven'[355] overcome all obstacles that our misguided and iniquitous choices present? Indeed, can this hound ever come home while the object of his hunt remains in the wilderness? So Barth: 'It would be a strange love [and that not holy] that was satisfied with the mere

[348] Ibid.
[349] Ibid.
[350] Ibid., p. 124.
[351] Karl Barth, *Church Dogmatics II.2* (ed. G. W. Bromiley and T. F. Torrance; trans. G. W. Bromiley et al.; Edinburgh: T&T Clark, 1957), p. 319.
[352] Dietrich Bonhoeffer, *Fiction from Tegel Prison* (ed. Clifford J. Green; trans. Nancy Lukens; Dietrich Bonhoeffer Works; vol. 7; Minneapolis: Fortress Press, 2000), 41.
[353] James I. Packer, *Knowing God* (Downers Grove: InterVarsity, 1973), p. 115.
[354] Hart, 'Universalism', p. 32.
[355] *Father* p. 8

existence and nature of the other, then withdrawing, leaving it to its own devices.'[356] Or, as Schlatter expresses it:

> Love does not work absorbingly. A Godhead which annihilates all the reality besides itself is power but never has the good will. Goodness gives, and it does so by making its gift the property of its recipient and by enriching, strengthening, and giving life to him through it. Only an egoistically distorted love brings about the weakening and abolition of its recipient. However, when love arises in us as the undistorted affirmation of the other, it has the power to overcome the logical mistake that we commit in perverting the unity into an empty one.[357]

Does the gospel really promise that the act of a loving shepherd could possibly be other than to finally pick up this lost sheep entangled in its own confusion, its utmost egotism, and lacking genuine freedom and *incurvatus in se* and carry it home – even 'kicking, struggling, resentful, and darting his eyes in every direction for a chance of escape' if he must[358] – not only guiding but also, in Forsyth's words, 'forcing every soul'[359] in order to bring it into the destiny of holy love and true freedom for which that sheep exists, and apart from which it cannot? Is this not the divine checkmate? That where holy love cannot draw us into sympathy with itself, 'it will change its face, and drive us', as Forsyth once argued.[360] And so Gregory of Nyssa's contention of 'the Divine force', who, 'for God's very love of man, drags that which belongs to Him from the ruins of the irrational and material'. By so doing, Gregory insists, God 'is only claiming and drawing to Himself whatever, to please Him, came into existence'.[361] And if this is the nature of God revealed in Jesus Christ, do we not then already have every reason why we *must* speak of holy love's 'guaranteed success', the victory of 'the strong One in the Universe'?[362] In fact, at different times Forsyth seems to point to no less when he insists that 'Christ had to save us from what we were too far gone to feel. Just as the man choked with damp in a mine, or a man going to sleep in arctic cold, does not realise his danger, and the sense of danger has to be created within him, so the violent action of the Spirit takes men by force'.[363]

Forsyth's reluctance to embrace dogmatic universalism, however, even while holding out *hope* for such a reconciliation, ultimately threatens to undermine the self-realization of, or impose limits (which we have no right to set) on, holiness. It also threatens to suggest that holiness might be other than what it is in Jesus Christ. Like Barth's, Forsyth's theology of grace incorporates a dialectical protest: he protests *both* against a system of universalism *and* against a denial of universalism. We have noted Forsyth's justified concern of overriding creaturely responsibility by hiding

356 Barth, *CD* III/1, p. 95.
357 Schlatter, *Das christliche Dogma*, p. 34. Translation mine.
358 C. S. Lewis, *Surprised by Joy* (New York: Harcourt Brace Jovanovich, 1955), p. 229.
359 *Justification*, p. 187.
360 *Mercy*, p. 12.
361 Schaff (ed.), *NPNF 2/5*, 'On the Soul and the Resurrection', p. 451; A crucial verb in John 6.44 is ἑλκύσῃ [lit. 'to drag', as with a net full of fish, Jn 21.6, 11; cf. Jn 12.32].
362 Brown, *The Doctrine of Annihilation*, p. 123.
363 *Work*, p. 18.

behind some notion of predestinarianism unnecessarily or terribly entangled with philosophical determinism. But Jacques Ellul's protest that the will does not – can not – cause the truth, but only recognize it and serve it is persuasive: 'We are not free to decide and choose to be damned . . . To take this point of view is to make us arbiters of the situation'.[364] While Forsyth is able to assert that God's eternal election is in Christ,[365] he falls short of acknowledging the radical implications of such a position, an implication helpfully articulated by Karl Rahner:

> Christ and his salvation are not simply one of two possibilities offering themselves to man's free choice; they are the deed of God which bursts open and redeems the false choice of man by overtaking it. In Christ God not only gives the possibility of salvation, which in that case would still have to be effected by man himself, but the actual salvation itself, however much this includes also the right decision of human freedom which is itself a gift from God. Where sin already existed, grace came in superabundance.[366]

The possibility of future final judgement

> *The Cross of Christ is God's last judgment on all sin, for its destruction by a realm of infinite grace and love. It is the last resource of the Almighty Holiness; and His last resource is the end of all things.*[367]

Forsyth's thinking on judgement is mostly commendable. The 'prophet of judgement'[368] vows: (i) judgement is restorative in character,[369] (ii) judgement is a necessary function of God's action as King,[370] (iii) judgement must be conceived christologically,[371] (iv) God's mercy and wrath are not co-eternal,[372] and (v) judgement helps us to make sense of our experiences in history.[373] One example of this final claim is Forsyth's prehension that Britain had a special role to play as a trustee of universal freedom in the economy

364 Jacques Ellul, *What I Believe* (trans. Geoffrey W. Bromiley; Grand Rapids: Wm. B. Eerdmans, 1989), p. 192.

365 *Authority*, p. 353.

366 Karl Rahner, *Theological Investigations, Volume 5* (trans. Karl-Heinz Krueger; New York: Crossroad, 1983), p. 124; cf. *Justification*, p. 122.

367 *Justification*, p. 183.

368 Simpson, 'The Prophet of Judgment', p. 148.

369 See *Mercy*, pp. 8–9, 12; *Justification*, pp. 173–74, 178–81, 189–90; *War*, p. 147; 'Revelation and Bible', p. 251; 'Sunday Schools', p. 127; *Prayer*, p. 73; Sermon on 1 Peter 4.19, in Goroncy (ed.), *'Descending on Humanity'*, 2013; *Work*, p. 243; *Cruciality*, p. 100; *passim*. Cf. Eberhard Jüngel, 'The Last Judgment as an Act of Grace', *Louvain Studies* 15 (1990), pp. 389–405; Christopher D. Marshall, *Beyond Retribution: A New Testament Vision for Justice, Crime, and Punishment* (Grand Rapids: Wm. B. Eerdmans, 2001), pp. 149–62.

370 See *Justification*, p. 174; *Cruciality*, pp. 69, 141, 173–74, 201–02, 207–10; *passim*.

371 See *Missions*, pp. 15, 73; *Father*, pp. 36, 53, 58, 87; *Authority*, p. 406; *Justification*, p. 187; *Person*, pp. 73–74; *Preaching*, p. 134; *passim*.

372 See *Mercy*, p. 14.

373 See *Work*, pp. 28–29, 242–43; *Justification*, pp. 178, 188–207; *War*, p. 55; 'Atonement', p. 81; *Missions*, p. 72; 'Church and Society', p. 43; cf. Friedrich Mildenberger, *Biblische Dogmatik. Eine Biblische Theologie in dogmatischer Perspektive. Band 3. Theologie als Oekonomie* (Stuttgart: Kohlhammer, 1993), pp. 279–80.

of sovereign grace. This included a responsibility to confront Germany during the Great War.[374]

When Forsyth does speak of future judgement, moreover, he contends that any judgement is the last of a long train, the last in an ascending series ending in a crisis of all the crises which closes one world and opens another. Forsyth rejects, however, the Hegelian tendency to interpret judgement in terms of evolutionary process or in terms of upward progression because such proposals offer no certainty of reconciliation's final goal.[375] Such proposals, he believes, destroy any sense of decisiveness or finality in eternity, and any sense of genuine accessibility in time. His response is to insist that God's final judgement is a decisive act which has already taken place in history, and through which God has constituted a new creation. By positing that the 'last judgement is past' in the cross, and that 'what we talk about as the last judgment is simply the working out of Christ's Cross in detail',[376] Forsyth is not denying eschatological judgement, however, so much as recognizing that the cross represents God's 'decisive word to history',[377] and that that word carries *results* which are to be worked out in history.

A question before us in this part of this study is whether future judgement might not occasion a way to universal salvation, whether negative judgement therefore is a penultimate and not the ultimate word, whether eschatological dualism will not finally be transcended in the all-embracing love of God on the way to the universal establishment of holiness.

Forsyth's second qualification against an *apokatastasis* introduces five difficulties into his soteriology: First, his instinct to concentrate and interpret judgement's decisiveness christologically is to be applauded. Without the judgement and destiny effected in Christ there can be no teleology of history. A philosophy of history cannot deal with the evil that is in the world, nor assure us that the holy will win the day at last. But it is precisely any sense of *coming* judgement that is practically circumvented. While Forsyth properly resists proposals to understand coming judgement as a *separate event* of God's righteous dealings with the world apart from the cross, and while he suitably rejects as fanatic those notions of impatient and reckless hope in a convulsive social *parousia*,[378] by so concentrating the final judgement almost exclusively as the event 'already by',[379] Forsyth has, as Terry observes, left Christ 'little judging still to do' – the final judgement serving 'largely as an appendix' – and so reversed the biblical accent on the final judgement as 'the great assize'.[380] Indeed, Forsyth's emphasis on the 'state' rather than 'date' of judgement sometimes reduces any future judgement to 'a thin spectre haunting the horizon'.[381] While minimal interest in future judgement may be indicative of a pastoral concern to reject those chiliast notions which so defer judgement that

[374] See 'Sects and Wars', p. 624; *War*, pp. 7, 191–92; *World-Commonwealth*, pp. 7–8, 16. On Nonconformist conceptions of Britain's role in the world, see Bebbington, *Nonconformist Conscience*, pp. 106–26.

[375] See *Justification*, pp. 201–02.

[376] *Work*, p. 160.

[377] Brown, *Prophet for Today*, p. 144.

[378] *Authority*, p. 243.

[379] *Father*, p. 72; cf. *War*, pp. 39, 84–85, 147; *Missions*, pp. 13–14; *Work*, p. 29; *Society*, p. 23.

[380] Terry, *The Justifying Judgement of God*, pp. 127–28.

[381] Howard L. Lawler, 'The Universalism of P. T. Forsyth: An Exposition to Indicate Particular Problems' (unpublished masters dissertation, Wheaton College, 1987), p. 120.

persons may 'go on sinning with defiant impunity and confidence',[382] Forsyth does not really assist his readers to interpret those New Testament texts that suggest a final division between the 'saved' and the 'lost', even if we interpret them as threats rather than predictions, and as threats which grace need not carry out.

Secondly, such ambiguity over future judgement leaves Forsyth's theology pregnable to the charge that in the face of ongoing injustices things may not be finally set right, leaving victims, perpetrators, and (presumably) God without the holy Sabbath for which creation was made and redeemed. Christ's 'last enemy' would remain undestroyed (1 Cor. 15.26), the Son's gift to the Father left incomplete, the universal manifestation of holiness frustrated, and God's promise of being 'all in all' left unfulfilled.[383] Then, the hunger for justice and righteousness for which holiness longs would remain a torment on both sides, granting (by default) triumph to the counter-history to the world perpetuated by history's evil-doers. Such a coda could only signify the failure of 'a faithful Creator' (1 Pet. 4.19) to be Redeemer to *this* creation. It would be entirely unacceptable for God to discard this creation precisely because it is this current creation that must be brought to its goal as new. This at least means being taken 'beyond the threat of evil and nothingness into an eternity of [God's] own presence'.[384] Here, on Forsyth's own terms, success means a fully sanctified creation, hallowed through the crucible of judgement. Yet by collapsing eschatology so radically, Forsyth leaves too shapeless what the new beginning of God's enduring kingdom for which the saints long and work might look like. The collapse also offers little by way of hope of release from the entanglements of this world. Only 'in my end is my beginning'.[385]

Thirdly, when Forsyth speaks of saving judgement, he imagines that 'salvation must be salvation not *from* judgment, but *by* judgment'.[386] Such judgement is no mere declaration of the finality of divine law, but is 'the actual final establishment of righteousness upon the wreck of sin'.[387] Few Christian theologians ought to have issue with the contention that there can be no salvation apart from judgement. But Forsyth also claims that there can be no 'judgment without salvation'.[388] Where the two claims become particularly obscure is in those passages where Forsyth appears to present a form of judgement that is exclusively negative and lacking any soteriological significance. Forsyth properly draws a distinction between punishment and judgement. The former, he argues, has no inherent saving power, though may serve as an 'indirect and collateral necessity', something akin to 'surgical pains that make room for nature's curing power'.[389] A problem arises, however, when Forsyth entertains the possibility that future judgement might in fact be *only* punitive; that type of punishment which

382 Pitt, *Church, Ministry and Sacraments*, p. 146.

383 Balthasar concedes this possibility. See Hans Urs von Balthasar, *Dare We Hope 'That All Men Be Saved'?: With a Short Discourse on Hell* (Fort Collins: Ignatius Press, 1988), p. 237.

384 Richard Bauckham, *The Theology of the Book of Revelation* (Cambridge: Cambridge University Press, 1993), p. 163.

385 T. S. Eliot, 'Four Quartets 2: East Coker', in *The Complete Poems and Plays, 1909–1950* (New York: Harcourt, Brace and World, 1971), p. 130.

386 'Atonement', p. 81.

387 *Missions*, p. 52.

388 *Justification*, p. 189.

389 *Work*, p. 135.

only 'hardens and hardens'.[390] Might that which is remedial and corrective here become uncorrective and merely punitive hereafter?

Fourthly, if Christ fully met both of holiness' demands – (i) an answering holiness in love and (ii) the judgement on those who refuse to answer but defy[391] – then one is at pains to understand how there might remain the possibility of a purely punitive experience of future judgement, especially one bereft of soteriological achievement. Rodgers' précis of Forsyth's position is that for those of us who remain in rebellion, the finality of the cross will come home only as justice.[392] But Forsyth is unclear about how such punitive experiences of future judgement relate to the universal and saving judgement born in Christ's substitutionary work. If the judgement at history's end is only the corollary of judgement at history's centre, as Forsyth claims,[393] then how can it be merely punitive? So Pitt: Forsyth seems to be seeking 'some synthesis which would allow some view of judgment past, present, and future, but he is not very sure of himself, especially with respect to a future judgment'.[394]

Finally, and most significantly for our argument, Forsyth's speculations on future judgement have unacceptable consequences for what he wants to affirm about the satisfaction of holiness. We have already noted Forsyth's conviction that 'an unsatisfied God, a dissatisfied God, would be no God. He would but reflect the distraction of the world, and so succumb to it'.[395] We have also noted that only holiness can adequately satisfy holiness: that a holy God can be satisfied by neither pain nor death, but by holiness alone: 'Justice may be satisfied with penalty: but the only satisfaction to holiness is holiness.'[396] Punishment is an insufficient vehicle for the re-establishment of holiness whose claim can be honoured only by 'personality of acknowledgement'.[397] This honouring, as I have outlined in this study, is a christological happening which reaches to the confession of holiness through the new humanity. Here we need only recall what we noted earlier in Chapter 3 about the satisfactionary and regenerative strands in the atonement's threefold cord – that Christ's holiness is satisfying to God not only because it is the means of our holiness but also because it carries by way of anticipation all humanity's future holiness. The alternative would sponsor, among other things, a Nestorian Christ isolated from human response. Although Forsyth is exiguous on the details of what future judgement will entail, he is adamant that no matter how much suffering might be an ingredient in God's sanctifying work, no amount of penalty, remorse, verbal acknowledgment or ritual can satisfy the claim of holy law. 'Nothing but holiness, actual holiness, and holiness upon the same scale as the one holy law which was broken' can hallow God's name.[398]

The problem is plain: Holiness must be satisfied, and no creature can do it. Neither can holiness be satisfied while its antithesis remains in creation. By denying both dogmatic

[390] Ibid., p. 161.
[391] See ibid., p. 206; *Cruciality*, p. 171.
[392] Rodgers, *Theology of P. T. Forsyth*, p. 72.
[393] *Missions*, p. 16.
[394] Pitt, *Church, Ministry and Sacraments*, p. 146.
[395] *Work*, p. 205.
[396] *Society*, p. 32.
[397] *Work*, p. 124.
[398] Ibid., p. 126.

universalism and annihilationism, Forsyth sets up both God and the universe for potential eternal frustration and insanity. We noted earlier that while annihilationism promises a universe without spot or blemish, it does so at the expense of granting evil a final victory. It also signals that God's capacity to create may be incommensurate with God's capacity to redeem. Most significantly for our argument, it falls short of the answering holiness that God seeks, what Forsyth identifies as the final certainty of the establishment of good in command of the world everywhere. Forsyth recalls that 'we are not dealing with a mere *élan*, nor a mere *nisus* in a certain direction'. God's moral action upon us is not a case of pressure but of imperative: 'It is not the flush and tide of a universal wave, making its slow and ebbless way through creation, with power to hold what it covers. It does not act by force but by authority.' And, when it is resisted, '*the resistance is not-simply to be overborne and erased; it must be converted and recovered, else the Holy is less than universal, infinite, and absolute*. The unholy *must* be restored to holiness. It is unmade but to be remade. And there is none but the Holy creative enough to do this. *And He must – by the necessity of His holiness*'.[399] The possibility of ongoing future judgement (whether as corrective or not), the combination of Forsyth's at-times over-realized eschatology, coupled with ambiguous articulations concerning future judgement, insufficiently press the certainty that future judgement might serve to occasion a way to universal salvation. Whether negative judgement is a penultimate and not the ultimate word, and whether eschatological dualism will not finally be transcended in the all-embracing love of God, are both questions demanded by what Forsyth himself wishes to assert about the necessity of holiness' full self-realization. That he vacillates here threatens to undermine those areas wherein he is more certain.

The possibility of a redeemed race without every member

> *True hope must be universal, because its healing future embraces every individual and the whole universe. If we were to surrender hope for as much as one single creature, for us God would not be God.*[400]

> *The love which won the sceptre on Calvary will wield it as a power, waxing ever, waning never, through all the ages; and that the Father will never cease from yearning over the prodigals, and Christ will never cease from seeking the lost, while one knee remains stubborn before the name of Jesus, and one heart is unmastered by His love.*[401]

Much we have explored thus far suggests that racial salvation – upon which Forsyth insists – requires the salvation of every individual. The material surveyed at the beginning of this chapter leaves little doubt that, for Forsyth, God's soteriological vision is universal in scope. We saw in Chapter 3, too, that the demands of holiness answered by Christ are likewise universal. And we noted in Chapter 4 that the human conscience reflects the ground of our racial consanguinity secured christologically. Given this,

[399] *Justification*, p. 67. Italics mine.
[400] Moltmann, *The Coming of God*, p. 132.
[401] Brown, *The Doctrine of Annihilation*, pp. 118–19.

Forsyth's posing of the possibility that some might not be redeemed is puzzling, particularly given all he affirms about holiness' desire to find its echo in *all* creation, and about the indispensable value of every soul. To be sure, Forsyth nowhere denies the possibility of an *apokatastasis*. Though while avoiding hasty conclusions, he does insist on the curious notion that racial redemption *does not* equate to the salvation of every person, that every individual is not indispensable to the race's solidarity. Not only does this move introduce the possibility that creation might reach its *telos* apart from all, but this notion is difficult to square with Forsyth's repudiation of modern individualism and his recognition that we are a 'moral organism, destined to a corporate personality' around Christ's public person.[402] Christ is, he insists, 'the universal personality in whom all individuals are saved, and gain their individuality by losing their individualism'.[403] And again:

> In the case of our neighbor we make the mistake of starting with an atomism, a discontinuity, between individuals. We ignore the fact that the other man's existence is a factor, and not merely a feature, in our own. *It is the other man that makes me possible.* I discover myself, possess myself, just as I come up against my limit in him. The individual is not a spiritual reality; he finds himself only in a society of individuals . . . We each partake, for our very existence, in a corporate personality.[404]

Preaching at the Primitive Methodist Conference in June 1909, Forsyth carefully distinguishes himself from 'Evangelicals' who equate a saved world with the harvesting of individual conversions, and from 'Unitarians' who insist that a saved world means the salvation 'at last of every last soul in it'. Given what Forsyth asserts – namely: (i) the value of the individual to God, (ii) that it is '*the world* that lay on God's heart, and not only the rebels or unfortunates within it', (iii) his rejection of limited atonement, and (iv) his insistence regarding the corporate nature of a world salvation – it does appear that the answer to Forsyth's soteriological question concerning the requirement of 'every soul' must finally be answered in the affirmative, however hesitant he may be to traverse there.[405]

Picking up on Forsyth's idea articulated above that it is the other person that makes me possible, we might also think here of some work by Paul Ricœur who convincingly contends that 'the selfhood of oneself implies otherness to such an intimate degree that one cannot be thought of without the other, that instead one passes into the other'.[406] We might also recall work by Gabriel Marcel, Martin Buber, Dietrich Bonhoeffer and others who argue that 'I' is never a self-contained, self-comprehending and self-sufficient

402 'Regeneration – I', p. 636.
403 'Sacramentalism', p. 230.
404 'Regeneration – II', p. 101. Individualism is properly exposed in Barth's criticism of Nietzsche, 'the prophet of that humanity without the fellow man . . . the man who is utterly inaccessible to others, having no friends and despising women . . .'. Barth, *CD* III/2, pp. 232, 240.
405 *Revelation*, p. 35.
406 Paul Ricœur, *Oneself as Another* (trans. Kathleen Blamey; Chicago: University of Chicago Press, 1992), p. 3.

referent but can exist only in the direction of a 'Thou' and a 'We' lest it become a hell for itself.[407] Only in community, it is argued, can one possibly exist as an individual. Who *I* am cannot be realized apart from the race. So understood, it is impossible to separate the eternal destiny of the individual from the destiny of the whole race and of being in all its manifestations. One's essence – and one's sanctification – is inextricably knotted into the whole, and all without loss of genuine personality. It is this notion that makes vicarious fulfilment meaningful, and gives currency to the belief that the joy of the redeemed is threatened while some remain lost.[408] It is not only, as Rowan Williams rightly argues, that 'our holiness is bound up with other people and with the things of the world'.[409] Equally true, it seems to me, is the claim by Nels Ferré that 'If hell were eternal . . . heaven would be an eternal place of mourning. All those truly in the Agape fellowship would identify their lot with the lost . . . Heaven can be only when it has emptied hell.'[410] Put otherwise, human community extends to the dead, apart from which the life of the living would be an absurdity.

Certainly if the race is an organic unity, as Forsyth claims, then salvation cannot mean salvation for only some of the family. In terms more specific to our study, it is simply not possible to be holy without the other, to be saved without the other, even to die without the other, but only with the other; indeed with the entire creation. So Forsyth: 'We are not absolute, solitary individuals. We are in a society, an organism . . . And our selfish, godless actions and influence go out, radiate, affect the organism as they could not do were we absolute units. They spread far beyond our memory or control . . . We are members one of another both for evil and for good'.[411] Commenting on 2 Corinthians 5.21, Forsyth suggests that one idea inherent in reconciliation is a change of relation not only between God and human persons, or two or three persons, or several groupings, but with the 'human race as one whole'.[412] This growing notion in Forsyth's theology can be partly attributed to the influence of Maurice who asserts (in 1843) that 'all attempts of men to reduce themselves into separate units are contradictory and abortive'.[413] So too John Neville Figgis (with whose work Forsyth was conversant) in his 1913 Bishop Paddock Lectures: 'In the name of personality there is asserted a freedom which is the very denial of personality; for personality can come to itself only in society, and that involves a measure of order and continuity.'[414]

407 Gabriel Marcel, 'Structure de l'Espérance', *Dieu vivante. Perspectives religieuses et philosophiques* 19 (1951), pp. 73–80; Bonhoeffer, *Sanctorum Communio*, pp. 51, 54–57; Jean-Paul Sartre, *Being and Nothingness: An Essay on Phenomenological Ontology* (trans. Hazel E. Barnes; London: Methuen, 1957), pp. 346–51.
408 See *Mercy*, p. 10; *Sacraments*, p. 44.
409 Williams, *Tokens of Trust*, p. 141.
410 Nels Ferré, *Evil and the Christian Faith* (Freeport: Books for Libraries Press, 1971), p. 119.
411 *Work*, p. 121.
412 Ibid., p. 57.
413 Frederick Denison Maurice, *The Kingdom of Christ; Or, Hints to a Quaker Respecting the Principles, Constitution and Ordinances of the Catholic Church, Volume 1* (ed. Alec R. Vidler; London: SCM Press, 1958), p. 275.
414 John Neville Figgis, *The Fellowship of the Mystery* (London: Longmans, Green, 1914), p. 141. Forsyth read Figgis' *Churches in the Modern State* in 1913, confessing in the 'Preface' to *Theology in Church and State* (pp. vii–viii) that 'this work of a historian highly erudite and spiritual acted . . . strongly on me' and that Figgis 'sprang up in the second portion of this book'.

Genuine self-discovery occurs in Christian community, both of which are a fruit of the gospel. As members of the Christian community, particularity is not swallowed up into universality (as in Hegel) so much as taken up into a shared history and a common memory that patiently waits its common *telos* in a fuller community.[415] Albeit all-too-rarely, Forsyth grounds this doctrine of community in God's Triunity.[416]

Sanctification never concerns the plucking of individuals from the web of relationships and history of existence that situates and graces meaning to every part of the whole. Because the faithful Creator values his whole work, nothing and no-one can finally be lost to God's purpose lest God fail to be true to himself. New Testament faith is that 'not one . . . escapes from [God's] leash, however long it may seem'.[417] So where modern individualism has sought to privatize death,[418] Jesus' resurrection announces the firstfruits of the raising of all life, the genesis of new creation. Only when all that is Christ's is made alive and subject to him will the end come for all and God be all in all (1 Cor. 15.28). Christian hope in bodily resurrection – which, as Forsyth notes, gives to the 'next life a realism drawn from its moral reality common and continuous with this'[419] – affirms that no individual can be saved apart from the race. It is the character of hope itself that is pertinent here, for there can be no particularism of hope. So Marcel: 'Hope loses all sense and all force if it does not imply the statement of an '"all of us" or an "all together"'.[420]

In light of Forsyth's (i) aversion to Hegelianism's sacrificing of the individual for the sake of the mass, (ii) positive voluntarism, and (iii) valuing of the individual soul, it is difficult to see how 'every member' of the race is not required for the race's redemption. Moreover, if the identity of every person is found in a common redeemed conscience, as Forsyth claims, and our unity is found in our corporate Head who represents 'a race, and not of a section of it',[421] then it becomes difficult to appreciate how Forsyth can entertain the grammar of a redeemed race that renders any person practically dispensable. Notwithstanding his important rejection of individual*ism*, his denial that racial redemption means the salvation of every individual creates a problem not only for anthropology (that we share one humanity in moral unity) but also for christology, for in Christ God is in covenant union with *humanity*. The loss of one therefore means loss to all (1 Cor. 12.21). Ironically, Forsyth's third qualification signals the triumph of individualism through the back door, contrary to his own assertions *against* individualism and *for* personalism within community.

415 See 'Conversion', p. 768: 'Christ judged in wholes and saved in wholes. In wholes, but not in masses. The individual has his place in a whole, but not in a mass. In the mass he is but a unit, in the whole he is a member'.

416 See *Theology*, p. 157; *Authority*, pp. 229–30. For Hegel too, 'an authentic politics was unimaginable without the doctrine of the Trinity'. Rowan Williams, 'Logic and the Spirit in Hegel', in *Post-Secular Philosophy: Between Philosophy and Theology* (ed. Phillip Blond; London: Routledge, 1998), p. 125.

417 *Justification*, p. 182.

418 On this matter see Philippe Ariès' seminal study *L'Homme devant la Mort* (Paris: Seuil, 1977), also available in English translation and published with the title *The Hour of Our Death* (trans. Helen Weaver; New York: Knopf, 1981).

419 *Life*, p. 78.

420 Marcel, 'Structure de l'Espérance', p. 80.

421 *Authority*, p. 354.

Yet there is an additional problem with Forsyth's qualification, one particularly germane to his insistence that holiness 'must . . . establish itself in command *everywhere*'.[422] If holiness' essence is God's perfect satisfaction and repose in eternal fullness,[423] then it becomes difficult to understand how holiness might be satisfied with less than the 'return to holiness'[424] of at least every human person, if not every part of creation. Indeed, there are places where Forsyth hints as much:

> Holiness is the eternal moral power which must do, and do, till it see itself everywhere. That is its only satisfaction and atonement, not the pound of flesh but entire absolute response in its own active kind. And that is what we have in Christ as our head.[425]
>
> If the holiness do not go out to cover, imbue, conquer, and sanctify all things, if it do not give itself in love, it is the less holy. It is but partial and not absolute. As holy He must subdue all and bless all.[426]

Of Forsyth's three qualifications, this one most lapses into incoherence and one is pained to see what value can be extracted from it. I have tried to show that Forsyth's denial of a dogmatic *apokatastasis* is inconsistent with his notion of retribution, with his doctrine of election, with his belief in the function and end of punishment, with his hope in post-mortem possibilities, and with his affirmation about the staurological shape and triumph of holy love. I also noted earlier Forsyth's concern that the necessary inclusion of every individual as part of a racial salvation equates to, in Forsyth's view, importing natural law into an equation where grace is the only valid ingredient. While I agree that grace remains God's free act and cannot be presumed upon (if it is in fact to be grace), it seems to me that we have no reason to believe that God's will (1 Tim. 2.4) for a universal *apokatastasis* has changed, and will not be fulfilled either in this age or in that to come. Indeed – as Forsyth himself insists – there is a 'must' about it. This too is the action of grace: '*that no speck of His world remain which is not covered, claimed, and cured by Him; no soul which is not judged and redeemed into His fellowship*'.[427] That said, Forsyth's tautological qualifications remain at best confusing. And at worst, they erode the 'must' of holiness upon which Forsyth's God insists, and towards the joy of which Forsyth's God moves.

VI. The self-realization, or the frustration, of holiness?

Is hope enough?

We noted earlier Forsyth's preservation of the New Testament's tension between universal restoration and final separation. Nowhere does he suggest the possibility,

422 *War*, p. 174. Italics mine.
423 See *Work*, p. 204.
424 Ibid., p. 202.
425 *Preaching*, p. 240.
426 *Life*, p. 29; cf. Hanna (ed.), *Letters of Thomas Erskine of Linlathen*, pp. 71, 428.
427 *Revelation*, p. 20. Italics mine.

however, that they are two sides of the one truth – the former as it is for God and the latter as it is for those facing the ultimate decision.[428] Neither does he describe Christ as both the chosen and the reprobate of our election.[429] Instead, the tension is left unresolved in Forsyth's theology. Perhaps this is, after all, as it should be. But we have suggested that such indecision undermines Forsyth's speech regarding the necessity for holiness' final self-realization in the other because it leaves history with (at least) two possible endings. Forsyth might reject such a conclusion, recalling that God's desire for universal restoration remains, in his theology, a christologically founded hope and so a genuine possibility. Here he finds support in Moltmann, whose theology does not however demand the sense of 'must' that Forsyth's does: 'Eschatology is not doctrine about history's happy end . . . no one can assure us that the worst will not happen . . . We can only trust that even the end of the world hides a new beginning if we trust the God who calls into being the things that are not, and out of death creates new life.'[430] However, Forsyth's moderate- or neo-Calvinism with its emphasis on divine sovereignty and its rejection of a twofold will makes it difficult to anticipate that any will ultimately be lost. This is certainly the impression gleaned from his friend A. E. Garvie:

> [Forsyth] does not expressly favour the 'larger hope', as resistance of grace may continue . . . But his theology seems to me to lend support to it. In the exercise of the sovereignty of God, in the election of individual men, not to eternal death, but life, in the finality and sufficiency and universality of the redemption of the world from sin, and reconciliation unto God in the Atoning Sacrifice of Christ on the Cross, there seems to be so great an assurance of God's absolute goodwill that although grace cannot coerce we may in my judgment believe that 'love will find some way to make the pile complete'.[431]

Clearly, Forsyth stood in that stream that ran through Maurice and Brown professing the 'possibility' of an *apokatastasis panton*. But the question I am posing is whether Forsyth's theological vision actually requires more dogmatism at this point. Put simply: Is hope enough? While God's mercy ought not be presumed upon, and there are sufficient warnings in Scripture against both postponing repentance as well as harbouring soteriological smugness, does not Forsyth's theology of divine hallowing demand a more unqualified dogmatic affirmation of holiness' complete achievement?

Holiness' 'Must'

> *When one day no other name stands over against the name of God any longer, when the One is the All One, and all created being acknowledges only him and him alone,*

[428] So Robinson, *In the End, God*, pp. 119–20.
[429] So Barth, *CD* II/2, p. 164.
[430] Moltmann, *The Coming of God*, p. 234.
[431] Garvie, 'A Cross-Centred Theology', p. 326.

then 'the act of sanctification has arrived at its rest', then everything has become holy.[432]

'However gently it may work, in harmony with our personal nature, disdaining all coercion, a grace of the Almighty – if it earnestly desires to win every sinful man – can scarcely do anything else than triumph in the end.'[433] So wrote Schleiermacher. Forsyth too understands that were God not determined to 'plant' himself in command universally, especially where most challenged, God would be less than holy.[434] That which has established itself out of the shock of human turpitude and has recovered 'all in principle', will at last cover 'all in fact'.[435] Put otherwise, there exists with holiness a necessary correspondence between ultimate veridicality and final actuality. This is holiness' 'genius and destiny',[436] and 'there can be no uncertainty [about] whether it will succeed'.[437]

> The supreme task for the last reality, if it be holy, is to assert and secure itself against the last challenge of it. It is to cope with moral evil, which is its absolute antithesis and mortal foe. If man can do that he is his own reality and his own God. If he cannot, his only footing is in the God who can – who indeed must, or He is not God.[438]

The erection of holiness' final kingdom recalls that there can be no consolation amidst tragedy if the ultimate truth about creation is tragic. It also recalls that nothing created in history is lost, but rather is 'liberated from the negative element with which it is entangled within existence'.[439] While pastorally imperative, this conviction is – if Forsyth's doctrine of God is to be subscribed to – ontologically necessary not merely for creation but especially *for God* who moves not from outer compulsion but freely from within the 'moral necessity' in his own 'Person' to establish holiness everywhere, and 'to cover existence with its response'.[440] Forsyth contends that there is something about holiness that 'must' find itself in all persons, things and places.

> Absolute holiness must secure universal holiness; i.e. it must recover and sanctify personality everywhere. But as the underlying reality of the world, this unity cannot be merely an *effort* for redemption, it cannot be merely conative [an attempt] and

[432] Moltmann, *The Coming of God*, p. 333.
[433] Friedrich Schleiermacher, *Der christliche Glaube nach den Grundsätzen der evangelischen Kirche im Zusammenhänge dargestellt* (ed. Martin Redeker; Berlin: Walter de Gruyter, 1960), 2:332; cf. Martinus C. de Boer, *The Defeat of Death: Apocalyptic Eschatology in 1 Corinthians 15 and Romans 5* (JSNTSup 22; Sheffield: JSOT Press, 1988), p. 175; Ernst Käsemann, *Commentary on Romans* (trans. Geoffrey W. Bromiley; Grand Rapids: Wm. B. Eerdmans, 1994), p. 157: '. . . all powerful grace is unthinkable without eschatological universalism'.
[434] *Jesus*, p. 75.
[435] *Society*, p. 22.
[436] 'Regeneration – II', 93.
[437] *Revelation*, p. 37.
[438] *Authority*, p. 185.
[439] Tillich, *Systematic Theology*, 3:424; cf. *Jesus*, p. 112.
[440] 'Regeneration – II', p. 89.

> tentative, with the result in more or less doubt. It must be, if it is reality, already accomplished in principle. It must be a foregone redemption, a redemption that has not now to be achieved but only actualised.[441]

That holiness is creation's *telos* gives to Christian eschatology a theological, sociological, ethical and aesthetic dimension, all of which are appropriately exploited by Forsyth who vows that holiness *must* and *will* find its correspondence through the transformative redemption of the disordered universe which God has for himself as his own universal end. As the last reality, holiness is realized and satisfied in, for and by God only as it is realized in and for all creation wherein God is 'working almightily'.[442] Forsyth is perhaps closer to Hegel here than at any other point; specifically, he echoes Hegel's belief that the history of the world equates to the self-realization of the absolute Mind/Spirit/Reason which not only provides the lens for interpreting world history as the course taken by God's own life but also creates the demand for eschatology. However, while Hegel can speak of all 'otherness' wholly vanishing in God, and therein God recognizing himself 'and in this way He maintains Himself for Himself as His own result through His own act',[443] Hegel's single subject modalism leads to either dialectical pantheism, an apotheosis of the world, or creation's end, rather than to its new vivification as creatures are drawn to participate in the divine space and life. Forsyth cannot follow Hegel here. Forsyth is, however, able to affirm, with Schlatter, that God realizes his own holiness in 'otherness', and even that there is a mutual *circumincessio* at work wherein God affects and is affected by the world. But God does so, Forsyth avers, in a way in which creation's dignity is both affirmed and assured rather than swallowed up in a pantheistic beclouding. Absolute holiness is the last reality of a loving God; not denying itself, it overcomes all that sin can do, and through it all loves the sinful unto itself.

So how literally must we take holiness' 'must'? I have argued that the comprehensiveness of Forsyth's vision of holiness is undermined by his three qualifications, even if the qualifications are only 'possibilities'. In order to sustain holiness' incontrovertible victory – what Forsyth names 'the victory of perfect holiness for an end of universal holiness'[444] – no such qualifications can remain. The gospel which 'argues the restoration of all things, a new heaven and a new earth' remains muffled while the regeneration of human society remains incomplete.[445] Here is the 'must' that holiness demands. Anything less may lay Christian truth claims regarding the triumph of grace open to the charge of 'mere illuminism',[446] bereft of any finality worthy of the name 'holy'.

Forsyth is confident that whatever else we might say – or not say – about how history will end, the last things will crown the first, 'the end will justify the means, and the goal glorify a Holy God'. He posits here an eschatology with inbuilt theodicy, a consummation

441 *Authority*, pp. 183–84.
442 *Justification*, p. 63.
443 Hegel, *Philosophy of Religion*, 1:199.
444 *Society*, p. 32.
445 *Work*, p. 171.
446 'Religion and Reality', p. 554.

of all things via holiness' triumph through gracious moral rescue which does full justice to holiness. Redemption is always more crucial than Meliorism.[447] Whenever the *finis creationis* may come, there can be no other end than that 'the holy will win the day at last'.[448] To assert such is neither daring speculation nor a mere possibility, but, in Robinson's words, 'a reality that shall and must be, because it already is. It already is, because it is grounded upon what has been, one decisive act of God, once for all, embracing every creature ... there cannot possibly be any other outcome'.[449] Here again, the relationship between time, eternity and divine patience comes to the fore. It also echoes Forsyth's contention that the perfectly faithful God's 'Yes' is the 'plan of the universe' and that the 'victory of the holy conscience on a world-scale is sure and certain – give it time; that the triumph of the soul is in principle won', and only remains to be worked through. Though for now the world lies in wickedness and apparent hopelessness,

> God is holy, God is love, God is grace, God is endless power for the purposes of His grace; ... the destiny of history is a forgone conclusion in Christ, and in the high spiritual places all is well ... We have the faith that history in its movement is the working out of man's conquest by this God and this God's man, and God is steadily working this out by teleology – immanent and irresistible.[450]

History so understood, the drums of the advancing future are not the throbs of human egotism swelled and inflamed but the 'beating of the Eternal Heart' who is himself among us as one who turns no one away, and whose own costly death provides dogmatic certainty for holiness' final victory.[451] Forsyth's staurology can lead to no other consequence.

The end of sin's hegemony

> *While sin remains in the universe, God is defeated; everlasting punishment involves His everlasting failure.*[452]
>
> *By destroying evil I do not mean locking it up by itself in a moral prison, which shall be enlarged through the ages and generations until it shall become the abode of countless millions of rebels, but its utter, final, everlasting extinction, so that at last the universe shall be 'without spot or wrinkle, or any such thing' – the pure home of a pure creation.*[453]

It is my view that the preservation of a doctrine of hell's permanence equates to a confession that despite God's best efforts to overcome sin, to sanctify creation and

[447] *Justification*, p. 69. Meliorism refers to the notion of creation's self-improvement, usually aided by humans.
[448] Ibid., p. 185.
[449] Robinson, *In the End, God*, p. 99.
[450] 'Gate', p. 181.
[451] Ibid.
[452] Campbell, *The New Theology*, p. 208.
[453] Parker, *The People's Bible*, p. 160.

transform rebels into enchanted children, a black line remains across a page that God has otherwise made clean. As Charles J. Ellicott argued in *The Ceylon Evangelist* (October, 1893): 'It seems inconceivable that when God is all in all, there should be some dark spot, where amid endless self-inflicted suffering, or in the enhancement of ever-enduring hate, rebel hands should be forever raised against the Eternal Father and God of Everlasting Love.'[454] The proposal by some[455] that there might be any ongoing compatibility between evil and holy love is, to my mind, both contumelious and blasphemous. Such a vision betrays a particular commitment to a version of reality in which hell and heaven share the same ontological rights, that hell is not simply the 'shutting up of the creature within the dungeon of its own mind'[456] but is as much reality as heaven is. Here I agree with Forsyth's claim that if eternity is arrested with the conflict and agony of 'eternally divided and warring halves, [it] would then be but the procession of an appalling tragedy'.[457] Indeed, it is difficult to imagine a more costly theological commitment. From (at least) 1879 until his death, Forsyth mostly avoids the implicit *ongoing* dualism in this account of a twofold end for humanity.[458] For Forsyth, we must remember, sin is not God's ontological opposite but God's antithesis, the supreme enemy with whom God can never be reconciled and which God must destroy lest eternity be marked by conflict and the hegemony of death. It is not enough that sin be quarantined in hell. Whatever sin is – and sin *is* a mystery – sin can never be granted its own independent reality. Sin is unjustifiable, unredeemable and unconvertible. Strictly speaking, sin is unforgivable. Sin is what God always leaves behind on the path to the sanctification of all things.[459]

Eternal hell can never, therefore, qualify as a triumph for divine justice precisely because an 'endless Hell is not reconcilable [*sic*] with the character of God as revealed by Christ . . . If God and his Love is to be all in all, then no place is left for Hell in the end'.[460] Were God to allow sin to remain – whether to vindicate his justice or otherwise – it could only concede to evil[461] a recognized place and function which *cannot* be. Evil

454 Cited in John Hancock Pettingell, *The Unspeakable Gift: The Gift of Eternal Life Through Jesus Christ Our Lord* (Yarmouth: I. C. Wellcome, 1887), p. 324.

455 See Henri Blocher, 'Everlasting Punishment and the Problem of Evil', in *Universalism and the Doctrine of Hell: Papers Presented at the Fourth Edinburgh Conference in Christian Dogmatics, 1991* (ed. Nigel M. de S. Cameron; Carlisle/Grand Rapids: Paternoster/Baker, 1992), pp. 293–94.

456 Lewis, *The Great Divorce*, p. 63.

457 *Mercy*, p. 13.

458 See 'Hell', p. 4; 'Paradise Lost', p. 4.

459 Forsyth never attempts to explain the origin of evil. Nor does he follow Augustine's attempt to describe evil as *privati boni*, as an unontological, anti-ontological and ante-ontological parasite upon creation's goodness, having no creative life-giving power or potential to determine reality. On Augustine's terms, evil has no rationality; so, strictly speaking, it is beyond explanation. What Augustine offers is a description, rather than an explanation, and one that, in a sense, continually advertises the fact that we cannot offer explanations at this point. Forsyth seems to share this basic sequitur when he favourably cites Schlatter who maintains reserve on 'the mystery of evil, on the worst corruptions of Humanity, [and] on the point where Satanic evil touches the will of Man'. 'Religious Strength', p. 577.

460 'Hell', p. 4.

461 While Forsyth often uses the words 'evil' and 'sin' interchangeably, it is 'sin' which is personified as God's antithesis. 'Evil' he understands in terms both of 'suffering' and of 'sin'. Although often 'closely connected', they are distinct. For while suffering can be transcended, even made into a means of salvation or converted into a sacrament, sin must be destroyed. No use can be made of it. 'God in

not only poses *the* challenge to philosophical and theological attempts towards logical coherence and of the 'failure of pure speculation',[462] but it is also a challenge to God and to God's purposes for creation. And such is the challenge that evil must not merely be responded to; it must be overcome, and so reduced to nought: 'Die sin must or God.'[463] And again: 'The holiness which condemns sin would be but a negative thing if it did not go on to destroy it, i.e., to destroy its power to come between God and man, and thus to thwart the universal empire of that holiness which makes the universal and infinite power to be truly God.'[464] At core here is Forsyth's contention that although sin has an inbuilt tendency to disorganize itself – to self-destruct – the only way of dealing fully with the race's moral quagmire is if Holiness personally intervenes on sin's stage, assumes all responsibility for sin once for all and destroys 'the vast and regnant personality of Satan'.[465] God has determined in Christ that evil has no future, that evil can never become a sort of 'naturalized or legitimated citizen of eternity',[466]and so its effects now, though very real, are short-lived. 'The world is [God's], whether in maelstrom or volcano, whether it sink to Beelzebub's grossness or rise to Lucifer's pride and culture.'[467]

> If evil is to be permanent in any part of the universe, then God is there foiled and the Cross of Christ of none effect . . . So long as evil lasts there will be Hell. If evil should cease Hell would be burned out. Now if Christ's cross means anything it means the destruction of evil everywhere and for ever. The work of the cross is not done while there is a single soul unwon to the mastery of Christ and uninfected by his spirit . . . If we believe in the cross then we believe there will come a time when evil shall everywhere cease and sin no longer be.[468]

Unlike (possibly) Origen,[469] Forsyth resists speculating on the salvation of Satan and demons. He does speak of punitive judgement in this context however.[470] He also intones

Christ is capable of suffering and of transmuting sorrow; but of sin He is incapable, and His work is to destroy it'. The one act of the cross constitutes both suffering's conversion and sin's destruction. Forsyth makes this distinction based on his understanding of God's holiness. It is sin, not suffering, that 'impugns the holiness which makes God God. A holy God might ordain the pain He took on Himself, but he could not ordain the sin'. *Justification*, pp. 135–36.

462 Paul Ricœur, 'Evil: A Challenge to Philosophy and Theology', in *Figuring the Sacred: Religion, Narrative, and Imagination* (ed. Mark I. Wallace; Minneapolis: Fortress, 1995), pp. 249, 258.

463 *Justification*, p. 147.

464 *Authority*, p. 355.

465 *War*, p. 40; cf. *Missions*, pp. 72–73; *Cruciality*, pp. 60–61. On the reality of a 'personal Satan', Forsyth trusts the witness of the Synoptics over 'our modern experience'. *Missions*, p. 10; cf. 'Effects of War', p. 18.

466 Fairbairn, *The Place of Christ*, p. 466.

467 *Justification*, p. 166; cf. *Father*, pp. 53–54, 72–73; *Justification*, p. 151; *Missions*, pp. 14, 17. Forsyth assigns to death the same end in *Missions*, p. 237.

468 'Hell', p. 4.

469 See Henry Chadwick, *Early Christian Thought and the Classical Tradition* (Oxford: Clarendon Press, 1966), p. 119; Balthasar, *Dare We Hope*, pp. 59–60, 244; Tom Greggs, *Barth, Origen, and Universal Salvation: Restoring Particularity* (Oxford: Oxford University Press, 2009); Tom Greggs, 'Apokatastasis: Particularist Universalism in Origen (c.185–c.254)', in '*All Shall Be Well': Explorations in Universalism and Christian Theology, from Origen to Moltmann* (ed. Gregory MacDonald; Eugene, OR: Cascade Books, 2010), pp. 29–46.

470 See *Missions*, pp. 60–61; *War*, p. 40; *Father*, pp. 53–54, 72–73.

in a sermon on Milton that if Satan is eternally Satan, then there 'seems no prospect of evil being destroyed – a requirement which must enter into the true justification of God to man'.[471] If, however, creation is for the reflection and communion of God's holiness then, while the personification and sponsor of evil (Satan) cannot be redeemed, Lucifer, 'the first of all the angels', must be.[472] We might reasonably conclude, therefore, that while Forsyth makes no such dogmatic statements about Lucifer's redemption per se, the thrust of his theology of holiness and his acceptance of the Lucifer tradition suggest a certain necessity about this creature's ultimate redemption. Again, there are hints here in Forsyth of Hegel's insistence that if God's goal of self-realization is to be attained, God's antithesis *must* be overcome, the negation of negation informing the essence of the divine nature ('negation itself is found in God'). Thus (as we noted in Chapter 3 in our discussion on Christ's confession of holiness in sin-bearing judgement) the necessity of God becoming fully exposed to sin's power, of even becoming the antithesis of God's self – in order to comprehensively bring God's antithesis (in all its political, economic and moral forms) to extinction, that God might maintain, even receive, himself in the process.[473] Only to the extent that we can confess that nothingness has been vanquished in the meeting, overcoming and struggling self-nihilation of Christ may we say that we 'know' something of sin and evil's reality, and be able to speak hopefully of its end. Articulated otherwise, because of the Resurrection and Pentecost, hell has become part of the good news.[474] Violence, sin and hatred have done their worst, but the Lord of Life will have the last word. Only as we are submerged into Golgotha's hellish depths do we discover the sureness of unbounded reconciliation. Hell now belongs to Christ. While Forsyth insists (as we have shown) on certain qualifications, his staurology affirms that hell cannot be the final destiny for God's creatures. The creation now stands in new light; its future is resurrection.

While we live in a redeemed world, sin – individual, corporate and cosmic – still informs our scene, however. Yet, as we have seen in this and in the preceding chapter, truth comes foremostly not in the world of experience nor through empirical enquiry but in the one gracious Word of God in whom sin has been judged. For now, human beings live under a veiled victory, certain only to faith which waits hopefully for judgement's effects to be worked out. While the Church, therefore, must be concerned about evil and battle against it, she is never to be overwhelmed by it. Perplexed, we do not despair. Indeed, we can be of good cheer, for the Lord has overcome the world by a 'complete judgment *and execution* of evil . . . effected through the perfect action of holiness' in the cross.[475] As Forsyth insists: 'The evil world will not win at last, because it failed to win at the only time it ever could. Be of good cheer. It is a vanquished world. Christ has overcome it. It can make tribulation, but desolation it can never make.'[476]

[471] 'Paradise Lost', p. 4.
[472] *Father*, p. 42.
[473] See Hegel, *Philosophy of Religion*, 3:91.
[474] See Anonymous, 'The Gospel of Nicodemus, or Acts of Pilate', in *The Apocryphal New Testament* (Oxford: Clarendon Press, 1924), p. 125.
[475] *Society*, p. 21.
[476] 'Conquest of Time', p. 108.

Primordial and consequent fulfilment

Again he speaks in thunder and in fire!/Thunder of Thought, & flames of fierce desire:/Even from the depths of Hell his voice I hear,/Within the unfathomd caverns of my Ear.[477]

The continuity/discontinuity of Jesus' resurrection provides the ontological basis for Christian hope, promising that of whatever post-resurrection life consists, it is hope in something other than endless continuity.[478] So Forsyth reproves those who look for a world just like this one 'only better oiled'. There is neither escape from this world nor a mere amelioration of it. Instead, believers look to the transformation of this world, a transformation which, like Jesus' ascended body, still bears the marks of the cross. And the looking is important because as meaningful as life's plots and subplots might be, it is the end (and the more improbable the better) that confers meaning on the whole. This *is not* to encourage a premature closure, or to circumvent grief and wrestling, or the devaluing of history, or 'the facile optimism which cannot recognise evil for what it is'.[479] It *is*, rather, to remind us that eschatology is constitutive of the Christian metanarrative, and that when disregarded or overreached sponsors disastrous effects. It is also to recall that it is eschatology which makes life so unlike a soap opera, and that no matter how many glimpses of hallowing activity we experience now, and no matter how much richer these experiences make creation and God for us, its full satisfaction awaits us – and God. This is not to suggest, however, that the narrative is not open-ended. It is instead to remind us that whatever form the new creation takes, the hallowing of God's name will be at its joyous centre. As Moltmann urges, it is precisely in the hallowing of God's name that God arrives at his identity and recognition in his world, emerges from his mystery and manifests himself and 'experiences the response and the correspondence of human beings to his manifested presence in the world'.[480] This is the reality of the future, the all-embracing and liberating puissance under the sway of which God calls us, for now, to live, labour and hope in the world.

VII. Amen – holiness, 'the last reality'[481]

That God, which ever lives and loves|One God, one law, one element|And one far-off divine event|To which the whole creation moves.[482]

477 William Blake, 'Jerusalem: The Emanation of The Giant Albion, Plate 3. To the Public', in *The Complete Poetry and Prose of William Blake* (ed. David V. Erdman; Berkeley/Los Angeles/London: University of California Press, 2008), p. 145.

478 See Eberhard Jüngel, *Death: The Riddle and the Mystery* (trans. Iain Nicol and Ute Nicol; Edinburgh: The Saint Andrew Press, 1975), pp. 119–20.

479 Bauckham and Hart, *Hope Against Hope*, p. 42.

480 Moltmann, *The Coming of God*, p. 332.

481 *Authority*, pp. 66, 154, 184, 185, 188, 196, 327, 418, 419. Elsewhere, Forsyth states that 'the last reality of the world is the righteousness of God in it and its tragedy'. 'Religion and Reality', p. 551. Forsyth here echoes François Fénelon whom he cites approvingly in *Justification*, p. 26. See Thomas C. Upham, *Life, Religious Opinions, and Experience of Madame de la Mothe Guyon: Together With Some Account of the Personal History and Religious Opinions of Fenelon, Archbishop of Cambray* (London: Sampson, Low, Son and Co., 1854), p. 429.

482 Tennyson, *In Memoriam*, p. 333.

> *The faith of a teleology in history protects us from the vagrancy of soul which dogs the notion that things are but staggering on, or flitting upon chance winds over a trackless waste.*[483]

One of the concerns of this chapter has been to argue that creation's consummation does not bypass the annihilation of the destructive powers set against it, nor is it reached apart from the forgiveness of sins. Eschatology is therefore concerned with a positive word: the last reality of creation is when God and creation find and indwell one another in holy communion, when Holiness sees his reflection in the other, and creation joyfully and completely participates in him. While it would be absurd to suppose that we could give detailed shape to how such an unprecedented happening might occur, we can believe that nothing will be lost, that creation's consummation will be attended by every soul forgiven, redeemed and settled 'in worship in the temple of a new heaven and earth full of holiness'.[484] Indeed, whereas the climax of God's work in creation is multi-faceted and much is uncertain, Forsyth consistently argues that the one certainty is that there will be a people who are holy and free from accusation. This is the goal for which God 'chose us in Christ before the foundation of the world' (Eph. 1.4). God's plan for the fullness of time is, it is clear, to 'present as a whole'[485] (ἀνακεφαλαιώσασθαι) all things, earthly and heavenly. All that is separated, isolated, forsaken and lost is, in Christ, sought out, gathered up, and delivered from the abyss of nothingness, fragmentation and hostility into the glory of hallowed life. This final beatitude is the Son's gift to the Father.

The theological schema outlined so attractively by Forsyth bespeaks of God's creating with a view to the sanctification of all things; that is, that all might belong *to* God, and exist *for* God, in holiness. And I have argued in this study that for Forsyth holiness is that which can do nothing less than cover, imbue, conquer and sanctify all things, harvesting all unto its domain of victorious love.

> The last reality of the world is . . . the historic holiness of God as the power fundamental, and at last irresistible, in all cosmic things, as their last authority, therefore, and their final wealth and fullness. 'Holy, Holy, Holy, is the Lord God of Hosts, the fullness of the whole earth is His Glory.' That holiness is not mere purity or saintliness; it is kingship, moral kingship, the moral absolute taking slow, costly, invincible possession of its own. It carries with it the patience which is sure of its achieved reversion of the world, the portentous meekness (not without irony) which inherits the earth and has the world in fee. The Gospel is not just a message that God is love; but it is the historic act in which God's holy love is installed as omnipotent for ever among the world's powers and affairs. It is not the cheery word of a great good comrade (who might be as helpless as we are in the last tragic push against Fate) but the decisive power and action of the royal, omnipotent, absolute Master of every fate, the last victorious Reality of history,

483 *Justification*, p. 120.
484 Ibid., p. 165.
485 G. Abbott-Smith, *Manual Greek Lexicon of the New Testament* (Edinburgh: T&T Clark, 1937), p. 30.

> with Whom we have for ever to do, and to Whom for ever we belong and we turn.[486]

This is consistent with Forsyth's claim that for Christian theology 'everything begins and ends . . . with the holiness of God'.[487] Holiness begins *and ends* in God. On the way, holiness goes out to sanctify all things so that holiness may be all in all. This is the doxology that holiness demands, creates, sustains and secures. Forsyth is acutely aware that God's call to creation – 'You must be holy as I am holy' – must be interpreted as that word which both asks for 'obedience at all costs' while guaranteeing 'in and through such asking the soul's ultimate succour'.[488] 'The final sanity is complete sanctity. And the Holiest is the Key to the whole', he writes.[489] He is also aware that to promulgate holiness as the last reality is to confess that holiness demands an eschatology commensurate with God's self, that all things end where they began – in God. But the divine movement which hallows all things is no mere metamorphosis of humanity via the advancement of humane civilization, philanthropy and social reform, as important as these may be. Rather, the discriminating, consuming, selective and reconstitutive principle which is holy love – brought to its most creative, decisive and ultimate head in the eternal act of God in his cross – arrives in one Man. In Jesus Christ, and in his ceaseless worship, all things have been taken up into the universal end of the Holy. In the triumph of God's true humility, holy love has made its way to all creation, has filled the earth. This is the last reality.

[486] 'Religion and Reality', pp. 551–52.

[487] *Work*, p. 78.

[488] Herbert Henry Farmer, *The World and God: A Study of Prayer, Providence and Miracle in Christian Experience* (London: Nisbet & Co., 1935), pp. 87–88.

[489] *Father*, p. 115.

By Way of Conclusion: Heaven's Laughter

'The last reality', Forsyth intones, 'is the eternal security of the moral and holy powers. It is the kingship of God as at once the prime mover at the interior of things, and the destiny at their close'.[1] This essay has sought to articulate that Forsyth's sight on the kingdom's 'deep and subtle command'[2] of history is concentrated in his unpacking of some of the radical implications of the first petition of the Lord's Prayer, and in his bearing witness to the depths to which a merciful God has descended in order to answer that petition. It has, that is to say, attended to the centre of Forsythian soteriology – as historic, christocentric, personal, creative and universal. The gospel's power, as Forsyth demonstrates, is 'the holy historic God in his act of judgment-grace' hallowing his own name from the side of sin, giving himself amid the flood of life's storm to justify himself, overcome his antithesis, 'meet our moral perdition',[3] and in so doing at once break all human delusions and guarantee creation's destiny on a finally impregnable footing. This is Holiness' *euangelion*, satisfying to God and coming home to us in experience, in action, in the moral region of humanity's centre.

The centrality of the notion of hallowing in Forsyth's soteriology clearly has implications beyond those attended to in this essay, and indeed beyond those attended to by Forsyth himself. If hallowing is about all that Forsyth insists it is – that the future not only of creation but also *of God* is determined by holiness' triumph as the all in all – then hallowing must have something crucial to say not only to issues of theology proper, or to theology more generally, but also to those broader conversations in which the human community is engaged.[4] Still, in an age when the Church's public discourse is more concerned with attending to the objects rather than to the Subject of the divine economy, when materialist props are more sought as the panacea for our ills than the forgiving love that makes us whole, when the word trumpeted from pulpits, fonts and tables sounds more like a greeting card than a witness to the paschal

1 'Public Impotence', p. 2.
2 'Religion and Reality', p. 549.
3 'Rallying Ground', pp. 830–31.
4 See, for example, Nico Koopman, 'Holiness and Public Life in South Africa: The Quest for Wholeness, Embrace and Justice', *Colloquium* 40, no. 2 (2008), pp. 166–81; Jürgen Moltmann, *The Church in the Power of the Spirit: A Contribution to Messianic Ecclesiology* (trans. Margaret Kohl; London: SCM, 1977), pp. 352–56; Walter Brueggemann, *The Word That Redescribes the World: The Bible and Discipleship* (Minneapolis: Augsburg Fortress, 2006), pp. 17–18, 192–211; Nicholas Wolterstorff, 'Liturgy, Justice, and Holiness', *Reformed Journal* 16 (1989), pp. 12–20.

mysteries, when a nation's economic decline or upsurge is discussed in isolation from the moral implications of being human community, Forsyth's theological perspicacity is as piercingly judicious today as it ever was.

During the centenary of Forsyth's birth, his student Sydney Cave appropriately recalled that 'No summary of [Forsyth's] theology can serve as a substitute for his books.'[5] I agree. Perhaps, therefore, the best service that any study on Forsyth can render is to whet readers' appetites in the hope that they might go and read Forsyth for themselves. It is hoped that this essay advances such interest, for

> [We] have much to learn from Forsyth, so long as we do not make him a fetish and think that he provides the answer to all our needs . . . Forsyth was almost exclusively concerned with the ultimate issues. He was trying to get the Church, which still retained a great hold on the community, to be anchored to the transforming power of the Gospel. We are in a radically different situation. But in the long run we need to be firm where Forsyth wants us to be firm.[6]

In few places is Forsyth more firm than in his confidence that for the Church to pray 'Hallowed be Thy name' is to be a community constituted by both hope and eucharistic mission: hope for the consummation, sanctification and final restitution of all things in Christ, and eucharistic mission insofar as it fulfils the community's priestly role among the nations of offering thanks and bearing witness to One who in hallowing his own name has acted to bring the hegemony of sin to ruin and the whole creation into the fullness of holy love.

We began by asking whether the notion of 'hallowing' provides a profitable lens through which to read and evaluate Forsyth's soteriology, proposing that to so read Forsyth is to engage with a commentary on the first petition of the Lord's Prayer. It is not a commentary without its blind spots and inconsistencies, as we have shown, but we can articulate with some confidence that to approach Forsyth's corpus thus is not only a way to fruitfully hear and evaluate his output, but that it also (and more importantly) informs the way Forsyth's readers participate prayerfully in the petition itself. It is appropriate, now, to conclude this discussion with Forsyth's own testimony:

> Heaven does not laugh loud but it laughs last – when all the world will laugh in its light. It is a smile more immeasurable than the ocean's and more deep; it is an irony gentler and more patient than the bending skies, the irony of a long love and the play of its sure mastery; it is the smile of the holy in its silent omnipotence of mercy.[7]

[5] Cave, 'Forsyth', p. 119.

[6] Hubert Cunliffe-Jones, 'P. T. Forsyth: Reactionary or Prophet?' *Congregational Quarterly* 27, October (1950), pp. 344–56 (354).

[7] *Justification*, p. 206.

Bibliography

'275th Commemoration', College Hall, New College (London: New College, London, 1948).

Abbott-Smith, G., *Manual Greek Lexicon of the New Testament* (Edinburgh: T&T Clark, 1937).

Abbott, Lyman et al. (eds), *That Unknown Country: Or, What Living Men Believe Concerning Punishment After Death Together with Recorded Views of Men of Former Times* (Springfield: C. A. Nichols & Co., 1889).

Adams, Marilyn McCord, 'The Problem of Hell: A Problem of Evil for Christians', in *Reasoned Faith: Essays in Philosophical Theology in Honor of Norman Kretzmann* (ed. Eleonore Stump; Ithaca: Cornell University Press, 1993), pp. 301–27.

Adamson, Thomas, *Studies in the Mind of Christ* (Edinburgh: T&T Clark, 1898).

'The Addresses Delivered at the Unveiling of the Tablet Erected in the College Library, to the Memory of Rev. Peter Taylor Forsyth, MA, DD, 11 May 1922' (unpublished, New College Library, University of London, 1922).

Aldwinckle, Russel F., *More Than Man* (Grand Rapids: Wm. B. Eerdmans, 1976).

Aletti, Jean-Noël, 'God made Christ to be Sin (2 Corinthians 5:21): Reflections on a Pauline Paradox', in *The Redemption: An Interdisciplinary Symposium on Christ as Redeemer* (ed. Stephen T. Davis, Daniel Kendall and Gerald O'Collins; Oxford: Oxford University Press, 2004), pp. 101–20.

Allen, Charlotte, *The Human Christ: The Search for the Historical Jesus* (Oxford: Lion Publishing, 1998).

Allen, Ray Maxwell, 'The Christology of P. T. Forsyth' (unpublished doctoral dissertation, Duke University, 1953).

Almond, Philip C., 'Rudolf Otto and the Kantian Tradition', *Neue Zeitschrift für Systematische Theologie und Religionsphilosophie* 25, no. 1 (1983), pp. 52–67.

—, 'Rudolph Otto: The Context of his Thought', *Scottish Journal of Theology* 36 (1983), pp. 347–62.

Andrews, Jessie F., 'Memoir', in *The Work of Christ* by P. T. Forsyth (London: Independent Press, 2nd edn, 1938), pp. vii–xxviii.

—, 'Jessie Forsyth Andrews to Wm. Bradley' (unpublished letter, 4 September 1948).

Ansell, Nicholas John, 'The Annihilation of Hell: Universal Salvation and the Redemption of Time in the Eschatology of Jürgen Moltmann' (unpublished doctoral dissertation, Vrije Universiteit/Institute for Christian Studies, 2005).

Anselm, *Cur Deus Homo?* (Edinburgh: John Grant, 1909).

—, *S. Anselmi Cantuariensis Archiepiscopi Opera Omnia* (ed. F. S. Schmitt; vol. 2; Edinburgh: Nelson, 1946).

Ariès, Philippe, *L'Homme devant la Mort* (Paris: Seuil, 1977).

—, *The Hour of Our Death* (trans. Helen Weaver; New York: Knopf, 1981).

Arnold, Matthew, 'Stanzas from the Grande Chartreuse', in *Dover Beach and Other Poems* (London: Dover, 1994), pp. 69–74.

'Autumnal Assembly', *British Weekly*, 19 October 1911, p. 90.

Badiou, Alain, *Saint Paul: The Foundation of Universalism* (trans. Ray Brassier; Palo Alto: Stanford University Press, 2003).
Baillie, Donald Macpherson, *God was in Christ. An Essay on Incarnation and Atonement* (London: Faber & Faber, 1948).
Baillie, John, *And the Life Everlasting* (New York: C. Scribner's Sons, 1936).
Balthasar, Hans Urs von, *Dare We Hope 'That All Men Be Saved'?: With a Short Discourse on Hell* (Fort Collins: Ignatius Press, 1988).
—, *You Crown the Year With Your Goodness: Sermons Through the Liturgical Year* (trans. Graham Harrison; San Francisco: Ignatius Press, 1989).
—, *Mysterium Paschale: The Mystery of Easter* (trans. Aidan Nichols; Edinburgh: T&T Clark, 1990).
Banks, J. S., *Words on Immortality* (London: Charles H. Kelly, 1902).
Barrett, C. K., *Epistle to the Romans* (Black's New Testament Commentaries, London: A&C Black, 1957).
Barth, Karl, *Church Dogmatics* (ed. Geoffrey W. Bromiley and Thomas F. Torrance; Edinburgh: T&T Clark, 1936–99).
—, 'A Theological Dialogue', *Theology Today* 19, no. 2 (1962), pp. 171–77.
—, *Table Talk* (ed. John D. Godsey; Scottish Journal of Theology Occasional Papers No. 10, Edinburgh: Oliver and Boyd, 1963).
—, *God Here and Now* (trans. Paul M. van Buren; Religious Perspectives Series, vol. 9; London: Routledge & Kegan Paul, 1964).
—, *The Epistle to the Romans* (trans. E. C. Hoskyns; Oxford: Oxford University Press, 2nd edn, 1968).
—, *Protestant Theology in the Nineteenth Century: Its Background and History* (trans. J. Bowden and B. Cozens; London: SCM Press, 1972).
Barth, Markus, 'P. T. Forsyth: The Theologian for the Practical Man', *Congregational Quarterly* 17 (1939), pp. 436–42.
Barton, Stephen C., 'Dislocating and Relocating Holiness: A New Testament Study', in *Holiness Past and Present* (ed. S. C. Barton; London/New York: T&T Clark, 2003), pp. 193–213.
Batho, Edith C. and Bonamy Dobrée, *The Victorians and After: 1830–1914* (London: The Cresset Press, 1950).
Bauckham, Richard, *The Theology of the Book of Revelation* (Cambridge: Cambridge University Press, 1993).
—, 'Eschatology in *The Coming of God*', in *God Will Be All In All: The Eschatology of Jürgen Moltmann* (ed. Richard Bauckham; Minneapolis: Fortress, 2001), pp. 1–34.
Bauckham, Richard and Trevor Hart, *Hope Against Hope: Christian Eschatology at the Turn of the Millennium* (Grand Rapids/Cambridge: Wm. B. Eerdmans, 1999).
Beasley-Murray, George R., *Baptism in the New Testament* (London/Grand Rapids: MacMillan/Wm. B. Eerdmans, 1962).
Bebbington, David, *The Nonconformist Conscience: Chapel and Politics, 1870–1914* (London: George Allen & Unwin, 1982).
—, *Evangelicalism in Modern Britain: A History from the 1730s to the 1980s* (London/New York: Routledge, 2005).
—, *Victorian Nonconformity* (Milton Keynes: Paternoster, 2007).
Bebbington, David W., Kenneth Dix and Alan Ruston (eds), *Protestant Nonconformist Texts, vol. 3: The Nineteenth Century* (ed. Alan P. F. Sell; Protestant Nonconformist Texts, vol. 3; 4 vols; Aldershot: Ashgate, 2006).
Beet, Joseph Agar, *The Last Things* (New York: Eaton and Mains, 3rd edn, 1898).

—, *The Immortality of the Soul: A Protest* (London: Hodder & Stoughton, 2nd edn, 1901).
Begbie, Jeremy S., *Voicing Creation's Praise: Towards a Theology of the Arts* (London/New York: T&T Clark, 1991).
—, 'The Ambivalent Rainbow: Forsyth, Art and Creation', in *Justice the True and Only Mercy: Essays on the Life and Theology of Peter Taylor Forsyth* (ed. Trevor A Hart; Edinburgh: T&T Clark, 1995), pp. 197–219.
Berdyaev, Nicholas A., *The Destiny of Man* (trans. Natalie Duddington; London: Centenary Press, 1937).
Berlin, Isaiah, *The Roots of Romanticism* (ed. H. Hardy; London: Chatto & Windus, 1999).
Binfield, Clyde, *So Down to Prayers: Studies in English Nonconformity 1780–1920* (London/Totowa: J. M. Dent & Sons/Rowman and Littlefield, 1977).
—, 'Peter Taylor Forsyth, 1848–1921, Minister of Emmanuel Church, Cambridge, 1894–1901: Sermon Preached to Mark the Sixtieth Anniversary of his Death' (unpublished sermon; Emmanuel Church, Cambridge, 1981).
—, 'Peter Taylor Forsyth: Pastor as Principal', in *P T Forsyth: Theologian for a New Millennium* (ed. Alan P. F. Sell; London: The United Reformed Church, 2000), pp. 7–40.
Bingham, Geoffrey C., *The Conscience – Conquering or Conquered?* (Blackwood: New Creation, 1987).
—, *Ah! Strong, Strong Love!* (Blackwood: New Creation, 1993).
—, *Everything in Beautiful Array* (Blackwood: New Creation, 1999).
Birks, Thomas Rawson, *The Victory of Divine Goodness* (London: Rivingtons, 1867).
—, *The Victory of Divine Goodness* (London: Rivingtons, 2nd edn, 1870).
Bishop, John, 'P. T. Forsyth: "Preaching and the Modern Mind"', *Religion in Life* 48 (1979), pp. 303–8.
Blake, William, *Blake: Complete Writings with Variant Readings* (ed. Geoffrey Keynes, Oxford: Oxford University Press, 1969).
—, 'Jerusalem: The Emanation of The Giant Albion, Plate 3, To the Public', in *The Complete Poetry and Prose of William Blake* (ed. David V. Erdman; Berkeley/Los Angeles/London: University of California Press, 2008), pp. 145–46.
Bleby, Martin, 'Publisher's Note', in *The Principle of Authority in Relation to Certainty, Sanctity and Society: An Essay in the Philosophy of Experimental Religion* by P. T. Forsyth (Blackwood: New Creation Publications, 2004), pp. vii–viii.
Blocher, Henri, 'Everlasting Punishment and the Problem of Evil', in *Universalism and the Doctrine of Hell: Papers Presented at the Fourth Edinburgh Conference in Christian Dogmatics, 1991* (ed. Nigel M. de S. Cameron; Carlisle/Grand Rapids: Paternoster/Baker, 1992), pp. 283–312.
Bloesch, Donald G., *Essentials of Evangelical Theology, Volume 2: Life, Ministry, and Hope* (San Francisco: Harper & Row, 1982).
—, *Jesus Christ: Saviour and Lord* (Christian Foundations, Carlisle: Paternoster Press, 1997).
Bockmuehl, Markus, *Seeing the Word: Refocusing New Testament Study* (ed. Craig G. Bartholomew, Joel B. Green and Christopher R. Seitz; Studies in Theological Interpretation, Grand Rapids: Baker, 2006).
Boer, Martinus C. de, *The Defeat of Death: Apocalyptic Eschatology in 1 Corinthians 15 and Romans 5* (JSNT Sup 22, Sheffield: JSOT Press, 1988).
Boettner, Loraine, 'Purgatory', in *Evangelical Dictionary of Theology* (ed. Walter A. Elwell; Grand Rapids: Baker, 1984), p. 897.
Bonhoeffer, Dietrich, *Life Together* (trans. John W. Doberstein; New York: Harper & Row, 1954).

—, *Ethics* (ed. E. Bethge; trans. N. H. Smith; London: SCM, 1955).
—, *The Cost of Discipleship* (trans. R. H. Fuller; London: SCM, 1959).
—, *Creation and Fall: A Theological Exposition of Genesis 1–3* (ed. John W. de Gruchy; trans. Douglas Stephen Bax; vol. 3; Dietrich Bonhoeffer Works, Minneapolis: Fortress Press, 2004).
—, *Christology* (trans. John Bowden, London: Collins, 1966).
—, *Sanctorum Communio: A Theological Study of the Sociology of the Church* (ed. Clifford Green; trans. Reinhard Krauss and Nancy Lukens; vol. 1; Dietrich Bonhoeffer Works, Minneapolis: Fortress Press, 1998).
—, *Act and Being* (ed. W. W. Floyd; trans. H. M. Rumscheidt; vol. 2; Dietrich Bonhoeffer Works, Minneapolis Fortress Press, 2000).
—, *Discipleship* (ed. G. B. Kelly; J. D. Godsey, B. Green and R. Krauss; vol. 4; Dietrich Bonhoeffer Works, Minneapolis: Fortress, 2000).
—, *Fiction from Tegel Prison* (ed. Clifford J. Green; trans. Nancy Lukens; vol. 7; Dietrich Bonhoeffer Works, Minneapolis: Fortress Press, 2000).
—, *Ethics* (ed. C. J. Green; trans. Ch. C. West, D. W. Stott, R. Krauss; Minneapolis: Fortress, 2005).
Bonnard, P., 'Holy', in *Vocabulary of the Bible* (ed. J.-J. von Allmen; London: Lutterworth, 1958), p. 166.
Bradley, William L., *P. T. Forsyth: The Man and His Work* (London: Independent Press, 1952).
—, 'Forsyth's Contributions to Pastoral Theology', *Religion in Life* 28 (1959), pp. 546–56.
—, 'Wm. Bradley to D. J. Carter' (Letter, 12 September 1990).
Bray, Gerald L., *Holiness and the Will of God: Perspectives on the Theology of Tertullian* (London: Marshall, Morgan & Scott, 1979).
Breidert, Martin, *Die kenotische Christologie des 19. Jahrhunderts* (Gütersloh: Gütersloher Verlagshaus Gerd Mohn, 1977).
Bridgewater, Francis H. E., *The Bridgewater Treatises on the Power, Wisdom and Goodness of God as Manifested in the Creation* (Philadelphia: Carey, Lea & Blanchard, 1836).
Bromiley, Geoffrey, 'Only God is Free', *Christianity Today* 46, no. 2 (2002), pp. 72–75.
Brown, D. Mackenzie, *Ultimate Concern – Tillich in Dialogue* (New York: Harper & Row, 1965).
Brown, David, 'No Heaven Without Purgatory', *Religious Studies* 21 (1985), pp. 447–56.
Brown, Elizabeth Baldwin (ed.), *In Memoriam: James Baldwin Brown* (London: James Clarke, 1884).
Brown, James, *The Restitution of All Things. An Essay* (London: R. Tullis, 1824).
Brown, James Baldwin, *Studies of First Principles, No. 1, Voluntaryism: An Appeal from the Custom to the Conscience of the Church* (London: The Author, 1848).
—, *Studies of First Principles, No. 3, First Principles of Politics* (London: M. Tayler, 1848).
—, *The Divine Life in Man* (London: Ward & Co., 1859).
—, *The Doctrine of the Divine Fatherhood in Relation to the Atonement* (London: Ward, 1860).
—, *Aids to the Development of the Divine Life* (London: Henry James Tresidder, 1862).
—, *The Soul's Exodus and Pilgrimage* (London: Smith, Elder and Co., 2nd edn, 1862).
—, *The Divine Mystery of Peace* (London: Jackson, Walford, & Hodder, 1863).
—, *The Divine Treatment of Sin* (London: Jackson, Walford, & Hodder, 1864).
—, 'Latter-Day Prophets', *The Evangelical Magazine, and Missionary Chronicle* 10 (1868), pp. 20–27.

—, *Misread Passages of Scripture* (London: Hodder & Stoughton, 1869).
—, *First Principles of Ecclesiastical Truth: Essays on the Church and Society* (London: Hodder & Stoughton, 1871).
—, *The Battle and Burden of Life* (London: Hodder & Stoughton, 1875).
—, *The Doctrine of Annihilation in the Light of the Gospel of Love* (London: Henry S. King & Co., 1875).
—, 'Letter'. *English Independent*, 22 November 1877, p. 1283.
—, *The Perfect Law of Liberty: An Address* (London: Unknown, 1878).
—, 'Our Theology in Relation to the Intellectual Movement of Our Times', *Congregational Yearbook* (1879), pp. 51–77.
—, *The Home: In Its Relation to Man and to Society* (London: James Clarke & Co., 1884).
—, *Light on the Way: Brief Discourses* (London: James Clarke & Co., 1886).
—, *The Risen Christ: The King of Men* (ed. Elizabeth Baldwin Brown; London: T. Fisher Unwin, 1887).
—, *Stoics and Saints: Lectures on the Later Heathen Moralists, and on Some Aspects of the Life of the Mediæval Church* (Glasgow/New York: James Maclehose and Sons/ Macmillan and Co., 1893).
Brown, John, *Gospel Truth Accurately Stated and Illustrated by the Rev. Messrs. Jamers Hog, Thomas Boston, Ebenezer and Ralph Erskine, and Others; Occasioned by the Republication of the Marrow of Modern Divinity. With Various Improvements* (Edinburgh: Archibald Fullarton and Co., 1817).
Brown, Robert McAfee, *P. T. Forsyth: Prophet for Today* (Philadelphia: Westminster Press, 1952).
—, 'P. T. Forsyth', in *A Handbook of Christian Theologians* (ed. Martin E. Marty and Dean G. Peerman; Cleveland: World Publishing, 1965), pp. 144–65.
Bruce, Alexander Balmain, *The Humiliation of Christ in its Physical, Ethical and Official Aspects* (Edinburgh: T&T Clark, 4th edn, 1895).
Brueggemann, Walter, *Theology of the Old Testament: Testimony, Dispute, Advocacy* (Minneapolis: Fortress Press, 1997).
—, *The Word That Redescribes the World: The Bible and Discipleship* (Minneapolis: Augsburg Fortress, 2006).
Brunner, Emil, *The Mediator: A Study of the Central Doctrine of the Christian Faith* (trans. Olive Wyon; London: Lutterworth Press, 1934).
—, *The Christian Doctrine of God, Dogmatics Volume 1* (trans. Olive Wyon; London: Lutterworth Press, 1949).
—, *The Christian Doctrine of Creation of Redemption, Dogmatics Volume 2* (trans. Olive Wyon; London: Lutterworth Press, 1958).
—, 'Emil Brunner on his Faith and Work: Television Interview with Vernon Sproxton', *The Listener* 65 (1961), pp. 307–08.
Buber, Martin, *Between Man and Man* (trans. Ronald Gregor-Smith; London/New York: Routledge, 2002).
Burton, Rufus Theodore, 'Glorious in Holiness: The Holiness of God in the Reformed Tradition' (unpublished doctoral dissertation, University of London, 2004).
Bushnell, Horace, *The Vicarious Sacrifice Grounded in Principles of Universal Obligation* (New York: Charles Scribner and Co., 1866).
Calvin, John, *Concerning the Eternal Predestination of God* (trans. J. K. S. Reid; London: James Clarke and Co., 1961).
—, *Institutes of the Christian Religion* (ed. John T. McNeill; trans. Ford Lewis Battles; The Library of Christian Classics, 2 vols; Philadelphia: The Westminster Press, 1977).

—, *Commentaries on the Epistles of Paul to the Galatians and Ephesians* (trans. W. Pringle; vol. 21; 22 vols; Grand Rapids: Baker, 2003).
—, *Commentaries on the Epistles to the Philippians, Colossians, and Thessalonians* (vol. 21; 22 vols; Grand Rapids: Baker, 2003).
—, *Commentaries on the Epistles to Timothy, Titus, and Philemon* (trans. William Pringle; vol. 21; 22 vols; Grand Rapids: Baker, 2003).
—, *Commentary on a Harmony of the Evangelists, Matthew, Mark, and Luke, Vol. 2* (vol. 16; 22 vols; Grand Rapids: Baker, 2003).
—, *Commentary upon the Acts of the Apostles, vol. I* (trans. H. Beveridge; vol. 18; 22 vols; Grand Rapids: Baker, 2003).
Camfield, F. W., 'Peter Taylor Forsyth', *The Presbyter* 6 (1948), pp. 3–10.
Campbell, John McLeod, *The Nature of the Atonement* (The Stables/Grand Rapids: Handsel/Wm. B. Eerdmans, 1996).
Campbell, Reginald J., *The New Theology* (London: Chapman & Hall, 1907).
—, *Thursday Mornings at the City Temple* (London: Macmillan, 1908).
—, *A Spiritual Pilgrimage* (New York: D. Appleton & Co., 1916).
—, *The Call of Christ: Sermons Preached on Various Occasions, Chiefly in Advent and Lent* (London: Skeffington & Son, 1932).
Carlyle, Thomas, *Past and Present* (Boston: Little, Brown, 1843).
Carpenter, Joseph Estlin, *The Historical Jesus and the Theological Christ* (London: Philip Green, 1911).
Carson, Don A., *The Gagging of God: Christianity Confronts Pluralism* (Grand Rapids: Zondervan, 1996).
Catholic Church, *Catechism of the Catholic Church* (Homebush: Society of St Pauls, 1994).
Cave, Sydney, *The Doctrine of the Work of Christ* (ed. Eric S. Waterhouse; London Theological Library, London: University of London Press, 1937).
—, *The Christian Estimate of Man* (London: Duckworth, 1944).
—, 'Dr. P. T. Forsyth: The Man and His Writings', *Congregational Quarterly* 26 (1948), pp. 107–19.
Chadwick, Henry, *Early Christian Thought and the Classical Tradition* (Oxford: Clarendon Press, 1966).
Chadwick, Owen, *The Victorian Church* (vol 2; 2 vols; London: Adam & Charles Black, 1970).
Clark, George K., *The Making of Victorian England* (Cambridge: Harvard University Press, 1962).
Clements, Keith W., *Lovers of Discord: Twentieth Century Theological Controversies in England* (London: SPCK, 1988).
—, 'P. T. Forsyth: A Political Theologian?', in *Justice the True and Only Mercy: Essays on the Life and Theology of Peter Taylor Forsyth* (ed. Trevor A. Hart; Edinburgh: T&T Clark, 1995), pp. 146–67.
Cocks, H. F. Lovell, 'The Message of P. T. Forsyth', *Congregational Quarterly* 26, July (1948), pp. 214–21.
—, 'P. T. Forsyth, "A Voice from a Better Future"', *British Weekly*, 6 May 1948, p. 7.
—, 'Books on the Person of Christ: P. T. Forsyth's *The Person and Place of Jesus Christ*', *Expository Times* 64 (1953), pp. 195–98.
—, *The Wondrous Cross* (London: Independent Press, 1957).
Coggan, F. D., '"Under-estimated Theological Books": A Review of *Positive Preaching and the Modern Mind* by P. T. Forsyth', *Expository Times* 72 (1961), pp. 324–26.

Colenso, John William, *St. Paul's Epistle to the Romans: Newly Translated and Explained from a Missionary Point of View* (Cambridge: Macmillan and Co., 1861).
Coleridge, Samuel Taylor, *The Table Talk and Omniana* (London: Oxford University Press, 1917).
Congregational Union of England and Wales, 'Declaration of the Faith, Church Order, and Discipline of the Congregational, or Independent Dissenters, Adopted at the Annual Meeting of the Congregational Union, May, 1833', in *Protestant Nonconformist Texts, vol. 3: The Nineteenth Century* (ed. David W. Bebbington, Kenneth Dix and Alan Ruston; Aldershot: Ashgate, 2006), pp. 39–44.
Cook, E. Albert, 'The Defense of God and Other Problems: A Review of *The Justification of God* by P. T. Forsyth', *American Journal of Theology* 22 (1918), pp. 303–05.
Cox, Samuel, *Salvator Mundi: or, Is Christ the Saviour of all Men?* (London: C. Kegan Paul and Co., 2nd edn, 1878).
Cranfield, Charles E. B., *First Epistle of Peter* (London: SCM, 1954).
—, 'The Interpretation of 1 Peter 3:19 and 4:6', *Expository Times* 69 (1958), pp. 369–72.
—, *The Epistle to the Romans* (vol 2; 2 vols; Edinburgh: T&T Clark, 2004).
Crowder, Colin, 'Rudolph Otto's *The Idea of the Holy* Revisited', in *Holiness Past and Present* (ed. Stephen C. Barton; London/New York: T&T Clark, 2003), pp. 22–47.
Cunliffe-Jones, Hubert, 'P. T. Forsyth: Reactionary or Prophet?', *Congregational Quarterly* 27, October (1950), pp. 344–56.
Dale, Alfred William Winterslow, Andrew M. Fairbairn and J. G. Rogers, *The Life of R. W. Dale of Birmingham* (London: Hodder & Stoughton, 1899).
Dale, Robert W., 'On Some Present Aspects of Theological Thought Among Congregationalists', *The Congregationalist* 6 (1877), pp. 1–15.
—, *The Atonement: The Congregational Union Lecture for 1875* (London: Hodder & Stoughton, 8th edn, 1881).
—, *Christian Doctrine: A Series of Discourses* (London: Hodder & Stoughton, 1894).
—, *Christ and the Future Life* (London: Hodder & Stoughton, 1895).
Das, A. Andrew, *Paul and the Jews* (Library of Pauline Studies, Peabody: Hendrickson, 2003).
Davies, Stephen T., 'Universalism, Hell and the Fate of the Ignorant', *Modern Theology* 6, no. 2 (1990), pp. 173–86.
Davis, Philip, *The Victorians* (Oxford: Oxford University Press, 2002).
'Death of Dr. W. H. Fremantle: Dean of Ripon for 20 Years', *The Times*, 26 December 1916, p. 4.
Denney, James, *Studies in Theology* (London: Hodder & Stoughton, 1906).
—, *The Second Epistle to the Corinthians* (London: Hodder & Stoughton, 4th edn, 1907).
—, *Jesus and the Gospel: Christianity Justified in the Mind of Christ* (London: Hodder & Stoughton, 1908).
—, *The Atonement and the Modern Mind* (London: Hodder & Stoughton, 1910).
—, *The Christian Doctrine of Reconciliation* (London: Hodder & Stoughton, 1917).
—, *Letters of Principal James Denney to W. Robertson Nicoll, 1893–1917* (London: Hodder & Stoughton, 1920).
—, *The Christian Doctrine of Reconciliation* (London: James Clarke & Co., 1959).
Derrida, Jacques, 'Faith and Knowledge: The Two Sources of "Religion" at the Limits of Reason Alone', in *Religion* (ed. Jacques Derrida and Gianni Vattimo; Cambridge: Polity Press, 1998), pp. 1–78.
Dodd, Charles Harold, *The Epistle to the Romans* (The Moffat New Testament Commentary, New York/London: Harper & Row, 1932).

—, *The Apostolic Preaching and its Developments: Three Lectures with an Appendix on Eschatology and History* (London: Hodder & Stoughton, 1936).
Dods, Marcus, 'The Atonement in Modern Religious Thought', in *The Atonement in Modern Religious Thought: A Theological Symposium* by Frédéric Louis Godet et al. (New York: Thomas Whittaker, 1901), pp. 175–92.
Donne, John, 'La Corona', in *The Poems of John Donne: Letters to Several Personages. Funeral Elegies. Divine Poems. Elegies upon the Author* (ed. Charles Eliot Norton and James Russell Lowell; vol. 2; 2 vols; New York: The Grolier Club, 1895), pp. 143–47.
Dorner, Isaak A., *A System of Christian Doctrine* (trans. Alfred Cave and J. S. Banks; 4 vols; Edinburgh: T&T Clark, 1880–82).
—, *System of Christian Ethics* (ed. A. Dorner; trans. C. M. Mead and R. T. Cunningham; Edinburgh: T&T Clark, 1887).
Douglas, Mary, *Purity and Danger: An Analysis of Concepts of Pollution and Taboo* (London: Routledge, 2002).
'Dr. Forsyth' (unpublished, Dr Williams's Library, London, nd).
Drummond, Henry, *Natural Law in the Spiritual World* (London: Hodder & Stoughton, 1883).
Due, Noel, *The Holiness of God in P. T. Forsyth's Theology of Atonement* (Blackwood: New Creation, 1986).
—, 'Foreword', in *The Preaching of Jesus and the Gospel of Christ* by P. T. Forsyth (Blackwood: New Creation Publications, 1987), pp. vii–viii.
—, 'Theodicy and Atonement' (paper presented at the P. T. Forsyth Colloquium, University of Aberdeen, 1993).
Dunn, James D. G., *The Epistle to the Colossians and to Philemon* (New International Greek Testament Commentary, Carlisle/Grand Rapids: Paternoster/Wm. B. Eerdmans, 1996).
Duthie, Charles S., 'A Review of *Faith, Freedom and the Future* by PT Forsyth', *Expository Times* 67 (1956), pp. 202–03.
—, 'The Faith of P. T. Forsyth', *British Weekly*, 17 December 1964, p. 9.
Edwards, Jonathan, *The Works of Jonathan Edwards* (2 vols; Edinburgh: Banner of Truth Trust, 1998).
Eichrodt, Walther, *Theology of the Old Testament* (trans. J. Baker; vol. 1; 2 vols; London: SCM, 1961).
Eliot, T. S., 'Four Quartets 2: East Coker', in *The Complete Poems and Plays, 1909–1950* (New York: Harcourt, Brace and World, 1971), pp. 123–30.
—, 'Ash Wednesday', in *The Waste Land and Other Poems* (ed. Helen Hennessy Vendler; New York: Signet Classic, 1998), pp. 66–76.
Ellul, Jacques, *The Politics of God and the Politics of Man* (trans. Geoffrey W. Bromiley; Grand Rapids: Wm. B. Eerdmans, 1972).
—, *What I Believe* (trans. Geoffrey W. Bromiley; Grand Rapids: Wm. B. Eerdmans, 1989).
—, *Perspectives on Our Age: Jacques Ellul Speaks on His Life and Work* (ed. William H. Vanderburg; trans. Joachim Neugroshel; Toronto: Canadian Broadcasting Corporation, 2004).
Erskine, Thomas, 'Letter to Mrs Schwabe, 14 December 1853' (National Library of Scotland, Manuscript), 9747–33.
—, *The Unconditional Freeness of the Gospel: In Three Essays* (Edinburgh: Waugh and Innes, 1873).
Escott, Harry (ed.), *Peter Taylor Forsyth (1848–1921), Director of Souls: Selections from His Practical Writings* (London: Epworth, 1948).

—, *P. T. Forsyth and the Cure of Souls: An Appraisement and Anthology of His Practical Writings* (London: George Allen & Unwin, 1970).
Fackre, Gabriel, 'Divine Perseverance', in *What About Those Who Have Never Heard?* (ed. John Sanders; Downers Grove: IVP, 1995), pp. 71–95.
Fairbairn, Andrew M., *The Place of Christ in Modern Theology* (London: Hodder & Stoughton, 2nd edn, 1893).
—, *The Philosophy of the Christian Religion* (London: Hodder & Stoughton, 1902).
Farmer, Herbert Henry, *The World and God: A Study of Prayer, Providence and Miracle in Christian Experience* (London: Nisbet & Co., 1935).
Feine, Paul, *Theologie des Neuen Testaments* (Leipzig: Hinrichs, 2nd edn, 1911).
Fergusson, David, 'Will the Love of God Finally Triumph?', in *Nothing Greater, Nothing Better: Theological Essays on the Love of God* (ed. Kevin J. Vanhoozer; Grand Rapids: Wm. B. Eerdmans, 2001), pp. 186–202.
Ferré, Nels, *The Christian Understanding of God* (New York: Harper, 1951).
—, *Evil and the Christian Faith* (Freeport: Books for Libraries Press, 1971).
Fiddes, Paul S., *Past Event and Present Salvation: The Christian Idea of Atonement* (London: Darton, Longman and Todd, 1989).
—, 'The Quest for a Place which is "Not a Place": The Hiddenness of God and the Presence of God', in *Silence and the Word: Negative Theology and Incarnation* (ed. Oliver Davies and Denys Turner; Cambridge: Cambridge University Press, 2002), pp. 35–60.
Figgis, John Neville, *The Fellowship of the Mystery* (London: Longmans, Green, 1914).
Fiori, Gabriella, *Simone Weil: An Intellectual Biography* (trans. J. R. Berrigan; Athens/London: University of Georgia Press, 1989).
'First Impressions: Dr. P. T. Forsyth at Cambridge. Signed, "A Country Cousin"', *The Rosebud*, 15 December 1898, np.
Flew, R. Newton, *The Idea of Perfection in Christian Theology: An Historical Study in the Christian Ideal for the Present Life* (Oxford: Oxford University Press, 1934).
Flew, R. Newton and Rupert E. Davies (eds), *The Catholicity of Protestantism, Being a Report Presented to His Grace the Archbishop of Canterbury by a Group of Free Churchmen* (London: Lutterworth, 1951).
Floyd, Richard L., *When I Survey the Wondrous Cross: Reflections on the Atonement* (San Jose: Pickwick Publications, 2000).
—, 'The Work of Christ in the Thought of PT Forsyth: Kenosis and Plerosis Revisited', in *PT Forsyth: Theologian for a New Millenium* (ed. Alan P. F. Sell; London: The United Reformed Church, 2000), pp. 131–52.
Foley, George Cadwalader, *Anselm's Theory of the Atonement: The Bohlen Lectures, 1908* (New York: Longmans, Green, & Co., 1909).
Forde, Gerhard O., 'The Work of Christ', in *Christian Dogmatics* (ed. Carl E. Braaten and Robert W. Jenson; vol. 2; 2 vols; Philadelphia: Fortress, 1984), pp. 5–99.
—, *Theology is for Proclamation* (Minneapolis: Fortress Press, 1990).
—, *On Being a Theologian of the Cross: Reflections of Luther's Heidelberg Disputation, 1518* (Grand Rapids: Wm. B. Eerdmans, 1997).
Forrest, David William, *The Christ of History and of Experience* (Edinburgh: T&T Clark, 1901).
Forster, John, 'Dr. Forsyth on the Authority of Grace', *Primitive Methodist Quarterly Review* 29 (1907), pp. 286–300.
Forsyth, Peter Taylor, 'An Allegory of the Resurrection', *Christian World Pulpit* 61 (1902), pp. 312–19.

—, 'The Argument for Immortality Drawn from the Nature of Love: A Lecture on Lord Tennyson's "Vastness"', *Christian World Pulpit*, 2 December 1885, pp. 360–64.
—, 'The Atonement in Modern Religious Thought', in *The Atonement in Modern Religious Thought: A Theological Symposium* by Frédéric Louis Godet et al. (New York: Thomas Whittaker, 1901), pp. 61–88.
—, 'The Attacks on the Churches', *British Weekly*, 23 and 30 March 1905, p. 614 and p. 38.
—, 'The Attitude of the Church to the Present Unrest', *British Congregationalist* (1910), pp. 214–15.
—, *Baldwin Brown: A Tribute, a Reminiscence, and a Study* (London: James Clarke, 1884).
—, 'Baldwin Brown: A Tribute, a Reminiscence, and a Study', in *In Memoriam: James Baldwin Brown* (ed. Elizabeth Baldwin Brown; London: James Clarke, 1884), pp. 133–42.
—, '"The Bible Doctrine of Hell and the Unseen": Sermon by the Rev. P. T. Forsyth, Preached in the Bradford Road Congregational Church, Shipley, Nov. 23rd', *Shipley and Saltaire Times*, 13 December 1879, p. 4.
—, 'The Chairman's Mantle: Dr Forsyth to Mr Jowett', *Examiner*, 11 January 1906, p. 28.
—, *The Charter of the Church: Six Lectures on the Spiritual Principle of Nonconformity* (London: Alexander & Shepherd, 1896).
—, 'The Charter of Missions', *Christian World Pulpit* 63 (1903), pp. 305–12.
—, 'Chinese Labour', *The Times*, Saturday, 20 January 1906, p. 12.
—, 'Chinese Labour', *The Times*, Friday, 26 January 1906, p. 7.
—, 'Chinese Labour in the Transvaal', *The Times*, Thursday, 18 January 1906, p. 4.
—, 'Chinese Labour', *The Times*, Saturday, 20 January 1906, p. 12.
—, 'Chinese Labour in the Transvaal', *The Times*, 25 January 1906, p. 11.
—, 'Chinese Labour in the Transvaal', *The Times*, 29 January 1906, p. 7.
—, 'Christ – King or Genius?' *The Methodist Review* 65, July (1916), pp. 433–47.
—, 'Christ and the Christian Principle', in *London Theological Studies* (ed. Members of the Faculty of Theology in the University of London; London: University of London Press, 1911), pp. 133–66.
—, 'Christ at the Gate', *Christian World Pulpit* 73 (1908), pp. 177–82.
—, *Christ on Parnassus: Lectures on Art, Ethic, and Theology* (London: Hodder & Stoughton, 1911).
—, 'Christ Our Sanctification', *Wesleyan Methodist Magazine* 134 (1911), pp. 732–34.
—, 'Christ's Person and His Cross', *The Methodist Review* 66 (1917), pp. 3–22.
—, *Christian Aspects of Evolution* (London: The Epworth Press, 1950).
—, *The Christian Ethic of War* (London: Longmans, Green, and Co., 1916).
—, 'Christianity and Nationality', *British Weekly*, 9 July 1914, pp. 385–86.
—, 'Christianity and Society', *Methodist Review Quarterly* 63, no. 1 (1914), pp. 3–21.
—, 'The Christianity of Christ and Christ Our Christianity', *Review and Expositor* 15, no. 3 (1918), pp. 249–65.
—, *The Church and the Sacraments* (London: Independent Press, 1947 [1917]).
—, 'The Church and Society – Alien or Allied?' *British Weekly*, 9 October 1913, p. 43.
—, *The Church, the Gospel and Society* (London: Independent Press, 1962).
—, 'Church, State, Dogma and Education', *Contemporary Review* 90 (1906), pp. 827–36.
—, 'Churches, Sects and Wars', *Contemporary Review* 107 (1915), pp. 618–26.
—, 'Congregationalism and the Principle of Liberty', *Constructive Quarterly* 1, September (1913), pp. 498–521.
—, *Congregationalism and Reunion: Two Lectures* (London: Independent Press, 1952).
—, 'The Conquest of Time by Eternity', *Christian World Pulpit* 87 (1915), pp. 104–08.

—, 'The Conversion of the "Good"', *Contemporary Review* 109 (1916), pp. 760–71.
—, 'The Cross as the Final Seat of Authority', *Contemporary Review* 76 (1899), pp. 589–608.
—, 'The Cross of Christ as the Moral Principle of Society', *Methodist Review* 99 (1917), pp. 9–21.
—, *The Cruciality of the Cross* (London: Hodder & Stoughton, 1910 [1909]).
—, 'The Distinctive Thing in Christian Experience', *Hibbert Journal* 6, no. 3 (1908), pp. 481–99.
—, '"Dr. Forsyth and Mr. Campbell", Letter', *British Weekly*, 19 May 1910, p. 172.
—, 'The Efficiency and Sufficiency of the Bible', *Biblical Review* 2 (1917), pp. 10–30.
—, 'The Empire for Christ', *Christian World Pulpit* 57 (1900), pp. 305–11.
—, 'The Evangelical Basis of Free Churchism', *Contemporary Review* 81 (1902), pp. 680–95.
—, 'The Evangelical Churches and the Higher Criticism', *Contemporary Review* 88, October (1905), pp. 574–99.
—, 'The Evangelical Churches and the Higher Criticism', in *The Gospel and Authority: A P. T. Forsyth Reader* (ed. Marvin W. Anderson; Minneapolis: Augsburg, 1971), pp. 15–52.
—, 'Faith and Mind', *Methodist Review Quarterly* 61 (1912), pp. 627–43.
—, *Faith, Freedom and the Future* (London: Hodder & Stoughton, 1912).
—, 'Faith, Metaphysic, and Incarnation', *Methodist Review* 97 (1915), pp. 696–719.
—, 'A Few Hints about Reading the Bible', *Biblical Review* 3 (1918), pp. 530–44.
—, 'The First and Second Adam', *Methodist Review* 98 (1916), pp. 347–51.
—, 'The Foolishness of Preaching', *Expository Times* 30 (1919), pp. 153–54.
—, 'The Fund and the Faith', *British Weekly*, 29 May 1913, p. 219.
—, *God the Holy Father* (London: Independent Press, 1957 [1897]).
—, 'God, Sin, and the Atonement', *British Weekly*, 28 March 1907, pp. 669–70.
—, 'The Healing of the Paralytic', *British Weekly*, 25 October 1894, p. 4.
—, 'Holy Father', *British Weekly*, 19 and 26 November 1896, pp. 74, 94–95.
—, 'Ibsen's Treatment of Guilt', *Hibbert Journal* 14 (1915), pp. 105–22.
—, 'Immanence and Incarnation', in *The Old Faith and the New Theology* (ed. C. H. Vine; London: Sampson Low Marston, 1907), pp. 48–61.
—, 'The Inner Life of Christ', *Constructive Quarterly* 7, no. 25 (1919), pp. 149–62.
—, 'The Insufficiency of Social Righteousness as a Moral Idea', *Hibbert Journal* 7 (1909), pp. 596–613.
—, 'Intellectualism and Faith', *Hibbert Journal* 11 (1913), pp. 311–28.
—, *Intercessory Services for Aid in Public Worship* (Manchester: John Heywood, 1896).
—, *The Justification of God: Lectures for War-Time on a Christian Theodicy* (London: Independent Press, 1957 [1916]).
—, 'Land Laws of the Bible', *Contemporary Review* 104 (1913), pp. 496–504.
—, 'Lay Religion', *Constructive Quarterly* 3, December (1915), pp. 767–89.
—, 'Letter', *British Weekly*, 26 October 1911, p. 100.
—, 'Letter', *English Independent*, 1 November 1877, pp. 1202–03.
—, 'Letter', *English Independent*, 8 November 1877, pp. 1231–32.
—, 'Letter to William Robertson Nicoll, 25 November' (unpublished, 1920).
—, 'Liberty and its Limits in the Church', *Contemporary Review* 101 (1912), pp. 502–12.
—, 'The Love of Liberty and the Love of Truth', *Contemporary Review* 93 (1908), pp. 158–70.
—, *'Maid, Arise': A Sermon to School Girls. Preached in Shipley Congregational Church, Sunday, 28 July 1878* (Bradford: T. Brear, 1878).
—, 'Majesty and Mercy', *Christian World Pulpit* 79 (1911), pp. 305–07.
—, *Marriage: Its Ethic and Religion* (London: Hodder & Stoughton, 1912).

—, *Mercy the True and Only Justice: A Sermon Preached in Shipley Congregational Church, on the Missionary Sunday, September 30, 1877* (Bradford: T. Brear, nd).
—, '"Milton's Paradise Lost": Lecture by the Rev. P. T. Forsyth, M.A.', *Shipley and Saltaire Times*, 22 March 1879, p. 4.
—, 'Ministerial Libraries: V. Principal Forsyth's Library at Hackney College', the *British Monthly* 4 (1904), pp. 267–70.
—, *Missions in State and Church: Sermons and Addresses* (London: Hodder & Stoughton, 1908).
—, 'Missions the Soul of Civilisation', *Christian World Pulpit*, 4 May 1910, pp. 273–77.
—, *Monism* (Letchworth: Garden City Press, 1909).
—, 'Moral Manhood', *Young Man* (Cambridge, After 1901), pp. 151–53.
—, 'The Moralization of Religion', *London Quarterly Review* 128 (1917), pp. 161–74.
—, 'Mystics and Saints', *Expository Times* 5 (1894), pp. 401–04.
—, 'The Need for a Positive Gospel', *London Quarterly Review* 101 (1904), pp. 64–99.
—, 'The Need of a Church Theory for Church Union', *Contemporary Review* 111, March (1917), pp. 357–65.
—, 'The "New Theology": Mr Campbell's Teaching Criticised: A Repudiation', *Daily Chronicle*, 4 February 1907, np.
—, 'A New Year Meditation', *Evangelical Magazine* 103, January (1895), pp. 29–35.
—, 'The Newest Theology', *British Weekly*, 7 March 1907, pp. 581–82.
—, *The Old Faith and the New* (Leicester, Birmingham, and Leamington/Manchester: Midland Educational Company/Brook & Chrsytal, 1891).
—, 'Ordination Address, 20 October' (unpublished, Dr Williams's Library, London, 1909).
—, 'Ordination Statement', *Shipley and Saltaire Times*, 25 November 1876, p. 4.
—, 'Orthodoxy, Heterodoxy, Heresy and Freedom', *Hibbert Journal* 8 (1910), pp. 321–29.
—, 'Our Experience of a Triune God', *Cambridge Christian Life* 1 (1914), pp. 240–46.
—, 'The Paradox of Christ', *London Quarterly Review* 102 (1904), pp. 111–38.
—, *The Person and Place of Jesus Christ: The Congregational Union Lecture for 1909* (London: Congregational Union of England and Wales/Hodder & Stoughton, 1910).
—, 'Pessimism', *Christian World Pulpit* 25 (1884), pp. 42–44.
—, 'The Pessimism of Mr Thomas Hardy', *London Quarterly Review* 118 (1912), pp. 193–219.
—, 'The Place of Spiritual Experience in the Making of Theology', *Christian World Pulpit* 69 (1906), pp. 184–87.
—, '"A Pocket of Gold", Review of *The Way, the Truth, and the Life*, by F. A. J. [sic] Hort', *Independent and Nonconformist*, 8 March 1894, p. 187.
—, *Positive Preaching and the Modern Mind* (London: Independent Press, 3rd edn, 1949 [1907]).
—, *The Preaching of Jesus and the Gospel of Christ* (Blackwood: New Creation Publications, 1987 [1915]).
—, 'The Preaching of Jesus and the Gospel of Christ. [VII:] The Meaning of a Sinless Christ', *The Expositor* 8th Series, 25 (1923), pp. 288–312.
—, 'Principal Forsyth on Preaching', *British Weekly*, 31 October 1907, p. 83.
—, *The Principle of Authority in Relation to Certainty, Sanctity and Society: An Essay in the Philosophy of Experimental Religion* (London: Independent Press, 1952 [1912]).
—, 'The Problem of Forgiveness in the Lord's Prayer', in *The Sermon on the Mount: A Practical Exposition of the Lord's Prayer* (ed. E. Griffith-Jones et al.; Manchester: James Robinson, 1903), pp. 181–207.
—, 'The Protestantism of the Protestant Religion', *Shipley and Saltaire Times*, 29 November 1879, p. 4.

—, 'The Public Impotence of Religion', *Westminster Gazette*, 21 February 1919, pp. 1–2.
—, *The Pulpit and the Age* (Manchester: Brook & Chrystal, 1885).
—, 'A Rallying Ground for the Free Churches: The Reality of Grace', *Hibbert Journal* 4 (1906), pp. 824–44.
—, 'The Reality of God: A War-time Question', *Hibbert Journal* 16 (1918), pp. 608–19.
—, 'Regeneration, Creation, and Miracle', *Methodist Review Quarterly* 64 (1914), pp. 627–43.
—, 'Regeneration, Creation, and Miracle: Second Article', *Methodist Review Quarterly* 64 (1915), pp. 89–103.
—, 'Religion and Reality', *Contemporary Review* 115 (1919), pp. 548–54.
—, *Religion in Recent Art: Being Expository Lectures on Rossetti, Burne Jones, Watts, Holman Hunt, and Wagner* (New York: AMS Press, 3rd edn, 1972 [1889]).
—, 'Religious Communion', *English Independent*, 1 November 1877, pp. 1202–03.
—, 'The Religious Strength of Theological Reserve', *British Weekly* (1913), pp. 577–78.
—, 'Rev. P. T. Forsyth on "The Workers of the Future"', *Shipley and Saltaire Times*, 28 July 1877, p. 4.
—, 'The Rev. P. T. Forsyth, MA, on "Contents of the [Saltaire] Institute Library"', *Shipley and Saltaire Times*, 19 October 1878, p. 4.
—, 'Revelation and Bible', *Hibbert Journal* 10 (1911), pp. 235–52.
—, 'Revelation and the Person of Christ', in *Faith and Criticism: Essays by Congregationalists* (ed. William Henry Bennett; London: Simpson Low Marston, 1893), pp. 95–144.
—, *Revelation Old and New: Sermons and Addresses* (ed. John Huxtable; London: Independent Press, 1962).
—, *Rome, Reform and Reaction: Four Lectures on the Religious Situation* (London: Hodder & Stoughton, 1899).
—, *The Roots of a World-Commonwealth* (London: Hodder & Stoughton, 1918).
—, 'Sacramentalism the True Remedy for Sacerdotalism', *The Expositor* 5th Series, 8 (1898), pp. 221–33, 262–75.
—, 'Self-Denial and Self-Committal', *Expositor* 4 (1912), pp. 32–43.
—, 'The Significance of the Church Fabric', *Christian World Pulpit* 59 (1901), pp. 415–18.
—, 'The Slowness of God', *Expository Times* 11 (1900), pp. 218–22.
—, *Socialism and Christianity in Some of Their Deeper Aspects* (Manchester: Brook & Chrystal, 1886).
—, *Socialism, the Church and the Poor* (London: Hodder & Stoughton, 1908).
—, 'Some Effects of the War on Belief', *Holborn Review* (1918), pp. 16–26.
—, 'The Soul of Christ and the Cross of Christ', *London Quarterly Review* 116 (1911), pp. 193–212.
—, *The Soul of Prayer* (London: Independent Press, 1951 [1916]).
—, 'The Spiritual Needs in the Churches', *Christian World Pulpit* 89 (1916), pp. 251–55.
—, 'The Strength of Weakness', *Christian World Pulpit* 13 (1878), pp. 85–87.
—, 'Sunday Schools and Modern Theology', *Christian World Pulpit* 31 (1887), pp. 123–27.
—, 'Teachers of the Century: Robert Browning', *Modern Church*, 15 October 1891, 451–52.
—, *Theology in Church and State* (London: Hodder & Stoughton, 1915).
—, 'Theology in the Future', *Independent and Nonconformist*, 10 June 1897, pp. 450–52, 454.
—, 'Things New and Old', *Christian World Pulpit* 84 (1913), pp. 273–76.
—, *This Life and the Next: The Effect on This Life of Faith in Another* (London: Independent Press, 1946 [1918]).

—, 'Unity and Theology: A Liberal Evangelicalism the True Catholicism', in *Towards Reunion: Being Contributions to Mutual Understanding by Church of England and Free Church Writers* (ed. John S. Lidgett et al.; London: Macmillan and Co., 1919), pp. 51–81.
—, '"Valedictory Address", Delivered in June, 1909, Based on 1 Corinthians 4:1' (unpublished, Dr Williams's Library, London, 1909).
—, 'Veracity, Reality, and Regeneration', *London Quarterly Review* 123 (1915), pp. 193–216.
—, 'The Way of Life', *Wesleyan Methodist Magazine* 120 (1897), pp. 83–88.
—, 'What is the Evangelical Faith?' *British Congregationalist*, 10, 17 and 24 September 1908, pp. 217–18, 239–40, 257–58.
—, *The Work of Christ* (London: Independent Press, 2nd edn, 1938).
—, 'Why am I a Liberal?' *Shipley and Saltaire Times*, 20 April 1878, p. 4.
Forsyth, Peter Taylor and J. A. Hamilton, *Pulpit Parables for Young Hearers* (Manchester/London: Brook & Chrystal/Simpkin, Marshall & Co./Hamilton, Adams & Co., 1886).
Forsyth Society, *Forsyth-kenkyu [Forsyth Studies]* (35 vols; Tokyo: Forsyth Society, 1932–35).
Fowler, Chas, H., 'Punishment Is Not the Great Aim or Design, but an Incident, of God's Moral Government; yet it is so Important, that the Doctrine Concerning Hell is Fundamental in Methodist Teaching', in *That Unknown Country: Or, What Living Men Believe Concerning Punishment After Death Together with Recorded Views of Men of Former Times* (ed. Lyman Abbott et al.; Springfield: C. A. Nichols & Co., 1889), pp. 303–22.
Franks, Robert S., *A History of the Doctrine of the Work of Christ in its Ecclesiastical Development* (Edinburgh: Thomas Nelson, 1918).
Fremantle, William Henry, 'The Atonement in Modern Religious Thought', in *The Atonement in Modern Religious Thought: A Theological Symposium* by Frédéric Louis Godet et al. (New York: Thomas Whittaker, 1901), pp. 157–74.
Froom, Le Roy Edwin, *The Conditionalist Faith of Our Fathers, Vol. 2: From Repression and Obscurity to Restoration, Gathering Momentum and Status, Accelerated Acceptance and Expansion Spiritualism Climaxes the Conflict* (Washington: Review and Herald, 1955).
Fudge, Edward William, *The Fire That Consumes: The Biblical Case for Conditional Immortality* (Carlisle: Paternoster, 1994).
Fuller, Peter, *Theoria: Art, and the Absence of Grace* (London: Chatto & Windus, 1988).
Furuya, Yasuo, *A History of Japanese Theology* (Grand Rapids: Wm. B. Eerdmans, 1997).
Garvie, Alfred Ernest, *The Christian Certainty Amid the Modern Perplexity: Essays Constructive and Critical Towards the Solution of Some Current Theological Problems* (London: Hodder & Stoughton, 1910).
—, *Revelation Through History and Experience: A Study of the Historical Basis of the Revelation of the Godhead* (London: Ivor Nicholson & Watson, 1934).
—, 'Freedom of the Church in Christ', *Congregational Quarterly* 20, no. 2 (1942), pp. 108–14.
—, 'Placarding the Cross: The Theology of P. T. Forsyth', *Congregational Quarterly* 21 (1943), pp. 343–52.
—, 'A Cross-Centred Theology', *Congregational Quarterly* 22 (1944), pp. 324–30.
Gaskell, G. A. (ed.), *Dictionary of the Sacred Languages of All Scriptures and Myths, Part 2* (Whitefish: Kessinger, 2003).
Gaunt, Alan, 'For PT Forsyth, 1848–1921', in *PT Forsyth: Theologian for a New Millenium* (ed. Alan P. F. Sell; London: The United Reformed Church, 2000), p. 5.
Gerrish, Brian Albert, *Tradition and the Modern World: Reformed Theology in the Nineteenth Century* (London: University of Chicago Press, 1978).

Gess, Wolfgang Friedrich, *Die Lehre von der Person Christi* (Basel: Bahnmaiers Buchhandlung [C. Detlof], 1856).
—, *Christi Person und Werk* (3 vols; Calw/Basel: Verlag der Vereinsbuchhanlung/ Bahnmaiers Buchhandlung [C. Detlof], 1870–87).
Gillespie, Neal C., 'Review of *P. T. Forsyth* by Archibald M. Hunter', *Church History* 44, no. 2 (1975), pp. 274–75.
Giorgiov, Adrian, 'The Kenotic Christology of Charles Gore, P. T. Forsyth and H. R. Mackintosh', *Perichoresis* 2, no. 1 (2004), pp. 47–66.
Gladstone, William E., *Studies Subsidiary to the Works of Bishop Butler* (Oxford: Clarendon Press, 1896).
Glaser, John F., 'Parnell's Fall and the Nonconformist Conscience', *Irish Historical Society* 12 (1960), pp. 119–38.
Gockel, Matthias, 'New Perspectives on an Old Debate: Friedrich Schleiermacher's Essay on Election', *International Journal of Systematic Theology* 6, no. 3 (2004), pp. 301–18.
—, *Barth and Schleiermacher on the Doctrine of Election: A Systematic-Theological Comparison* (Oxford: Oxford University Press, 2006).
Goodwin, Thomas, *The Works of Thomas Goodwin* (ed. Thomas Smith; Nichol's Series of Standard Divines, Puritan Period, 12 vols; Edinburgh/London/Dublin: James Nichol/ James Nisbet and Co./W. Robertson, 1845–63).
Gordon, James M., *James Denney (1856–1917): An Intellectual and Contextual Biography* (ed. David Bebbington et al.; Studies in Evangelical History and Thought, Milton Keynes: Paternoster, 2006).
Gore, Charles, *The Incarnation of the Son of God; Being the Bampton Lectures for the Year 1891* (London: John Murray, 1891).
—, *Dissertations on Subjects Connected with the Incarnation* (London: John Murray, 1895).
Gore, Charles (ed.), *Lux Mundi: A Series of Studies in the Religion of the Incarnation* (10th edn, London: John Murray, 1890).
Goroncy, Jason A., 'Bitter Tonic for Our Time – Why the Church Needs the World: Peter Taylor Forsyth on Henrik Ibsen', *European Journal of Theology* 15, no. 2 (2006), pp. 105–18.
—, 'Fighting Troll-Demons in Vaults of the Mind and Heart – Art, Tragedy and Sacramentality: Some Observations from Ibsen, Forsyth and Dostoevsky', *Princeton Theological Review* 13, no. 1 (2007), pp. 61–85.
—, 'The Elusiveness, Loss, and Cruciality of Recovered Holiness: Some Biblical and Theological Observations', *International Journal of Systematic Theology* 10, no. 2 (2008), pp. 195–209.
—, '"That God May Have Mercy Upon All": A Review-Essay of Matthias Gockel's *Barth and Schleiermacher on the Doctrine of Election*', *Journal of Reformed Theology* 2, no. 2 (2008), pp. 113–30.
—, 'The Final Sanity is Complete Sanctity: Universal Holiness in the Soteriology of P. T. Forsyth (1848–1921)', in '*All Shall Be Well*': *Explorations in Universalism and Christian Theology, From Origen to Moltmann* (ed. Gregory MacDonald; Eugene, OR: Cascade Books, 2010), pp. 249–79.
—, 'Preaching *sub specie crucis*: An Introduction to the Preaching Ministry of P. T. Forsyth', in *Descending on Humanity and Intervening in History: Notes from the Pulpit Ministry of P. T. Forsyth* (ed. Jason A. Goroncy; Eugene, OR: Pickwick Publications, 2013).

—, '"Tha mi a' toirt fainear dur gearan": J. McLeod Campbell and P. T. Forsyth on the Extent of Christ's Vicarious Ministry', in *Evangelical Calvinism: Essays Resourcing the Continuing Reformation of the Church* (ed. Myk Habets and Bobby Grow; Eugene, OR: Pickwick Publications, 2012), pp. 253–86.
Goroncy, Jason A. (ed.), 'Descending on Humanity and Intervening in History': Notes from the Pulpit Ministry of P. T. Forsyth (Eugene, OR: Pickwick Publications, 2013).
'The Gospel of Nicodemus, or Acts of Pilate', in *The Apocryphal New Testament* (Oxford: Clarendon Press, 1924), pp. 94–146.
Gossip, A. J., 'P. T. Forsyth: A Review of *Peter Taylor Forsyth (1848–1921); Director of Souls* by Harry Escott', *Expository Times* 60 (1949), p. 149.
Grant, John W., *Free Churchmanship in England 1870–1940: With Special Reference to Congregationalism* (London: Independent Press, 1955).
Gray, James Michael, 'An Atonement Theology for South Africa: Preaching the Cross Using Insights from the Atonement Theology of P. T. Forsyth' (unpublished doctoral dissertation, University of St Andrews, 2000).
Gray, Ronald D., *Goethe: A Critical Introduction* (Cambridge: Cambridge University Press, 1967).
Greggs, Tom, *Barth, Origen, and Universal Salvation: Restoring Particularity* (Oxford: Oxford University Press, 2009).
—, 'Apokatastasis: Particularist Universalism in Origen (c.185–c.254)', in '*All Shall Be Well*': *Explorations in Universalism and Christian Theology, from Origen to Moltmann* (ed. Gregory MacDonald; Eugene, OR: Cascade Books, 2010), pp. 29–46.
Green, Alan, 'Personal Memories of P. T. Forsyth', *British Weekly*, 13 May 1948, p. 11.
Greene-McCreight, Katherine, *Ad Litteram: How Augustine, Calvin, and Barth Read the 'Plain Sense' of Genesis 1–3* (New York: Peter Lang, 1998).
Griffith-Jones, Ebenezer, 'Dr Forsyth on the Atonement', *The Expositor*, 7th Series, 9 (1910), pp. 307–19.
—, *Faith and Immortality: A Study of the Christian Doctrine of the Life to Come* (London: Duckworth, 1917).
Griffith-Thomas, W. H., 'Notices of Recent Publications', *Bibliotheca Sacra* 75 (1918), pp. 604–07.
Griffith, Gwilym O., 'Peter Taylor Forsyth', *The Christian World*, 13 May 1948, pp. 1–2.
—, *The Theology of P. T. Forsyth* (London: Lutterworth Press, 1948).
Gundry, Stanley N., *Love Them In: The Life and Theology of D. L. Moody* (Chicago: Moody Press, 1999).
Gunton, Colin E., *Yesterday and Today: A Study of Continuities in Christology* (London: Darton, Longman and Todd, 1983).
—, *The Actuality of Atonement: A Study of Metaphor, Rationality and the Christian Tradition* (Edinburgh: T&T Clark, 1988).
—, 'Foreword', in *Justice the True and Only Mercy: Essays on the Life and Theology of Peter Taylor Forsyth* (ed. Trevor A. Hart; Edinburgh: T&T Clark, 1995), pp. xiii–xv.
—, 'The Real as the Redemptive: Forsyth on Authority and Freedom', in *Justice the True and Only Mercy: Essays on the Life and Theology of Peter Taylor Forsyth* (ed. Trevor A. Hart; Edinburgh: T&T Clark, 1995), pp. 37–58.
—, 'Authority and Freedom: P. T. Forsyth's *The Principle of Authority*', in *Theology Through the Theologians: Selected Essays 1972–1995* (Edinburgh: T&T Clark, 1999), pp. 221–42.

—, 'The Nature of Systematic Theology: Anselm of Canterbury, Samuel Taylor Coleridge and the Possibility of an English Systematic Theology', in *Theology Through the Theologians: Selected Essays 1972–1995* (Edinburgh: T&T Clark, 1999), pp. 1–18. [First published as 'An English Systematic Theology?', in *Scottish Journal of Theology* 46 (1993), pp. 479–96].

—, *The Christian Faith: An Introduction to Christian Doctrine* (Oxford: Blackwell, 2002).

—, *Father, Son, and Holy Spirit: Essays Toward a Fully Trinitarian Theology* (London: T&T Clark, 2003).

—, *The Barth Lectures* (ed. Paul H. Brazier; London/New York: T&T Clark, 2007).

Hall, Lindsey, *Swinburne's Hell and Hick's Universalism: Are We Free to Reject God?* (Aldershot: Ashgate, 2003).

Hamilton, H., 'A Review of *Lectures on the Church and the Sacraments* by P. T. Forsyth', *Journal of Theological Studies*, no. 19 (1917), pp. 91–94.

Hamilton, Kenneth, 'Love or Holy Love? Nels Ferré Versus P. T. Forsyth', *Canadian Journal of Theology* 8 (1962), pp. 229–36.

Hanna, William (ed.), *Letters of Thomas Erskine of Linlathen* (Edinburgh: David Douglas, 4th edn, 1884).

Hanson, A. T., *The Wrath of the Lamb* (London: SPCK, 1957).

Hanson, R. P. C., *God: Creator, Saviour, Spirit* (London: SCM, 1960).

Häring, Theodor, *The Christian Faith: A System of Dogmatics* (trans. John Dickie and George Ferries; vol. 1; 2 vols; London: Hodder & Stoughton, 1915).

Harnack, Adolf von, *History of Dogma* (ed. Alexander Balmain Bruce; trans. N. Buchanan; Theological Translation Library, 7 vols; London: Williams & Norgate, 1894–99).

Hart, Trevor A., 'Universalism: Two Distinct Types', in *Universalism and the Doctrine of Hell: Papers Presented at the Fourth Edinburgh Conference in Christian Dogmatics, 1991* (ed. Nigel M. de S. Cameron; Carlisle/Grand Rapids: Paternoster/Baker, 1992), pp. 1–34.

—, 'Atonement and Worship', *Anvil* 11, no. 3 (1994), pp. 203–14.

—, 'Morality, Atonement and the Death of Jesus: The Crucial Focus of Forsyth's Theology', in *Justice the True and Only Mercy: Essays on the Life and Theology of Peter Taylor Forsyth* (ed. Trevor A. Hart; Edinburgh: T&T Clark, 1995), pp. 16–36.

—, 'Imagination for the Kingdom of God? Hope, Promise, and the Transformative Power of an Imagined Future', in *God Will Be All In All: The Eschatology of Jürgen Moltmann* (ed. Richard Bauckham; Minneapolis: Fortress, 2001), pp. 49–76.

—, 'Systematic – In What Sense?', in *Out of Egypt: Biblical Theology and Biblical Interpretation* (ed. Craig G. Bartholomew and Anthony Thiselton; Milton Keynes/ Grand Rapids: Paternoster/Zondervan, 2004), pp. 341–51.

Hart, Trevor A. (ed.), *Justice the True and Only Mercy: Essays on the Life and Theology of Peter Taylor Forsyth* (Edinburgh: T&T Clark, 1995).

Hashimoto, Akio, 'An Analysis of the Theology of Pain of God', *ATA Journal* 3, no. 2 (1995), pp. 49–69.

Hastings, Adrian, *A History of English Christianity 1920–1990* (London: SCM Press, 3rd edn, 1991).

Hattersley, Roy, *The Edwardians* (London: Abacus, 2004).

Hebblethwaite, Brian, *The Christian Hope* (Basingstoke: Marshall, Morgan & Scott, 1984).

Hegel, Georg Wilhelm Friedrich, *Encyclopedia of the Philosophical Sciences. Part 3: The Philosophy of Spirit* (trans. William Wallace and A. V. Miller; vol 3; 3 vols; Oxford: Clarendon Press, 1892).

—, *Lectures on the Philosophy of Religion* (trans. E. B. Speirs and J. Burdon Sanderson; 3 vols; London: Kegan Paul, Trench, Trübner, & Co., 1895).
—, *Elements of the Philosophy of Right* (trans. H. B. Nisbet; Cambridge Texts in the History of Political Thought, Cambridge: Cambridge University Press, 1991).
—, *Phenomenology of Spirit* (trans. A. V. Miller; New Delhi: Motilal Banarsidass, 1998).
Heim, Karl, *Jesus the World's Perfector: The Atonement and the Renewal of the World* (trans. D. H. van Daalen; Edinburgh/London: Oliver and Boyd, 1959).
Helmstadter, Richard J. and Bernard Lightman (eds), *Victorian Faith in Crisis: Essays on Continuity and Change in Nineteenth-Century Religious Belief* (Houndmills: Macmillan, 1990).
Herbert, George, 'Love (3)', in *George Herbert: The Complete English Poems* (ed. John Tobin; London: Penguin, 1991), p. 178.
Hermann, E., 'Studies of Representative British Theologians: VI.–Peter Taylor Forsyth, D.D.', *Homiletic Review* 66 (1913), pp. 179–85.
Herrmann, Wilhelm, *Systematic Theology (Dogmatik)* (trans. Nathaniel Micklem and Kenneth A. Saunders; London: George Allen & Unwin, 1927).
Heschel, Abraham Joshua, *The Prophets*, (vol. 1; New York: Harper & Row, 1962).
Hick, John, *Evil and the God of Love* (London/New York: Macmillan & Co./Harper & Row, 1966).
—, *Death and Eternal Life* (London: Collins, 1976).
Higgins, D. L., *Is it Christianity?: An Examination of a Book Entitled 'The New Theology,'* by the Rev. R. J. Campbell (London: G. Morrish, 1911).
Higginson, R. E., 'Peter Taylor Forsyth: Prophet and Pastor, 1848–1921', *English Churchman and St James' Chronicle*, 1 July 1955, pp. 309, 315.
—, 'The Theology of P. T. Forsyth and its Significance for Us Today', *The Churchman* (1959), pp. 66–75.
Hilary of Poitiers and John of Damascus, *Hilary of Poitiers, John of Damascus* (ed. Philip Schaff and Henry Wace; trans. E. W. Watson and L. Pullan; A Select Library of the Nicene and Post-Nicene Fathers of the Christian Church, Second Series, vol. 9; Edinburgh: T&T Clark, 1898).
Hilborn, David and Don Horrocks, 'Universalistic Trends in the Evangelical Tradition: An Historical Perspective', in *Universal Salvation? The Current Debate* (ed. Robin A. Parry and Christopher H. Partridge; Carlisle: Paternoster, 2003), pp. 219–44.
Hinchliff, Peter, *God and History: Aspects of British Theology, 1875–1914* (Oxford/New York: Clarendon Press/Oxford University Press, 1992).
Hinton, John Howard, 'Strictures on Some Passages in the Rev. J. B. Brown's *Divine Life in Man*', *Baptist Magazine* 52 (1868), pp. 134–37.
Hodge, Charles W., 'Review of *The Person and Place of Jesus Christ*', *Bibliotheca Sacra* 67 (1910), pp. 363–64.
—, 'Review of *The Person and Place of Jesus Christ*', Princeton Theological Review 8 (1910), pp. 688–93.
Holmes, Stephen R., 'British (and European) Evangelical Theologies', in *The Cambridge Companion to Evangelical Theology* (ed. Timothy Larsen and Daniel J. Treier; Cambridge: Cambridge University Press, 2007), pp. 214–58.
Hopkins, Mark, *Nonconformity's Romantic Generation: Evangelical and Liberal Theologies in Victorian England* (ed. David Bebbington et al.; Studies in Evangelical History and Thought, Milton Keynes: Paternoster, 2004).
Horne, Silvester, *A Popular History of the Free Churches* (London: James Clarke & Co., 1903).

Hudson, Charles Frederic, *Debt and Grace: As Related to the Doctrine of a Future Life* (Boston: John P. Jewett and Company, 5th edn, 1859).
Hughes, Thomas Hywel, 'Dr. Forsyth's View of the Atonement', *Congregational Quarterly* 18 (1940), pp. 30–37.
—, *The Atonement: Modern Theories of the Doctrine* (London: George Allen & Unwin, 1949).
Hunter, Archibald M, 'P. T. Forsyth Neutestamentler', *Expository Times* 73 (1962), pp. 100–06.
—, *P. T. Forsyth: Per Crucem ad Lucem* (London: SCM Press, 1974).
Hunter, John, 'Alexander John Scott', *Expositor* 21 (1921), pp. 386–400, 450–62.
Hunter, Leslie Stannard and John Hunter, *John Hunter, D.D., A Life* (London: Hodder & Stoughton, 1921).
Huntley, G. Haydn, 'Notes on Victorian Art', *College Art Journal* 4, no. 3 (1945), pp. 127–31.
Huxtable, John, 'Forsyth, Peter Taylor (1848–1921)', in *Oxford Dictionary of National Biography* (ed. H. C. G. Matthew and Brian Howard Harrison; vol. 20; 60 vols; Oxford: Oxford University Press, 2004), p. 442.
Huxtable, W. J. F., 'P. T. Forsyth: 1848–1921', *Journal of the United Reformed Church History Society* 4 (1987), pp. 72–78.
Ibsen, Henrick, *Peer Gynt* (trans. K. McLeish; London: Royal National Theatre/Nick Hern, 1990).
Inagaki, Hisakazu and J. Nelson Jennings, *Philosophical Theology and East-West Dialogue* (Currents of Encounter: Studies on the Contact between Christianity and Other Religions, Beliefs, and Cultures, Amsterdam/Atlanta: Rodopi, 2000).
Irenaeus, *Adversus haereses* (ed. Adelin Rousseau and Louis Doutreleau; Sources chrétiennes, vol. 211; Paris: Éditions du Cerf, 1974).
Ishijima, Saburo, *Gaisetsu Forsyth-shingaku* (Tokyo: Nagasaki-shoten, 1938).
Iverach, James, *Christianity and Evolution* (London: Hodder & Stoughton, 3rd edn, 1900).
Jackson, George D., 'The Biblical Basis of the Theology of P. T. Forsyth' (unpublished doctoral dissertation, Princeton Theological Seminary, 1952).
—, 'The Interpreter at Work: XIV. P. T. Forsyth's Use of the Bible', *Interpretation* 7 (1953), pp. 323–37.
James, William, *The Varieties of Religious Experience: A Study in Human Nature, Being The Gifford Lectures on Natural Religion Delivered at Edinburgh in 1901–1902* (New York: Longmans, Green, and Co., 1920).
Jennings, J. Nelson, *Theology in Japan: Takakura Tokutaro (1885–1934)* (Lanham: University of America Press, 2005).
—, 'Who Did They Say That He Is?: Four Hopeful and Suffering Generations of Japanese-Reformed Christologies', *Global Missiology* 4, no. 8 (2011), http://ojs.globalmissiology.org/index.php/english/article/view/610/1533.
Jenson, Robert W., 'Reconciliation in God', in *The Theology of Reconciliation* (ed. Colin E. Gunton; Edinburgh: T&T Clark, 2003), pp. 158–66.
Johnson, Dale A., 'Fissures in Late-Nineteenth-Century English Nonconformity: A Case Study in One Congregation', *Church History* 66, no. 4 (1997), pp. 735–49.
—, *The Changing Shape of English Nonconformity 1825–1925* (New York/Oxford: Oxford University Press, 1999).
Johnson, George, 'A Review of *A Principle of Authority* by P. T. Forsyth', *Princeton Theological Review* 12 (1914), pp. 125–27.
Johnson, Robert Clyde, *Authority in Protestant Theology* (Philadelphia: Westminster Press, 1959).

Jones, Frank F., 'The Christological Thought of Peter Taylor Forsyth and Emil Brunner: A Comparative Study' (unpublished doctoral dissertation, University of St Andrews, 1970).
Jones, Owen Rogers, *The Concept of Holiness* (London: George Allen & Unwin, 1961).
Jukes, Andrew John, *The Second Death and the Restitution of All Things* (London: Longmans, Green, and Co., 1867).
Jung, Carl Gustav, *Collected Works: The Archetypes and the Collective* (trans. R. F. C. Hull; Bollingen Series, vol. 9, part 1; 20 vols; London: Princeton University Press, 2nd edn, 1968).
Jüngel, Eberhard, *Death: The Riddle and the Mystery* (trans. Iain Nicol and Ute Nicol; Edinburgh: The Saint Andrew Press, 1975).
—, *God's Being Is in Becoming: The Trinitarian Being of God in the Theology of Karl Barth* (trans. John Webster; Grand Rapids: Wm. B. Eerdmans, 1976).
—, 'The Last Judgment as an Act of Grace', *Louvain Studies* 15 (1990), pp. 389–405.
—, *Justification: The Heart of the Christian Faith – A Theological Study with an Ecumenical Purpose* (trans. J. F. Cayzer; Edinburgh: T&T Clark, 2001).
Kaftan, Theodor, *Vier Kapitel von der Landeskirche* (Schleswig: Julius Bergas, 1903).
—, *Moderne Theologie des alten Glaubens* (Schleswig: Julius Bergas, 1905).
Kähler, Martin, *The So-Called Historical Jesus and the Historic Biblical Christ* (trans. Carl E. Braaten; Philadelphia: Fortress Press, 1964).
Kaiser, Walter C., '(shem) name', in *Theological Wordbook of the Old Testament* (ed. Gleason L. Archer, R. Laird Harris and Bruce K. Waltke; vol. 1; 2 vols; Chicago: Moody, 1980), pp. 934–35.
Kant, Immanuel, *The Metaphysic of Ethics* (trans. J. W. Semple; Edinburgh: Thomas Clark, 1836).
—, *Lectures on Ethics* (ed. P. Heath and J. B. Schneewind; trans. P. Heath; Cambridge: Cambridge University Press, 1997).
Käsemann, Ernst, *Commentary on Romans* (trans. Geoffrey W. Bromiley; Grand Rapids: Wm. B. Eerdmans, 1994).
Kawakami, Naoya, 日本におけるフォーサイス受容の研究　-神学の現代的課題の探求 (Tokyo: Christian Literature Society of Japan, 2012).
Keats, John, 'This Living Hand, Now Warm and Capable', in *Selected Poems* (trans. John Barnard; London: Penguin, 2007), p. 237.
Kendall, Guy, *Charles Kingsley and His Ideas* (London: Hutchinson & Co., 1947).
Kierkegaard, Søren, *Christian Discourses and The Lilies of the Field and the Birds of the Air and Three Discourses at the Communion on Fridays* (trans. Walter Lowrie; London: Oxford University Press, 1939).
—, *Fear and Trembling and The Sickness Unto Death* (trans. Walter Lowrie; Princeton: Princeton University Press, 1954).
—, *Gospel of Sufferings* (trans. A. S. Aldworth and W. S. Ferrie; London: James Clarke & Co., 1955).
—, *The Concept of Anxiety* (trans. Reider Thomte; Princeton: Princeton University Press, 1980).
—, *Practice in Christianity* (trans. Howard V. Hong and Edna V. Hong; Princeton: Princeton University Press, 1991).
Kitamori, Kazoh, *Theology of the Pain of God* (Richmond: John Knox Press, 1965).
Knight, Harold, *The Hebrew Prophetic Consciousness* (London: Lutterworth Press, 1947).
Köhnke, Klaus Christian, *The Rise of Neo-Kantianism: German Academic Philosophy between Idealism and Positivism* (ed. Richard Rorty et al.; trans. R. J. Hollingdale; Ideas in Context, Cambridge: Cambridge University Press, 1991).

Koopman, Nico, 'Holiness and Public Life in South Africa: The Quest for Wholeness, Embrace and Justice', *Colloquium* 40, no. 2 (2008), pp. 166–81.

Kroner, Richard, *Kant's Weltanschauung* (trans. John E. Smith; Chicago: University of Chicago Press, 1956).

Küng, Hans, *The Incarnation of God: An Introduction to Hegel's Theological Thought as Prolegomena to a Future Christology* (trans. J. R. Stephenson; Edinburgh: T&T Clark, 1987).

Lambert, D. W., 'The Missionary Message of P. T. Forsyth', *Evangelical Quarterly* 21 (1949), pp. 203–08.

Lane, Tony, 'The Wrath of God as an Aspect of the Love of God', in *Nothing Greater, Nothing Better: Theological Essays on the Love of God* (ed. Kevin J. Vanhoozer; Grand Rapids: Wm. B. Eerdmans, 2001), pp. 138–67.

Larson, Timothy, *Crisis of Doubt: Honest Faith in Nineteenth-Century England* (Oxford: Oxford University Press, 2006).

Lawler, Howard L., 'The Universalism of P. T. Forsyth: An Exposition to Indicate Particular Problems' (unpublished masters dissertation, Wheaton College, 1987).

Leckie, Joseph H., *The World to Come and Final Destiny* (Edinburgh: T&T Clark, 2nd edn, 1922).

Leembruggen, W. H., 'The Witness of P. T. Forsyth – A Theologian of the Cross', *Reformed Theological Review* (1945), pp. 18–46.

Leow, Theng Huat, '"The Cruciality of the Cross": P. T. Forsyth's Understanding of the Atonement', *International Journal of Systematic Theology* 11, no. 2 (2009), pp. 190–207.

—, *The Theodicy of Peter Taylor Forsyth: A 'Crucial' Justification of the Ways of God to Man* (Eugene, OR: Wipf and Stock, 2011).

Lessing, Gotthold Ephraim, *Theological Writings* (trans. Henry Chadwick; London: Adam & Charles Black, 1956).

Lewis, C. S., *The Great Divorce* (London: Geoffrey Bles, 1946).

—, *Mere Christianity* (New York: Macmillan, 1952).

—, *Surprised by Joy* (New York: Harcourt Brace Jovanovich, 1955).

—, *The Problem of Pain* (New York: Macmillan, 1962).

—, *Letters to Malcolm: Chiefly on Prayer* (Orlando: Harcourt, 2002).

Lewis, Warren H. (ed.), *Letters of C. S. Lewis* (London: Geoffrey Bles, 1966).

Lidgett, John S., *The Fatherhood of God in Christian Truth and Life* (Edinburgh: T&T Clark, 1902).

—, *The Spiritual Principle of the Atonement: As a Satisfaction Made to God for the Sins of the World: Being the Twenty-Seventh Fernley Lecture Delivered in Leeds, July, 1897* (London: Chas. H. Kelly, 4th edn, 1907).

Lieber, W., *The New Theology or the Rev. R. J. Campbell's Main Conclusions Refuted* (London: R.&T. Washbourne, 1907).

Lincoln, Andrew T., 'The Letter to the Colossians', in *The New Interpreter's Bible: Second Corinthians – Philemon* (*The New Interpreter's Bible*, vol. 11; 12 vols; Nashville: Abingdon, 2000), pp. 551–669.

Lindbeck, George, *The Nature of Doctrine: Religion and Theology in a Postliberal Age* (Philadelphia: Westminster Press, 1984).

Livingstone, David N., *Darwin's Forgotten Defenders: The Encounter Between Evangelical Theology and Evolutionary Thought* (Grand Rapids: Wm. B. Eerdmans, 1987).

Loetscher, Lefferts Augustine, 'Brown, James Baldwin', in *The New Schaff-Herzog Encyclopedia of Religious Knowledge* (ed. Johann Jakob Herzog, Philip Schaff and Albert Hauck; vol. 1; 12 vols; Grand Rapids: Baker, 1977), p. 276.

Loofs, Friedrich, 'Kenosis', in *Encyclopedia of Religion and Ethics* (ed. James Hastings; vol. 7; 13 vols; Edinburgh: T&T Clark, 1914), pp. 680–87.
Lord, F. Townley, *Conquest of Death: A Christian Interpretation of Immortality* (London: SCM, 1940).
Lowrie, Walter, 'Fear and Trembling: Translator's Introduction', in *Fear and Trembling and The Sickness Unto Death* by Søren Kierkegaard (Princeton: Princeton University Press, 1954), pp. 9–19.
Ludlow, Morwenna, 'Universalism in the History of Christianity', in *Universal Salvation? The Current Debate* (ed. Robin A. Parry and Christopher H. Partridge; Carlisle: Paternoster, 2003), pp. 191–218.
Luther, Martin, *Reading in Luther for Laymen* (ed. Charles S. Anderson; Minneapolis: Augsburg, 1967).
—, *Luther's Works, vol. 48: Letters I* (ed. Helmut T. Lehmann; 55 vols; Philadelphia: Fortress Press, 1999).
Maas, A. J., 'Kenosis', in *The Catholic Encyclopedia: An International Work of Reference on the Constitution, Doctrine, Discipline, and History of the Catholic Church* (ed. Charles G. Herbermann et al.; vol. 8; 15 vols; New York: Robert Appleton Company, 1913), p. 617.
MacDonald, George, *Unspoken Sermons: Series I, II and III* (Whitefish: Kessinger, 2004).
MacDonald, Gregory, *The Evangelical Universalist* (Eugene: Cascade Books, 2006).
MacKinnon, Donald M., 'Philosophy and Christology', in *Essays in Christology for Karl Barth* (ed. T. H. L. Parker; London: Lutterworth, 1956), pp. 269–97.
—, *Borderlands of Theology and Other Essays* (ed. George W. Roberts and Donovan E. Smucker; Philadelphia/New York: J. B. Lippincott Company, 1968).
—, 'Kenosis and Establishment', in *The Stripping of the Altars* (Suffolk: Collins, 1969), pp. 13–40.
—, 'Aspects of Kant's Influence on British Theology', in *Kant and His Influence* (ed. G. M. Ross and T. McWalter; Bristol: Thoemmes, 1990), pp. 348–66.
—, 'Teleology and Redemption', in *Justice the True and Only Mercy: Essays on the Life and Theology of Peter Taylor Forsyth* (ed. Trevor A. Hart; Edinburgh: T&T Clark, 1995), pp. 105–09.
Mackintosh, Hugh Ross, *The Person of Jesus Christ* (Edinburgh: T&T Clark, 1912).
—, *The Doctrine of the Person of Jesus Christ* (Edinburgh: T&T Clark, 1913).
—, *The Christian Experience of Forgiveness* (London: Nisbet, 1927).
Mackintosh, Robert with annotations by Dr. P. T. Forsyth, 'The Authority of the Cross', *Congregational Quarterly* 21 (1943), pp. 209–18.
Macquarrie, John, 'Kenoticism Reconsidered', *Theology* 77 (1974), pp. 115–24.
Madden, William A., 'Victorian Morality: Ethics Not Mysterious', *The Review of Politics* 23, no. 4 (1961), pp. 458–71.
Manson, T. W., 'The Lord's Prayer: II', *Bulletin of the John Rylands University Library of Manchester* 38 (1955–56), pp. 436–48.
Marcel, Gabriel, 'Structure de l'Espérance', *Dieu vivante. Perspectives religieuses et philosophiques* 19 (1951), pp. 73–80.
Marsh, James, *Select Practical Works of Rev. John Howe and Dr. William Bates* (New York/Burlington: G. & C. & H. Carvill/Chauncey Goodrich, 1830).
Marshall, Christopher D., *Beyond Retribution: A New Testament Vision for Justice, Crime, and Punishment* (Grand Rapids: Wm. B. Eerdmans, 2001).
Marshall, I. Howard, 'Universal Grace and Atonement in the Pastoral Epistles', in *The Grace of God, the Will of Man: A Case for Arminianism* (ed. Clark H. Pinnock; Grand Rapids: Zondervan, 1989), pp. 51–70.

—, *The Work of Christ* (Carlisle: Paternoster, 1994).
Martin, A., 'Peter Taylor Forsyth', *The Messenger* (1942), p. 557.
Mason, Arthur James, *The Conditions of Our Lord's Life on Earth: Being Five Lectures Delivered on the Bishop Paddock Foundation, in the General Seminary at New York, 1896; to Which is Prefixed Part of a First Professorial Lecture at Cambridge* (London/New York/Bombay: Longmans, Green and Co., 1896).
Maurice, Frederick Denison, *The Lord's Prayer* (London: John W. Parker, 1851).
—, *Lectures on the Apocalypse; or, Book of Revelation of St. John the Divine* (London: Macmillan and Co., 1861).
—, *The Conscience. Lectures on Casuistry, Delivered in the University of Cambridge* (London: Macmillan and Co., 1872).
—, *The Life of Frederick Denison Maurice, Chiefly Told in His Own Letters* (vol. 1; 2 vols; London: Macmillan and Co., 3rd edn, 1884).
—, *The Kingdom of Christ; Or, Hints to a Quaker Respecting the Principles, Constitution and Ordinances of the Catholic Church, vol. 1* (ed. Alec R. Vidler; London: SCM Press, 1958).
McCurdy, Leslie C., 'Bibliography', in *Justice the True and Only Mercy: Essays on the Life and Theology of Peter Taylor Forsyth* (ed. Trevor A. Hart; Edinburgh: T&T Clark, 1995), pp. 256–330.
—, *Attributes and Atonement: The Holy Love of God in the Theology of P. T. Forsyth* (Carlisle: Paternoster, 1998).
McDonald, Hugh Dermot, *Theories of Revelation: An Historical Study, 1860–1960* (London: George Allen & Unwin, 1963).
McGrath, Alistair E., *T. F. Torrance: An Intellectual Biography* (Edinburgh: T&T Clark, 1999).
McIntyre, John, *The Shape of Soteriology: Studies in the Doctrine of the Death of Christ* (Edinburgh: T&T Clark, 1992).
McKay, Clifford A., 'The Moral Structure of Reality in the Theology of Peter Taylor Forsyth' (unpublished doctoral dissertation, Vanderbilt University, 1970).
Meadley, Thomas D., 'The "Obscurity" of P. T. Forsyth', *Congregational Quarterly* 24 (1946), pp. 308–17.
—, 'A Preacher's Theologian: P. T. Forsyth', *Preacher's and Classleader's Magazine* 22 (1949), pp. 149–53, 157.
Mellone, Sydney Herbert, *Eternal Life Here and Hereafter* (London: The Lindsey Press, 1916).
Menn, Esther M., 'Sanctification of the (Divine) Name: Targum Neofiti's "Translation" of Genesis 38.25–26', in *The Function of Scripture in Early Jewish and Christian Tradition* (ed. C. A. Evans and J. A. Sanders; Sheffield: Sheffield Academic Press, 1998), pp. 206–40.
Mikolaski, Samuel J., 'The Nature and Place of Human Response to the Work of Christ in the Objective Theories of the Atonement Advanced in Recent British Theology by R. W. Dale, James Denney and P. T. Forsyth' (unpublished doctoral dissertation, University of Oxford, 1958).
—, 'The Theology of P. T. Forsyth', *Evangelical Quarterly* 36 (1964), pp. 27–41.
—, *The Grace of God* (Grand Rapids: Wm. B. Eerdmans, 1966).
—, 'P. T. Forsyth', in *Creative Minds in Contemporary Theology* (ed. Philip Edgcumbe Hughes; Grand Rapids: Wm. B. Eerdmans, 1969), pp. 306–39.
Mildenberger, Friedrich, *Biblische Dogmatik. Eine Biblische Theologie in dogmatischer Perspektive. Band 3. Theologie als Oekonomie* (Stuttgart: Kohlhammer, 1993).
Miller, Donald G., Browne Barr and Robert S. Paul, *P. T. Forsyth: The Man, the Preachers' Theologian, Prophet for the 20th Century: A Contemporary Assessment* (The Pittsburgh Theological Monograph Series, vol. 36; Pittsburgh: Pickwick Press, 1981).

Milton, John, *The Paradise Lost* (ed. James Robert Boyd; New York: A. S. Barnes & Co., 1867).
Moberly, Robert Campbell, *Atonement and Personality* (London: John Murray, 1901).
Moffatt, James (ed.), *Letters of Principal James Denney to His Family and Friends* (London: Hodder & Stoughton, 1921).
Moltmann, Jürgen, *The Crucified God: The Cross of Christ as the Foundation and Criticism of Christian Theology* (trans. R. A. Wilson and John Bowden; London: SCM, 1974).
—, 'Creation and Redemption', in *Creation, Christ and Culture: Studies in Honour of T. F. Torrance* (ed. Richard W. A. McKinney; Edinburgh: T&T Clark, 1976), pp. 119–34.
—, *The Church in the Power of the Spirit: A Contribution to Messianic Ecclesiology* (trans. Margaret Kohl; London: SCM, 1977).
—, *The Trinity and the Kingdom: The Doctrine of God* (trans. Margaret Kohl; Minneapolis: Fortress, 1993).
—, 'Hope and Reality: Contradiction and Correspondence', in *God Will Be All In All: The Eschatology of Jürgen Moltmann* (ed. Richard Bauckham; Minneapolis: Fortress, 2001), pp. 77–85.
—, 'The Logic of Hell', in *God Will Be All In All: The Eschatology of Jürgen Moltmann* (ed. Richard Bauckham; Minneapolis: Fortress, 2001), pp. 43–47.
—, *The Coming of God: Christian Eschatology* (trans. Margaret Kohl; Minneapolis: Augsburg Fortress, 2004).
—, *In the End – The Beginning: The Life of Hope* (trans. Margaret Kohl; Philadelphia: Fortress, 2004).
Moore, James R., *The Post-Darwinian Controversies: A Study of the Protestant Struggle to Come to Terms with Darwin in Britain and America, 1870–1900* (Cambridge: Cambridge University Press, 1979).
Morgan, D. Densil, *Barth Reception in Britain* (London/New York: T&T Clark, 2010).
Morgan, Richard C., *The Life of Richard Weaver, the Converted Collier* (London: Morgan and Chase, 1861).
Morgan, Sue, '"Wild Oats or Acorns?": Social Purity, Sexual Politics and the Response of the Late-Victorian Church', *Journal of Religious History* 31, no. 2 (2007), pp. 151–68.
Morishima, Yutaka, 'God's Holiness in P. T. Forsyth: Through [the] Influence of R. W. Dale', *Theological Studies in Japan* 46 (2007), pp. 101–18.
Moule, C. F. D., 'The Manhood of Jesus in the New Testament', in *Christ, Faith and History* (ed. S. W. Sykes and J. P. Clayton; Cambridge: Cambridge University Press, 1972), pp. 95–110.
Moule, Handley C. G., '"Detached Remarks on the Doctr[ine] of Future Punishment", Lecture Notebook, Handley Moule Papers' (unpublished, Ridley Hall, Cambridge, nd).
Mozley, John Kenneth, 'A Review of *The Person and Place of Jesus Christ*, by P. T. Forsyth', *Journal of Theological Studies* 12 (1911), pp. 298–300.
—, *The Doctrine of the Atonement* (New York: Charles Scribner's Sons, 1916).
—, 'The Theology of Dr Forsyth', *Expositor*, 8th Series, 23 (1922), pp. 81–98, 161–80.
—, *The Heart of the Gospel* (London: SPCK, 1925).
—, *The Impassibility of God: A Survey of Christian Thought* (Cambridge: Cambridge University Press, 1926).
—, 'Christology and Soteriology', in *Mysterium Christi: Christological Studies by British and German Theologians* (ed. G. K. A. Bell and D. Adolf Deissmann; London: Longmans, Green, 1930), pp. 167–90.

—, 'Preface by the Rev. Dr. J. K. Mozley', in *The Church and the Sacraments* by P. T. Forsyth (London: Independent Press, 1947), pp. vii–xiii.
Muir, Edwin, 'The Transfiguration', in *Collected Poems* (London: Faber and Faber, 1960), pp. 198–200.
Müller-Fahrenholz, Geiko, *The Kingdom and the Power: The Theology of Jürgen Moltmann* (trans. John Bowden; Minneapolis: Fortress Press, 2000).
Mursell, Gordon, *English Spirituality from 1700 to the Present Day* (London/Louisville: SPCK/Westminster John Knox, 2001).
'The New Theology', *Wairarapa Daily Times*, 30 October 1911, p. 2.
Newman, John Henry, *Discourses on the Scope and Nature of University Education* (Dublin: James Duffy, 1852).
Newton, Fort, 'Dr Fort Newton's Reminiscences', *The Southern Cross* (1921), p. 659.
Nicoll, W. R., 'City Temple Theology', *British Weekly* 24 (1907), pp. 437–38.
Nicholls, Angus, *Goethe's Concept of the Daemonic: After the Ancients* (Rochester: Camden House, 2006).
Nietzsche, Friedrich, *Thus Spoke Zarathustra: A Book for Everyone and No One* (trans. R. J. Hollingdale; London: Penguin, 1969).
Nygren, Anders. *Agape and Eros* (vol. 1; 3 vols; London: SPCK, 1932–39).
O'Donovan, Oliver, *Resurrection and Moral Order: An Outline for Evangelical Ethics* (Leicester/Grand Rapids: IVP/Wm. B. Eerdmans, 1986).
Oden, Thomas, *Life in the Spirit, Systematic Theology: Volume 3* (Peabody: Prince, 2001).
Odgers, James Edwin, 'Universalism', in *The Encyclopedia of Religion and Ethics, Volume 12: Suffering – Zwingli* (ed. James Hastings and John A. Selbie; vol. 12; 13 vols; Edinburgh: T&T Clark, 1970 (1928), pp. 529–34.
Ōmiya, Hiroshi, *Fōsaisu Shohan, Hito to shisō shirīzu* (Tōkyō: Nihon Kirisuto Kyōdan Shuppanbu, 1965).
Ōmiya, Hiroshi (ed.), *Fōsaisu shingaku gairon: jūjika no shingaku* (Tōkyō: Kyōbunkan, 2011).
Orr, James, *The Christian View of God and the World, as Centring in the Incarnation: Being the Kerr Lectures for 1890–1891* (New York: Anson D. F. Randolph and Co., 1893).
—, *The Ritschlian Theology and the Evangelical Faith* (London: Hodder & Stoughton, 1897).
—, *The Progress of Dogma: Being the Elliot Lectures, Delivered at the Western Theological Seminary, Alleghany, Penns, U.S.A., 1897* (London: Hodder & Stoughton, 1901).
Ottley, Robert Lawrence, *The Doctrine of the Incarnation* (2 vols; London: Methuen, 1895).
Otto, Rudolph, 'Foreword by the Author', in *The Idea of the Holy: An Inquiry into the Non-Rational Factor in the Idea of the Divine and its Relation to the Rational* (London: Oxford University Press, 1931), p. vii.
'Our Photograph', *The Wyvern* (1892), p. 67.
Owen, Wilfred, *The Collected Letters of Wilfred Owen* (ed. Harold Owen and John Bell; Oxford: Oxford University Press, 1967).
Packer, James I., *Knowing God* (Downer's Grove: InterVarsity, 1973).
Paddison, Angus, 'P. T. Forsyth, Scripture, and the Crisis of the Gospel' (unpublished, University of Nottingham, 2008).
—, 'P. T. Forsyth, "the Positive Gospel", and the Church', *Ecclesiology* 5 (2009), pp. 28–47.
Pannenberg, Wolfhart, *Jesus – God and Man* (trans. Duane Priebe and Lewis L. Wilkins; Philadelphia: Westminster Press, 1968).

Parker, Joseph, *The People's Bible: Discourses upon Holy Scripture* (vol 1; 25 vols; London: Hazell, Watson and Viney, 1897).
Pascal, Blaise, *Letters* (ed. Charles W. Eliot; trans. M. L. Booth; vol. 48/2; 51 vols; New York: P. F. Collier & Son, 1909–14).
Pattison, George, *Art, Modernity and Faith* (London: SCM Press, 1988).
Paul, Robert Sydney, *The Atonement and the Sacraments: The Relation of the Atonement to the Sacraments of Baptism and the Lord's Supper* (London: Hodder & Stoughton, 1961).
Peake, A. S., *Recollections and Appreciations* (ed. W. F. Howard; London: The Epworth Press, 1938).
Peel, David R., 'PT Forsyth on Ministry: A Model for Our Time?', in *P T Forsyth: Theologian for a New Millennium* (ed. Alan P. F. Sell; London: The United Reformed Church, 2000), pp. 171–207.
Peels, H. G. L., *The Vengeance of God* (Leiden: Brill, 1995).
Pelikan, Jaroslav, 'Foreword', in *Christus Victor: An Historical Study of the Three Main Types of the Idea of the Atonement* by Gustaf Aulén (New York: Macmillan, 1969), pp. xi–xix.
Perowne, J. J. Stewart, *Immortality: Four Sermons Preached Before the University of Cambridge* (Cambridge: Deighton, Bell, and Co., 1869).
Peterson, David, *Hebrews and Perfection: An Examination of the Concept of Perfection in the 'Epistle to the Hebrews'* (Cambridge: Cambridge University Press, 1982).
Peterson, Eugene H., 'Foreword', in *The Soul of Prayer* by P. T. Forsyth (Vancouver: Regent College Publishing, 2002), pp. 2–5.
Pettingell, John Hancock, *The Theological Trilemma. The Threefold Question of Endless Misery, Universal Salvation, or Conditional Immortality (i.e., the Survival of the Fittest), Considered in the Light of Reason, Nature, and Revelation* (New York: Sherwood & Co., 1878).
—, *The Unspeakable Gift: The Gift of Eternal Life Through Jesus Christ Our Lord* (Yarmouth: I. C. Wellcome, 1887).
Phillips, Ann, *The Bond Memorial Windows* (Cambridge: Emmanuel United Reformed Church, Cambridge, 2002) [Revised from 1987 version by Andrew A. Smith].
Pinnock, Clark H., 'The Finality of Jesus Christ in a World of Religions', in *Christian Faith and Practice in the Modern World: Theology from an Evangelical Point of View* (ed. Mark A. Noll and David F. Wells; Grand Rapids: Wm. B. Eerdmans, 1988), pp. 152–68.
Pitt, Clifford S., *Church, Ministry and Sacraments: A Critical Evaluation of the Thought of Peter Taylor Forsyth* (Washington: University Press of America, 1983).
Plantinga Jr., Cornelius, *Not the Way It's Supposed to Be: A Breviary of Sin* (Grand Rapids/Leicester: Wm. B. Eerdmans/Apollos, 1995).
Plumptre, Edward Hayes, *The Spirits in Prison* (London: Isbister, 2nd edn, 1893).
Polkinghorne, John, 'Kenotic Creation and Divine Action', in *The Work of Love: Creation as Kenosis* (ed. John Polkinghorne; Grand Rapids: Wm. B. Eerdmans, 2001), pp. 90–106.
Pope, William Burt, *The Person of Christ: Dogmatic, Scriptural, Historical. The Fernley Lecture of 1871, with Two Additional Essays on the Biblical and Ecclesiastical Development of the Doctrine, and Illustrative Notes* (London: Wesleyan Conference Office, 2nd edn, 1875).
Powicke, Frederick J., 'Frederick Denison Maurice (1805–1872): A Personal Reminiscence', *Congregational Quarterly* 8 (1930), pp. 169–84.
Powys, David J., *'Hell': A Hard Look at a Hard Question: The Fate of the Unrighteous in New Testament Thought* (Carlisle: Paternoster, 1998).

Pringle-Pattison, Andrew Seth, *The Idea of God in the Light of Recent Philosophy* (Oxford: Clarendon Press, 1917).
—, *The Idea of Immortality* (Oxford: Clarendon Press, 1922).
Pryce, R. Vaughan, 'The Redemptive Work of the Lord Jesus Christ', in *The Ancient Faith in Modern Light* (ed. T. Vincent Tymms et al.; Edinburgh: T&T Clark, 1897), pp. 193–226.
Purkiser, Westlake Taylor, *Sanctification and its Synonyms* (Kansas City: Beacon Hill Press, 1961).
Rahner, Karl, 'On the Theology of the Incarnation', in *Theological Investigations, Volume 4*, (London: Darton, Longman & Todd, 1966), pp. 105–20.
—, *Theological Investigations, Volume 5* (trans. K.-H. Krueger; New York: Crossroad, 1983).
Rashdall, Hastings, *Doctrine and Development: University Sermons* (London: Methuen & Co., 1898).
—, *The Idea of Atonement in Christian Theology* (London: Macmillan, 1919).
Ratzinger, Joseph, *Eschatology: Death and Eternal Life* (ed. Aidan Nichols; trans. Michael Waldstein; Washington, DC: The Catholic University of America Press, 2nd edn, 1988).
—, 'Encyclical Letter Spe Salvi of the Supreme Pontiff Benedict XVI to the Bishops Priests and Deacons Men and Women Religious and all the Lay Faithful on Christian Hope, Given in Rome, at Saint Peter's, on 30 November, the Feast of Saint Andrew the Apostle, in the Year 2007, the Third of My Pontificate'. No pages. Cited 5 December 2007. Online: www.vatican.va/holy_father/benedict_xvi/encyclicals/documents/hf_ben-xvI_enc_20071130_spe-salvI_en.html.
—, *Jesus of Nazareth* (trans. Adrian J. Walker; New York: Doubleday, 2007).
Reardon, Bernard M. G., *From Coleridge to Gore: A Century of Religious Thought in Britain* (London: Longman, 1971).
Rees, Thomas, *The Racovian Catechism, with Notes and Illustrations* (London: Longman, Hurst, Rees, Orme, and Brown, 1818).
Reitan, Eric, 'Human Freedom and the Impossibility of Eternal Damnation', in *Universal Salvation? The Current Debate* (ed. Robin Parry and Chris Partridge; Carlisle: Paternoster, 2003), pp. 125–42.
'A Review of *Positive Preaching and the Modern Mind* by P. T. Forsyth', *Expository Times* 19 (1907), pp. 98–99.
Ricœur, Paul, *Oneself as Another* (trans. Kathleen Blamey; Chicago: University of Chicago Press, 1992).
—, 'Evil: A Challenge to Philosophy and Theology', in *Figuring the Sacred: Religion, Narrative, and Imagination* (ed. Mark I. Wallace; Minneapolis: Fortress, 1995), pp. 249–61.
Rieber, Robert W. and David Keith Robinson (eds), *Wilhelm Wundt in History: The Making of a Scientific Psychology* (New York: Kluwer Academic, 2nd edn, 2001).
Riglin, Keith G., 'The Saints' Everlasting Rest – the Reformed Position', in *Mary for Earth and Heaven* (ed. William McLoughlin and Jill Pinnock; Leominster: Gracewing, 2002), pp. 62–74.
Ringer, Fritz K., *The Decline of the German Mandarins: The German Academic Community, 1890–1933* (Hanover/London: Wesleyan University Press, 1990).
Ringgren, Helmer, *The Prophetical Conception of Holiness* (Uppsala: A.-B. Lundequistska Bokhandeln, 1948).
Ritschl, Albrecht, *The Christian Doctrine of Justification and Reconciliation: The Positive Development of the Doctrine* (trans. Hugh Ross Mackintosh and Alexander Beith Macaulay; Edinburgh: T&T Clark, 1900).

Robbins, Keith, 'The Spiritual Pilgrimage of the Rev. R. J. Campbell', in *History, Religion, and Identity in Modern Britain* (London/Rio Grande: The Hambledon Press, 1993), pp. 133–48.
Robinson, John Arthur Thomas, *In the End, God: A Study of the Christian Doctrine of the Last Things* (London: James Clarke & Co., 1950).
Robinson, N. H. G., 'The Importance of P. T. Forsyth', *Expository Times* 64 (1952), pp. 76–79.
—, *Christ and Conscience* (London: James Nisbet, 1956).
Rodgers, John H., *The Theology of P. T. Forsyth: The Cross of Christ and the Revelation of God* (London: Independent Press, 1965).
Rogerson, John, 'What is Holiness?', in *Holiness Past and Present* (ed. Stephen C. Barton; London/New York: T&T Clark, 2003), pp. 3–21.
Rowell, Geoffrey, *Hell and the Victorians: A Study of the Nineteenth-Century Theological Controversies Concerning Eternal Punishment and the Future Life* (Oxford: Clarendon Press, 1974).
Russell, Bertrand, *Mysticism and Logic, and Other Essays* (London: Longmans, Green and Co., 1918).
Russell, Stanley, 'Spoiling the Egyptians: P. T. Forsyth and Hegel', in *Justice the True and Only Mercy: Essays on the Life and Theology of Peter Taylor Forsyth* (ed. Trevor A. Hart; Edinburgh: T&T Clark, 1995), pp. 220–36.
Ruston, Alan, 'Protestant Nonconformist Attitudes Towards the First World War', in *Protestant Nonconformity in the Twentieth Century* (ed. Alan P. F. Sell and Anthony R. Cross; Milton Keynes: Paternoster, 2003), pp. 240–63.
Sanders, Matthew Lee, 'Subordinate but Equal: The Intra-Trinitarian Subordination of the Son to the Father in the Theologies of P. T. Forsyth and Jürgen Moltmann' (unpublished doctoral dissertation, University of St Andrews, 2010).
Saramago, José, *The Gospel According to Jesus Christ* (trans. G. Pontiero; San Diego: Harcourt Brace & Co., 1994).
Sartre, Jean-Paul, *Being and Nothingness: An Essay on Phenomenological Ontology* (trans. Hazel E. Barnes; London: Methuen, 1957).
Schafer, T. A., 'Jonathan Edwards and Justification by Faith', *Church History* 20 (1951), pp. 55–67.
Schaff, Philip (ed.), *Gregory of Nyssa: Dogmatic Treatises, etc.* (ed. Philip Schaff and Henry Wace; Nicene and Post-Nicene Fathers Series II, vol. 5; Edinburgh/Grand Rapids: T&T Clark/Wm. B. Eerdmans, 1997).
Schlatter, Adolf, 'Genesis' (unpublished, Landeskirchliches Archiv Stuttgart, 1881).
—, 'Wesen und Quellen der Gotteserkenntnis' (unpublished, Landeskirchliches Archiv Stuttgart, 1883).
—, *Die Theologie des Neuen Testaments, vol. 2: Die Lehre der Apostel* (vol. 2; 2 vols; Calwer: Verlag der Vereinsbuchhandlung, 1909).
—, 'Die Unterwerfung unter die Gotteswirklichkeit', *Die Furche: Akademische Monatsschrift zur Förderung einer Deutschen christlichen Studentenbewegung* (1911), pp. 6–17.
—, *Einleitung in die Bibel* (Stuttgart: Calwer Verlag, 4th edn, 1923).
—, *Gesunde Lehre: Reden und Aufsätze* (Velbert: Freizeiten-Verlag, 1929).
—, *Das christliche Dogma* (Stuttgart: Calwer Verlag, 1977).
—, *Die philosophische Arbeit seit Cartesius: Ihr ethischer und religiöser Ertrag* (Giessen: Brunnen-Verlag, 5th edn, 1981).
—, *Die christliche Ethik* (Stuttgart: Calwer Verlag, 5th edn, 1986).

—, *Romans: The Righteousness of God* (trans. Siegfried S. Schatzmann; Peabody: Hendrickson, 1995).
—, *The History of the Christ: The Foundation for New Testament Theology* (trans. Andreas J. Köstenberger; Grand Rapids: Baker, 1997).
—, *The Theology of the Apostles: The Development of New Testament Theology* (trans. Andreas J. Köstenberger; Grand Rapids: Baker, 1998).
Schleiermacher, Friedrich, *The Christian Faith* (ed. H. R. Mackintosh and J. S. Stewart; trans. D. M. Baillie; Edinburgh: T&T Clark, 1928).
—, *Der christliche Glaube nach den Grundsätzen der evangelischen Kirche im Zusammenhänge dargestellt* (ed. Martin Redeker, 2 vols, Berlin: Walter de Gruyter, 7th edn, 1960).
—, *Brief Outline on the Study of Theology* (trans. Terrence N. Tice; Richmond: John Knox Press, 1966).
Schmöle, Klaus, *Läuterung nach dem Tode und pneumatische Auferstehung bei Klemens von Alexandrien* (Münster: Aschendorff, 1974).
Schopenhauer, Arthur, *The World as Will and Idea* (trans. R. B. Haldane and J. Kemp; vol. 1; 3 vols; London: Routledge & Kegan Paul, 1883).
—, *The World as Will and Idea* (trans. R. B. Haldane and J. Kemp; vol. 3; 3 vols; London: Kegan Paul, Trench, Trübner, 6th edn, 1909).
Schwarz, Hans, *Theology in a Global Context: The Last Two Hundred Years* (Grand Rapids: Wm. B. Eerdmans Publishing, 2005).
Schweitzer, Albert, *Geschichte der Leben-Jesu-Forschung* (Tübingen: JCB Mohr [Paul Siebeck], 1913).
Scullard, H. H., 'Principal Forsyth', *London Quarterly Review* 137 (1922), pp. 104–06.
Seitz, Christopher R., *Word Without End: The Old Testament as Abiding Theological Witness* (Grand Rapids/Cambridge: Wm. B. Eerdmans, 1998).
Selbie, W. B. (ed.), *The Life of Charles Silvester Horne, M.A., M.P.* (London: Hodder & Stoughton, 1920).
Sell, Alan P. F., *The Philosophy of Religion 1875–1980* (London: Croom Helm, 1988).
—, 'P. T. Forsyth as Unsystematic Systematician', in *Justice the True and Only Mercy: Essays on the Life and Theology of Peter Taylor Forsyth* (ed. Trevor A. Hart; Edinburgh: T&T Clark, 1995), pp. 110–45.
—, 'P T Forsyth: Theologian for a New Millennium?', in *P T Forsyth: Theologian for a New Millennium* (ed. Alan P. F. Sell; London: The United Reformed Church, 2000), pp. 237–59.
—, 'The Theological Contribution of Protestant Nonconformists in the Twentieth Century: Some Soundings', in *Protestant Nonconformity in the Twentieth Century* (ed. Alan P. F. Sell and Anthony R. Cross; Milton Keynes: Paternoster, 2003) pp. 33–62.
—, *Testimony and Tradition: Studies in Reformed and Dissenting Thought* (Aldershot: Ashgate, 2005).
—, *Nonconformist Theology in the Twentieth Century: The Didsbury Lectures 2006* (Milton Keynes: Paternoster, 2007).
Sell, Alan P. F. (ed.), *PT Forsyth: Theologian for a New Millennium* (London: The United Reformed Church, 2000).
Sellers, Ian, *Nineteenth-Century Nonconformity* (Foundations of Modern History; London: Edward Arnold, 1977).
Shakespeare, William, *The Complete Works of William Shakespeare* (ed. Williams Aldis Wright; Garden City: Garden City Publishing Company, 1936).
Shaw, J. M., 'The Theology of P. T. Forsyth', *Theology Today* (1946), pp. 358–70.

Shelley, Percy B., *Works of P. B. Shelley* (Hertfordshire: Wordsworth Editions, 1994).
Simpson, A. F., 'P. T. Forsyth: The Prophet of Judgment', *Scottish Journal of Theology* 4 (1951), pp. 148–56.
Sloan, Walter B., *These Sixty Years: The Story of the Keswick Convention* (London: Pickering & Inglis, 1935).
Smail, Thomas A., *Once and For All: A Confession of the Cross* (Eugene: Wipf and Stock, 2005).
Smith, Gerald B., 'The Modern-Positive Movement in Theology', *The American Journal of Theology* 13 (1909), pp. 92–99.
Smith, Hannah Whitall, *The Unselfishness of God and How I Discovered It: A Spiritual Autobiography* (Victoria: Shirley Sloan, 2008).
Snaith, Norman H., *The Distinctive Ideas of the Old Testament* (London: Epworth Press, 1947).
Söderblom, Nathan, 'Holiness', in *Encyclopædia of Religion and Ethics* (ed. James Hastings; vol. 6; 24 vols; Edinburgh: T&T Clark, 1913), pp. 731–41.
Söding, Thomas, 'Heilig, heilig, heilig. Zur politischen Theologie der Johannes-Apokalypse', *Zeitschrift für Theologie und Kirche* 96 (1999), pp. 49–76.
Spengler, Oswald Arnold Gottfried, *The Decline of the West: Form and Actuality* (vol. 1; 2 vols; London: George Allen & Unwin, 1922).
Spurgeon, Charles H., 'Preface', in *The Duration of Future Punishments: Two Lectures to the Students at the Metropolitan Tabernacle* by William Barker (London: Passmore & Alabaster, 1865), pp. iii–vii.
Steffen, Bernhard, *Das Dogma vom Kreuz. Beitrag zu einer staurozentrische Theologie* (Gütersloh: Bertelsmann, 1920).
Stewart, R. W., 'Old Soldiers Never Die', *Expository Times* 58 (1947), p. 289.
—, 'Unrusted Claymore', *Expository Times* 63 (1952), pp. 329–30.
Storr, Vernon F., *The Problem of the Cross* (London: John Murray, 1919).
Stott, John R. W., *The Cross of Christ* (Leicester: IVP, 1986).
Strauss, David Friedrich, *Das Leben Jesu kritisch bearbeitet* (2 vols; Tübingen: C. F. Osiander, 1835–36).
—, *Die christliche Glaubenslehre in ihrer geschichtlichen Entwicklung und im Kampfe mit der modernen Wissenschaft dargestellt* (2 vols; Tübingen: C. F. Osiander, 1840–41).
—, *Das Leben Jesu für das deutsche Volk bearbeitet* (Leipzig: Brockhaus, 1864).
—, *The Christ of Faith and the Jesus of History: A Critique of Schleiermacher's Life of Jesus* (trans. Leander E. Keck; Philadelphia: Fortress, 1977).
Stump, Eleanore, 'Dante's Hell, Aquinas' Moral Theory, and the Love of God', *Canadian Journal of Philosophy* 16 (1986), pp. 181–96.
Swinburne, Richard, 'A Theodicy of Heaven and Hell', in *The Existence of God* (ed. Alfred J. Freddoso; Notre Dame: University of Notre Dame Press, 1983), pp. 37–54.
—, *Providence and the Problem of Evil* (Oxford: Clarendon Press, 1998).
—, *Responsibility and Atonement* (Oxford: Oxford University Press, 1998).
Sykes, Stephen W., 'P. T. Forsyth on the Church', in *Justice the True and Only Mercy: Essays on the Life and Theology of Peter Taylor Forsyth* (ed. Trevor A. Hart; Edinburgh: T&T Clark, 1995), pp. 1–15.
—, 'Theology Through History', in *The Modern Theologians: An Introduction to Christian Theology in the Twentieth Century* (ed. David F. Ford; Oxford: Blackwell, 1997), pp. 229–51.
Symonds, Alfred Radford, *The Ultimate Reconciliation and Subjection of all Souls to God Under the Kingdom of Christ* (London: Hamilton, Adams, R. Gladding, 1873).

Symondson, Anthony (ed.), *The Victorian Crisis of Faith* (London: SPCK, 1970).
Takemori, Masaichi, 'Scottish Theology and the Church and Theology in Japan', *Theological Studies in Japan* 14 (1975), pp. 16–17, 161–77.
Talbott, Thomas, *The Inescapable Love of God* (Boca Raton: Universal, 1999).
—, 'Reply to My Critics', in *Universal Salvation? The Current Debate* (ed. Robin Parry and Chris Partridge; Carlisle: Paternoster, 2003), pp. 247–73.
Taylor, John Randolph, *God Loves Like That!: The Theology of James Denney* (London: SCM, 1962).
Tenbruck, Friedrich H., 'Geschichte und Geschichtsschreibung der Philosophie am Beispiel des Neukantianismus', *Philosophische Rundschau* 35 (1988), pp. 1–15.
Tennyson, Alfred, *In Memoriam* (Boston: Ticknor and Fields, 1861).
Terry, Justyn, 'The Justifying Judgement of God', *Anvil* 22, no. 1 (2005), pp. 29–39.
—, *The Justifying Judgement of God: A Reassessment of the Place of Judgement in the Saving Work of Christ* (Milton Keynes: Paternoster, 2007).
Thayer, Thomas Baldwin, *Theology of Universalism: Being an Exposition of its Doctrines and Teachings, in Their Logical and Moral Relations; Including a Criticism of the Texts Cited in Proof of the Trinity, Vicarious Atonement, Natural Depravity, a General Judgment, and Endless Punishment* (Boston: Universalist Publishing House, 1882).
Thielicke, Helmut, *Encounter with Spurgeon* (trans. John W. Doberstein; London: James Clarke & Co., 1964).
Thom, David, *The Assurance of Faith: Or Calvinism Identified with Universalism* (London: Simpkin and Marshall, 1833).
Thomasius, Gottfried, *Christi Person und Werk. Darstellung der evangelisch-lutherischen Dogmatik vom Mittelpunkte der Christologie aus* (vol. 3; Erlangen: Bläsing, 2nd edn, 1857–63).
—, 'Christ's Person and Work. Part II: The Person of the Mediator', in *God and Incarnation in Mid-Nineteenth Century German Theology* (ed. Claude Welch; *A Library of Protestant Thought* (New York: Oxford University Press, 1965), pp. 31–101.
Thompson, John, 'Was Forsyth Really a Barthian Before Barth?', in *Justice the True and Only Mercy: Essays on the Life and Theology of Peter Taylor Forsyth* (ed. Trevor A. Hart; Edinburgh: T&T Clark, 1995), pp. 237–55.
Thompson, Robert Franklin, 'Peter Taylor Forsyth: A Pre-Barthian' (unpublished doctoral dissertation, Drew University, 1940).
Thompson, Thomas R., 'Nineteenth-Century Kenotic Christology: The Waxing, Waning, and Weighing of a Quest for a Coherent Orthodoxy', in *Exploring Kenotic Christology: The Self-Emptying of God* (ed. C. Stephen Evans; Oxford: Oxford University Press, 2006), pp. 74–111.
Tillich, Paul, *Systematic Theology* (vol. 1; 3 vols; London: Nisbet & Co., 1955).
—, *Systematic Theology* (vol. 3; 3 vols; Digswell Place: James Nisbet and Co., 1964).
Torrance, Iain R., 'Dominated by His Own Illustrations? P. T. Forsyth on the Lord's Supper', in *Justice the True and Only Mercy: Essays on the Life and Theology of Peter Taylor Forsyth* (ed. Trevor A. Hart; Edinburgh: T&T Clark, 1995) pp. 59–66.
Torrance, Thomas Forsyth, 'The Goodness and Dignity of Man in the Christian Tradition', in *Christ in Our Place – The Humanity of God in Christ for the Reconciliation of the World: Essays Presented to Professor James Torrance* (ed. Trevor Hart and Daniel Thimell; Exeter/Allison Park: Paternoster Press/Pickwick Publications, 1989), pp. 369–87.
—, *The Christian Doctrine of God, One Being Three Persons* (Edinburgh: T&T Clark, 2001).

—, *Divine and Contingent Order* (Edinburgh: T&T Clark, 2005).
Troeltsch, Ernst, 'Zur Frage des religiösen Apriori', in *Gesammelte Schriften* (vol. 2; 3 vols; Tübingen: J. C. B. Mohr [Paul Siebeck], 1913), pp. 754–68.
—, 'The Ideas of Natural Law and Humanity in World Politics', in *Natural Law and the Theory of Society, 1500 to 1800* (ed. Otto Gierke; vol. 1; 2 vols; Boston: Beacon Press, 1957), pp. 201–22.
—, *The Christian Faith* (ed. G. von le Fort; trans. G. E. Paul; Minneapolis: Fortress, 1991).
Turner, Frank M., 'The Victorian Conflict Between Science and Religion: A Professional Dimension', *Isis* 69, no. 3 (1978), pp. 356–76.
Turner, John M., 'Theologian of Righteousness: Peter Taylor Forsyth (1848–1921)', *Methodist Sacramental Fellowship Bulletin* 199 (1990), pp. 1–14.
Tuttle, George M., *So Rich a Soil: John McLeod Campbell on Christian Atonement* (Edinburgh: Handsel, 1986).
Tymms, Thomas Vincent, *The Christian Idea of Atonement: Lectures Delivered at Regent's Park College, London, in 1903* (London: Macmillan, 1904).
Upham, Thomas C., *Life, Religious Opinions, and Experience of Madame de la Mothe Guyon: Together With Some Account of the Personal History and Religious Opinions of Fenelon, Archbishop of Cambray* (London: Sampson, Low, Son and Co., 1854).
Varley, Henry, *The New Theology and Mr. R. J. Campbell's Teachings Examined and Criticised* (London: A. Holness, London Bible and Book Saloon, 1907).
Volf, Miroslav, 'The Final Reconciliation: Reflections on a Social Dimension of the Eschatological Transition', *Modern Theology* 16, no. 1 (2000), pp. 91–113.
Waddell, H. C., 'Is P. T. Forsyth Coming to His Own?', *Biblical Theology* 7 (1957), pp. 35–39.
Waddington, Norah, *The First Ninety Years* (Leicester: Clarendon Park Congregational Church, Leicester, nd).
Walker, W. L., *The Spirit and the Incarnation in the Light of Scripture, Science, and Practical Need* (Edinburgh: T&T Clark, 3rd edn, 1907).
Wallace, Ronald S., *The Atoning Death of Christ* (London: Marshall Morgan and Scott, 1981).
Ware, Kallistos, *Through the Creation to the Creator* (London: Friends of the Centre Papers, 1997).
Ware, Owen, 'Rudolph Otto's *Idea of the Holy*: A Reappraisal', *The Heythrop Journal* 48, no. 1 (2007), pp. 48–60.
Warfield, Benjamin B., 'Modern Theories of the Atonement', in *Studies in Theology* (*The Works of Benjamin B. Warfield*, vol. 9; 10 vols; Grand Rapids: Baker, 2003), pp. 281–97.
Warschauer, James, 'Liberty, Limited: A Rejoinder to Dr. Forsyth', *Contemporary Review* 101 (1912), pp. 831–39.
—, 'Theology and the Church', *Expository Times* 24 (1913), p. 213.
Warschauer, Joseph, *The New Evangel: Studies in the 'New Theology'* (London: James Clarke, 1907).
Watts, Michael R., *Why Did the English Stop Going to Church?* (London: Dr Williams's Trust, 1995).
Weber, Otto, *Foundations of Dogmatics* (trans. D. L. Guder; vol. 2; 2 vols; Grand Rapids: Wm. B. Eerdmans, 1983).
Webster, Douglas, 'P. T. Forsyth's Theology of Missions', *International Review of Missions* 44 (1955), pp. 175–81.
Webster, John, *Word and Church: Essays in Christian Dogmatics* (Edinburgh: T&T Clark, 2001).

—, *Holiness* (Grand Rapids/Cambridge: Wm. B. Eerdmans, 2003).
—, 'Discipleship and Obedience', *Scottish Bulletin of Evangelical Theology* 24, no. 1 (2006), pp. 4–18.
—, 'God and Conscience', in *The Doctrine of God and Theological Ethics* (ed. Alan J. Torrance and Michael Banner; London/New York: T&T Clark, 2006), pp. 147–65.
Weinel, Heinrich, *Biblische Theologie des Neuen Testaments. Religion Jesu und des Urchristentums* (Tübingen: J. C. B. Mohr, 1911).
Wells, David F., *The Person of Christ: A Biblical and Historical Analysis of the Incarnation* (Westchester: Crossway Books, 1984).
Wenham, Gordon J., *The Book of Leviticus* (Grand Rapids: Wm. B. Eerdmans, 1979).
Wenham, John W., 'The Case for Conditional Immortality', in *Universalism and the Doctrine of Hell: Papers Presented at the Fourth Edinburgh Conference in Christian Dogmatics, 1991* (ed. Nigel M. de S. Cameron; Carlisle/Grand Rapids: Paternoster/Baker, 1992), pp. 161–91.
Westphal, Merold, *Hegel, Freedom, and Modernity* (Albany: State University of New York, 1992).
Whately, Richard, *A View of the Scripture Revelations Concerning a Future State* (Philadelphia: Lindsay & Blakiston, 3rd edn, 1857).
Whatley, A. R., 'Review of P. T. Forsyth, *The Principle of Authority in Relation to Certainty, Sanctity and Society: An Essay in the Philosophy of Experimental Religion*', *Hibbert Journal* 12 (1914), pp. 936–41.
White, Edward, *Life in Christ: A Study of the Scripture Doctrine on the Nature of Man, the Object of the Divine Incarnation, and the Conditions of Human Immortality* (London: Elliot Stock, 1875).
Wickens, G. Glen, *Thomas Hardy, Monism, and the Carnival Tradition: The One and the Many in the Dynasts* (Toronto: University of Toronto Press, 2002).
Wicks, Sidney F., 'He Loved the Children in Cheetham Hill: A Tribute to Dr Peter Taylor Forsyth, Great Theologian', *Manchester City News*, 23 September 1949, np.
Widdicombe, D. W., 'Theology and Experience: Methodological Issues in the Theology of P. T. Forsyth' (unpublished doctoral dissertation, Oxford University, 2000).
Wiersbe, Warren, 'Theologian for Pastors', *Moody Monthly* (1975), pp. 97–101.
Wilkerson, Albert H., *The Rev. R. J. Campbell, the Man and His Message* (London: np, 1907).
Willey, Thomas E., *Back to Kant: The Revival of Kantianism in German Social and Historical Thought, 1860–1914* (Detroit: Wayne State University Press, 1978).
Williams, Rowan, *The Wound of Knowledge: Christian Spirituality from the New Testament to St. John of the Cross* (Cambridge: Cowley Publications, 2nd edn, 1991).
—, *Open to Judgement: Sermons and Addresses* (London: Darton, Longman & Todd, 1994).
—, 'Logic and the Spirit in Hegel', in *Post-Secular Philosophy: Between Philosophy and Theology* (ed. Phillip Blond; London: Routledge, 1998), pp. 116–30.
—, *On Christian Theology* (Oxford: Blackwell, 2000).
—, *Ponder These Things: Praying with Icons of the Virgin* (Norwich: Canterbury Press, 2002).
—, *Tokens of Trust: An Introduction to Christian Belief* (Norwich: Canterbury Press, 2007).
Williams, T. Charles, 'A Tribute from Wales, by the Rev. T. Charles Williams, M.A.', *British Weekly*, 17 November 1921, p. 154.
Williams, T. Rhondda, *The Evangel of the New Theology* (London: Percy Lund, Humphries, 1905).

Wilson, Henry Bristow, 'Seances Historiques de Genève. The National Church', in *Essays and Reviews* (ed. John William Parker; London: John W. Parker and Son, 1860) pp. 145–206.

Wilson, William E., *Dr. Forsyth and the War: A Pacifist's Reply* (London: Headley Bros., 1917).

Windelband, Wilhelm, *Die Geschichte der Neueren Philosophie in ihrem Zusammenhange mit der Allgemeinen Cultur und den besonderen Wissenschaften, Erster Band: Von der Renaissance bis Kant* (vol. 1; 2 vols; Leipzig: Druck und Verlag von Breitkopf und Härtel, 1878).

—, *Präludien – Aufsätze und Reden zur Einleitung in die Philosophie* (vol. 1; 2 vols; Tübingen: Verlag von J. C. B. Mohr [Paul Siebeck], 1907).

—, 'Was ist Philosophie? (Über Begriff und Geschichte der Philosophie)', in *Präludien – Aufsätze und Reden zur Einleitung in die Philosophie* (Tübingen: Verlag von J. C. B. Mohr [Paul Siebeck], 1907), pp. 24–77.

—, 'Pessimismus und Wissenschaft', in *Präludien – Aufsätze und Reden zur Einleitung in die Philosophie* (vol. 2; 2 vols; Tübingen: Verlag von J. C. B. Mohr [Paul Siebeck], 1911), pp. 195–220.

—, *Einleitung in die Philosophie* (Tübingen: J. C. B. Mohr [Paul Siebeck], 1914).

—, *An Introduction to Philosophy* (trans. Joseph McCabe; London: T. Fisher Unwin, 1921).

Wolterstorff, Nicholas, 'Liturgy, Justice, and Holiness', *Reformed Journal* 16 (1989), pp. 12–20.

Wood, Ralph C., 'Christ on Parnassus: P. T. Forsyth Among the Liberals', *Literature and Theology* 2 (1988), pp. 83–95.

Woods, Charlotte E., *Memoir and Letters of Canon Hay Aitken* (London: C. W. Daniel Co., 1928).

Worrall, B. G., 'The Authority of Grace in the Theology of P. T. Forsyth', *Scottish Journal of Theology* 25 (1972), pp. 58–74.

—, 'R. J. Campbell and His New Theology', *Theology* 81 (1978), pp. 342–48.

Wright, N. T., 'Towards a Biblical View of Universalism', *Themelios* 4, no. 2 (1978), pp. 54–58.

—, *Evil and the Justice of God* (Leicester: IVP, 2006).

—, *Surprised by Hope* (London: SPCK, 2007).

Wright, Nigel, *The Radical Evangelical: Seeking a Place to Stand* (London: SPCK, 1996).

Yasukata, Toshimasa, *Lessing's Philosophy of Religion and the German Enlightenment: Lessing on Christianity and Reason* (New York: Oxford University Press, 2002).

Zachman, Randall C., *The Assurance of Faith: Conscience in the Theology of Martin Luther and John Calvin* (Minneapolis: Fortress, 1993).

Ziegler, Robert E., 'P. T. Forsyth and His Theology', *Methodist Quarterly Review* 62 (1913), pp. 455–63.

Žižek, Slavoj, 'Foreword: Hallward's Fidelity to the Badiou Event', in *Badiou: A Subject to Truth* by Peter Hallward (Minneapolis: University of Minnesota Press, 2003), pp. ix–xiv.

—, *The Puppet and the Dwarf: The Perverse Core of Christianity* (Cambridge: MIT Press, 2003).

Index

19172044R00171

Printed in Great Britain
by Amazon